Saṅgītaratnākara of Śārṅgadeva, vol. II

The present volume of the annotated translation of *Saṅgītaratnākara* contains the second, third and fourth chapters of the text dealing with *rāga*, miscellaneous topics pertaining to vocal music and *prabandha* (vocal compositional forms), respectively. These chapters deal with topics that are directly related to current practice.

The format of the first volume has been followed in this volume, except a small deviation in the word-index, where a glossary has not been attempted on account of the special nature of the terms contained in the chapters presented here. The vast expanse of terms which is mostly comprised of nomenclature of *rāga*-s, varieties of melodic rendering, *prabandha*-s and *tāla*-s prescribed therein has been thoroughly scanned and thus the index is a mirror of the totality of contents.

While the first volume was preceded by an earlier attempt at translation (without annotation), the second volume presents the above-noted three chapters in English for the first time. This long awaited volume will be a welcome addition to the primary source-material for a study of the rich textual tradition of Indian music.

Dr. R.K. Shringy received the degree of Doctor of Philosophy in Indian Philosophy and Religion from Banaras Hindu University in 1974. He worked as Research Assistant in the Department of Musicology, Banaras Hindu University. His published work is *Philosophy of J. Krishnamurti: A Systematic Study* (1977, 1988). He died in 1983.

Dr. Prem Lata Sharma was Professor of Musicology, Banaras Hindu University (retired in 1987) and Vice-Chancellor, Indira Kala Sangeet Vishwavidyalaya, Khairagarh. She also published the Critical editions of *Rasavilāsa* (1972) and *Ekaliṅgamāhātmyam* (1976).

SAṄGĪTARATNĀKARA
OF
ŚĀRṄGADEVA

Sanskrit text and English Translation with
Comments and Notes

Chapters II-IV

English translation by
Dr. R.K. SHRINGY
Under the Supervision of
Dr. PREM LATA SHARMA

Vol. II

Munshiram Manoharlal
Publishers Pvt Ltd

ISBN 81–215–0466–X (vol. II)
This edition 2007

Published by Munshiram Manoharlal Publishers Pvt. Ltd.,
Post Box 5715, 54 Rani Jhansi Road, New Delhi 110 055.

Contents

Transliteration Code vii

Abbreviations viii

Introduction ix

Acknowledgements xv

Detailed Contents

Sanskrit xvii

English xxv

CHAPTER II

The Discernment of Rāga-s (Rāgavivekādhyāya) 1-144

CHAPTER III

Miscellaneous Topics (Prakīrṇakādhyāya) 145-208

CHAPTER IV

The Prabandha-s (Prabandhādhyāya) 209-324

Half-line Śloka-Index 325-47

Word-Index 348-97

Transliteration Code

Devanāgari script	***Roman script***
1. Vowels:	
(i) short—अ, इ, उ, ऋ, ऌ	**a, i, u, ṛ, lṛ**
(ii) long—आ, ई, ऊ	ā, ī, ū
(iii) dipthongs—ए, ऐ, ओ, औ	**e, ai, o, au**
(iv) anusvāra— ं, and visarga— :	**ṁ, and ḥ**
2. Consonants:	
(i) gutturals—क्, ख्, ग्, घ्, ङ्	**k, kh, g, gh, ṅ**
(ii) palatals—च्, छ्, ज्, झ्, ञ्	c, ch, j, jh, ñ
(iii) linguals—ट्, ठ्, ड्, ढ्, ण्	ṭ, ṭh, ḍ, ḍh, ṇ
(iv) dentals—त्, थ्, द्, ध्, न्	t, th, d, dh, n
(v) labials—प्, फ्, ब्, भ्, म्	p, ph, b, bh, m
Semivowels—य्, र्, ल्, व्	y, r, l, v
Sibilants—श्, ष्, स्	ś, ṣ, s
Sonant aspirate—ह	h

Metrical symbols	*Tonal symbols*
(i) *laghu*—I short	*Ṣaḍja*—sa, *Madhyama*—ma,
(ii) *guru*—S long	*Ṛṣabha*—ri, *Pañcama*—pa,
(iii) *pluta*—Ś prolonged or elongated	*Gāndhāra*—ga, *Dhaivata*—dha, *Niṣāda*—ni

Abbreviations

Ad. ed.	Adyar edition of *Saṅgītaratnākara*
Bṛ. D.	*Bṛhaddeśī* of Mataṅga, Trivandrum Sanskrit Series, 94, 1928
G. O. S.	Gaekwad Oriental Series
I. M. J.	*Indian Music Journal*, Delhi
K.	*Kalānidhi*, commentary of Kallinātha on *S. R.*
Lit.	Literally
N. S.	*Nāṭyaśāstra* of Bharata, G.O.S.
P. L. S.	Prem Lata Sharma
S	*Sudhākara*, commentary of Siṁhabhūpāla on *S. R.*
S. R.	*Saṅgītaratnākara*
S. Rāj.	*Saṅgītarāja* of Kumbhakarṇa, (Rāṇā Kumbhā) Banaras Hindu University, vol. I, 1963
S.S. Sāra	*Saṅgita-samayasāra* of Pārśvadeva, Trivandrum Sanskrit Series, 1925

Introduction

Prefatory Note

The second volume of the translated and annotated edition of *Saṅgīta-ratnākara* is being presented with a mixed feeling of sorrow and joy; sorrow due to the sad demise of Dr. R.K. Shringy in December 1983, while the book was in the press and joy because the book is at last seeing the light of the day after being in press for about six years. Scholars and students have been eagerly awaiting the second volume for ten years ever since the publication of the first volume in 1978. This volume contains the second, third and fourth chapters of the text dealing with *rāga-s*, miscellaneous topics and *prabandha-s* respectively. Observations on these three chapters are presented here in the same sequence.

Rāga-s

The name of the chapter dealing with *rāga-s* is *Rāga-viveka* i.e. discernment of *rāga-s* and this nomenclature implies that the author felt the need of discriminating between those *rāga-s* that were current in his times and those that had becomes obsolete. This title is justified by his treatment of this topic; he has tried to strike a balance between the dual responsibility of recording earlier tradition on the one hand and current practice on the other. Mataṅga's *Bṛhaddeśi* is the main source of earlier material for Śārṅgadeva, the author of *S. R.* and in comparison to the former, the latter text bears the following distinctive features.

(a) While Mataṅga accepts seven *giti-s*, Śārṅgadeva speaks of only five, excluding *Bhāṣā* and *Vibāṣā*. This is a more rational approach because the first five *giti-s* stand for stylistic differences in the rendering of *Grāma-rāga-s* and *Grāma-rāga-s* are classified according to them, *Bhāṣā-s* and *Vibhāṣā-s* are derivative varieties of *Grāma-rāga-s* and hence they could not be categorised at par with the first five *gīti-s* viz. *Śuddhā*, *Bhinnā*, *Gauḍi*, *Rāga* or *Vesarā* and *Sādhāraṇī*.

(b) Mataṅga's *Bṛ. D.* describes *Grāma-rāga*-s according to their grouping under the five *gīti-s*; i.e. *Śuddha*, *Bhinna*, *Gauḍa*, *Vesara* and *Sādhāraṇa rāga-s* of both the *Grāma-s* are described in the order of the five *giti-s*.

S. R. follows the above scheme only partially. Seventeen *Grāma-rāga-s* i.e. three each of the *Śuddhā*, *Bhinnā*, *Gauḍi* and *Vesarā gīti-s* and five of the *Sādhāraṇī gīti* are described in the accepted order. The remaining thirteen out of the thirty *Grāma-rāga-s* enumerated in *S. R.*, 2.1.8-14, are described alongwith their derivative varieties and the order of their treatment is not in accordance with that of the *gīti-s* or the *grāma-s*. This treatment mixes these thirteen *Grāma-rāga-s* with two *upa-rāga-s* which are also the origin of *rāgāṅga-s* (and are described at par with *Grāma-rāga-s*) as well as with *bhāṣāṅga-s* and *bhāṣā-s*. The author has treated these thirteen *rāga-s* not in their own right, but as the origin of current *rāga-s* of his times in the categories of *rāgāṅga*, *bhāṣāṅga* and *upāṅga* as well as one *Bhāṣā* and one *Vibhāṣā*. Hence their sequence is determined by the relative importance of their derivative *rāga-s* rather than by their own position according to *gīti* or *grāma*. Thus, *S. R.* has virtually divided the thirty *Grāma-raga-s* handed down by textual tradition into two categories, one of those that had lost relevance in the current practice of his time and the other of those which stood out as the origin of some of the current *rāga*-forms.

(c) *S. R.* adds another dimension to the description (*lakṣaṇa*) of *Grāma-rāga-s* viz. the prescription of season and specific part of the day in their usage as well as *devatā* at the esoteric level in addition to the specific juncture (*sandhi*) or situation of drama which was already prescribed in *Bṛ. D.* Notated *ākṣiptikā-s* are also added by *S. R.* for each *Grāma-rāga*.

(d) *S. R.* enumerates eight *upa-rāga-s*, although it describes only two of them without specifying them as such. *Bṛ. D.* does not mention this category; three out of these eight viz. *takkasaindhava*, *revagupta* and *pañcamaṣāḍava* are, however, described in that text under *Grāma-rāga-s*.

(e) The section of *Bṛ. D.* dealing with *Deśī-rāga-s* breaks off in its very beginning. But *S. R.* gives a detailed treatment of *Deśī-rāga-s* in four categories, viz. *rāgāṅga*, *bhāṣāṅga*, *kriyāṅga* and *upāṅga*. The citation from *Bṛ. D.* found in Kallinātha's commentary on *S. R.*, 2.2.1—enumerates only three categories omitting the last one viz. *upāṅga*. Thus *upāṅga* could be taken as a later addition.

(f) *S. R.* adds a new (unqualified) category by way of *rāga* which is neither put under *Mārga* nor *Deśī*. Twenty names are given under this category, but only ten are described. Curiously enough, most of these *rāga-s* (that are described) are derived directly from *jāti-s* and are assigned to a specific *grāma*. This would suggest that they were designed as being parallel to *Grāma-rāga-s* and were the product, so to say, of an attempt to retrieve a lost tradition. *S. Rāj.*, 2.2.1.20 c d-23, however, discards this category, saying that it has no specific characteristic that would justify its distinctive entity.

(g) Although *S. R.* describes a much smaller number of *Bhāṣā-s*, *Vibhāṣā-s* etc. it adds a new dimension to their description and this is the mention of specific *gamaka-s* like *āhata*, *kampita*, *sphurita* etc. *Deśi-rāga-s* grouped under the four categories viz. *rāgāṅga*, *bhāṣāṅga*, *kriyāṅga* and *upāṅga* are also described in similar terms. The following references would confirm this point:

Name	*Category*	*Descriptive phrase*
Toḍī	*Rāgāṅga*	*Kampra-pañcamā* (with a shakeful *pañcama)*
Gurjarī	*Rāgāṅga*	*Tāḍitā* (a synonym of *āhata*, name of a gmaka)
Deśākhyā	*Rāgāṅga*	*Sphurita-gāndhāra* (with *sphurita gamaka* on *gāndhāra)*
Ragantī	*Bhāṣāṅga*	*Sphurita-dhaivatā* (with *sphurita gamaka* on *dhaivata)*
Siṁhalī-kāmodā	*Upāṅga*	*Kampra-dhaivatā*
Chāyānaṭṭā	*Upāṅga*	*Kampita-niṣāda-gāndhārā*
Kolāhalā	*Bhāṣā*	*Gamakānvitā* (full of *gamaka)*
Chevāṭī	*Bhāṣā*	*Gamaka-saṁyutā* (full of *gamaka)*
Malhārī	*Upāṅga*	*Tāḍitā* (see *gujrarī* above)
Deśavāla-gauḍa	*Upāṅga*	*Āndolita-ṣaḍja* (*āndolita gamaka* on *ṣaḍja)*
Turuṣka-gauḍa	*Upāṅga*	*Mandra-tāḍitā* (*āhata gamaka* in the lower register)
Drāviḍa-gauḍa	*Upāṅga*	*Prasphurat-ṣaḍja-pañcama* (*sphurita gamaka* on *ṣaḍja-pañcama)*
Saurāṣṭrī	*Bhāṣā*	*Gamkānvitā* (full of *gamaka)*
Saindhavī	*Bhāṣā*	*Gamaka-sāndrā* (dense with *gamaka-s)* and *laṅghita* (skipped) *svara-s*

The seven points given above presenting a comparative view of the treatment of *rāga-s* in *Bṛ. D.* and *S. R.* evince two definite trends of the post-Mataṅga period viz. (1) inclusion of non-dramatic elements like season, time of the day, *devatā* etc. in the description of *Grāma-rāga-s* and (2) description of *Deśī rāga-s* and *Bhāṣā-s* in terms of generic and specific *gamaka-s*. Both these trends are very significant. The author's complete silence about *rāga-dhyāna* (visual contemplation of *rāga-s)* is also notable.

Miscellaneous Topics

The third chapter dealing with miscellaneous topics evinces a definite bias towards vocal music. The *vāggeyakāra* (composer of text and music of song), the good and bad qualities of a singer, five types of singers, threefold singers (solo, duet and ensemble), songstresses, types of voice, excellences of voice, blemishes of voice, *śārīra* (gifted voice), *gamaka*, *sthāya*, *ālapti*, the ensembles of male and female vocalists, all these are directly related to vocal music. The good and bad qualities of instrumentalists are dealt with in the sixth chapter. The main source of the treatment of most of these topics is Someśvara's *Mānasollāsa*. (Gaekwad Oriental Series, no.

138). For *sthāya-s* Pārśvadeva's *Saṅgita-samayasāra* which is most probably more or less a contemporary of *S. R.* could be said to be a source or a parallel document of this excellent analysis of melodic phrasing and rendering. The main difference between these two texts in this context is that while *S. R.* represents the Sanskritised version of the terms forming part of this concept, *S.S. Sāra* represents the Prākṛta version. The word *sthāya* itself is a Sanskritised version of *ṭhāya.* This chapter is of great relevance to our contemporary music. The description of *sthāya-s* under two categories viz. those that were known earlier (*pūrva-prasiddha*) and those that were known in the author's time (*adhunā-prasiddha*) bears testimony to the author's concern for recording earlier tradition and current practice.

Prabandha-s

S. R. equates *prabandha* with *gāna* of *N. S.* which is contra-distinct from *Gāndharva* and *gāna* in its turn is identified with *Deśī*, while *Gāndharva* is identified with *Mārga.* This identification is not quite valid because the earlier pair of *Gāndharva-gāna* is not identical with the later pair of *Mārga-Deśī,* the former being more closed and guarded and the latter being comparatively wider in comprehension and more loose. Anyway, *prabandha* is accepted as part of *Deśī* and this fact is handed down by *Bṛ. D. S. R.*'s treatment of *prabandha* is nearer to that of Nānyadeva's *Bharata-bhāṣya* and Someśvara's *Mānasollāsa* than to *Bṛ. D.* which, of course, is the first extant text to speak of *prabandha-s.*

Three names of *nibaddha-gāna* (composed or pre-determined music) are given in *S. R.* viz. *prabandha*, *vastu* and *rūpaka*; but they are not defined. *S. Rāj.* (2.4.2.3 c d-6) tries to distinguish the three as follows, although he concedes that they are synonymous.

Prabandha—that composition which is comprised of all the six *aṅga-s* and four *dhātu-s.*

Vastu—that composition which has a lesser number of *aṅga-s* and *dhātu-s* i.e. some of them are omitted.

Rūpaka—that composition where the dramatic element is predominant.

Neither *S. R.*, nor any other text (not even *S. Rāj.*) makes a specified use of these three names. *Prabandha* is the name that is widely used and *S. R.* uses the word *rūpaka* only in two contexts viz. in the compound *Rūpakālapti* standing for the improvised elaboration alongwith the composition and while analysing the elements of novelty in a composition It is not clear as to why the word *rūpaka* has been used there instead of *prabandha* which has otherwise dominated the scene without exception. *Vastu* has not been used at all.

The basis of the threefold division of *prabandha* as *Sūḍa* (including its sub-type *Sālaga sūḍa*), *Ālikrama* or *Ālisaṁśrita* and *Viprakirṇa* is not clear and the same has not been indicated at all in *S. R. S. Raj.* (2.4.2.36 a b) says for *Viprakīrṇa prabandha-s* that they were fit to be sung as unconnected pieces i.e. each one is self-sufficient. This suggests that the other two categories viz. *Sūḍa* and *Ālikrama* imply a series of compositions that are interlinked like the 24 songs in *Gīta-Govinda* of Jaideva. But it is not possible to verify this suggestion on account of paucity of illustrative material; whatever little is available in *Mānasollāsa* is not adequate for this purpose. If this question of presence or absence of interlinking among compositions is set aside, then the following characteristic features of these categories collectively or individually stand out on close scrutiny.

(a) The various combinations of six *aṅga-s* viz. *svara* i.e. solfa syllables, *tāla*, *pada* (verbal structure), *tena* (the syllabic unit '*tena*' standing for 'That' =Ultimate Reality), *pāṭa* (drum-syllables), *biruda* (eulogistic epithets) do not at all play a part in the *Sūḍa prabandha-s*. All the eight varieties in this category are made up of only two *aṅga-s* viz. *pada* and *tāla*. Hence the arrangement of other *aṅga-s* is not responsible for the creation of variety in the *Sūḍa* category, whereas it is so in the other two categories viz. *Ālikrama* and *Viprakīrṇa*. In the varieties of *Sūḍa* however, *gāna-bheda* (the order of repetition of the *dhātu-s* or sections) does play an important role.

(b) The *udgrāha* (introductory section) is generally bigger than the *dhruva* (the section that is constant due to repetition or due to being indispensable) or it is at least of equal length with the *dhruva*, very seldom it is smaller. Hence *dhruva* tends to find a position almost in the middle of a composition and not in the beginning, as is the case today with the *sthāyī* which could be equated with *dhruva*. The *Sālaga-sūḍa prabandha-s* embody a marked deviation from this location of *dhruva*. The first *prabandha* of this category is known as *dhruva* and there the first half of *udgrāha* is treated as *dhruva*, thus shifting the location of *dhruva* from the middle to the beginning. Thus the *Sālaga-sūḍa-s* are closer to our contemporary practice. It should be noted here that *Sālaga-sūḍa prabandha-s* were later accorded a separate category called *gīta* in the scheme of *caturdaṇḍī* or four rods viz. *ālāpa*, *ṭhāya*, *gīta* and *prabandha* (see *Caturdaṇḍi Prakāśika*, 8.1-4).

(c) Although four *dhātu-s* (sections) are spoken of with a fifth one called *antara* prescribed for *Sālaga-sūḍa-s*, really speaking the maximum number of *dhātu-s* that could find place in a *prabandha* is four, because *melāpaka* is forbidden where *antara* is prescribed. Even so, the majority of *prabandha-s* has only three *dhātu-s* viz. *udgrāha*, *dhruva* and *ābhoga*, because *melāpaka* is generally optional even when it is prescribed.

(d) Inscription (*aṅkana*) of the name of the composer (*gātā*-singer), the *nāyaka* (hero) or *stutya* (the object of eulogy) and of the *prabandha* is prescribed in the *ābhoga*. Even when the text omits this prescription, Kallinātha invariably supplies it. Because of the requirement of inscription, the *ābhoga* is prescribed to be composed of *pada* (unspecified verbal text). Inscription of the name of *prabandha* is prescribed only in two cases, viz. *gadya-prabandha* and *pañcatāleśvara*, but the illustrations found in Someśvara's *Mānasollāsa* contain this inscription in many cases.

(e) The *Ela prabandha*, the first in the *Sūda* category (qualified as *Śuddha-sūda* with reference to *Sālaga-sūḍa*) is given a special treatment, the origin of its four primary varieties is traced to the four Veda-s, *devatā-s* (presiding deities) are mentioned for its sixteen *pada-s* or components, ten *prāṇa-s* are allocated to ten of its sixteen components etc. Similarly, *dhruva*, the first out of the seven *Sālaga-sūḍa-s* is given a special and elaborate treatment; its sixteen varieties are described in terms of number of syllables of text, *tāla*, *rasa*, benefit accruing to the singer (composer) and his patron.

(f) Numerous varieties of many *prabandha-s* have been spoken in terms of a corresponding variety of *tāla-s* and both have been given identical names. Metre (*chandas*) also plays an important role in the creation of many varieties and sub-varieties of *prabandha-s*.

(g) Although *prabandha* belongs to a category of music independent of drama, it has inherited the tradition of *viniyoga* (specific application) in terms of *rasa-s*, private or public situations, and seen benefit (*dṛṣṭa phala*).

(h) Although *prabandha* is said to be composed in *Deśi-rāga-s* and *Deśī-tāla-s*, hangovers of the *Mārga* tradition are strewn here and there. For example, the *Pañcatāleśvara prabandha* is described in terms of all the five *Mārga-tāla-s*.

The chapter ends with a short discussion of the factors responsible for novelty in a given composition. This is a very interesting and significant part of the treatment of *prabandha*.

Reference is invited to the following research papers on some of the points made out here.

1. '*Sūlādi-s* and *Ūgābhoga-s* of Karnataka Music' by R. Sathyanarayana, published by Varalakshmi Academy, Mysore.
2. '*Dhruva* in *Dhrupad*'—Prem Lata Sharma.
3. 'Signature in *Dhrupad* Song-texts and the Problems Arising Therefrom'—Prem Lata Sharma.

(No. 2 and 3 published in *Dhrupad*, Annual no. 2, 1987 by All India Kashiraj Trust, Fort, Ramnagar, Varanasi).

Word-Index

The subject matter of the present volume is different from that of the first volume because it is abundant with nominal terms that do not involve an elaboration of the concepts they stand for. Hence a word-index indicating the context(s) of each term has been prepared, but a glossary in English has not been attempted. This departure from the pattern of word-index-cum-glossary adopted in the first volume has been dictated by the contents of this volume. It is hoped that the readers will find this index useful.

Acknowledgements

Grateful acknowledgements are due to the following:

The University Grants Commission for granting a fellowship under the Book-writing scheme.

Members of the Department of Musicology, Banaras Hindu University for their direct and indirect help.

Sri Devendra Jain of Munshiram Manoharlal Publishers for taking up the publication of this volume.

Varanasi
January 1989

PREM LATA SHARMA

विस्तृत विषयसूची

द्वितीयो रागाध्यायः

ग्रामरागोपरागरागभाषाविभाषान्तरभाषाविवेकाख्यं प्रथमं प्रकरणम्

श्लोक संख्या

(i) ग्रन्थकृत्प्रतिज्ञा — १
(ii) पञ्चधा ग्रामरागाः — २ क ख
(iii) पञ्चगीतयः — २ ग-७
(iv) ग्रामरागोद्देशः — ८-१४
(v) उपरागोद्देशः — १५, १६ क ख
(vi) रागोद्देशः — १६ ग-१८
(vii) भाषाजनकरागोद्देशः — १९-२१ ख
(viii) भाषाविभाषान्तरभाषोद्देशः — २१ ग-४३
(ix) भाषाभेदाः — ४४-४७

रागाङ्गादिनिर्णयाख्यं द्वितीयं प्रकरणम्

(i) उपोद्घातः — १-३
(ii) प्राक्प्रसिद्धरागाः — ४-९ ख
(iii) अधुनाप्रसिद्धरागाः, रागाणां सम्मिलितसङ्ख्या, निरूपणक्रमश्च — ९ ग-२०
(iv) प्राक्प्रसिद्ध-ग्रामराग-निरूपणम् — २१-६७ ख

1. शुद्धसाधारितः — २१-२७ ख
   - (क) तल्लक्षणम् — २१-२३ ख
   - (ख) रागालापलक्षणम् — २३ ग-२४
   - (ग) रूपकलक्षणम् — २५ क ख
   - (घ) आक्षिप्तिकालक्षणम् — २५ ग, २६ ख
   - (ङ) करणवर्तन्योः प्रबन्धान्तर्गतिः — २६ ग घ
   - (च) रूपकनिरूपणप्रतिज्ञा — २७ क ख
2. षड्जग्रामः — २७ ग-३० ख
3. शुद्धकैशिकः — ३० ग-३२

4. भिन्नकैशिकमध्यमः ३३, ३४
5. भिन्नतानः ३५-३७ ख
6. भिन्नकैशिकः ३७-३९
7. गौडकैशिकमध्यमः ४०-४२ ख
8. गौडपञ्चमः ४२ ग-४५ ख
9. गौडकैशिकः ४५ ग-४७
10. वेसरषाडवः ४८-५० ख
11. बोट्टः ५० ग-५२
12. मालवपञ्चमः ५३-५५ ख
13. रूपसाधारः ५५ ग-५७
14. शकः ५८, ५९
15. भम्माणपञ्चमः ६०, ६१ ख
16. नर्तः ६२ ग-६५ ख
17. षड्जकैशिकः ६५ ग-६७ ख

(v) सहेतवोऽधुनाप्रसिद्धरागाः (अधुनाप्रसिद्धरागास्तद्धेतुभूत—प्राक्प्रसिद्धरागाश्च) ६७ ग-१०६ ख
1. मध्यमग्राम-मध्यमादिः ६८-७० ग
2. मालवकैशिक-मालवश्रीः ७० घ-७३
3. षाडव-तोडिका-बङ्गालः ७४-७८
4. भिन्नषड्ज-भैरवः ७९-८२ ख
5. भिन्नपञ्चम-वराटी ८२ ग-८६ ख
6. पञ्चमषाडव-गुर्जरी ८६ ग-८९
7. टक्क-गौड-कोलाहलः ९०-९३ ख
8. हिन्दोल-वसन्तः ९३ ख-९६
9. शुद्धकैशिक मध्यम—धन्नासी ९७-१०० ख
10. रेवगुप्त-देशी १०० ख-१०३ ख
11. गान्धारपञ्चम-देशाख्या १०३ ग-१०६ ख

(vi) भाषाङ्गाणि, कतिपय हेतुभूतरागाश्च १०६ ग-१२६
1. त्रवणा-डोम्बकृतिः १०६ ग-१०८ ख
2. ककुभ-रगन्ती-सावरी १०८ ग-११२ ख
3. भोगवर्धनी-वेलावली-प्रथममञ्जरी ११२ ग-११५
4. बाङ्गाली-आडीकामोदिका ११६, ११७
5. वैगरञ्जी-नागध्वनिः ११८, ११९
6. सौवीर-सौवीरी-वराटी १२०-१२४ ख
7. पिञ्जरी-नट्टा-कर्णाटबङ्गालः १२४ ग-१२६

(vii) क्रियाङ्गाणि १२७-१२९
1. रामकृतिः १२७
2. गौडकृतिः १२८
3. देवकृतिः १२९

(viii) उपाङ्गानि १३०-१५८
1. वराट्युपाङ्गानि १३०-१३३
(i) कौन्तली वराटी १३०
(ii) द्राविडी वराटी १३१ क ख
(iii) सैन्धवी वराटी १३१ ग-१३२ ख
(iv) उपस्थानवराटी १३२ ग घ
(v) हतस्वरवराटी १३३ क ख
(vi) प्रतापवराटी १३३ ग घ
2. तोड्युपाङ्गे १३४
(i) छायातोडी १३४ क ख
(ii) तुरुष्कतोड़ी १३४ ग घ
3. गुर्जर्युपाङ्गानि १३५-१३७ ख
(i) महाराष्ट्रगुर्जरी १३५
(ii) सौराष्ट्रगुर्जरी १३६ क ख
(iii) दक्षिणगुर्जरी १३६ ग घ
(iv) द्राविडगुर्जरी 137 क ख
4. वेलावल्युपाङ्गानि १३७ ख-१४० ख
(i) भुच्छी १३७ ग, १३८ ख
(ii) खम्भाइतिः १३८ ग, १३९ ख
(iii) छायावेलावली १३९ ग घ
(iv) प्रतापवेलावली १४० क ख
5. भैरवोपाङ्गम् १४० ग, १४१ ख
भैरवी १४० ग-१४२ ख
6. कामोदोपाङ्गम् १४१ ग, १४२ ख
सिंहलीकामोदा १४१ ग, १४२ ख
7. नट्टोपाङ्गम् १४२ ग, १४३ ख
छायानट्टा १४२ ग, १४३ ख
8. कोलाहला—रामकृतिः १४३ ग-१४५
9. छेवाटी—वल्लाता १४६-१४८ ख
10. शुद्धपञ्चमस्तज्जनिता रागाश्च १४८ ग-१५५
(i) शुद्धपञ्चमः १४८ ग-१५० ख
(ii) दाक्षिणात्या (भाषा) १५१, १५२ क
(iii) आन्धाली (भाषा) १५१ ख-१५३
(iv) मल्हारी (उपाङ्गम्) १५४
(v) मल्हारः १५५
11. गौडोपाङ्गानि १५६-१५८
(i) कर्णाटगौडः १५६ क ख
(ii) देशवालगौडः १५६ ग घ
(iii) गुरुष्कगौडः १५७

(iv) द्राविड़गोड: १५८
(ix) अधुनाप्रसिद्धदेशीरागा: १५९-१६९
1. श्रीराग: १५९-१६० ख
2. प्रथमबङ्गाल: १६० ग-१६१ ख
3. द्वितीयबङ्गाल: १६१ ग-१६२ ख
4. मध्यमषाडव: १६२ ग-१६३ ख
5. शुद्धभैरव: १६३ ग-१६४ ख
6. मेघराग: १६४ ग-१६५ ख
7. सोमराग: १६५ ग-१६६ ख
8. प्रथमकामोद: १६६ ग-१६७ ख
9. द्वितीयकामोद: १६७ ग-१६८ ख
10. आम्रपञ्चम: १६८ ग-१६९
(x) प्रकीर्ण-भाषा: १७०-१८९
1. कैशिकी १७०, १७१
2. सौराष्ट्री १७२-१७४ ख
(i) प्रथमसौराष्ट्री १७२, १७३ ख
(ii) द्वितीयसौराष्ट्री १७३ ग-१७४ ख
3. ललिता १७४ ग-१७७ ख
(i) प्रथमललिता १७४ ग, १७५
(ii) द्वितीयललिता १७६, १७७ ख
4. सैन्धवी १७७ ग-१८२
(i) प्रथमसैन्धवी १७७ ग-१७८
(ii) द्वितीयसैन्धवी १७९-१८० ख
(iii) तृतीयसैन्धवी १८० ग-१८१
(iv) चतुर्थसैन्धवी १८२
5. गौडी १८३-१८५
(i) प्रथमगौडी १८३, १८४ख
(ii) द्वितीयगौडी १८४ ग, १८५
6. त्रावणी १८६, १८७
7. हर्षपुरी १८८
8. भम्माणी १८९
(xi) टक्ककैशिक-मालवा-द्राविडी १९०-१९४
(i) टक्ककैशिक: १९०-१९२
(ii) मालवा (भाषा) १९३
(iii) द्राविडी (विभाषा) १९४

तृतीयः प्रकीर्णकाध्यायः

(i) ग्रन्थकृत्प्रतिज्ञा

(ii) वाग्गेयकारलक्षणम्, तद्भेदाश्च २-१२ ख
(iii) गान्धर्व-स्वरादि-लक्षणम् १२ ग-१३ ख
(iv) गामकलक्षणम्, तद्भेदाश्च १३ ग-२४
(क) उत्तमगायकः १३-१८ ख
(ख) मध्यमगायकः १८ ग घ
(ग) अधमगायकः १९ क ख
(घ) पञ्चविधगायकाः १९ ग-२४ ख
(ङ) त्रिविधगायकाः २२ ग-२३
(च) गायन्यः २४
(v) निन्दित-(सदोष)-गायकाः २५-३८
(vi) शब्दभेदाः ३९-६७
(क) चतुर्विधशब्दः ३९-४५
(ख) मिश्रस्य भेदचतुष्टयम् ४६-५६ ख
(i) द्वन्द्वजभेदाः ५० ग-६० ग
(ii) सांनिपातिकभेदाः ६० घ-६६ क
(ग) उपसंहारः ६६ ख-६७
(vii) शब्दगुणाः ६८-७७
(viii) शब्ददोषाः ७८-८१
(ix) शारीरम् ८२-८६
(क) शारीरलक्षणम् ८२
(ख) शारीरगुणाः ८३-८४ ख
(ग) शारीरदोषाः ८४ ग-८५
(घ) सुशारीरप्राप्त्युपायाः ८६
(x) गमकलक्षणम्, तद्भेदाश्च ८७-९७ ख
(xi) स्थायलक्षणम्, तद्भेदाश्च ९७ ग-११२ ग
(क) लक्षणम्, उद्देशयश्च ९७ ग-११२ ख
(ख) प्रसिद्धस्थायाः ११२ ग-१५१
(i) तत्रासंकीर्णलक्षणाः स्थायाः ११२ ग-१२७
(ii) तत्र संकीर्णलक्षणाः स्थायाः १२८-१५१
(ग) अप्रसिद्धस्थायाः १५२-१७६ ख
(i) तत्रासङ्कीर्णलक्षणाः स्थायाः १५२-१६२ ख
(ii) तत्र सङ्कीर्णलक्षणाः स्थायाः १६२ ग-१७६ ख
(घ) मिश्रस्थायाः १७६ ग-१८९ ख
(xii) आलप्तिस्तद्भेदाश्च १८९ ग-२०२
(क) आलप्तिलक्षणम्, भेदद्वयोद्देशश्च १८९ ग-१९० ख
(ख) रागालप्तिः १९० ग-१९६
(ग) रूपकालप्तिः १९७-२०१
(घ) आलप्तेः सामान्यलक्षणम् २०२
(xiii) वृन्दम्, तद्भेदाश्च २०३-२२३

(क) वृन्दलक्षणम् २०३
(ख) गायनवृन्दम् २०४-२०६
(ग) गायनवृन्दगुणाः २१०-२११ ख
(घ) कुतपः २११ ग-२२३

चतुर्थः प्रबन्धाध्यायः

प्रथमप्रकरणम्, उपोद्घातः
(i) गीतलक्षणम्, तद्भेदाश्च १-३
(ii) गानभेदद्वयम् ४-६
(iii) धातवः ७-११
(iv) धातुसङ्ख्यानुसारेण प्रबन्धभेदाः १२ क-ग
(v) प्रबन्धाङ्गानि १२ ग-१६ ख
(vi) प्रबन्धजातयः १६ ग-२१ ख
(vii) प्रबन्धभेदाः २१ ग-२३ ग
(viii) त्रिविधप्रबन्धभेदानामुद्देशः २३ ग-३३ ख

द्वितीयप्रकरणम्, सूडप्रबन्धाः
(i) एलाप्रबन्धाः ३३ ग-१३२ ख
(क) सामान्यलक्षणम् केचिद्विशेषाश्च ३३ ग-६५
(ख) गणैला ६६-६४ ख
(ग) मात्रैला ६४ ग-१०५ ख
(घ) वर्णैला १०५ ग-११३
(ङ) देशैला ११४-१३२ ख
(ii) करणप्रबन्धः १३२ ग-१४४
(iii) ढेङ्कीप्रबन्धः १४५-१५२ ख
(iv) वर्तनीप्रबन्धः १५२ ग-१५४
(v) झोम्बड-प्रबन्धः १५५-१६८
(vi) लम्भ-प्रबन्धः १६९-१७५ ख
(vii) रासकप्रबन्धः १७५ ग-१७९
(viii) एकताली-प्रबन्धः १८०, १८१ ख

तृतीयप्रकरणम्, आलिप्रबन्धाः
(i) वर्णप्रबन्धः १८१ ग-१८२ ख
(ii) वर्णस्वरप्रबन्धः १८२ ग-१८३
(iii) गद्यप्रबन्धः १८४-१९८
(iv) कैवाडप्रबन्धः १९९, २०० ख
(v) अङ्कचारिणीप्रबन्धः २०० ग-२०४ ख
(vi) कन्दप्रबन्धः २०४ग-२०९ ख

(vii) हयलीलाप्रबन्धः २०९ ग-२१२ ख
(viii) गजलीलाप्रबन्धः २१२ ग, २१३ ख
(ix) द्विपदीप्रबन्धः २१३ ग-२१९ ख
(x) चक्रवालप्रबन्धः २१९, २२०
(xi) क्रौञ्चपदप्रबन्धः २२१
(xii) स्वरार्थप्रबन्धः २२२, २२३
(xiii) ध्वनिकुट्टनीप्रबन्धः २२४, २२५ ख
(xiv) आर्याप्रबन्धः २२५ ग-२३१ ख
(xv) गाथाप्रबन्धः २३१ ग-२३२ ख
(xvi) द्विपथप्रबन्धः २३२ ग-२४१
(xvii) कलहंसप्रबन्धः २४२, २४३
(xviii) तोटकप्रबन्धः २४४, २४५
(xix) घटप्रबन्धः २४६ क ख
(xx) वृत्तप्रबन्धः २४६ ग-२४८ ख
(xxi) मातृकाप्रबन्धः २४८ ग-२५२
(xxii) रागकदम्बप्रबन्धः २५३-२५६ ख
(xxiii) पञ्चतालेश्वरप्रबन्धः २५६ ग-२६४
(xxiv) तालार्णवप्रबन्धः २६५ क ख

चतुर्थप्रकरणम्, विप्रकीर्णप्रबन्धनिरूपणम्

(i) श्रीरङ्गप्रबन्धः २६५ ग घ
(ii) श्रीविलासप्रबन्धः २६६ क ख
(iii-v) पञ्चभङ्गिपञ्चाननोमातिलकप्रबन्धाः २६६ ग, २६७
(vi) त्रिपदीप्रबन्धः २६८-२७०
(vii) चतुष्पदीप्रबन्धः २७१-२७२ ख
(viii) षट्पदीप्रबन्धः २७२ ग-२७४
(ix) वस्तुप्रबन्धः २७५, २७६
(x) विजयप्रबन्धः २७७
(xi) त्रिपथप्रबन्धः २७८ क ख
(xii) चतुर्मुखप्रबन्धः २७८ ग-२७९ ख
(xiii) सिंहलीलप्रबन्धः २७९ ग, २८० ख
(xiv) हंसलीलप्रबन्धः २८० ग घ
(xv) दण्डकप्रबन्धः २८१
(xvi) झम्पटप्रबन्धः २८२ क ख
(xvii) कन्दुकप्रबन्धः २८२ ग घ
(xviii) त्रिभङ्गिप्रबन्धः २८३, २८४
(xix) हरविलासप्रबन्धः २८५ क ख
(xx) सुदर्शनप्रबन्धः २८५ ग घ
(xxi) स्वराङ्कप्रबन्धः २८६

(xxii) श्रीवर्धनप्रबन्धः २८७
(xxiii) हर्षवर्धनप्रबन्धः २८८ क ख
(xxiv) वदनप्रबन्धः २८८ ग-२८९
(xxv) चच्चरीप्रबन्धः २९०-२९२ ख
(xxvi) चर्याप्रबन्धः २९२ ग-२९४
(xxvii) पद्धडीप्रबन्धः २९५
(xxviii) राहडीप्रबन्धः २९६
(xxix) वीरश्रीप्रबन्धः २९७ क ख
(xxx) मङ्गलाचारप्रबन्धः २९७ ग-२९८ ख
(xxxi) धवलप्रबन्धः २९८ ग-३०४ ख
(xxxii) मङ्गलप्रबन्धः ३०३ ग-३०४ ख
(xxxiii) ओवीप्रबन्धः ३०४ ग-३०६
(xxxiv) लोलीप्रबन्धः ३०७
(xxxv) ढोल्लरीप्रबन्धः ३०८
(xxxvi) दन्तीप्रबन्धः ३०९

पञ्चमप्रकरणम्, सालगसूडप्रबन्धनिरूपणम्
उपोद्घातः ३११-३१४
(i) ध्रुवप्रबन्धः ३१५-३३२ ख
(ii) मण्ठप्रबन्धः ३३२ ग-३३८ ख
(iii) प्रतिमण्ठप्रबन्धः ३३८ ग-३४३ ख
(iv) निःसारुकप्रबन्धः ३४३ ग-३४७
(v) अड्डतालप्रबन्धः ३४८-३५२ ख
(vi) रासकप्रबन्धः ३५२ ग-३५६ ख
(vii) एकतालीप्रबन्धः ३५६ ग-३६१ ख

षष्ठप्रकरणम्, प्रबन्धानामुत्तमादिविभागः
(क) रूपकविभागः ३६१ ग-३७३
(i) उत्तमरूपकम् ३६१ ग-३६५
(ii) मध्यमरूपकम् ३६६
(iii) अधमरूपकम् ३६७ क ख
(iv) मध्यमरूपकभेदाः ३६७ ग-३७१
(v) अधमरूपकभेदाः ३७२, ३७३
(ख) गीतगुणदोषाः ३७४-३८०
(i) गीतगुणाः ३७४-३७९
(ii) गीतदोषाः ३७९, ३८०

Detailed Contents

CHAPTER II
The Discernment of *Rāga-s*
(*Rāgavivekādhyāya*)

SECTION 1: The discernment of *grāma-rāga-s, uparāga-s, rāga-s, bhāṣā-s, vibhāsā-s* and *antara-bhāṣā-s.*

verse no.

(i) Announcement of the subject matter 1
(ii) The fivefold *grāma-rāga-s* 2 a b
(iii) The five *gīti-s* 2 c-7
(iv) The *grāma-rāga-s* 8-14
(v) The *uparāga-s* 15, 16 b
(vi) The *rāga-s* 16 c-18
(vii) The *bhāṣā-janaka* (parent) *rāga-s* 19-21 b
(viii) The *bhāṣā-s, vibhāṣā-s* and *antarabhāṣā-s* 21 c-43
(ix) The classification of *bhāṣā-s* 44-47

SECTION 2: The identity of the *rāgāṅga-s*, the *bhāṣāṅga-s*, the *kriyāṅga-s* and the *upāṅga-s*.

(i) Introduction 1-3
(ii) The well-known ancient *rāga-s* 4-9 b
(iii) The current well-known *rāga-s*, the total number of *rāga-s* and the scheme of their description 9 c-20
(iv) The characteristic features of the ancient *rāga-s* 21-67 b
1. *Śuddhasādhārita* (21-27 b)
(a) The definition of *rāga* (21-23 b)
(b) The definition of *rāgālāpa* (23 c-24)
(c) The definition of *rūpaka* (25 a b)
(d) The definition of *ākṣiptikā* (25 c-26 b)
2. *Ṣaḍjagrāma* (27 c-30 b)
3. *Śuddhakaiśika* (30 c-32)
4. *Bhinnakaiśikamadhyama* (33-35 b)
5. *Bhinnatāna* (35 c-37 b)
6. *Bhinnakaiśika* (37 c-39)

7. *Gauḍakaiśikamadhyama* (40-42 b)
8. *Gauḍapañcama* (42 c-45 b)
9. *Gauḍakaiśika* (45 c-47)
10. *Vesaraṣāḍava* (48-50 b)
11. *Boṭṭa* (50 c-52)
12. *Mālavapancama* (53-55 b)
13. *Rūpasādhāra* (55 c-57)
14. *Śaka* (58, 59)
15. *Bhammāṇapañcama* (60-62 b)
16. *Narta* (62 c-65 b)
17. *Ṣaḍjakaiśika* (65 c-67 b)

(v) The characteristic features of the ancient *rāga-s* recognised as sources of popular *rāgāṅga-rāga-s*. 67 c-106 b
1. *Madhyamagrāma-madhyamāḍi* (68-70 c)
2. *Mālavakaiśika-mālavaśrī* (70 d-73)
3. *Ṣāḍava, toḍi-baṅgāla* (74-78)
4. *Bhinnaṣaḍja-bhairava* (79-82 b)
5. *Bhinna-pañcama-varāṭī* (82 c-86 b)
6. *Pañcamaṣāḍava-gurjari* (86 c-89)
7. *Ṭakka—gauḍa* and *kolāhala* (90-93 b)
8. *Hindola-vasanta* (93 c-96)
9. *Śuddhakaiśikamadhyama-dhannāsi* (97-100 b)
10. *Revagupta-deśī* (100 c-103 b)
11. *Gāndhārapañcama-deśākhyā* (103 c-106 b)

(vi) *Bhāṣāṅga-s* and some source *rāga-s* 106 c-126
1. *Travaṇā* and *ḍombakṛti* (106 c-108 b)
2. *Kakubha—ragantī* and *sāvarī* (108 c-112 b)
3. *Bhogavardhanī, velāvalī* and *prathama-mañjarī* (112 c-115)
4. *Bāṅgālī* and *Āḍikāmodikā* (116-117)
5. *Vegarañji* and *Nāgadhvani* (118-119)
6. *Sauvīra—sauvirī* and *varāṭī* (120-124 b)
7. *Piñjarī, Naṭṭā* and *Karṇāṭabaṅgāla* (124 c-126)

(vii) The *Kriyāṅga-s* 127-129
Rāmakṛti, Gauḍakṛti and *Devakṛti* (127-129)

(viii) The *Upāṅga-s* 130-158
1. The *Upāṅga-s* of *varāṭī* (130-133)
(i) *Kauntalīvarāṭi* (130)
(ii) *Drāviḍivarāṭī* (131 a b)
(iii) *Saindhavīvarāṭī* (131 c-132 b)
(iv) *Apasthānavarāṭī* (132 c d)
(v) *Hatasvaravarāṭī* (133 a b)
(vi) *Pratāpavarāṭi* (133 c d)
2. The *Upāṅga-s* of *toḍī* (134)

(i) *Chāyātoḍī* (134 a b)
(ii) *Turuṣkatoḍī* (134 c d)
3. The *Upāṅga-s* of *Gurjarī* (135-137 b)
(i) *Mahārāṣṭra-gurjari* (135)
(ii) *Saurāṣṭra-gurjarī* (136 a b)
(iii) *Dakṣiṇa-gurjari* (136 c d)
(iv) *Drāviḍa-gurjari* (137 a b)
4. The *Upāṅga-s* of *Velāvali* (137 c-140 b)
(i) *Bhucchi* (137 c, 138 b)
(ii) *Khambhāitiḥ* (138 c, 139 b)
(iii) *Chāyāvelāvalī* (139 c d)
(iv) *Pratāpavelāvali* (140 a b)
5. The *Upāṅga* of *Bhairava—Bhairavi* (140 c-141 b)
6. The *Upāṅga* of *Kāmoda—Siṁhalīkāmodā* (141 c-142 b)
7. The *Upāṅga* of *Naṭṭā—Chāyānaṭṭā* (142 c, 143 b)
8. *Kolāhalā* and *Rāmakṛti* (143 c-145)
(i) *Kolāhalā* (143 c-144 b)
(ii) *Rāmakṛti* (144 c-145)
9. *Chevāṭī* and *Vallātā* (146-148 b)
(i) *Chevāṭī* (146, 147 b)
(ii) *Vallātā* (147 c, 148 b)
10. *Śuddhapañcama* and its offshoots (148 c-155)
(i) *Śuddhapañcama* (148 c-150)
(ii) *Dākṣiṇātyā* (151, 152 a)
(iii) *Āndhālikā* (152 b-153)
(iv) *Malhāri* (154)
(v) *Malhāra* (155)
11. The *Upāṅga-s* of *Gauḍa* (156-158)
(i) *Karṇāṭagauḍa* (156 a b)
(ii) *Deśavālagauḍa* (156 c d)
(iii) *Turuṣkagauḍa* (157)
(iv) *Drāviḍagauḍa* (158)
(ix) The current well-known *rāga-s* 159-169
1. *Śrīrāga* (159, 160 b)
2. *Prathama-baṅgāla* (160 c, 161 b)
3. *Dvitiya-baṅgāla* (161 c, 162 b)
4. *Madhyamaṣāḍava* (162 c, 163 b)
5. *Śuddhabhairava* (163 c, 164 b)
6. *Megharāga* (164 c, 165 b)
7. *Somarāga* (165 c, 166 b)
8. *Prathama-kāmoda* (166 c, 167 b)
9. *Dvitiya-kāmoda* (167 c, 168 b)
10. *Āmrapañcama* (168 c, 169)

(x) Miscellaneous *Bhāṣāṅga-s* 170-187
1. *Kaiśikī* (170, 171)
2. *Saurāṣṭrī* (172-174 b)
(i) *Prathama-saurāṣṭrī* (172, 173 b)
(ii) *Dvitīya-saurāṣṭrī* (173 c, 174 b)
3. *Lalitā* (174 c-177 b)
(i) *Prathama-lalitā* (174 c, 175)
(ii) *Dvitīya-lalitā* (176, 177 b)
4. *Saindhavī* (177 c-182)
(i) *Prathama-saindhavī* (177 c, 178)
(ii) *Dvitīya-saindhavī* (179, 180 b)
(iii) *Tṛtīya-saindhavī* (180 c, 181)
(iv) *Caturtha-saindhavī* (182)
5. *Gauḍī* (183-185)
(i) *Prathama-gauḍī* (183, 184 b)
(ii) *Dvitīya-gauḍī* (184 c, 185)
6. *Trāvaṇī* (186, 187)
7. *Harṣapurī* (188)
8. *Bhammāṇī* (189)
(xi) *Ṭakkakaiśika*, *Mālavā* and *Drāviḍī* 190-194
(i) *Ṭakkakaiśika* (190-192)
(ii) *Mālavā* (*bhāṣā*) (193)
(iii) *Drāviḍī* (*vibhāṣā*) (194)

CHAPTER III
Miscellaneous Topics
(*Prakīrṇakādhyāya*)

(i) Author's announcement of the subject 1
(ii) The definition and classification of *Vāggeyakāra* 2-12 b
(iii) The definition of *gāndharva* and *svarādi* 12 c, 13 b
(iv) The definition and classification of vocalists 13 c-24
(a) The best singer (13 c-18 b)
(b) The average singer (18 c d)
(c) The bad singer (19 a b)
(d) Five types of singers (19 c-22 b)
(e) Threefold singers (22 c, 23)
(f) Songstresses (24)
(v) The censured singers 25-38
(vi) Kinds of voice 39-67
(a) The fourfold voice (39-45)
(b) The four varieties of *miśra* (46-66 b)
(i) The varieties of double combine (50 c-60)

(ii) The varieties of triple combine (61-66 b)
(c) Conclusion (66 c-67)
(vii) Excellences of voice 68-77
(viii) The blemishes of voice 78-81
(ix) *Śārīra* (Gifted voice) 82-86
(a) The definition of *śārīra* (82)
(b) The excellences of *śārīra* (83, 84 b)
(c) The blemishes of *śārīra* (84 c, 85)
(d) Means of attaining the gifted voice (86)
(x) The definition and varieties of *gamaka* 87-97 b
(xi) The definition and varieties of *sthāya* 97 c-189 b
(a) Definition and enumeration (97 c-112 b)
(b) The well-known (*prasiddha*) *sthāya-s* (112 c-151)
(i) The distinctly defined *sthāya-s* (112 c-127)
(ii) The indistinctly defined *sthāya-s* (128-151)
(c) The obscure (*aprasiddha*) *sthāya-s* (152-176 b)
(i) The distinctly defined *sthāya-s* (152-162 b)
(ii) The indistinctly defined obscure *sthāya-s* (162 c-176 b)
(d) The mixed (*miśra*) *sthāya-s* (176 c-189 b)
(xii) *Ālapti* and its types 189 c-202
(a) The definition of *ālapti* (189 c, 190 b)
(b) *Rāgālapti* (190 c, 196)
(c) *Rūpakālapti* (197-201)
(d) The general definition of *ālapti* (202)
(xiii) The ensemble (*vṛnda*) and its types 203-223
(a) The definition (203 a b)
(b) The (vocal) ensemble (203 c-209)
(c) The excellences of the vocal ensemble (210, 211 b)
(d) The *kutapa* (211 c-223)

CHAPTER IV
The *Prabandha-s*
(*Prabandhādhyāya*)

SECTION 1: Introductory

(i) The definition and classification of *gīta* 1-4 b
(ii) Classification of *gāna* 4 c-6
(iii) *Dhātu-s* (sections) 7-11

(iv) Classification of *prabandha-s* 12 a b
(v) The *aṅga-s* of *prabandha-s* 12 c-19 b
(vi) The *jāti-s* (families) of the *prabandha-s* 19 c-21 b
(vii) The classification of *prabandha-s* 21 c-23 b
(viii) The three classes of *prabandha-s* 23 c-33 b

SECTION 2: *Sūḍa-prabandha-s*
(i) The *elā-prabandha-s* 33 c-132 b
(a) General description and other features (33 c-65)
(b) *Gaṇa-elā* (66-94 b)
(c) *Mātrā-elā* (94 c-105 b)
(d) *Varṇa-elā* (105 c-113)
(e) *Deśa-elā* (114-132 b)
(ii) *Karaṇa-prabandha-s* 132 c-144
(iii) *Ḍheṅki-prabandha-s* 145-152 b
(iv) *Vartanī-prabandha* 152 c-154
(v) *Jhombaḍa-prabandha-s* 155-168
(vi) *Lambha-prabandha-s* 169-175 b
(vii) *Rāsaka-prabandha-s* 175 c-179
(viii) *Ekatāli-prabandha-s* 180, 181 b

SECTION 3: *Āli-prabandha-s*
(i) *Varṇa-prabandha* 181 c-182 b
(ii) *Varṇa-svara-prabandha* 182 c, 183
(iii) *Gadya-prabandha* 184-198
(iv) *Kaivāḍa-prabandha* 199, 200 b
(v) *Aṅkacāriṇi-prabandha* 200 c, 204 b
(vi) *Kanda-prabandha* 204 c-209 b
(vii) *Hayalīlā-prabandha* 209 c-212 b
(viii) *Gajalilā-prabandha* 212 c, 213 b
(ix) *Dvipadi-prabandha* 213 c-219 b
(x) *Cakravāla-prabandha* 219 c, 220
(xi) *Krauñcapada-prabandha* 221
(xii) *Svarārtha-prabandha* 222, 223
(xiii) *Dhvanikuṭṭanī-prabandha* 224, 225 b
(xiv) *Āryā-prabandha* 225 c-231 b
(xv) *Gāthā-prabandha* 231 c, 232 b
(xvi) *Dvipatha-prabandha* 232 c-241
(xvii) *Kalahaṁsa-prabandha* 242, 243
(xviii) *Toṭaka-prabandha* 244, 245
(xix) *Ghaṭa-prabandha* 246 a b
(xx) *Vṛtta-prabandha* 246 c-248 b
(xxi) *Mātṛkā-prabandha* 248 c-252
(xxii) *Rāgakadamba-prabandha* 253-256 b

(xxiii) *Pañcatāleśvara-prabandha* 256 c-264
(xxiv) *Tālārṇava-prabandha* 265 a b

SECTION 4: *Viprakīrṇa-prabandha-s*
(i) *Śrīraṅga-prabandha* 265 c d
(ii) *Śrīvilāsa-prabandha* 266 a b
(iii-v) *Pañcabhaṅgi, Pañcānana* and *Umātilaka prabandha-s* 266 c, 267
(vi) *Tripadī-prabandha* 268-270
(vii) *Catuṣpadī-prabandha* 271-272 b
(viii) *Ṣaṭpadī-prabandha* 272 c-274
(ix) *Vastu-prabandha* 275, 276
(x) *Vijaya-prabandha* 277
(xi) *Tripatha-prabandha* 278 a b
(xii) *Caturmukha-prabandha* 278 c, 279 b
(xiii) *Siṁhalīla-prabandha* 279 c, 280 b
(xiv) *Haṁsalīla-prabandha* 280 c d
(xv) *Daṇḍaka-prabandha* 281
(xvi) *Jhampaṭa-prabandha* 282 a b
(xvii) *Kanduka-prabandha* 282 c d
(xviii) *Tribhaṅgi-prabandha* 283, 284
(xix) *Haravilāsa-prabandha* 285 a b
(xx) *Śudarśana-prabandha* 285 c d
(xxi) *Śvarāṅka-prabandha* 286
(xxii) *Srīvardhana-prabandha* 287
(xxiii) *Harṣavardhana-prabandha* 288 a b
(xxiv) *Vadana-prabandha* 288 c, 289
(xxv) *Caccarī-prabandha* 290-292 b
(xxvi) *Caryā-parbandha* 292 c-294
(xxvii) *Paddhaḍi-prabandha* 295
(xxviii) *Rāhaḍi-prabandha* 296
(xxix) *Vīraśri-prabandha* 297 a b
(xxx) *Maṅgalācāra-prabandha* 297 c, 298 b
(xxxi) *Dhavala-prabandha* 298 c-303 b
(xxxii) *Maṅgala-prabandha* 303 c-304 b
(xxxiii) *Ovī-prabandha* 304 c-306
(xxxiv) *Lolī-prabandha* 307
(xxxv) *Ḍhollari-prabandha* 308
(xxxvi) *Dantī-prabandha* 309

SECTION 5: *Sālagasūḍa-prabandha-s*
Introductory 311-314
(i) *Dhruva-prabandha* 315-332 b
(ii) *Maṇṭha-prabandha* 332 c-338 b

(iii) *Pratimaṇṭha-prabandha* 338 c-343 b
(iv) *Niḥsāruka-prabandha* 343 c-347
(v) *Aḍḍatāla-prabandha* 348-352 b
(vi) *Rāsaka-prabandha* 352 c-356 b
(vii) *Ekatāli-prabandha* 356 c-361 b

SECTION 6: Criteria of Critical Evaluation of *Prabandha-s*
(a) Critical classification of *Rūpaka* 361 c-373
(i) *Uttama-rūpaka-s* (361 c-365)
(ii) *Madhyama-rūpaka* (366)
(iii) *Adhama-rūpaka* (367 a b)
(iv) Varieties of *Madhyama-rūpaka* (367 c-371)
(v) Varieties of *Adhama-rūpaka* (372, 373)
(b) The Excellences and blemishes of song (*gita*) 374-380
(i) The excellences of song (374-379 b)
(ii) The blemishes of melody (379 c-380)

Chapter II

The Discernment of Rāga-s

द्वितीयो रागविवेकाध्यायः

ग्रामरागोपरागरागभाषाविभाषान्तरभाषाविवेकाख्यं प्रथमं प्रकरणम्

(i) ग्रन्थकृत्प्रतिज्ञा

अथ ग्रन्थेन संक्षिप्तप्रसन्नपदपङ्क्तिना ।
निःशङ्को निखिलं रागविवेकं रचयत्यमुम् ॥१॥

SECTION 1

The discernment of *grāma-rāga-s, uparāga-s, rāga-s, bhāṣā-s, vibhāṣā-s* and *antara-bhāṣā-s :*

(i) Announcement of the subject-matter : 1

Śārṅgadeva,[1] now, proposes to deal[2] comprehensively[3] with the discernment[4] of *rāga-s*, composing in a succinct and lucid style.[5] (1)

Comments

In the first chapter the author has dealt with all those factors of tonal phenomenon that go to constitute music, and also with the primary forms of melody. the melodic types (*jāti-s*) and the rules and regulations of *jāti*-songs. Now, the author proposes to deal with the melodic forms that came into being subsequent to the *jāti-gāna*, and which are generally considered to be derived from it. The chapter is aptly entitled *rāga-viveka-adhyāya*, i.e. the discernment of *rāga-s*. It cannot be definitely asserted that *rāga-s* or the melodic forms signified by the term *rāga* were known to Bharata, though such a possibility cannot, on the other hand, be ruled out abso-

[1]*Niḥśaṅka* of the text meaning 'free from doubts' is an appellation of the author.

[2]*Racayati* of the text literally means 'composes,' but in this context it means 'is going to compose'. It has been rendered as 'proposes to deal with' in view of the fact that he is making an announcement (*pratijñā*) of the subject-matter of this chapter.

[3]*Nikhilam* of the text literally means, 'entirely,' without a part (undiscussed).

[4]*Raga-viveka* literally means 'the discernment of *rāga-s*' but as pointed out by 'S', it implies not only the classification but also the specific characterisation of different *rāga-s*.

[5]The phrase '*Saṅkṣipta-prasanna-pada-paṅktinā*' has been rendered as 'in a succinct and lucid style.' *Pada* stands for a word and *paṅkti* literally means a line, i.e. a sentence.

lutely. The word *rāga* is used by Bharata in its general connotation of emotional colour, or aesthetic enjoyment, or pleasure (*rakti*) and in the compound *grāma-rāga* at certain places. The word *rāga* is used by Mataṅga for the first time in a technical sense. He as quoted by 'S', defines *rāga*: "That particular sound (formation) which is embellished by musical tones and the movement of tonal patterns and is (thereby) delightful to the people's minds, is called *rāga* by the wise."[1] He derives the word *rāga* from the root *rañj*, 'to colour' and brings out the significance of this derivation grammatically, as well as by usage.[2] 'K' points out that, though the word *rāga* can be derived grammatically as shown above, yet it seems to have acquired a different meaning in usage, such as when one says, "I don't like this or that *rāga*."

Rāga, as such, implies a particular melodic configuration, and not merely '*rakti*,' its literal meaning. That is why Mataṅga says: "The particular form of the traditional technique of *rāga* which is not recorded by Bharata and others (following him) is demonstrated by us by the description of the *lakṣya* (characterised music) and its *lakṣaṇa* (characteristic features).[3]

This shows that the technique of *rāga* was being evolved in the tradition since the time of Bharata and had acquired a definite shape and was prevalent sometime before Mataṅga.

Discernment of *rāga-s* implies the classification, differentiation and the definition of tenfold *rāga-s* viz. *grāmarāga-s, uparāga-s, rāga-s, bhāṣā-s, vibhāṣā-s, antara-bhāṣā-s, rāgāṅga-s, bhāṣāṅga-s, kriyāṅga-s* and *upāṅga-s*, 'K' interprets *rāga-viveka* as the relative differentiation of the ten types of *rāga-s*, while 'S' primarily defines it as a classification of *rāga-s* including their characterisation and definition as a secondary meaning. Thus, 'S' thinks that the author proposes to deal with the entire subject-matter concerning the study of the sum and substance of *rāga-s*.

The author explicitly proposes to deal with the subject of *rāga-s* quite comprehensively, succinctly and lucidly. This statement merits a few observations. 'K' interprets that Śārṅgadeva proposes to make a succinct and lucid presentation of the subject-matter that is expounded in an extended style by Mataṅga and other ancient teachers. This leads to the inference that Śārṅgadeva undertakes not only to compile the extant literature of his times on the subject in a systematic and abridged form but, also

[1]योऽसौ ध्वनिविशेषस्तु स्वरवर्णविभूषितः ।
रञ्जको जनचित्तानां स रागः कथितो बुधैः ॥ *S.R.*, II, p. 3.

[2]रञ्जनाज्जायते रागो व्युत्पत्तिः समुदाहृता ।
अश्वकर्णादिवद्रूढो यौगिको वापि वाचकः ।
योगरूढोऽथवा रागो ज्ञेयः पङ्कजशब्दवत् ॥ *Br.D.*, 283, 284.

[3]रागमार्गस्य यद्रूपं यन्नोक्तं भरतादिभिः ।
निरूप्यते तदस्माभिर्लक्ष्यलक्षणसंयुतम् ॥ *Br.D.*, 279.

intends to deal with it comprehensively, which shows that the earlier treatises on the subject were not considered adequate for its study in his times. In other words, the task of Śārṅgadeva has been twofold, viz. to compile the earlier literature on the subject in a systematic and abridged form, and to deal with the subject adequately so as to include the later developments in his work. This view is amply evidenced by the treatment of this chapter, as it will be observed in due course.

(ii) पञ्चधा ग्रामरागाः

पञ्चधा ग्रामरागाः स्युः पञ्चगीतिसमाश्रयात् ।

(ii) The fivefold *grāma-rāga-s* : 2ab

The *grāma-rāga s* are five-fold as they conform to five *gīti-s*[1]. (2ab)

Comments

Grāma-rāga-s are related to the two *grāma-s* with the intervention of *jāti-s* only, and therefore are more closely affiliated to them as compared to the *bhāṣā-s* and the later *rāga-s*. Mataṅga raises the question as to why these *rāga-s* are related to *grāma-s* and are called *grāma-rāga-s*, and in reply quotes Bharata who says, "because the *grāma-rāga-s* are derived from *jāti-s*" (as quoted by 'K'). This statement however, is not to be found in any of the available recensions of N.S.

This classification of *grāma-rāga-s* is based on the five *gīti-s*. The author has already spoken of *gīti-s* (*S.R.*, I,8.14cd-16b) as based on *pada* (verbal text) and *tāla*. Presently he is talking of *gīti-s* that are based on tonal peculiarities, i.e. *svarāśrita-gīti*.

Bharata has spoken of the four *pada-gīti-s* viz. *māgadhī*, *ardhamāgadhī*, *sambhāvitā* and *pṛthulā*. However, *gīti-s* as associated with *rāga-s* are first mentioned by Mataṅga, and he describes seven *gīti-s* viz. *śuddhā*, *bhinnā*, *gauḍī*, *rāga-gīti*, *sādhāraṇī*, *bhāṣā* and *vibhāṣā*. Yāṣṭika has spoken of three *gīti-s* viz. *bhāṣā*, *vibhāṣā* and *antara-bhāṣā* only, while Śārdūla recognises *bhāṣā* as the only *gīti*. (see Mataṅga's *Bṛ.D.*, 285-90). Durgāśakti accepts five *gīti-s* viz. *śuddhā*, *bhinnā*, *gauḍī*, *vesarā* and *sādhāraṇī*.

Śārṅgadeva obviously accepts the views of Durgāśakti and this fact is noticed by 'S'. Among the seven *gīti-s* of Mataṅga, the last two viz. *bhāṣā* and *vibhāṣā* represent the derived varieties of *grāma-rāga-s*. For the purpose of classifying the *grāma-rāga-s* only the first five *gīti-s* have been used. Śārṅgadeva rationalises this confusion of categories by eliminating *bhāṣā* and *vibhāṣā* from the list of *gīti-s* and by accepting only five *gīti-s* into which the *grāma-rāga-s* are classified. Thus, the source *rāga-s* and their derived varieties have been put in different categories.

Gīti, in general, signifies the act of singing, i.e. the tonal, rhythmic and

[1]These are known as *rāga-gīti-s* in contrast with the *pada-gīti-s*.

the verbal structure of a musical piece; the specific distinguishing features of the five melodic *gīti-s* are described presently (2cd-7).

(iii) पञ्च गीतयः

गीतयः पञ्च शुद्धा च भिन्ना गौडी च वेसरा ॥२॥ सा.
साधारणीति, शुद्धा स्यादवक्रैर्ललितैः स्वरैः ।
भिन्ना वक्रैः स्वरैः सूक्ष्मैर्मधुरैर्गमकैर्युता ॥३॥
गाढैस्त्रिस्थानगमकैरोहाटीललितैः स्वरैः ।
अखण्डितस्थितिः स्थानत्रये गौडी मता सताम् ॥४॥
ओहाटी कम्पितैर्मन्द्रैर्मृदुद्रुततरैः स्वरैः ।
हकारौकारयोगेन हृन्यस्ते चिबुके भवेत् ॥५॥
वेगवद्भिः स्वरैर्वर्णचतुष्केऽप्यतिरक्तितः ।
वेगस्वरा रागगीतिर्वेसरा चोच्यते बुधैः ॥६॥
चतुर्गीतिगतं लक्ष्म श्रिता साधारणी मता ।
शुद्धादिगीतियोगेन रागाः शुद्धादयो मताः ॥७॥

(iii) The five *gīti-s* : 2c-7

There are five *gīti-s* viz. *śuddhā*, *bhinnā*, *gauḍī*, *vesarā* and *sādhāraṇī* (2c-3a)

Śuddhā is (characterised) by captivating[1] and straight[2] notes. *Bhinnā* is (marked) by fine[3] and curved[4] notes taken along with sweet sounding *gamaka-s.*[5] *Gauḍī* is considered by the wise to have an unbroken stay[6] among the three registers by ohatiased[7] captivating notes and closely knit *gamaka-s* of the three registers. (3b-4)

Ohāṭī is (produced) by low, soft and quick[8] notes taken with *kampita*[9] *gamaka-s* in (a posture obtained in) an effort to (pronounce) the letter *ha*

[1] *Lalita* is interpreted by 'K' as *manohara* (literally that which steals the mind) i.e. captivating attention. Nijenhuis identifies it with the *alaṅkāra* of the same name. cf. *Dattilam*, p. 179. Eng. tr.

[2] *Avakra* literally means 'not twisted or curved' i.e. even or straight. 'S' interprets it as *sarala* (simple).

[3] *Sūkṣma* of the text.

[4] *Vakra* is literally twisted or curved.

[5] *Gamaka* is defined by the author as a 'shake' of the note that is pleasing to listeners' minds.

[6] *Sthiti* is literally 'stay' indicating, prevalence. In this context it shows that *gauḍi* prevails in all the three registers.

[7] That is made captivating through the use of *ohāṭi*.

[8] *Drutatara* literally means 'faster' which implies a comparison with other *gīti-s*.

[9] *Kampita* is one of the *gamaka-s*. to be explained in chapter III.

in combination with the letter *au* by keeping the chin over the chest.[1] (5)

Vegasvarā,[2] also called *rāga*[3] or *vesarā* by the learned, employs notes in quick succession[4] so as to be delightful in all the four *varṇa-s*,[5] while *Sādhāraṇī*[6] is considered to be based on the characteristic features of all the four *gīti-s*. (6-7b)

Rāga-s are considered to be *śuddha*[7] and so on accordingly as they are associated with *śuddhā* and other *gīti-s*. (7cd)

[1]This signifies the posture obtained in an effort to sing the syllable *auha*.

[2]*Vegasvarā* literally means 'one having the notes in quick succession', so that its very name reflects its significance.

[3]The other name given to this *gīti* is *rāga*, which too is literally significant as 'S' derives it from the word *rāga* in its literal meaning of aesthetic colour or delight. He says : "Being extremely delightful among the four *varṇa-s* (patterns of tonal movement) it is called *rāga*. And he quotes Kāśyapa in support of his interpretation: "The *rāga* that is delightful (lit. beautiful) in the four *varṇa-s* and that is seen among them in its entirety is, by that reason known as *rāga* (*gīti*). That is (also) known as *vesarā* because the notes in it move swiftly"*. Thus, the name *vesarā* too is literally significant. The word *vesarā* in its Prākṛta connotation denotes a class name. Literally it signifies 'mule', the crossbreed of horse and donkey. In the terminology of architecture *vesara* (as derived from *dvi+aśra*) signifies the cave-like structure with two corners (or angles) only, that progressively widens as it goes deeper from a narrow mouth having an arch-like curved formation over a flat base. This may be suggestive of the melodic form assumed by this *gīti*. Technically, in the context of the above observations it may be inferred that Śārṅgadeva has adopted the name *vega-svarā* for *vesarā* on the basis of Kāśyapa's definition. It is gathered from the Dhrupad singers of repute that even to this day the dhrupads that are sung in *vesarā gīti*, begin with quick tempo and progress into middle and then into the slow tempo. Such a procedure seems to provide a common concept signified by the name *vesarā* in music and architecture. However, 'K' offers a slightly different interpretation. He says, "*Rāga gīti* is that (or is so called) which functions as the foundation (literally support) of rāga." (*Rāgā-śraya-bhūtā gīti*). But since this entire classification pertains to *svarāśrita gīti-s*, the interpretation of 'S' seems to be much more consistent.

*चतुर्णामपि वर्णानां यो रागः शोभनो भवेत् ।
स सर्वो दृश्यते येषु तेन रागा इति स्मृताः ।
स्वराः सरन्ति यद्वेगात्तस्माद्वेसरका स्मृता ॥

[4]The sense of 'succession' is taken by implication,

[5]Namely *Sthāyī*, *ārohī*, *avarohī* and *sañcārī*.

[6]*Sādhāraṇī* literally means general or the *gīti* that unreservedly partakes of the characteristic features of all the previous four types of *gīti*. So the name by itself signifies its character. Mataṅga defines it as under (as quoted by 'S') :**

"*Sādhāraṇī*, which is known as taking resort to all the *gīti-s* is composed with notes that are straight, lilting somewhat subtle and subtler, sweet sounding, a little bit swift, soft and captivating and are arranged with fine and smooth intonations in practice."

**ऋजुभिर्ललितैः किंचित् सूक्ष्मात्सूक्ष्मैश्च सुश्रवैः ।
ईषद् द्रुतैश्च कर्तव्या मृदुभिर्ललितैस्तथा ॥
प्रयोगे मसृणैः सूक्ष्मैः काकुभिश्च सुयोजितैः ।
एवं साधारणी ज्ञेया सर्वगीतिसमाश्रया ॥

[7]As the *śuddhā* and other *gīti-s* are *svarāśrita-gīti-s* the *rāga-s* that are associated

Comments

'K' observes that the name *ohāṭī* is derived semantically to indicate 'that which wallows between *au* and *ha* (*aukāra-hakārau-aṭati*)'. He further points out that the syllable *auha* (*au+ha*) is not literally to be sung. What is implied is that, by adopting the posture obtained in an effort to pronounce softly (i.e. in the low register) the syllable *auha* viz. by keeping the chin over the chest when low, soft and quick notes are taken with *kampita gamaka-s*, *ohāṭī* is produced. 'The notes of *gauḍī* are embellished by *ohāṭī*,' would therefore mean that they are sung with the particular effort called *ohāṭī*. Thus, *ohāṭī* is the name of a technique of producing notes.

(iv) ग्रामरागोद्देशः

षड्जग्रामसमुत्पन्नः शुद्धकैशिकमध्यमः ।
शुद्धसाधारितः षड्जग्रामो, ग्रामे तु मध्यमे ॥८॥
पञ्चमो मध्यमग्रामः षाडवः शुद्धकैशिकः ।
शुद्धाः सप्तेति, भिन्नाः स्युः पञ्च कैशिकमध्यमः ॥९॥
भिन्नषड्जश्च षड्जाख्ये, मध्यमे तानकैशिकौ ।
भिन्नपञ्चम इत्येते, गौडकैशिकमध्यमः ॥१०॥
गौडपञ्चमकः षड्जे मध्यमे गौडकैशिकः ।
इति गौडास्त्रयः, षड्जे टक्कवेसरषाडवौ ॥११॥
ससौवीरौ, मध्यमे तु बोट्टमालवकैशिकौ ।
मालवः पञ्चमान्तोऽथ द्विग्रामष्टक्ककैशिकः ॥१२॥
हिन्दोलोऽष्टौ वेसरास्ते, सप्त साधारणास्ततः ।
षड्जे स्याद्रूपसाधारः शको भम्माणपञ्चमः ॥१३॥
मध्यमे नर्तगान्धारपञ्चमौ षड्जकैशिकः ।
द्विग्रामः ककुभस्त्रिंशद् ग्रामरागा अमी मताः ॥१४॥

(iv) *The grāma-rāga-s* : 8-14

Śuddha-kaiśika-madhyama, *śuddha-sādhārita* and *ṣaḍja-grāma* as derived from the *ṣaḍja-grāma*[1], and *pañcama*, *madhyama-grāma*, *ṣāḍava* and *śuddha-kaiśika* as derived from the *madhyma-grāma* constitute the seven *śuddha*[1]

with them are qualified by them as *śuddha*, *bhinna*, *gauḍi(a)*, *vesara* and *sādhāraṇa* as will be seen subsequently. The *māgadhī* and other *gīti-s* spoken of in Section eight of chapter I are primarily based on *pada* (verbal structure) and *tāla*. These are however based on the tonal structure of and the style of rendering the *rāga*.

[1]The *grāma-rāga-s* are derived from the *jāti-s* which are necessarily associated with the *grāma-s*; therefore, they too are associated with them (*grāma-s*), and it seems, this is one of the factors that gives them the prime place among the derived *rāga-s*. Indeed the *jāti-s* and the *grāma-rāga-s* are very closely associated in their melodic form as well as in history.

(pure) *grāma-rāga-s*. (8-9c)

Bhinna-s are five viz. *Kaiśika-madhyama* and *bhinna-ṣaḍja* in the *ṣaḍja-grāma*, and *tāna, kaiśika* and *bhinna-pañcama* in the *madhyama-grāma*. (9c-10c)

Gauḍa-s are three viz. *gauḍa-kaiśika-madhyama* and *gauḍa-pañcama* in the *ṣaḍja-grāma* and *gauḍa-kaiśika* in the *madhyama-grāma*. (10d-11c)

There are eight *vesara-s* viz. *ṭakka, vesara-ṣāḍava* and *sauvīra* in the *ṣaḍja-grāma, boṭṭa, mālavā-kaiśika* and *mālava-pañcama* in the *madhyama-grāma*, and *ṭakka-kaiśika* and *hiṇḍola* pertaining to both the *grāma-s*.[1] (11d-13a)

Then, there are seven *sādhāraṇa-s* viz. *rūpa-sādhāra, śaka* and *bhammāṇa-pañcama* in the *ṣaḍja-grāma, narta, gāndhāra-pañcama* and *ṣaḍja-kaiśika* in the *madhyama-grāma* and *kakubha* pertaining to both the *grāma-s*. (13b-14c)

These thirty[2] (*rāga-s*) are considered to be the *grāma-rāga-s*.[3] (14d)

Comments

'K' quotes Mataṅga[4] and gives the definitions of the five types of *rāga-s* in his (Mataṅga's) words as under :

(i) The *śuddha rāga-s* :

"The *rāga-s* that proceed in accordance with their own *Jāti*, that do not look to others and manifest their own *Jāti* are known as *śuddha-s*."

(ii) The *bhinna rāga-s* :

"*Bhinna* (literally differentiated) is so called because it is differentiated with reference to four (factors) viz. *śruti, jāti*, purity and tone (*svara*)".

He further explains how it is differentiated with reference to each of these four factors which may be referred to in his commentary on *śuddha-sādhārita* (following its *Ākṣipṭikā*, pp. 25-26).

(iii) The *gauḍa rāga-s* :

"Being related to the aforesaid *gauḍi gīti*, (such *rāga-s*) are called *gauḍa-s*.

[1]Since these two belong to *jāti-s* associated with both the *grāma-s*, they have been so described, explains 'K'. There are other similar instances following.

[2]Seven *śuddha-s*, five *bhinna-s*, three *gauḍa-s*, eight *vesara-s* and seven *sādhāraṇa-s* (7+5+3+8+7=30) make a total of thirty *rāga-s* in all.

[3]'K' explains why the name *grāma-rāga* is applied to these *rāga-s* and on the authority of Mataṅga he assigns two reasons enunciated by Bharata viz. (i) "all that is sung in the contemporary and regional music subsists in the *jāti-s* and (ii) because the *grāma-rāga-s* are derived from *jāti-s*." It may, however, be noted that no such reference is found in the available recensions of Nāṭyaśāstra. cf. *Dattilam*, 97ab for the corroboration of (i) above.

He further points out the immediate proximity of the *grāma-rāga-s* to *jāti-s* with reference to the other derived melodic forms such as *bhāṣā-s* and *antarabhāṣā-s* as an additional reason lending significance to the name *grāma-rāga*.

[4]See 'K's commentary on verses 23-26 of Sec. 2.

(iv) The *vesara rāga-s :*

"Since notes move rapidly (in these *rāga-s,* they are called *vesara-s.*"

(v) The *sādhāraṇa rāga-s* :

"I (am to) describe the seven *sādhāraṇa rāga-s* that are other than the *śuddha-s, bhinna-s, gauḍa-s,* and the *vesara-s* and yet are the combination of these all."

(v) उपरागोद्देश:

अष्टोपरागास्तिलकः शकादिष्टक्कसैन्धवः ।
कोकिलापञ्चमो रेवगुप्तः पञ्चमषाडवः ॥१५॥
भावनापञ्चमो नागगान्धारो नागपञ्चमः ।

(v) The *Uparāga-s* : 15-16b

There are eight *Uparāga-s*[1] viz. *Śakatilaka, ṭakka-saindhava, kokilā-pañcama, revagupta, pañcama-ṣāḍava, bhāvanāpañcama, nāgagāndhāra and nāgapañcama.* (15-16b)

(vi) रागोद्देश:

श्रीरागनट्टौ बङ्गालौ भासमध्यमषाडवौ ॥१६॥
रक्तहंसः कोल्लहासः प्रसवो भैरवो ध्वनिः ।
मेघरागः सोमरागः कामोदौ चाम्रपञ्चमः ॥१७॥
स्यातां कन्दर्पदेशाख्यौ ककुभान्तश्च कैशिकः ।
नट्टनारायणश्चेति रागा विंशतिरीरिताः ॥१८॥

(vi) The *rāga-s* : 16c-18

Twenty *rāga-s* are known to be there viz. *Śrī, naṭṭa, baṅgāla* of two varieties, *bhāsa madhyama, ṣāḍava, rakta haṁsa, kohlahāsa, prasava, bhairava, dhvani, megha, soma,* two varieties of *kāmoda, āmra-pañcama kandarpa, deśākhya, kaiśika-kakubha* and *naṭṭa-nārāyaṇa.* (16c-18)

(vii) भाषाजनकरागोद्देश:

सौवीरः ककुभष्टक्कः पञ्चमो भिन्नपञ्चमः ।
टक्ककैशिकहिन्दोलबोट्टमालवकैशिकाः ॥१९॥
गान्धारपञ्चमो भिन्नषड्जो वेसरषाडवः ।
मालवः पञ्चमान्तश्च तानः पञ्चमषाडवः ॥२०॥
भाषाणां जनकाः पञ्चदशैते याष्टिकोदिताः ।

[1] *Upa-rāga* literally implies approximate (*grāma*) *rāga,* 'K' says, the *upa-rāga-s* nearly approach the *grāma-rāga-s* and that is why they are so-called.

(vii) The *bhāṣā-janaka* (parent) *rāga-s* : 19-21b

There are fifteen *rāga-s* declared by Yāṣṭika[1] to be the progenitors[2] of *bhāṣa-s* viz. *sauvīra, kakubha, ṭakka, pañcama, Bhinna-pañcama, ṭakka-kaiśika, hiṇḍola, boṭṭa, mālava-kaiśika, gāndhāra-pañcama, bhinna-ṣaḍja, vesara-ṣāḍava, mālava-pañcama, tāna* and *pañcama-ṣāḍava.* (19-21b)

(viii) भाषाविभाषाऽन्तरभाषोद्देशः

भाषाश्चतस्रः सौवीरे सौवीरी वेगमध्यमा ॥२१॥
साधारिता च गान्धारी, ककुभे भिन्नपञ्चमी ।
काम्भोजी मध्यमग्रामा रगन्ती मधुरी तथा ॥२२॥
शकमिश्रेति षट्, तिस्रो विभाषा भोगवर्धनी ।
आभीरिका मधुकरी, तथैकान्तरभाषिका ॥२३॥
शालवाहनिका, टक्के त्रवणा त्रवणोद्भवा ।
वैरञ्जी मध्यमग्रामदेहा मालववेसरी ॥२४॥
छेवाटी सैन्धवी कोलाहला पञ्चमलक्षिता ।
सौराष्ट्री पञ्चमी वेगरञ्जी गान्धारपञ्चमी ॥२५॥
मालवी तानवलिता ललिता रविचन्द्रिका ।
तानाम्बाहेरिका दोह्या वेसरीत्येकविंशतिः ॥२६॥
भाषाः स्युरथ देवारवर्धन्यान्ध्री च गुर्जरी ।
भावनीति विभाषाः स्युश्चतस्रः ; पञ्चमे पुनः ॥२७॥
कैशिकी त्रावणी तानोद्भवाभीरी च गुर्जरी ।
सैन्धवी दाक्षिणात्यान्ध्री माङ्गली भावनी दश ॥२८॥
इति भाषा, विभाषे द्वे भम्माण्यान्धालिके ततः ।
चतस्रः पञ्चमे भिन्ने भाषा धैवतभूषिता ॥२९॥
शुद्धभिन्ना च वाराटी विशालेत्यथ कौशली ।
विभाषा ; मालवाभिन्नवलिते टक्ककैशिके ॥३०॥
भाषे द्वे, द्राविडीत्येका विभाषा ; प्रेङ्खके नव ।
भाषाः स्युर्वेसरी चूतमञ्जरी षड्जमध्यमा ॥३१॥

[1]According to 'K' Mataṅga speaks of six such *grāmarāga-s*, Kāśyapa of twelve and Śārdūla of four only. Since the school of Yāṣṭika comprehends all these schools, with its fifteen *grāma-rāga-s*, the author seems to have adopted his views (with one subsequent addition of his own) which, incidentally happens to be the most comprehensive one. It may however be noted that *pañcama-sādava* is listed by Śārṅagadeva as an *uparāga*. See note no. 3 on verse 41b-42b.

[2]*Bhāṣā* (lit. language) is explained by 'K' as the manner (or type) of *ālāpa* of the *grāmarāga-s*. *Vibhāṣā* and *antarabhāṣā* are also to be understood in this sense.

मधुरी भिन्नपौराली गौडी मालववेसरी ।
छेवाटी पिञ्जरीत्येका बोट्टे भाषा तु माङ्गली ॥३२॥
बाङ्गाली माङ्गली हर्षपुरी मालववेसरी ।
खञ्जनी गुर्जरी गौडी पौराली चार्धवेसरी ॥३३॥
शुद्धा मालवरूपा च सैन्धव्याभीरिकेत्यमूः ।
भाषास्त्रयोदश ज्ञेया विज्ञैर्मालवकैशिके ॥३४॥
विभाषे द्वे तु काम्भोजी तद्वद्देवारवर्धनी ।
गान्धारपञ्चमे भाषा गान्धारी ; भिन्नषड्जके ॥३५॥
गान्धारवल्ली कच्छेल्ली स्वरवल्ली निषादिनी ।
त्रवणा मध्यमा शुद्धा दाक्षिणात्या पुलिन्दका ॥३६॥
तुम्बुरा षड्जभाषा च कालिन्दी ललिता ततः ।
श्रीकण्ठिका च बाङ्गाली गान्धारी सैन्धवीत्यमूः ॥३७॥
भाषाः सप्तदश ज्ञेयाश्चतस्रस्तु विभाषिकाः ।
पौराली मालवा कालिन्द्यपि देवारवर्धनी ॥३८॥
वेसरे षाडवे भाषे द्वे नाद्या बाह्यषाडवा ।
विभाषे पार्वती श्रीकण्ठ्यथ मालवपञ्चमे ॥३९॥
भाषास्तिस्रो वेदवती भावनी च विभावनी ।
ताने तानोद्भवा भाषा ; भाषा पञ्चमषाडवे ॥४०॥
पोता ; भाषां शकामेके रेवगुप्तं विदुर्विदः ।
विभाषा पल्लवी, भासवलिता किरणावली ॥४१॥
शकाद्या वलितेत्येतास्तिस्रस्त्वन्तरभाषिकाः ।
चतस्रोऽनुक्तजनका बृहद्देश्यामिमाः स्मृताः ॥४२॥
एवं षण्णवतिर्भाषा विभाषा विंशतिस्तथा ।
चतस्रोऽन्तरभाषाः स्युः शार्ङ्गदेवस्य संमताः ॥४३॥

(viii) The *bhāṣā-s*, *vibhāṣā-s* and *antara-bhāṣā-s* : 21c-43

There are four *bhāṣā-s*[1] of *sauvīra* viz. *sauvīri*, *vegamadhyamā*, *sādhārītā* and *gāndhārī*. (21c-22a)

In *kakubha* there are six *bhāsā-s viz. bhinna-pañcamī*, *Kāmbhojī*, *madhya-*

[1]It has already been said that the *Bhāsā's* represent different forms of *ālāpa* of the *Bhāsā-janaka* (parent) *rāga-s*. Thus, as observed by 'S', they manifest the essence of the *rāga* (*rāgatva*) in different ways, so that they are not essentially different from their parent *rāga-s*.

magrāmā, ragantī, madhurī and *śaka-miśrā*, three *vibhāṣā-s* viz. *bhoga-vardhanī, ābhīrikā*[1] and *madhukarī* and one *antarabhāṣā* (named) *Śālavāhanī* (22b-24a)

Ṭakka has twentyone *bhāṣā-s* viz. *travaṇā, travaṇ-o-dbhavā, vairañjī, madhyama-grāma-dehā, mālava-vesarī, chevāṭī, saindhavī, kolāhalā, pañcama-lakṣitā, saurāṣṭrī, pañcamī, vegarañjī, gāndhāra-pañcamī, mālavī, tāna-valitā, lalitā, ravi-candrikā, tānā, ambāherī dohyā* and *vesarī*, and four *vibhāṣā-s* viz. *devāra-vardhanī, āndhrī, Gurjarī*, and *bhāvanī*. (24b-27c)

Pañcama has ten *bhāṣā-s* viz., *Kaiśikī, trāvaṇī, tān-o-dbhavā, ābhīrī, gurjarī, saindhavī, dākṣiṇātyā, āndhrī, māṅgalī* and *bhāvanī*, and two *vibhāṣā-s* viz. *bhammāṇī* and *āndhālī*. (27d-29b).

Bhinna-pañcama has four *bhāṣā-s* viz. *dhaivatā-bhūṣitā, Śuddha-bhinnā, vārāṭī* and *viśālā*, and one *vibhāṣā* (called) *Kauśalī*. (29c-30c)

Ṭakka-kaiśika has two *bhāṣā-s* viz., *mālavā* and *bhinna-valitā*, and one *vibhāṣā* (called) *drāviḍī*. (30d-31b).

Preṅkhaka[2] has nine *bhāṣā-s* viz. *vesarī, cūta-mañjarī, ṣaḍja-madhyamā, madhurī, bhinna-paurālī, gauḍī, mālava-vesarī, chevāṭī*, and *piñjarī*. (31b-32c)

Boṭṭa has only one *bhāṣā* viz. *māṅgalī*. (32d).

Bāṅgālī, māṅgalī, harṣapurī, mālava-vesarī, khañjanī, gurjarī, gauḍī, paurālī, ardhavesarī, śuddhā, mālava-rūpā, saindhavī and *ābhīrī*—these are the thirteen *bhāṣā-s* of *mālava-kaiśika* as known to the experts. It has two *vibhāṣā s* viz. *kāmbhojī* and likewise *devāra-vardhanī*. (33-35b).

Gāndhārī is the only *bhāṣā* of *gāndhāra-pañcama*. (35cd).

Seventeen *bhāṣā-s* are known to be in *bhinna-ṣaḍja* viz. *gāndhāra-vallī, kacchelī, svara-vallī, niṣādinī, travaṇā, madhyamā, śuddhā, dākṣiṇātyā, pulindakā, tumburā, ṣaḍja-bhāṣā, kālindī, lalitā, Śrīkaṇṭhikā, bāṅgālī, gāndhārī* and *saindhavī*. It has four *vibhāṣā-s* as well viz. *Paurālī, mālavā, kālindī* and *devāra-vardhanī*. (35d-38)

Vesara-ṣāḍava has two *bhāṣā-s* viz. *nādyā* and *bāhya-ṣāḍavā* and also two *vibhāṣā-s* viz. *Pārvatī* and *śrīkaṇṭhī*. (39a-39c).

Mālava-pañcama has three *bhāṣā-s*-viz. *vedavatī, bhāvanī* and *vibhāvanī*. (39d-40b)

Tāna has only *tān-o-dbhavā bhāṣā* and (similarly) *pañcama-ṣāḍava* has one viz. *potā*. (40c-41a).

In *Revagupta*[3] the experts know of one *bhāsā* viz. *sakā*, one *vibhāṣā, viz. pallavī* and three *antara-bhāṣā-s* viz. *bhāsavalitā, kiraṇāvalī* and *śaka-valitā*. (41b-42b)

Four of these are mentioned in the *Bṛhaddeṣī* without reference to their

[1]That is, *ābhīrī*.

[2]Another name for *hiṇḍola* according to 'K' and 'S'.

[3]Even though *revagupta* is not counted among the fifteen parent *rāga-s* enumerated according to the school of Yāṣṭika, it has been described by Śārṅgadeva as it gives rise to *śaka-bhāṣā*.

parent, *rāgā-s*.[1] Thus there are ninety-six *bhāṣā-s*, twenty *vibhāṣā-s* and four *antara-bhāṣā-s* as accepted by Śārṅgadeva.[2] (42c-43).

Parent Rāga-s

and their *bhāṣā-s*, *vibhāṣā s*, and *antara-bhāṣā-s*.

Sl. No.	Name of the parent *rāga*	No. of *bhāṣā-s*	No. of *vibhāṣā-s*	No. of *antara-bhāṣā-s*
1.	*Sauvīra*	4	—	—
2.	*Kakubha*	6	3	1
3.	*Ṭakka*	21	4	—
4.	*Pañcama*	10	2	—
5.	*Bhinna-pañcama*	4	1	—
6.	*Ṭakka-kaiśika*	2	1	—
7.	*Preṅkhaka* (*Hiṇḍola*)	9	—	—
8.	*Boṭṭa*	1	—	—
9.	*Mālava-kaiśika*	13	2	—
10.	*Gāndhāra-Pañcama*	1	—	—
11.	*Bhinna-ṣadja*	17	4	—
12.	*Vesara-ṣāḍava*	2	2	—
13.	*Mālava-Pañcama*	3	—	—
14.	*Tāna*	1	—	—
15.	*Pañcama-ṣāḍava*	1	—	—
16.	*Revagupta*	1	1	3
		96	20	4

(ix) भाषाभेदा:

भाषा मुख्या स्वराख्या च देशाख्या चोपरागजा ।
चतुर्विधा मतङ्गोक्ता, मुख्यानन्योपजीवनी ॥४४॥
स्वरदेशाख्यया ख्याता स्वराख्या देशजा क्रमात् ।
अन्योपरागजा ताभ्यो, याष्टिकेनोदिताः पुनः ॥४५॥
संकीर्णा देशजा मूला छायामात्रेति नामभिः ।
शुद्धाभीरी रगन्ती च त्रिधा मालववेसरी ॥४६॥
मुख्याः षडिति शेषाः स्युर्विज्ञेयाः स्फुटलक्षणाः ।
नामसाम्यं तु कासांचिद् भिन्नानामपि लक्ष्मतः ॥४७॥

[1] *Pallavi* and others enumerated by Mataṅga without being associated with any particular parent *rāga*.

[2] All these are respectively shown in the above chart.

(ix) The classification of *bhāṣā's* : 44-47

Bhāṣā-s are of four types as classified by Mataṅga viz. *mukhyā*, *svarākhyā*, *deśākhyā* and *uparāgajā*. *Mukhyā* is that which does not depend for its being on another,[1] *svarākhyā*[2] is named after a *svara* (tone), *deśākhyā*[3] is named after the province of its origin, while that which is different from these (three) is *uparāgajā*.[4] (44-45c)

Again, these (four types) according to Yāṣṭika, are called *saṅkīrṇā*, *deśajā*, *mūlā* and *chāyāmātrā*.[5] (45d-46b).

Mukhyā is sixfold viz. *śuddhā*, *ābhīrī*, *ragantī* and the three varieties of *mālava-vesarī*. The rest (of these) are well known with their distinct features. However, similarity of nomenclature is (observed) despite their different characteristic features. (46c-47).

Comments

Śārṅgadeva here adopts the classification of Mataṅga, even though he mentions Yāṣṭika's nomenclature as well. The *bhāṣā-s* probably were well known in his time so that he does not consider it necessary to dwell upon their details. It might be observed that *bhāṣā-s* of similar names have been enumerated as associated with different parent *rāga-s*. But the author makes it abundantly clear that they must not be confounded to be the same as they are different in their tonal structure.

[1]'K' elucidates that *mukhyā* is self-dependent in the sense that it has an independent origin with reference to tone and region, which is not the case with *svarākhyā* and *deśākhyā*.

[2]Such as *gāndhārī*, as pointed out by 'S'.

[3]Such as *āndhrī*.

[4]'S' does not read *anyo* with *tābhyo* and consequently interprets *tābhyo* quite differently. According to him the *uparāgajā* is born of any one of the first three.

[5]These four names correspond to the four names of Mataṅga.

रागाङ्गादिनिर्णयाख्यं द्वितीयं प्रकरणम्

(i) उपोद्घातः

अथ रागाङ्गभाषाङ्गक्रियाङ्गोपाङ्गनिर्णयम् ।
केषाञ्चिन्मतमाश्रित्य कुरुते सोढलात्मजः ॥१॥
रञ्जनाद्रागता भाषारागाङ्गादेरपीष्यते ।
देशीरागतया प्रोक्तं रागाङ्गादिचतुष्टयम् ॥२॥
प्रसिद्धा ग्रामरागाद्याः केचिद्देशीत्यपीरिताः ।
तत्र पूर्वप्रसिद्धानामुद्देशः क्रियतेऽधुना ॥३॥

SECTION 2

The identity of the *rāgāṅga s, the bhāṣāṅga's* the *kriyāṅga-s* and the *upāṅga-s.*

(i) *Introduction* : 1-3

Now, the son of Soḍhala (Śārṅgadeva) attempts to establish[1] the identity[2] of the *rāgāṅga-s*, the *bhāṣāṅga-s, the kriyāṅga s* and the *upāṅga s* on the basis of some[3] of the (extant) views. Delightfulness is the essence of *rāga*, and that obtains also among the *bhāṣā-s* and the *rāgāṅga-s*,[4] but these four viz. *rāgāṅga* etc. are described by way of *deśīrāga-s*. Some *grāmarāga-s* etc.[5] are also known as *deśī*. Hence, those that are known for a long time past[6] are to be dealt with in the first instance. (1-3)

[1]*Kurute* lit. means does or establishes, but it has been rendered as 'attempts to establish' in view of the fact that the author is making an announcement for writing or presenting this Section.

[2]*Nirṇayam* lit, means 'judgement' or 'decision', and by implication suggests that the author is going to establish the identity, or in other words, judge the different types of *deśi-rāga-s* and so he classifies them.

[3]'S' points out that, by implication the author is referring to the fact that such a classification is not to be based on Bharata, but on some other views.

[4]'S' infers from the use of etc. (*ādi*) that along with the *bhāṣā-s, vibhāṣā-s* and *antara-bhāṣā-s* are also implied.

[5]According to 'S' some of the *grāma-rāga-s* such as *pañcama, revagupta* and *naṭṭa-nārāyaṇa* etc. are also enumerated among the *deśi-rāga-s* as they do not strictly conform to the rules.

[6]The *deśi-rāga-s* are twofold viz. *pūrva-prasiddha*, i. e. known from ancient time and *adhunā-prasiddha*, well known in the present time, i.e. contemporary to Sārṅgadeva.

In the first Section of this chapter the author has dealt with the *grāma-rāga-s*, *rāga-s*, *uparāga-s* and their *bhāṣā s*, *vibhāṣā-s* and *antarabhāṣā-s*, and these melodic forms were proximately or remotely related to the system of *jāti* and *grāma-rāga-s*. Now, in the second Section he proposes to deal with a different class of derived melodic forms which bear the generic name *aṅga* as it may be observed from their nomenclature viz. *rāgāṅga*, *bhāṣāṅga*, *kriyāṅga* and *upāṅga*. It will be seen that the word *aṅga* (lit. an organ) is suffixed to *rāga*, *bhāṣā*, *kriyā* and *upa*. Bharata has not included *rāga* in the list of subjects dealt with by him. Mataṅga divided the music of his time as *mārga* and *deśī* and consequently classified the prevalent *rāga-s* as *grāma-rāga-s* and *deśī-rāga-s*. The *aṅga-rāga-s* comprising the above four types are the varieties of *deśī-rāga-s*. Although Mataṅga, as quoted by 'K', has spoken of the first three only. Śārṅgadeva has added one more category viz. that of *upāṅga-s*. Even these *deśī-rāga-s* are related in some measure to the *grāma-rāga-s*, but they do not strictly conform to their technical features which are more or less fixed, and to their strict rules. Mataṅga, as quoted by 'K', defines the essential feature characterising *deśī rāga-s* as under :

"The rule already laid down with respect to the *grāma-rāga-s* may or may not apply to the *deśī-rāga-s* and also to *bhāṣā-s*."

The significance of these four types of *deṣī-rānga-s* is briefly indicated as under :

(i) *Rāgāṅga—Deśī-rāga-s* that were found to be associated with some of the *grāma-rāga-s*.

(ii) *Bhāṣāṅga—Daśī-rāga-s* that were linked with the *bhāṣa-s*, *vibhāṣā-s* and the *antara-bhāṣā s* of the *grāma-rāga-s*.

(iii) *Kriyāṅga—Deśī-rāga-s* that were related to specific emotive situations and

(iv) *Upāṅga—Deśī-rāga-s* that could not be classified in the above three categories. 'S', however, says that these are based on the *aṅga-s* (lit. organs) implying the parts of the above three.

(ii) प्राक्प्रसिद्ध रागा:

शङ्कराभरणो घण्टारवो हंसकदीपकौ ।
रीतिः कर्णाटिका लाटी पाञ्चालीति बभाषिरे ॥४॥
रागाङ्गाण्यष्ट, गाम्भीरी वेहारी श्वसितोत्पली ।
गोली नादान्तरी नीलोत्पली च्छाया तरङ्गिणी ॥५॥
गान्धारगतिका वैरञ्जीत्येकादश मेनिरे ।
भाषाङ्गाण्यथ भावक्रीस्वभावक्रीशिवक्रियः ॥६॥
मकरक्रीत्रिनेत्रक्रीकुमुदक्रीरनुक्रियः ।
ओजक्रीन्द्रक्रियौ नागकृतिर्धन्यकृतिस्तथा ॥७॥

विजयक्री: क्रियाङ्गाणि द्वादशेति जगुर्बुधाः ।
वीण्युपाङ्गानि पूर्णाटी देवालश्च गुरुञ्जिका ॥८॥
चतुस्त्रिंशदिमे रागाः प्राक्प्रसिद्धाः प्रकीर्तिताः ।

(ii) The well-known ancient[1] *rāga-s* : 4-9b

Śaṅkarābharaṇa, ghaṇṭārava, haṁsaka, dīpaka, riti, karṇāṭikā, lāṭī and *pāñcālī*, are said to be the eight *rāgāṅga-s.* (4-5a)

Gāmbhīrī, vehārī, śvasitā, utpalī, golī, nādāntarī, nīlotpalī, chāyā, taraṅgiṇī, gāndhāragatikā and *vairañjī* are accepted to be the eleven *bhāṣāṅga's.* (5b-6c)

Bhāvakrī, svabhāvakrī. śivakrī, makarakṛī, trinetrakrī, kumudakrī, raāniku, ojakrī, indrakrī, Nāgakṛti, dhanyakṛti and *vijayakrī* are declared by the learned to be the twelve *kriyāṅga-s.* (6d-8b)

Pūrṇāṭī, devāla, and *guruñjikā* are the three *upāṅga-s.* (8cd)

These are considered to be the thirty-four well-known ancient *rāga-s.* (9ab)

(iii) अधुनाप्रसिद्धरागाः, रागाणां सम्मिलित सङ्ख्या, निरूपणक्रमश्च

(क) अधुनाप्रसिद्धरागोद्देशः

अथाधुनाप्रसिद्धानामुद्देशः प्रतिपाद्यते ॥९॥
मध्यमादिर्मालवश्रीस्तोडी बङ्गालभैरवौ ।
वराटी गुर्जरी गौडकोलाहलवसन्तकाः ॥१०॥
धन्यासीदेशिदेशाख्या रागाङ्गाणि त्रयोदश ।
डोम्बक्री सावरी वेलावली प्रथममञ्जरी ॥११॥
आडि[2]कामोदिका नागध्वनिः शुद्धवराटिका ।
नट्टा कर्णाटबङ्गालो भाषाङ्गाणि नवाब्रुवन् ॥१२॥
क्रियाङ्गत्रितयं रामकृतिर्गौडकृतिस्तथा ।
देवक्रीरित्यथोपाङ्गसप्तविंशतिरुच्यते ॥१३॥
कौन्तली द्राविडी सैन्धव्युपस्थानवराटिका ।
हतस्वरवराटी च स्यात्प्रतापवराटिका ॥१४॥
वराट्यः षडिति च्छायातुरुष्काद्ये तु तोडिके ।
महाराष्ट्री च सौराष्ट्री दक्षिणा द्राविडीत्यमः ॥१५॥
उक्ताश्चतस्रो गुर्जर्यो भुञ्जिका स्तम्बतीथिका ।
छायाप्रतापोपपदे वेलावल्यौ च भैरवी ॥१६॥

[1] *Prākprasiddha* of the text literally means "well-known for a long time past."

[2] Ad. Ed. reads आदि—etc.

कामोदासिंहली छायानट्टा रामकृतिस्तथा ।
भल्लातिका च मल्हारी मल्हारो गौडकास्ततः ॥१७॥

कर्णाटो देशवालश्च तौरुष्कद्राविडाविति ।
एतेऽधुनाप्रसिद्धाः स्युर्द्वापञ्चाशन्मनोरमाः ॥१८॥

(ख) सर्वरागाणां सम्मिलितसङ्ख्या

सर्वेषामपि रागाणां मिलितानां शतद्वयम् ।
चतुःषष्टयधिकं ब्रूते शार्ङ्गी श्रीकरणाग्रणीः ॥१९॥

(ग) रागनिरूपणक्रमाख्यानम्

तत्रादौ ग्रामरागाणां केषाञ्चिल्लक्ष्म चक्ष्महे ।
देशीरागादिहेतूनां शेषाणां तत्र तत्र तु ॥२०॥

(iii) The current[1] well known *rāga-s,* total number of rāga-s and the scheme of their description : 9c-20.

(*a*) ***Current well-known rāga-s*** :

Now, (the *rāga-s*) that are well known at present are listed as under.[2] (9cd)

Madhyamādi, mālavaśrī, toḍī, baṅgāla, bhairava, varāṭī,[3] *gurjarī, gauḍa, kolāhala, vasanta, dhanyāsī, deśī* and *deśākhyā* are the thirteen *rāgāṅga-s.* (10-11b)

Ḍombakrī[4], *sāvarī velāvalī, prathamamañjarī, ādikāmodikā, nāgadhvani. śuddhavarāiṭkā, naṭṭā* and *karṇāṭa-baṅgāla* are said to be the nine *bhāṣāṅga-s.* (11c-12)

Rāmakṛti, gauḍakṛti, and *devakrī* are the three *kriyāṅga-s.* (13a-c)

Now, the twenty-seven *upāṅga-s* are stated (as under) : the six *varāṭī-s* viz. *Kauntalī, drāviḍī, saindhavī, upasthānavarāṭikā, hatasvaravarāṭī* and *pratāpavarāṭikā* ; two *toḍi-s* viz. *chāyātoḍī* and *turuṣkatoḍī* ; four *gurjarī-s*[5] viz. *mahārāṣṭrī, saurāṣṭrī, dakṣiṇā* and *drāviḍī* ; *bhuñjikā, stambatīrthikā, chāyāvelāvalī, pratāpavelāvalī, bhairavī, kāmodasiṁhalī, chāyānaṭṭā, rāmakṛti*[6], *bhallātikā, malhārī, malhāra, gauḍa, karṇāṭa, deśavāla,*[7] *turuṣka*[8], and *drāviḍa.* (13c-18b)

These are the fifty-two[9] captivating (*rāga-s*) well-known at present.

[1]Lit. 'well known at present'.

[2]This represents a free rendering of the text.

[3]*Varāli* is a text variant for *varāṭī.*

[4]According to 'K' *ḍombakrī* is another name for *bhūpālī.*

[5]*Uktāḥ* (are said to be) of the text has been dropped out in view of the construction of the sentence.

[6]Among the *Upāṅga s,* according to 'K', *rāmakṛti* is another name for bauli.

[7]According to 'K' *deśavāla* is *kedāragaula.*

[8]Similarly 'K' says, *tauruṣka* is *mālavagauḍa.*

[9]That is, 13 *rāgāṅga-s*, 9 *bhāṣāṅga-s*, 3 *Kriyāṅga-s* and 27 *Upāṅga-s* (13+ 9+3+27 =52).

(b) *The total number of rāga-s* :

Śārṅgadeva, the forerunner[1] of Śrikaraṇa describes the sum total of two hundred and sixty four *rāga-s* in all. (18c-19)

(c) *The scheme of description of rāga-s* :

From amongst these we shall deal with[2] the characteristic features of some[3] of the *grāma-rāga-s* in the first place and then with the rest of them that are the sources of the *deśī-rāga-s* and so on in the context (of the latter).[4] (20)

Comments

In this section the author has mentioned thirty-four well known ancient *rāga s* and fifty-two *rāga-s*, well known in his time. Thus the well known *rāga-s*, ancient as well as contemporary, mentioned by him number eighty-six in all. In the first Section he has mentioned thirty *grāma-rāga-s*, eight *uparāga-s*, twenty *rāga-s*, *ninety-six bhāṣā-s*, twenty *vibhāṣā-s* and four-*antarabhāṣā-s* making a total of one hundred and seventy-eight *rāga-s* in all. Thus, the total No. of *rāga-s* mentioned in both the sections comes to (34+52)+(30+8+20+96+20+4)=86+178=264, two hundred and sixty-four. Obviously the fifteen *bhāṣā-janaka-rāga-s* are not to be included in this total since they are already contained in these categories.

It may, however, be noted that, the author has mentioned only such *rāga-s* in this Section that are well known, implying thereby that many *rāga-s* that were prevalent but not so well known, have not been taken into account. 'K' quotes Mataṅga who says, "The *rāga-s* pertaining to different regions, i.e. *deśī-rāga-s* being infinite and undefined (*anibaddha*) are numberless."

Now, from amongst 264 *rāga-s* mentioned above, the author proposes to deal with *grāma-rāga-s* some of which are related to *deśī-rāga-s* as their sources and thus in terms of Mataṅga belong to *Mārga-saṅgīta*. *Deśī-rāga-s* are the *rāgāṅga-s* and so on mentioned above and, according to 'K', include the *bhāṣā-s*, *vibhāṣā-s* and the *antara-bhāśās* as well. Since these *rāga-s* were more or less prevalent during the time of the author, they were so commonplace that the author does not consider it necessary to define them all in their entirety. He will therefore deal with them, in relation to their parent *rāga-s* in due proportion to their relative importance. In short, as observed by 'K', he means to deal with only such of them that were well known in his time.

(iv) प्राक्प्रसिद्ध-ग्रामराग-निरूपणम्

1. शुद्धसाधारित:

(क) तल्लक्षणम्

षड्जमध्यमया जातस्तारषड्जग्रहांशकः ।
निगाल्पो मध्यमन्यासः पूर्णः षड्जादिमूर्छनः ॥२१॥

[1]*Śrikaraṇāgraṇī* indicates that Śārṇgadeva was accountant-general of the king.

[2]Lit. 'we shall describe'.

[3]That is, the *grāma-rāga-s* that are not the origins of *deśī-rāga-s*.

[4]That is, while describing the *deśī-rāga-s* derived from them.

अवरोहिप्रसन्नान्तालङ्कृतो रविदैवतः ।
वीरे रौद्रे रसे गेयः प्रहरे वासरादिमे ॥२२॥
विनियुक्तो गर्भसन्धौ शुद्धसाधारितो बुधैः ।

(ख) रागालापलक्षणम्

ग्रहांशमन्द्रताराणां न्यासापन्यासयोस्तथा ॥२३॥
अल्पत्वस्य बहुत्वस्य षाडवौडुवयोरपि ।
अभिव्यक्तिर्यत्र दृष्टा स रागालाप उच्यते ॥२४॥

(ग) रूपकलक्षणम्

रूपकं तद्वदेव स्यात्पृथग्भूतविदारिकम् ।

(घ) आक्षिप्तिकालक्षणम्

चच्चत्पुटादितालेन मार्गत्रयविभूषिता ॥२५॥
आक्षिप्तिका स्वरपदग्रथिता कथिता बुधैः ।

(च) करणवर्तन्योः प्रबन्धान्तर्गतिः

नोक्ते करणवर्तन्यौ प्रबन्धान्तर्गतेरिह ॥२६॥

(छ) रूपकनिरूपणप्रतिज्ञा

मतङ्गादिमताद् ब्रूमो भाषादिष्वेव रूपकम् ।

सां पां धां रीपापाधारी पाधा सासा पाध्रानीधा पामांमां रींपा धारीं पाधारीं पाधापाधापापा सासा मा। सां गां रीं मां। मगरि सासा सरिग पाधारीपाधारीपाधापाधासासा सारीगामाधापानीधापानीधापा सां सां-इत्यालापः।

सस पप धध रिरि पप धस सां २ रिरि पप धनि पप रिप धस सा सा २ धध मंमं गारी गंमं रिग मम मगरिग सासा २ सस धस रिंगं सासा पाधा निधप मंमं—इति करणम् ।

१.	सा	सा	धा	नी	पा	पा	पा	पा
	उ	द	य	गि	रि	शि	ख	र
२.	धा	धा	नी	नी	रीं	रीं	पा	पा
	शे	ख		र	तु	र	ग	खु
३.	री	पा	पा	पा	धा	नी	पा	मा
	र		क्ष	त	वि	भि		न्न
४.	धा	मा	धा	सा	सा	सा	सा	सा
	ध	न	ति	मि	रः			

५.	धा	धा	सा	धा	सा	री	गा	सा
	ग	ग	न	त	ल	स	क	ल
६.	री	गा	पा	पा	पा	पा	पा	पा
	वि	लु	लि	त	स	ह		स्त्र
७.	धा	मा	धा	मा	सा	सा	सा	सा
	कि	र		णो	ज	य		तु
८.	पा	धा	निध	पा	मा	पा	मा	मा
	भा					नुः		

—इत्याक्षिप्तिका ।

इति शुद्धसाधारितः ।

तत्र साकल्येन पदयोजना

उदयगिरिशिखरशेखरतुरगखुरक्षतविभिन्नघनतिमिरः ।
गगनतलसकलविलुलितसहस्रकिरणो जयतु भानुः ॥

(iv) The characteristic features of the ancient *rāga-s* : 21-67b

1. *Śuddhasādhārita* : (21-27b)

(a) The definition of the *rāga* :

Born of the *ṣaḍja-madhyamā*[1](*jāti*) with the upper[2] *ṣaḍja* for its initial and[3] the fundamental notes, having a weak[4] *niṣāda* and *gāndhara*, and *madhyama* as its final (note), complete with the *mūrcchanā* initiated[5] by *śaḍja* and embellished by the *prasannānta*[6] in the descending pattern (of tonal movement),[7] having the Sun for its presiding deity and meant to

[1]One of the *sansargajā vikṛtā* (associate modified) *jāti-s Śuddhasādhārita* is derived from this *jāti*.

[2]*Tāra-ṣaḍja* denotes the *ṣaḍja* of the upper register.

[3]The initial note and the fundamental note is generally the same in *jāti-gāna* but in the *rāga-s*, it is not necessarily so, the two can be different; therefore 'K' observes that the rule, "the mention of either of the two implies the other one", as applied to *jāti*-songs, does not hold good with respect to *rāga-s*.

[4]Though *alpa*, in the terminology adopted here, is rendered as 'rare' elsewhere, this being a complete (*pūrṇa*) formation, employing all the notes, it has been rendered as 'weak' in this context.

[5]That is, having *ṣaḍja* as its first note, i.e *Uttaramandrā* since *ṣaḍja-madhyamā* belongs to *saḍja-grāma*.

[6]An *alaṅkāra* (pattern of tonal phrase).

[7]*Varṇa* has been rendered as 'pattern of tonal movement' which is said to be of four types viz. ascending and so on. For the sake of brevity an *ārohī* (*varṇa*) will henceforth be rendered as the 'ascending pattern' and so on, not mentioning 'tonal movement,' which may be taken as understood.

be sung in (the context of) the sentiments of valour and wrath[1] in the first quarter of the day, the *Śuddhasādhārita* is employed by the wise in the *garbha-sandhi.*[2] (21-23b)

(b) The definition of *rāgālāpa :*

The (melodic pattern) that makes possible[3] the manifestation of the initial and the fundamental notes, the extent of the low and the high (pitch), the final and the semifinal notes, the rarity and the profusion (of the notes employed), and the hexatonic and the pentatonic formations[4] is called *rāgālāpa*[5]. (23c-24)

(c) The definition of *rūpaka* :

Rūpaka is just the same[6] with the (only) difference that the sections are distinctly separated[7] (in singing). (25ab)

(d) The definition of *ākṣiptikā* :

As declared by the learned, *ākṣīptikā*[8] is composed with verbal text set to notes and *tāla-s* such as caccatpuṭa and so on[9] employed[10] in the three *mārga-s*[11]. (25c-26b)

(e) Inclusion of *Karaṇa* and *Vartanī* in *prabandha-s* :

Karaṇa and *vartanī* are not mentioned here as they are dealt with

[1]*Vīra* and *raudra* respectively. *Rasa* is aesthetic delight created through an emotive situation depicted in drama ; as such it has roughly been rendered as 'sentiment' though that is not the exact translation of the term.

[2]Since the *grāma-rāga-s* were sung in the production and the staging of dramas, they were designed to serve a useful purpose in the development of the plot and were therefore associated to one of the five *sandhi-s* (junctural subdivisions of the plot in sanskrit drama) viz. *mukha, pratimukha, garbha, vimarśa* and *upasamhṛti* in due order.

[3]*Dṛṣṭā* : of the text lit. means "is seen to be".

[4]All these terms have been defined in Chapter I, Sec. 7.

[5]*Rāgālāpa* (*rāga-ālapa*) lit. means "vocalisation of *rāga*", and is a variety of *ālapti to* be defined later.

[6]Same as *rāgālāpa*. *Rūpaka* as explained by 'K', being a variety of *ālāpa* is not a synonym of *prabandha*, in this context.

[7]"K' explains the distinction between *ālāpa* and *rūpaka* : *ālāpa* is singing in an uninterrupted continuum without resting on the semifinal notes, and *rūpaka* is the same section taken with a pause stopping on the semifinal note." 'S' reads *vivādikam* instead of *vidārikam* which is a text variant given in the Adyar Edition of S. R., and interprets *rūpaka* accordingly : "from the *ālāpa* as defined above, if the dissonants are dropped it becomes *rūpaka*." It may be observed that as per the definition of *rāgālāpa*, *apanyāsa* is also to be manifested as much as the other factors mentioned in this context. So 'K's' interpretation does not seem to be fully warranted by the text. This contention is supported by the definition of *rūpaka* as given by Kumbhā who is considered to be a commentator of Śārṅgadeva ; he also purports to be representing this view. He says : "In *rūpaka* the consonant and other notes are differentiated from the dissonants". (*S. Raj*, II. 2.1.154). There is no mention of *vidārī* here. Thus it seems that, the reading *vivādikam* is more authentic.

[8]*Ākṣiptikā* is a variety of composed songs (*nibaddha-gīta*).

[9]Other *mārgatāla-s* such as *cācapuṭa*.

[10]Lit. embellished.

[11]*Citra, vārttika* and *dakṣiṇa* spoken of in Chapter I, Sc. 7.

in the context of *prabandha s.*[1] (26cd)

(f) The scheme of dealing with *rūpaka*:

We shall speak of *rūpaka* as well in the case of *bhāṣā-s* and the like[2] in accordance with *Mataṅga.* (27ab)

1. *Ākṣiptikā* :

1.	sā	sā	dhā	nī	pā	pā	pā	pā
	U	*da*	*ya*	*gi*	*ri*	*śi*	*kha*	*ra*
2.	dhā	dhā	nī	nī	rī	rī	pā	pā
	śe	*kha*		*ra*	*tu*	*ra*	*ga*	*khu*
3.	rī	pā	pā	pā	dhā	nī	pā	mā
	ra		*kṣa*	*ta*	*vi*	*bhi*		*nna*
4.	dhā	mā	dhā	sā	sā	sā	sā	sā
	gha	*na*	*ti*	*mi*	*raḥ*			
5.	dhā	dhā	sā	dhā	sā	rī	gā	sā
	ga	*ga*	*na*	*ta*	*la*	*sa*	*ka*	*la*
6.	rī	gā	pā	pā	pā	pā	pā	pā
	vi	*lu*	*li*	*ta*	*sa*	*ha*		*sra*
7.	dhā	mā	dhā	mā	sā	sā	sā	sā
	ki	*ra*		*ṇo*	*ja*	*ya*		*tu*
8.	pā	dhā	ni-dha	pā	mā	pā	mā	mā
	bhā				*nuḥ*			

The purport of the song is as under :

Victory be unto the Sun, who, having dispelled the intense darkness rent asunder by the hoofs of the horses (of his chariot galloping) over the crest of the top of the mountain (of the rising sun) elegantly breaks forth into a thousand rays through the entire firmament.

Thus ends *Śuddhasādhārita.*

2. षड्जग्राम:

षड्जमध्यमया सृष्टस्तारषड्जग्रहांशकः ॥२७॥
सम्पूर्णो मध्यमन्यासः षड्जापन्यासभूषितः ।
अवरोहिप्रसन्नान्तभूषः षड्जादिमूर्छनः ॥२८॥
काकल्यन्तरसंयुक्तो वीरे रौद्रेऽद्भुते रसे ।
विनियुक्तः प्रतिमुखे वर्षासु गुरुदैवतः ॥२९॥
गेयोऽह्नः प्रथमे यामे षड्जग्रामाभिधो बुधैः ।

[1]See Chapter IV.
[2]Such as *vibhāṣā* and *antarabhāṣā*.

संसंरी गधगरिस सनिधापाधाधारीगासां । री गा सा सग पनिधनिस सा सा । गसरिग पधनिप मामा—इत्यालापः ।

रीं रीं गाधा गरि सासा नींधपापा । रीं रीं गध परि सां सां सां सां । सां सां गानिधा रीरीगा । धा गारी सां सां निधपापा । री री पापा निधनि सां सां सां । सरि सरि पधनिध पमामामामा—इति करणम् ।

१. री री गा सा गा री गा सा
स ज य तु भू ता

२. नी धा पा पा री री गा धा
धि प तिः प रि क र

३. गा री सा सा सा सा सा सा
भो गीं द्र कुं ड

४. सा सा गा धनि नी नी नी नी
ला भ र णः

५. गा रिग धा धा गा गरि सा सा
ग ज च र्मं प ट नि

६. नी धा पा पा री री पा पा
व स नः श शां क

७. नी धा नी सा सा सा सा रिसरि
चू डा म णिः

८. पा धा निध पा मां मां मां मां—
शं भुः

इत्याक्षिप्तिका ।

इति षड्जग्रामः ।

तत्र साकल्येन पदयोजना

स जयतु भूताधिपतिः परिकरभोगीन्द्रकुण्डलाभरणः ।
गजचर्मपटनिवसनः शशाङ्कचूडामणिः शम्भुः ॥

2. *Saḍjagrāma* : (27c-30b)

The *rāga* named by the learned as '*ṣaḍjagrāma*' is derived[1] from the *ṣaḍja-madhyamā* (*jāti*), has the upper *ṣaḍja* for its initial and the fundamental note, is complete, has *madhyama* as the final and *ṣaḍja* as the semifinal note[2]' and is embellished by the descending *prasannānta*; its

[1]Literally, created.
[2]*Bhūṣita*, 'embellished' is not literally translated.

mūrcchanā commences with *ṣaḍja*; it is served by *kākali* and *antara*, is employed in the sentiments of valour[1], wrath[2] and wonder[3] in (the junctural sub-division called) *pratimukha* during the rainy season, has Jupiter[4] for its presiding deity, and is sung in the first quarter of the day. (27c-30b)

Ākṣīptikā :

1.	rī	rī	gā	sā	gā	ri	gā	sā
	Sa	*ja*	*ya*	*tu*	*bhū*		*tā*	
2.	nī	dhā	pā	pā	rī	ri	gā	dhā
	dhi	*pa*	*tiḥ*		*pa*	*ri*	*ka*	*ra*
3.	gā	rī	sā	sā	sā	sā	sā	sā
	bho		*gīn*	*dra*		*kuṇ*		*ḍa*
4.	sā	sā	gā	dha-ni	nī	nī	nī	nī
	lā		*bha*	*ra*	*ṇaḥ*			
5.	gā	ri-ga	dhā	dhā	gā	ga-ri	sā	sā
	ga	*ja*	*ca*		*rma*	*pa*	*ṭa*	*ni*
6.	nī	dhā	pā	pā	rī	rī	pā	pā
	va	*sa*	*naḥ*		*śa*	*śāṅ*	*ka*	
7.	nī	dhā	nī	sā	sā	sā	sā	ri-sa-ri
	cū		*ḍā*	*ma*	*ṇiḥ*			
8.	pā	dhā	ni-dha	pā	mā	mā	mā	mā
	śaṁ				*bhuḥ*			

The purport of the song is as under :

Let that Lord of creatures (Śiva) be victorious who is adorned by the ear-rings of the attending serpents, who is clad in the fabric of the elephant's skin and who has the moon for his crest jewel.

Thus ends *Śaḍjagrāma.*

3. शुद्धकैशिक:

कार्मारव्याश्च कैशिक्याः संजातः शुद्धकैशिकः ॥३०॥
तारषड्जग्रहांशश्च पञ्चमान्तः सकाकली ।
सावरोहिप्रसन्नान्तः पूर्णः षड्जादिमूर्छनः ॥३१॥
वीररौद्राद्भुतरसः शिशिरे भौमवल्लभः ।
गेयो निर्वहणे यामे प्रथमेऽह्नो मनीषिभिः ॥३२॥

सांसां गामा गारी गामां सांनी सांरी साधा माधा माधा नीधा पामा गामा पापा—इत्यालापः ।

[1]*Vīra.*
[2]*Raudra.*
[3]*Adbhuta,*
Guru is the name of Bṛhaspati, the preceptor of gods and also the planet Jupiter.

सांसांसांसां रीरीसासारीरी गागा सांसांसांसां मामा गारी गारी सासारीरी पनि सांसांसांसां रीरी मामा पापाधामा मामाधानी सासासासा रीरीगामा सासापापा धामागामा पामा पापापापा—इति वर्तनी ।

१.	सा	सा	सा	सा	सा	सा	नी	धा
	अ		ग्नि		ज्वा		ला	शि
२.	सा	सा	री	मा	सा	री	गा	मा
	खा		के		शि			
३.	सा	गा	री	सा	सा	सा	सा	सा
	मां		स	शो				णि
४.	सा	सा	सा	सा	नी	सा	नी	नी
	त	भो				जि	नि	
५.	मा	मा	गा	री	मा	मा	पा	पा
	स		र्वा		हा		रि	णि
६.	धा	नी	पा	मा	धा	मा	धा	सा
	नि		मां		से			
७.	सा	सा	सा	सा	नी	धा	पा	पा
	च		र्म	मुं	ण्डे		न	
८.	धा	नी	गा	मा	पा	पा	पा	पा
	मो			स्तु	ते			

—इत्याक्षिप्तिका ।

इति शुद्धकैशिकः ॥

तत्र साकल्येन पदयोजना

अग्निज्वालाशिखाकेशि मांसशोणितभोजिनि ।
सर्वाहारिणि निर्मांसे चर्ममुण्डे नमोऽस्तु ते ॥

3. *Śuddhakaiśika* : (30c-32)

Śuddhakaiśika is produced jointly from *Karmāravī* and *Kaiśikī* (*jāti-s*) : it has the upper *ṣaḍja* for its initial and the fundamental note, *pañcama* as the final note, and has *kākalī* and the descending *prasannānta*; it is complete and its *mūrcchanā* commences with *ṣaḍja*; it has Mars for its presiding deity and is employed in the sentiments of valour, wrath and wonder in the winter season. It is sung by the proficient in the forenoon in the denouement (*nirvahaṇa*).[1] (30c-32)

Ākṣiptikā :

1.	sā	sā	sā	sā	sā	sā	nī	dhā
	A		*gni*		*jvā*		*lā*	*śi*
2.	sā	sā	rī	mā	sā	rī	gā	mā
	khā		*ke*		*śi*			
3.	sā	gā	rī	sā	sā	sā	sā	sā
	māṁ				*sa*	*śo*		*ṇi*
4.	sā	sā	sā	sā	nī	sā	nī	nī
	ta	*bho*				*ji*	*ni*	
5.	mā	mā	gā	rī	mā	mā	pā	pā
	sa		*rva*		*hā*		*ri*	*ṇi*
6.	dha-ni	pā	mā		dhā	mā	dhā	sā
	ni	*rmāṁ*			*se*			
7.	sā	sā	sā	sā	nī	dhā	pā	pā
	ca			*rma*	*muṇ*	*ḍe*	*na*	
8.	dhā	nī	ga	ma	pā	pā	pā	pā
	mo'			*stu*	*te*			

The purport of the song is as under :

Salutations to you Oh ! the fleshless Cāmuṇḍā (Durgā) with the flames of blazing fire for the locks of hair, the devourer of flesh and blood, the destroyer of all.

Thus ends *Śuddhakaiśika*.

4. भिन्नकैशिकमध्यम:

षड्जमध्यमिकोत्पन्नो भिन्नकैशिकमध्यमः ।
षड्जग्रहांशो मन्यासो मन्द्रसान्तोऽथवा भवेत् ॥३३॥
षड्जादिमूर्छनः पूर्णः संचारिणि सकाकली ।
प्रसन्नादियुतो दानवीरे रौद्रेऽद्भुते रसे ॥३४॥
दिनस्य प्रथमे यामे प्रयोज्यः सोमदैवत: ।

सां निधा सामां । मम धम मम धम गामाधाधा नीधा सस सां गां माधानीधा सां सां धमा मगा स गास साधा मामा । सां गां माधानीधा सांसां मधा पमाप मामा—इत्यालापः ।

सस निध सस मम मध मग मध निमम । निधांनीमधनिस । निधनि

[1] *Nirvahaṇa* is another name for *upasaṁhṛti* i e. the last *sandhi*.

संसंसंसंसं धध। मम गसं सं गमा सांग गधांधांधधममधंमगममधसंसं। संसंधम-धपमापा मामा—इति वर्तनिका।

१.	सा	सा	नी	धा	सा	सा	मा	मा
	बृ	ह	दु	द	र	वि	क	ट
२.	मा	धा	मा	गा	मा	धा	नी	मा
	ग		म	न	ज	ठ	र	वि
३.	मा	नी	धा	नी	मा	धा	नी	नी
	भ		क्तं		सु	वि	पु	ल
४.	नी	धा	नी	सा	सा	सा	सा	सा
	पी		नां		गं			
५.	मा	मस	सा	सा	नी	धा	पा	पा
	अ	रि	द	म	न	वि	ष	म
६.	धा	नी	मा	मा	गा	री	मा	मा
	लो		च	नं	सु	र	न	मि
७.	मा	मा	मा	मा	धा	नी	मा	मा
	तं	वि	ना		य	कं		
८.	सा	सा	धा	नी	मा	मा	मा	मा
	वं				दे			

—इत्याक्षिप्तिका।

इति भिन्नकैशिकमध्यमः।

तत्र साकल्येन पदयोजना

बृहदुदरविकटगमनजठरविभक्तं सुविपुलपीनाङ्गम्।
अरिदमनविषमलोचनं सुरनमितं विनायकं वन्दे॥

4. *Bhinnakaiśikamadhyama* : (33-36b)

Formed[1] out of *ṣaḍja-madhyamā* (*jāti*), *bhinnakaiśikamadhyama* has *ṣaḍja* for its initial and the fundamental note and *madhyama* or the lower *ṣaḍja* as its final note; (its) *mūrcchanā* commences with *ṣaḍja*, (it) is complete, having *kākalī* in the *sañcārī* (circulatory) *varṇa*; (embellished) with *prasannādi*, it is employed in (the context of) the sentiment of heroism in

[1]Lit. 'born of'.

phillanthropy,[1] wrath[2] and wonder[3] in the first quarter of the day; and it has *soma* (the mc on) for its presiding deity. (33-36b)

Ākṣiptikā:

1.	sā	sā	ni	dhā	sā	sā	mā	mā
	Bṛ	*ha*	*du*	*da*	*ra*	*vi*	*ka*	*ṭa*
2.	mā	dhā	mā	gā	mā	dhā	ni	mā
	ga		*ma*	*na*	*ja*	*ṭha*	*ra*	*vi*
3.	mā	ni	dhā	ni	mā	dhā	ni	ni
	bha		*ktam*		*su*	*vi*	*pu*	*la*
4.	ni	dhā	ni	sā	sā	sā	sā	sā
	pī		*nāṅ*	*gam*				
5.	mā	ma-sa	sā	sā	ni	dhā	pā	pā
	a	*ri*	*da*	*ma*	*na*	*vi*	*ṣa*	*ma*
6.	dhā	nī	mā	mā	gā	ri	mā	mā
	lo		*ca*	*naṁ*	*su*	*ra*	*na*	*mi*
7.	mā	mā	mā	mā	dhā	ni	mā	mā
	taṁ	*vi*	*nā*		*ya*	*kam*		
8.	sā	sā	dhā	ni	mā	mā	mā	mā
	van				*de*			

The purport of the song is as under :

I bow down to Vināyaka (Gaṇeśa) who, (on account of his) difficult movement (caused by his) vast stomach, dissipates hardships; who has stout fleshy limbs, is capable of vanquishing the foes, has three eyes and is adored by the gods.

Thus ends *Bhinnakaiśikamadhyama*.

5. भिन्नतान:

मध्यमापञ्चमीजात: पञ्चमांशग्रहोऽल्परि: ॥३५॥
रिहीनो वा मध्यमान्तो मध्यमाल्प: सकाकली ।
संचारिणि प्रसन्नादिमण्डितोऽन्तिममूर्छन: ॥३६॥
प्राग्यामे करुणे गेयो भिन्नतान: शिवप्रिय: ।

पां नीं सागा मापा धापागामांमां । ममध ममग सां सां संसं सं मागम पापापानी सांगांमां धापाम गंमंमां । मम धप धध संसं पांपां संसंसं मागम पापा मंमं पप धध निनि पध मध मग गंसां सां गंसगससम पापापानी

[1] *Dānavīra* (*Dāna* + *vira*) extremely generous in giving charity.

[2] *Raudra* of the text.

[3] *Adbhuta* of the text.

सांगांपापा धापामगमामा—इत्यालापः ।

पापा नीनी संसं गंगं पापानीपांनी सांगंगं सांगामा पाधा पाम गामापापा (पञ्चम) पापा सांसां धामापापापा (षड्ज) सस गम (पञ्चम) नी सांगां मापाधाम गां मामा—इति वर्तनी ।

१.	पा	पा	नी	नी	सां	सां	गा	गा
	ह	र	व	र	मु	कु	ट	ज
२.	सा	गां	मप	मग	सां	सां	सां	सां
	टा		लु	लि	तं			
३.	सा	गा	मा	पा	धा	पा	मप	मग
	अ	म	र	व	धू		कु	च
४.	सा	गा	मा	पा	पा	पा	पा	पा
	प	रि	म	लि	तं			
५.	धा	पा	सा	मा	पा	पा	धा	धा
	ब	हु	वि	ध	कु	सु	म	र
६.	सा	सा	पा	पा	धा	पा	मा	गा
	जो		रु	णि	तं			
७.	धा	पा	पम	मपग	सां	गां	मां	पां
	वि	ज	य	ते	गं		गा	
८.	धा	पा	मग	मा	मा	मा	मा	मा
	वि	म	ल	ज	लं			

—इत्याक्षिप्तिका ।

इति भिन्नतानः ॥

तत्र साकल्येन पदयोजना

हरवरमुकुटजटालुलितं, अमरवधूकुचपरिमलितम् ।
बहुविधकुसुमरजोरुणितं, विजयते गङ्गाविमलजलम् ॥

5. ***Bhinnatāna*** : (35c-37b)

Born of *Madhyamā* and *Pañcamī* (*jāti-s*), having *pañcama* for its initial and the fundamental note and a weak[1] *ṛṣabha* which may even be omitted, with *madhyama* as its final note which is otherwise rare, taking *kākalī* and embellished by *prasannādi* in the *sañcārī* (circulatory) *varṇa*, with its

[1]Lit., 'rare'.

mūrcchanā commencing with *pañcama*,[1] *bhinnatāna*, loved (as it is) by Lord Śiva, is sung in the first quarter of the day in (the context of) pathos.[2] (35c-37b)

Ākṣiptikā :

1.	pā	pā	nī	nī	sȧ	sȧ	gā	gā
	Ha	*ra*	*va*	*ra*	*mu*	*ku*	*ṭa*	*ja*
2.	sā	gȧ	ma-pa	ma-ga	sȧ	sȧ	sȧ	sȧ
	ṭā		*lu*	*li*	*tam*			
3.	sā	gā	mā	pā	dhā	pā	ma-pa	ma-ga
	a	*ma*	*ra*	*va*	*dhu*		*ku*	*ca*
4.	sā	gā	mā	pā	pā	pā	pā	pā
	pa	*ri*	*ma*	*li*	*tam*			
5.	dhā	pā	sā	mā	pā	pā	dhā	dhā
	ba	*hu*	*vi*	*dha*	*ku*	*su*	*ma*	*ra*
6.	sā	sā	pā	pā	dhā	pā	mā	gā
	jo		*ru*	*ṇi*	*tam*			
7.	dhā	pā	pa-ma	ma-pa-ga	sā	gā	mā	pā
	vi	*ja*	*ya*	*te*	*gaṅ*		*gā*	
8.	dhā	pā	ma-ga	mā	mā	mā	mā	mā
	vi	*ma*	*la*	*ja*	*lam*			

The purport of the song is as under :

Victory be to the pure waters of the Ganges that are rendered tremulous by the crown of the locks of hair on Śiva's head, and are fragrant by the washing of the breasts of the wives of gods (in heaven) and by carrying the pollen of the flowers of many types (on earth).

Thus ends *Bhinnatāna*.

6. भिन्नकैशिकः

कैशिकीकार्मारवीभ्यामुद्भूतो भिन्नकैशिकः ॥३७॥
षड्जग्रहांशापन्यासः सम्पूर्णः काकलीयुतः ।
मन्द्रभूरिः ससञ्चारी प्रसन्नादिविभूषणः ॥३८॥
षड्जादिमूर्छनो दानवीरे रौद्रेऽद्भुते रसे ।
गेयोऽह्नः प्रथमे यामे शिशिरे शिववल्लभः ॥३९॥

साधा मांधासा निधस नीसां सां सांरीं मांपांधांमांधांसां निध सनि सासा

[1] *Antima-mūcchanaḥ* is interpreted by 'S' a commencing with *ṛṣabha*. He seems to have taken Bhinnatāna as belonging to the *ṣadja-grāma*, though actually it belongs to the *madhyama-grāma*. cf. *S.Raj.*, II.2. 1.279-281. Pañcama is the last note of the *madhyama-grāma*.

[2] *Karuṇa* of the text.

सारीं सामा धानी साधा सा मपांमापापा--इत्यालापः ।

सासाधा माधापा मारी मापा धामाधासांसां सां । सांसां रीरी गांगां सारी गांगां सारी सासामाधा पापा सारी मापा धासा धापा मापापापा—इति वर्तनी ।

१.	सा	सा	सा	सा	री	री	मा	मा
	इं			द्र	नी			ल
२.	मा	मा	पम	पा	पा	पा	पा	पा
	स			प्र	भं			म
३.	मा	धा	सा	पा	धा	मा	री	सा
	दां			धं	गं			ध
४.	मा	मा	सनि	सां	सां	सां	सां	सां*
	वा			सि	तं			
५.	सा	सा	सा	सा	सा	सा	सा	सा
	ए			क	दं			त
६.	नी	गा	सा	सा	धा	पा	मा	पा
	शो			भि	तं			न
७.	मा	धा	सा	पा	धा	मा	री	मा
	मा			मि	तं			वि
८.	मा	मा	पम	पा	पा	पा	प	प
	ना			य	कं			

—इत्याक्षिप्तिका ।

इति भिन्नकैशिकः ।।

तत्र साकल्येन पदयोजना

इन्द्रनीलसप्रभं मदान्धगन्ध वासितम् ।
एकदन्तशोभितं नमामि तं विनायकम् ।।

6. *Bhinnakaiśika* : (37c-39)

Arising[1] from *Kaiśiki* and *kārmāravī* (*jāti-s*), *bhinnakaiśika* takes *ṣaḍja* for its initial, fundamental and the semi-final note; it is complete, takes *kākalī*, has a profusion of the low (notes) and is embellished by *prasannādi* in the *sañcārī* (circulatory) *varṇa*; with *ṣaḍja* as the commencing note of its

*The fifth sā in this line is inadvertautly omitted from the second edition of Adyar, though it is duly supplied in the first-edition.

[1]*Udbhūta* of the text is literally 'arisen'.

mūrcchanā, it is sung in (the context of) the sentiments of philanthropy,[1] wrath[2] and bewilderment[3], in the first quarter of the day in winter to the endearment of Lord Śiva[4]. (37c-39)

Ākṣiptikā :

1.	sā	sā	sā	sā	rī	rī	mā	mā
	In			***dra***	***nī***			***la***
2.	mā	mā	pa-ma	pā	pā	pā	pā	pā
	sa			***pra***	***bham***			***ma***
3.	mā	dhā	sā	pā	dhā	mā	rī	sā
	dān			***dha***	***gan***			***dha***
4.	mā	mā	sa-ni	sȧ	sȧ	sȧ	sȧ	
	vā			***si***	***tam***			
5.	sā	sā	sā	sā	sā	sā	sā	sā
	e			***ka***	***dan***			***ta***
6.	nī	gā	sā	sā	dhā	pā	mā	pā
	śo			***bhi***	***tam***			***na***
7.	mā	dhā	sā	pā	dhā	mā	rī	mā
	mā			***mi***	***taṁ***			***vi***
8.	mā	mā	pa-ma	pā	pā	pā	pa	pa
	nā			***ya***	***kaṁ***			

The purport of the song is as under :

My salutations to that Vināyaka (who is) resplendent like a sapphire and is scented by the aroma of his rut and who displays only one tooth.

Thus ends *bhinnakaiśika*.

7. गौडकैशिकमध्यमः

षड्जमध्यमया सृष्टो गौडकैशिकमध्यमः ।
षड्जग्रहांशो मन्यासः पूर्णः काकलिना युतः ॥४०॥
प्रसन्नमध्येनारोहिवर्णः षड्जादिमूर्छनः ।
भयानके च वीरादौ रसे शीतांशुदैवतः ॥४१॥
यामद्वये मध्यमेऽह्नो गेयो निःशङ्ककीर्तितः ।

सां सां सधस सधसा सधस रिमागामामा मम धमधरिधधधध धनिधनि धमाधमा गधरि धनिध (षड्ज) ससध धससससधसरिसा सधधससससरिगरिमरि

[1] ***Dānavira*** lit. extremely generous.

[2] ***Raudra*** of the text.

[3] ***Adbhuta*** of the text.

[4] ***Śivavallabha*** lit. dear to Śiva, the grammatical forms of the text have been transformed to suit the English diction.

गसगसधसस (मध्यम) मममधमध (ऋषभ) रिरिरिधरिधधनिधध धसपधमामा। रीरीरिरिगरिगगधां सासाधधसधधरिधरि। ममधारि रिधानि धनिमधामा। गधारिधानिधा (षड्ज) ससधधससस। रिगरिमरिगसगसां धसासं (मध्यम) मममधमध (ऋषभ) रिरिरिधरिधधनिधधधस पधमामा। रीरीरिरिगरिगगधासा-साधधसधसधधरिधरिममधारिरिधानिधनिमधमा। गधारिधानि धाध (षड्ज) ससधधसमसस। रिगरिगरिगंस गसांनिनिनिसनिससससससससससधसधसारि-मममममधाधाध गसगसा। धाधाधमपधमामा—इत्यालापः।

धाधाध (षड्ज) सधसासा धध धस धाममाध मध मां (मध्यम) ममध मग निध धध रिधधा। रिधधा निधध सांसांध धधसं संसं धध सामधरिम रिग सांसंसंधससा। (षड्ज) समामाममधामधाधनिधाधा धनिध गधा सगधा धधधस पप मधमारीगाग (धैवत) धासाधाध रिरिरि (ऋषभ) रिगा मामधमधानिध-निधधा (धैवत) रिधधाधधा। धनिसांसा। सधधधधसंसंसंसांधधधसं ममम रिरिरिग। संगंधा संधध सां सग (षड्ज) स धा सस धसरि। रिमं मधध मधा। मध धध रिधधा धनि (धैवत) धधधगं ससस गं धधधसपधधधमामाम रिग गमा म (षड्ज) पधमा मधमा मामधा (धैवत) रीरीधाधरिधा (षड्जमध्यमधैवत) धासपधमा ममगामामा—इति करणम्।

१.	स	सा	धा	सा	सां	सां	सां	सां
	त	रु	ण	र	वि	स	ट्ट	श
२.	मां	मां	सा	सा	धा	सा	री	मा
	भा		सु	र	वि	क	ट	ज
३.	मम	री	सा	सा	सा	सा	गरि	सम
	टा		जू		ट	शि	ख	र
४.	मां	मां	मां	मां	सां	सां	सां	सां
	प	रि	र	च्चि	ता			
५.	मा	धा	मा	गा	मा	धा	मा	गा
	हि	म	शि	ख	रि	शि	ख	र
६.	मा	धा	सा	सा	नी	धा	सा	सा
	मा		ला		श	र	ण	ग
७.	सां	सां	मा	मग	री	गा	सा	सनि
	ता		पा		तु	वः		स

८. धा सा पा धा मग मा मा मा
दा गं गा

इत्याक्षिप्तिका ।

(तत्र साकल्येन पदयोजना)

(तरुणरविसदृशभासुरविकटजटाजूटशिखरपरिरचिता ।
हिमशिखरिशिखरमालाशरणगता पातु वः सदा गङ्गा ॥)
इति गौडकैशिकमध्यमः ।

(*vi*) *Gauḍakaiśikamadhyama* : 40-42b

Derived[1] from *Saḍjamādhyamā*, *Gauḍakaiśikamadhyama* has *ṣaḍja* for its initial and the fundamental note, and *madhyama* as its final note; it is complete and includes *kākalī*, has *prasannamadhya*[2] in the ascending *varṇa* and its *mūrcchanā* commences with *ṣaḍja*; it is employed in the sentiment of terror[3] and valour[4], and with the moon[5] for its presiding deity, it is sung in the two middle quarters of the day as declared by Śārṅgadeva[6]. (40-42b)

Ākṣiptikā :

1.	sā	sā	dhā	sā	sā̇	sā̇	sā̇	sā̇
	Ta	*ru*	*ṇa*	*ra*	*vi*	*sa*	*dṛ*	*śa*
2.	mā̇	mā̇	sā	sā	dhā	sā	rī	mā
	bhā		*su*	*ra*	*vi*	*ka*	*ṭa*	*ja*
3.	ma-ma	rī	sā	sā	sā	sā	ga-ri	sa-ma
	ṭā		*jū*		*ṭa*	*śi*	*kha*	*ra*
4.	mā̇	mā̇	mā̇	mā̇	sā̇	sā̇	sā̇	sā̇
	pa	*ri*	*ra*	*ci*	*tā*			
5.	mā	dhā	mā	gā	mā	dhā	mā	gā
	hi	*ma*	*śi*	*kha*	*ri*	*śi*	*kha*	*ra*
6.	mā	dhā	sā	sā	nī	dhā	sā	sā
	mā		*lā*		*śa*	*ra*	*ṇa*	*ga*

[1] Lit. 'created'.
[2] Name of an *alaṅkāra*.
[3] *Bhayānaka* of the text.
[4] *Vīra* of text.
[5] Lit., "(the celestial body) having cool rays."
[6] *Niḥśaṅka* (of the text) literally signifies 'one who is free from doubt', and is used as an epithet of Śārṅgadeva.

7.	ṡā	ṡā	mā	ma-ga	ri	gā	sā	sa-ni
	tā		*pā*		*tu*	*vaḥ*		*sa*
8.	dhā	sā	pā	dhā	ma-ga	mā	mā	mā
	dā		*gaṅ*		*gā*			

The purport of the song is as under :

May the Gaṅgā ever protect you, the Ganges that was formed in the cluster of the immense locks of hair (of Lord Śiva), shining like the nascent dawn, and that took refuge among the series of the snow-capped peaks of the Himālayas.

Thus ends *gauḍakaiśikamadhyama.*

(viii) गौडपञ्चम:

धग्रहो धैवतीषड्जमध्यमाजातिसम्भवः ॥४२॥
धांशो मान्तस्तथा गौडपञ्चमः पञ्चमोज्झितः ।
काकल्यन्तरसंयुक्तो धैवतादिकमूर्छनः ॥४३॥
प्रसन्नमध्येनारोहिवर्णः शौरिस्मरप्रियः ।
भयानके च बीभत्से विप्रलम्भे रसे भवेत् ॥४४॥
उद्भटे नटने गेयो ग्रीष्मेऽह्नो मध्ययामयोः ।

धामा धधमधधधनिधनिध धधनिधनिधसरिगगरिगरिगगधधनिधनिधधमगम-मगामाम (धैवत) धधधधधनिधनिधधधधसधनिधसरिगधनिधधधनि ममनि धगससमग (मध्यम) मममधधधधनिधनिधमाधधमाधधनिध निध धधध ममधा मधध धनि धनिमधमगागससगसा । धधनि ममनि धनिसाधाधा (धैवत) धधध-धधनिधनिधधधधसधनी धसरिगधनिध धधनि ममनि धग सगमगम (मध्यम) मममध ममध ममध धनि धनि धमामध निध निधनिधधसधधधधसधधनिधनिध-निधमधमगागसगमगमधधधधधनिधनिधगं ससमगममधसरिमधमगधाधमधधा-धा। धधनि धधस धधनि धधध धधनिधधधमधसरिमगामामामाधधधमधधध-धधधधधधधधनिधनिमधमगामामा—इत्यालापः ।

मध मध धाधनिधास धनिधा धस रिगा धनि धामगामामा। धमधमा धमधमा। मध्यम) मनि धध रिध धाममममधागमधानिध धनि धाममसं गम धाधनि धनि धनि धाध धधस। धनिधा धसरिग धनिधा मधसरि मधमधधा धधधनि धनि धनि धनि मधमा मागामामा—इति करणम् ।

१.	धा	धा	मा	धा	सां	सां	सां	सां
	घ	न	च	ल	न	खिं		न
२.	धा	धा	धा	धा	धा	धा	सा	धा
	पं		न	ग	वि	ष	म	वि

३.	सां	सां	मां	मां	मां	धा	धा	धा
	नि		श्वा		स	धू		म
४.	धा	धा	मा	गा	मा	मा	मा	मा
	धू		स्र	श	शि			
५.	मा	मा	मा	गा	मा	धा	धा	धा
	वि	र	चि	त	क	पा		ल
६.	धा	नी	धा	मा	मा	मा	मा	गा
	मा		लं		ज	य	ति	ज
७.	मा	धा	धा	धा	मा	मा	मा	मा
	टा		मं	ड	लं			
८.	धा	धा	धा	धनि	गा	मा	मा	मा
	श				भोः			

इत्याक्षिप्तिका ।

(तत्र साकल्येन पदयोजना)

(घनचलनखिन्नपन्नगविषमविनिश्वासधूमधूस्रशशि ।
विरचितकपालमालं जयति जटामंडलं शम्भोः ।।

इति गौडपञ्चमः ।

(*viii*) *Gauḍapañcama* : 42c-45b.

Brought into being by *dhaivati* and *ṣaḍja-madhyamā* (*jāti-s*), *Gauḍapañcama* has *dhaivata* for its initial and the fundamental note, and *madhyama* for its final (note); it is devoid of *pañcama*[1] and takes (both) *kākalī* and *antara*[2] ; its *mūrcchanā* commences with *dhaivata*; and embellished by *prasannamadhya*[3] in the ascending *varṇa*, dear to Viṣṇu[4] and cupid, it is employed in (the context of) terror,[5] abhorence[6] and love in separation[7] for being sung to (the accompaniment of) brisk dancing in the two middle quarters of the day during the summer season. (42c-45b)

[1]That implies that it is hexatonic.

[2]That is *Kākalī-niṣāda* and *antara-gāndhāra*.

[3]An *alaṅkāra*.

[4]*Śauri* is Viṣṇu, but *sauri* is a text varient for it and means Saturn. 'S' takes both the readings into account. Obviously Viṣṇu or Saturn and Cupid are the presiding deities of this *rāga*.

[5]*Bhayānaka* of the text.

[6]*Bībhatsa* of the text.

[7]*Vipralambha* of the text.

Ākṣiptikā :

1.	dhā	dhā	mā	dhā	sā̇	sā̇	sā̇	sā̇
	Gha	*na*	*ca*	*la*	*na*	*khin*		*na*
2.	dhā	dhā	dhā	dhā	dhā	dhā	sā	dhā
	pan		*na*	*ga*	*vi*	*s*	*ma*	*vi*
3.	sā̇	sā̇	mā̇	mā̇	mā̇	dhā	dhā	dhā̇
	ni		*śvā*		*sa*	*dhu*		*ma*
4.	dhā	dhā	mā	gā	mā	mā	mā	mā
	dhu		*mra*	*śa*	*śi*			
5.	mā	mā	mā	gā	mā	dhā	dhā	dhā
	vi	*ra*	*ci*	*ta*	*kà*	*pā*		*la*
6.	dhā	ni	dhā	mā	mā	mā	mā	gā
	mā		*lam*		*ja*	*ya*	*ti*	*ja*
7.	mā	dhā	dhā	dhā	mā	mā	mā	mā
	ṭā		*maṇ*	*ḍa*	*lam*			
8.	dhā	dhā	dhā	dha-ni	gā	mā	mā	mā
	śam				*bho*			

The purport of the song is as under :

Victory be unto the crown of the locks of hair of Lord Śiva, which is forming as it were a garland of skulls by the dint of the moon beclouded by smoky uneven breath exhaled by the serpents tired of excessive movement.

Thus ends *gàuḍapañcama*.

(ix) गौडकैशिक:

उद्धृतः कैशिकीषड्जमध्यमाभ्यां-ग्रहांशसः ॥४५॥
सकाकलिः पञ्चमान्तः पूर्णः षड्जादिमूर्छनः ।
आरोहिणि प्रसन्नादिभूषितः करुणे रसे ॥४६॥
वीरे रौद्रेऽद्धृते गेयः शिशिरे शंकरप्रियः ।
दिनस्य मध्यमे यामे द्वितीये गौडकैशिकः ॥४७॥

सासा सग सनिसरी मगगसमम पम निप पगम गरि रिगम मस । गसां संनि सरिम गपम पपरिमपाधारी मापाधानि रिमापा धास नि सासा । सासा (षड्ज) ससससस ससस मगसं गसनि सासा । सासा सस ग ससस मगमरि गसग सधस । पधप मापमापापा । पमपापापधपधपापप पधरिरिरि मरि मसरि मधासनिसासा । सासा (षड्ज) ससससससससस सग सग सनिसासा । सासा ससगस समग मरिगस गसधसपध पमा पापा धभ पापा गम गगम (पञ्चम) पप गग मम गग गमग । निनिपनिपागमगस सनिपनिप । गमग पम मगमग गरीरी

रिगमम (षड्ज) स ससससस ससगसधसा गध सरीमामापम-पापा—इत्यालापः ।

निस निध सस रिम रिगम ममगपपनिगा पमगारि परीरीरिमरिम समरी मरिगसा मवधस रिमापमापांपांरिमरिम रिमपापारिम पनि रीरीरिमसा पध सससनिसा समरिगा सग सनिनीनिनि निनि सधध सध मम पपपा गागगनि पपधनी गगगप गमागा रीरी रिगामाम (षड्ज) स सनी निसा गारी रिम गम सागा मापा पनि धनि गमग धधम रिस गा सग सनि धसा धसरि मा पम पापा पम धमा रिमा रीसध सारी रिम मम मग साधध सस मम पप मम पापा पप गग मम पापापा—इति करणम् ।

१.	सा	सा	सा	सा	नी	नी	नी	नी
	भ		स्मा		भ्यं		ग	वि
२.	नी	नी	सा	री	री	गा	सा	सा
	भू		षि	त		दे		हं
३.	सा	सा	री	सा	री	सा	री	सा
	सु	र	व	र	मु	नि	स	हि
४.	री	री	री	री	मा	मा	मा	मा
	तं				भी		म	भु
५.	सा	सा	सा	सा	री	री	री	री
	जं		ग	म	वे		ष्टि	त
६.	सा	सा	सा	सा	मा	मा	री	मा
	बा		हुं		सु	र	व	र
७.	री	मा	मा	मा	पा	पा	पा	पा
	न	मि	त	प	दं			
८.	री	री	री	री	पा	पा	पा	पा
	चं		द्र	क	ला		क	र
९.	सा	री	री	री	सा	सा	नी	नी
	सं		त	ति	ध	व	लं	
१०.	नी	नी	सा	नी	री	मा	री	गा
	सु	र	स	रि	दं	बु	ध	

११.	सा	सा	सम	गरि	सा	सा	सध	धनि
	रं				प्र	ण	म	त
१२.	पध	पध	पप	पप	मप	मप	पा	पा
	स	त	तं		नि	ष्क	लं	
१३.	पध	पध	रिम	पम	धा	सा	सा	सा
	स	क	लं		प	र	म	
१४.	धा	नी	पध	मा	पा	पा	पा	पा
	शि	व	म	जे	यं			

—इतिध्रुवाक्षिप्तिका ।

(तत्र साकल्येन पदयोजना)

(भस्माभ्यङ्गविभूषितदेहं सुरवरमुनिसहितं,
भीमभुजङ्गमवेष्टितबाहुं सुरवरनमितपदम् ।
चन्द्रकलाकरसन्ततिधवलं सुरसरिदम्बुधरं,
प्रणमत सतत निष्कलं सकलं परमशिवमजेयम् ॥)

इति गौडकैशिकः

(*ix*) *Gauḍakaiśika* : 45c-47

Arising from *kaiśikī* and *ṣaḍja-madhyamā* with *ṣaḍja* as its initial and the fundamental note and endowed with *kākalī-gauḍakaiśika* has *pañcama* as its final note, it is complete, and its *mūrcchanā* commences with *ṣaḍja*. Embellished by *prasannādi*[1] in the ascending *varṇa* it is (employed) in (the depiction of) pathos[2], valour[3], wrath[4], and bewilderment[5]; and dear to Lord Śiva, it is sung in the second quarter of the mid-day in the winter season[6]. (45c-57)

Ākṣiptikā :

1.	sā	sā	sā	sā	nī	nī	nī	nī
	Bha		*smā*		*bhyaṅ*		*ga*	*vi*
2.	nī	ni	sā	ri	ri	gā	sā	sā
	bhū		*śi*	*ta*		*de*		*ham*

[1]An *alaṅkāra*.
[2]*Karuṇa* of the text.
[3]*Vira* of the text.
[4]*Raudra* of the text.
[5]*Adbhuta* of the text.
[6]*Śiśira* implies the first half of the writer season, the other being called *hemanta*.

3.	sā	sā	ri	sā	ri	sā	ri	sā
	su	*ra*	*va*	*ra*	*mu*	*ni*	*sa*	*hi*
4.	ri	ri	ri	ri	mā	mā	mā	mā
	tam				*bhī*		*ma*	*bhu*
5.	sā	sā	sā	sā	ri	ri	ri	ri
	jam		*ga*	*ma*	*ve*		*ṣṭi*	*ta*
6.	sā	sā	sā	sā	mā	mā	ri	mā
	bā		*hum*		*su*	*ra*	*va*	*ra*
7.	ri	mā	mā	mā	pā	pā	pā	pā
	na	*mi*	*ta*	*pa*	*dam*			
8.	ri	ri	ri	ri	pā	pā	pā	pā
	can		*dra*	*ka*	*lā*		*ka*	*ra*
9.	sā	rī	ri	ri	sā	sā	ni	nī
	saṁ		*ta*	*ti*	*dha*	*va*	*la*	
10.	ni	ni	sā	ni	ri	mā	ri	gā
	su	*ra*	*sa*	*ri*	*dam*		*bu*	*dha*
11.	sā	sā	sa-ma	ga-ri	sā	sā	sa-dha	dha-ni
	ram			*pra*		*ṇa*	*ma*	*ta*
12.	pa-dha	pa-dha	pa-pa	pa-pa	ma-pa	ma-pa	pā	pā
	sa	*ta*	*ta*		*ni*	*ṣka*	*lam*	
13.	pa-dha	pa-dha	ri-ma	pa-ma	dhā	sā	sā	sā
	sa	*ka*	*la*	*pa*	*ra*	*ma*		
14.	dhā	nī	pa-dha	mā	pā	pā	pā	pā
	Śi	*va*	*ma*	*je*	*yam*			

The purport of the song is as under :

Worship the great invincible Lord Śiva, who is eternally the whole and is yet fragmented (in manifestation), who bears the waters of the heavenly river (*Gaṅgā*), that are sparkling white in (the light of) the streaks of the rays of the moon, whose feet are adored by the best of the gods, whose arms are surrounded by serpents and who has his whole body decorated with the application of *bhasma* (sacrificial ashes).

Thus ends *gauḍakaiśika*.

(x) वेसरषाडवः

वेसरः षाडवः षड्जमध्यमाजातिसम्भवः ।
मध्यमांशग्रहन्यासः काकल्यान्तरराजितः ॥४८॥
सारोही सप्रसन्नादिर्मध्यमादिकमूर्छनः ।

सम्पूर्णः शान्तश्रृङ्गारहास्येषूशनसः प्रियः ॥४६॥

दिनस्य पश्चिमे यामे गेयः श्रीशार्ङ्गिणोदितः ।

मांमारीगांसांरीं गांमां मागा मासां । मामारीमांपाधानी पनी धामां नीधासासा । सांधा सारीगाधा सनी धानीध (पञ्चम) पापा सधा सगा मरीगांरीमामामरीगारीधामा मरी मगागमासासासरि गमा मग सनि धनि धस धस निधनिधा (पञ्चम) पस धग सम गरी मगां मां मांमांमांसां मधा नीसा रीगा मम गसा नीधनि धसनिधा नीध (पञ्चम) पापा । पपनि धधनि पापा पपनि धधनि मांमां । मम निधा धध गसा । ससमरी री गामामा । मरिरिग सांसां । सरिरिग मां मां मरि रिग रिरिधामा मरिरि गरि रिधस रिरि सांरिग सगा सधनि धसस धनि धगगधनि धधस धनि धमंमं मस समध मंरिरि मरिग सगसा धनिधसनि धानिधा (पञ्चम) पापा पप पपनि धनि धधनि धनि ममनि धधस ससग धधस धधमा रिग सगस धसरिगम रिगमांमां । मरि गसां रिगमां मां मरी गरिगमा । मदिगरि धरि रिरि धरि रिरि मांमां । गममग धधम धम रिरिम रिग सगस धनिध सनि धनिधा । (पञ्चम) पापा । पंपं पंपं पंपं पंपं । निध निध धनि धनि ममनि निध निध धमां गंस गस धनिध सनि धनी धसरि गगरि सनिधासां पधासरी मं गा मं मां—इत्यालापः ।

मंधामम गंमांयां मम गम मां । संसंमरिमांमं ममरि मं मां धधांनि धनिधा धस धनिधा धाधा म रिग मग मांमां (ऋषभ) रि धरीरीरीरी धरीरीरीरीग रिग मांमांनि पधा मा रिग रिग रिग सा । संमं (धैवत) निध धस धनि धापापा । पप (धैवत) धनींनींमांमां । मांरि मरिग मनि धा धा धा (धैवत) धनिधग (षड्ज) सा नीधा सारीं गां मां मं मधारि रि रि गग मंमं रिग रिनि पध मंमं रिग रिम रिगा ससा धनि धस धनि धध (पञ्चम) पा । (धैवत) धग सस मग रिग मांमांगामांमां—इति करणम्

१.	मा	गा	री	सा	री	गा	री	सा
	इं		द	गो		व	म	णि
२.	रो	सा	री	गा	मां	मां	मां	मां
	दा		म	सं		चि	अं	
३.	मा	री	गा	सा	नी	धा	सा	सा
	फु	ल्ल	कं		द	ल	मि	
४.	पा	धा	सा	री	गा	मा	मा	मा
	लिं		ध	सो		हि	अं	

५.	री	री	पा	पा	मा	पा	धा	नी
	म		त्त	द		द्दु	र	णि
६.	पा	धा	मा	गा	री	गा	री	सा
	णा		अ	सो		हि	अं	
७.	मा	री	गा	सा	नी	धा	सा	सा
	का		ण	णं		सु	र	हि
८.	पा	धा	सा	री	गा	मा	मा	मा
		गं	ध	सी		अ	लं	

—इत्याक्षिप्तिका।

(तत्र साकल्येन पदयोजना)

(इन्दगोवमणिदामसंचिअं, फुल्लकन्दलमिलिन्दसोहिअम्।
मत्तदद्दुरणिणाअसोहिअं, काण्णं सुरहिगन्धसीअलम्॥)

इति वेसरषाडवः।

10. *Vesaraṣāḍava* : 48-50b

Derived from *ṣaḍja-madhyamā* (*jāti*) *vesaraṣāḍava* has *madhyama* for its initial, fundamental and the final note; it is embellished by *kākalī* and *antara* with *prasannādi*[1] in the ascending *varṇa*, and the *mūrcchanā* commences with *madhyama*; it is complete and is employed in the sentiments of tranquility[2], conjugal love[3], and mirth;[4] dear to Jupiter, it is sung in the last quarter of the day as declared by Śārṅgadeva (48-60b),

Ākṣiptikā :

1.	mā	gā	ri	sā	ri	gā	ri	sā
	In		*da*	*go*		*va*	*ma*	*ṇi*
2.	ri	sā	rī	gā	mȧ	mȧ	mȧ	mȧ
	dā		*ma*	*saṅ*		*ci*	*aṁ*	
3.	mā	rī	gā	sā	nī	dhā	sā	sā
	phu	*lla*	*kan*		*da*	*la*	*mi*	
4.	pā	dhā	sā	ri	gā	mā	mā	mā
	lin		*da*	*so*		*hi*	*aṃ*	

[1]Name of an *alaṅkāra*.
[2]*Śānta* of the text.
[3]*Śṛṅgāra* of the text.
[4]*Hāsya* of the text.

5.	ri	ri	pā	pā	mā	pā	dhā	nī
	ma		*tta*	*da*		*ddu*	*ra*	*ṇī*
6.	pā	dhā	mā	gā	ri	gā	ri	sā
	ṇā		*a*	*so*		*hi*	*aṅ*	
7.	mā	ri	gā	sā	ni	dhā	sā	sā
	kā		*ṇa*	*ṇam*		*su*	*ra*	*hi*
8.	pā	dhā	sā	ri	gā	mā	mā	mā
		gan	*dha*	*si*		*a*	*lam*	

The purport of the song is as under:

The forest that has put on a garland of gems in (the form of red) silk worms, and that is lovely with the black bees settled on the fully developed leaves of the trees, and with the 'love-intoxicated' croaks of the frogs, is cool and fragrant.

Thus ends *vesaraṣāḍava*.

(xi) बोट्टः

बोट्टः स्यात्पञ्चमीषड्जमध्यमाभ्यां ग्रहांशपः ॥५०॥
मान्तोऽल्पगः काकलिमान् पञ्चमादिकमूर्छनः ।
आरोहिणि प्रसन्नान्तालङ्कृतः सकलस्वरः ॥५१॥
अन्त्येऽह्नः प्रहरे गेयो हास्यशृङ्गारयोः स्मृतः ।
उत्सवे विनियोक्तव्यो भवानीपतिवल्लभः ॥५२॥

पंनिसासा धगारि पानी धा पामा गरी ममा मामा । मं पांपां पंनिनिमां-मंधांसासनि धा धमगा मगारिरिसा री पंमापांपांपंसा सपपमपपं मंपंमंपंपंमां । पधनि पध मधस गरि रिरिपं रिरिप रिपपप (षड्ज) सा । सस गरि पां (पञ्चम) पपपपमगरि मगां मां मां मधा धा धा धध निध निसा मम धध सस रिरि गग रिगा ग (पञ्चम) पप सप धस निध धधधमसमां मगा री रिध रिरिध रिरि (ऋषभ) रिरिप रिरिप पां पनिधा पामा गरि मगामा मा। गाम । मगममगा ममगप ममगागरी रिरिरि ध धस गागारी। रिस मम गग पमपपमपपापा पमप ध नि धनि मामामधाधामा मामामधाधमामधासारीगागाया परि पापमपधनिपधमधमां गारी। रिगमपाधापामागारिपगामाम (मध्यम) मगाममगममगमपमगागपमागामापापा पनिधधनिधनिनिपानिधधससधधगरी-गरिरि गपापपधपधापधससधधगसग । साससमरिंरिंरपंमपममपापापममपपधधस सपा । ससममसमरिरिगागससपपपपधधनिपधमधमगरिमगाग । सगसधस पपधधससरिरिपपपपपमगरीमगागगा । मामांगमम (मध्यम) मा पनिधनिरिधा धनिपपपधममरिगरिमरिग । ससाससगससगधधधगसससमरिरिरिपरिपाप ।

पापसधसासपाप (षड्ज) रिसरिरिपाप। पममपपधधधधनिपधमामरिरि ममरिरिगरिपरिपपपपपप (षड्ज) ससासधधगधमगरिपा। पापाधाधापापा-सासापापाधध पपममगगागारिधारिरिधरिरि (ऋषभ) रिरिपा (पञ्चम) पधापामागारी गारीसगामामा—इत्यालापः।

धाममगममाममगममा (पञ्चम) पगममारमगमसाधधधनिप धमाधनिप-धसारिगरिमरिमसाममगरिसा। रिगरिग (पञ्चम) पपपपनिनिधामामा। माममधधाधममधधासरिधगाधगगधरिग (पञ्चम) पापपपनिनिध ससधगसमा-गारीमारीमा (मध्यम) निधाधाधधनि। पांमागारीरिपारीनिधा (षड्ज) ससससममारिरिरिरिपमभमनिधापामागारीरिमांगामांमांधरिरि धरीरिधरिरिरिप-परिपपरिपपमनिनिधनिधानिनिधाधधध निधधमधमाभाममधध (षड्ज) स (ऋषभ) रि (पञ्चम) पपनिनिनिनिधधनिनि निपधधधरिपपमधममरिरिगरि (पञ्चम) पनिनिधधर्वपंमंमगगरिरिमग मामानिधनिधाधधधनिपपधगमरीगरि-रिपरिपामगागामामा—इति करणम्।

१.	सा	धा	सा	सा	सा	सा	सा	सा
	प	व	न	वि	लु	लि	त	
२.	धा	पा	मा	पा	धा	पा	मा	मा
	भ्र	मि	त	म	धु	क	र	
३.	धा	पा	मा	गा	री	गा	सा	निध
	ज	ल	ज	रे		णु	प	रि
४.	सा	री	मा	पा	पा	पा	पा	पां
	पिं		ज	रि	ते			
५.	सा	री	मा	पा	पा	पा	पा	धा
	म		द	मं		द	ग	ति
६.	सा	सा	पा	पा	धा	पा	मा	गा
	हं		स	व	धू			
७.	धा	पा	मा	गा	री	गा	सा	निध
	वि	च	र	ति	वि	क	सि	त
८.	पा	पा	पम	गम	मा	मा	मा	मा
	कु	मु	द	व	ने			

—इत्याक्षिप्तिका।

(तत्र साकल्येन पदयोजना)

(पवनविलुलितभ्रमितमधुकरजलजरेणुपरिपिञ्जरिते।
मदमन्दगति हंसवधूर्विचरति विकसितकुमुदवने ॥)

इति बोट्टः

(xi) Boṭṭa : 50c-52

Boṭṭa is derived from *pañcamī* and *ṣaḍja-madhyamā* (*jāti-s*) with *pañcama* for its initial and the fundamental note and *madhyama* for its final note; with weak *gāndhāra* it takes *kākalī*, and its mūrcchanā commences with *pañcama*. Embellished by *prasannānta*[1] in the ascending *varṇa*, it employs all the notes[2], and dear to Lord Śiva[3], it is known to be sung in the last quarter of the day in (the context of) mirth[4] and conjugal love[5] during festive occasions. (50c-52).

Ākṣiptikā :

1.	sā	dhā	sā	sā	sā	sā	sā	sā
	pa	va	na	vi	lu	li	ta	
2.	dhā	pā	mā	pā	dhā	mā	mā	mā
	bhra	mi	ta	ma	dhu	ka	ra	
3.	dhā	pā	mā	gā	rī	gā	sā	ni-dha
	ja	la	ja	re	ṇu	pa	ri	
4.	sā	rī	mā	pā	pā	pā	pā	pā
	piñ		ja	ri	te			
5.	rī	rī	mā	pā	pā	pā	pā	dhā
	ma		da	man		da	ga	ti
6.	sā	sā	pā	pā	dhā	pā	mā	gā
	haṁ		sa	va	dhū			
7.	dhā	pā	mā	gā	rī	gā	sā	ni-dha
	rvi	ca	ra	ti	vi	ka	si	ta
8.	pā	pā	pa-ma	ga-ma	mā	mā	mā	mā
	ku	mu	da		va		ne	

The purport of the song is as under :

A goose sports with her love-afflicted and slow gait in the grove of white water lilies in full bloom, which is surrounded by black bees displaced by the wind, while the water around is strewn with the pollen of the (lotus) flowers.

Thus ends *boṭṭa*.

[1] An *alaṅkāra*.
[2] That means, it is complete.
[3] Lit. the husband of *Bhavānī*.
[4] *Hāsya* of the text.
[5] *Śṛṅgāra* of the text.

(xii) मालवपञ्चमः

मध्यमापञ्चमीजातिजातो मालवपञ्चमः ।
पञ्चमांशग्रहन्यासो हृष्यकामूर्छनान्वितः ॥५३॥
सारोहिसप्रसन्नान्तो गान्धाराल्पः सकाकलिः ।
विप्रलम्भे कञ्चुकिनः प्रवेशे केतुदैवतः ॥५४॥
गेयोऽङ्कः पश्चिमे यामे हास्यश्रृङ्गारवर्धनः ।

पामारिगासाधानिधपाधधानिसरीमागागपा धामारिगासानिर्धनिमामाधनिसारिगाममगससाधानीधपापधानीसारी । मांमांगगपांधामारीगासानिधनिमामाधनिसारिगामगगसनिध निपां । पां पां सधाधासगसासंमगारिरिरिमांमांपमासारीमापाधनीधापाधमासाधानीधापां रिरिरिगामापारीरीगामापारीरीरीगामापानिधा मापानिधा मारीरिगमाममासरिगमामगसनिधानिपा । पापा पपस धधग ससग गरिप ममप मपपांपां । धाम मप धमामा पांधानीनिमामापाधासासमामा पांधागासांधानि धापां धमासधनि धापा मामा (मध्यम) गागं मगंम री रिरीरिरिमसासससससमरीरिरिरिप मापमामपापापपधामाममनिनिधधपपपधमासमससधधनिनिधधपपममगगरिरीनिनीधधपारीरीधरिरिगामापारीरीधरिरिगमापा । रीरीधरीधरिरिगामापारिगमरिगमपधनिधमां मरिरिरिगगससससधसरिगगरिसनिधमपपरिम्मसंधनिधापाधामांगासांधानीधापा धमसधनिधपाः—इत्यालापः ।

मापाधामा मरिगसा धनिमा धनिसा रिगमा धनि धधसधनिधापापा । धधधनिधनिरि मापधनिधगसधानीधासाधानी (पञ्चम) पापधसधाधधगसासससामगारीरीपमांमांपनिधनिधसनिधपांपां रिगमापा धनिधस धनिपंपपधममपमधसधधनिममनिनिधधपापधमनिधपापा—इति करणम् ।

१.	गा	री	सनि	सा	मग	रिग	सा	पम
	ध्या		न	म	यं	न	वि	
२.	पा	पा	सा	मा	गम	गा	निध	नो
	मं		च	ति	दी	नं		
३.	री	मग	पा	पम	पा	पा	धप	मा
	व्या	ह	र		ति	वि	श	ति
४.	रिम	गस	धम	धनि	पा	पा	पा	पा
	स	रः	स	लि	ले			
५.	पम	धम	सा	सा	सा	गा	सा	निध
	वि	धु	नो		ति	प		क्ष

६.	निध	सा	सा	सा	सा	री	गा	मा
	यु	ग	लं		न	रे		न्द्र
७.	धा	मा	रिग	सा	निध	सा	पा	मा
	हं		सो		नि		ज	
८.	मरि	गम	धस	निध	पा	पा	पा	पा
	प्रि	या	वि	र	हे			

—इत्याक्षिप्तिका ।

(तत्र साकल्येन पदयोजना)

(ध्यानमयं न विमुञ्चति दीनं व्याहरति विशति सरःसलिले ।
विधुनोति पक्षयुगलं नरेन्द्रहंसो निजप्रियाविरहे ॥)

इति मालवपञ्चमः ।

(*xii*) *Mālavapañcama* : 53-55b

Originating from the *madhyamā* and *pañcamī jāti-s*, *mālavapañcama* has *pañcama* for its initial, fundamental and the final note; it is incorporated in the *mūrcchanā* called *hṛśyakā*[1], and has *prasannānta*[2] in the ascending *varṇa*, a weak *gāndhāra* and *kākalī*; it is sung in the event of the chamberlain entering (the stage) in (the depiction of) love in separation in the last quarter of the day and having *Ketu*[3] as its presiding deity, it is conducive to mirth[4] and conjugal love[5]. (53-55b)

Ākṣiptikā :

1.	gā	rī	sa-ni	sā	ma-ga	ri-ga	sā	pa-ma
	Dhya		*na*	*ma*	*yam*	*na*	*vi*	
2.	pā	pā	sā	mā	ga-ma	gā	ni-dha	nī
	muñ		*ca*	*ti*	*dī*	*nam*		
3.	rī	ma-ga	pā	pa-ma	pā	pā	dha-pa	mā
	vyā	*ha*	*ra*		*ti*	*vi*	*sā*	*ti*

[1]That is, the seventh *mūrcchanā* of *madhyama-grāma*,

[2]An *alaṅkāra*.

[3]Astronomically ketu is the name given to the ninth planet. Mythologically it is the co-product of Rahu (cf. note 80 on Rahu verse 103-105b). It is said that on the occasion of the distribution of nectar among the goods the demon Saiṁbikeya stealthly joined the goods and drank of it. Coming to know of it, Viṣṇu cut his throat off, but since he had already taken nectar, his head was transformed into Rahu and his body into ketu.

[4]*Hāsya* of the text.

[5]*Śṛṅgāra* of the text.

4.	ri-ma	ga-sa	dha-ma	dha-ni	pā	pā	pā	pā
	sa	*raḥ*	*sa*	*li*	*le*			
5.	pa-ma	dha-ma	sā	sā	sā	gā	sā	ni-dha
	vi	*dhu*	*no*		*ti*	*pa*		*kṣa*
6.	ni-dha	sā	sā	sā	sā	rī	gā	mā
	yu	*ga*	*lam*		*na*	*ren*		*dra*
7.	dhā	mā	ri-ga	sā	ni-dha	sā	pā	mā
	haṁ		*so*		*ni*		*ja*	
8.	ma-ri	ga-ma	dha-sa	ni-dha	pā	pā	pā	pā
	pri	*yā*	*vi*	*ra*	*he*			

The purport of the song is as under:

This 'royal' swan, separated from his beloved, does not give up (her) thought and expresses misery, moves into the pond and tosses his wings in despair.

Thus ends *mālavapāñcama.*

(xiii) रूपसाधारः

जातो नैषादिनीषड्जमध्यमाभ्यां ग्रहांशसः ॥५५॥
मन्यासो रूपसाधारोऽल्परिपः काकलीयुतः ।
प्रसन्नमध्यालङ्कारः पूर्णः षड्जादिमूर्छनः ॥५६॥
अवरोहिणि वर्णे स्याद्वीरे रौद्रेऽद्भुते रसे ।
प्रयोज्यो वीरकरुणे सवितुः प्रीतये सदा ॥५७॥

सानिधा सनि सा सामा पामापापामपा मगामनी निधाधधा सधनि धासनी संसंपा धा सा री गाधा सापा धमा माधा निधानीनी मागा मागा मसा —इत्यालापः ।

साधा सनिधनी सा सा पामा पममा गसं नीधाधाध सधनिधध (षड्ज) सा साधाधासारी गमगरिसधाधपसाधधनिसा (मध्यम) मगमसा । सगमधमनिधा सगस सधनिध धमा मगामा मामा (मध्यम) (पञ्चम) पगगम माग ममनि निधपपमपा । गममम (षड्ज) सध सससा निधम पप धध स रिरि मरि ग सा धधधधगसा (धैवत) निधमा (मध्यम) म सा सगगध मम पस सग सस धनि धध मा मग मामा—इति करणम् ।

अथ वा—सा धा सा धा पा पधा सासा सगाम गासगांधा पां धा सां सां सां गा मं निधा सां ससनि सा सं मां सं गां ग सा धा पाप धप ध सां सां सा गा मा नी सासा (षड्ज) स सगा सगा ग सासा धापा धाप मामा —इत्यालापः

१.	मा	मा	नी	नी	धा	धा	सा	सा
	स	द्यो			जा	तं		
२.	नी	नी	धा	सा	सा	सा	सा	सा
	वा		म	म	घो	रं		
३.	सा	सा	नी	धा	पा	मा	मा	मा
	त		त्पु	रु	ष	मी		
४.	सां	रीं	सां	नीं	नी	धा	सा	सा
	शा				नं			
५.	मा	मा	मा	मा	नी	नी	धा	धा
	वि		श्वं		वि	ष्णुं		
६.	सा	सा	पा	पा	मा	मा	मा	मा
	वे		द	प	दं			
७.	मा	मा	नी	नी	नी	धा	सा	सा
	सू	क्ष्म	म	चिं		त्य	म	
८.	नी	नी	धा	सा	सा	सा	सा	सा
	ज	न	क	म	जा	तं		
९.	मा	मा	मा	मा	सा	सा	सा	सा
	प्र	ण	मा		मि	ह	रं	
१०.	सा	सा	नी	धा	सा	सा	सा	सा
	स	द्गु		रुं				
११.	मा	मा	नी	नी	नी	धा	सा	सा
	श	र	ण		म	भ	व	म
१२.	सा	सा	पा	धा	मा	मा	मा	मा
	हं		प	र	मं			

—इत्याक्षिप्तिका ।

(तत्र साकल्येन पदयोजना)

(सद्योजातं वाममघोरं तत्पुरुषमीशानं विश्वं विष्णुं वेदपदम् ।
सूक्ष्ममचिन्त्यमजनकमजातं, प्रणमामि हरं सद्गुरुं शरणमभवमहं परमम् ॥)

इति रूपसाधारः ।

13. *Rūpasādhāra* : 55c-57

Having originated from *naiṣādī*[1] and *ṣaḍjamadhyamā* (*jātis*), *rūpasādhāra* has *ṣaḍja* for its initial as well as the fundamental note, and *madhyama* as the final note; it has weak *ṛṣabha* and *pañcama* and takes *kākalī*; it is complete and is (embellished) by the pattern of tonal phrase (*alaṅkāra*) called *prasanna-madhya* in the ascending *varṇa*, and its *mūrcchanā* commences with *ṣaḍja*: it is always employed in the sentiments of valour[2], wrath[3], bewilderment[4], and heroic pathos[5] for propitiating the Sun[6]. (55c-57)

Ākṣiptikā :

1.	mā	mā	nī	nī	dhā	dhā	sā	sā
	Sa	*dyo*			*jā*		*tam*	
2.	ni	ni	dhā	sā	sā	sā	sā	sā
	vā		*ma*	*ma*	*gho*		*ram*	
3.	sā	sā	ni	dhā	pā	mā	mā	mā
	ta		*tpu*	*ru*	*ṣa*	*mī*		
4.	sā̇	rī̇	sā̇	nī̇	ni	dhā	sā	sā
	śā				*nam*			
5.	mā	mā	mā	mā	ni	ni	dhā	dhā
	vi		*śvam*		*vi*		*ṣṇum*	
6.	sā	sā	pā	pā	mā	mā	mā	mā
	ve		*da*	*pa*	*dam*			
7.	mā	mā	ni	ni	ni	dhā	sā	sā
	sū	*kṣma*	*ma*	*cin*		*tya*	*ma*	
8.	ni	ni	dha	sā	sā	sā	sā	sā
	ja	*na*	*ka*	*ma*	*jā*		*tam*	
9.	mā	mā	mā	mā	sā	sā	sā	sā
	pra	*ṇa*	*mā*		*mi*	*ha*	*ram*	
10.	sā	sā	nī	dhā	sā	sā	sā	sā
	sa	*dgu*		*rum*				
11.	mā	mā	ni	nī	ni	dhā	sā	sā
	śa	*ra*	*ṇa*		*ma*	*bha*	*va*	*ma*

[1] *Naiṣādinī* of the text.
[2] *Vīra* of the text.
[3] *Raudra* of the text.
[4] *Adhbuta* of the text.
[5] *Vīrakaruṇa* of the text.
[6] 'S' is provided capital in view of the fact that the sun is embodying a divinity here.

12. sā sā pā dhā mā mā mā mā
ham pa ra mam

The purport of the song is as under:

I bow down to Lord Śiva who is the true preceptor and the highest refuge, the unborn one, and to His five faces viz. *sadyojāta*, *vāma*, *aghora* *tatpuruṣa* and *īśāna*, to Śiva who is all-pervasive and perfect, the source of the Veda-s, subtle, beyond imagination, uncreating and uncreated.

Thus ends *rūpasādhāra*.

१४. शकः

षाड्जीधैवतिकोत्पन्नो ग्रहांशन्यासषड्जकः ।
काकल्यन्तरसंयुक्तः पूर्णः षड्जादिमूर्छनः ॥५८॥
प्रसन्नमध्येनारोहिवर्णे वीरादिके रसे ।
वीरहास्ये निर्वहणे गेयो रुद्रप्रियः शकः ॥५९॥

सा निधनी पापाधनी सारीगासासारी गाधा धानी सासा निधसासा निधसानी धापानिसा गमा धध निनिरिगा सासा—इत्यालापः ।

(षड्ज) ससनि मम मम पप धध गगा सरिरीरी गमगम माधधधस गगससगासनि सासससनि रिरिरिरिनिरिरिधानिमपधामा (गांधार) ग (षड्ज) सनिनि पनिसासा सससनि रिरि गरिरि धापापनिनिधासासा सरिरिरिधधधमधममा। धसरिममरिमधधपप मम गग (षड्ज) सस निसासा—इति करणम् ।

अथवा—सा सनिमा मप धम पंगंगां मम मग माध साम पगसमासनि सससम निरिनिरि रिरि धनि मामपाधा मागासासनि सां संनी सास। रिरिरिरि गा रिधाधा पानिनिनि निध सासा सरि रिरि धंधंधं मं धं मा धस रिमं मरि। मां धापामा मागासास री सासा—इत्यालापः ।

(षड्ज) सनि धनि सांसांसां स ससा। सरिरिरिरिम (षड्ज) (धैवत) धध (षड्ज) सस मां गा गगगमा गगनिस (षड्ज) सनिनिनि स रिरिगगमा —इति करणम् ।

इति शकः ।

14. *Śaka*: 58-59

Originating from *ṣāḍjī* and *dhaivatī*, having *ṣaḍja* for its initial, fundamental and the final note, *śaka* includes *kākalī* and *antara*, is complete, and its *mūrcchanā* commences with *ṣaḍja;* (embellished) with *prasanna-madhya*[1] in the ascending *varṇa*, dear to Lord Śiva, it is sung in the denouement (*nirvahaṇa*) in the depiction of valour[2] and the sentiment of mirth[3]. (58—59)

१५. भम्माणपञ्चमः

शुद्धमध्यमया सृष्टो रागो भम्माणपञ्चमः ।
ग्रहांशन्यासषड्जश्च मन्यासः काकलीयुतः ॥६०॥
गाल्पः पूर्णः सषड्जादिमूर्छनारोहिवर्णकः ।
प्रसन्नमध्यालंकारो वीरे रौद्रेऽद्भुते रसे ॥६१॥
पथि भ्रष्टे वनभ्रान्ते विनियुक्तः शिवप्रियः ।

सा रिरिस रिरि सारी रिपा धाधधध धपाधपाप धपधप म मा ममा। गारी रिधा धप धासा धासा धासा सरी रीसा सस मग रिसा सनिनि (धैवत) (पञ्चम) पप धप धप पपप ममप मप मा मगमामा—इत्यालापः।

सस रिरिरि सरीरीरी। पापा धप धधा धध पधधा। पापाप मपमपपा पापा धधध मामा माम ध रीरीरीरीरी धरिरि धा। धापा पापा पाप पपप धाधधा सध धसा सां सां। स रिरिरि ससममसमरिग स पधध धापमपनि पपाप पाप पध मधपध पाध पध पाधपपापपमगसा—इति करणम्।

अथवा—सासा सधा सरी मा पां पं (पञ्चम) पां पां सां सां सरीं पापां मंपं धंसं निध पांमां पंमां पांपां मांधां सांनी धापां मांपं मांपां मां मम पम प (मध्यम) मा—इत्यालापः।

सस रिरि सासा धध रिरि सासा धंधंधं सरिम मग सासरि गरिस रिरि मपधससनि धास रिगामा (पञ्चम) पम धम मम पग पां पां मां मां—इति करणम्।

१.	री	गा	मा	सा	रिग	सा	धा	मा
	गु	रु	ज	घ	न	ल	लि	तं
२.	पा	धा	पध	पम	पा	पा	धा	पम
	मृ	दु	च	र	ण	प	त	नं
३.	सा	री	मा	पा	पा	धा	पम	मप
	ग	ति	सु	भ	ग	ग	म	नं

[1] An *alaṅkāra*.
[2] *Vira* of the text.
[3] *Vīra-hāsya* of the text, which actually refers to mirth created in the context of valour.

४.	पा	धनि	पम	धस	सा	सा	सा	सा
	म	द	य	ति				
५.	री	री	मा	पम	रिग	सा	धा	मा
	प्रि	य	मु	दि	ता	म	धु	र
६.	पा	पा	पध	पध	पा	पा	पा	पा
	म	धु	म	द	प	र	व	श
७.	मा	मा	पा	धस	रिग	सा	धनि	पम
	हृ	द	या		भृ	शं		
८.	पा	धा	पा	धप	मा	मा	मा	मा
	त				न्वी			

—इत्याक्षिप्तिका ।

(तत्र साकल्येन पदयोजना)

(गुरुजघनललितं मृदुचरणपतनं, गतिसुभगगमनं मदयति
प्रियमृदिता मधुरमधुमदपरवशहृदया भृशं तन्वी ॥)

इति भम्माणपञ्चमः ।

15. *Bhammāṇapañcama*: 60-62b

Created from *śuddhamadhyamā* (*jāti*), *rāga bhammāṇapañcama* has *ṣaḍja* for its initial, fundamental, and the final note, and also *madhyama* as the final; it includes *kākalī*, has a weak *gāndhāra*, is complete, and its *mūrcchanā* commences with *ṣaḍja;* having the *prasannamadhya alaṅkāra* in the ascending varṇa, dear to Lord Śiva, it is employed in the sentiments of valour, wrath[1] and bewilderment[82] in the context of the (traveller) who has lost his way, being confounded in the woods. (60—62b)

Ākṣiptikā :

1.	ri	gā	mā	sā	ri-ga	sā	dhā	mā
	Gu	*ru*	*ja*	*gha*	*na*	*la*	*li*	*tam*
2.	pā	dhā	pa-dha	pa-ma	pā	pā	dhā	pa-ma
	mṛ	*du*	*ca*	*ra*	*ṇa*	*pa*	*ta*	*nam*
3.	sā	rī	mā	pā	pā	dhā	pa-ma	ma-pa
	ga	*ti*	*su*	*bha*	*ga*	*ga*	*ma*	*nam*

[1]*Vira* and *raudra* of the text.

4.	pā	dha-ni	pa-ma	dha-sa	sā	sā	sā	sā
	ma	*da*	*ya*	*ti*				
5.	ri	ri	mā	pa-ma	ri-ga	sā	dhā	mā
	pri	*ya*	*mu*	*di*	*tā*	*ma*	*dhu*	*ra*
6.	pā	pā	pa-dha	pa-dha	pā	pā	pā	pā
	ma	*dhu*	*ma*	*da*	*pa*	*ra*	*va*	*śa*
7.	mā	mā	pā	dha-sa	ri-ga	sā	dha-ni	pa-ma
	hṛ	*da*	*yā*		*bhṛ*		*śam*	
8.	pā	dhā	pā	dha-pa	mā	mā	mā	mā
	ta				*nvī*			

The purport of the song is as under:

The beautiful gait of the slender damsel, gladdened by her beloved, with her heart overpowered by the sweet passionate stimulation, rendered lovely by her heavy hips and distinguished by the soft landing of her feet, greatly intoxicates (the mind).

Thus ends *Bhammāṇapañcama*.

१६. नर्तः

मध्यमापञ्चमीजातो नर्तोऽंशग्रहपञ्चमः ॥६२॥
मन्यासः काकलीयुक्तः पञ्चमादिकमूर्च्छनः ।
गाल्पः प्रसन्नमध्येन भूष्यः संचारिवर्णभाक् ॥६३॥
धीरैरुद्धटचारीकमण्डलाजौ प्रयुज्यते ।
हास्यशृङ्गारयोरेष रसयोः कश्यपोदितः ॥६४॥
धैवतीमपि तद्धेतुं दुर्गाशक्तिरभाषत ।

पापसा मगामापापगामा नोधापापमानीनी सांसां सागा सानि धनी नीनी । नि निध धमपध ममगा गसा समं मगा गनी निनि धधप पधममगामा इत्यालापः ।

पापमगापा (पञ्चम) ससगगं निनिधापा (पञ्चम) नीनीधा (षड्ज) सनिनिध सनी धापा मापा पमगा गनिनि पधनि गम गम पाम धाममामा—इति करणम् ।

अथवा—पामागम मापापग पापा । पगापानीनिधाधा । नीनी सांगांसां सं धा नीनि नींनीं निनि मसा संसंसं धानीनीनी निनिनि धधनि पपध मामगागसा समा गगागरी निंनी निध धधनी प (पञ्चम) मागामामा इत्यालापः ।

पपप मपपप मपप मग समग मामग सा। मगा मपापनी निधनि (षड्ज) सनि सनि निधनिधा निनि धधधनि पधपा पपधपाप धामम गमसा ससमससा (पञ्चम) धमा नीधापा। मामानी धधसा धधधध निपाधा पापागा गमसा सासा गपमा धनिधा धनि (पञ्चम) पधप मममनि धनि पधमम षड्ज सगामामा—इति करणम्।

पापा (षड्ज) सघामा (पञ्चम) पापापा पधमा मगमा (मध्यम) मामा। ममम निधा धध निधमा पपधमा गमगमां मां (षड्ज) स मापपाधप मास मनि धरिधगं (षड्ज) सं धांनी निनि नीधधधनि। पापपध पामा सामा। गां (पञ्चम) धधम मनिधनि पध पमामा गामामामा—इति द्वितीयकरणम्।

१.	पा	पा	मा	गा	पा	पा	बा	सा
	अ	न	व	र	त	ग	लि	त
२.	सा	सा	सां	सां	सा	मा	गा	सा
	म	द	ज	ल	दु		र्दि	न
३.	गा	मा	पा	मा	गा	मा	मा	मा
	धा		रौ		ध	सि		क्त
४.	मा	गा	मा	पा	मा	पा	पा	पा
	भु	व	न	त	ल			
५.	नी	सां	नी	सा	सा	सा	सा	सा
	म	धु	क	र	कु	लां		ध
६.	सा	गा	नी	धा	पा	पा	पा	पा
	का		रि	त	दि	न		दि
७.	नी	सा	नी	सा	मा	धा	पा	धा
	ङ्मु	ख	ग	ज	मु		ख	
८.	मा	पा	गा	गा	मा	मा	मा	मा
	न		म		स्ते			

—इत्याक्षिप्तका।

(तत्र साकल्येन पदयोजना)

(अनवरतगलितमदजलदुर्दिनधारौघसिक्तभुवनतल।
मधुकरकुलान्धकारितदिनदिङ्मुखगजमुख नमस्ते ॥)

इति नर्तः।

16. *Narta*: 62c-65b

Derived[1] from *madhyamā* and *pañcamī* (*jāti-s*) *narta* has *pañcama* for its initial and the fundamental note and *madhyama* for its final note; it incorporates *kākalī*, its *mūrcchanā* commences with *pañcama* and it has a weak *gāndhāra*. To be embellished by *prasannamadhya*[2] in the *sañcārī* (circulatory) *varṇa*, it is used by valiant (dancers) in the *cārīmaṇḍala*[3] formation, and in the battle-field. As declared by Kaśyapa (it is to be employed in the context of) the sentiments of mirth[4] and conjugal love[5]. However, Durgaśakti has said that *dhaivatī* too is the parent (*jāti*) for this (*rāga*). (62c-65b)

Ākṣiptikā :

1.	pā	pā	mā	gā	pā	pā	gā	sā
	A	*na*	*va*	*ra*	*ta*	*ga*	*li*	*ta*
2.	sā	sā	sȧ	sȧ	sā	mā	gā	sā
	ma	*da*	*ja*	*la*	*du*		*rdi*	*na*
3.	gā	mā	pā	mā	gā	mā	mā	mā
	dhā		*rau*		*gha*	*si*		*kta*
4.	mā	gā	mā	pā	mā	pā	pā	pā
	bhu	*va*	*na*	*ṭa*	*la*			
5.	ni	sā	ni	sā	sā	sā	sā	sā
	ma	*dhu*	*ka*	*ra*	*ku*	*lān*		*dha*
6.	sā	gā	ni	dhā	pā	pā	pā	pā
	kā		*ri*	*ta*	*di*	*na*		*di*
7.	ni	sā	ni	sā	mā	dhā	pā	pā
	ṅmu	*kha*	*ga*	*ja*	*mu*		*kha*	
8.	mā	pā	gā	gā	mā	mā	mā	mā
	na		*ma*		*ste*			

The purport of the song is as under:

Salutations to you O ! the elephant-faced one (Gaṇeṣa); the swarms of bees (hovering over) the face of the earth soiled by the incessant flow of the stream of rut have darkened the day and veiled the directions in the sky (as it were).

Thus ends *Narta*.

[1] *Adbhuta* of the text.
[2] Lit. 'born of'.
[3] An *alaṅkāra*.
[4] 'S' observes that the *maṇḍala-s* are dealt with, by the author, in Chapter VII.
[5] *Hāsya* of the text.
[6] *Śṛṅgāra* of the text.

१७. षड्जकैशिकः

षड्जर्षभांशग्रहः स्यात् कैशिकीजातिसंभवः ॥६५॥
ऋषभोऽल्पो निगन्यासो मन्द्रगान्धारषड्जकः ।
प्रसन्नाद्यवरोहिभ्यां युक्तः षड्जादिमूर्छनः ॥६६॥
वीररौद्राद्भुतरसः शांभव षड्जकैशिकः ।

सांसनि रिसामा पामं पाप ममगा । मं निनि धाधामा । मधाधममधा सा समा मधा गसस । धमा मसा समा मधा सासधा धमध नीनी—इत्यालापः

(षड्ज) सनिध समा ससनि सांसां निनिस त्रिरिसाममपमम पपापप-मपपा (मध्यम) । मम गगाममममगम गा (गान्धार) गगगनिधम निधम मामामा धाम धमामाधा गंगं सगं सगंसा । (षड्ज) ससधधधनि समम निधानीनि । (निषाद) निधनिनिनिनी (षड्ज) सधनि नी निनिधनिगा । मामपम पापप (मध्यम) मगम ग (षड्ज) सस संसंसं गधरिग गनिध निनिनिधमा । मम धध गग रिग (षड्ज) स सधनिधधमा पधानीनीनी (निषाद) निनि—इति करणम् ।

अथवा—सासास नीनी सनिनी मपानीनीपापा रीरिग रीरी गगरिरि पापा मप पमगम गरीगागरीसा । सनीमपनीनी धधमप निरिरिग । सा (षड्ज) स निरी सानीसा (षड्ज) स निरीसानी—इत्यालापः ।

सा (षड्ज) सनि री सानिसा (षड्ज) समापा नीपा नीधा (पञ्चम) पापारीधरीरी पमा मारी रिगरिग (षड्ज) सरिस निधप निसनि सनीनी—इति करणम् ।

१.	सा	री	सा	री	सा	सा	सा	सा
	दी		हु	र	फ	णि		द
२.	सा	नी	नी	नी	नी	सा	नी	री
	ना		ले		म	हि	ह	र
३.	री	री	री	री	री	गा	सा	सा
	के		स	र	दि	सा		मु
४.	नी	सा	नी	री	री	री	री	री
	ह	द	लि		ल्ले			
५.	मा	मा	पा	पा	मा	मा	सग	री
			पि	अ	इ	का		ल
६.	रिस	सा	नी	नी	पा	पा	नी	नी
	भ	म	रो		ज	ण	म	अ

७.	सा	सा	सा	सा	सा	नी	नी	नी
	रं		दं	पु	ह	वि		
८.	री	री	रिस	नी	नी	नी	नी	नी
	प	उ		मे				

—इत्याक्षिप्तिका ।

(तत्र साकल्येन पदयोजना)

(दीहरफणिन्दनाले महिहरकेसरदिसामुहदलिल्ले ।
पिअइ कालभ्रमरो जणमअरन्दं पुहविपउमे ॥)

इति षड्जकैशिकः ।

17. *Śaḍjakaiśika* : 65c-67b

Having *ṣadja* and *ṛaṣabha* as the fundamental and the initial notes respectively, born of *kaiśikī jāti* with a weak *ṛṣabha* and *niṣāda* (or) *gāndhāra* as its final note[1], *ṣaḍjakaiśika* takes low *gāndhāra* and *ṣaḍja*, is embellished by *prasannādi*[2] in the descending (*varṇa*) and has *ṣaḍja* as the commencing note of its *mūrcchanā*; it has Lord Śiva as its presiding deity and is (employed) in the sentiments of valour[3], wrath[4] and bewilderment[5]. (65c-67b)

Ākṣiptikā :

1.	sā	ri	sā	ri	sā	sā	sā	sā
	Dī		*ha*	*ra*	*pha*	*ṇin*		*da*
2.	sā	ni	nī	ni	nī	sā	nī	ri
	nā		*le*		*ma*	*hi*	*ha*	*ra*
3.	ri	ri	rī	rī	ri	gā	sā	sā
	ke		*sa*	*ra*	*di*	*sā*		*mu*
4.	ni	sā	ni	ri	ri	ri	ri	ri
	ha	*da*	*li*		*lle*			
5.	mā	mā	pā	pā	mā	mā	sa-ga	ri
			pi	*a*	*i*	*kā*		*la*
6.	ri-sa	sā	ni	ni	pā	pā	ni	ni
	bha	*ma*	*ro*		*ja*	*ṇa*	*ma*	*a*

[1] The text reads that it (*ṣaḍjakaiśika*) has *niṣāda*, *gāndhāra* for its final note and 'S' interprets that they are to be taken as alternative finals.

[2] An *alaṅkāra*.

[3] *Vīra* of the text.

[4] *Raudra* of the text.

[5] *Adbhuta* of the text.

7. sā sā sā sā sā nī nī nī
ran *dan* *pu* *ha* *vi*
8. rī rī ri-sa nī nī nī nī nī
pa *u* *me*

The purport of the song is as under:

The black bee of time drinks of the honey of man's life in the lotus flower of earth having the directions for its leaves, the mountains for its pollen, and the king of serpents (Śeṣa) with its long hood for its stalk.

Thus ends *ṣadjakaiśika*.

Comments :

Incidentally, the author is introducing a few concepts in relation to *rāga*. A *rāga* is fully manifested through five stages of the mode of singing called, *ālāpa*, *rūpaka*, *karaṇa*, *vartanī* and *ākṣiptikā* In the words of 'K', "the author is introducing the reader to all the elements common to the *rāga-s*". Thus, the *rāga-s* are characterised in this way and may therefore be distinguished from the melodic compositions called *prabandha-s* that are characterised by *dhātu-s* (sections) and *aṅga-s* (integral parts) dealt with in chapter IV. (23c-27b).

Before proceeding to the characteristic features of other *rāga-s*, 'K' points out some discrepancies between the definitions of certain *rāga-s* as given in Section two and their indications as given in Section one of this Chapter, and also he tries to resolve the inheren tcontradictions and explains them in the light of Mataṅga.

However, it is proposed to deal with such cases individually, while describing the *rāga-s* concerned. It may be noted here that these discrepancies are indicative of structural changes in the practical rendering of these *rāga-s* with reference to their original enunciation. (30c-32)

It has been stated (cf. *S.R.*, II 1, 11) that *Gauḍakaiśika* belongs to the *madhyama-grāma*; but here it is said to have arisen from *kaiśikī* and *ṣaḍja-madhyamā jāti-s*, which indicates that it belongs to both the *grāma-s* since the two parent *jāti-s* respectively belong to the *madhyama-grāma* and the *ṣaḍja-grāma*. Therefore, there seems to be an obvious contradiction, as pointed out by 'K' (cf. his commentary on verses 30-32 in this Section), which is resolved by him in the light of Mataṅga who says, "Even though derived from the *jāti-s* of both *grāma-s* it is related to *Madhyama-grāma* only, since in practice its *pañcama* and *dhaivata* are respectively found to be of three and four *śruti-s*. Its advent from *ṣaḍja-madhyamā* is however inferred from the statement of Mataṅga (as quoted by 'K'), "its initial note is *mandra* (low) and not *madhyama* which indicates that its *mūrcchanā* commencing with *ṣaḍja* is probably meant to be *uttaramandrā*, and thus its relationship to *ṣaḍja-grāma* is implied." That is how 'K' attempts to explain the above contradiction.

'K' points out an apparent contradiction in the statement, ""*Boṭṭa* and

Mālavakaiśika belong to the *Madhyama-grāma*" (*S.R.*, II 1.12) and the above statement that it is derived from *pañcamī* and *ṣaḍja-madhyamā* (*jāti-s*) which respectively belong to *madhyama* and *ṣaḍja-grāma-s*. He resolves this anomaly in the light of Mataṅga who says, "Though *boṭṭa rāga* is derived from *jāti-s* belonging to both the *grāma-s*, it is related to the *madhyama-grāma* because its pañcama is (found in practice) to be of three *śruti-s*."[1] 'K' further infers the *mūrcchanā* of *boṭṭa* to be that of *ṣaḍja-grāma* on the basis of its origin in the *ṣaḍjamadhyamā jāti*. Thus, the *mūrcchanā* commencing with *pañcama* is to be taken as *śuddha-ṣāḍjī* of *ṣaḍja-grāma* and not *hṛṣyakā* of *madhyama-grāma*. (50c-52)

(v) सहेतवोऽधुनाप्रसिद्धरागाः (अधुनाप्रसिद्धरागास्तद्धेतुभूतप्राक्प्रसिद्ध-रागाश्च) (तत्र रागाङ्गाणि)

१. मध्यमग्राम-मध्यमादिः

(i) मध्यमग्रामः

लक्ष्माधुनाप्रसिद्धानां सहेतूनां ब्रुवेऽधुना ॥६७॥
गान्धारीमध्यमापञ्चम्युद्भवः काकलीयुतः ।
मन्यासो मन्द्रषड्जांशग्रहः सौवीरमूर्छनः ॥६८॥
प्रसन्नाद्यवरोहिभ्यां मुखसन्धौ नियुज्यते ।
मध्यमग्रामरागोऽयं हास्यश्रृङ्गारकारकः ॥६९॥
ग्रीष्मेऽह्नः प्रथमे यामे ध्रुवप्रीत्यै,

सां नीधापांधां धांधरि । गांसां । रिगानीसां । सगपांपपप निनिपनि सां सां गपसानिधनिनि निरिगासा । पां मं पं निधामा—इत्यालापः ।

निनिपपगंगंसंसंसंरिगं । निं सं सासा । संसंगंगंपंपंधंधं मधनिसनिध पापा-पापा पनी पनी सांसांसांगागासागासनी धनीनीनिनि रिगांसांसांपापामापानिधपा-मामा—इति करणम् ।

१. सां सां गां गां पां पां मा मा ।
अ म र गु रु म म र
२. गां मा मां मा धा नी सां सा
प ति म ज यं

[1]Cf. SR., II 2.1. 453-455 where Kumbha seems to disagree with Śarṅgadeva and prefers to relate boṭṭa to the saḍjagrāma. It is also notable that K's version of Mataṅga does not quite agree with the available text of Br. D. (See prose portion after verse no. 343 i.e. p. 96).

३. सां सां मां मां पां पां सां सां
जि त म द् नं स क ल

४. री गा नी सा सां सां सां सां
श शि ति ल कं

५. नीं नीं नीं नीं धा पा मा मा
ग ण श त प रि वृ त

६. गां मां गां मां धा नी सा सा
म शु भ ह रं

७. नीं रीं गां नीं सां सां पां पां
प्र ण म त सि त वृ ष

८. सा सा निध पा मा मा मा मा
र थ ग म नं

—इत्याक्षिप्तिका ।

(तत्र साकल्येन पदयोजना)

(अमरगुरुममरपतिमजयं जितमदनं सकलशशितिलकम् ।
गणशतपरिवृतमशुभहरं प्रणमत सितवृषरथगमनम् ।।)
इति मध्यमग्रामः ।

(v) The characteristic features of the ancient *rāga-s* recognised as the sources of popular *rāgāṅga-rāga-s* (67c-106b).

Now, I shall describe the characteristic features of the current well-known *rāga-s* along with their progenitors. [67cd].

1. *Madhyamagrāma-Madhyamādi ; 68-70*

(*i*) *Madhyamagrāma*

Arising from *gāndhārī*, *madhyamā* and *pañcamī* [*jāti-s*], taking *kākalī*, having *madhyama* as its final note, low *ṣadja* as its fundamental and the initial note, and *sauvīrī*[1] as its *mūrchanā*, *madhyamagrāma* is (embellished) by *prasannādi*[2] in the descending (*varṇa*), and is employed in the first

[1]The first *mūrcchanā* of the *madhyma-grāma* which commences with *madhyama*.
[2]An *alaṅkāra*.

(*mukha*) *sandhī*[1] in creating mirth[2] and conjugal love[3]; it is sung in the first quarter of the day in summer for the propitiation of Lord Śiva[4]. (68-70b).

Ākṣiptikā :

1.	sȧ	sȧ	gȧ	gȧ	pȧ	pȧ	mā	mā
	A	*ma*	*ra*	*gu*	*ru*	*ma*	*ma*	*ra*
2.	gȧ	ma	mȧ	mā	dhā	nī	sȧ	sa
	pa	*ti*	*ma*	*ja*	*yam*			
3.	sȧ	sȧ	mȧ	mȧ	pȧ	pȧ	sȧ	sȧ
	ji	*ta*	*ma*	*da*	*nam*	*sa*	*ka*	*la*
4.	rī	gā	nī	sā	sȧ	sȧ	sȧ	sȧ
	śa	*śi*	*ti*	*la*	*kam*			
5.	nī	nī	nī	nī	dhā	pā	mā	mā
	ga	*ṇa*	*śa*	*ta*	*pa*	*ri*	*vṛ*	*ta*
6.	gȧ	mȧ	gȧ	mȧ	dhā	nī	sā	sā
	ma	*śu*	*bha*	*ha*	*ram*			
7.	nī	rī	gȧ	nī	sȧ	sȧ	pȧ	pȧ
	pra	*ṇa*	*ma*	*ta*	*si*	*ta*	*vṛ*	*ṣa*
8.	sā	sā	nir-dha	pā	mā	mā	mā	mā
	ra	*tha*	*ga*	*ma*	*nam*			

The purport of the song is as under :

Worship the best of and the invincible protector of the gods, the conqueror of the cupid, holding the full moon for the mark of *tilaka,* who is surrounded by a hundred hordes, is the destroyer of evil and whose chariot is drawn by a white bull (*i.e.*: Lord Śiva).

Thus ends *madhyamagrāma* :

(ii) मध्यमादि :

तदुद्भवा ।
मध्यमादिर्मग्रहांशा,

(ii) *Madhyamādi* :

Derived out of it is *madhyamādi*[5] with *madhyama*[6] for its initial and fundamental notes. (70b—70)

[1]See note on *sandhi-s* (no. 9) vide verses 21-23 b ante.
[2]*Hāsya.*
[3]*Śṛṅgāra*
[4]*Dhruva* is a common name for Brahmā, Vṇu and Śiva. But Śiva is the personal God of the author.
[5]Name of the *rāga.*
[6]Name of a note.

२. मालवकैशिक—मालवश्रीः

(i) मालवकैशिकः

—अथ मालवकैशिकः ॥७०॥

कैशिकीजातिजः षड्जग्रहांशान्तोऽल्पधैवतः ।

सकाकलीकः षड्जादिमूर्छनारोहिवर्णवान् ॥७१॥

प्रसन्नमध्यालङ्कारो वीरे रौद्रेऽद्भुते रसे ।

विप्रलम्भे प्रयोक्तव्यः शिशिरे प्रहरेऽन्तिमे ॥७२॥

दिनस्य केशवप्रीत्यै,

सासपामामामारीसनीसासरी मापासां नीनीरीरिसारिपामासनिसां । सनिरीरिपासनीसामगामापासनीसासनिपापनी सधनीपापनीनीनीरींपापनी मां मां गंगरीरीसासनिं निपापगामापाधनिससनिपममामगमपपमगागरिरिरि मससससम रीरिरिपममममनिपापप सनीनीरीरिसरिमपनिपपसनी सांपापानीसपनिपपसनि सानीससनिसनिसनि सपपनीपनिगगनीपपनिगंगंगंमरिरिमससंमगगरिरिपरिपपनीपपसनी सांसांनीनीससनीसनिससनिसंसपापानीससनिसनिसंसंनिरीरीपा पानीससनिमम गरिरिससनिनि पनिपमगमगपमगमगरिससरिमपनिपापसनिसां सां गाममागाममगमगमगममगमा गपपगपगनिनिगमगपपगमगसां । सससधनिपमा सस निसनिरिरिससमगमा गपमगगरिमासससधनीपानि पगमगपगममगरिमा । समगरिपपनि पपसनि पमगमगपमगमगरि मासरिमपनीपपसनी रीरीरीपप सनीसा इत्यालापः ।

गागपमगपापनि मापापमनी गपापमन्नी गपापमनी सं सनीसा (षड्ज) ससा । नीरिरि (ऋषभ) रिममपपनीनिनिरीसनीसा (षड्ज) ससानिनिरिरिरिनिपानि (पञ्चम) गगगससधनि पपगमगपगमगारीरिगमांममरीरि (षड्ज) सससमगारिरि सापापपनीनि (पञ्चम) निरिरि (पञ्चम) नि मां मां मगिस सधनिपपगम गरीसरी मपानी रिसनी सा सं नीरिसनिसा इति करणम् ।

१.	सा	सा	पा	पा	गा	मा	गा	पा
	चं		द्रा		भ	र	णं	
२.	धा	नी	पा	पा	धा	नी	गा	गा
	ह	र	नी	ल	कं		ठ	
३.	सा	पां	सां	सां	सा	नी	पा	नी
	म	हि	व	ल	यं			

४.	री	धा	सनि	सा	सा	सा	सा	सा
	त्रि	पु	र	ह	रं			
५.	पा	नी	री	पा	नी	री	री	सनि
	मृ	गां		क	न	य	नं	
६.	पा	नी	री	गम	री	गा	री	सनि
	गि	रि	नि	ल	यं			
७.	सा	सा	पा	पा	नी	नी	पम	नी
	न	म	त	स	दा		म	द
८.	सां	सां	सां	सां	सां	सा	सा	सा
	नां		ग	ह	रं			

—इत्याक्षिप्तिका ।

(तत्र साकल्येन पदयोजना)

(चन्द्राभरणं हरनीलकण्ठमहिवलयं त्रिपुरहरम् ।

मृगाङ्कनयनं गिरिनिलयं नमत सदा मदनाङ्गहरम् ॥)

इति मालवकैशिकः ।

2. *Mālavakaiśika-mālavaśrī* (*70b-73*)

(*i*) *Mālavakaiśika*

Malavakaiśika is derived[1] from *kaiśikī jāti*, has *ṣadja* for its initial, fundamental and the final notes, and takes weak *dhaivata* a d *kākalī*: its *mūrcchanā is ṣadja*, it (is embellished by) *prasannc-madhya alaṅkāra*[2] in the ascending *varṇa* and is employed[3] in the sentiments of valour,[4] wrath,[5] bewilderment[6] and love in separation,[7] and is sung in the last quarter of the day in winter to the endearment of Viṣṇu.[8] (70d – 73a)

[1] Lit. 'born'

[2] Pattern of tonal phrases.

[3] Lit. 'should be employyd'

[4] *Virā* of the text.

[5] *Rudra* of the text.

[6] *Adhuta* of the text.

[7] *Vipralambha* os the text.

[8] *Keśvara* is a name for Viṣṇu (or Kṛṣṇa)

Ākṣiptikā :

1.	sā	sā	pā	pā	gā	mā	gā	pā
	Can		*drā*		*bha*	*ra*	*ṇam*	
2.	dhā	nī	pā	pā	dhā	nī	gā	gā
	ha	*ra*	*nī*	*la*	*kaṇ*		*ṭha*	
3.	sā	pā̇	sā̇	sā̇	sā	ni	pā	nī
	ma	*hi*	*va*	*la*	*yam*			
4.	rī	dhā	sa-ni	sā	sā	sā	sā	sā
	tri	*pu*	*ra*	*ha*	*ram*			
5.	pā	nī	rī	pā	nī	rī	rī	sa-nī
	mṛ	*gāṅ*		*ka*	*na*	*ya*	*nam*	
6.	pā	nī	rī	ga-ma	rī	gā	rī	sa-nī
	gi	*ri*	*ni*	*la*	*yam*			
7.	sā	sā	pā	pā	nī	nī	pa-ma	nī
	na	*ma*	*ta*	*sa*	*dā*	*ma*	*da*	
8.	sā̇	sā̇	sā̇	sā̇	sā̇	sā	sā	sā
	naṅ		*ga*	*ha*	*ram*			

The purport of the song is as under :

Bow down ever to the destroyer of cupid's body (Lord Śiva) who has the moon for his decoration, whose throat is blue with poison, who has a snake for his bracelet, the vanquisher of the three towns of Tripurāsura, the fawn-eyed dweller of the mountain (Himālaya).

Thus ends *mālavakaiśika*.

(ii) मालवश्री:

मालवश्रीस्तदुद्भवा
समस्वरा तारमन्द्रषड्जांशन्यासषड्जभाक् ॥७३॥
इति मालवश्रीः ।

(*ii*) *Mālavaśrī*

Mālavaśrī, which is derived from it has equipoised[1] notes and the high

[1]*Samasvara*-Lit. the one having equipoised notes. 'K' defines *samasvaratā* as the absence of profusion or rarity (*bahutva* and *alpatva*) of notes. Thus even though *ṣadja* is the fundamental note, it will note be profusely used and the absence of its profūsion as such, contrary to the general rule, wiil not mar its beauty. 'S' gives an alternative interpretation as well. He says, *samasvaratā* means that all the notes employed should belong to one register.

or low[1] *ṣaḍja* as its fundamental note and also *ṣaḍja* as its final note.[2] (73b—73d),

३. षाडव-तोडिका-बङ्गालः

(i) षाडवः

> विकारिमध्यमोद्भूतः षाडवो गपदुर्बलः ।
> न्यासांशमध्यमस्तारमध्यमग्रहसंयुतः ।।७४।।
> काकल्यन्तरयुक्तश्च मध्यमादिकमूर्छनः ।
> अवरोह्यादिवर्णेन प्रसन्नान्तेन भूषितः ।।७५।।
> पूर्वरङ्गे प्रयोक्तव्यो हास्यशृङ्गारदीपकः ।
> शुक्रप्रियः पूर्वयामे,

मां सारी नीधा साधानी माधा सारीगां धां सां धांमांरिगामां माधामारी गारीनीधा सांधानीमांमां—इत्यालापः ।

ममरिग मम सस धनि सस धनि मां मां पपपपनि धममध धससरि गांगामां-रिगामांमां—इति करणम् ।

साधनि पध मारि मानि धधाधधससरि मासासाधनी धपमां मां गारी गारी गासामाधामां गारीगा गमारिगा सांसाधनी मां धनि धगसाधनी मां मांमां—इति वर्तनिका ।

१.	मां	मां	धां	धां	सा	धा	नी	पा
	पृ	थु	गं		ड	ग	लि	त
२.	धा	नीं	मां	मां	मां	री	मां	री
	म	द	ज	ल	म	ति	सौ	
३.	धां	नीं	सां	सां	गा	रिग	धा	धा
	र	भ	ल		ग्न		षट्	प
४.	सा	धा	सा	मग	मां	मां	मां	मां
	द	स	मू		हं			

[1]'K' interprets "the one having the high and the low *ṣaḍja-s* which indicates the range of the high and low." It may be noted that 'K' also understands *ṣaḍja* to be its fundamental note. 'S', on the other hand, thinks that this indicates that middle *ṣaḍja* is not to be used.

[2]The other characterstic features may be inferred from the parent *rāga* viz. *mālava-kaiśika*.

५. मग री गा मा मा मा पम गा

मु ख मिं द्र नी ल

६. री गा सां सां भां मां मां मां

श क लै र्भू षि त

७. नी धां नी धां सां सां सां सां

मि व ग ण प ते

८. गा री री गा मां मां मां मां

र्जं य तु

इत्याक्षिप्तिका ।

(तत्र साकल्येन पदयोजना)

(पृथुगण्डगलितमदजलमतिसौरभलग्नषट्पदसमूहम् ।
मुखमिन्द्रनीलशकलैर्भूषितमिव गणपतेर्जयितु ॥)

इति षाडवः ।

3. *Sāḍava, todī baṅgāla 74-78*

(i) *Sāḍava*

Arising[1] from a modification[2] of *madhyamā* (*jāti*), *ṣāḍava*[3] has weak *gāndhāra* and *pañcama*, *madhyama* as its final and the fundamental note. and high *madhyama* for its initial note : it takes *kākalī* and *antara*, has *madhyma* as the commencing note of its *mūrcchanā*, is embellished by *prasannānta* in the descending *varṇa*, and is employed in the prelude highlighting mirth[4] and conjugal love[5] in the first quarter of the day and is dear to Venus[6]. (J4-76c).

[1]Lit. 'arisen'

[2]That is, not from its *śuddhā*-variety. *Madhyamā* has one *śuddhā* (pure) form and 23 modified forms. Thus *ṣāḍava* is derived from one of these modified forms.

[3]'S' interprets that *ṣāḍava* is devoid of *ga* and *ni*, He further quotes Matṅga explaining why this *rāga* is called *ṣāḍava*-(lit having six or being among the six)-"Because it is the chief among the six *rāga-s*. It cannot literally be taken as hexatonic, since it employs all the seven notes. True, but how then is it to be considered the chief among the six *ragā*-s ? Because it has been laid down (by Bharata) that *ṣāḍava* should be used in the prelude." (Matnga as quoted by 'S' in his commentary on the above text)

[4]*Hāsya* of the text.

[5]*Śṛṅgāra* of the text.

[6]*Śukra* is said to be the preceptor of the demons (*asura-s*)

Āsiptikā :

1.	mā̇	mā̇	dhā̇	dhā̇	sā	dhā	nī	pā
	Pṛ	*thu*	*gam*		*ḍa*	*ga*	*li*	*ta*
2.	dhā	nī̇	mā̇	mā̇	mā̇	rī	mā	rī
	ma	*da*	*ja*	*la*	*ma*	*ti*	*sau*	
3.	dhā̇	nī	sā̇	sā̇	gā	ri-ga	dhā	dhā
	ra	*bha*	*la*		*gna*		*ṣaṭ*	*pa*
4.	sā	dhā	sā	ma-ga	mā̇	mā̇	mā̇	mā̇
	da	*sa*	*mū*		*ham*			
5.	ma-ga	rī	gā	mā	mā	mā	pa-ma	gā
	mu	*kha*	*min*		*dra*	*ni*		*la*
6.	ri	gā	sā̇	sā̇	mā̇	mā̇	mā̇	mā̇
	śa	*ka*	*lai*		*rbhū*	*ṣi*		*ta*
7.	nī	dhā̇	nī	dhā̇	sā̇	sā̇	sā̇	sā̇
	mī	*va*	*ga*	*ṇa*	*pa*	*te*		
8.	gā	rī	rī	gā	mā̇	mā̇	mā̇	mā̇
		rja	*ya*	*tu*				

The purport of the song is as under :

Victory be unto Gaṇapati's face which looks beautiful with precious stones (*Nīlamaṇi*) in the form of the swarms of bees hovering around it, attracted by the aroma of the rut oozing out of his broad temple.

Thus ends *ṣāḍava.*

(ii) तोडी

तोडिका स्यात्तदुद्भवा ॥७६॥

(मध्यमांशग्रहन्यासा सतारा कम्प्रपञ्चमा ।

समेतरस्वरा मन्द्रगान्धारा हर्षकारिणी ॥७७॥)

इति तोडी ।

(ii) ***Toḍī*** (*toḍikā*)

Toḍī, which is derived from it, has *madhyama* for its fundamental, initial and the final note : it employs high *ṣaḍja* and a shakeful *pañcama*, while the other notes in it are equipoised[1]. It has a low *gāndhāra* and creates gladness. (76 d-77).

[1]That is *madhyama* being the fundamental note, as pointed out by 'K', has to be used profusely, while other notes are of equal stress.

(iii) बङ्गाल:

(षाडवादेव बङ्गालो ग्रहांशन्यासमध्यमः ।
प्रहर्षे विनियोक्तव्यः प्रोक्तः सोढलसूनुना ॥७८॥)

इति बङ्गालः ।

(iii) *Baṅgāla*

Baṅgāla too is (derived) from *ṣāḍava.* It has *āmadhyama* for its initial, fundamental and the final note and should be employed for (creating) joy as declared by Śārṅgadeva.[1] (78)

४. भिन्नषड्ज-भैरव:

(i) भिन्नषड्ज:

षड्जोदीच्यवतीजातो भिन्नषड्जो रिपोज्झितः ।
धांशग्रहो मध्यमान्त उत्तरायतया युतः ॥७९॥
संचारिवर्णरुचिरः प्रसन्नान्तविभूषितः ।
काकल्यन्तरसंयुक्तश्चतुराननदैवतः ॥८०॥
हेमन्ते प्रथमे यामे बीभत्से सभयानके ।
सार्वभौमोत्सवे गेयो,

इति भिन्नषड्ज

(ii) भैरव :

भैरवस्तत्समुद्भवः ॥८१॥
धांशो मान्तो रिपत्यक्तः प्रार्थनायां समस्वरः ।

धां धां माम गा सां सां सगम धधा धा निधमगगमा मम मध मग सां सां ससं ग सं । ग मधा धा धा सनिस सां सानि गनि सनिधाधा । सनिसां सां सं सं सं ग सग सं ग मधा धानि धम गमा माधा । धंनिनीं नीं गाम गा मामा —इत्यालापः ।

धा धगा मामध मम सां सां । सगम धधा धा धनिध पामामा मा मा मम धम गसां सां सा मप मध गसां सां गसगध धा धा धनि पध मागा मा मा । मग सां सां सग धम धधा धाध निध पम गा मामा इति वर्तनी ।

१.	धा	धा	धा	नी	धा	पा	मा	गा
	च	ल		त्त	रं			ग

[1]Lit. the son of Soḍhala.

२.	सा	गां	मा	नो	धां	धां	धां	नीं
	भं			गु	रं			अ
३.	धा	पा	मा	गा	सा	गा	सा	धा
	ने			क	रे			णु
४.	धा	धा	नी	गा	मां	मां	मां	मां
	पिं			ज	रं			सु
५.	मा	नी	धा	नी	सां	सां	सां	सां
	रा			सु	रंः			सु
६.	नीं	गां	सा	नी	धां	धां	धा	नी
	से			वि	तं			पु
७.	धा	पा	मा	गा	सा	गा	मा	धा
	ना			तु	जा		ह्न	
८-	धा	धा	नी	मा	मा	मा	मा	मा
	वी			ज	लं			

—इत्याक्षिप्तिका।

(तत्र साकल्येन पदयोजना)

(चलत्तरङ्गभङ्गुरमनेकरेणुपिञ्जरम्।
सुरासुरैः सुसेवितं पुनातु जाह्नवीजलम्॥)

इति भिन्नषड्जः।

4. *Bhinnaṣaḍja-bhairava* (79-82b)

(i) *Bhinnaṣaḍja*

Born of *ṣaḍjodicyav*[1] (*jāti*), *bhinnaṣaḍja* is devoid of *ṛṣabha* and *pañcama*, has *dhaivata* as its fundamental and initial note and *madhyama* for its final note : it takes *uttarāyatā*[2] and is embellished by *prasannānta*[3] as beautified in the circulatory (*sañcārī*) *varṇa* and employes *kākalī* and *antara*. Having Brahmā for its presiding deity, it is sung on the occassions of universal

[1] *Saḍjodīcyavatī* of the text,
[2] The third *mūrcchanā* of *Sa-grāma* which commences with *dhaivata*.
[3] *Alaṁkāra*

festivity in the first quarter of the day in winter to (express) terror[1] and disgust.[2] (79-81c)

Ākṣiptikā

1.	Dhā	dhā	dhā	ni	dhā	pā	mā	gā
	Ca	*la*		*tta*	*raṅ*			*ga*
2.	sā	gȧ	mā	ni	dhȧ	dhȧ	dhȧ	ni
	bhaṅ			*gu*	*ram*			*a*
3.	dhā	pā	mā	gā	sā	gā	sā	dhā
	ne			*ka*	*re*			*ṇu*
4.	dhā	dhā	nī	gā	mȧ	mȧ	mȧ	mȧ
	pin			*ja*	*ram*			*su*
5.	mā	ni	dhā	ni	sȧ	sȧ	sȧ	sȧ
	rā			*su*	*raih*			*su*
6.	ni̇	gȧ	sā	ni	dhā	dhā	dhā	ni
	se			*vī*	*tam*			*pu*
7.	dhā	pā	mā	gā	sē	gā	mā	dhā
	nā			*tu*	*jā*		*hna*	
8.	dhā	dhā	ni	gā	mā	mā	mā	mā
	vī			*ja*	*lam*			

The purport of the song is as under :

Let the water of the Ganges, tremulous with the moving waves, tawny with the innunmerable particles of pollen and partaken of by gods as well as demons, purify with its drops.

Thus ends *bhinnaṣaḍja.*

(i) *Bhairava*

Bhairava, which is derived from it, has *dhaivata* for its fundamental note, and *madhyama* for its final note, it is devoid of *ṛṣabha* and *pañcama*, and with equipoised notes, it is (sung in) a prayer. (81d-82b)

५. भिन्नपञ्चमः वराटी

(i) भिन्नपञ्चमः

मध्यमापञ्चमीजात्योः संजातो भिन्नपञ्चमः ॥८२॥

[1]*Bhayānaka* of the text.

[2]*Bībhatsa* of the text.

धग्रहांशः पञ्चमान्तः पौरवीमूर्छनायुतः ।
काकल्या कलितः क्वापि निषादेनाप्यलङ्कृतः ॥८३॥
प्रसन्नाद्येन सञ्चारिवर्णः शौरिप्रियो रसे ।
भयानके सबीभत्से सूत्रधारप्रवेशने ॥८४॥
ग्रीष्मे प्राक्प्रहरे गेयो,

धा पा धामा नीधा पानी धामा गा मा पा पा पम मग पम मगस मगा गा रीं रीं री माधा पाधा मानोधा धप धनो (धैवत) धा धा मा धा सां (षड्ज) सामारिगसांसां गां गसां मनीं नि (धैवत) धा निध पधा धाम धा मा गा मा पा पा—इत्यालापः ।

(धैवतषड्ज) सा गा रि (ऋषभ) मनिध पप धपनि (धैवत) धा धप धनी पधम परि गरि निधाधा पा मागा मा पा (पञ्चम) (ऋषभ) रि मध मम मधा पा (धैवत) धप पनी धनी (षड्ज) समा रीरी निधा (धैवत) धधा मधा मधा ममा गामा मा मगनी धा (पञ्चम) नी धा पां मागा मां पा पा—इति वर्तनी ।

१. धा मा धप धा धा धनि धप मा
वि म ल श शि खं ड

२. धा सा नी धा पा निध मां मा
धा रि ण

३. मा री मा धा धप धा धप मा
म म र ग ण न मि त

४. नो धा पध धनि धा धा धा धा
म भ व भ यं

५. री मा धा मा नी गां मां नीं
वं दे त्रि लो क

६. धा पनि धा धा धा मा री मा
ना थं गं गा

७. धा पम गरि मां धप धा धप मा
स रि त्स लि ल

८. नी धा धप धनि धा मा पा पा
धौ त ज टं
—इत्याक्षिप्तिका ।

(तत्र साकल्येन पदयोजना)

(विमलशशिखण्डधारिणममरगणनमितमभवभयम् ।
बन्दे त्रिलोकनाथं गङ्गासरित्सलिलधौतजटम् ॥)

इति भिन्नपञ्चमः ।

5. *Bhinnapañcama-varaṭī* (82c-86b)

(i) *Bhinnapañcama* :

Produced by *madhyamā* and *pañcamī jāti-s* together, *bhinnapañcama* has *dhaivata* for its initial and the fundamental note and *pañcama* for its final note ; it takes the *mūrcchanā* called *pauravī*,[1] and *kākalī* or some times (standard) *niṣāda*[2] in its place, and is embellished by *prasannādi*[3] in the circulatory (*sañcārī*) *varṇa*. Dear to Viṣṇu[4], it is sung for (expressing) terror[5] and disgust[6] at the time of the stage manager's entrance in the first quarter of a summer day. 82c-85a)

Ākṣiptikā :

1.	dhā	mā	dha-pa	dhā	dhā	dha-ni	dha-pa	mā
	Vi	*ma*	*la*	*śa*	*śi*	*khaṇ*		*ḍa*
2.	dhā	sā	nī	dhā	pā	ni-dha	mā̊	mā
	dhā			*ri*	*ṇa*			
3.	mā	rī	mā	dhā	dha-pa	dhā	dha-pa	mā
	ma	*ma*	*ra*	*ga*	*ṇa*	*na*	*mi*	*ta*
4.	ni	dhā	pa-dha	dha-nı	dhā	dhā	dhā	dhā
	ma	*bha*	*va*	*bha*	*yam*			

[1]The sixth *mūrcchanā* of *ma-grāma* which commences with *dhaivata*.

[2]'K' explains the alternative use of these two notes which is not permissible. He says, "*kākalī* is to be used in the low and the middle registers, but not in the high ; because in *ma-grāma* standard *niṣāda* is the highest note. So *śuddha niṣada* has to be taken in the *tāra* (high) *saptaka* (heptad)".

[3]An *alaṁkāra*.

[4]*Śauri* is a name of Viṣṇu (or Kṛṣṇa).

[5]*Bhayānaka* of the text.

[6]*Bībhatsa* of the text.

5.	rī	mā	dhā	mā	nī	gā̇	mā̇	nī̇
	van		*de*		*tri*	*lo*		*ka*
6.	dhā	pa-ni	dhā	dhā	dhā	mā	ri	mā
	nā		*tham*		*gaṅ*	*gā*		
7.	dhā	pa-ma	ga-ri	mā	dha-pa	dhā	dhā-pa	mā
	sa	*ri*		*tsa*	*li*	*la*		
8.	nī	dhā	dha-pa	dhā-ni	dhā	mā	pā	pā
	dhau		*ta*	*ja*	*ṭam*			

The purport of the song is as under :

Obeisance to the Lord of the three worlds (Śiva), whose locks of hair are washed by the waters of the Ganges, who bears the spotless (shining) arc of the moon, who is worshipped by the hordes of Gods, and is the destroyer of fear (of becoming).

Thus ends *bhinnapañcama*.

(ii) वराटी

वराटी स्यात् तदुद्भवा ।
धांशा षड्जग्रहन्यासा ममन्द्रा तारधैवता ॥८५॥
समेतरस्वरा गेया शृङ्गारे शार्ङ्गसंमता ।
इति वराटी ।

(ii) *Varāṭī*

Varāṭī, which is born of it, has *dhaivata* as its fundamental note, *ṣaḍja* for its initial and the final note, a low *madhyama* and a high *dhaivata* and is equipoised with regard to other notes. It is sung in (the context of conjugal love as understood by Śārṅgadeva. (85c-86b).

६. पञ्चमषाडव-गुर्जरी

(i) पञ्चमषाडव:

मध्यमग्रामसंबन्धो धैवतयार्षभिकोद्भवः ॥८६॥
रिन्यासांशग्रहः क्वापि मान्तः पञ्चमषाडवः ।
विलसत्काकलीकोऽपि कलोपनतयान्वितः ॥८७॥
प्रसन्नाद्यन्तकलितारोहिवर्णः शिवप्रियः ।
वीररौद्राद्भुतरसो नारीहास्ये नियुज्यते ॥८८॥

रीरीरिगारि सानी रीरीरीरि निरिरिरि मगामाम धामाम मामामामम मरि मग पप गम मगामम गममप पग मम गा गरिरि गरि मम रि गमम सधं निध सनि धसनिधाध (पञ्चम) निपां पनि सनी रीरीं रिनीरीम गामाम धामम माम गा गम गम गप पग मम नींनि धाधपापमाम गागरीरीरिम सरिग सगसंध निनिध सनिध धनिधाध (पञ्चम) निपापरीरी रिग मां पां धनीरी रीरिनीरि ममामाम गरि सगा मागरीरि मगा मामा —इत्यालापः।

रीमामाम मगारि (ऋषभ) रिमापानीनी निमम धामपा गामागा मरीरी गारी मगारिगा (षड्ज) सनिधा (पञ्चम) पंनो (पञ्चम) मधा ममा (ऋषभ) रीं मापानी पासानी मारि (ऋषभ) रि (षड्ज) सनी सरि रिगाग सामगाग-रीरी—इति करणम्।

१.	री	गा	मा	मा	गा	री	री	री
	स	क	ल	सु	र	न	मि	त
२.	मा	गा	री	मा	गा	री	री	री
	वि	म	ल	मृ	दु	च	र	ण
३:	री	गा	री	धा	नी	मा	नी	नी
	द्व	य		स	रो		ज	यु
४.	धा	मा	धा	नी	गा	रीं	रीं	रीं
	ग	ल	म	म	र	गु	रूं	श
५.	री	री	री	गा	री	री	री	री
	र	ण	म	म	ल	मु	प	
६.	री	री	री	गा	नी	नी	नी	नी
	या		मि	द		या		लु
७.	मा	नी	मा	मा	नी	मा	मा	री
	म	सु	र	सु	र		ज	यि
८.	मा	गा	मा	मा	री	री	री	री
	न	म	जे		यं			

—इत्याक्षिप्तिका।

(तत्र साकल्येन पदयोजना)

(सकलसुरनमितविमलमृदुचरणद्वयसरोजयुगलममरगुरुम् ।
शरणममलमुपयामि दयालुमसुरसुरजयिनमजेयम् ॥)

इति पञ्चमषाडवः

6. *Pañcamaṣāḍava-gurjarī*

(*i*) *Pañcamaṣāḍava* :

Related to *madhyama-grāma*, arisen from *dhaivatī* and *ārṣabhī* (*jāti-s*), having *ṛṣabha* for its final, fundamental and the initial notes with *madhyama* also being sometimes[1] used as the final (note), *pañcamaṣāḍava* is beautified by *kākalī* even though set in *kalopanatā*.[2] Embellished by *prasannādyanta*[3] in the ascending *varṇa* and dear to Lord Śiva, it is employed in (the expression of) valour,[4] wrath,[5] bewilderment[6] and in female comics.[7] (89c—88)

Ākṣiptikā :

1.	ri	gā	mā	mā	gā	ri	ri	ri
	Sa	*ka*	*la*	*su*	*ra*	*na*	*mi*	*ta*
2.	mā	gā	ri	mā	gā	ri	ri	rī
	vi	*ma*	*la*	*mṛ*	*du*	*ca*	*ra*	*na*
3.	ri	gā	rī	dhā	ni	mā	ni	ni
	dva	*ya*		*sa*	*ro*		*ja*	*yu*
4.	dhā	mā	dhā	nī	gā	ṙī	ṙī	ṙī
	ga	*la*	*ma*	*ma*	*ra*	*gu*	*ruṁ*	*śa*
5.	ri	ri	ri	gā	ri	rī	ri	ri
	ra	*ṇa*	*ma*	*ma*	*ha*	*mu*	*pa*	
6.	ri	rî	ri	gā	ni	ni	ni	ni
	yā		*mi*	*da*		*yā*		*lu*

[1]'K' quotes Mataṅga while explaining the alternative use of *madhyama* as the final note, who says, "As it is in vogue, when *madhyama* is employed as the fundamental, it also serves for the final "(Mataṅga as quoted by 'S'). In other words, normally when *ṛṣabha* is the fundamental note it also serves as the final.

[2]*Kalopantā* (*ri ga ma pa dha ni sa* is the third *mūrcchanā* of *ma-grama* and its high range ought to be limited to the standard *nisāda*. So, 'K' explains that *kākalī* is to be used in the low and the middle heptads only, and standard *niṣāda* in the high heptad, though *rāga* pervades the three registers.

[3]An *alaṁkārā*.

[4]*Vīra* of the text.

[5]*Raudra* of the text.

[6]*Adbhuta* of the text.

[7]*Nārī-hāsya* of the text.

7.	mā	nī	mā	mā	nī	mā	mā	rī
	ma	su	ra		su	ra	ja	yi
8.	mā	gā	mā	mā	rī	rī	rī	rī
	na	*ma*	*je*		*yaṁ*			

The purport of the song is as under :

I simply take refuge unto the invincible conqueror of the demons, who is mereiful. whose pair of tender spotless lotus feet is worshiped by ail the gods, and who is best among the gods.

Thus ends *pañcamaṣāḍava*.

(ii) गुर्जरी

तज्जा गुर्जरिका मान्ता रिग्रहांशा ममध्यभाक् ।
रितारा रिधभूयिष्ठा श्रृङ्गारे ताडिता मता ॥८९॥

इति गुर्जरी ।

(ii) *Gurjarī* :

Born of it, *gurjarī*[1] has *madhyama* for its final note, *ṛṣabha* for its initial and the fundamental note, middle *madhyama*, high *ṛṣabha* and a profusion of *ṛṣabha* and *dhaivata*. It is accepted to be employed with shakes[2] in erotics.[2] (89)

७. टक्क-गौड-कोलाहल:

(i) टक्क:

षड्जमध्यमया सृष्टो धैवत्या चाल्पपञ्चमः ।
टक्कः सांशग्रहन्यासः काकल्यन्तरराजितः ॥९०॥
प्रसन्नान्तान्वितश्चारुसंचारी चाद्यमूर्छनः ।
मुदे रुद्रस्य वर्षासु प्रहरेऽह्नश्च पश्चिमे ॥९१॥
वीररौद्राद्भु‌ुतरसे युद्धवीरे नियुज्यते ।

साधा मारी मागा गस गध निसारी गसारी गम मास निध मध मरीरी रिमागागसा सासग मधनिधासाधामरि गसा गधनि सा । सा सा ससंगसासस-समरिगसाससगधाधध गसा सस धध निधाधम धमंनिमरिगरिरिरि निधममधमरी गरीमरिगसा ससग सासरिगधाधनि निसासा सांसांसंगससममगधममनिधध सास-

[1]*Gurjarikā* of the text.

[2]Plural is inferred from the past participle '*tāditā*.' Also see note 7 on verse 134 of this chapter.

[3]*Sṛṅgāra* of the text.

धाधमामधा मरिगसा गधनि स। मामामधामामधानिधानि मामधा धनिधमगाम-रिग साधधनिसासासासासधा गममनि गगमध मरीरिमगागसा सासाससगसस-मगमसगमगनि धासा। सासा (षड्ज) सससरि धमगगसनिधाधमा मामा धमधमंमं मममधमधमाधनि सरिगमगमगरिमगागसागगंनिसाममगमगमम गगममगग निनिमम गगमम ससममगगगमस सममरिरि गससगगससधधनिनि मममधधधधधध निधनिधमधधधधध मधधसध निधामधधमधधधधधधमसगस-धनिधा। मममममममध सगारि मागागमग धनी सासा—इत्यालापः।

(षड्ज) सधा मारिगरिनिधाम मधमारिगसासगधाध (षड्ज) सधाधा-सांध गरि गरीरीरीनिरिमा। मामधनिधा ममध धससधधगरिमासगसनि मनिमाधासाधानी सासामासनिधनिधानी सागाधनी सामा साधा मागांरीरी (ऋषभ) रिगामा निधानी सां सां सं गं मधधनिगा धासासासमरिगसगसनिधा नीधाधाध सा सासा सासा मगामगागनिगपमागा। सामामामा धामरि गसांस-गसागनी गासा मामा गानी (षड्ज) सं सां सा सा गागा गामा सां सां। सगासासा गामगा ममगममामा। गासागारि मारि मारि मारि गसागनि (षड्ज) ससा—इति करणम्।

१.	सा	सा	धा	धा	मा	मा	मा	मा
	सु	र	मु	कु	ट	म	णि	ग
२,	सा	सनि	धा	सा	सा	सा	सा	सा
	णा	र्चि	त		च	र	णं	
३.	सा	सा	गा	गा	सा	मा	गा	मा
	सु	र	वृ	क्ष		कु	सु	म
४.	धा	सा	निध	सा	सा	सा	सा	सा
	वा		सि	त	मु	कु	ट	
५.	धा	नी	सा	गा	मा	धा	मा	गा
	श	शि	श	क	ल	कि	र	ण
६,	सा	सा	धा	नी	सनि	धा	धा	धा
	वि	च्छु	रि		त	ज	टं	
७.	सा	सा	पा	नी	मा	गा	मा	गा
	प्र	ण	म	त	प	शु	प	ति

८. गा गा धा नी सा सा सा सा
म ज म म रं
—इत्याक्षिप्तिका ।

(तत्र साकल्येन पदयोजना)

(सुरमुकुटमणिगणार्चितचरणं सुरवृक्षकुसुमवासितमुकुटम् ।
शशिशकलकिरणविच्छुरितजटं प्रणमत पशुपतिमजममरम् ॥)

(इति टक्कः ।)

7. *Ṭakka-gauḍa* and *Kolāhala* (90-93b)

(i) *Ṭakka* :

Produced by *ṣaḍja-madhyamā* and *dhaivatī* (jāti-s), with a weak *pañcama*, *ṭakka* has *ṣaḍja* for its fundamental, initial and final notes, and is bestowed with *kakalī* and *antara*. Graced with *prasannānta*[1] in the circulatory (*sañcārī*) *varṇa*, it is set in the first[2] *mūrcchanā*, and is employed in (the expression of) valour,[3] wrath[4] and bewilderment[5] as (depicted) by a battle hero.[6] It is sung in the last quarter of the day during the rains to the propitiation of Lord Śiva.[7] (90—92b).

Ākṣiptikā :

1.	sā	sā	dhā	dhā	mā	mā	mā	mā
	Su	*ra*	*mu*	*ku*	*ṭa*	*ma*	*ṇi*	*ga*
2.	sā	sa-ni	dhā	dhā	sā	sā	sā	sā
	ṇā	*rci*	*ta*		*ca*	*ra*	*ṇam*	
3.	sā	sā	gā	gā	sā	mā	gā	mā
	su	*ra*	*vṛ*	*kṣa*		*ku*	*su*	*ma*
4.	dhā	sā	nī-dhā	sā	sā	sā	sā	sā
	vā		*si*	*ta*	*mu*	*ku*	*ṭam*	

[1]An *alaṅkāra*.

[2]'S' interprets it to be the *uttaramandrā*, obviously because the initial note etc. being *ṣaḍja*, it should commence with *ṣaḍja*.

[3]*Vīra* of the text.

[4]*Raudra* of the text.

[5]*Adbhuta* of the text.

[6]*Yuddha-vīra* of the text. Valour is conceived to be of three types (observes 'K'), characterising three types of heroes viz. *dāna-vīra*, *dayā-vīra* and *yuddha-vīra*, i.e. valiant in generosity, valiant in compassion and valiant in warfare.

[7]*Rudra* is a name of Lord Śiva.

5.	dhā	nī	sā	gā	mā	dhā	mā	gā
	śa	*śi*	*śa*	*ka*	*la*	*ki*	*ra*	*ṇa*
6.	sā	sā	dhā	nī	sa-ni	dhā	dhā	dhā
	vi	*cchu*	*ri*		*ta*	*ja*	*ṭam*	
7.	sā	sā	pā	nī	mā	gā	mā	gā
	pra	*ṇa*	*ma*	*ta*	*pa*	*śu*	*pa*	*ti*
8.	gā	gā	dhā	nī	sā	sā	sā	sā
	ma	*ja*	*ma*	*ma*	*ram*			

The purport of the song is as under :

Bow down to the Lord of creatures (Śiva), the unborn and immortal one, whose feet are worshipped by the crest jewels of the gods, whose crown is fragrant with the aroma of the (five) heavenly trees, and whose locks of hair are filled with the rays of the arc of the moon.

Thus ends *ṭakka*.

(ii) गौड:

गौडस्तदङ्गं निन्यासग्रहांशः पञ्चमोज्झितः ॥९२॥
इति गौडः ।

(ii) *Gauḍa* :

Gauḍa is an integral part[1] of *ṭakka* with *niṣāda* for its final, initial and the fundamental notes, and it is devoid of *pañcama*. (92 cd).

(iii) कोलाहल:

टक्काङ्गं टक्कवत्तारैः स्वरैः कोलाहलोऽखिलैः ।

इति कोलाहलः ।

(iii) *Kolāhala*

Kolāhala is an integral part of *ṭakka* and is like *ṭakka* (in all respects) but all the notes are in the high (register). (93 ab)

८. हिन्दोल-वसन्त:

(i) हिन्दोल:

धैवत्यार्षभिकावर्जस्वरनामकजातिजः ॥९३॥
हिन्दोलको रिधत्यक्तः षड्जन्यासग्रहांशकः।
आरोहिणि प्रसन्नाद्ये शुद्धमध्याख्यमूर्छनः ॥९४॥

[1]*Aṅga* of the text.

काकलीकलितो गेयो वीरे रौद्रेऽद्भुते रसे।
वसन्ते प्रहरे तुर्ये मकरध्वजवल्लभः ॥९५॥
संभोगे विनियोक्तव्यो,

सानीपापमागागपापसागनी सासासासा गामापापनीनीनी गागपपापनीसा। सनींमागागपापनीसनीसनीगसा। पनीं[1]सामपनी सगासासामां मगगससनि गसासनीसनी पपसममामगसनिसासंगाममा पापनीसा मनीमगामपापनीसनी सनि गसा पनि सागानी सा गासासमं गमा गसा सनिसनि निपापमगामा। ससगगममपपनिनि सनिमगा गपापनिसा। गासगसनीसनो सागा मम गम मग मगमप मगापाप सगासामा मगममनीपा पापममगागसगपापनी निसनि सस। नीपा मागागमा पापनी सा। सनि मगा गपापनी सागासमसनीसनी स। नि ससनी सा सा सासागसासनी साससगमसगपमा गपापस गगमगनी पापमम गा। गससमगगपा। ममनीप पसनिनिमगापापनी सागासगसनी सनी सा (षड्ज) ससा। पापानी सासापपनी पनिपापनी सासापापनि पनी पनि सगासम मगसगसनीसनी पनी मगमगासासनी। पनी पमगम गमा गस गसानिसनिपनी पमगमगामा। मगमग सागासस निनि पपमम गमपनीनिपम। गाममपनीनि पमगाममपनी ससनिमगाससगासगामपनीपापनी मगागपनी सनींसनीगसानी सापनीमपागममगागससनि सा (षड्ज) सससगसस। मगामगम मगनी पापापस निनिगसा। ससमा (गान्धार) पा (पञ्चम) पपनिनि गागस गसनी सनीसा (षड्ज) ससगससमगमा सस गा। निनि सपानी ममापगमा सससगगससगसगम पापासनि मगागपापनी सागासगासनिसनीसा (पञ्चम) पपनि पनि पापनि ससनि ससपापनीपगनीगगपापनी मंमंमं। गगगनिनिनि पपपनिनिनि सस। पागगम ससगसगसगमपनिपस निमगागापापनिं[2] सासाससमगसगसनीनी सा—इत्यालापः।

सगापमगापा (पञ्चम) (षड्ज) समागसागनीनिपानि पपगगपमगगांगांगां (षड्ज) ससगागम पाधमम (पञ्चम) पानिनि सनिसां सं। निनिनि सासासनिसासानिगपानी। सांसांसांससनि ससं निमगगगस ससनिसगमनिसनि निपनीनिपानीपपगगपगमंमां गांग (षड्ज) ससंसंसंमपम। पानिसनिमा। मामा (पञ्चम) यिसनिनि सनि ससा। सस निससनी सासापनी। पनि पापपनि सनि ससस पपपपनी। नीमम निपनिप पगसग गमगामास सनिमम गम गापप गमगानीगांगां (षड्ज) ससमग मगागमगागमगागमससग सनिसनीपागपागमांमाससगगपापस (षड्ज) ससगंगं ममपपनिनि सनीससगगसगसनिसासा—इति करणम्।

[1]Adyar edn., न्नीं।
[2]Ibid., न्नि।

१.	सा	सा	मा	गा	सा	गा	मा	पा
	स	मु	प	न	त	स	क	ल
२.	पम	गा	सा	सा	सा	गा	मा	मा
	म	भि	ग	त	ज	नौ		घ
३.	नी	सा	पा	नी	पा	नी	गा	पा
	प	रि	तु		ष्ट	मा		न
४.	नी	सां	सां	सा	सनि	गा	सप	नी
	स		हं		सं			
५.	नी	नी	सा	गा	सा	नी	पा	पा
	प्रि	य	त	म	स	ह	च	र
६.	पम	गा	सा	सा	गम	गा	मा	पा
	स	हि	तं		म	द	नां	
७.	नी	सा	पा	नी	पा	नी	गा	पा
	ग		वि		ना	श	नं	
८.	निस	निस	सा	गा	सा	सा	सा	सा
	नौ			मि				

इत्याक्षिप्तिका।

(तत्र साकल्येन पदयोजना)

(समुपनतसकलमभिगतजनौघ परितुष्टमानसहंसम्।
प्रियतमसहचरसहितं मदनाङ्गविनाशनं नौमि ॥)

इति हिन्दोलः।

8. *Hindola-Vasanta 93c-96*

(i) *Hindola*

Derived from *jāti-s* named after the *svara-s*[1] (notes) excepting *dhaivati* and *ārṣbbhī*, devoid of *ṛṣabha* and *dhaivata*, and having *ṣaḍja* for its final, initial and fundamental notes, *hiṇḍola*[2] is set in the *mūrchhanā* called *śuddha-madhyā*[3] with *prasannādi* in the ascending *varṇa*. Served by *kākalī*, it is to be sung for (depicting) the sentiments of valour,[4] wrath[5] and bewil-

[1] The seven *śuddhā jāti-s* bear the names of seven notes. It seems, therefore, that the rest of the five *śuddhā jāti-s* are meant. However, 'S' thinks that *vikṛtā* (modified) *jāti-s* such as *ṣaḍja-kaiśikī* bearing the names of the notes in part are also to be included.

[2] *Hindolaka* of the text.

[3] The fourth *mūrchanā* of the *ma-grāma* that commences with *ṣaḍja*.

[4] *Vīra* of the text.

[5] *Raudra* of the text.

derment[1] in the fourth quarter of the day in the spring season. It is employed in the context of the enjoyment of erotic love[2] to the endearment of cupid.[3] (93c-96a)

Ākṣiptikā :

1.	sā	sā	mā	gā	sā	gā	mā	pā
	Sa	*mu*	*pa*	*na*	*ta*	*sa*	*ka*	*la*
2.	pa-ma	gā	sā	sā	sā	gā	mā	mā
	ma	*bhi*	*ga*	*ta*	*ja*	*nau*		*gha*
3.	ni	sā	pā	nā	pā	ni	ga	pa
	pa	*ri*	*tu*		*ṣṭa*	*mā*		*na*
4.	nī	sā̇	sā̇	sā	sa-ni	gā	sa-pa	nī
	sa		*haṁ*		*saṁ*			
5.	nī	ni	sā	gā	sā	ni	pā	pā
	pri	*ya*	*ta*	*ma*	*sa*	*ha*	*ca*	*ra*
6.	pa-ma	gā	sā	sā	ga-ma	gā	mā	pā
	sa	*hi*	*tam*		*ma*	*da*	*nāṅ*	
7.	ni	sā	pā	ni	pā	ni	gā	pā
	ga		*vi*		*nā*	*śa*	*nam*	
8.	ni-sa	ni-sa	sā	gā	sā	sā	sā	sạ̄
	nau			*mi*				

The purport of the song is as under :

I bow down to Śiva who has satisfied the wishes (lit. the mind swans) of all the people who have taken refuge in him, and who, accompanied by his consort, is the destroyer of the body of the cupid.

Thus ends *hiṇḍola*.

(ii) वसन्तः

वसन्तस्तत्समुद्भवः ।

पूर्णस्तल्लक्षणो देशीहिन्दोलोऽप्येष कथ्यते ॥९६॥

इति वसन्तः ।

(ii) *Vasanta*

Vasanta, which is derived from it, bears all the same characteristic features (of *hindola*), but is complete.[4] It is also called as *deśī-hindola*. (96 bcd)

[1] *Adbhuta* of the text.

[2] *Sambhoga* (lit. copulation) is a technical sub-division of conjugal love (*Śṛṅgāra*).

[3] Lit. one who has a flsg with a fish on it.

[4] That is, it takes all the seven notes and this is what distinguishes it from *hindola*.

६. शुद्धकैशिकमध्यम·धन्नासी

(i) शुद्धकैशिकमध्यमः

षड्जमध्यमया सृष्टः कैशिक्या च रिपोज्झितः ।
तारसांशग्रहो मान्तः शुद्धकैशिकमध्यमः ॥६७॥
प्रसन्नान्तावरोहिभ्यामाद्यमूर्छनया युतः ।
गान्धाराल्पः काकलीयुग्वीरे रौद्रेऽद्भुते रसे ॥६८॥
चन्द्रप्रियः पूर्वयामे संधौ निर्वहणे भवेत् ।

सां धांमां धां सनि धसनी सां सां । सा धानी मां मां सां गां सां गां माधा माधा सां निध सनि सां सां धांमां मधमगागमा सासाधामासगासागामाधास निधसांनी सां सासाधानी मा मां—इत्यालापः ।

ससममधधममधसनिधसासांसांसां । संसंगंम गमं मधमसानिधसां सां सां सां धंधं मंमं धम सगसगमस गग धध सस गंसं मम धमध सधनि मामा मामा —इति करणम् ।

१.	सां	सां	धा	पा	मा	धां	पां	मां
	ओं		का		र	मू		र्ति
२.	धा	पा	मा	पा	री	री	मा	मा
	सं		स्थं		मा		त्रा	
३.	नी	धा	मा	नी	धा	नी	सां	सां
	त्र	य	भू		षि	तं		क
४.	नी	धा	नी	सां	सां	सां	सां	सां
	ला		ती		तं			
५.	धा	धा	मां	मां	री	री	सा	सा
	व	र	दं		व	रं		व
६.	धा	धा	मा	मा	गां	गां	मां	गां
	रे		ण्यं		गो		विं	
७.	नी	धा	मा	नी	धा	नी	सा	सा
	द	क	सं		स्तु		तं	

८. धां सा धां नी मां मां मां मां
वं दे

—इत्याक्षिप्तिका ।

(तत्र साकल्येन पदयोजना)

(ओङ्कारमूर्तिसंस्थं मात्रात्रयभूषितं कलातीतम् ।
वरदं वरं वरेण्यं गोविन्दसंस्तुतं वन्दे ॥)

इति शुद्धकैशिकमध्यमः

9. *Śuddhakaiśikamadhyama-dhannāsī* : (97-100b)

(*i*) *Śuddhakaiṣikamadhayma* :

Produced by *ṣaḍjamadhyamā* and *kaiśikī* (*Jāti-s*), devoid of *ṛṣabha* and *pañcama*, having high *ṣaḍja* for its fundamental and initial note, and *madhyama* as its final note, *śuddha-kaiśikamadhyama* has *prasannānta*[1] in the descending *varṇa;* set in the first *mūrcchanā*, it has weak *gāndhāra*, and takes *kākalī*. Dear to the moon, it is employed[2] in the sentiments of valour[3], wrath[4] and bewilderment[5] in the first quarter (of the day) in the denounment[6]. (97-99b).

Ākṣiptikā :

1.	sā̇	sā̇	dhā	pā	mā	dhā̇	pā̇	mā̇
	Oṁ		*kā*		*ra*	*mū*		*rti*
2.	dhā	pā	mā	pā	rī	rī	mā	mā
	saṁ		*sthaṁ*		*mā*		*trā*	
3.	nī	dhā	mā	nī	dhā	nī	sā̇	sā̇
	tra	*ya*	*bhū*		*ṣi*	*tam*		*ka*
4.	nī	dhā	nī	sā̇	sā̇	sā̇	ṣā̇	sā̇
	lā		*tī*		*taṁ*			
5.	dhā	dhā	mā̇	mā̇	rī	rī	sā	sā
	va	*ra*	*daṁ*		*va*	*raṁ*		*va*

[1] An *alaṅkāra*.
[2] *Bhavet*, lit. means 'may become'.
[3] *Vīra* of the text.
[4] *Raudra* of the text.
[5] *Adbhuta* of the text.
[6] *Nirvahaṇa* is the name of the last of the five *sandhi-s* i.e. the junctural sub-divisions.

6.	dhā	dhā	mā̇	mā̇	gȧ	gā̇	mā̇	gā̇
	re		*ṇyam*		*go*		*vin*	
7.	ni	dhā	mā	ni	dhā	nī	sā	sā
	da	*ka*	*saṁ*		*stu*		*tam*	
8.	dhā̇	sā	dhā̇	ni	mā	mā̇	mā̇	mā̇
	vaṅ				*de*			

The purport of the song is as under :

Obvesance to Him who is represented by the symbol of *Oṁkāra*, is adorned by three *mātrā-s*, is indivisible, is the best bestower of blissful blessings, is the Beloved and is worshipped by Govinda.

Thus ends *śuddhakaiśikamadhyama*,

(ii) धन्नासी

तज्जा धन्नासिका षड्जग्रहांशन्यासमध्यमा ॥९९॥
रिवर्जिता गपाल्पा च वीरे धीरैः प्रयुज्यते ।
इति धन्नासी ।

(ii) *Dhannāsī*

Dhannāsī, which is born of it, has *ṣaḍja* for its initial and the fundametal note, and *madhyama* for its final note. Devoid of *ṛṣabba*, it has a weak *gāndhāra* and *pañcama* and is employed in (the expression) of valour[1] by the wise (99c-100b)

१०. रेवगुप्त-देशी

(i) रेवगुप्तः

षड्जग्रामे रेवगुप्तो मध्यमार्षभिकोद्भवः ॥१००॥
रिग्रहांशो मध्यमान्तः प्रसन्नाद्यन्तभूषितः ।
बुधैरुद्भटचारीकमण्डलाजौ नियुज्यते ॥१०१॥
वीररौद्राद्भुतरसः पार्वतीपतिवल्लभः ।

रीसंनीरिसं मगा मामा गा मा माम ग मम ग पप ग ममगा गरी । रिगा ममगाधरी रि निनिनाध (पञ्चम) पपनि पनि म ममनि पापगसनि निनिरीरी रि सनो निरिम (गान्धार) रिरिनि । निनिरिनिरिरिमगामधा मामा (मध्यम)

[1]*Vīra* of the text.

गमधम मगागरिरि गाममगा गरि रि गाममगागरि रि निनि धनी सारी मगामा —इत्यालापः ।

रि (ऋषभ) रि निधा (पञ्चम) निध धा (मध्यम) मपरी (ऋषभ) री धापा (पञ्चम) नी नी सा नी री सानि रि (ऋषभ) री री गसनिधनि (पञ्चम) धनि मा (मध्यम) म (पञ्चम) पपप सनी नि निगरि रिग रिग सारिरि सानी नी (गान्धार) रि गा गारी सानी नि रि पगमामा मि रि मगरी समगरि सनि (ऋषभ) रि री रिमा (मध्यम) गं मर्नीं[1] पा (पञ्चम) नी नी री री गामा मम मध मगग म री री नी नी गप (षड्ज) स (पञ्चम) माप मध धस मासमरि पाप मग नोरी रि गसनी निनि मरिरि गम गरी रि मसानी पमम मग मरी री। रिरि नि निगम मरिमग गरिरि मा माध निधा। धम धनि पा पाम पा। पसनी नि सनी नि ग रि रि गरि नी रिरि स नि नि रि गा रि गरी रि रि गारि सनी निरी मारि सनी नि रि नि निध पम मप गरी मम गमा निरि गम-गारी मानी निम गामामा –इति करणम्।

(ऋषभ) रि गमा (मध्यम) गा रीं नि पापनि पापनि पापमा सा नि पाप नि री रि गा पां। पनि स नि रि ग नि रि री री रि रि नि मागां रीं रीं रीं रि रि मापां धामा गांरीं री री ममा मारिग निधधनि पाप निगा रि। ग निधसध-नि पधमप म मरीरी गमपनि पधसनि रि धधा म पगरि मग पा मा सां मां गां मं मं पां सां सां गां पं मां। मम पम। ध पाध धपमरी री नीरीगामरिगम रिगमां मां (मध्यम) गा धा री री स स रि रि मानी नि नि स सरि रि नि नि नि स सग गनी नि नि स स रि सनी नि ससस रि धरि नि पगम मरि ग सरि नि सनि धस धनि सनि मधा गरि म गरि मा मारी स नी रि मधामामा-इति द्वितीयकरणम्।

रीरी (षड्ज) स री री मम मागामप। ग ममाम मग मनी गम गप गम मग री रि ग री ग (मध्यम) म (गान्धार) ग (ऋषभ) री निध धनि (पञ्चम) मपमधनि (मध्यम) ममनि धनि पा पसनि नि स नी नि रि रि सनी। वि रि सा सनी नि नि नि रि रि नि नि रि रि रि रि रि रि मम (मध्यम) (गान्धार) गमगाग (मध्यम) ग गग मम रि धम मध मग गरीरी। रि रि गगग म गरि मगग रि रि नि नि धधनि नि ससरि रि ग ग मगमगमां मां मां –इति तृतीय करणम्।

१. नी धा पा पा नी नी नी नी

ग रु अ णि अं ब म

[1]Adyar edn. र्नीं।

२.	सा	नी	सा	री	री	री	री	री
	णो		ह	रि	आ		त	णु
३.	सा	गा	री	री	मा	गा	री	री
	अं		गी		पी		ण	प
४.	गा	री	सा	सा	नी	सा	नी	नी
	ओ		ह	रि	आ			
५.	मां	मां	गां	गां	पा	पा	नी	धा
	म	अ	ण	वि	ला		सि	णी
६.	पा	मा	गा	री	गा	री	सा	नी
	र		क्ख	उ	अ		म्हु	उ
७.	सा	सा	री	वी	सा	नी	सा	री
	गो		री		म	हि	स	वि
८.	गा	री	गा	मग	मा	मा	मा	मा
	आ		र	णि	आ			

—इत्याक्षिप्तिका ।

(तत्र साकल्येन पदयोजना)

(गुरुअणिअंवमणोहरिआ तणुअंबी पीणपओहरिआ ।
मअणविलासिणीरक्खउ अम्हउ गोरी महिसविआरणिआ ।।)

इति रेवगुप्तः ।

10. *Revagupta-deśī* : (100c-103b)

(i) *Revagupta*

Revagupta springs from *madhyamā* and *ārṣabhi* (*jāti-s*) in the *ṣaḍja-grāma* with *ṛṣabha* as its initial and the fundamental note and *madhyama* as its final note, it is embellished by *prasannādyanta*[1] and is employed by the proficient in the *cārimaṇḍala*[2] formation of valiant heroes on the battle-field for

[1]An *alaṁkāra*.

[2]'S' has observed (vide his commentary on *narta* 62c-65 b ante) that the author deals with the *maṇḍala-s* in chapter VII. *Maṇḍala* refers to circular movements in dance.

(the expression of) the sentiments of valour,[1] wrath,[2] and bewilderment.[3] It is dear to Śiva, the Lord of Pārvatī. (100c-102b)

Ākṣiptikā :

1.	nī	dhā	pā	pā	ni	nī	ni	nī
	Ga	*ru*	*a*	*ṇi*	*aṁ*		*ba*	*ma*
2.	Sā	ni	sā	ri	ri	ri	ri	ri
	ṇo		*ha*	*ri*	*ā*		*ta*	*ṇu*
3.	sā	gā	ri	ri	mā	gā	ri	ri
	aṅ		*gi*		*pī*		*ṇa*	*pa*
4.	gā	rī	sā	sā	ni	sā	ni	nī
	o	*ha*		*ri*	*ā*			
5.	mȧ	mȧ	gȧ	gȧ	pā	pā	ni	dhā
	ma	*a*	*ṇa*	*vi*	*lā*		*si*	*ṇī*
6.	pā	dhā	gā	ri	gā	ri	sā	ni
	ra		*kkha*	*u*	*a*		*mha*	*u*
7.	sā	sā	ri	nī	sā	ni	sā	rī
	go		*rī*		*ma*	*hi*	*sa*	*vi*
8.	gā	ri	gā	ma-ga	mā	mā	mā	mā
	ā		*ra*	*ṇi*	*ā*			

The purport of the song is as under :

Protect us O ! Gaurī, the devourer of Mahiṣāsura, appearing beautiful with the heavy hips, and the slender body, bearing massive breasts and taking delight in the intoxication of love, as it were.

Thus ends *revagupta.*

(ii) देशी

तज्जा देशी रिग्रहांशन्यासा पञ्चमवर्जिता ॥१०२॥

गान्धारमन्द्रा करुणे गेया मनिसभूयसी ।

इति देशी

(ii) *Deśī*

Deśī, which is derived from it, has *ṛṣabha* for its initial, fundamenta! and final notes; it is devoid of *pañcama*, takes a low *gāndhāra*, has a profusion

[1] *Vīra* of the text.

[2] *Raudra* of the text.

[3] *Adbhuta* of the text.

of *madhyama, niṣāda* and *ṣaḍja* and is sung in (the context of) pathos. (102c-103b)

११. गान्धारपञ्चम-देशाख्या

(i) गान्धारपञ्चमः

गान्धारीरक्तगान्धारीजन्यो गान्धारपञ्चमः ॥१०३॥
गान्धारांशग्रहन्यासो हारिणाश्वाख्यमूर्छनः ।
प्रसन्नमध्यालङ्कारः संचारिणि सकाकलिः ॥१०४॥
राहुप्रियोऽद्भुते हास्ये विस्मये करुणे भवेत् ।

गा सा सा नि सनि स गम गा गा । पामा गा सा सा नि सनि स समम गा गानी धानी सा नीधा पानो मा पा मा । गा स नि स नि सग मगा—इत्यालापः ।

गममग निगमापपपनिममपामप पा पानी नि मधा मम धम ममा गा गा गम मम गामा (षड्ज) सनि स स ग ग मग मम मगागा री गा नी स सनी पानो नी मप मा गम पा पग मम गं निधनि सम पपप मम । गा स गनि मसा सा सा गम धप धम ममा धा नी पनी नि म मप नि मगा (षड्ज) स नि सा सां सम गपमग । इति करणम् ।

अथवा—गागारोरी सनी सपनीसगागा (पञ्चम) सगा मामग पाधानि धानि मपनि धनि स पनि निध निधपापमगागा मसास साम गमधगम गा गागरी सनिपनि सगापमपसगागा—इत्यालापः ।

मगरिरि ससनि निससगागाग ममगगममस गसगा गममगमनि धधधनि मध ममापपधनि नीधा (पञ्चम) पा ममपा मम निधसाम ममपा मपपममा मा सां ससगागा—इति करणम् ।

१.	सा	नी	सा	गा	सा	गा	गा	गा
	पिं		ग	ल	ज	टा		क
२.	मा	पा	मा	पा	गा	गा	गा	गा
	ला		पे		नि	प	तं	
३.	गा	पा	सा	गा	गा	गा	गा	गनि
	ती		ज	य	ति	जा		ह्ल
४.	नी	पा	मा	पम	गा	गा	गा	गा
	वी		स	त	तं			

५. गा गा गा गनि नी नी नी निस
पू र्णा हु ति रि व

६. नी पा मा पम गा गा गा गा
हु त भु जि सु स मि धि

७. मा पा सा गा गा गा मा गनि
प य सः क प र्दि

८. नी पा मा पम गा गा गा गा
नो प(घ) नु दे

—इत्याक्षिप्तिका ।

(तत्र साकल्येन पदयोजना)

(पिङ्गलजटाकलापे निपतन्ती जयति जाह्नवीसततम् ।
पूर्णाहुतिरिव हुतभुजि सुसमिधि पयसः कर्पर्दिनोऽप(घ)नुदे ॥)

इति गान्धारपञ्चमः । इति रागाङ्गानि ।

11. *Gāndhāra pañcama-deśākhyā* : (103c-106b)

(i) *Gandhāra-pañcama*

Produced by *gāndhārī* and *rakta-gāndhārī* (*jāti-s*) *gāndhārapāñcama* has *gāndhāra* for its fundamental, initial and the final notes and (is set in) the *mūrcchanā* called *hāriṇāśvā*[1]; it is (embellished) by the *alaṅkāra*[2] called *prasannmadhya* in the circulatory (*sañcārī*) *varṇa* and takes *kākalī*. Dear to Rāhu[3] it is (used)in (the sentiments of) mirth[4], wonder[5] and pathos[6]. (103-105b)

[1] *Hāriṇāśvā* is the second *mūrcchanā* of *ma-grāma* and commences with *gāndhāra*.

[2] A pattern of tonal phrases.

[3] *Rāhu* in pauranic mythology, is the name of a demon who was the son of Vipracitti and Simhikā and who deceitfully partook of nectar in the guise of a god, but was recognised by the Sun and the moon on whose behest Viṣṇu cut his throat off. But having drunk the nectar he had become immortal and so he was fixed in the stellar wherefrom he periodically oppresses the sun and the moon by causing eclipses. Astronomically, *Rāhu* is a planet, (cf. note 7 on verse 54d antefor Rāhu's association with Ketu).

[4] *Hāsya* of the text.

[5] *Vismaya* of the text.

[6] *Karuṇa* of the text.

Ākṣiptikā :

1.	sā	ni	sā	gā	sā	gā	gā	gā
	Pīṅ		*ga*	*la*	*ja*	*ṭā*		*ka*
2.	mā	pā	mā	pā	gā	gā	gā	gā
	lā		*pe*		*ni*	*pa*	*tan*	
3.	gā	pā	sā	gā	gā	gā	gā	ga-ni
	tī		*ja*	*ya*	*ti*	*jā*		*hna*
4.	ni	pā	mā	pa-ma	gā	gā	gā	gā
	vī		*sa*	*ta*		*tam*		
5.	gā	gā	gā	ga-ni	ni	nī	ni	ni-sa
	pū	*rṇā*			*hu*	*ti*	*ri*	*va*
6.	ni	pā	mā	pā-ma	gā	gā	gā	gā
	hu	*ta*	*bhu*	*ji*	*su*	*sa*	*mi*	*dhi*
7.	mā	pā	sā	gā	gā	gā	mā	ga-ni
	pa	*ya*	*saḥ*		*ka*	*pa*	*rdi*	
8.	ni	pā	mā	pa-ma	gā	gā	gā	gā
	no		*pa(gha)*	*nu*	*de*			

The purport of the song is as under :

Victory be to the Ganges that pours into the tawny locks of hair of Śiva like the final oblation of milk in the well ignited fire for the removal (of evil).

Thus ends *gandharapañcama.*

(ii) देशाख्या

तज्जा स्फुरितगान्धारा देशाख्या वर्जितर्षभा ॥१०५॥

ग्रहांशन्यासगान्धारा निमन्द्रा च समस्वरा ।

इति देशाख्या ।

(ii) *Deśākhyā*

Derived from it with a shaken *gāndhāra, deśākhyā* is devoid of ṛṣabha and has *gāndhāra* for its initial, fundamental and final notes, with a low *niṣāda* and equipoised[1] notes (105c-106b)

[1] *Sama-svaratā* has already been explained (see note 17 ante).

Now, from here onwards the author is going to characterise those *rāga-s* among the *deśī rāga-s* that were contemporarily well known i.e., popular in the author's time. Alongwith the characteristic features of such *rāga-s*, he is also to mention their progenitor *grāma-rāga* and so on. However, in case of the derived *rāga-s*, he is mentioning only such of their features that distinguish them from their parent *rāga-s*. It may be observed here that, though the author has declared to focus his attention mainly on the *desī rāga-s* and incidentally on the *grāma-rāga-s* that give rise to them, in actual description he characterises the latter in the first instance and then goes on to described the former as derived from them. This procedure enables him to economise on space, but incidentally at places its rationale becomes vague.

The other features of such derived *rāga-s* have to be inferred from the nature of their parent *rāga-s* and are to be determined by the rule, "the unsaid may be inferred from elsewhere." For example, the *rāga madhyamādi* is derived from the *raga madhyamagrāma* and has *madhyama* for its initial and the fundamental note, as stated in the text, it will be observed that these features have been explicitly given by the author because they differ from the corresponding details of the parent *rāga*, the rest of the features, however, since they are similar, have not been stated in the text. Therefore, *madhyamādi* shares all other features with *madhyama-grāma* except the initial and the fundamental notes.

Furthermore, 'K' points out that its *mūrcchanā* (*sauvīrī*), even though taken in the descending *varṇa* (i.e. *ga, ri, sa, ni, dha, pa, ma*), is not incompatible with *prasannādi alaṅkāra* (*ṁa ṁa ma* i.e. two low notes followed by a high one) following it,

By. It definition, observes 'K' (vide his commentary on 30–32 ante), "*hinḍola* is derived from *ṣāḍji*, *gāndhāri madhyamā*, *pañcamī* and *naiṣāḍī*; thereby it belongs to both the *grāma-s*. Because *ri* and *dha* are omitted from its note-series (*tāna-s*), its relation to *madhyama-grāma* is quite obvious. Thus, it is proper to consider it as belonging to both the *grāma-s* (as stated in the first Section). But, however, acoording to the view in which *dha* should not be omitted, and *pa* instead should be omitted, is should belong to *ṣaḍja-grāma* only. If only *ṛṣabha* is desired to be omitted, then too, since the four *śruti-pañcama* is available, it indicates its relation to *ṣaḍja-grāma*. He further supports this contention by quoting Mataṅga as well.

'K' observes (cf. his commentary on *śuddha-kaiśika* 30–32 ante.) *Śuddhakaiśikamadhyama* is said to have been produced by *ṣaḍja-madhyamā* and *kaiśiki jāti-s* which respectively belong to *sa-grāma* and *ma-grāma*. Thus it belongs to both the *grāma-s*, whereas it has been previously stated that it is born of *sa-grāma* (of. II 1.8 ante). This obviously presents a contradiction." And he resolves the contradiction as follows : ("Mataṅga has observed that, "Since *ri* and *pa* are omitted in it, it is obviously related to *sa-grāma* i.e in other words, *pañcama* cannot be eliminated in *madhyama-grāma*" (Mataṅga as quoted by 'K'). He elucidates it further when he points out that it has been said, "The seven (*mūrcchanā-s*) of *ṣaḍja-grāma* being deprived of *sa* and *pa*, *ga* and *ni*, and *ri* and *pa* respectively from twenty-one pentatonic note-series." (S. R. I. 4.29 c–30 b). So by the definition of *auḍuva*, *śuddha-tāna* (pure pentatonic note series), it has been demonstrated that the omission of *ri* and *pa* is related to *ṣaḍja-grāma* which will be discernible even in the absence of *pañcama* that differentiates between the two *grāma-s* by the dint of the pentatonic note-series mentioned above. Well, if that be so, then how could it be said to be produced from *kaiśikī* ? It has been provided in the definition that *śuddha-kaiśika-madhyama* is set in the first *mūrcchanā*, by which it is the *sauvīrī* of *ma-grāma* and not the *matsarīkṛt* of the *sagrāma* that is to be taken; for otherwise, the rule pertaining to the high *ṣaḍja* being its initial and the fundmental note 'cannot' be observed in practice, since it would be irregular to place a note used as the fundamental and the initial towards the end of the *mūrcchanā*. Thus, even though *pañcama* is omitted in it, due to the relation of the range of high (pitch) its relationship to *madhyama-grāma* is inferred, 'and on this basis, as well as because it is ordained by Bharata, this *rāga* is accepted to be produced also by *kaiśikī*."

'K' points out (vide his commentary cn *śuddha-kaisika* 30–32 ante) that "*Revagupta* is derived from *madhyamā* and *ārṣabhī* in *ṣaḍja-grāma*. Here too, since the *pañcama* of *revagupta* is of four *śruti-s* its relation to *ṣaḍja-grāma* is obvious. Its relation to *madhyama-grāma*, however, is only with reference to the high pitch range.

(vi) भाषाङ्गाणि कतिपयहेतुभूतरागाश्च

१. त्रवणा-डोम्बकृतिः

(i) त्रवणा

त्रवणा भिन्नषड्जस्य भाषा धनिसभूयसी ॥१०६॥
धनिसंबलिता धांशग्रहन्यासा रिपोज्झिता ।
गमद्विगुणिता मन्द्रधैवता विजये मता ॥१०७॥

धाधाधामानी सा नी सासनी सा सासनी धाध सासस्नि सासनि धानी नि धानी सासा सनि सनी निधाधा मां गा गं सां स । सगिधाध मां गां मां मां नी धामां मगाग सा स सनि धानी धानी निध निध निध गागमां ससनी नीनि-धानीनिधानि धानि सनि । धाधधमाधाधा—इत्यालापः ।

---

[1]Cf. Mataṅg's Br. D. prose following verse 320 where he prescribes the *mūrcchanā* commencing with *ṣaḍja*, implying the *ṣaḍjagrāma* thereby.

धनिधगगांग सानीनी निनिसनिसनिधनी निधा धा । समनी निध निधा धा धसगमा मगमगा सासा । निनिनि गसनि धनि निधा धा । गाधनि सनि धनिधग समसनि धनि मम धनिधा...इति रूपकम् ।

इतित्रवत्रा ।

(vi) *Bhāṣāṅga-s* and some source *rāga-s* : 106c-126

1. *Travaṇā* and *Dombakṛti* : 106c-108b

(i) *Travaṇā*

Travaṇā, a *bhāṣā* of *bhinnaṣaḍja*, has a profusion of *dhaivata*, *niṣāda* and *ṣaḍja* taken with a shake,[1] and *dhaivata* as its fundamental, initial and the final notes; it is devoid of *ṛṣabha* and *pañcama*; its *gāndhāra* and *madhyama* are doubled[2], it takes a low *dhaivata* and (is employed) in (the context of) victory. (106e-107)

(ii) डोम्बकृति:

तज्जा डोम्बकृतिः सांशा धान्ता दैन्येरिपोज्झिता ।

इति डोम्बकृतिः

(ii) *Ḍombakṛti*

Derived from it, *ḍombakṛti* has *ṣaḍja* for its fundamental note : and dhaivata for its final note; it is devoid of *ṣabha* and *pañcama* and (is employed) in (the expression of) misery. (108 ab)

२. ककुभ-रगन्ती-सावेरी

(i) ककुभः

मध्यमापञ्चमीधैवत्युद्भवः ककुभो भवेत् ॥१०८॥

धांशग्रहः पञ्चमान्तो धैवतादिकमूर्छनः ।

प्रसन्नमध्यारोहिभ्यां करुणे यमदैवतः ॥१०९॥

गेयः शरदि,

[1]*Valtaim* is a variety of *gamaka* (shake) which will be dealt with in the next chapter.

[2]*Dvigunitā* lit. doubled (in pitch), is interpreted by 'K' to the effect that *ga* and *ma* (taken as belonging to the middle register) are doubled in pitch i,e. are used in the high register. Thus this rule incidentally lays down in the operational range of the high register which is limited to *madhyama*, since *dhaivata* is initial note. So, according to 'K', the purport of this statement is to indicate the range of the high (pitch). *Gāndhāra* is also spoken of along with, *madhyama* which, alone was otherwise sufficient for this purpose, to indicate its profusion in the high register as compared to other high tones.

धमां मं मगारी रिरि ससनि निधा गामापापगामा धा धगामाममनी सगि निधानिधनि निगा धागधागा रिसासगि मगाग रिरिसासनिनि। धधधपाधपा इत्यालापः ।—

धा (धैवत) नीधा (पञ्चम) गामा (ऋषभ) रिरि रि गारि (षड्ज) सधनी नी (धैवत) धाधाधानीरीं रिसानि रिसनि सनि सधा नीनी (धैवत) धा धा । धनी रिरिसा रिरिसानिधानी ममगमगारी रिसानी रिसानी धानिपपमग-पमधाधा । नी निसनि निधध (षड्ज) सगधरिग (मध्यम) मनींनि मानि निधध (पञ्चम) मपनि मगागरी ममपमगमधाधा । गाधाम गमरिमागा (ऋषभ) रिमाग षड्ज सा। धानी नि (धैवत) धा। धामाध सरिगमगपगमगिधानी पधापनि पधमगरि ममपगरि गां मां रि (ऋषभ) रिमाग (षड्ज) स । धानी म । (धैवत) धा माधसरि गमगपगमनि निधानिप धापनीप धमगरिममपगारि-गामांमां ऋषभ सधनिम धैवत । गा पमपमा षड्ज सधनि धनि सनिधाधपा इति करणम् ।

अथवा—धाधाधसं ससससधाध साध साधससधारीरी ममरिग सासंधाधाध पधसधपधधममामा । मरि मारि मां माधा धाधाधाधपधनिध पधामां मधापाधा सारीं मरी सं गंसां ग गांध पधपमपापा —इत्यालापः ।

धधसासमधधधसरींगा सांधा पाधापापा मामापा मापाधा पामां मां। सरि मरि ममाधप धापप मां मां पध सरि मरि तासां धामा पारीमा पां पां—इति करणम् ।

१.	धा	धा	सा	सा	धा	धा	री	री
	यो		ना		म	य		त्र
२.	घा	धा	धा	धा	पा	धा	पा	मा
	नि	व	स	ति	क		रो	ति
३.	री	री	मा	मा	पा	धा	पा	मा
	प	रि	र		क्ष	णं		स
४.	पा	धा	पा	मा	मा	मा	मा	मा
	ख	लु	त		स्य			
५.	री	री	मा	मा	धा	धा	पा	मा
	मु		ग्धे		व	स	सि	च

६. पा मा पा पा धा धा पा मा

हृ द ये द ह सि च

७. पा धा पा मा सा री सा री

स त तं नृ शं

८. गा सा पा पा पा पा पा पा

सा सि

—इत्याक्षिप्तिका ।

(तत्र साकल्येन पदयोजना)

(यो नाम यत्र निवसति करोति परिरक्षणं स खलु तस्य ।
मुग्धे वससि च हृदये दहसि च सततं नृशंसासि ।।)

इति ककुभः ।

(ii) रगन्ती

तज्जाता भवेद्भाषा रगन्तिका ।
धन्यासांशग्रहा भूरिधैवतैः स्फुरितैर्युता ॥११०॥
अतारमध्यमा पापन्यासा श्रीशार्ङ्गिणोदिता ।

इति रगन्ती ।

(iii) सावरी

तद्भवा सावरी धान्ता गतारा मन्द्रमध्यमा ॥१११॥
मग्रहांशा स्वल्पषड्जा करुणे पञ्चमोज्झिता ।

इति सावरी ।

2. *Kakubha—raganti* and *sāvarī* : (108c—112b)

(*i*) *Kakubha* :

Produced from *madhyamā*, *pañcamī* and *dhaivatī* (*jāti-s*), *kakubha* has *dhaivata* for its fundamental and initial notes, and *pañcama* for its final note and it *mūrcchanā* commences with *dhaivata*. Having Yama[1] for its presiding

[1]God of death.

deity, it is (embellished) by *prasannamadhya*[1] in the ascending (*varṇa*) and is sung in the autumn for (expressing) pathos.[2] (108c—110a).

Ākṣiptikā :

1.	dhā	dhā	sā	sā	dhā	dhā	rī	rī
	Yo		*nā*		*ma*	*ya*		*tra*
2.	dhā	dhā	dhā	dhā	pā	dhā	pā	mā
	ni	*va*	*sa*	*ti*	*ka*	*ro*		*ti*
3.	rî	rī	mā	mā	pā	dhā	pā	mā
	pa	*ri*	*ra*		*kṣa*	*ṇam*		*sa*
4.	pā	dhā	pā	mā	mā	mā	mā	mā
	kha	*lu*	*ta*		*sya*			
5.	rī	rī	mā	mā	dhā	dhā	pā	mvā
	mu		*gdhe*		*va*	*sa*	*si*	*ca*
6.	pā	mā	pā	pā	dhā	dhā	pā	mā
	hṛ	*da*	*ye*		*da*	*ha*	*si*	*ca*
7.	pā	dhā	pā	mā	sā	rī	sā	rī
	sa	*ta*	*tam*		*nṛ*	*śaṁ*		
8.	gā	sā	pā	pā	pā	pā	pā	pā
	sā				*si*			

The purport of the song is as under :

One naturally protects the place one lives in, but how heartless you are, Oh ! tender lass, that dwelling in (my) heart, you never tire of burning the same.

Thus ends *kakubha*.

(*ii*) *Ragantī*

There is a *bhāṣā* derived from it (called) *ragantikā* which has *dhaivata* for its final, the fundamental and the initial notes and a profusion of *dhaivata-s*[3] employed with shakes. As declared by Śārṅgadeva, it does not take high *madhyama* and has *pañcama* for its semi-final note. (110a-111b)

[1] An *alaṁkāra*.

[2] *Karuṇa* of the text.

[3] 'S' interprets the plural in the sense that "it is accompanied with many *dhaivata-s* having many shakes." "बहुभि: स्फुरितै र्धैवतैर्युक्ता". *Dhaivata-s* of the different registers may also be implied.

(*iii*) *Sāvarī*.

Sāvarī which is born of it, has *dhaivata* for its final note, a high *gāndhāra*, a low *madhyama*, and a weak *ṣaḍja*; with *madhyama* as its initial and the fundamental note, it is devoid of *pañcama* and is employed in (the expression of) pathos.[1] (111c-112b)

३. भोगवर्धनी-वेलावली-प्रथममञ्जरी

(i) भोगवर्धनी

विभाषा ककुभे भोगवर्धनी तारमन्द्रगा ॥११२॥

धैवतांशग्रहन्यासा गापन्यासा रिवर्जिता ।

धनिभ्यां गमपैर्भूरिर्वैराग्ये विनियुज्यते ॥११३॥

धाधाधाध गामापा पप मम पापापम मा गा मानी धासनी गासनी । धा पामागामानीधा पामा धाधप मध पममधा धाधगापामागा मापापापपगा मपगम-नी धासनी गासनी धापमा गामानीधाधा । धपमधपमधाधा—इत्यालापः ।

गामधापामगा मगममध धनि निनि (षड्ज) सधध धनि पपपगगा मधा पा मधापा मधनि धाधानी साधधनि धमपप ममधगागा । मगममधनि निनि (षड्ज) सधधनी निनि धमपपपगगामधा पामधापम धनिधा—इति रूपकम् ।

इति भोगवर्धनी ।

(ii) वेलावली

तज्जा वेलावली तारधा गमन्द्रा समस्वरा ।

धाद्यन्तांशा कम्प्रषड्जा विप्रलम्भे हरिप्रिया ॥११४॥

इति वेलावली ।

(iii) प्रथममञ्जरी

पञ्चमांशग्रहन्यासा धरितारा गमोत्कटा ।

गमन्द्रा चोत्सवे गेया तज्ज्ञैः प्रथममञ्जरी ॥११५॥

इति प्रथममञ्जरी ।

[1]*Karuṇa* of the text.

3. *Bhogavardhanī*, *velāvalī* and *prathamāmañjarī*

(*i*) *Bhogavardhanī*

Bhogavardhanī, a *vibhāṣā* of *kakubha* has a high as well as low *gāndhāra*[1] and *dhaivata* for its fundamental, initial and the final notes; it has *gāndhāra* as its semi-final note and is devoid of *ṛṣabha*. With a profusion of *dhaivata*, *niṣāda*, *gāndhāra*, *madhyama* and *pañcama*, it is employed (in depicting) detachment.[2] (112c-113)

(*ii*) *Velāvalī*

Velāvalī, which is derived from it, has a high *dhaivata*, a low *gāndhāra* and equipoised notes. With *dhaivata* as its initial, final and fundamental note and a shaky *ṣaḍja*, dear to Viṣṇu[3], it is employed in (portraying) conjugal love in separation.[4] (114)

(*iii*) *Prathamamañjari*

Having *pañcama* for its fundamental, initial and final notes, high *dhaivata* and *ṛṣabha*, acute[5] *gāndhāra* and *madhyama* and a low *gāndhāra*, *prathamamañjarī* is sung on the festive occasions by the proficient[6] (vocalists). (115)

४. बाङ्गाली-आडिकामोदिका

(i) बाङ्गाली

धन्यासांशग्रहा भाषा बाङ्गाली भिन्नषड्जजा।
गापन्यासा दीर्घरिमा धमन्द्रोद्दीपने भवेत् ॥११६॥

धा गा गा धध निगां ध गांगागमसा मा मा माम मा धामागा मागा स स री गा मा पम गरि सनी री मरी गासनी सा सा। ध स धा नी नी धा ध मा धा धा धधनी मा धा नी गा। गा गागममा सस मा सा सा सा पमा धा माम गा गा स स री गा माप म गरी सनी रि गारी सनी सा सा। स धानी नीधा धा धमा धा धा—इत्यालापः।

धम गमम ध धधा मा मा गामा (षड्ज) सस धा धा धानि सनी साममध मधा। धा धा धनी नी गा धमास स री री गगम मपप ममपपरी री स स री री

[1]The implication seems to be that middle *gāndhāra* is avoided.
[2]*Vairāgya* is a state of mind that is free from attachment and partiality.
[3]Hari is a name of Viṣṇu.
[4]*Vipralambha* of the text.
[5]'S' interprets *utkaṭa* as profuse.
[6]*Tajjña* (of the text) lit. means the proficient in that (subject).

गग री री (षड्ज)ससनी नी सनि सासाधमगम धगम स नी धा धा धा नी सानी साम मध मधा धा—इति रूपकम् ।

इति बाङ्गाली ।

(ii) आडिकामोदिका

आडिकामोदिका तज्जा ग्रहांशन्यासधैवता ।
समन्द्रा तारगान्धारा गुर्वाज्ञायां समस्वरा ॥११७॥

इत्याडिकामोदिका ।

4. *Bāṅgālī* and *Āḍikāmodikā*

(*i*) *Bāṅgālī*

Having *dhaivata* for its final, fundamental and initial notes, the *bhāṣa* (called) *bāṅgālī* is derived from *bhinnaṣaḍja*. With *gāndhāra* as its semi-final note, prolonged[1] *ṛṣabha* and *madhyama* and a low *dhaivata* it is used for stimulating[2] (a sentiment). (116)

(*ii*) *Āḍikāmodikā*

Āḍikāmodikā, which is derived from it, has *dhaivata* for its initial, fundamental and final notes, a low *madhyama*, hight *gāndhāra* with equipoised notes and (is used) in (the context of) preceptor's command. (117)

५. वेगरञ्जी-नागध्वनिः

(i) वेगरञ्जी

टक्कभाषा वेगरञ्जी निमन्द्रा धपवर्जिता ।
सांशग्रहान्ता माने स्यान्निषड्जरिगमैर्बहुः ॥११८॥

सा सा सनी सा रिगा नीगगम स नी गा सगसा सनी सारी नी सारी नी सारी सनी सासा मामागागा गा री सनि सानी सारी सारी सारी सारी सनी सनी समागारी सनी नी सरि गानी गागमासनी सासा—इत्यालापः ।

ममगगरी री स सनी नी सनी (षड्ज) सनी सरी गरि गगगनी सगरि

[1]*Dīrgha* lit. means long.

[2]*Uddīpana* in rhetorics is the situation that feeds the prevailing sentiment (*rasa*), or in other words, stimulates it. The word lit. means 'stimulant'.

मासामागा गा री री सा रि ग री सनी नी नी नी नी (षड्ज) सस (ऋषभ) रि गमरि स रिगम म री गसमरी गरी नी सा ममरी गा सा सा—इति रूपकम् ।

इति वेगरञ्जी भाषा ।

(ii) नागध्वनि:

नागध्वनिं तदुद्भूतं षड्जन्यासग्रहांशकम् ।
धपत्यक्तं रसे वीरे शार्ङ्गदेवः समादिशत् ॥११९॥

इति नागध्वनिः ।

5. *Vegarañjī* and *Nāgadhvani*

(*i*) *Vegarañjī*

Vegarañjī, a *bhāṣā* of *ṭakka* (*rāga*) has a low *niṣāda*, is devoid of *dhaivata* and *pañcama*, and has *ṣaḍja* for its fundamental, initial and final notes. It has a profusion of) *niṣāda*, *ṣaḍja*, *ṛṣabha*, *gāndhāra* and *madhyama* and is (used) in (the context of) wounded pride.[1] (118)

(*ii*) *Nāgadhvani*

Nāgadhvani, which is produced from it and indicated by Śārṅgadeva, has *ṣaḍja* for its final, initial and the fundamental notes, is devoid of *dhaivata* and *pañcama*, and is employed in the sentiment of valour.[2] (119)

६. सौवीरः-सौवीरी-वराटी

(i) सौवीर:

षड्जमध्यमया सृष्टः सौवीरः काकलीयुतः ।
गाल्पः षड्जग्रहन्यासांशकः षड्जादिमूर्छनः ॥१२०॥
प्रसन्नाद्यवरोहिभ्यां संयतानां तपस्विनाम् ।
गृहिणां च प्रवेशादौ रसे शान्ते शिवप्रियः ॥१२१॥
प्रयोज्यः पश्चिमे यामे वीरे रौद्रेऽद्भुते रसे ।

सां सपा पधानी धापा पधा सा सपाप धा सा सपापधा ध गारि मा गा रि सनि स पा धा सनि सां । मां मां मगारी रि मा म पा प ध निधा पापधा सां स

[1]*Māna* is a sense of wounded self-respect or honour and has a technical significance in *Śṛṅgāra rasa* (conjugal love).

[2]*Vīra* of the text.

पापधा धगा रि मा गा री सनिधा धपा सा सनी सां सां। मम समम (षड्ज) ससं सां ग सं ग ग री ग सा सं सं स ध ध नि निध सनि धनि धा ध प। पपपधध ध स नि सां सां सं सं सं सम (षड्ज) ससं ससं ग सस मरि रिग सस गध धनि ध ध ग सं सं सं धनि ध सनि धनि धध (पञ्चम) पापप रि पपनि ध ध स सा सस धम रि रि धम रि रि धप सप। धध नि ग धध सस धध नि ध स नि धनि धधपा। पापपप (गान्धार) गा गग मरि स ग सनिध सस। पपधध सनिसा। स सं स प पप नि नि नि (षड्ज) स स स रि रि रि रि परि पा धध स निसा। सध म रि रि धम मा रि रि ग सस ग धध नि धध गस सस धध निध सनि धनि ध धप धध रि नि धधध ग रि म ग रि स निध स निध निध पपंध रि निध सध गरि मगरि मगरि सनि ध समापपधध सनिसा—इत्यालापः।

(षड्ज) स (पञ्चम) नीधा धा धा नी (पञ्चम) नीधा धा धनी (षड्ज) ससारी रि रि पपनि धाधा धधस स धनि ध पा। पप नि ध पं पं निं रिं रिं ग रि मरि सासा मम रि ग सा स स्स स रि ग सा ससनि ध (पञ्चम) धा नि (षड्ज) स स। मम स सस स मस सां ससरि ग गसं ग सां ग सं गां सस गसनिधनिधाधध निपा। पगां धगां धगां गगगसमारी (षड्ज) सनिधापा पापा-धापा धनिनि (षड्ज) समां मां गगारी (ऋषभ) रिरि मममधमम। मासांस (पञ्चम) धासाधनिनिपानीधपारीपपपपध धध सं सं सं धं धं धध ममम रि रि रि रि गरि गरि गस सधनि धसा धनिधधरि पपपप। पधधधध निनि (पञ्चम) पम धध धनि (षड्ज) ससां—इति करणम्।

१.	सां	सां	सां	सां	सां	सां	सां	सां
	त	रु	ण	त	रु	शि	ख	र
२.	नी	नी	धा	धा	पा	पा	पा	मा
	कु	सु	म	भ	र	न	मि	त
३.	नी	धा	सा	धा	नी	धा	पा	पा
	मृ	दु	सु	र	भि	प	व	न
४.	धा	गा	धा	सा	सा	सां	सां	सां
	धु	त	वि	ट	पे			

५. सां सां सां नी सा सा री गा

का न ने

६. सा गा धा धा नी धा पा पा

कुं ज रो

७. नी धा सा धा नी धा पा पा

भ्र म ति म द ल लि त

८. गां गां धा सां सां सां सां सां

ली ला ग तिः

—इत्याक्षिप्तिका ।

(तत्र साकल्येन पदयोजना)

(तरुण-तरुशिखर-कुसुमभरनमित-मृदुसुरभिपवन-धुतविटपे ।
काननने कुञ्जरो भ्रमति मदललितलीलागतिः ॥)

इति सौवीरः ।

(ii) सौवीरी

सौवीरी तद्भवा मूलभाषा बहुलमध्यमा ॥१२२॥
षड्जाद्यन्तात्र संवादः सधयो रिधयोरपि ।

सा गा सा सा नी धा सा सा मा धानी धा पा पाधा मा धा समधानि धानिरिगा रिमामा गारीसा सा माधानीधासासा ।

इति सौवीरी ।

(iii) वराटी

तज्जा वराटिका सैव नटुको धनिपाधिका ॥१२३॥
सन्यासांशग्रहा तारसधा शान्ते नियुज्यते ।

इति वराटी ।

6. *Sauvīra—Sauvīrī* and *Varāṭī*

(*i*) *Sauvīra*

Created by *ṣaḍja-madhyamā* (*jāti*), *sauvīra* incorporates ***kaklī*** and a weak *gāndhāra*; it has *ṣaḍja* for its initial, final and the fundamental notes, and its *mūrcchanā* commences with *ṣaḍja*. Having *prasannādi*[1] in the descending (*varṇa*) and dear to Lord Śiva, it is (incidental) to the entrance[2] of the self-disciplined hermits and house-holders, and is employed in (depicting) the sentiments of tranquillity[3] valour,[4] wrath,[5] and bewilderment[6] in the last quarter (of the day). (120-122b)

Ākṣiptikā

1.	sȧ	sȧ	sȧ	sȧ	sȧ	sȧ	sȧ	sȧ
	Ta	*ru*	*ṇa*	*ta*	*ru*	*śī*	*kha*	*ra*
2.	nī	nī	dhā	dhā	pā	pā	pā	mā
	ku	*su*	*ma*	*bha*	*ra*	*na*	*mi*	*ta*
3.	nī	dhā	sā	dhā	nī	dhā	pā	pā
	mṛ	*du*	*su*	*ra*	*bhi*	*pa*	*va*	*na*
4.	dhā	gā	dhā	sā	sā	sȧ	sȧ	sȧ
	dhu	*ta*	*vi*	*ṭa*	*pe*			
5.	sȧ	sȧ	sȧ	ni	sā	sā	rī	gā
	kā			*na*	*ne*			
6.	sā	gā	dhā	dhā	nī	dhā	pā	pā
	kuñ			*ja*	*ro*			
7.	nī	dhā	sā	dhā	nī	dhā	pā	pā
	bhra	*ma*	*ti*	*ma*	*da*	*la*	*li*	*ta*
8.	gȧ	gȧ	dhā	sȧ	sȧ	sȧ	sȧ	sȧ
	lī		*lā*	*ga*	*tiḥ*			

The purport of the song is as under :

An elephant strolls elegantly with the grace of love-sticken gait through a forest wherein the twigs of the young trees, the tops of which are bending downwards due to the weight of the flowers, are shaken by the soft fragrant breeze.

Thus ends *sauvīra*.

[1] An *alamkāra*.
[2] That is, entrance to the stage.
[3] *Śānta* of the text.
[4] *Vīra* of the text.
[5] *Raudra* of the text.
[6] *Adbhuta* of the text.

(*ii*) *Sauvīrī*

Sauvīrī, which is originally a *bhāṣā* derived from it,[1] has a profusion of *madhyama*, takes *ṣaḍja* for its initial and final notes. The consonance of *ṣaḍja-dhaivata* and *ṛṣabha-dhaivata*, as well[2] is (found) here. (122c 123b)

(*iii*) *Varāṭī*

Varāṭī, also called *baṭukī*, which is born of it,[3] has a profusion of *dhaivata*, *niṣāda* and *pañcama*, takes *ṣaḍja* for its final, fundamental and initial notes, and has high *ṣaḍja* and *dhaivata*. It is employed in the (sentiment of) tranquillity.[4] (123c-124b)

७. पिञ्जरी-नट्टा-कर्णाटबङ्गाल:

(i) पिञ्जरी

हिन्दोले पिञ्जरी भाषा गांशा सान्ता निर्वजिता ।।१२४।।

गागारि सा धारि सा सारी गां मां मामा रीरि साधासापामागापाधासारी गापामागारी सा सानि साधारीसासारीगासारी गागामामागारीसारी रि गरि रीस रि मां । पां धापासारि गामारि रीसा ।

इति पिञ्जरी ।

(ii) नट्टा

तज्जा समस्वरा नट्टा तारगान्धारपञ्चमा ।
सन्यासांशग्रहा मन्द्रनिषादा तारधैवता ।।१२५।।

इति नट्टा ।

(iii) कर्णाटबङ्गाल:

अङ्गं कर्णाटबङ्गालं वेगरञ्ज्याः पवर्जितम् ।
गांशं सान्तं च शृङ्गारे वक्ति श्रीकरणेश्वरः ।।१२६।।

इति कर्णाटबङ्गालः । इति भाषाङ्गाणि ।

7. *Piñjarī*, *naṭṭā* and *karṇāṭabaṇgāla*

(*i*) *Piñjarī*

Piñjarī, a *bhāṣā* of *hindola* (*rāga*), has *gāndhāra* for its fundamental note, *ṣaḍja* for its final note and is devoid of *niṣāda*. (124cd)

[1]Obviously from *sauvīra*.

[2]'S' interprets that the consonance of *ri-dha* is offered as an alternative to that of *sa-dha*.

[3]Obviously from *sauvīrī*.

[4]*Śānta* of the text.

(*ii*) *Naṭṭā*

Naṭṭā, which is derived from it,[1] has equipoised notes, high *gāndhāra*, *pañcama* and *dhaivata*, takes *ṣaḍja* for its final, fundamental and initial notes, and has a low *niṣāda*. (125)

(*iii*) *Karṇāṭabaṅgāla*

An integral part of *vegarañjī*,[2] *karṇāṭabaṇgāla* is devoid of *pañcama*, has *gāndhāra* as its fundamental note and *ṣaḍja* as its final note. As declared[3] by Śārṅgadeva, it is employed in the (context of) conjugal love.[4] (126)

Now, according to 'K' (cf. his comments on 30-33 ante), "though it has been declared (cf. *SR.*, II 1.14 ante) that *kakubha* belongs to both the *grāma-s* and also it is said in the (above) definition to be produced from the *jāti-s* of the two *grāma-s*, its relation to *sa-grāma* is quite obvious because of its *pañcama* which is of 4 *śruti-s*, its relation to *ma-grāma* is not so obvious from the application of the definition. He resolves the difficulty by pointing out that, "Mataṅga, while giving the *prastāra* (delineation in notation), even though not so explicitly provided in the definition, omits *niṣāda* and *gāndhāra* in forming the pentatones (*auḍuva-s*). Thus, in practice the relation of *kakubha* to *ma-grāma* is obvious too." The validity of this reasoning, however, is not clearly intelligible in view of the fact that such an omission is also permissible in the *sa-grāma* (cf. *S.R.*, I 4. 29 30).

(vii) क्रियाङ्गाणि

१. रामकृति:

आपञ्चमं तारमन्द्रा षड्जन्यासांशकग्रहा ।
रिषड्जाभ्यधिका धीरैरेषा रामकृतिर्मता ॥१२७॥

इति रामकृतिः

२. गौडकृति:

षड्जांशग्रहणन्यासां मतारां मपभूयसीम् ।
रिधत्यक्तां पमन्द्रां च तज्ज्ञा गौडकृतिं जगुः ॥१२८॥

इति गौडकृतिः ।

[1]That is, from *piñjarī*.
[2]*Vegarañjī* is a *bhāṣā* of *ṭakka* (*rāga*).
[3]Lit. "says Śrīkaraṇeśvara" which is an epithet of the author meaning accountant general.
[4]*Śṛṅgāra* of the text.

३. देवकृतिः

निमन्द्रा मध्यमव्याप्ता रिपत्यक्ता समस्वरा ।

सन्यासांशा धग्रहा च वीरे देवकृतिर्भवेत् ॥१२९॥

इति देवकृतिः । इति क्रियाङ्गाणि ।

(vii) *Kriyāṅga-s*

Rāmakṛti, gauḍakṛti and *devakṛti*

1. *Rāmakṛti*

Rāmakṛti is accepted by the wise to be having high and low (notes) upto *pañcama*,[1] *ṣaḍja* for its final, fundamental and the initial notes and a profusion of *ṛṣabha* and *ṣaḍja.* (127)

2. *Gauḍakṛti*

Gauḍakṛti is declared by the experts to have *ṣadja* for its fundamental, initial and final notes, high *madhyama*, low *pañcama* and a profusion of the two (i.e. *madhyama* and *pañcama*), and to be devoid of *ṛṣabha* and *dhaivata.* (128)

3. *Devakṛti*

Devakṛti has a low *niṣāda*, and a prevalence[2] of *madhyama.* It is devoid of *ṛṣabha* and *pañcama* and has equipoised notes with *ṣaḍja* as its final and the fundamental note and *dhaivata* as its initial note, and is employed in (the expression of) valour.[3]

(viii) उपाङ्गानि

१. वराट्युपाङ्गानि

(i) कौन्तली वराटी

स्युर्वराट्या उपाङ्गानि सन्यासांशग्रहाणि षट् ।

समन्द्रा कौन्तली तत्र निभूरिः कम्प्रधा रतौ ॥१३०॥

इति कौन्तली वराटी ।

[1]'S' interprets that from *Ṣaḍja* to *pañcama*, the notes in it are high and low i.e. they do not occur in the middle register.

[2]'S' interprets vyāpti (lit. prevalence) in the sense of profusion (bahulatā)

[3]*Vīra* of the text.

(ii) द्राविडी वराटी

वराटी द्राविडी भूरिनिमन्द्रा स्फुरितर्षभा ।

इति द्राविडी वराटी ।

(iii) सैन्धवी वराटी

वराटी सैन्धवी भूरिगान्धारा सधकम्पिता ॥१३१॥

शार्ङ्गदेवेन गदिता श्रृंगारे मन्द्रमध्यमा ।

इति सैन्धवी वराटी ।

(iv) अपस्थानवराटी

मण्डिता मनिधैर्मन्द्रैरपस्थानवराटिका ॥१३२॥

इत्यपस्थानवराटी ।

(v) हतस्वरवराटी

हतस्वरा धमन्द्रा कम्प्रपसा हतपञ्चमा ।

इति हतस्वरवराटी ।

(vi) प्रतापवराटी

स्यात् प्रतापवराटी तु धमन्द्रा कम्प्रसोरुपा ॥१३३॥

इति प्रतापवराटी । इति वराट्युपाङ्गानि ।

(viii) The *Upāṅga-s*

1. The *upāṅga-s* of *varāṭī*

There are six *upāṅga-s* of *varāṭī* that have *ṣaḍja* for their final, the fundamental and the initial notes,[1] (130 a b) viz.

(i) *Kauntalī-varāṭī*

Among them,[2] *kauntalī* has a low *ṣaḍja*, a profusion of *niṣāda*, and with a shaky *dhaivata*, it is employed in an erotic situation.[3] (130 c d)

(ii) *Drāviḍī-varāṭī*

Drāviḍī-varāṭī has a profusion of low *niṣāda* and a shaky *ṛṣabha*. (131 a b)

[1]This feature is common to all the six varieties, the uncommon features are set forth separately.

[2]That is, the six varieties.

[3]*Rati*, in Rhetorics, signifies the *sthāyī bhāva* (i.e. the stahle disposition or state of being) of conjugal love and also means sexual pleasure or the delight of love making.

(iii) *Saindhavī-varāṭī*

Saindhavī-varāṭī as declared by Śārṅgadeva has profuse *gāndhāra* and employs *ṣaḍja* and *dhaivata* with a shake. It has a low *madhyama* and is employed in (the context of) conjugal love.[1] (131 c-132 b)

(iv) *Apasthāna-varāṭī*

Apasthāna-varāṭī is embellished by low *madhyama* and *niṣāda* and *dhaivata.* (132 c d)

(v) *Hatasvara-varāṭī*

Hatasvara-varāṭī has a low *dhaivata*, shakable *pañcama* and *ṣaḍja* and an *āhata*[2] on *pañcama*. (133 a b)

(vi) *Pratāpa-varāṭī*

Pratāpa-varāṭī has a low *dhaivata*, shakable *ṣaḍja* and extensive *pañcama.*[3] (133 c d)

२. तोड्युपाङ्गे

(i) छायातोडी

रिपत्यक्ता तु तोड्येव छायातोडीति कीर्तिता ।

इति छायातोडी ।

(ii) तुरुष्कतोडी

तोड्येव ताडिता गाल्पा तौरुष्की निधभूयसी ।।१३४।।

इति तुरुष्कतोडी । इति तोड्युपाङ्गे ।

2. The *upāṅga-s* of *toḍī* (134)

(i) *Chāyā-toḍī*

Toḍī, when devoid of *ṛṣabha* and *pañcama* is known as *chāyā-toḍī.* (134 a b)

(ii) *Turuṣka-toḍī*

Toḍī with *āhata gamaka-s*[4] and having a weak *gāndhāra* and a profusion of *niṣāda* and *dhaivata* (becomes) *turuṣka-toḍī* (134 c d)

[1] *Śṛṅgāra* of the text.

[2] *Hata* refers to *āhata gamaka*. See note 7 below and also cf. S. Sudhā 2. 379.

[3] *Uru* (lit. extensive) is interpreted by 'S' ās profuse.

[4] *Tāḍitā* of the text literally means beaten. Technically, *tāḍita* is a synonym of *āhata* which is a variety of *gamaka* as described in Chapter III (verse 93). The word *tāḍita*, as may be observed from the metrical construction, is used by the author in place of the word *āhata* due to the exigency of the metre. A reference is invited to Kallinātha's commentary on *S.R.* III 6. 344 on the technical meaning of *āhata* (lit. having struck) in the sense of *āhata gamaka.*

३. गुर्जर्युपाङ्गानि

(i) महाराष्ट्रगुर्जरी

पञ्चमेनोज्झिता मन्द्रनिषादा ताडितोत्सवे ।
गीयतामृषभान्तांशा महाराष्ट्री तु गुर्जरी ॥१३५॥
इति महाराष्ट्रगुर्जरी ।

(ii) सौराष्ट्रगुर्जरी

गुर्जर्येव रिकम्प्रा स्यात् सौराष्ट्री गुर्जरी भवेत् ।
इति सौराष्ट्रगुर्जरी ।

(iii) दक्षिणगुर्जरी

दक्षिणा गुर्जरी कम्प्रमध्यमा ताडितेतरा ॥१३६॥
इति दक्षिण गुर्जरी

(iv) द्राविडगुर्जरी

रिमन्द्रतारा स्फुरिता हर्षे द्राविडगुर्जरी ।
इति द्राविडगुर्जरी । इति गुर्जर्युपाङ्गानि ।

3. The *upāṅga-s* of *gurjarī* (135-137 b)

(i) *Mahārāṣṭra-gurjarī*

Devoid of *pañcama*, having a low *niṣāda* and *āhata-gamaka, mahārāṣṭra-gurjarī* is sung with *ṛṣabha* as the final and the fundamental notes on festive occasions. (135)

(ii) *Saurāṣṭra-gurjarī*

If the *ṛṣabha* in *gurjarī* is shakable it becomes *saurāṣṭra-gurjarī*. (136 ab)

(iii) *Dakṣiṇa-gurjarī*

If the *madhyama* is shaky and the other notes have *āhata gamaka-s* it is *dakṣiṇa-gurjarī*. (136 cd)

(iv) *Drāviḍa-gurjarī*

Drāviḍa-gurjarī has low and high *ṛṣabha*, is replete with shakes[1] and is (employed) on joyous occasions.[2] (137 ab)

[1]*Sphurita* of the text lit. means throbbing.
[2]*Harṣa* lit. means gladness.

४. वेलावल्युपाङ्गानि

(i) भुच्छी

मत्यक्तान्दोलितसपा धन्यासांशग्रहान्विता ॥१३७॥
विप्रलम्भे भवेद्भुच्छीत्यवोचत् सोढलात्मजः ।
इति भुच्छी ।

(ii) खम्भाइतिः

मध्यमेन निषादेनान्दोलिता त्यक्तपञ्चमा ॥१३८॥
खम्भाइतिस्तदंशान्ता शृङ्गारे विनियुज्यते ।
इति खम्भाइतिः ।

(iii) छायावेलावली

छायावेलावली वेलावलीवत् कम्प्रमन्द्रमा ॥१३९॥
इति छायावेलावली ।

(iv) प्रतापवेलावली

सैव प्रतापपूर्वा स्यादाहता रिपवर्जिता ।
इति प्रतापवेलावली । इति वेलावल्युपाङ्गानि ।

4. The *upāṅga-s* of *velāvalī*

(i) *Bhucchī*

Bhucchī,[1] as declared by Śārṅgadeva, is devoid of *madhyama,*[2] has swinging *ṣaḍja* and *pañcama* with *dhaivata* for its final, fundamental and initial notes, and is (used) in the (context of) love in separation. (137 c-138 b)

(ii) *Khamhbā-itiḥ*

Swung by *madhyama* and *niṣāda*[3] and devoid of *pañcama, khambhā-iti* has *niṣāda* for its fundamental and the final notes and is employed in (the context of) conjugal love. (138 c-139 b)

(iii) *Chāyāvelāvalī*

Chāyāvelāvalī is like *velāvalī*[4] except that it has a low and shakable *madhyama.* (139 cd)

[1]Also known as *bhuñchī* (comp. *SR*, II 2.2 140-141).

[2]The omission of *madhyama,* as pointed out by *Kumbhā* (*SR.*, ibid) is notable, for it is considered to be immutable.

[3]That is, with a swing on *ma* and *ni.*

[4]*Velāvalī* is derived from *bhogavardhanī* which is a *vibhāṣā* of *kakubha.*

(iv) *Pratāpa-velāvalī*

That itself,[1] with *āhata gamaka-s*[2] and deprived of *ṛṣabha* and *pañcama* becomes *pratāpa-velāvalī*. (140 ab)

५. भैरवोपाङ्गम्

भैरवी

धांशन्यासग्रहा तारमन्द्रगान्धारशोभिता ॥१४०॥
भैरवी भैरवोपाङ्गं समशेषस्वरा भवेत् ।
इति भैरवी ।

5. The *upāṅga of Bhairava*

Bhairavī

Having *dhaivata* for its fundamental, final and the initial notes and embellished by the high as well as the low *gāndhāra*,[3] *bhairavī*, an *upāṅga* of *bhairava*, has the rest of its notes[4] equipoised. (140c-141b)

६. कामोदोपाङ्गम्

सिंहलीकामोदा

कामोदोपाङ्गमाख्याता कामोदा सिंहली बुधैः ॥१४१॥
कामोदलक्षणोपेता समन्द्रा कम्प्रधैवता ।
इति सिंहलीकामोदा ।

6. The *upāṅga of kāmoda*

Siṁhalī-kāmodā

Being an *upāṅga* of *kāmoda*, called as *siṁhalī-kāmoda* by the learned, and having all the features of *kāmoda*, it has a low *madhyama* and a shakable *dhaivata*. (141 c-142 c)

७. नट्टोपाङ्गम्

छायानट्टा

छायानट्टा तु नट्टैव मन्द्रपञ्चमभूषिता ॥१४२॥
नट्टोपाङ्गं निषादेन गान्धारेण च कम्पिता ।
इति छायानट्टा ।

[1]That is *chāyāvelāvalī*.
[2]See note on *tāḍitā* (verse 134 cd) ante.
[3]The implication seems to be that the middle *gāndhāra* is excluded.
[4]That is, leaving aside *dhaivata* and *gāndhāra*.

7. The *upāṅga of naṭṭa*

Chāyānaṭṭā

Chāyānaṭṭā is almost *naṭṭā* (itself). Embellished by a low *pañcama* and shaken by *niṣāda* and *gāndhāra*, it is an *upāṅga* of *naṭṭā*. (142 c-143 b)

८. कोलाहला—रामकृतिः

(i) कोलाहला

कोलाहला टक्कभाषा सग्रहांशा पवर्जिता ॥१४३॥
सधमन्द्रा मभूयिष्ठा कलहे गमकान्विता ।

सासा सासा मासा सास सरी गामा मामगरी सरीरीध मारीगरी धममग-मामारीधा साधासागा रीमाधगा मरी गसा सासा सास निग सारी मागामामा रीगरीध मधममारीधा सागा साधा सामा रीमाधा गासा—इत्यालापः ।

रीगसध सरीमम धमगम गामसरी सनी धासा रीगरीग माधध ससस सगरी ममधमगरिस नीधासरी गामाधमरी गमसाधनी धसरीगा माम गमधम गारी सनि धासरी गासरी गासा मागरी मा रीगा सासा—इति रूपकम् ।

इति कोलाहला ।

(ii) रामकृतिः

तज्जा रामकृतिर्वीरे मांशा सान्ता पवर्जिता ॥१४४॥
भाषाङ्गत्वेऽप्युपाङ्गत्वमतिसामीप्यतोऽत्र च ।
शार्ङ्गदेवेन निर्णीतमन्यत्वाप्यूह्यतां बुधैः ॥१४५॥

इति रामकृतिः ।

8. *Kolāhalā* and *rāmakṛti*

(*i*) *Kolāhalā*

Kolāhalā,[1] which is a *bhāṣā* of *ṭakka*, has *ṣaḍja* for its initial and the fundamental note, is devoid of *pañcama*, takes low *ṣaḍja* and *dhaivata*, and is profuse with *madhyama*. Employing *gamaka-s* (shakes),[2] it is used in (the context of) strife.[3] (143c-144b)

[1]*Kolāhala* literally means a loud and confused noise.
[2]*Gamaka-s* are dealt with in Chapter III.
[3]*Kalaha* of the text. Its use is appropriate to its very name.

(*ii*) *Rāmakṛiti*

Rāmakṛiti, which is born of it,[1] is (employed in depicting) valour.[2] It has *madhyama* for its fundamental note and *ṣaḍja* for its final note, and is devoid of *pañcama.* Even though (constitutionally) it is a *bhāṣāṅga*[3] because of close proximity,[4] Śārangadeva adjudges it as *upāṅga* as well. This is, however, open to further investigation by the learned. (144c-145)

९. छेवाटी-वल्लाता

(i) छेवाटी

हिन्दोलभाषा छेवाटी गापन्यासा धभूयसी ।
रिहीनांशग्रहन्यासषड्जा सगममन्द्रभाक् ॥१४६॥
सगतारोत्सवे हास्ये गेया गमकसंयुता ।

सासा सासगम पापा पापम गापमगापाधागा धानी पापगम नीधापापामग-पगा गसासासा सगमधपापा पमगापमगा धानीपापमगपम गपमगागसा सपा-नीसा सासागासा मगाभप पनि सासा—इत्यालापः ।

सम गम गपा पाम पमपम गागा गागससासगमनि निसनिससगस मम निनि सनि सासमगसगमपपसनिसागासा धानि पानी नीपा मगा गपमम गामसां-सां गांगां पानी मासा गासनी सासा—इति रूपकम् ।

इति छेवाटी ।

(ii) वल्लाता

वल्लाता तदुपाङ्गं स्याद् रिहीना मन्द्रधैवता ॥१४७॥
सन्यासांशग्रहा गेया श्रृङ्गारे शार्ङ्गिणोदिता ।

इति वल्लाता ।

9. *Chevāṭī* and *vallātā*

(*i*) *Chevāṭī*

Chevāṭi, which is a *bhāṣā* of *hindola*, has *gāndhāra* as its semi-final note and a profusion of *dhaivata*, is devoid of *ṛṣabha* and takes *ṣaḍja* for its

[1]That is *kolāhalā*.

[2]*Vīra* of the text.

[3]*Bhāṣāṅgatva* is an abstract noun.

[4]'S' thinks that similarity of *sthāya-s* (to be dealt with in Chapter III) is meant by proximity.

fundamental, initial and the final notes. It partakes of low *ṣaḍja*, *gāndhāra* and *madhyama*, with high *ṣaḍja* and *gāndhāra*, and is sung with *gamaka-s* (shakes) on festive occasions (expressing) mirth.[1] (146-147b)

(*ii*) *Vallātā*

Vallātā is its[2] *upāṅga* and is devoid of *ṛṣabha*. It takes a low *dhaivata*, has *ṣaḍja* for its final, fundamental and initial notes, and as declared by Śārṅgadeva, is sung in the (context of) conjugal love. (147c-148b)

१०. शुद्धपञ्चमस्तज्जनिता रागाश्च

(i) शुद्धपञ्चमः

मध्यमापञ्चमीजातः काकल्यन्तरसंयुतः ॥१४८॥
पञ्चमांशग्रहन्यासो मध्यसप्तकपञ्चमः।
हृष्यकामूर्छनोपेतो गेयः कामादिदैवतः ॥१४९॥
चारुसंचारिवर्णश्च ग्रीष्मेऽह्नः प्रहरेऽग्रिमे।
शृङ्गारहास्ययोः संधाववमर्शे प्रयुज्यते ॥१५०॥

पाधा मांधा नीधापापा। पधनीरिमपधामा घनि ध पापारींगां सांसां। मांपमागां रीरीं। रींमांपधा मा पनिधपापा। सांगां नीधा पप निरी मां पाधामाध निध पापा – इत्यालापः।

पापधपधमधधनिध पापा। पापाधनि रिगपापा मधनिध पापा पपधनि रीरी गंगं संसं गग रींरीं रींरीं मम पप धम धध निध पा—इति करणम्।

१.	सां	सां	सां	सां	रीं	रीं	गां	सां
	ज	य	वि	ष	म	न	य	न
२.	मा	गा	पम	गा	रीं	रीं	रीं	रीं
	म	द	न	त	नु	द	ह	न
३.	मां	सां	सां	सां	रीं	रीं	गां	सां
	व	र	वृ	ष	भ	ग	म	न
४.	मा	गां	पम	गा	रीं	रीं	रीं	रीं
	पु	र	द	ह	न			

[1]*Hāsya* of the text.
[2]That is—of *Chevāṭī*.

५. रीं रीं मां मां पा मा धा मा

न त स क ल भु व न

६. मा धा सां सां नी धा पा मा

सि त क म ल व द न

७. धां नीं रीं मां रीं मां पा पा

भ व म म भ य ह र

८. धा मां धा नीं पा पा पा पा

भ व श र णं

—इत्याक्षिप्तिका।

इति शुद्धपञ्चमः।

(तत्र साकल्येन पदयोजना)

(जय विषम नयन मदनतनुदहन वरवृषभगमन पुरदहन
नत सकलभुवन सितकमल वदन भवमम भयहरभव शरणम्)

(ii) दाक्षिणात्या (भाषा)

तद्भाषा दाक्षिणात्या स्याद् ग्रहांशन्यासधैवता।
ऋषभोऽस्यामपन्यासस्तारा निपमधैवताः ॥१५१॥
प्रियस्मृतौ नियोगोऽस्या,

पापा धासा निरीरीरी गरिमरि गपगग नीसानीमा नीधा पापा पाधा सनी रीरीरीरी गरी सगारीसनी रीरीरी नीनी गपनीध नीनी सानी सनी सागरीरी रीरी मरी सनी नीध निधा पानी निधापापमधा पासा पाधासनी रीरी रीरीरीरी गरीगग पापानीधा पापापा—इत्यालापः।

पपधधसनी रीरी गरी सनी धनी नीप पध धस नीरी रीग नीस नीरी रीग नीस निधा नीनी पापा—इति रूपकम्।

इति दाक्षिणात्या भाषा।

(ii) आन्धालिका, विभाषाऽऽन्धालिका मता।
पञ्चमांशग्रहन्यासा न्यल्पा भूरीतरस्वरा ॥१५२॥
तारधा मन्द्रषड्जा च धापन्यासा गर्वाजता।
वियुक्तबन्धने गेया शार्ङ्गदेवेन कीर्तिता ॥१५३॥

पापामामसरी मापा धापा धाप धध पध धपपसा मास सारी रीमा पाधा पध मास निधा पापधपधपपमा मासा सारी साधा पाधा पप धध पध धध धम पापा मसा रीमा सारी मासारी मा सारी मासारीमाधाप धधधधा पधधप नम-माम सारीमापा धाप धपा धासा नीधा पाप धप पपापा—इत्यालापः ।

रीरीसारीरी सरीरीसरी रीस रीप रीस रीस धध पाधधप धधधध पममा ममा पमधा पधामामपपमाधसधसधपमधा—इति रूपकम् ।

इत्यान्धाली विभाषा ।

(iv) मल्हारी (उपाङ्गम्)

मल्हारी तदुपाङ्गं स्याद् गहीना मन्द्रमध्यमा ।
पञ्चमांशग्रहन्यासा शृङ्गारे ताडिता मता ॥१५४॥

इति मल्हारी ।

(v) मल्हारः

आन्धाल्युपाङ्गं मल्हारः षड्जपञ्चमवर्जितः ।
धन्यासांशग्रहो मन्द्रगान्धारस्तारसप्तमः ॥१५५॥

इति मल्हारः ।

10. *Śuddhapañcama* and its offshoots

(*i*) *Śuddhapañcama*

Born of *madhyamā* and *pañcamī* (*jāti-s*), taking *kākalī* and *antara* and having *pañcama* for its fundamental, initial and final notes i.e., the *pañcama* of the middle heptad,[1] *Śuddhapañcama*[2] is set in *hṛṣyakā mūrcchanā*.[3] With cupid for its presiding deity and beautified with the circulatory (*sañcārī*) *varṇa*, it is to be sung in the first quarter of the summer day in (depicting) conjugal love and mirth[4] in the *vimarśa*[5] (epitasis). (148c-150)

[1]That is, *saptaka*.

[2]The name is not found in the text.

[3]The seventh *mūrcchanā* of *ma-grāma* commencing with *pañcama*.

[4]*Śṛṅgāra* and *hāsya* respectively of the text.

[5]*Vimarśa* (also written as *vimarṣa*) is the fourth *sandhi* (junctural subdivision of a drama) out of the five already mentioned (cf. notes on verses 21-23 b ante). Here the seed of the plot, which is already sufficiently developed, is exposed to greater hazards engendering some serious calamity. It manifests a change in the prosperous course of the love story caused by some unforeseen reverse. This episode generally closes with the possibilities of future union.

Ākṣiptikā

1.	sā̇	sā̇	sā	sā̇	rī̇	rī̇	gā̇	sā̇
	ja	*ya*	*vi*	*ṣa*	*ma*	*na*	*ya*	*na*
2.	mā	gā	pa-ma	gā	rī̇	rī̇	rī̇	rī
	ma	*da*	*na*	*ta*	*nu*	*da*	*ha*	*na*
3.	mā̇	sā̇	sā̇	sā̇	rī̇	rī̇	gā̇	sā̇
	va	*ra*	*vṛ*	*ṣa*	*bha*	*ga*	*ma*	*na*
4.	mā	gā̇	pa-ma	gā	rī̇	rī̇	rī̇	rī̇
	pu	*ra*	*da*	*ha*	*na*			
5.	rī̇	rī̇	mā̇	mā̇	pā	mā	dhā	mā
	na	*ta*	*sa*	*ka*	*la*	*bhu*	*va*	*na*
6.	mā	dhā	sā̇	sā̇	nī	dhā	pā	mā
	si	*ta*	*ka*	*ma*	*la*	*va*	*da*	*na*
7.	dhā̇	nī̇	rī̇	mā̇	rī̇	mā̇	pā	pā
	bha	*va*	*ma*	*ma*	*bha*	*ya*	*ha*	*ra*
8.	dhā	mā̇	dha	nī̇	pā	pā	pā	pā
	bha	*va*	*śa*	*ra*	*ṇam*			

The purport of the song is as under :

Victory be unto thee, the three-eyed one (Śiva) the destroyer of the body of the cupid, the rider of the best white bull, the destroyer of Tripurāsura; thou, who are worshipped by the entire world, Oh ! the lotus-faced one, be the destroyer of my fear and refuge from the process of becoming (*saṁsāra*).

Thus ends *śuddhapañcama*.

(*ii*) *Dākṣiṇātyā*

Its *bhāṣā* is (called) *dākṣiṇātyā*. With *dhaivata* as its initial, fundamental and the final notes, it has *ṛṣabha* for its semi-final note, high *niṣāda*, *pañcama*, *madhyama* and *dhaivata* and is used in the fond memory of the beloved. (151-152a)

(*iii*) *Āndhālikā*

Andhālikā is considered to be its *vibhāṣā*. It has *pañcama* for its fundamental, initial and final notes, a weak *niṣāda*, and a profusion of the remaining notes. It takes high *dhaivata*, low *ṣaḍja*, has *dhaivata* as its semi-final note and is devoid of *gāndhāra*. As declared by Śāṅgadeva, it is to be sung at the meeting of separated lovers.[1] (152b-153)

(*iv*) *Malhārī*

Malhārī is its[2] *upāṅga*. It is devoid of *gāndhāra* and has a low *madhyama* with *pañcama* for its fundamental, initial and the final notes. With notes stressed as the *āhata gamaka* it is accepted to be (used) in conjugal love.[3] (154)

(*v*) *Malhāra*

Malhāra is an *upāṅga* of *āndhālī* and is devoid of *ṣaḍja* and *pañcama*. It has *dhaivata* for its final, fundamental and initial notes, a low *gāndhāra* and a high *niṣāda*. (155)

११. गौडोपाङ्गानि

(i) कर्णाटगौड:

गेयः कर्णाटगौडस्तु षड्जन्यासग्रहांशकः ।

इति कर्णाटगौडः ।

(ii) देशवालगौड:

स एवान्दोलितः षड्जे देशवालो रिपोज्झितः ॥१५६॥

इति देशवालगौडः ।

(iii) तुरुष्कगौड:

गान्धारबहुलो मन्द्रताडितो रिपवर्जितः ।
निषादांशग्रहन्यासस्तुरुष्को गौड उच्यते ॥१५७॥

इति तुरुष्कगौडः ।

(iv) द्राविडगौड:

गान्धाररतिरिपोपेतः प्रस्फुरत्षड्जपञ्चमः ।
गेयो द्राविडगौडोऽयं ग्रहांशन्याससप्तमः ॥१५८॥

इति द्राविडगौडः । इति गौडोपाङ्गानि ।

(इत्युपाङ्गानि)

[1]The compound वियुक्तबन्धने is analysed as वियुक्तानां बन्धने

[2]*Tad* (its) probably refers to *Śuddhapañcama* and not *āndhālikā* which it follows. Cf. S. Raj II. 2. 3. 98 where it is associated with *āndhālikā*.

[3]*Śṛṅgāra* of the text.

11. The *upāṅga-s* of *gauḍa*

(*i*) *Karṇāṭagauḍa*

Karṇāṭagauḍa is to be sung with (the difference[1] that it takes) *ṣaḍja* for its final, initial and the fundamental notes. (156a b)

(*ii*) *Deśavālagauḍa*

When that[2] itself is swung upon *ṣaḍja* and is deprived of *ṛṣabha* and *pañcama*, it becomes *deśavālagauḍa*. (156c d)

(*iii*) *Turuṣkagauḍa*

Turuṣkagauḍa is said to have *niṣāda* for its fundamental, initial and final notes, a profusion of *gāndhāra* and with the *āhata gamaka* in the low register, and it is devoid of *ṛṣabha* and *pañcama*. (157)

(*iv*) *Drāviḍagauḍa*

Drāviḍagauḍa is sung with a terse[3] *gāndhāra*, shaky *ṣaḍja* and *pañcama* and has *niṣāda* for its initial, fundamental and final notes. (158)

'S' enumerates the total of fifty-two *rāga-s* including the parent *rāga-s* so far described.

१२ अधुनाप्रसिद्धदेशीरागाः

१. श्रीरागः

षड्जे षाड्जीसमुद्भूतं श्रीरागं स्वल्पपञ्चमम् ।
सन्यासांशग्रहं मन्द्रगान्धारं तारमध्यमम् ॥१५९॥
समशेषस्वरं वीरे शास्ति श्रीकरणाग्रणीः ।

इति श्रीरागः ।

(*ix*) The current[4] well known *rāga-s*

1. *Śrīrāga*

Śrīrāga has sprung from *ṣāḍjī* (*jāti*) of the *ṣaḍja-grāma*.[5] It has a weak

[1] The phrase put into brackets brings out the implication of the indeclinable *tu* of the text.

[2] That refers to *karṇāṭagauḍa*.

[3] 'S' interprets *Tiripeṇa* as *vakroccāritena gāndhāreṇa* i.e. by the *gāndhāra* sung in a crooked or zigzag way.

[4] *Adhunāprasiddha* lit. 'presently well known.'

[5] 'S' points out that *grāma* has been explicitly indicated despite the fact that *ṣāḍjī* being the parent *jāti* is by itself indicative of the *ṣaḍja-grāma*, because *deśi-rāga-s*. as a rule, are not governed by the relation of the parent and the derived structure.

pañcama, ṣadja for its final, fundamental and the initial notes, a low *gāndhāra* and high *madhyama* with the remaining[1] notes equipoised. As ordained by Śārṅgadeva, it is (employed) in (the expression of) valour.[2] (159-160b)

२. प्रथमबङ्गाल:

षड्जग्रामे मन्द्रहीन: षड्जमध्यमया कृत: ॥१६०॥
बङ्गालोंऽशग्रहन्यासषड्जस्तुल्याखिलस्वर: ।

इति प्रथमबङ्गाल: ।

2. *Prathama-baṅgāla* (First *baṅgala*)

Produced[3] from *ṣadja-madhyamā* (*jāti*) in *ṣaḍjagrāma* and devoid of the lower octave,[4] *baṅgāla* has *ṣaḍja* for its fundamental, initial and the final notes, with all the other notes equipoised. (160c-161b).

३. द्वितीयबङ्गाल:

मध्यमे कैशिकीजात: षड्जन्यासांशकग्रह: ॥१६१॥
बङ्गालस्तारमध्यस्थपञ्चम: स्यात् समस्वर: ।

इति द्वितीयबङ्गाल: ।

3. *Dvitīya-baṅgāla* (Second *baṅgāla*)

Born of *kaiśikī* (*jāti*) in the *madhyama-grāma* and having *ṣaḍja* for its final, fundamental and initial notes, *baṅgāla* has the *pañcama* of the higher and the middle octave[5] with equipoised notes. (161c-162b)

४. मध्यमषाडव:

ऋषभांश: पञ्चमान्त: स्यादपन्यासधैवत: ॥१६२॥
वीररौद्राद्भुतरस: पाल्पो मध्यमषाडव: ॥

इति मध्यमषाडव: ।

4. *Madhyamaṣāḍava*

Madhyama-ṣāḍava has *ṛṣabha* as the fundamental note, *pañcama* as the

[1]'S', significantly mentions *ṛṣabha, pañcama, dhaivata* and *niṣāda* (see the above comments).

[2]*Vīra* of the text.

[3]*Kṛtaḥ* of the text lit. means 'done' or 'fashioned' so to say.

[4]The word octave is used for hepted (*saptaka*) for the convenience of the readers.

[5]'S' interprets that it is devoid of the low *pañcama*.

final note and *dhaivata* as the semifinal note. It has a week *pañcama* and is employed in (the context of) the sentiments of valour,[1] wrath[2] and bewilderment,[3] (162c-163b)

५. शुद्धभैरवः

धैवतांशग्रहन्यासंयुतः स्यात् समस्वरः॥१६३॥
तारमन्द्रोऽयमाषड्जगान्धारं शुद्धभैरवः।

इति शुद्धभैरवः।

5. *Śuddhabhairava*

Śuddhabhairava takes *dhaivata* for its fundamental, initial and final notes with equipoised notes within the pitch range[4] of high *ṣaḍja* and low *gāndhāra*. (163c-164b)

६. मेघरागः

षड्जे धैवतिकोद्भूतः षड्जतारसमस्वरः॥१६४॥
मेघरागो मन्द्रहीनो ग्रहांशन्यासधैवतः।

इति मेघरागः।

6. *Megharāga*

Sprung from *dhaivatī* (*jāti*) in the *ṣaḍjā-grāma* with high *ṣaḍja*[5] and equipoised notes, *megharāga* has *dhaivata* for initial, fundamental and the final notes and has no lower octave. (164c-165b)

७. सोमरागः

षड्जे षाड्जीभवः षड्जग्रहांशान्तो निगोत्कटः॥१६५॥
सोमरागः स्मृतो वीरे तारमध्यस्थमध्यमः।

इति सोमरागः।

7. *Somarāga*

Produced from *ṣāḍjī* (*jāti*) in the *ṣaḍjagrāma* with *ṣaḍja* for its initial,

[1] *Vīra* of the text.

[2] *Raudra* of the text.

[3] *Adbhuta* of the text.

[4] *Tāramandra* is interpreted by 'S' to mean that it is devoid of the middle octave, or alternatively, he says, the high and the low pitch range may be taken upto *ṣaḍja* or *gāndhāra* starting from the fundamental note *dhaivata*.

[5] 'S' interprets that in this rāga only high *ṣaḍja* is taken i.e., the low and the middle *ṣaḍja* are absent.

fundamental and the final notes, *somarāga* takes acute[1] *niṣāda* and *gāndhāra*, and *madhyama* as placed in the upper and the middle octaves,[2] and is employed[3] in (the expression of) valour.[4] (165c-166b)

८. प्रथमकामोद:

तारषड्जग्रहः षड्जे षड्जमाध्यमिकोद्भवः ॥१६६॥
गतारमन्द्रः कामोदो धांशः सान्तः समस्वरः ।
इति प्रथमकामोदः ।

8. *Prathama kāmoda* (The first *kāmoda*)

Born of *ṣaḍja-madhyamā* (*jāti*) in the *ṣaḍjagrāma*, with the high *ṣaḍja* for its initial note, *dhaivata* for its fundamental note and *ṣaḍja* for its final note, *kāmoda* takes high and low *gāndhāra*[5] and has equipoised notes. (166c-167b)

९. द्वितीयकामोद:

षड्जे षाड्जीभवः षड्जग्रहांशन्याससंयुतः ॥१६७॥
समस्वरोऽन्यः कामोदो मन्द्रगान्धारसुन्दरः ।
इति द्वितीयकामोदः

9. *Dvitīya kāmoda* (The second *kāmoda*)

Born of *ṣāḍjī* (*jāti*) in the *ṣaḍja grāma* with *ṣaḍja* for its initial, fundamental and final notes and having equipoised notes, (there is) another *kāmoda* that is graceful with low *gāndhāra*. (167c-168b)

१०. आम्रपञ्चमः

गान्धारांशग्रहन्यासो मन्द्रमध्यसमुद्भवः ॥१६८॥
निगतारो मन्द्रहीनो रागः स्यादाम्रपञ्चमः ।
शार्ङ्गदेवेन गदितो हास्याद्भुतरसाश्रयः ॥१६९॥
इत्याम्रपञ्चमः । इति प्रसिद्धरागाः ।

[1] 'S' interprets *utkaṭa* (lit. acute) as *bahula* (profuse).

[2] In other words, the *madhyama* of the middle register is absent. The word octave is used for *saptaka*.

[3] *Smṛtaḥ* of the text lit. means 'is remembered', or 'is known to be (used)'.

[4] *Vīra* of the text.

[5] In other words, the middle *gāndhāra* is absent.

10. *Āmrapañcama*

Having *gāndhāra* for its fundamental, initial and final notes, arising out of the middle and the low (notes)[1] with high *niṣāda* and *gāndhara*, or (alternatively) being completely devoid of the low (notes),[2] *āmrapañcama* is a *rāga* declared by Śārṅgadeva to be the substratum of the sentiments of mirth[3] and bewilderment.[4] (168c-169)

Here, in the context of *deśīrāga-s*, kallinātha offers a few observations and comments with regard to the discrepancies found in the theory (*lakṣaṇa* i.e. the definition of the characteristic features of the particular rāga) and the practice (*lakṣya*) of some of the *rāga-s*. These are briefly represented here as the value of their implications seems to be far reaching.

For example, it has been said in the above definition of the formal structure of *Śrīrāga* that its *pañcama* is weak and so on. It has also been laid down that the remaining notes are equipoised. 'K' observes (and accordingly interprets) that the general implication in such cases is that the weakness (*alpatva*) of *pañcama* is accompanied with the equal profusion (*bahutva*) of the rest of the notes.

So he rather deduces a general rule, "wherever a particular note is rare (or weak) and the other notes are said to be equipoised, the equality of the other notes relates to their profusion with reference to the weak note." This is quite intelligible, but as in the present case, it may be observed that the note which becomes the initial, the fundamental and or the final note should also be excluded from the expression, "the remaining notes" which are said to be equipoised; for, in terms of profusion, it is bound to excell all others ; 'S' has interpreted it like that at several places.

'K' also observes that among the *deśī-rāga-s,* wherever the highest or the lowest pitch range has not been laid down, it has to be taken as discretionary. Then, he goes on to offer tentative solutions to some of the seeming contradictions to be observed between the theoretical definitions of some of the well-known *rāgāṅga-s* and the like and their actual practice.

The general premise of such seeming contradictions arises, he says, from the fact that, although it should be possible to begin with the *mūrcchanā-s* of the respective *rāga-s* from the *ṣaḍja* or *madhyama* of the middle register according to their indirect origin in the *ṣaḍja-grāma* or *madhyama-grāma* respectively through the *jāti-s* and the like (*grāma-rāga-s*, *bhāṣā s* etc.), it is seen that in practice *rāga-s* like *madhyamādi* and *toḍī* which are (in-

[1]Literally rendered the text would read "which has its origin in the *mandra* (low) and the *madhya* (middle) ('S' interprets that the terms low and middle refer to notes (of these particular registers). Also see the following note.

[2]*Mandrahīna* i.e. 'It is devoid of the low (notes), is in contradiction with the first statement that it arises out of the low and the middle notes. Therefore 'S' is led to interpret that it is an alternative structure permissible.

[3]*Hāsya* of the text.

[4]*Adbhuta* of the text.

directly) born of *madhyama-grāma* commence with middle *ṣaḍja* and not middle *madhyama* (as they should in theory).

Kallinātha considers the high *pañcama* and high *niṣāda* as the highest limit for the pitch-range of the high register in *ṣaḍja* and *madhyama grāma* respectively. *Madhyama-grāma* is the parent *rāga* of *madhyamādi* and *toḍi* in which *kākalī* is used. If the initial note is taken according to the definition, the high *niṣāda* has necessarily to be taken in *madhyamādi* and *toḍī*. But in Kallinātha's time these two *rāga-s* were already commencing with *ṣaḍja*, therefore, at that time high *pañcama* was used as the last note in the higher pitch range in these two *rāga-s*, and because of that high *kākali niṣāda* was out of use. *Uttarasvara sādhāraṇnā mabhāvaśca* of 'K'may thus be interpreted as the non-availability of the usage of the high *kākalī niṣāda*.

Pañcama of 3 and 4 *śruti-s* being the distinguisher of *grāma* and also being used as immutable, is used without such distinction. The commencement of *rāga-s* with *ṣaḍja* in spite of the ancient theory prescribing different points of commencement and use of one *pañcama* are pointers to a change in the entire *grāma-mūrcchanā* system that seems to have been already breeding by Kallinātha's time. Some of the typical features of this process are highlighted by him as follows.

In the *kriyāṅga*, *rāmakrī*; *madhyama* gains two *śruti-s* of *pañcama*; and similarly, in *naṭṭā*, *devakrī* etc. *ṛṣabha* and *dhaivata* gain the first two *śruti-s* of *antara* and *kākalī*, and thus each obtains five *śruti-s*, which is quite contrary to the rule.[1] In *Śrīrāga*, *gāndhāra* and *niṣāḍa* take resort to the first one *śruti* each of *madhyama* and *sadja* respectively, and thereby secure an extension to three *śruti-s* each, Though such extension is secured in accordance with rules, the three *śruti*-measure of *ṣaḍja* and *madhyama* thus obtained is somewhat unhappy. In that context, as he further observes, *ṛṣabha* and *dhaivata* also gain the first one *śruti* each of *gāndhāra* and *niṣāda* and thereby extend to four *śruti-s* each. Is this as well in accordance with the rules ?

In *āndhālī*, *pañcama* is given to be the initial and the fundamental note, as per the definition, and also it has been demonstrated as such in the *prastāra*; but in actual practice, *madhyama* is used instead. Similarly, in *karṇāṭagauḍa*, *ṣadja* is said to be the initial and the fundamental note in definition; but in actual practice, *niṣāda* is used as such. Among the *grāma-rāga-s*, *hindola* is said to be devoid of *ṛṣabha* and *dhaivata* in the definition, but in actual practice *ṛṣabha* and *pañcama* are dropped. Among the hexatones and the pentatones as well, at places the omitted note is taken in practice. In some cases there is no correspondence in the relation of the parent and the derived *rāga*-s or there is discrepancy with regard to the relevant sentiment (*rasa*) or its proper application and so on. In this way

[1]The commentary of 'K' as printed in the Adyar ed. of S.R. reads शास्त्रविवक्षिता instead of शास्त्रविवक्षिता as read by us. It is a matter of common knowledge that four *śruti* interval is the biggest in the *grāma-s*.

there are to be found, he says, many discrepancies between the theory and the practice as far as the *deśī-rāga s* are concerned.

But all the same, as he points out, it is no fault with *deśī-rāga-s* for they are purposefully so composed as to cater to the popular taste of various regions. And he quotes Āñjaneya in support of his view.

येषां श्रुतिस्वरग्रामजात्यादिनियमो न हि ।
नानादेश-गतिच्छाया देशीरागास्तु ते स्मृताः ॥

"The *rāga-s* that do not follow any particular rule with regard to *śruti, svara, grāma* and *jāti*, but that follow the trend prevalent in the different regions are called *deśī-rāga-s*,"

Incidentally, this furnishes us with a good definition of *deśī-rāga*. Discretion, says, Kallinātha, is the hallmark of whatever is *deśi* in *sangīta*, vocal or instrumental music or even dance. Wherever rules are strictly applied, it becomes *mārga*. Even though 'K' is obviously presenting one aspect of the divergence between *mārga* and *deśi* in defense as it were of the departures of practice of his times from the traditional theory, he does not wish to conceal the fact that the gap between the two was too wide to be bridged.

(x) प्रकीर्ण-भाषा

१. कैशिकी

शुद्धपञ्चमभाषा स्यात् कैशिकी मपभूयसी ।
पन्यासांशग्रहा मापन्यासा सगमतारभाक् ॥१७०॥
ईर्ष्यायां विनियोक्तव्या भाषाङ्गं केचिदूचिरे ।
समस्वरा रितारा सा ममन्द्रा चोत्सवे भवेत् ॥१७१॥

पापापा समधा सानी सासासाधा माससम धास नीसरी गासासा सधम मामासस धसमनी नीधा मामगमा पाप समधासा मा धासा । पाधासामाधास-माधासनि रीसनी गसा । सधमागा गस सास धमासस धसमनी नीधामाम गामा पापा—इत्यालापः ।

पामामा धससनि धसनि धसनिधा माध गाग स सनिध पापारिगसरिग मा रिगसधनिधा मानिधससास ममा निधा सपा धमरिग रिमाधमधनिधनि धनि ध (मध्यम) मनिधा सास ममा निध स पापा—इति रूपकम् ।

इति कैशिकी ।

(*vii*) Miscellaneous *bhāṣāngas*

1. *Kaiśikī*

Kaiśikī is a *bhāṣā* of *Śuddhapañcama* (*rāga*). Profuse with *madhyama* and *pañcama*, it has *pañcama* for its final, fundamental and initial notes, *madhyama* as the semifinal, note and high *ṣaḍja*, *gāndhāra* and *madhyama*, and is to be used in (the expression of) envy. However, some have declared it to be a *bhāṣāṅga* with epuipoised notes, high *ṛṣabha*, low *ṣaḍja* and *madhyama* and to be used on festive occasions. (170-171)

२. सौराष्ट्री

(ii) प्रथमसौराष्ट्री

पञ्चमादेव सौराष्ट्री भाषा पान्तग्रहांशका ।
रिहीना सगधैस्तारा ममन्द्रा सपभूयसी ॥१७२॥
नियुक्ता सर्वभावेषु मुनिभिर्गमकान्विता ।

पापापापमधनी सासासनीग सासासनि गानी गानी धाधा धध सास पापा पपधा पा धापामापा । मधनी मांधानी मां धनीसा सा । सनी गानी गां सासा स नी गा नी धा धाधधसा धममपा पप धापा धापामामा । मधनी मधनी । मां धनि सा सापमानी निधापम धापमध पापा—इत्यालापः ।

पा पम स नीसा सनी गग सस नी गगनी नीगमग नीधाधाध धध मध सस । पाधा पाधा पामा मामा ममधम धधनी सा सनि गग सास । निधधस निधमपा पमधध पमधस पमधध धग मनी धध पा । पमनी नी नीधा पम धध पम धध पा --इति रूपकम् ।

इति प्रथमसौराष्ट्री ।

(ii) द्वितीय सौराष्ट्री

सांशग्रहान्ता सौराष्ट्री टक्करागेऽतिभूरिनिः ॥१७३॥
भूरीतरा ममन्द्रा च पहीना करुणे भवेत् ।

सा सा सानी धनी नीध नीनी मां नी धनी धानी धानी धनी नी मां नीधा नीसा साध नीधमध नीधनीध माधनीध मं गागाग मंगां सगा सनी धनी नीध नी नी धनी नी नी मां नीधा नीसा सा—इत्यालापः ।

सनि धनि नी नी मां नी धनि सासा धनी नी मां नी धनीसा धससध रीरी रीध मम । धममं (मध्यम) म (गान्धार) ग (षड्ज) ससा गासागाध नी नी नी धनी मधास नीसा गानी धध सासा—इति रूपकम् ।

इति द्वितीयसौराष्ट्री । इति सौराष्ट्री ।

2. *Saurāṣṭrī*

(*i*) [1]*Prathama-saurāṣṭrī*

Saurāṣṭrī-bhāṣā is (derived) from *pañcama* (*rāga*) and has *pañcama* for its final, initial and fundamental notes. Devoid of *ṛṣabha*, it takes high *ṣaḍja*, *gāndhāra* and *dhaivata*, low *madhyama* and a profusion of *ṣaḍja* and *pañcama*. Provided with *gamaka-s* (shakes) it is employed in (the expression of) all the emotions[2] as ordained by the sages. (172-173b)

(*ii*) [3]*Dvitīya-saurāṣṭrī*

(The second) *saurāṣṭrī*, (a bhāṣā) of *ṭakka rāga* has *ṣaḍja* for its fundamental, initial and final notes, a great profusion of *niṣāda* and a profusion of the other[4] notes, and a low *madhyama*. Devoid of *pañcama*, it is (used) in pathos[5]. (173c-174b)

३. ललिता

(i) प्रथमललिता

टक्कभाषैव ललिता ललितैरुत्कटैः स्वरैः ॥१७४॥

षड्जांशग्रहणन्यासा षड्जमन्द्रा रिपोज्झिता ।

धीरैर्वीरोत्सवे प्रोक्ता तारगान्धारधैवता ॥१७५॥

सासा सास मम धधा धधमधा माम गाग मसा सग मसगम धधा धाधा धमधनी नोधामाम गाग मां सां सधनीनी धनी नोध नीगागस सागासनी धनी सासा सासममसा मसगम धधा धाध मधानीनी धामामगा गमसास धानी नोध नीनीधध नीगागसा। सागां सनी धानी सासा—इत्यालापः ।

सममध धाधामंध धमामा (गान्धार) गसासासग मधधनी नीधामा। धामामध गापागस सासस गगसग मसगम धाधाधनी धधनीम मपधमा गससमस गसासाससनीधधनी धनीगागागसां ग धानीं सासा—इति रूपकम् ।

[1]*Prathama* lit. means 'the first'.

[2]*Bhāva* is technically rendered as 'emotive situation'.

[3]*Dvitīya* lit. means 'the second'.

[4]That is, other than *niṣāda* which is said to be very profuse and *ṣaḍja* which is the fundamental note.

[5]*Karuṇa* of the text.

इति प्रथमललिता ।

(ii) द्वितीयललिता

भिन्नषड्जेऽपि ललिता ग्रहांशन्यासधैवता ।
रिगमैर्लंलितैस्तारमन्द्रैर्युक्ता धमन्द्रभाक् ॥१७६॥
प्रयोज्या ललिते स्नेहे मतङ्गमुनिसंमता ।

धाधाधाध सनी धाधाधध नीरी गासनीसा नोधाधाध सनो रीगामा। गरी मागा री री री री री रो गमपधाधप नींधा पामा गारी। मागारी। रीगरीग मगमरी गामागारी धनी रीगासनी। धाधाधम धाधाधध नीरी रीधा नीरी धानी रीगा सनी सनी धाधाधध सरिग मगरि मामा रीरीरीरीरी मगपधा पधनीधापामा गारी मागा रीरी गमगमं रीगामागा रीधानीरीमा सनी सनी धाधा—इत्यालापः ।

(धैवत) सनिगनिस रिग रिम सनि धनि धममाध धमनिनि धधधध रीरी-रीरी गम । मंमं गारी धापा-मगरीमागारी सनी धधनी गगा। सनी सनी धानीमाधा सनीनीधाधा—इति रूपकम् ।

इति द्वितीयललिता । इति ललिता ।

3. *Lalitā*

(*i*) *Prathama-lalitā:*

Lalitā is a *bhāṣā* of *ṭakka* (*rāga*) having smooth[1] and acute notes. It takes *ṣaḍja* for its fundamental, initial and the final notes and a low *ṣaḍja*. Devoid of *ṛṣabha* and *pañcama*, it has high *gāndhāra* and *dhivata* and is declared by the experts to be (used) in (the expression of) valour and festivities. (174c-175)

(*ii*) *Dvitīya-lalitā* :

Lalitā, as conceived by Mataṅga, is also (accepted to be) in *bhinnaṣaḍja*.[2] With *dhaivata* for its initial, fundamental and final notes, it is provided with

[1] *Lalita* (adj.) is interpreted by 'S' in this context as *masṛṇa* i.e. smooth.
[2] The use of the word *api* in the text suggests that, as the first *lalitā* is a *bhāṣā* of *ṭakka*, the second *lalitā* is also a *bhāṣā* of *bhinna-ṣaḍja*.

slightly twisted,[1] high and middle *ṛṣabha, gāndāra* and *madhyama*, and with a low *dhaivata*. It is employed for (expressing) tenderness and affection. (176-177b).

४. सैन्धवी

(i) प्रथमसैन्धवी

चतुर्धा सैन्धवी तत्र टक्कभाषा रिपोज्झिता ॥१७७॥

सन्यासांशग्रहा सान्द्रा गमकैर्लङ्घितस्वरैः ।

सगतारा षड्जमन्द्रा गेया सर्वरसेष्वसौ ।१७८॥

सासासासा मांसा मांसा सा । मंस गामा गासा सागां सामां सासमम गामा गममस नीगससा सनी मांस नीगां नीधांधां । धमाधांधाधं मानी नीनी धमाधाधा धाध मनी नीनीं धनी धनी सासा—इत्यालापः ।

(मध्यम) म (षड्ज) स सागाससा । नीनीनीनी सधंनीस नीधाधा धमा धममनी धाधाधममनि नीनोनीनीनीनो सनी सनी गगसासा ममगममम धग गग-सम नोनीधध ममधम धनीनीनी मधनीनी नीधनीसगमधध गध मग सनी सनी ससनीध नोनीनीसनीधमनन धध नीनी समगग नीनीनीम नीधममधधनीनीगगसा सा—इति रूपकम् ।

इति प्रथमसैन्धवी ।

(ii) द्वितीयसैन्धवी

सैन्धवी पञ्चमेऽप्यस्ति ग्रहांशन्यासपञ्चमा ।

रिपापन्यासंयुक्ता रम्या सगमकैः स्वरैः ॥१७९॥

नितारा रिबहुस्तारपा पूर्वविनियोगिनी ।

पापापा स पध सरी री री री री पमधपम धपापास पधसरी रीरीरीसरी-गारी । मारी पाधा सारी गासा रीरीरीरी गापां रीं री गाससरी रीमाधा पम-धपमध पापासपधम पधमपध मपधसनीरीरी मरीसरी रीपमध पमधपापा ।

[1]Here, in this context 'S' interprets *lalita* as *kiñcidvakra* i.e. slightly twisted. It is worthwhile to bear his interpretation as given in note-6 above. The usage of this word in the phrase *lalite snehe* is quite non-technical.

सपधसरी। रीरीरीस रीरीरीस रीगारीमाधापाधासारी गासारीरीधरीरी गां पां रीरी माससरी रीसा धापमधापमधापापा—इत्यालापः।

पधसधसरी गसरिगरीसरी। गरीसध मधं धंप पसरीरी रीरीपारी पपपारी रिममामांमाससारी सरीरीरी रीससधा धपपपधधसग पंधं सरी सरीगम धधपाधा पमधध पमधधप।पा—इति रूपकम्।

इति द्वितीयसैन्धवी।

(iii) तृतीयसैन्धवी

मालवे कैशिकेऽप्यस्ति सैन्धवी मृदुपञ्चमा ॥१८०॥
समन्द्रा निगनिर्मुक्ता षड्जन्यासग्रहांशिका।
प्रयोज्या सर्वभावेषु श्रीसोढलसुतोदिता ॥१८१॥

सासासासा समरीमा पापापप धापधापा मा रीरी मा रीरी सां सां समरीमा पापा पप धापामा। पप धापा मा पापा पपधा सा पप धासा धारी। रीमपाधापम रीरी मरीरीसरीसारीससासारी मासारीमामारी मापापापपधापाधापधापा मारीरीमारीमासा। समरीमा पापा पप धापापामा धापामापा पप पधा सां पपधा पमारींरीं मपाधापमरीमारी रीसासा—इत्यालापः।

सम रीरी ममरिरि पप रिप पपाधाप मरीरी सममरि पप पप धध (षड्ज) सं पाधापामारी मरीमरीसरीसाधधसध (षड्ज) सस मम रिरि पप रिरि स रिस रि सास धस ससं मं रिरि मम रिरि पाधापम रिरिसरिसामरिरिरिसा—इति रूपकम्।

इति तृतीयसैन्धवी।

(iv) चतुर्थसैन्धवी

सैन्धवी भिन्नषड्जेऽपि न्यासांशग्रहधैवता।
उद्दीपने नियोक्तव्या धमन्द्रा रिपवर्जिता ॥१८२॥

धाधा धध गमधनि निनि धानी सानी सनि सधा नीधा नीनी धाधमामगमा सानी धाधा पमा धाधाधगसधगमगधमधनीनी। नीनीनी। धनीसधानीनीमधासानीधाधमधाधा—इत्यालापः।

धाध गम धनी नीनी सनी धनी नीनीनीध (षड्ज) सं सनीनी सनी धध गम धग मध नीनी मनी धनी नीध नीध गां सगमा नीसनी धनीधगमधगमधनीनीमनी-धनीनीध धासा धमनी सनी धनीध गमधगमधनीं। नीमनीधनीनीधनीधाधा

—इति रूपकम् ।

इति चतुर्थसैन्धवी । इति सैन्धवी ।

4. *Saindhavī*

(*i*) *Prathama-saindhavī*:

Saindhavī is fourfold. The one that is a *bhāṣā* of *ṭakka* (*rāga*), is devoid of *ṛṣabha* and *pañcama*, has *ṣaḍja* for its final, the fundamental and the initial notes and is replete with graceful shakes (*gamaka-s*) and swift[1] notes. With high *ṣaḍja* and *gāndhāra* and low *ṣaḍja* it is to be sung in (the context of) all the sentiments. (177c-178)

(*ii*) *Dvitīya-saindhavī*:

Saindhavī is also (a *bhāṣā*) in *pañcama* (*rāga*) with *pañcama* for its initial, fundamental and final notes, and *ṛṣabha* and *pañcama* for its semifinal notes. Graced with shakeful notes[2] it takes high *niṣāda* and *pañcama* and profuse *ṛṣabha*, and is employed like the first one.[3] (179-180b)

(*iii*) *Tritīya*[4]*-saindhavī*:

Saindhavī is also (a *bhāṣā*) of *mālavakaiśika* (*rāga*) which has a soft *pañcama* and a low *ṣaḍja*, and which is devoid of *niṣāda* and *gāndhāra*. It has *ṣaḍja* for its final, initial and fundamental notes, and is meant to be used for (the expression of) all the emotions,[5] as declared by *Śārṅgadeva*.[6] (180c-181)

[1]*Laṅghita-svara* lit. is 'an overstepped note' (cf *S.R.*, II 3. 126 cd); obviously the expression is metaphorically used in the sense of 'notes swiftly taken' as interpreted by 'S'.

[2]'S' interprets 'graceful with *gamaka-s* (shakes) on *niṣāda, dhaivata* and *pañcama*, which does not accord with the text available to us.

[3]That is, in all the sentiments.

[4]*Tritīya* lit. means 'the third'.

[5]*Bhāva* is technically an emotive situation.

[6]*Soḍhala-suta* lit. 'the son of Soḍhala'.

(iv) *Caturtha*[1]*-saindhavī*:

Saindhavī is (again a *bhāṣā*) of *bhinna-ṣaḍja* (*rāgā*) as well which has *dhaivata* for its final, fundamental and the initial notes. It takes a low *dhaivata*, is devoid of *ṛṣabha* and *pañcama* and is to be used in order to stimulate[2] (the prevailing mood). (182).

५. गौडी

(i) प्रथमगौडी

हिन्दोलभाषा गौडी स्यात् षड्जन्यासग्रहांशिका ।
पञ्चमोत्पन्नगमकवहुला धरिवर्जिता ॥१८३॥
षड्जमन्द्रा प्रयोक्तव्या प्रियसम्भाषणे बुधैः ।

सां मां सां स मगामापापामापामापा मागामसांसां सस सगामापापागमगा मगापगामपापा । मागागसासनीसागामामगासनीसामास सगासासा सस गामा सागामाप मगा सापा पापा मामा गाग सासा समगा । मापा मापा पा पमगा । पमागम पगापमा गमपगा पमापगा पासासासगसामागासनिसां सां—इत्यालापः ।

(षड्ज) सगमग पममगगसां (षड्ज) ससागामा मामा पाप मगापम पगा गगसापानी सनीस मगम गमपम पम गम मम गन्सिं गगसगसनिसामगागसासा —इति रूपकम् ।

इति प्रथमगौडी ।

(ii) द्वितीयगौडी

ग्रहांशन्यासषड्जान्या गौडी मालवकैशिके ॥१८४॥
मतङ्गोक्ता तारमन्द्रषड्जा भूरिनिषादभाक् ।
प्रयोज्या रणरणके वीरे त्वन्यैः प्रयुज्यते ॥१८५॥

सांसां सानि धासां पमा गामानी नीधनी धधमपममगम मगा गसासगारी सागामगमनीनी धम पम पाप मम मगरीमं सां सनी नीरीपा । सनीरीस नीसा-सा । मगमनी गा मा नीगा मानी । नीधसापा मागामनी नीधधनी धमपमगमगा-

[1]*Caturtha* lit. means 'the fourth'.

[2]*Uddīpana* is technically a *vibhāva* i.e. the external situation that stimulates and feeds the *sthāyi-bhāva* (the prevailing stable state of being as experienced by a subject usually the hero of a dramatic performance). Thus, *uddipana* is not just a stimulant.

मपाम गरी री मपगमानीधनींस पामगमापाप सां ममगारीरीं सास नीरीरी पास नीरीसनी रीसनी सासा—इत्यालापः ।

सांनीधससपापममगाधनिधनि धनिध मपम गमम सा मगरीरी सांसनी रीरी पांसनी रीरी पां स नीरीरीसागममा गानीधपममपममगमगरी सनिसास नीसासनि रिरि सासा—इति रूपकम् ।

इति द्वितीयगौडी । इति गौडी ।

5. *Gauḍī*

(*i*) *Prathama-gauḍī:*

Gauḍī is a *bhāṣā* of *hindola* with *ṣaḍja* for its final, initial and fundamental notes and profuse *gamaka-s* (shakes) arising from *pañcama.* Devoid of *dhaivata* and *ṛṣabha* it takes a low *ṣaḍja* and is employed by the learned in the dialogue of lovers[1]. (183-184b)

(*ii*) *Dvitīya-gauḍī:*

Another *gauḍī* with *ṣaḍja* for its initial, fundamental and the final notes is (a *bhāṣā*) of *mālavakaiśika* (*rāga*), which is enunciated by Mataṅga. It has high and low *ṣaḍja* and a profusion of *niṣāda* and is to be used in (the expression of) longing (of lovers) in separation, or in (the context of) valours according to others. (184c-185)

६. त्रावणी

याष्टिके त्रावणी भाषा पञ्चमस्य ग्रहांशसा ।
पान्ता सरिपमैर्भूरिः संगतद्विश्रुतिर्मता ॥१८६॥
एषा भाषाङ्गमन्येषां धग्रहांशा निपोज्झिता ।
अतारा प्रार्थने मन्द्रधगव्याप्तोरुमध्यमा ॥१८७॥

सासांसापा पापाधाधानीनी सानिधानिधा सारी सासानीधनीध सारी गारी मासनी पापाधानीसा सनीमध धससनिमधमधसनिधामागामा सानीससासंसं सनिसांसां निगास निधामा मामां सरि सासा साधानिधापापा—

इति त्रावणी ।

[1]*Priyasambhāṣaṇa* lit. would mean' conversation with the beloved.

6. *Trāvanī*

According to Yāṣṭika, *trāvaṇī* is a *bhāṣā of pañcama* (*rāga*) having *ṣaḍja* for its initial and the fundamental note, *pañcama* for its final note and a profusion of *ṣaḍja*, *ṛṣābha*, *pañcama* and *madhyama* with *niṣāda* and *gāndhāra*[1] in concert. According to others, however, it is a *bhāṣāṅga*. With *dhaivata* for its initial and the fundamental note, it is devoid of *niṣāda* and *pañcama* and of the higher octave Pervaded by low *dhaivata* and *gāndhāra*, it is profuse with madhyama and is employed in prayer. (186-187)

७. हर्षपुरी

भाषा हर्षपुरी षड्जमन्द्रा मालवकैशिके ।
सन्यासांशग्रहा तारमपा हर्षे धवर्जिता ॥१८८॥

सासासासनिसनिस रिस नीसासा । मगमापापापा । समपापा पममाम मगाग री । रीसांसनि निपां सनि ममगारी नी नी पासनीसांसां सरि रीरी पांसनिरी सनिरीस निसासा । सनिसांरी निसानीनी निसारी । सनिसां सां । मगामा पापा । समपापमगा गममारीरीसा मनीपांसनी सासागगरी नी नीपासनी-सांसां । सनिरीरी पांसनिरी सनिरी सनीसां सां—इत्यालापः ।

सानी रीसा नी नीगरी सा । नीरीरीग रीमरीग नीरीगरी नीस (मध्यम) म (गान्धार) गारी गगरीसारीगरीपागरी सनी रीग रीनीसासा—इति रूपकम् ।

इति हर्षपुरी ।

7. *Harṣapurī*

Harṣapurī, a *bhāṣā* in *mālavakaiśika* (*rāga*) with a low *ṣaḍja*, has *ṣaḍja* for its final, fundamental and initial notes and high *madhyama* and *pañcama*. Devoid of *dhaivata* it is used in (the expression of) joy. (188)

८. भम्माणी

पञ्चमस्य विभाषा स्याद्भम्माणी मन्द्रषड्जभाक् ।
पान्तांशादिः समनिपैस्तारत्यक्तरिरुत्सवे ॥१८९॥

पापा पाम गामा पापा । मामा नीधा मामगमा पापा । पगा गमा सनीधपा

[1] *Dviśruti*-lit. the notes having two *śruti-s*.

पापमनी नीधनीसां सां गममापा पापमपमनीसनीधापापापमपमनीसनिधां पा पापा पम निनिधागां मां पमनि निधापसधापमधपमधापापा—इत्यालापः।

पां (पञ्चम) पंग गम पामम गग मम गग ममनि धधमगा पापा। पपगम-समसनिधसनिधपापमनिनिनि धनि निसमम गपमपमनि सानि मनिध पापा पम नि पानि निधनी सस पममममाधांधमधधपमधधसमधधपापा—इति रूपकम्।

इति भम्माणी।

(xi) टक्ककैशिक-मालवा-द्राविडी

(i) टक्ककैशिकः

धैवत्या मध्यमायाश्च संभूतष्टक्ककैशिकः।
धैवतांशग्रहन्यासः काकल्यन्तरराजितः ॥१६०॥
सारोही सप्रसन्नादिरुत्तरायतयान्वितः।
उद्भटे नटने कामग्रस्ते कञ्चुकिकर्तृके ॥१६१॥
प्रवेशे तुर्ययामेऽह्नो बीभत्से सभयानके।
प्रयोक्तव्यो महाकालमन्मथप्रीतये बुधैः ॥१६२॥

धासा धपा धमामगारीमगाग सासनीम गरीगसा धाधाधसा गरीरीमा माध-धधरीरीरी गागमाम धाधाधासागारीरी धाधाधास पाधममगरी गसासधधसस-रीरीग गममधधरी गगसस सनीनीनी सरीगस निसां सां धांधांधांधां। ससमाम धागसासनिसधाधा धाधाधाधा ससस मरी धम ममससरि मरिमधपमसा धासासासा सागधासगध सधधसधपरिरि ममसरि ममधपमधा धाधाधस सधसस सस ससारिमधासनिगा सासा निनिधा—इत्यालापः।

सागरिम मारिममाधापा धापा धामा धाध धधसास धासामाधापामा धापा-माप धम धधपामारिमा धमधास मामधाधा सागारी। मम गग धध पम धाधा-धधसा धससा धपसास गधरीरी रीरी मम ममरीम मममाम ममरिम धपमध मधमध मधपधाधा रीधध रिधाधारि धधाधपा पामा रिस रिरिमम ममधप धाधासधा सासागम मधमध सधसम मसधम धाधा—इति करणम्।

१.	धा	धा	धा	धा	धा	मा	पा	पा
	श्री		म		त्क	ट	त	ट
२.	धा	धा	री	गा	सां	सां	री	गा
	वि	ग	लि	त	म	द	म	दि
३.	धां	धां	मां	धां	धां	धां	धां	धां
	रा		मो		द	म		त्त
४.	मां	धां	मां	धां	धां	धां	धां	धां
	म	धु	प	कु	लं			
५.	धां	धां	सां	सां	गा	री	मा	मा
	कु	लि	श	ध	र	क	म	ल
६.	री	री	मा	मा	धा	री	मा	मा
	यो		नि		प्र	भू	ति	नु
७.	धा	धा	धा	धा	धा	धा	धा	सा
	तं			ग	ण		प	
८.	धा	पा	मा	धा	धा	धा	धा	धा
	तिं		वं		दे			

—इत्याक्षिप्तिका

इति टक्कैशिकः ।

(ii) मालवा (भाषा)

मालवा तस्य भाषा स्याद् ग्रहांशन्यासधैवता ।

षड्जधौ संगतौ तत्र स्यातामृषभपञ्चमौ ॥१६३॥

धाधासारि सामापामा गारीमाधा पाधाधानी धासाधा ।

इति मालवा ।

(iii) दाविडी (विभाषा)

गान्धारांशग्रहा धान्ता द्राविडी तद्विभाषिका ।
द्विश्रुती संगतौ तत्र भवेतां षड्जधैवतौ ॥१६४॥

गासागामा धाधा पामा धाधा गास निधाधास गासनि धापनिमागा मनिधा ।

इतिद्राविडी

इति रागाङ्गादिनिर्णयाख्यं द्वितीयं प्रकरणम्

॥इति श्रीमदनवद्यविद्याविनोदश्रीकरणाधिपतिश्रीसोढलदेवनन्दन-
निःशङ्कश्रीशार्ङ्गदेवविरचिते संगीतरत्नाकरे रागविवेकाध्यायो द्वितीयः ॥

8. *Bhammāṇī*

Bhammāṇī is a *vibhāṣā* of *pañcama* (*rāga*) with a low *ṣaḍja*, It has *pañcama* for its final, fundamental and initial notes, and high *ṣaḍja, madhyama, niṣāda, and pañcama.* Devoid of *ṛṣabha*, it is employed on festive occasions (189).

Ṭakkakaiśika-malavā and *drāviḍī*:

(*i*) *Ṭakkakaiśika*:
Produced from *dhaivatī* and *madhyamā* (*jāti-s*) *ṭakkakaiśika* has *dhaivata* and its fundamental, initial and final notes and is graced by *kākalī* and *antara*. Set in the *uttarāyatā*[1] with *prasannādi*[2] *in the ascending varṇa* it is to be employed, according to the experts[3], in the fourth quarter of the day, to the endearment of Lord Śiva and the Cupid for (expressing) disgust[4] accompanied with terror[5], in an amorous and brisk dance, while the chamberlain enters[6] (the stage). (190-192)

[1]The third *mūrcchanā* of the *sa-grāma*, commencing with *dhaivata.*
[2]Name of an *alaṅkāra.*
[3]*Budhaiḥ* lit. means 'by the learned or wise'.
[4]*Bībhatsa* of the text is also rendered as abhorrence by some.
[5]*Bhayānaka* of the text is lit. an adjective but in rhetorics is used for a noun.
[6]We are once again reminded that the *rāga*-s were sung in dramatic performances.

Ākṣiptikā:

1.	dhā	dhā	dhā	dhā	dhā	mā	pā	pā
	Śrī		*ma*		*tka*	*ṭa*	*ta*	*ṭa*
2.	dhā	dhā	rī	gā	sȧ	sȧ	rī	gā
	vi	*ga*	*li*	*ta*	*ma*	*da*	*ma*	*di*
3.	dhȧ	dhȧ	mȧ	dhȧ	dhȧ	dhȧ	dhȧ	dhȧ
	rā		*mo*		*da*	*ma*		*tta*
4.	mȧ	dhȧ	mȧ	dhȧ	dhȧ	dhȧ	dhȧ	dhȧ
	ma	*dhu*	*pa*	*ku*	*lam*			
5.	dhȧ	dhȧ	sȧ	sȧ	gā	rī	mā	mā
	ku	*li*	*śā*	dha	*ra*	*ka*	*ma*	*la*
6.	rī	rī	mā	mā	dhā	rī	mā	mā
	yo		*ni*		*pra*	*bhṛ*	*ti*	*nu*
7.	dhā	dhā	dhā	dhā	dhā	dhā	dhā	sā
	taṃ			*ga*	*ṇa*		*pa*	
8.	dhā	pā	mā	dhā	dhā	dhā	dhā	dhā
	tiṃ		*vān*		*de*			

The purport of the song is as under:

Obeisance to Gaṇapati, who is saluted by gods like Brahmā and Indra and who has intoxicated a swarm of black bees by the fragrance of the rut oozing out by the sides of his charming temples.

Thus ends *ṭakkakaiśika*.

(*ii*) *Mālavā* (*bhāṣā*):

Mālavā which is its *bhāṣā*, has *dhaivata* for its initial, fundamental and the final notes. *Ṣaḍja* and *dhaivata*, and *ṛṣabha* and *pañcama* are here in concert with each other. (193)

(*iii*) *Drāviḍī* (Vibhāṣā)

Drāviḍī, its *vibhāṣā*, has *gāndhāra* for its fundamental and initial notes and *dhaivata* for its final note. *Gāndhāra* and *niṣāda* as well as *ṣaḍja* and *dhaivata* are here in concert with each other. (19+)

In his commentary on *Ṣuddhakaiśika* (30c-32 ante) 'K' observes that even though keeping in view the principle of Metaṅga, *ṭakkakaiśika* is related to *śaḍja-grāma* only despite the fact that it is derived from *dhaivatī* and *madhyamā jāti-ś* that belong to the two *grāma-s*, because the *pañcama*, of four *śruti-s* is available with it in practice and because it takes all the seven notes in theory as well, yet Ṣārṅgadeva has rightly classified it as belonging to both the *grāma-s* (S.R. II. 1. 12). This happens to be so because according to Kāśyapa (as quoted by Mataṅga) *ṭakkakaiśika* becomes pentatonic by the omission of *niṣaḍa* and *gāndhāra*; and it has been laid down (vide S.R. I. 4. 30c-31a) that deprived of *ṛṣabha* and *dhaivata*, and *niṣāda* and *gāndhāra* fourteen pentatoni Śuddhatcās (specific combinational note-series) pertaining to *madhyama-grāma* are formed. Thus, Śārṅgadeva's definition is obviously based on the validity of both the authorities.

It will be observed that the author has not described the characteristic features of all the *rāga-s* mentioned in section one of this chapter, specially of those that are not known to be the parent *rāga-s* of the well-known *rāga-s* of his time. But Kallinātha has endeavoured to give in some detail the characteristic features of many more *rāga-s* on the basis of the traditions of the schools of Mataṅga and Āñjaneya. Here it is proposed to enumerate such *rāga-s* in association with their parent *rāga-s*.[1]

[1]See appendix I.

Appendix I

List of *rāga-s* defined by Kallinātha[1]

(*a*) ***As derived from parent rāga-s:***

No.	Name of parent *rāga*	Name of derived *bhāṣā*	Name of the derived *vibhāṣa* and *antarabhāṣā* (A-B)
1.	***Sauvīra***	*Vegamadhyamā, sādhāritā gāndhārī*	———
2.	*Kakubha*	*Bhinnapañcamī, Kāmbhojī. madhyamagrāmī, madhurī śakamiśrā.*	*Ābhīrikā madhukarī-Śālavāhanī*[2]
3.	*Ṭakka*	*Travaṇā, travaṇodhavā, verañjī, madhyamagrāmad, ehā, mālavavesarī, chevāṭī, pañcamalakṣitā, pañcamī, gāndhāra-pañcamī, mālavī, tānavalitā, ravicandrikā, tānā, ambāherī, dohyā, vesarī.*	*Devāravardhnī, āhdhrī, gurjarī, bhāvanī.*
4.	*Śuddhapañcama*	*Tānodbhavā, ābhīrī, gurjarī, āndhrī, māṅgalī, bhāvanī.*	
5.	*Bhinnapañcama*	*Dhaivatabhūṣitā, śuddhabhinnā varāṭī, viśālā.*	*Kauśalī*
6.	*Ṭakkakaiśika*	*Mālavā, bhinnavalitā, drāviḍī.*	

1. Spoken of by Mataṅga and Āñjaneya.
2. An *antarabhāṣā*.

No.	Name of parent *rāga*	Name of derived *bhāṣā*	Name of the derived *vibhāṣa* and *antarabhāṣā* (A-B)
7.	*Hindola*	*Vesarī, cūtamañjarī, ṣaḍja-madhyamā, madhurī, bhinna-paurālī, mālavavesarī*	
8.	*Boṭṭa*	*Māṅgali*	
9.	*Mālavakaiśika*	*Bāṅgālī, māṅgālī, mālava-vesarī,, khañjanī, gurjarī, paurālī, ardhavesarī, śuddhā, mālavarūpā, ābhīrī.*	*Kāmbhojī, devāra-vardhanī*
10.	*Gāndhāra-pañcama*	*Gāndhārī*	
11.	*Bhinna-ṣaḍja*	*Gāndhāravallī, kacchelī, svara-vallikā, niṣādinī madhyamā, śuddhā, dākṣiṇātyā, pulindī, tumburā, ṣaḍja-bhāṣā, kālindī, śrīkaṇṭhī, gāndārī.*	*paurālī, mālavī, kālindī, devāravar-dhanī.*
12.	*Vesaraṣāḍava*	*Nādyā, bāhyaṣāḍavā*	*Pārvatī, śrīkaṇṭhī*
13.	*Mālava-pañcama*		*Vegavatī, bhāvanī, vibhāvanī*
14.	*Bhinnatāna*	*Tānodbhavā*	
15.	(*Pañcamaṣaḍja*)	*Potā*	
16.	*Revagupta*[1]	*Śakā*	
17.			*Pallavī*[2]
18.			*Bhāsavalitā*[3]
19.			*Kiraṇāvalī*[3]
20.			*Śākavalitā*[3]

[1] According to another school.

[2] The parent *rāga* is not known.

[3] These are *antarabhāṣā-s* that are not assigned to any particular parent *rāga*.

No.	Name of parent *rāga*	Name of derived *bhāṣā*	Name of the deriven *vibhāṣa* and *antarabhāṣā* (A-B)

(*b*) *Other forms*:

Uparāga-s

1. *Śakatilaka*	:	4. *Bhāvanāpañcama*
2. *Ṭakkasaindhava*	:	5. *Nāgagāndhāra*
3. *Kokilāpañcama*	:	6. *Nāgapañcama*

Rāga-s belonging to no sub-division.

1. *Naṭṭa*	:	6. *Dhvani*
2. *Bhāsa*	:	7. *Kandarpa*
3. *Raktahaṁsa*	:	8. *Deśākhya*
4. *Kolhāsa*	:	9. *Kaiśikakakubha*
5. *Prasava*	:	10. *Naṭṭanārāyaṇa*

The ancient well known *deśī rāgas:*

Rāgāṅga-s:

1. *Śaṅkarābharāṇa*	:	5. *Rīti*
2. *Ghaṇṭārava*	:	6. *Pūrṇāṭikā*
3. *Haṁsaka*	:	7. *Lāṭī*
4. *Dīpaka*	:	8. *Pallavī*

Bhāṣāṅga-s :

1. *Gāmbhīrī*	:	7. *Nīlotpalī*
2. *Vehārī*	:	8. *Chāyā*
3. *Śvasitā*	:	9. *Tarāṅgiṇi*
4. *Utpalī*	:	10. *Gāndhāragati*
5. *Golī*	:	11. *Verañjī*
6. *Nādāntarī*:	:	

Kriyāṅga-s

The definition of the twelve *kriyāṅga-s* such as *bhāvakrī* etc. is the samc as defined.

*Upāṅga-*s:

1. *Pūrṇāṭa* 2. *Devāla* 3. *Kurañjī*

Chapter III

Miscellaneous Topics

(*Prakīrṇakādhyāya*)

तृतीयः प्रकीर्णकाध्यायः

(i) ग्रन्थकृत्प्रतिज्ञा

अथ प्रकीर्णकं कर्णरसायनमनाकुलम् ।
देशीमार्गाश्रयं वक्ति शाङ्र्गदेवो विदां वरः ॥१॥

SECTION 3

(i) Author's announcement of the subject:[1]

Śārṅgadeva, the best of the learned, now relates the miscellany[1], the excellent[2] elixir[3] of the ears and the substratum of *deśī* and *mārga* (*saṅgīta*)[4].

[1]'K' explains that its miscellaneous character consists in the fact the topics dealt with in this chapter fall outside the classified division of the subject-matter of the book. For example Chapter—I deals with *svara* (tone) Chapter—II with the *rāga-s*, Chapter—IV with the *prabandha-s* and so on.

[2]*Anākulam* (*an* + *ākulam*) lit. unobscure, or in detail (*viśadam*) as interpreted by 'S'. It is explained by 'K' as the capacity to signify the meaning without narrowing it,' i.e. in other words,' the capacity of being heard clearly.' However, the expression is negative even though it refers to a positive content, since it employs a double negative, so to say. Moreover, it is a part of a metaphor—' the excellent elixir of the ears', which will be elucidated in the following note. It may be pointed out, however, that the original double negative has been rendered as a single positive in view of the English idiom. The word excellent is not the literal equivalent of the original *anākulam* but it is expressive of the metaphorical significance implied.

[3]*Rasāyanam* is a medicine that enables the organism to overcome physical decay and is the elixir that prolongs life. Here, the miscellany (i.e. the collection of miscellaneous topics to be dealt with in this chapter) is metaphorically described as the excellent elixir of the ears. In other words, the author's description of such topics is not only well ordered but also essential to the understanding of his exposition of music, and at the same time it is interesting as well.

[4]The topics such as the definitions of the master composer and the like, forming part of this chapter (as well as the entire work) are common to the exposition of the *mārga* and *deśī* music, and therefore the miscellany of this chapter is described as their substratum.

In the last chapter the author has presented the definitions and the characteristic features of various *rāga-s* classified as *grāma—rāga-s, rāga-s, uparāga-s* etc. However, the music so described depends for its manifestation on the composers and the performers, their medium of expression, talent and so on. Therefore, the author now deals with such topics as these, brought together under the heading *prakīrṇaka,* that are of miscellaneous character. He begins with the characteristic features that mark out a master composer.

(ii) वाग्गेयकारलक्षणम्, तद्भेदाश्च

वाङ् मातुरुच्यते गेयं धातुरित्यभिधीयते ।

वाचं गेयं च कुरुते यः स वाग्गेयकारकः ॥२॥

शब्दानुशासनज्ञानमभिधानप्रवीणता ।

छन्दःप्रभेदवेदित्वमलङ्कारेषु कौशलम् ॥३॥

रसभावपरिज्ञानं देशस्थितिषु चातुरी ।

अशेषभाषाविज्ञानं कलाशास्त्रेषु कौशलम् ॥४॥

तौर्यत्रितयचातुर्यं हृद्यशारीरशालिता ।

लयतालकलाज्ञानं विवेकोऽनेककाकुषु ॥५॥

प्रभूतप्रतिभोद्भेदभाक्त्वं सुभगगेयता ।

देशीरागेष्वभिज्ञानं वाक्पटुत्वं सभाजये ॥६॥

रोषद्वेषपरित्यागः सार्द्रत्वमुचितज्ञता ।

अनुच्छिष्टोक्तिनिर्बन्धो नूत्नधातुविनिर्मितिः ॥७॥

परचित्तपरिज्ञानं प्रबन्धेषु प्रगल्भता ।

द्रुतगीतविनिर्माणं पदान्तरविदग्धता ॥८॥

त्रिस्थानगमकप्रौढिर्विविधालप्तिनैपुणम् ।

अवधानं गुणैरेभिर्वरो वाग्गेयकारकः ॥९॥

विदधानोऽधिकं धातुं मातुमन्दस्तु मध्यमः ।

धातुमातुविदप्रौढः प्रबन्धेष्वपि मध्यमः ॥१०॥

रम्यमातुविनिर्माताप्यधमो मन्दधातुकृत् ।

वरो वस्तुकविर्वर्णकविर्मध्यम उच्यते ॥११॥
कुट्टिकारोऽन्यधातौ तु मातुकारः प्रकीर्तितः ।

(ii) The definition and classification of *vāggeyakāra* (master composer): 2-12b.

The literary composition[1] is said to be *mātu* and the tonal structure is called *dhātu*.[2] One who composes the verbal text[3] as well as the melodic form is (known as) *vāggeyakāra*[3] (the master composer). (2)

(a) The best *vāggeyakāra*:

The best *vāggeyakāra* is (possessed) of these excellences: a thorough knowledge of grammar[4], proficiency in lexicography, knowledge of prosody (lit. differentiating among the various meters), proficiency in the use of (different) figures of speech, comprehension of aesthetic delight (*rasa*) as related to (different) emotive states of being (*bhāva*), intelligent familiarity with local custom,[5] knowledge of many languages, proficiency in the scientific[6] theories of fine arts, expert knowledge of the three musical arts[7], a lovely tone-quality[8], good knowledge of *laya* (tempo), *tāla* (musical time)[9] and *kalā*[10], discrimination of different intonations, a versatile genius, a beautiful musical rendering, acquaintance with regional (*deśi*) *rāga-s*, cleverness in conversation for victory in debates, freedom from like and

[1]'S' defines *mātu* as poetic composition coming to prominence through a singer or a musician. *Vāk* is lit. speech and therefore by context implies the verbal text or the verbal structure of a musical composition.

[2]*Geyam* lit. that which is the object of singing, i.e. *dhātu*, the tonal rhythmic structure of melody. 'S' defines it as *gānayogyam* lit. worthy of being sung.

[3]*Vāggeyakāra* (*Vāk+geya+kāra*) one who composes the verbal as well as the tonal-rhythmic structure of the song.

[4]'K' says that this is indicative of the ability for the appropriate use of words.

[5]'S' observes that this is necessary to grasp the intonations (*kāku*) peculiar to particular regions.

[6]The text literally means the sciences of the many fine arts.

[7]The three musical arts included in the concept of *saṅgīta* viz. the vocal music, the instrumental music and dancing.

[8]*Śārīra* is to be defined in this chapter; it refers to that specific quality of voice that is characteristic of the individual body as the medium of voice-production.

[9]The terms *laya* and *tāla* are to be properly defined in Chapter V (*Tālādhyāya*). For the time being, it may be understood that *tāla* signifies 'sounding' and 'silent' action in cyclic order designed to measure musical time, and *laya* (in the ancient theory) is the interval of time in between such actions.

[10]*Kalā* has more than one denotation, but in this context it signifies a unit of *tāla*, 'sounding' or 'unsounding'. These will be dealt with in Chapter V.

dislike,[1] aesthetic sensitivity,[2] a sense of propriety in expression and new melodic forms, knowledge of another's mind, maturity in the understanding of different (varieties of) *prabandha-s*, the ability to compose songs at short notice,[3] the expert knowledge of composing different verbal structures for particular melodic forms, maturity in producing *gamaka-s* (shakes and graces) pervading the three registers, proficiency in (the presentation of) different (forms of) *ālāpa* and attention.[4] (3-9)

(b) The average *vāggeyakara*:

An average[5] *vāggeyakāra* excels in composing the tonal structure (*dhātu*), but is relatively not so good[5] at composing the verbal structure (*mātu*). Even though able to compose both the tonal as well as the verbal structure (of a melody), he is immature in the *prabandha-s*. (10)

(c) The bad *vāggeyakāra*:

A bad *vāggeyakāra* is a composer of beautiful verbal structure and poor tonal structure. (11 a b)

(d) Another criterion of classification as best and average:

The poet who excels in (the presentation of) the substance is best and the one who excels in form is average. (11 c d)

(e) The unworthy *vāggeyakāra*:

(The *vāggeyakāra*) who composes verbal structures and sets them to the melodic forms of others is (called) *kuṭṭikāra*.[6] (12 a b)

A musical composition comprises some verbal text, usually poetic and of literary excellence or even verbal phrases (meaningful or meaningless syllables) which is set in tonal rhythmic structure or melodic form. Thus,

[1]*Rāga* is a text variant available to 'S' and seems to be more in line with *dveṣa* which is its opposite. The Adyar Ed. text reads *roṣa* instead, which 'K' elucidates as *vācika-amarśa* (Lit. jealous anger expressed in words). As against that, he interprets *dveśa* as mental violence.

[2]*Sārdratā* lit. having moisture, is a metaphorical expression for a sympathetic and a sensitive heart.

[3]Lit. quickly, implying ready wit.

[4]'S' defines *avadhāna* as the power of determining the order of succession. *pūrvāpara-viniściti*'.

[5]Lit. the middle one.

[6]Seems to have been used in the sense of a bad name.

two specific capacities are involved in the composition of a musical piece viz. its verbal structure and its tonal-rhythmic structure. Correspondingly, an excellent blending of these two different capacities is required of a person who is expected to be an independent artist and a real composer. The author here classifies the calibre of *vāggeyakāra-s* (master composer) into three grades viz. ordinary, average and extraordinary which correspond to the Sanskrit notion of *adhama*-(lit. the lowest) *madhyama* (lit. the middle one) and *uttama* or *vara* (lit. the best).

The best *vāggeyakāra* besides having other excellences enumerated in the text, is equally proficient in both the arts viz. the art of composing the verbal structure and that of the tonal-rythmic structure of melody. The average *vāggeyakāra* is proficient in the art of composing the tonalrhythmic structure but is dull at composing the verbal structure, while the ordinary one, who is of the lowest capacity, is good at composing the verbal structure. but poor at composing the tonal-rhythmic structure. Obviously, for a music composer proficiency at tonal composition is of greater value. This fact is pointed out by the author through a simile. Just as, he says, the best poet is concerned more with the meaning of the words used by him and the thought and feeling and the beauty of the emotion that they are designed to express, than the words themselves, so also the best *vāggeyakāra* is most concerned with the tonal rhythmic structure and not with the words on which it is built. Similarly he says that, like a mediocre poet who pays greater attention to words than to the meaning, the substance, the *vāggeyakāra* who composes poetry which he sets to the tunes composed by another is a *kuṭṭikāra* i.e., he is neither a poet nor a music composer; he is a blot on the name of both. Thus, he is unworthy of being called a *vāggeyakāra*.

(iii) गान्धर्व—स्वरादि—लक्षणम्

मार्गं देशीं च यो वेत्ति स गान्धर्वोऽभिधीयते ॥१२॥
यो वेत्ति केवलं मार्गं स्वरादिः स निगद्यते ।

(iii) The definition of *gāndharva* and *svarādi*: 12c-13b

One[1] who knows both, the *mārga* and *deśī* (*suṅgīta*) is called *gāndharva*, while one[2] who knows only *mārga* (*saṅgīta*) is said to be *svarādi*, (12 c-13 b).

It has already been said (cf. I 1. 21 c-24 b) that "*gītam* (vocal melody), *vādyam* (playing on instruments) and *nṛtyam* (dancing), all the three together constitute *saṅgīta* which is two-fold viz. *mārga* and *deśī*. That which was

[1-2]The Musicians.

discovered by Brahmā and (first) practised by Bharata and others in the audience of Lord Śiva is known as *mārga* which definitely bestows prosperity, while the *saṅgīta* that entertains people according to their taste in different regions is known as *deśī*."

This history of the concepts of *mārga* and *deśī* reveals that these terms were mainly associated with *rāga-s*, *tāla-s* and *prabandha-s*. Kallinātha's observations on II. 159-160 indicate that the main distinction between *mārga* and *deśī* in the context of *rāga* is that, while the former is strictly bound by the rules and regulations of the *grāma-mūrcchanā* system, the latter is, by and large, free from it. Therefore, the melodic structures from *jātī-s* and *grāma-rāga-s* to *antarabhāṣā-s* are roughly included in the *mārga saṅgīta,* while the *deśī rāga-s* dealt with by Śārṅgadeva in Section two are included by him in *deśī saṅgīta.* This indicates an approximate division. Another important point is that Kallinātha also identifies the concepts of *gāndharva* and *gāna* with *mārga* and *deśī* (cf. his observations on the first two verses of chapter IV). Obviously, in his time the earlier distinction of these concepts was no more considered to be significant.

(iv) गायकलक्षणं, तद्भेदाश्च

(क) उत्तमगायक:

हृद्यशब्दः सुशारीरो ग्रहमोक्षविचक्षणः ॥१३॥
रागरागाङ्गभाषाङ्गक्रियाङ्गोपाङ्गकोविदः ।
प्रबन्धगाननिष्णातो विविधालप्तितत्त्ववित् ॥१४॥
सर्वस्थानोत्थगमकेष्वनायासलसद्गतिः ।
आयत्तकण्ठस्तालज्ञः सावधानो जितश्रमः ॥१५॥
शुद्धच्छायालगाभिज्ञः सर्वकाकुविशेषवित् ।
अनेकस्थायसंचारः सर्वदोषविवर्जितः ॥१६॥
क्रियापरो युक्तलयः सुघटो धारणान्वितः ।
स्फूर्जन्निर्जवनो हारिरहःकृद्भजनोद्धुरः ॥१७॥
सुसंप्रदायो गीतज्ञैर्गीयते गायनाग्रणीः ।

(ख) मध्यमगायक:

गुणैः कतिपयैर्हीनो निर्दोषो मध्यमो मतः ॥१८॥

(ग) अधमगायकः

महामाहेश्वरेणोक्तः सदोषो गायनोऽधमः ।

(घ) पञ्चविधगायकाः

शिक्षाकारोऽनुकारश्च रसिको रञ्जकस्तथा ॥१९॥

भावकश्चेति गीतज्ञाः पञ्चधा गायनं जगुः ।

अन्यूनशिक्षणे दक्षः शिक्षाकारो मतः सताम् ॥२०॥

अनुकार इति प्रोक्तः परभङ्ग्यनुकारकः ।

रसाविष्टस्तु रसिको रञ्जकः श्रोतृरञ्जकः ॥२१॥

गीतस्यातिशयाधानाद्भावकः परिकीर्तितः ।

(ङ) त्रिविधगायकाः

एकलो यमलो वृन्दगायनश्चेति ते त्रिधा ॥२२॥

एक एव तु यो गायेदसावेकलगायनः ।

सद्वितीयो यमलकः सवृन्दो वृन्दगायनः ॥२३॥

(च) गायन्यः

रूपयौवनशालिन्यो गायन्यो गातृवन्मताः ।

माधुर्यधुर्यध्वनयश्चतुराश्चतुरप्रियाः ॥२४॥

(iv) The definition and classification of 'vocalists': 13c-24

(a) The best singer:

The vocal experts[1] declare[2] him to be the best among the singers who has an attractive[3] voice of good tone quality[4], who is an adept in initiating

[1]*Gitajña*: Lit. one who is an expert singer, but technically it implies the knowledge of both the theory and the practice of vocal music at the highest level.

[2]Lit. 'is sung' used in a passive construction.

[3]*Hṛdya* lit. that which appeals to the heart.

[4]*Śārīra*: The specific quality of the tone that is native to the medium of the particular voice-production.

and finishing[1] (a *rāga*); who is well versed in (singing) the *rāga-s*, *rāgāṅga-s*, *bhāṣāṅga-s*, *kriyāṅga-s* and *upāṅga-s*, an expert in singing *prabandha-s* and knows the essentials of the different forms of *ālapti*[2]; who commands a natural access to the *gamaka-s* (shakes and graces) arising from all the (three) registers, and a self-controlled voice[3]; who is aware of musical time (*tāla*), and is attentive[4] and indefatigable[5], who knows *śuddha*[6] and *chāyālaga*[7] (compositions), who is an expert in all the specific intonations[8] (*kāku*), who commands the movement[9] of different *sthāya-s*; who is free of all blemishes, given to regular exercise,[10] mindful of *laya* (tempo), versatile[11] and retentive;[12] who has the capacity to hold his breath while singing[13] with great passion and to arrest the attention of the audience,[14] and who

[1] *Graha-mokṣa* is defined by 'K' here as the beginning and the end of a song. The point of being an adept consists, as observed by 'K', in synchronising the initial note with *tāla* or *laya*.

[2] *Ālapti* is to be defined in this chapter. It refers to the action of exposing and concealing the image of *rāga* alternatively.

[3] *Āyattakaṇṭha*: 'S' interprets it as *svādhīna-kaṇṭha* i.e. self-dependent voice (lit. throat) and 'K' as *svādhīnadhvani* i.e. self-dependent tone.

[4] *Sāvadhāna* is interpreted by 'S' as *śrutiniścayajña* i.e. expert in determining *śruti-s*.

[5] 'S' interprets *jitaśrama* (lit. one who can work tirelessly) to be 'one who is not tired even after singing many *prabandha-s*'.

[6] That is, *mārga-sūḍa* according to 'S'.

[7] That is, *sālagasūḍa*.

[8] *Kāku* is to be defined in this chapter.

[9] *Sañcāra* of the text. The *sthāya-s* are to be defined in this chapter.

[10] 'S' quotes *Saṅgīta-samayasāra* who defines *kriyāpara* as under :

"One who sings without blemishes both *mārga* and *deśī* (*saṅgīta*) practising according to the theory laid down in the scientific works, is said to be in regular practice (*kriyāpara*)."

[11] *Sughaṭa* is defined by 'K' as one who performs with excellence i.e. one whose movement is well organised. 'S' quotes *Saṅgītasamayasāra* as under :

"One who causes the manifestation of tone, verbal text and *tāla* to the accompaniment of a beautiful voice is called *sughaṭa*." In other words, one who is able to command the excellence in the manifestation of the three elements of music viz. *svara, tāla* and *pada* through the beauty of his voice is a versatile artist.

[12] *Dhāraṇā* is defined by *saṅgītasamayasāra* (as quoted by 'S') as the capacity of retaining the thickness (*pragāḍhatā*) of voice, while descending from a high pitch.

[13] 'S' quotes *saṅgītasamayasāra* to explain *nirjavana*. "Singing with controlled breath is called *nirjavanam*."

[14] This is according to 'K'. 'S' reads it as *rahaḥ-kṛt* find interprets it as "a fast singer."

excels in the exposition of *rāga*[1] and belongs to a good tradition.[2] (13c – 18b)

(b) The average singer:

One who is lacking in some of the above excellences but is free from blemishes is considered to be the average[3] singer. (18 c d)

(c) The bad singer:

However, as declared by Mahāmāheśvara, the singer who is not free from blemishes is a bad singer.[4] (19 ab)

(d) Five types of singers:

Five types of vocalists are recognised by the vocal experts viz. *śikṣākāra*,[5] *anukāra*,[6] *rasika*,[7] *rañjaka*[8] and *bhāvaka*[9] One who is capable of imparting flawless instructions is considered by the wise to be *śikṣākāra* (the educator). The imitator of another's style is called *anukāra* (the imitator). One who gets absorbed in the aesthetic delight (*rasa*) is *rasika* (the aesthete), and one who entertains the listeners is *rañjaka* (entertaining), and one who is extremely expressive in the delineation of the song is known as *bhāvaka* (the inspirer of emotion). (19c-22b)

(e) Threefold singer:

The singer is also (conceived as) threefold viz. solo, duet and chorus. When a person sings alone, he is a solo singer (*ekala*).[10] When he sings

[1] 'S' says, this excellence is due to the native tone quality (*śārīra*) of voice.

[2] 'K' defines *sampradāya* as "Instruction imparted through the tradition of teacher and taught which, even though not explicitly propounded in *śāstra* (the oral or written tradition of the theoretical understanding) with regard to a particular subject-matter, is yet endorsed by it (in principle) and is not against it (see Kallinātha's commentary on *S.R.* VII. 91). The modern *Gharānā* of the Hindustani music represents the teacher-taught tradition confined to a particular family line of musicians which is not (necessarily) related to a tradition of theory or *śāstra*. Thus, *gharānā* is not an adequate substitute for *sampradāya*.

[3] *Madhyama* lit. means the middle one.

[4] *Adhama* lit. means the lowest or poor.

[5] *Śikṣākāra* lit. means 'educator'.

[6] *Anukāra* lit. means 'imitator'.

[7] *Rasika* lit. means 'aesthete'.

[8] *Rañjaka* lit. means 'entertaining'.

[9] *Bhāvaka* lit. means 'inspirer of emotion'.

[10] *Ekala* lit. means 'alone' or single.

alongwith another, he is a duet-singer (*yamala*);[1] and when he sings with a group, he is a chorus-singer. (22c-23)

(f) Songstresses:

Songstresses possessed of youth and beauty, excelling in sweetness of voice, (clever and loved by the clever, are considered[2] in the same way as the singers.

Like the *vāggeyakāra*, the singers are also classified in three categories viz. the best, the middle (average) and the inferior. Therefore, the same terms have been used in the English version despite their literal meaning.

In the first instance, the author classifies singers on the basis of their individual talent and distinguishes them into three categories viz. the first-rate artists who are classified as the best, the second-rate singers who are classed as the average, and the third-rate singers who are considered to be poor in achievement and talent and are classed as such. Then he classifies them on the basis of their predominant function viz. instruction, imitation, aesthetic delight, entertainment and emotional inspiration. Thereafter, he classifies the singers on the basis of the number of performers, viz. one, two or many. Thus, in all, he gives three different classifications of singers based on talent and attainment, function and number respectively.

The vocalists have been classified into five types of which the educator and the imitator are unique in their essential functions. But the other three viz. the *rasika*, the *bhāvaka* and the *rañjaka* are indicative of the aesthetic value of their function. According to Dr. Premlata Sharma," *Rasika* is the highest category represented by those musicians who are immersed in *Rasa*, and are replete with *Sāttvika Bhāvas* such as *aśru* (tears) and *pulaka* (thrill-making hair stand on end). *Bhāvaka* is the intermediary category represented by those singers who infuse their music with *Bhāva* and who sing with a knowledge of *citta* (feelings) of the audience. *Rañjaka* is the lowest category represented by those who lend *Raṅga* (emotional colour) to their music." (See Levels of Aesthetic Experience in Music—Indian Music Journal April 1964, p. 19-20).

These three categories represent, according to her, the three stages of aesthetic delight. She further opines that the *rasika*, who reflects the highest level of the aesthetic experience is guided by the taste of the audience in the least, in the creation of aesthetic delight in which he gets immersed through the universalised *bhāva*. The *bhāvaka* takes due note of the mental propensities of the audience and the *rañjaka*, who represents the lowest category, is mindful of the taste of the audience to the utmost.

[1] *Yamalaka* lit. means 'twin' or double.
[2] That is, 'classified' by implication.

As far as the female singers are concerned he says that they are to be similarly classified, but they have, in addition, to be possessed of youth and beauty and so on. This marks the specific role of the songstresses.

(v) निन्दित (सदोष)—गायकाः

संदष्टोद्घुष्टसूत्कारिभीतशङ्कितकम्पिताः ।
कराली विकलः काकी वितालकरभोद्भटाः ॥२५॥

झोम्बकस्तुम्बकी वक्री प्रसारी विनिमीलकः ।
विरसापस्वराव्यक्तस्थानभ्रष्टाव्यवस्थिताः ॥२६॥

मिश्रकोऽनवधानश्च तथान्यः सानुनासिकः ।
पञ्चविंशतिरित्येते गायना निन्दिता मताः ॥२७॥

संदश्य दशनात् गायन् संदष्टः परिकीर्तितः ।
उद्घुष्टो विरसोद्घोषः सूत्कारी सूत्कृतैर्मुहुः ॥२८॥

भीतो भयान्वितो गाता त्वरया शङ्कितो मतः ।
कम्पितः कम्पनाज्ज्ञेयः स्वभावाद्गात्रशब्दयोः ॥
कराली गदितः सद्भिः करालोद्घाटिताननः ।
विकलः स तु यो गायेत् स्वरान् न्यूनाधिकश्रुतीन् ॥

काकक्रूररवः काकी वितालस्तालविच्युतः ।
दधानः कंधरामूर्ध्वां करभोऽभिहितो बुधैः ॥३१॥

छागवद्वहनीं कुर्वन्नुद्भटोऽधमगायनः ।
सिरालभालवदनग्रीवो गाता तु झोम्बकः ॥३२॥

तुम्बकी तुम्बकाकारोत्फुल्लगल्लस्तु गायनः ।
वक्री वक्रीकृतगलो गायन् धीरैरुदीरितः ॥३३॥

प्रसारी गीयते तज्ज्ञैर्गात्रगीतप्रसारणात् ।
निमीलको मतो गायन् निमीलितविलोचनः ॥३४॥
विरसो नीरसो वर्ज्यस्वरगानादपस्वरः ।
गद्गदध्वनिरव्यक्तवर्णस्त्वव्यक्त उच्यते ॥३५॥

स्थानभ्रष्टः स यः प्राप्तुमशक्तः स्थानकत्रयम् ।

अव्यवस्थित इत्युक्तः स्थानकैरनवस्थितैः ॥३६॥
शुद्धच्छायालगौ रागौ मिश्रयन् मिश्रकः स्मृतः ।
इतरेषां च रागाणां मिश्रको भूरिमिश्रणात् ॥३७॥
स्थायादिष्ववधानेन निर्मुक्तोऽनवधानकः ।
गेयं नासिकया गायन् गीयते सानुनासिकः ॥३८॥

(v) The censured singers: 25-38

The (following) twenty-five (types of) singers are considered 'censured': *Sandaṣṭa, udghuṣṭa, sūtkāri, bhīta, śaṅkita, kampita, karālī, vikala, kākī, vitāla, karabha, udbhaṭa, jhombaka, tumbakī, vakrī, prasārī, vinimīlaka, virasa, apasvara, avyakta, sthānabhraṣṭa, avyavasthita, miśraka, anavadhāna*, and *sānunāsika*. (25—27)

1. *Sandaṣṭa*—one who compresses his teeth while singing is known as *sandaṣṭa*.[1] (28 ab).

2. *Udghuṣṭa*—(one) having a loud spreading voice is (called) *udghuṣṭa*[2] (28 c).

3. *Sūtkāri*—again *sūtkāri* is so called because of the whistling voice.[3] (28 d)

4. *Bhīta*—the singer who is seized with fear is (called) *Bhīta*.[4] (29 a)

5. *Śaṅkita*—and with haste (he) is considered as *śaṅkita*.[5] (29 b)

6. *Kampita*—is known by the natural (involuntary) shaking of limbs and voice. (29 cd)

7. *Karāli*—one, who sings with his mouth frightfully wide open is declared by the wise to be *karālī*.[8] (30 ab)

8. *Vikala*—one who sings the notes inaccurately with less or more *śruti-s* is (called) *vikala*.[9] (30 cd)

9. *Kākī*[10]—is the one whose voice is as hoarse as that of a crow. (31 a)

[1]*Sandaṣṭa*—lit. means compressed. *Sandanśa* is technically explained as too great a compression of the teeth in the pronunciation of the vowels. In musical parlance it is applicable to singers who are seen to compress their teeth particularly in ālāpa.

[2]*Udghuṣṭa*—lit. pronounced or publicly declared.

[3]*Sūtkāri* is one who produces the sound *sū* i.e. a whistling sound while singing.

[4]*Bhīta*—lit. frightened.

[5]*Śaṅkita*—lit. doubtful or apprehensive.

[6]*Kampita*—lit. shaken.

[7]That is, involuntary, beyond one's control, or even unconscious and habitual.

[8]*Karālī* who is associated with *karāla*, lit. yawning (opening the mouth widely).

[9]*Vikala*—lit. imperfect or unsound.

[10]*Kākī*=crow-like.

10. *Vitāla*[1]—is inept with regard to *tāla*. (31 b)

11. *Karabha*—one who holds his neck upwards is called *karabha*[2] by the learned. (38 cd)

12. *Udbhaṭa*—one whose voice is shaky like a lamb while doing *vahanī*[3] is (called) *udbhaṭa*, the inferior singer. (32 ab)

13. *Jhombaka*—the singer who has a large number of veins (displayed while singing) on his forehead, face and neck is (called) *jhombaka*. (32 c d)

14. *Tumbakī*—the singer who inflates his throat like a gourd is (called) *tumbakī*[4]. (33 ab)

15. *Vakrī*—one who twists his neck while singing is declared by the wise to be *vakrī*[5]. (33 cd)

16. *Prasārī*—one who stretches his limbs while projecting his song is called *prasārī*[6] by the experts. (34 ab)

17. *Nimīlaka* one who is given to closing his eyes while singing is considered to be *nimīlaka*.[7] (34 cd)

18. *Virasa*—is the one who is devoid of *rasa* (aesthetic delight or the enjoyment of beauty). (35 a)

19. *Apasvara*—is by singing the omitted note. (35 a)

20. *Avyakta*—one having a faltering voice and an indistinct pronunciation[8] is said to be *avyakta*. (35 cd)

21. *Sthānabhraṣṭa*[9]—is one who is unable to reach the three registers. (36 ab)

22. *Avyavasthita*[10]—is so called because of disorganised (singing) with reference to the registers. (36 cd)

23. *Miśraka*[11]—is known to be one who mixes up the *śuddha* and *chāyālagā rāga-s*, and also when he intermixes (confuses) other *rāga-s* he is known to be *miśraka*. (37)

24. *Anavadhāna* - one who does not observe due order in the use of *sthāya-s* etc.[12] is (called) *anavadhānaka*.[13] (38 ab)

[1] *Vitāla*—lit. without *tāla* i.e. not keeping due time.

[2] *Karabha*—lit. camel.

[3] *Vahanī* is one of the well known (*prasiddha*) *sthāya-s* defined (vide 114 c-115b) in this chapter as the shake on the notes in the four *varṇa-s*) (tone-patterns).

[4] *Tumba*—lit. means a gourd, and *tumbakī* is one who has gourd.

[5] *Vakrī*—having a twist (in the neck).

[6] *Prasāri*—lit. one who extends or outstretches (his limbs).

[7] *Nimīlaka*—lit. one who closes (his eyes)

[8] *Avyaktavarṇa*—lit. having unmanifest letters (indistinct in pronunciation).

[9] *Sthānabhraṣṭa*—lit. imperfect in commending the (three) registers.

[10] *Avyavasthita*—lit. means 'unsystematic'.

[11] *Miśraka*—lit. one who intermixes.

[12] *Sthāya-s*—are to be defined in this very chapter, 'etc.' is suggestive of *gamaka-s* and the like.

[13] *Anavadhānaka*—lit. one who is inattentive.

25. *Sānunāsika*—one who sings the melody[1] through the nose is called *sānunāsika*.[2] (38 cd)

Having defined the different types or classes of singers, male as well as female, the author is now, under this topic, describing the blemishes of singing. Though he is pointing out the defects in singing, he is doing so by attributing them to the singers. Thus, blemishes appear in the form of adjectival noun—the adjectives qualifying their substratum viz. the singer. Whatever is said with respect to the singers is applicable to the female singers as well.

(vi) शब्दभेदाः

(क) चतुर्विधशब्दः

चतुर्भेदो भवेच्छब्दः खाहुलो नारटाभिधः ।
बोम्बको मिश्रकश्चेति तल्लक्षणमथोच्यते ॥३९॥

कफजः खाहुलः स्निग्धमधुरः सौकुमार्ययुक् ।
आडिल्ल एष एव स्यात् प्रौढश्चेन्मन्द्रमध्ययोः ॥४०॥
त्रिस्थानघनगम्भीरलीनः पित्तोद्भवो ध्वनिः ।
नाराटो बोम्बकस्तु स्यादन्तर्निःसारतायुतः ॥४१॥

परुषोच्चैस्तरः स्थूलो वातजः शार्ङ्गिणोदितः ।
एतत्संमिश्रणादुक्तो मिश्रकः सांनिपातिकः ॥४२॥

ननु रूक्षगुणो बोम्बः खाहुलः स्निग्धतायुतः ।

कथं तयोर्मिश्रणं स्याद्विरुद्धगुणयोगिनोः ॥४३॥

अत्रोच्यते परित्यागात् पारुष्यस्य विरोधिनः ।

अविरुद्धस्य माधुर्यं स्थौल्यादेर्मिश्रणं मतम् ॥४४॥

एतेन घननिःसारगुणनाराटबोम्बयोः ।

विरुद्धगुणताक्षेपसमाधाने निवेदिते ॥४५॥

[1] *Geya* refers to the content of a vocal rendering.
[2] *Sānunāsika*—lit. nasal.

(ख) मिश्रस्य भेदचतुष्टयम

मिश्रस्य भेदाश्चत्वारो युक्तौ नाराटखाहुलौ ।
नाराटबोम्बकौ बोम्बखाहुलौ मिश्रितास्त्रयः ।।४६।।
निःसारतारूक्षताभ्यां हीनस्त्रितयमिश्रणात् ।
उत्तमोत्तम इत्युक्तः सुराणामिव शंकरः ।।४७।।
नाराटखाहुलोन्मिश्र उत्तमः खाहुलः पुनः ।
बोम्बयुक्तो मध्यमः स्याद्बोम्बो नाराटसंयुतः ।।४८।।
शब्दानामधमः प्रोक्तः श्रीमत्सोढलसूनुना ।
निःसारतारूक्षताभ्यां युक्तः सर्वाधमो मतः ।।४९।।
भवन्ति बहवो भेदा नानातद्गुणमिश्रणात् ।

१. द्वन्द्वजभेदाः

कश्चित् स्यान्मधुरस्निग्धघनोऽन्यः स्निग्धकोमलः ।।५०।।
धनोऽपरस्तु मधुरमृदुत्रिस्थानकोऽन्यकः ।
मृदुत्रिस्थानगम्भीरोऽपरः स्निग्धो मृदुर्घनः ।।५१।।
त्रिस्थानोऽन्यस्तु मधुरमृदुत्रिस्थानको घनः ।
अन्यस्तु मधुरस्निग्धमृदुत्रिस्थानकोऽपरः ।।५२।।
मधुरस्निग्धगम्भीरघनत्रिस्थानकोऽपरः ।
स्निग्धकोमलगम्भीरघनत्रिस्थानलीनकः ।।५३।।
अपरः स्निग्धमधुरकोमलः सान्द्रलीनकः ।
त्रिस्थानशोभी गम्भीर इति भेदा दशोदिताः ।।५४।।
खाहुलोन्मिश्रनाराटे ततः खाहुलबोम्बयोः ।
स्निग्धकोमलनिःसार एकोऽन्यो मधुरो मृदु ।।५५।।
रूक्षोऽन्यस्तु मृदुस्निग्धनिःसारोच्चतरः परः ।
कोमलः स्निग्धनिःसारः स्थूलोऽन्यः स्निग्धकोमलः ।।५६।।
निःसारोच्चतरस्थूलः परो मधुरकोमलः ।

रूक्षनिःसारपीनश्च भेदाः षडिति कीर्तिताः ॥५७॥

नाराटे बोम्बभेदाः स्युर्धनत्रिस्थानरूक्षकः ।

एकोऽन्यो घनगम्भीररूक्षोऽन्यो लीनपीवरः ॥५८॥

निःसाररूक्षोऽन्यो लीनघनोच्चतरपीवरः ।

त्रिस्थानघनगम्भीरलीनरूक्षोऽपरः परः ॥५९॥

त्रिस्थानलीननिःसाररूक्षः स्थूलः षडित्यमी ।

एते द्वन्द्वजभेदाः स्यु—

२. सांनिपातिकभेदाः

रथैते सांनिपातिकाः ॥६०॥

स्निग्धत्रिस्थाननिःसारोऽन्यो मृदुर्मधुरो घनः ।

गम्भीरोच्चतरो रूक्षः परस्तु स्निग्धकोमलः ॥६१॥

घनलीनः पीवरोच्चतरोऽन्यः स्निग्धकोमलः ।

त्रिस्थानलीननिःसारपीवरोच्चतरोऽपरः ॥६२॥

कीर्तितो मधुरो लीनस्त्रिस्थानो रूक्षपीवरः ।

निःसारोच्चतरोऽन्यस्तु मधुरस्निग्धकोमलः ॥६३॥

त्रिस्थानघनगम्भीरलीनः उच्चतरः परः ।

मधुरो मृदुगम्भीरलीनत्रिस्थानरूक्षकः ॥६४॥

निःसारोच्चतरोऽन्यस्तु कोमलो मधुरो घनः ।

लीनत्रिस्थानरूक्षोच्चतरपीवरतायुतः ॥६५॥

अष्टाविति त्रिमिश्रस्य भेदाः,

(ग) उपसंहारः

सर्वेतु मिश्रजाः ।

मिलिता मुग्धबोधाय त्रिंशन्निःशङ्ककीर्तिताः ॥६६॥

अन्येषां सूक्ष्मभेदानां नान्तोऽस्ति गुणसंकरात् ।
ते ग्रन्थविस्तरत्रासादस्माभिर्न समीरिताः ॥६७॥
इति शब्दभेदाः ।

(vi) Kinds of voice: 39-67

(a) The fourfold voice:

Voice is distinguished[1] into four kinds viz. *khāhula*, *nārāṭa*, *bombaka*, and *miśraka* which are now defined as under[2]: (39)

(1) *Khāhula*:

Arising from (the predominance of) phlegm (*Kapha*), *khāhula* is creamy, sweet and soft. When it matures[3] in the lower and the middle registers it becomes *āḍilla*. (40)

(2) *Nārāṭa*:

The voice arising from (the predominance of) bile (*pitta*) which is full[4] (*ghana*), deep (*gambhīra*)[5], clear (līna)[6] with the range of three registers is *nārāṭa*[7]. (41 a-c)

(3) *Bombaka*:

***Bombaka*, however, as declared by Śārṅgadeva, is (the voice) that arises from (the predominance of) wind (*vāta*) and is hollow[8], harsh[9], high sounding[10] and rich (*sthūla*)[11]. (41c-42b)**

[1]*Caturbheda* (Catur+bheda lit. classified into four) points to a fourfold division.
[2]'As under' is implied in the text.
[3]*Prauḍha* of the text in form of *prauḍhi* is interpreted by 'S' as *vyāpti* (lit. prevalence). However, it has been rendered as mature in its literal sense. The expression seems to be a figurative one.
[4]*Ghana* is interpreted by 'S' as *antaḥsāra* which may properly be understood with reference to its opposite *antar-niḥsāra* (lit. hollow). Thus it has been rendered as 'full' in the sense of 'solid'.
[5]*Gambhīra* of the text is interpreted by 'S' as *nirhrādī* lit. noiseless.
[6]*Līna* of the text is interpreted by 'S' as '*asphuṭita*,' lit. uncracked, absorbed or dissolved.
[7]*Nārāṭa* is the same as above *nāraṭa*.
[8]*Antar-niḥsāratāyuta* of the text, lit. having no substance within.
[9]*Parusa* of the text is lit. harsh and is opposed to the softness of *khāhula*.
[10]*Uccaistara* of the text.
[11]*Sthūla* is lit. gross or fat i.e. not fine.

(4) *Miśraka*:

Miśraka is said to be (arising) by the admixture of these (three and is therefore called) *sānnipātika*[1].

Indeed *bomba*[2] is characterised by dryness (of voice) while *khāhula* is creamy; how then can there be the combination of the two characterised as they are by opposite qualities? (43)

To explain, it is thought to be (possible) by the elimination of the opposite (quality) of harshness and the combination of the unopposed (qualities of) sweetness and grossness etc. This (explanation) also holds good with reg rd to the similar objection concerning the opposition of qualities obtaining in-between the solidity of *nārāṭa* and the hollowness of *bomba*. (44 45)

(b) The four varieties of *Miśra* (combine):

There are four varieties of *miśra* viz. the respective combines of (1) *nārāṭa* and *khāhula*, (2) *nārāṭa* and *bombaka*, (3) *bombaka* and *khāhula* and (4) all the three put together. (46)

The combine of all the three, being free from hollowness and harshness is said to be the finest among the fine (voices) like Lord Śiva (God) among the gods. (47)

The combine of *nārāṭa* and *khāhula* is the best, while that of *khāhula* and *bombaka* is of average standard.[3] *Bomba* in combination with *nārāṭa* is declared by Śarṅgadeva to be of low grade among (the different kinds of) voice; but of these all (the voice) that combines hollowness with harshness is considered to be the lowest. (48-49)

Many varieties (of voice) come into being by the intermixture of the different qualities of these (types). (50 ab)

1. The varieties of double combine:

Khāhula-nārāṭa combine:

One (of these) is sweet, creamy and full[4]; the other is creamy, soft and full; another is sweet and soft having the range of three registers; and yet another is soft with a range of three registers and deep; the other one is

[1] *Sannipātika* lit. 'pertaining to *sannipāta*' the combination of the three humours.
[2] *Bomba* is the same as *bombaka*.
[3] Lit. the middle one.
[4] Though *ghana* is literally 'soid', in the context of voice it implies the sense of fulness. So it is rendered as such.

soft, full and with the range of three registers; another is sweet, soft, having the range of three registers and full; while another is sweet, creamy and soft with the range of three registeres; yet another is sweet, creamy, deep and full with the range of three registers; while another is creamy, soft, de·p, intense and unbroken in the range of three registers; and also the other which is creamy, sweet, soft, full, clear, radiant in the three registers and deep. These are the ten varieties said to be arising out of the *khāhula-nārāṭa* combine. (50c-55a)

Khāhula-bomba combine:

Thereafter, among the combines of *khāhula* and *bomba*, one is creamy, soft and hollow; the other is sweet, soft and dry[1]; while another is soft, creamy, hollow and high sounding; the other one is soft, creamy, hollow and rich; yet another is creamy, soft, hollow, high sounding and rich, and also the other which is sweet, soft, dry, hollow and rich. (These) are known to be the six varieties. (55b-57)

Nārāṭa-bomba combine:

There are six varieties of *nārāṭa* in combination with *bomba* One is ranging in three registers and dry; another is clear, rich, hollow and dry; another one is clear, high sounding and rich; and yet another is ranging in the three registers, full, deep, clear and dry; and also the other that is ranging in three registers, clear, hollow, dry and rich. (58-60b)

These (varieties) arise out of the pair combines, while the following pertain to the triple combines.[2] (60 cd)

2. The varieties of triple combine:

Creamy, ranging in three registers and hollow;[3] soft, sweet, full, deep, high sounding and dry; creamy, soft, full, clear, rich and high sounding; creamy, soft, ranging in the three registers, clear, hollow, rich and high sounding; sweet, clear, ranging in the three registers, dry, rich, hollow and high sounding; sweet, creamy, soft, ranging in the three registers, full, deep,

[1] *Rūkṣa* (lit. dry) is the opposite of *snigdha* (creamy). It seems the word *rūk ṣa* is used subsequently for the original *paruṣa* (harsh). vide 41c-42b ante.

[2] A product of a combination has been called a combine. The product of *sannipāta* (a combination of the three on the model of the three humours of the body) has been expressed as triple combine.

[3] Some of conjunctive words such as *anya* (other and so on) of the text have been left out of the translation, being unnecessary in this form.

clear and high sounding; sweet, soft, deep, clear, ranging in the three registers, dry, hollow and high sounding; soft, sweet, full, clear, ranging in the three registers, dry, high sounding and rich—these are the eight varieties of triple combines. (61-66b)

Conclusion:

All the different varieties of combines[1] put together are declared by Śārṅgadeva for the understanding of the unwitting to be thirty[2]. There is no end to the subtle differentiations caused by the entermixing of (different) qualities; therefore apprehending undue elaboration of the work, they are not described by us. (66c-67)

Analysing the qualities of voice, the author distinguishes altogether four different kinds of voice viz. *khāhula*, *nārāṭa*, *bombaka* and *miśṛaka* (lit. an admixture or combination). The particular qualities of the first three of these are traced to the predominance of the three different humours of the body viz. phlegm, bile and wind which, according to the Āyurvedic theory of medicine, are the basic constituents of human organism (cf. *S. R.* I 2. 71). Though the author has attributed the cause of each of these three kinds of voice to the respective humours in the body, what he actually means is their respective predominance, for they are not conceived to function in isolation. The fourth kind is conceptually divided to include such voices as are not very distinctly marked by the exclusive qualities of any one of the main three types. Thus, this class which is appropriately called *miśraka* (lit. compounded) comprehends the combination of the individual characteristic qualities of the first three kinds.

There can obviously be a possible objection to this concept of a mixed class since it may be contended that some the characteristic qualities of the first three kinds are responsible for their mutual exclusiveness and are therefore opposed to each other. They cannot as such combine to form a distinct homogeneous class of *miśraka*. The author, foreseeing this objection, explains, that *miśraka* is not a theoretical or a mechanical combination; it is an intelligent admixture of unopposed and mutually unexclusive qualities combined together. This is adequately demonstrated by the author when he points out that in the combination of *bomba* and *khāhula*, the mutually exclusive and opposite qualities of dryness (*paruṣa*) or harshness and the softness of voice are left out of the combination and only the voice that is characterised by sweetness and grossness, the other two mutually unexclu-

[1]*Miśraka* (lit. derived from or born of combinations) are the products of the combinations of different qualities of the different kinds of voice, designated here as combine.

[2]This includes 10 varieties of the *khāhula-nārāṭa* combine, 6 of *khāhula-bomba*, 6 of *nāraṭa-bomba* and 8 of the triple combine (10+6+6+8=30).

sive and unopposed qualities of the two kinds, is classified as *miśraka*. Similarly, while forming a *miśraka* by the combination of *nārāṭa* and *bomab*, the mutually exclusive and opposite qualities of the two viz. the solidity of the one and the hollowness of the other are excluded from the combination. In this way *miśraka* provides a richer voice and is, therefore, distinguished further in four varieties.

By the intermixture of the three main kinds, the fourth general category of *miśra* is obtained, which is further subdivided into the varieties formed out of the intermixture of their qualities. Among all these kinds of voice the combination of all the three kinds viz. *nārāṭa*, *khāhula* and *bomba* is said to be the best.

The varieties of voice as characterised by the qualities of *khāhula* and *nāraṭa* are given as the different combines of the two. All these and the varieties of the other combines that follow belong to the *miśra* class.

(vii) शब्दगुणाः

मृष्टो मधुरचेहालत्रिस्थानकसुखावहाः ।
प्रचुरः कोमलो गाढः श्रावकः करुणो घनः ॥६८॥

स्निग्धः श्लक्ष्णो रक्तियुक्तश्छविमानिति सूरिभिः ।
गुणैरेभिः पञ्चदशभेदः शब्दो निगद्यते ॥६९॥

श्रोत्रनिर्वापको मृष्टस्त्रिषु स्थानेष्वनश्वरः ।[1]
मधुरः कीर्तितस्तारः प्रौढो मधुररञ्जकः ॥७०॥

नातिस्थूलो नातिकृशः स्निग्धश्चेहालको घनः ।
आकण्ठकुण्ठनं स स्यात् पुंसां स्त्रीणां तु सर्वदा ॥७१॥

त्रिषु स्थानेष्वेकरूपश्छविरक्त्यादिभिर्गुणैः ।
त्रिस्थानो मनसो यस्तु सुखदः ससुखावहः ॥७२॥

श्रीशंकरप्रियेणोक्तः प्रचुरः स्थूलतायुतः ।
कोमलोऽन्वर्थनामैव कोकिलाध्वनिवन्मतः ॥७३॥

गाढस्तु प्रबलो दूरश्रवणाच्छ्रावको मतः ।
करुणः श्रोतृचित्तस्य करुणारसदीपकः ॥७४॥

[1] Ad. ed. स्थानेष्वविस्तरः

दूरश्रवणयोग्यस्तु धनोऽन्तःसारतायुतः ।

अरूक्षो दूरसंश्राव्यो बुधैः स्निग्धो ध्वनिः स्मृतः ॥७५॥

श्लक्ष्णस्तु तैलधारावदच्छिद्रो धीरसंमतः ।

अनुरक्तेस्तु जनको रक्तिमानभिधीयते ॥७६॥

धातुर्विमलकण्ठत्वाद्यः प्राज्ञैरुपलक्ष्यते ।

उज्ज्वलोऽयमिति प्रोक्तश्छविमानिति स ध्वनिः ॥७७॥

इति शब्दगुणाः ।

(vii) Excellences of voice: 68-77

Voice as qualified by these excellences is differentiated by the learned into fifteen varieties viz. *mṛṣṭa*, *madhura*, *cehāla*, *tristhānaka*, *sukhāvaha*, *pracura*, *komala*, *gāḍha*, *śrāvaka*, *karuṇa*, *ghana*, *snigdha*, *ślakṣṇa*, *raktiyukta* and *chavimān*. (68-69)

1. *Mṛṣṭa*[1] is that (voice) which is refreshing to the ears. (70 a)

2. *Madhura*[2] is that which is undecaying[3] in all the three registers. (70 bc)

3. *Cehāla* is known to be of a high pitch, mature, sweet[4], delightful, neither very gross nor too feeble, creamy and full. It is (manifest) among the males till the breaking of voice[5] and always among the females. (70c-71)

4. *Tristhānaka* is uniformly endowed with the qualities of lustre[6] and delightfulness[7] in the three registers. (72 a-c)

[1]*Mṛṣṭa*-lit. a greeable, pleasing.

[2]*Madhura*-lit. sweet.

[3]*Anaśvara* is the reading availble to 'S' and is surely better than *avistara* (unvitiated) of the Ad. ed. of *S. R.*, and hence it has been adopted in our text. However, it appears that most probably the original version might have been something like *avisvara* implying thereby that *madhura* is never out of tune in all the three registers.

[4]*Madhura*, in this context has a literal meaning.

[5]When boys are in the age of attaining adolescence, *cehāla* is no longer manifest in them. That stage is marked by the breaking of their voice.

[6]*Chavi*-lit. colour, splendour, beauty.

[7]*Rakti*-lit. delight.

5. *Sukhāvaha*[1] is that which comforts the mind (i.e. soothing). (72cd)

6. *Pracura*[2] as declared by Śārṅgadeva,[3] is (the voice) full of richness. (73 ab)

7. *Komala*[4] is significant by its name (i.e. tender) believed to be like the voice of the Indian cuckoo. (73 cd)

8. *Gāḍha*[5] is strong. (74 a)

9. *Śrāvaka*[6] is so called[7] because of being audible from a distance. (74 ab)

10. *Karuṇa*[8] inspires the aesthetic delight of pathos in the minds of the listeners.[9] (74 cd)

11. *Ghana*[10] is capable of being heard at a distance and full of intensity (75 ab)

12. *Snigdha*[11] is accepted by the learned to be the voice that is not dry (or hoarse), and is capable of being heard at a distance. (75 cd)

13. *Ślakṣṇa*, according to the wise, is continuous like the (vertical) flow of oil.[12] (76 ab)

14. *Raktimān* is that which creates interest (among the listeners).[13] (76 cd)

15. When a tonal structure emerging from a faultless[14] throat, is characterised by the experts as bright, that voice is called *chavimān*.[15] (77)

Having classified voice into four basic varieties viz. *khāhula*, ***nārāṭa***, ***bomba*** and *miśra* based on the three hunours of the human body, **the author now** goes on to give us a different classification which represents **a qualitative** analysis of voice. Incidentally, he introduces us **to the terms in which** voice may be distinctly perceived as qualified by different ***guṇa-s*** **(excellen-**

[1]*Sukhāvaha*-lit. comforting.
[2]*Pracura*-lit. profuse. 'S' elucidates it as full of richness '*sthūlatāyukta*'.
[3]*Śrīśaṅkarapriya*, the lover of Lord Śiva i.e. Śārṅgadeva.
[4]*Komala*-lit. soft or tender.
[5]*Gāḍha*-lit. thick, dense and deep.
[6]*Śrāvaka*-lit. the pronouncer.
[7]*Mataḥ* of the text literally means 'is accepted, is believed'.
[8]*Karuṇa*-lit. pathetic or pathos.
[9]The plural is supplied; the text literally rendered would be 'the mind of the audience'.
[10]*Ghana*-lit. dense.
[11]*Snigdha*-lit. creamy, unctuous or emollient.
[12]The flow of oil is characterised by an indistinct process of continuity, of imperceptible change. *Acchidra*-lit. having no vacuum, i.e. in other words continuous. *Chidra* is an empty space, a hole.
[13]Literally the passage would read, "the voice that creates (interest) is called *raktimān*." *Anurakti* lit. means love, attachment.
[14]*Vimala*-lit. devoid of impurity.
[15]*Chavimān*-lit. lusturous, colourful.

ces). But instead of describing the qualities individually, he is describing voice as qualified by them. *Guṇa*, in this context, is a value concept; it represents a good quality rather than a property and may be understood with reference to its opposite *doṣa*, which is a bad quality. So, the author now describes the excellences and the blemishes of voice, or in other words, classifies voice as characterised by them.

(viii) शब्ददोषाः

रूक्षस्फुटितनिःसारकाकोलीकेटिकेणयः ।
कृशो भग्न इति प्रोक्ता दुष्टस्याष्टौ भिदा ध्वने ॥७८॥
रूक्षः स्निग्धत्वनिर्मुक्तः स्फुटितोऽन्वर्थनामकः ।
एरण्डकाण्डनिःसारो निःसार इति कीर्तितः ॥७९॥
काकोलिकाख्यः काकोलकुलनिर्घोषनिष्ठुरः ।
स्थानत्रयव्याप्तियुक्तो निर्गुणः केटिरुच्यते ॥८०॥
कृच्छ्रोन्मीलन्मन्द्रतारः केणिरित्यभिधीयते ।
अतिसूक्ष्मः कृशो भग्नः खरोष्ट्रध्वनिनीरसः ॥८१॥

इति शब्ददोषाः ।

(viii) The blemishes of voice : 78-81

Eight varieties are spoken of for the defective voice viz. *rūkṣa, sphuṭita, niḥsāra, kākolī, keṭi, keṇi, kṛśa* and *bhagna.* (78)

1. *Rūkṣa*[1] is devoid of viscosity. (79 a)
2. *Sphuṭita*[2] is significant by its name (i.e. it is broken). (79 b)
3. *Niḥsāra*[3] is said to be hollow like the seed of the caster oil plant (79 cd)
4. *Kākolī* is hoarse like the cawing of a group of ravens.[4] (80 ab)
5. *Keṭi* is said to be ranging in the three registers without any excellence.[5]

[1]*Rūkṣa*-lit. dry, the opposite of *snigdha* (creamy).
[2]*Sphuṭita*-lit. broken.
[3]*Niḥsāra*-lit. devoid of substance. It has been rendered as hollow. It is not understood how it is compared to the seed of the castor oil plant, since that is not without substance.
[4]Crow with glossy, black plumage.
[5]Such as sweetness and so on.

6. *Keṇi* is known to be (the voice) that approaches[1] the high and the low registers with difficulty. (81 ab)

7. *Kṛśa* is extremely frail.[2]

8. *Bhagna*[3] is hard and unpleasant like the braying of an ass and grunting of a camel. (81 d)

(ix) शारीरम्

(क) शारीरलक्षणम्

रागाभिव्यक्तिशक्तत्वमनभ्यासेऽपि यद्ध्वनेः ।
तच्छारीरमिति प्रोक्तं शरीरेण सहोद्भवात् ॥८२॥

(ख) शारीरगुणाः

तारानुध्वनिमाधुर्यरक्तिगाम्भीर्यमार्दवैः ।
घनतास्निग्धताकान्तिप्राचुर्यादिगुणैर्युतम् ॥८३॥
तत् सुशारीरमित्युक्तं लक्ष्यलक्षणकोविदैः ।

(ग) शारीरदोषाः

अनुस्वानविहीनत्वं रूक्षत्वं त्यक्तरक्तिता ॥८४॥
निःसारता विस्वरता काकित्वं स्थानविच्युतिः ।
कार्श्यं कार्कश्यमित्याद्यैः कुशारीरं तु दूषणैः ॥८५॥

(घ) सुशारीरप्राप्त्युपायाः

विद्यादानेन तपसा भक्त्या वा पार्वतीपतेः ।
प्रभूतभाग्यविभवैः सुशारीरमवाप्यते ॥८६॥

इति शारीरम् ।

[1] *Unmilan*-lit. opening.
[2] *Sūkṣma*-lit subtle, may imply a frail voice as the opposite of *sthūla* (full),
[3] *Bhogna*-lit. broken.

(ix) *Śārīra* (gifted voice): 82-86

(a) The definition of *Śārīra*:

The (inherent) capability[1] of voice for the delineation of a *rāga* even without (any) practice is called *śārīra*[2], since it comes into being along with the body. (82)

(b) The excellences of *Śārīra*:

The voice having such excellences as (access to) the higher register, resonance, sweetness, delightfulness, depth, softness, fulness[3], creaminess, brilliance and volume etc. is considered, by the experts in theory and practice, to be well gifted[4]. (83-84b)

(c) The blemishes of *śārīra*:

The voice charactcrised by such blemishes as lack of resonance, dryness, lack of delightfulness, lack of fulness[5], inaccurate tonality[6], hoarseness[7] inaccessibility to the (three) registers[8], frailty and harshness etc. is (considered to be) poorly gifted[9]. (84c-85)

(d) Means of attaining the gifted voice:

A well gifted voice is obtained through great fortune, imparting of knowledge, penance or devotion to Lord Śiva[10]. (86)

The concept of *Śārīra* is perhaps unique to musicological thinking in India As it has been defined, what is meant by *śārīra* is the original and the natural capability of the voice of a person. Thus, *śārīra* is not a general

[1]The capability of voice for singing that is not dependent on practice.

[2]*Śārīra*-lit. pertaining to the body.

[3]*Ghanatā* is an abstract noun from *ghana* which, hitherto, has been rendered as full.

[4]It would be clear from the comments that *śārīra* implies a natural gift of musical voice. *Suśārīra* is good *śārīra*, a voice that is well gifted, as opposed to being poorly gifted.

[5]See note 3 above.

[6]*Visvaratā*-lit. bad tonality, signifies "being out of tune." Tonality mainly signifies "loyalty to a tonic."

[7]*Kākitva* consists in the hoarseness of voice, as found in the cawing of the crows The word *kākitva* is the abstract noun from *kākī* (lit. crow).

[8]*Sthānavicyuti* (sthāna+vicyuti)-lit. inadequate approach to the range of three egisters.

[9]*Kuśārīra* is the opposite of *suśārīra* explained in note 4 above.

[10]Literally, the Lord (the husband) of Pārvati.

property of sound like timbre or intensity, but represents the personal capacity of a singer to sing and to render a *rāga* without prior practice. In other words, it denotes the personal power of the singer to grasp and reproduce a tonal structure merely by listening and not by training. That is why it has been described as co-existent with the body or born along with the body.

'K' emphasises another aspect of it. He says that given the singer's capability and practice, a *rāga* is always delineated, but without the capability it cannot be rendered merely by practice. Thus, *śārīra* refers to the musicality of voice gifted by nature to the singer, which cannot be produced by any amount of practice subsequent to birth.

'S' quotes from the Saṅgītasamayasāra the definition and the fourfold classification of *śārīra*. He says "the capacity of exposing a *rāga*, apart from the element of practice that arises along with the body is said to be *śārīra*." He further distinguishes this capability into four types, the details of which we need not enter here. 'S' interprets it as the capability inherent in voice to delineate *rāga-s* without any practice.

(x) गमकलक्षणम्, तद्भेदाश्च

स्वरस्य कम्पो गमकः श्रोतृचित्तसुखावहः ।
तस्य भेदास्तु तिरिपः स्फुरितः कम्पितस्तथा ॥८७॥
लीन आन्दोलितवलित्रिभिन्नकुरुलाहताः ।
उल्लासितः प्लावितश्च हुंफितो मुद्रितस्तथा ॥८८॥
नामितो मिश्रितः पञ्चदशैते परिकीर्तिताः ।
लधिष्ठडमरुध्वानकम्पानुकृतिसुन्दरः ॥८९॥
द्रुततुर्यांशवेगेन तिरिपः परिकीर्तितः ।
वेगे द्रुततृतीयांशसंमिते स्फुरितो मतः ॥९०॥
द्रुतार्धमानवेगेन कम्पितं गमकं विदुः ।
लीनस्तु द्रुतवेगेनान्दोलितो लघुवेगतः ॥९१॥
वलिर्विविधवक्रत्वयुक्तवेगवशाद्भवेत् ।
त्रिभिन्नस्तु त्रिषु स्थानेष्वविश्रान्तघनस्वरः ॥९२॥
कुरुलो वलिरेव स्याद् ग्रन्थिलः कण्ठकोमलः ।
स्वरमग्रिममाहत्य निवृत्तस्त्वाहतो मतः ॥९३॥

उल्लासितः स तु प्रोक्तो यः स्वरानुत्तरोत्तरान् ।
क्रमाद्गच्छेत्, प्लावितस्तु प्लुतमानेन कम्पनम् ॥९४॥
हृदयंगमहुंकारगर्भितो हुंफितो भवेत् ।
मुखमुद्रणसंभूतो मुद्रितो गमको मतः ॥९४॥
स्वराणां नमनादुक्तो नामितो ध्वनिवेदिभिः ।
एतेषां मिश्रणान्मिश्रस्तस्य स्युर्भूरयो भिदाः ॥९३॥
तेषां तु स्थायवागेषु विवृतिः संविधास्यते ।
इति गमकभेदाः ।

(x) The definition and varieties of *kampa* (shake): 87-97b

The shaking of tone that is delightful to the listener's mind is (called) *gamaka*. Its varieties are: *Tiripa*, *sphurita*, *kampita*, *līna*, *āndolita*, *vali*, *tribhinna*. *kurula*, *āhata*, *ullāsita*, *plāvita*, *humphita*, *mudrita*, *nāmita* and *miśrita*—these are known to be fifteen. (87a-89b)

1. *Tiripa*-The shake (of a note) that is delightful [1]like the sound of a small ḍamaru speeding in a quarter *druta*[2] is called *tiripa*. (90 ab)

2. *Sphurita*[3]-If it[4] is produced speeding in one third of a *druta*, it is considered to be *sphurita*. (90 cd)

3. *Kampita*[5]-The *gamaka* speeding in half a *druta* is known as *kampita*. (91 ab)

4. *Līna*[6]-is speeding (the shake) in (the period of) a *druta*. (91 c)

5. *Āndolita*[7] is by the speed of a *laghu*[8]. (91 d)

[1]*Anukṛti* of the text literally means resembling (the sound of a small ḍamaru) in beauty.

[2]*Druta* is a half *mātrā* (cf. *S. R.*, V 238). In terms of *tāla*, *mātrā* is equal to five short syllables (*laghu akṣara-s*); *laghu* is of one *mātrā*, *guru* of two and *pluta* of three.

[3]*Sphurita*-lit. trembling, throbbing, shaken.

[4]That is, the shake.

[5]*Kampita*-lit. shaken.

[6]*Līna*-lit. absorbed or dissolved.

[7]*Āndolita*-lit. swung

[8]See note 2 above.

6. *Vali* take place while speeding (the shake) through various curves. (92 ab)

7. *Tribhinna* is the (shake) with uninterrupted and full tone in the three registers. (92 cd)

8. *Kurula* is crooked, being the same as *vali* in a soft voice. (93 ab)

9. *Āhata*[1] is accepted as that which touches the succeeding note and returns. (93 cd)

10. *Ullāsita*[2] is said to be that (shake) which approaches the succeeding notes in due order. (9 ac)

11. *Plāvita* is shaking in the measure of *pluta*. (94 cd)

12. *Humphita*[3] is (the shake) with heart-captivating (tone) sounding *huṁ*. (95 ab)

13. *Mudrita*[4] is considered to be the shake that is produced by closing the mouth. (95 cd)

14. *Nāmita*[5] is so called by the expert musicologists[6] because of the descendance of notes (that produce it). (96 ab)

15. *Miśra*[7] (conjoint) is (produced) by the admixture of these[8] (1-14) and there are many varieties in it which will be expounded in the context of *sthāya-s*[9]. (96c-97b)

Now, the author is defining *gamaka* in general terms, as well as in terms of its specific varieties. *Gamaka*, as defined by the author, in the widest sense, is the shaking of a tone, or it may be said to be a tonal shake that is musically delightful. 'S' quotes Pārśvadeva who defines it as follows:

"In a melodic structure, the formulation of a tonal shade arising out of a *svara's* own *śruti* and resorting to that of another *śruti*, is demonstrated to

[1]Āhata—lit. struck.
[2]*Ullāsita*-lit. delighted.
[3]*Humphita*-lit. embodying the sound huṁ.
[4]*Mudrita*-lit. closed.
[5]*Nāmita*-lit. lowered.
[6]*Dhvanivedi*-lit. the sound experts.
[7]*Miśra* or *miśrita*-lit. mixed.
[8]'K' observes that it is not the intention of the author to imply that all the varieties (1 to 14) put together would make for *miśra* for, he has further said that there are many varieties of *miśra*.
[9]*Sthāya* is shortly to be defined.

be *gamaka*[1]." Obviously, this definition is more precise and gives a better idea of what it means.

Historically, Śārṅgadeva seems to be the first writer known to us who has consolidated the concept of *gamaka* and formulated it as such in some detail. It is well known that Bharata does not distinguish between *alaṁkāra* and *gamaka*; he rather includes the latter in the former.

(xi) स्थायलक्षणम्, तद्भेदाश्च

(क) लक्षणम्, उद्देशश्च

रागस्यावयवः स्थायो वागो गमक उच्यते ।।९७।।

तत्रोक्तं लक्ष्म वागानां स्थायानां तूच्यतेऽधुना ।
वागानामपि केषांचित् प्रसङ्गाद्ब्रूच्मि लक्षणम् ।।९८।।
ते च शब्दस्य ढालस्य लवन्या वह्नेरपि ।
वाद्यशब्दस्य यन्त्रस्य छायायाः स्वरलङ्घितः ।।९९।।
प्रेरितस्तीक्ष्ण इत्युक्ता व्यक्तासंकीर्णलक्षणाः ।
भजनस्य स्थापनाया गतेर्नादध्वनिच्छवेः ।।१००।।
रक्तेर्द्रुतस्य शब्दस्य भृतस्यांशावधानयोः ।
अपस्थानस्य निकृतेः करुणाविविधत्वयोः ।।१०१।।
गात्रोपशमयोः काण्डारणानिर्जवनान्वितौ ।
गाढो ललितगाढश्च ललितो लुलितः समः ।।१०२।।
कोमलः प्रसृतः स्निग्धचोक्षोचितसुदेशिकाः ।
अपेक्षितश्च घोषश्च स्वरस्यैते प्रसिद्धितः ।।१०३।।
स्थायानां गुणभेदेन व्यपदेशा निरूपिताः ।
वहाक्षराडम्बरयोरुल्लासिततरङ्गिते ।।१०४।।
प्रलम्बितोऽवस्खलितस्त्रोटितः संप्रविष्टकः ।
उत्प्रविष्टो निःसरणो भ्रामितो दीर्घकम्पितः ।।१०५।।
प्रतिग्राह्योल्लासितश्च स्यादलम्बविलम्बकः ।
स्यात् त्रोटितप्रतीष्टोऽपि प्रसृताकुञ्चितः स्थिरः ।।१०६।।

[1]स्वश्रुतिस्थानसंभूतां छायां श्रुत्यन्तराश्रयाम् ।
स्वरूपं गमयेद्गीते गमकोऽसौ निरूपितः ।। (Pārśvadeva as quoted by 'S')

स्थायुकः क्षिप्तसूक्ष्मान्ताविव्यसंकीर्णलक्षणाः ।

प्रकृतिस्थस्य शब्दस्य कलाक्रमणयोरपि ॥१०७॥

घटनायाः सुखस्यापि चालेर्जीवस्वरस्य च ।

वेदध्वनेर्घनत्वस्य शिथिलोऽवघटः प्लुतः ॥१०८॥

रागेष्टोऽपस्वराभासो बद्धः कलरवस्य च ।

छान्दसः सुकराभासः संहितो लघुरन्तरः ॥१०९॥

वक्रो दीप्तप्रसन्नश्च स्यात् प्रसन्नमृदुर्गुरुः ।

ह्रस्वः शिथिलगाढश्च दीर्घोऽसाधारणस्ततः ॥११०॥

साधारणो निराधारो दुष्कराभासनामकः ।

मिश्रश्चैतेऽपि संकीर्णा गुणैर्भिन्नाश्च पूर्ववत् ॥१११॥

इति षण्णवतिः स्थायाः शाङ्र्गदेवेन कीर्तिताः ।

(xi) The definition and varieties of *sthāya*: (97c-189 b)

(a) Definition and enumeration: (97c-112b)

Sthāya is an organic component[1] of *rāga*. *Vāga* is said to be *gamaka*. Of these (two), the characteristic features of *vāga-s* (*gamaka-s*) have already been described; and now those of *sthāya-s* are being related. Incidentally I am also to describe the characteristic features of some[2] of the *gamaka-s*. (97c-98)

Those (of the *sthāya-s*) that are related to *śabda*, *ḍhāla*, *lavanī*, *vahanī*, *vādyaśabda*, *yantra*, *chāyā*, *svaralaṅghita*, *prerita* and *tīkṣṇa* are quite well known and also distinctly defined. (99-100b)

The (*sthāya-s*) related to *bhajana*, *sthāpanā*, *gati*, *nāda*, *dhvani*, *chavi*, *rakti*, *druta*, *bhṛta*, *aṁśa*, *avadhāna*, *apasthāna*, *nikṛti*, *karuṇā*, *vividhatva*, *gātra*. *upaśama*, *kāṇḍāraṇā*, *nırjavana*, *gāḍhaṇā*, *lalitagāḍha*, *lalita*, *lulita*, *sama*, *komala*, *prasṛta*, *snigdha*, *cokṣa*, *ucita*, *sudeśika*, *apekṣita*, *ghoṣa* and *svara*

[1]*Sthāya* is defined by the author as an *avayava* (lit. a limb) of a *rāga*. 'S' interprets *avayava* as *ekadeśa*, probably in the sense of a portion; and that, he says, rests on a tone other than *saṁnyāsa* and *vinyāsa*. It is a melodic pattern constituted by the fundamenta and such other few notes, 'C' interprets *avayava* as *bhāga* (part of a *rāga*) P.I.L.S. concludes that *Sthāya* comprises an analysis of the elements of *rañjakatā* (delightfulness) in music and delineation of *rāga*. She also further concludes, "*Sthāya* includes *gamaka-s* and all characteristic features in the rendering of *rāga* as also time measure." (cf. *I.M.J.* no. 3,4-"The Concept of *Sthāya*").

[2]'K' elucidates that the *gamaka-s* dealt with here are the varieties of *miśra* (conjoin *gamaka-s*) spoken of earlier.

rana, bhra·nita, dirgñākampita, pratigrāhyollāsita, alambavilambaka, troṭitapratīṣta, praṣrtakuṇcita, ṣthira, sthātruka, ksipta, and *sūkṣmānta*, (104c-107b)[1]

Besides, these are the indistinctly[2] defined (*sthāya-s*) distinguished by their character as (mentioned) before, viz. as related to *pr·k·tistha śabda, kalā, ākramaṇa, ghaṭanā, sukha, cāli, jīvasvara, vedadhvani, ghanatva, sithila, avaghaṭa, pluta, rāgeṣta, apasvarābhāsa, baddha, kalnrava, chāndasa, sukkarābhāsa, saṁhita, laghu, antara, vakra, dīptaprasanna, prasannamṛdu, guru, hrava, sithila, gāḍha, dīrgha, aṣādhāraṇa. sādhāraṇa, nirādhāra, duṣkarābhāsa* and *miśra.* (107c-111)[3]

Thus, ninety-six[4] *sthāya-s* are enumerated by Sārngadeva. (112 a b)

(b) The well known (*prasiddha*) *sthāya-s.* (112c-151)

(i) The distinctly defined *sthāya-s:*

1. *Śabda:* The *sthāya-s* that hold upon the previous[5] tone are known as related to *śabda.* (112 c d)

2. *Dhāla* is a rolling movement like that of a pearl. The *sthāya-s* in which this (movement) is found pertain to *ḍhāla.* (113 a b)

[1] 'K' says "Well known to the musicologists."

[2] *Guṇabhedana*—lit. by differentiating them according to their qualities, or on the basis of their (tonal) character. 'K' elucidates that they are named on the basis of their potency to enrich the delineation of *rāga* (*rāgātiśayādhānarupabhajanādiguṇānām bhedena*).

[3] 'S' defines *asaṅkīrṇa* as "those (*sthāya-s*) that are distinctly defined." He further points out that "if this be the significance of what is called *asaṅkīrṇa*, then the first group of *sthāya-s* too is similarly defined; what then differentiates them?" And he replies that, "the difference lies in the fact that the preceding ones are well known but these are obscure." That is why, while defining these, they have been categorised as *aprasiddha* (obscure), even though distinctly defined.

[4] This comprises—

(i) The wellknown and distinctly defined *sthāya-s*	10
(ii) The well-known and indistinctly defined *sthāya-s*	33
(iii) The obscure and distinctly defined *sthāya-s*	20
(iv) The obscure and indistinctly defined *sthāya-s*	33
Total number of *sthāya-s*	96

[5] *Mukta*—lit. released. 'S' reads it as *yukta* i.e. 'proper', and interprets, "The *sthāya-s* that commence with the proper' tone (lit. word) are related to *śabda.*" But 'K' seems to have the better reading' *mukta* and he interprets that, if the tone that ends the preceding *sthāya* begins the succeeding one in cycle, such *sthāya-s* are related to *sābda. Śubda* literally means sound, as well as word but in this context it implies tone. *Pratigrahaṇa* literally means' catching' in already released thing. P.Ḷ.S. illustrates it on the analogy of the *alaṁkāra* 'as ri ga ri, ri ga ma ri' where the preceding phrase ends with the note with which the succeeding phrase begins. (*I. M.J.*, no. 4, p. 34)

(ख) प्रसिद्धस्थायाः

(i) तत्रासङ्कीर्णलक्षणाः स्थायाः

मुक्तशब्दप्रतिग्राह्याः स्थायाः शब्दस्य कीर्तिताः ।।११२।।

ढालो मुक्ताफलस्येव चलनं लुण्ठनात्मकम् ।

स येषु ते स्युर्ढालस्य, नमनं त्वतिकोमलम् ।।११३।।

लवनी, तद्युजः स्थाया लवन्याः परिकीर्तिताः ।

यत्तु कम्पनमारोहिण्यवरोहिणि वा भवेत् ।।११४।।

वहनी साथ संचारिण्यपि वा स्थिरकम्पनम् ।

सा गीतालप्तिसंबन्धभेदेन द्विविधा मता ।।११५।।

पुनर्द्विधा स्थिरा वेगाढ्या पुनस्त्रिविधोदिता

हृद्या कण्ठ्या शिरस्या च देहस्था हृदयोद्भवा ।।११६।।

वहनी स्यात् पुनर्द्वेधा खुत्तोत्फुल्लेति भेदतः ।

यस्यामन्तर्विशन्तीव स्वराः खुत्तेति सा मता ।।११७।।

सोत्फुल्लेत्युदिता यस्यां निर्यान्तीवोपरि स्वराः ।

वलिर्या गमकेषूक्ता साप्येवंविधभेदभाक् ।।११८।।

वहनी येषु ते स्थाया वहन्याः परिभाषिताः ।

रागमग्ना वाद्यशब्दा येषु ते वाद्यशब्दजाः ।।११९।।

ये यन्त्रेष्वेव दृश्यन्ते बाहुल्यात्ते तु यन्त्रजाः ।

छाया काकुः षट्प्रकारा स्वररागान्यरागजा ।।१२०।।

स्याद्देशक्षेत्रयन्त्राणां तल्लक्षणमथोच्यते ।

श्रुतिन्यूनाधिकत्वेन या स्वरान्तरसंश्रया ।।१२१।।

स्वरान्तरस्य रागे स्यात् स्वरकाकुरसौ मता ।

या रागस्य निजच्छाया रागकाकुं तु तां विदुः ।।१२२।।

सा त्वन्यरागकाकुर्या रागे रागान्तराश्रया ।

सा देशकाकुर्या रागे भवेद्देशस्वभावतः ।।१२३।।

शरीरं क्षेत्रमित्युक्तं प्रतिक्षेत्रं निसर्गतः ।

रागे नानाविधा काकुः क्षेत्रकाकुरिति स्मृता ॥१२४॥
वीणावंशादियन्त्रोत्था यन्त्रकाकुः सतां मता ।
अन्यच्छायाप्रवृत्तौ ये छायान्तरमुपाश्रिताः ॥१२५॥
छायायास्ते मताः स्थाया गीतविद्याविशारदैः ।
मध्ये मध्ये स्वरान् भूरीँल्लङ्घयन् स्वरलङ्घितः ॥१२६॥
तिर्यगूर्ध्वमधस्ताच्च प्रेरितः प्रेरितैः स्वरैः ।
स्वरः पूर्णश्रुतिस्तारे तीक्ष्णवत्तीक्ष्ण उच्यते ॥१२७॥

3. *Lavanī*[1] is a very soft[2] descending movement, and the *sthāya-s* associated with it are known as pertaining to *lavanī*. (113 c-114 b)

4. *Vahanī*[3] is the shaking (of notes) either in the ascent or in the descent and also in the *sancārī* (*varṇa*) with a constant tremor. It is considered to be twofold viz. as related to *gīta* (composition) and to *ālapti* (improvisation). Again it is twofold viz. *sthirā* (stable or constant), and *vegāḍhyā* (speeding). Again it is said to be threefold viz. *hṛdyā*, *kaṇṭhyā*, *śirasayā* i.e. (pertaining to the heart, the throat and the head respectively) in the body.[4] That which arises from the heart (*hṛdyā*) is again twofold viz. *khuttā* and *utphullā*. *Khuttā* is thought as that in which the notes appear to be moving in[5]. *Utphullā* is said to be that in which the succeeding notes appear to be moving out.[6] (114 c-118 b)

Vali, which has been described among the *gamaka-s*, is also differentiated on these lines. (118 c d)

The *sthāya-s* associated to *vahanī* are defined as pertaining to *vahanī*. (119 a b)

[1]P.L.S. defines it as—"Rendering of *svara-s* with extra tenderness in descent is *lavani*."

[2]*Namanam* is interpreted by 'S' as *adha* + *ucchāraṇam* (lit. singing downwards) i.e. descending movement (of tones). However, Pārśvadeva lends it a technical meaning: "The shaking of creamy and tender notes without effort and alongwith *laghutva* (lit. smallness) is said by the musicologists to be *namanam*. (*S.S. Sāra* II 103, 104). *Nāmitam* has already been mentioned as a *gamaka* with descending notes."

[3]The classification of *vahanī* may be illustrated as follows: '*Vahanī* is divided as *gītavahanī* and *ālaptivahanī* each of which is sub-divided as *Sthirā* and *vegāḍhyā*. Again each of these is subdivided into *hṛdyā*, *kaṇṭhyā* and *śirasyā*. Of these, only *hṛdyā* is subdivided as *khuttā* and *utphullā*.'

[4]These three correspond to the three registers arising respectively in the heart, the throat and the cerebrum.

[5]That is, "where the succeeding note appears to be getting into the preceding one e.g. sa ri, sa, ri ga ri, ga ma ga, etc." (cf. P.L.S. in *I.M.J.*, no. 4, p. 35).

[6]That is, "where the notes appear to be coming out, or the succeeding notes naturally follow out of the preceding ones; e.g. sa ri, ri ga, ga ma, ma pa, pa dha, etc." (cf. P.L.S. in *I.M.J.*, no. 4, p. 35)

5. *Vādyaśabda*: The *sthāya-s* incorporating delightful[1] instrumental sound-syllables[2] are born of *vādyaśabda* (lit. instrumental sound). (119 c d)

6. *Yantra*: Those (however) that are found in abundance among the instruments only[3] are born of *yantra* (instrument). (120 a b)

7. *Chāyā* is *kāku* (intonation) which is of six types viz. ***svarakāku***, *rāgakāku, anyarāgakāku, deśakāku, kṣetrakāku* and ***yantrakāku***, and their definitions follow: (120 c-121 b)

(a) *Svarakāku*:[4] When in a *rāga* the reflection (*chāyā*) of one note by the decrease or the increase of its *śruti*-measure is cast upon another it is considered[5] to be *svarakāku*[6] (tonal inflection). (121 c-122 b)

(b) *Rāgakāku*: However, the particular shade of a ***rāga***, which is its own, is known as *rāgakāku*[7] (inflection of *rāga*). (122 c d)

(c) *Anyarāgakāku*: But, if in a *rāga* (the *chāyā*) of another ***rāga*** is reflected, it is *anyarāgakāku* (the inflection of another *rāga*). (123 a b)

(d) *Deśakāku*: That (i e. the *chāyā*) which in a *rāga* is reflected in the regional practice[8] is *deśakāku* (regional inflection). (123 c d)

(e) *Kṣetrakāku*: The body is said to be the *kṣetra* (field) and in the singing of *rāga*, naturally there are various tonal inflections (***kāku-s***) related to every *kṣetra* (producing organism). This (shade of ***rāga***) is known as *kṣetrakāku*[9] (individual inflection of tone). (124)

[1] *Rāgamagna*—lit. immersed in *rāga*, in its primary meaning of delight, therefore delightful.

[2] *Vādyaśabda*—P.L.S. cites *Saṅgītasudhā* of Raghunātha Bhūpa who identifies it with *pāṭākṣara* i.e. "syllables associated with an instrument, e.g. the modern ***jhālā*** in sitar, *tatkāra* in wind instruments or where the syllables of an instrument are used in vocal music, e.g. *tana, ri nom* etc. in *ālāpa* of *dhrupada* style, *tānam* of karnaṭaka music, ***tarānā*** or *tillānā* and similar compositions." (cf. *I.M.J.*, no. 4, p. 36)

[3] Such as modern "*ghasīṭa, sūta* etc. of plucked stringed instruments or special bow-techniques of bowed instruments." (cf. P.L.S. in *I.M.J.*, no. 4, p. 36)

[4] The word *chāyā* (lit. shade or shadow and also lustre or beauty or so on) is used in a technical sense, since it is identified with *kāku* which implies tonal inflection or intonation. Here it has been translated either as reflection or shade according to the context.

[5] *Ucyate* of the text lit. 'is spoken of'.

[6] P.L.S. observes that, "*Svarakāku* pertains to *vikṛta svara-s* where one note enters the sphere of another and thus adopts its shadow by getting nearer." (cf. *I.M.J.*, no. 4, p. 36).

[7] Compare the surmise of P.L.S. "The special characteristic of a ***rāga*** which distinguishes it from others is a *rāga-kāku*." (cf. *I.M.J.*, no. 4, p. 36)

[8] *Deśāsvabhāvataḥ* of the text may literally be rendered as "in accordance with regional nature" which seems to include regional aesthetic taste and ethnic structure.

[9] *Kṣetrakāku* has been identified by P.L.S. mainly with timber of human voices which distinguishes one voice from another." The relation of personal timbre to the rendering of a *rāga* seems to be incomprehensible, but is not yet insignificant. As observed by P.L.S., "Serious thought reveals that the timbre of the human voice has its own importance in the aesthetic atmosphere created by a *rāga*." (cf. *I.M.J.*, no. 4, p. 37)

(f) *Yantrakāku*: The (shade of a *rāga*) arising out of the instruments such as *vīṇā*, flute etc. is considered by the experts to be *yantrakāku*[1] (instrumental inflection). (125 a b)

The *sthāya-s* involved in the shade (of a *rāga*) other than the one which they reflect are considered by the expert vocalists and instrumentalists to be related to *chāyā* (shade).[2] (125 c-126 b)

8. *Svaralanghita*[3] is by frequent overstepping of intermediary notes (126 c d)

9. *Prerita*:[4] is that (*sthāya*) which is stimulated by the upward, downward and the oblique (movement of) notes. (127 a b)

10. *Tīkṣṇa*:[5] The note that is complete in the *śruti*-measure and yet is quite sharp in the upper register is said to be *tīkṣṇa*. (127 c d)

(ii) तत्र संकीर्णलक्षणाः स्थायाः

रागस्यातिशयाधानं प्रयत्नाद्भजनं मतम् ।
तद्युक्ता भजनस्य स्युः स्थापनायास्तु ते मताः ॥१२८॥
स्थापयित्वा स्थापयित्वा येषां प्रतिपदं कृतिः ।
सविलासास्ति गीतस्य मत्तमातङ्गवद्गतिः ॥१२९॥
तद्युक्तास्तु गतेः स्थायाः स्निग्धो माधुर्यमांसलः ।
बहुलो येषु नादः स्यात्ते नादस्य प्रकीर्तिताः ॥१३०॥

[1]*Yantrakāku* (instrumental inflection) too is significant in the rendering of a *rāga*, from the aesthetic point of view. For example, as pointed out by P.L.S., "*Bina* of north India is specially suitable for solemn and grave *rāga-s* like *darbārikāthaḍā* and *malhāra*, but *jalataranga* is just the opposite."

[2]In the preceding few verses the author has defined six varieties of *chāyā*. Now, he is defining the *sthāya-s* pertaining to it. *Chāyā* (lit. shade or shadow, lustre etc.) has been defined by Kumbhā as a tonal modification in a *rāga* which is identified with *kāku* (*Dhvaner vikāro yaḥ kākuḥ sā chāyā S. Rāj.* II 3. 4. 7.). If the *chāyā* a specific characteristic of one *rāga*, is transferred, in singing, to another, the *sthāya-s* involved in the *chāyā* of one *rāga* and reflected or transferred to that of another are said to be pertaining to *chāyā*.

[3]*Svaralaṅghita*—lit. that which oversteps notes. *Laṅghana* is omission by overstepping; when notes are frequently omitted, that *sthāya* is *svaralaṅghita*, 'S' interprets *bhūri* (many) of the text as three or four.

[4]*Prerita*—lit. stimulated. The oblique movement of notes is elucidated by P.L.S. as "*vakragati* i.e. curved or winding movement of notes, e.g. sa ga ri ga—ma ga ri ga—ri ga ma ri—sa ri ni sa." (*I.M.J.*, no. 4, p. 38)

[5]*Tīkṣṇa*—lit. sharp, compared by 'S' with the point of a needle. Also sec P.L.S. (*I.M.J.*, no. 4, p. 38) who quotes *Saṅgīta-sudhā* and says, "The sharpness of the whole tone used in the *tāra-sthāna* (upper register) has been given here the analogy of a needle point, e.g. *antara-gāndhāra* in *tāra-sthana*."

अतिदीर्घप्रयोगाः स्युः स्थाया ये ते ध्वनेर्मताः ।
युक्ताः कोमलया कान्त्या छबेः स्थाया निरूपिताः ॥१३१॥
रक्तेरुत्कर्षतो रक्तेरुक्ताः स्थाया मनीषिभिः ।
द्रुतस्यान्वर्थनामानो भृतस्य भरणाद्ध्वनेः ॥१३२॥
रागान्तरस्यावयवो रागेंऽशः स च सप्तधा ।
कारणांशश्च कार्यांशः सजातीयस्य चांशकः ॥१३३॥
सदृशांशो विसदृशो मध्यमस्थांशकोऽपरः ।
अंशांशश्चेति यो रागे कार्योंऽशः कारणोद्भवः ॥१३४॥
कारणांशस्त्वसौ रामकृतौ कोलाहलांशवत् ।
कारणे कार्यरागांशः कार्यांशो भैरवे यथा ॥१३५॥
भैरव्यंशः, समां जातिं गौडत्वाद्यां समाश्रिताः ।
कर्णाटाद्याः सजातीयास्तेष्वेकांशोऽपरत्र यः ॥१३६॥
सजातीयांशकः स स्यादंशः सदृशरागयोः ।
सदृशांशो यथा नट्टावराट्योः शुद्धयोर्मिथः ॥१३७॥
सादृश्यशून्ययोरंशोऽत्यन्तं विसदृशांशकः ।
वेलावल्याश्च गुर्जर्याः परस्परगतौ यथा ॥१३८॥
मध्यस्थरागौ सादृश्यवैसादृश्यविवर्जितौ ।
मध्यस्थांशस्तयोरंशो नट्टादेशाख्ययोरिव ॥१३९॥
अंशोंऽशान्तरसंचारादंशांश इति कीर्तितः ।
येष्वंशो दृश्यते स्थायास्तेंऽशस्य परिकीर्तिताः ॥१४०॥
मनसा तद्गतेनैव ये ग्राह्यास्तेऽवधानजाः ।
आयासेन विना यत्र स्थाने स्यात् प्रचुरो ध्वनिः ॥१४१॥
स्वस्थानं तदपस्थानं त्वायासेन तद्द्गतेः ।
अपस्थानस्य ते स्थाया येऽपस्थानसमुद्भवाः ॥१४२॥
निकृतेः करुणायाश्च स्थायास्त्वनर्थनामकाः ।
स्थाया नानाविधां भङ्गीं भजन्तो विविधत्वजाः ॥१४३॥

गात्रस्य, गात्रे नियताः कृत्वा तीव्रतरं ध्वनिम् ।
येषूपशान्तिः क्रियते भवत्युपशमस्य ते ॥१४४॥
काण्डारणा प्रसिद्धैव तस्याः स्थायास्तदुद्भवाः ।
सरलः कोमलो रक्तः क्रमान्नीतोऽतिसूक्ष्मताम् ॥१४५॥
स्वरः स्याद्येषु ते स्थायाः प्रोक्ता निर्जवनान्विताः ।
गाढः शैथिल्यनिर्मुक्तः स एव मृदुतान्वितः ॥१४६॥
भवेल्ललितगाढस्तु ललितस्तु विलासवान् ।
मार्दवाघूर्णितः प्रोक्तो लुलितः स्यात् समः पुनः ॥१४७॥
हीनो वेगविलम्बाभ्यां, यथार्थः कोमलो मतः ।
प्रसृतः प्रसरोपेतः स्निग्धो रूक्षत्ववर्जितः ॥१४८॥
उज्ज्वलो गदितश्चोक्ष उचितस्तु यथार्थकः ।
सुदेशिको विदग्धानां वल्लभोऽपेक्षितस्तु सः ॥१४९॥
स्थायः स्थायेन पूर्वेण पूर्त्यर्थं योऽभिकाङ्क्षितः ।
वलौ वहे वहन्यां च यः स्निग्धमधुरो महान् ॥१५०॥
मन्द्रे ध्वनिः स घोषः स्यात्तद्युक्ता घोषजा मताः ।
गम्भीरमधुरध्वाना मन्द्रे ये स्युः स्वरस्य ते ॥१५१॥

(128-151) (ii) The indistinctly defined *sthāya-s* —

1. *Bhajana* is considered to be the creation of excessive delightfulness in a *rāga* through conscious effort. The (*sthāya-s*) associated with it are 'related to *Bhajana*'[1] (128 a b c)

2. *Sthāpanā*: The *sthāya-s* that are produced by stopping and reawakening[2] at every step are thought to be related to *sthāpanā*,[3] (128 d-129 b)

[1]Comp. P.L.S., "It is common experience that a performing musician has some special pieces in his performance where he puts in greater effort in creating *rakti* (delightfulness). Thus strain or effort cannot and should not remain constant throughout a performance. (*I.M.J.*, no. 4, p. 38)

[2]*Sthāpayitvā* lit. 'having firmly laid' signifies the arresting and the releasing of the movement of notes alternatively.

[3]*Sthāpanā*—lit. establishment or consolidation of a certain step in the tonal movement.

3. *Gati*: The *sthāya-s* that are associated with the majestic movement[1] of the song resembling the *gati* of the intoxicated elephant, are related to *gati*'. (129 c-130 a)

4. *Nāda*: The *sthāya-s* in which the *nāda* (musical sound that is creamy and heavily sweetened) is profuse, are known as 'related to *nāda*'. (c 130 b-130 d)

5. *Dhvani*: The *sthāya-s* that are full of elongated phrases[2] are considered 'related to *dhvani*'. (131 a b c)

6. *Chavi*: The *sthāya-s* that are associated with tender lustre are demonstrated[3] as 'related to *chavi*'. (131 c d)

7. *Rakti*: Because of heightened delightfulness *sthāya-s* are described by the experts as 'related to *rakti*'.[4] (132 a b)

8. *Druta*: The *sthāya-s* related to *druta* are significant by the name (itself)[5]. (132 c)

9. *Bhṛta*: (The *sthāya-s*) 'related to *bhṛta*' are associated with the filling up[6] of voice. (132 d)

10. The constituent part of another *rāga*, when adopted in a *rāga* is (called) *aṁśa*[7] which is sevenfold viz. *kāraṇāṁśa*, *kāryāṁśa*, *sajātīyāṁśa*, *sadṛśāṁśa*, *visadṛśāṁśā*, *madyhasthāṁśa* and *aṁśāṁśa*. (133-134 c)

[1] 'S' says that this particular movement known as *gati* is well known to the singers.

[2] *Prayoga* is interpreted by 'S' as a phrase full of *gamaka-s*. Comp. P.L.S., "*Dhvani* can be taken to imply the use of long phrases full of *gamaka-s*" (*I.M.J.*, no. 4 p. 38).

[3] Śārṅgadeva has already defined *chavi* (lustre) in describing *chavimān* (vide S.R. III verse 77 ante). There too, he associates the qualities or excellences of softness and brightness with it.

[4] *Rakti*—lit. delightfulness.

[5] That is, they are related to fast tempo (cf. P.L.S. in *I.M.J.*, no. 4, p. 40). *Druta*, as already mentioned, is equal to one half of *laghu*.

[6] *Bhṛta*—lit. filled up. P.L.S. identifies it with modern *bharāv*, "implying fulness of volume or intensity" (cf. *I.M.J.*, no. 4, p. 40)

[7] *Aṁśa* in this context has a specific meaning and should not be confused with the fundamental note. When in *a rāga* a phrase of another *rāga* is imported, it is called *aṁśa*.

This bears a close resemblance to *anyarāgakāku* i.e. tonal inflection already dealt with in this chapter (vide 123 a b ante). The question is how to differentiate the two. 'K' points out, "When the *chāyā* of another *rāga* comes to subsist in a given *rāga* in the relation of *samavāya* (inherence) for enhancing its beauty, it is called *anyarāgakāku*; but here the *aṁśa* (constituent part) of another *rāga*, when applied to a given *rāga* for enhancing its delightfulness, is borrowed from it temporarily and is incorporated into it in the relation of *saṁyoga* (combination). Thus *aṁśa* does not inhere in the given *rāga* as is the case with *chāyā* in the *anyarāgakāku*." It is perceptible as a foreign element.

Moreover, as pointed out by 'S', *aṁśa* is constituted by a group of notes that form an *avayava* (constituent part) of another *rāga*; whereas, *anyarāgakāku* depends on the *chāyā* of another *rāga*. Comp. P.L.S. "*Anyarāgakāku* denotes the *chāyā* of one *rāga* being inseparably woven into another *rāga* and *aṁśa* denotes a solitary phrase of a *rāga* being used in another *rāga* merely as an arbitrary embellishment." (cf. *I.M.J.* no. 4, p. 40).

(a) *Kāraṇāṁśā;* (Parental constituent). When the *aṁśa* (constituent part) of a parent *rāga* becomes a part of the derived *rāga*, it is called *kāraṇāṁśā* e.g., the constituent part of *kolāhala* applied to *rāmakṛti*. (134 c-135 b)

(b) *Kāryāṁśa;* (derived constituent): When the constituent part of a derived *rāga* is applied to the parent *rāga* it is called *kāryāṁśa* e.g. the constituent part of *bhairavī* applied to *bhairava*. (135 c-136 a)

(c) *Sajātīyāṁśa* (family constituent): The *rāga-s* such as *karṇāṭa* and others that are based on the same generic features such as *gauḍatva*[1] and so on are (said to be) of the same family (*sajātīya*). Among them, if a constituent part of one is applied to the other it is (considered as) having *sajātīyaṁśa*. (136 a-137 a)

(d) *Sadṛśāṁśa* (similar constituent): The (transferred) constituent part of similar *rāga-s* is (called) *sadṛśāṁśa* e.g. in between *śuddha-naṭṭa* and *varāṭī*. (137 b-137 d)

(e) *Visadṛśāṁśā* (dissimilar constituent). The (transferred) constituent part of two extremely dissimilar[2] *rāga-s* makes for *visadṛśāṁśa*; as for example, the constituent parts of *velāvalī* and *gurjarī* transferred to each other. (138)

(f) *Madhyasthāṁśa* (neutral constituent): The constituent part (transferable) in between two neutral *rāga-s* that are devoid of similarity and dissimilarity is (called) *madyasthāṁśa*[3] like the constituent part obtained in between *naṭṭa* and *deśākhya*. (139)

(g) *Amśāṁśa* (constituting constituent)[4] The movement of one constituent part into another is called *aṁśāṁśā*. (140 a b)

Aṁśa is the constituent part of a *rāga* that is transferred to another *rāga*. When the movement of one *āṁśa* into another is spoken of, obviously the mixture of more than one *aṁśa-s* seems to be applied.

The *sthāya-s* in which *aṁśa* (a transferred constituent part) is perceived, are known as 'related to *aṁśa*.' (140 c d)

11. *Avadhāna*: Those (*sthāya-s*) that are taken with a fully absorbed mind are born of *avadhāna* (undistracted attention). (141 a b)

[1]*Gauḍatva* is the essence of the characteristic features that go to make up *rāga gauḍa*. The *sajātīyatā* (the relation of belonging to the same family) is based on the same generic features shared by *rāga-s*. Therefore 'S' warns us not to confuse it with the relation of belonging to the same *jāti* such as *ṣāḍjī* and so on.

[2]Literally, the expression is negative i.e. 'devoid of similarity in the extreme.'

[3]*Madhyasthāṁśa*—lit. the aṁśa obtained inbetween the two neutral *rāga-s*. This is the reading given by 'S'. Ad. Ed. reads *madhymasya* etc. which does not seem to be techinically so good.

[4]*Aṁśa* is the constituent part of a *rāga* that is transferred to another *rāga*. When the movement of one *aṁśa* into another is spoken of, obviously the mixture of more than one *aṁsā* seems to be implied in what is called *aṁśāṁśa* which sounds rather enigmatic.

12. *Apasthāna*: The *sthāna* (pitch-range) in which sound[1] is produced in great volume without effort is known as *Svasthāna* (normal range). But if it is produced with effort, it is (called) *apasthāna* (abnormal range). The *sthāya-s* that are produced from *apasthāna* are related to it. (141 c-142)

13. 14. *Nikṛti* and *karuṇā:* The *sthāya-s* pertaining to *nikṛti*[2] (resolution) and *karuṇā*[3] (compassion) are significant by their names. (143 a b)

15. *Vividhatā:* The *sthāya-s* taking resort to a variety of undulation[4] are (said to be) born of *vividhatā* (variety). (143 c d)

16. *Gātra*: (The *sthāya-s*) that are body-oriented are 'related to *gātra*'[5] (body). (144 a)

17. *Upaśama:* (The *sthāya-s*) in which the pitch having been heightened,[6] a calm[7] is obtained, are 'related to *upaśama*' (calm). 144 b-144 d)

18. *Kāṇḍāraṇā* is of course well known. The *sthāya-s* arising out of it pertain to *kāṇḍāraṇā*[8]. (145 a b)

19. *Nirjavana:* The *sthāya-s* in which the tone is even, soft, delightful

[1] *Dhvani* (musical sound) is common to vocal and instrumental music, but in this context voice seems to be prominently in view. In this connection P.L.S. observes, "It is a well known fact that each voice and instrument has a special pitchrange which may be called *svasthāna.* If that range is violated i.e. the tonic is not in confermity with that range, the result will be that the voice will be strained and some extra effort may have to be put in while singing or playing on an instrument." (*I.M.J.*, no. 4, p. 41).

[2] P.L.S. identifies *nikṛti* with resolution, and suggests *niṣkṛti* as a better reading for it, which she says, "would imply restoration to the original position after the use of various *sthāya s*" and quotes *Saṅgita-sudhā* and *Saṅgitasamayasāra* in support of her interpretation. (cf. *I M.J.*, no. 4, p. 41)

[3] The *sthāya-s* that arouse compassion among the listeners are said to be related to *karuṇā.*

[4] PLS cites *moḍāmoḍī* and *gumphāgumphī*, *gūnthagūnthī* as examples of *bhaṅgi* (lit. undulation) and quotes *Saṅgitasamayasāra* in support. (*I.M.J.*, no. 5, p. 29)

[5] *Gātra* – lit. body or limb. See P.L.S. who observes that "these (*sthāya-s*) are related to the characteristic features of the music of each vocalist associated with the peculiarities of (his) physiological set up. Obviously the *gātrasthāya* bears a close resemblance to *kṣetrakāku.* 'S' differentiates them as follows, "*kṣetrakāku* is merely the *chāyā* (personal shade) appertaining to each individual body, whereas in the case of the *gātra-sthāya*, it is the character of the *sthāya-s* that varies with the individual body." In other words, some singers have greater facility with certain *sthāya-s* and others with quite different *sthāya-s*.

[6] *Tīvratara* is interpreted by 'S' as *atitāra* i.e. the pitch-range beyond the upper heptad (*saptaka*).

[7] *Upaśānti* signifies release of tension. 'S' interprets it as a sudden descent from the higher to the lower range. Literally, it indicates calm or may be even resolution.

[8] *Kāṇḍāraṇā* seems to be a concept familiar to Śārṅgadeva, and therefore he does not define it. 'K' derives the word from '*kāṇḍa*,' a division, and interprets "*kāndāraṇa* to be that which moves in all the three registers," as it were. 'S' elucidates it on the analogy of the art of engraving. He says, "the engraving of the forms of lotus and so on is known in the every day life as *kāndāraṇā.* The *sthāya-s* related to it are considered as pertaining to *kāṇḍārāṇa*."

and gradually reduced[1], are said to involve *nirjavana*[2] (successful control). (145 c-146 b)

20. *Gāḍha* is free from slackness.[3] (146 c)

21. *Lalitagāḍha:* When it (*gādha*) involves softness, it becomes *lalitagāḍha*.[4] (146 d-147 a)

22. *Lalita* (graceful) is sportive[5]. (147 b)

23. *Lulita* (rolled) is said to be (characterised) by softness and a swinging movement[6]. (147 c d)

24. *Sama*[7] is free from the (extremities of) fast and slow (tempo) (147 d-148 a)

25. *Komala*[8] is considered to be significant by its name i. e. tender. (148 b)

26. *Prasṛta*[9] is that which is extended. (148 c)

27. *Snigdha*[10] is devoid of dryness. (148 d)

28. *Cokṣa*[11] is said to be bright. (149 a)

29. *Ucita*[12] is significant by its very name (i.e., proper or appropriate). (149 b)

[1]*Sūkṣmatāṁ-nītāḥ*—lit. led to subtlety; in the context of tone implies reduction in volume.

[2]*Nirjavana* is derived from *nirjṛ*, to control, to conquer, to subdue etc. P.L.S. quotse *Saṅgītasamayasāra* who uses the word *nirjavana* in the technical sense of singing that implies breath control.

[3]From *gāḍha* onwards the names of the *sthāya-s* of this class have been named in the nominative case instead of the genetive case applied to the foregoing *sthāya-s* (see 102 c d-104 a b). *Gāḍha* lit. means thick or substantive. Here it is indicated in the negative terms of being free from slackness (*śaithilya*).

[4]*Lalita-gāḍha* is *gāḍha* qualified by softness (*lalita* lit. means soft, tender, beautiful, charming etc.)

[5]PLS opines that *lalita* implies special skill or graceful movement. (*I.M.J.*, no. 5, p. 30).

[6]'S' links softness to swinging in a casual relation. He says "because of softness it is swung to and fro."

[7]*Sama*—lit. even i.e. the middle tempo or that which is neither fast nor slow; it can also be interpreted as the tonal embellishments used in the original tempo of the song or composition known as '*barābar kī lay*'. (*I.M.J.*, no. 5. p. 30).

[8]*Komala*—lit. tender or delicate.

[9]Comp. P.L.S. who says, "*Prasṛta* is widespread; it seems to imply a long-spread-out musical phrase" (*I.M.J.*, no. 5, p. 30)

[10]*Snigdha*—lit. unctuous or creamy; and is understood to be the opposite of *rūkṣa* (dry).

[11]*Cokṣa*—lit. pure, spotless.

[12]*Ucita*—lit. proper, apt, appropriate or suitable. Comp. P.L.S. who says, "*Aucitya* is a general quality which is an essential feature of all artistic creation. Its absence has been pronounced as the greatest cause of *rasabhaṅga* i.e. violation of aesthetic principles" (*I.M.J.*, no. 5, p. 31). *Aucitya* is propriety which implies the awareness of aesthetic principles that makes for a sense of proportion in the application of the mind to the execution of an artistic theme.

30. *Sudeśika* is dear to the connoisseurs[1] (of music). (149 cd)

31. *Apekṣita* (expected) is that *sthāya* which is wanted for the completion of the preceding *sthāya*. (149 d-150 b)

32. *Ghoṣa*: The tone that is creamy, sweet, big[2] and is used in the lower register in (the application of the *gamaka-s*) *vali, vaha* and *vahanī* is (called) *ghoṣa*. The *sthāya-s* related to it are considered to be arising out of *ghoṣa*[3] (150 c-151 b)

33. *svara*: The *sthāya-s* that are (couched) in deep and sweet tones in the lower register, pertain to *svara*.[4] (15 ic d)

(ग) अप्रसिद्धस्थायाः

(i) तत्रासङ्कीर्णलक्षणाः स्थायाः

वहन्त इव कम्पन्ते स्वरा येषु वहस्य ते ।
अक्षराडम्बरो येषु मुख्यास्ते स्युस्तदन्विताः ॥१५२॥
वेगेन प्रैरितैरूर्ध्वं स्वरैरुल्लासितो मतः ।
यत्र गङ्गातरङ्गन्ति स्वराः स स्यात्तरङ्गितः ॥१५३॥
परितोऽर्धभृते कुम्भे जलं डोलायते यथा ।
गीते तथाविधः स्थायः प्रोक्तस्तज्ज्ञैः सलम्बितः ॥१५४॥
अवस्खलति यो मन्द्रादवरोहेण वेगतः ।
सोऽवस्खलित इत्युक्तस्त्रोटितस्तु स्वरे क्वचित् ॥१५५॥
चिरं स्थित्वाग्निवत्तारं स्पृष्ट्वा प्रत्यागतो भवेत् ।
घनस्वरोऽवरोहे स्यात् संप्रतिष्ठस्तथाविधः ॥१५६॥
आरोहिण्युत्प्रविष्टः स्यादन्वर्थाः स्युः परे त्रयः ।
प्रतिग्राह्योल्लासितः स्यादसौ य. प्रतिगृह्यते ॥१५७॥
उत्क्षिप्योत्क्षिप्य निपतन् केलिकन्दुकसुन्दरः ।
द्रुतपूर्वो विलम्बान्तः स्यादलम्बविलम्बकः ॥१५८॥
स्यात् त्रोटितप्रतीष्टोऽसौ यत्र स्यात्तारमन्द्रयोः ।
प्रथमं त्रोटयित्वैकमपरस्य प्रतिग्रहः ॥१५९॥
प्रसृताकुञ्चितः स्थायः प्रसार्याकुञ्चितध्वनिः ।
स्थायिवर्णस्थितिः कम्पः स्थिर इत्याभिधीयते ॥१६०॥
एकैकस्मिन् स्वरे स्थित्वा स्थित्वा वाथ द्वयोर्द्वयोः ।
त्रिषु त्रिष्वथवा स्थायो रचितः स्थायुको मतः ॥१६१॥
ऊर्ध्वं प्रसारितः क्षिप्तः सूक्ष्मान्तोऽन्तेऽल्पतां गतः ।

[1]Comp. P.L.S. who says, "There are some fine features of musical rendering which appeal only to an aesthete and not to the common man." (*I.M.J.*, no. 5, p. 31)

[2]'S' interprets *mahān* (lit. big) as *sthūla* (hitherto rendered as rich).

[3]*Ghoṣa* is lit. noise, tumult or sound in general.

[4]*Svara* is lit. tone.

(c) The obscure (*aprasiddha*) *sthāya-s:* (152-176 b)

(i) The distinctly defined *sthāya-s*:

1. *Vaha*: The *sthāya-s* in which the notes tremble, as if under a heavy burden, are related to *Vaha* [1] (152 a b)

2. *Akṣarāḍambara*: Those (*sthāya-s*) which abound in the display of syllables[2] appertain to them (the *akṣara-s*, i. e. syllables). (152 c d)

3. *Ullāsita*[3] is associated with fast ascending notes. (153 a b)

5. *Taraṅgita* is that (*sthāya*) wherein the notes move like the waves of the Ganges (153 c d)

5. *Salambita*: When the *sthāya* is so construed in a song as to sound like the swirling of water in a half- filled jar, it is said by the experts to be *salambita*.[4] (154)

6 *Avaskhalita* is said to be that (*sthāya*) which involves a speedy reversal from the lower register while descending.[5] (155 a-155 c)

7. *Troṭita* is that wherein having stayed on a certain note for some time its octave note having been touched (slightly) like the flame,[6] there is a return (to the starting point). (155 d-156 b)

8. *Sampraviṣṭa* is that which has its notes closely knit in the descent.[7] (156 c d)

9. *Utpraviṣṭa* is similarly (close knit) with notes in the ascent. (156 d-157 a)

[1]*Vahantaḥ*—lit. carrying (a burden). The purport is that the tones in the *sthāya-s* related to *vaha* tremble like the man oppressed by a heavy burden on his head.

[2]*Āḍambara*—lit. show or display (of syllables) in this context, implies the profusion of solfa syllables or verbal phrases forming part of the text of the song. Cf. P.L.S. who says, "the abundance of *akṣara-s* or syllables referred to here can come about in two ways i) by pronouncing the solfa syllables in quick successions and ii) by pronouncing the syllables of the verbal structure of *gita* in a similar way". (*I.M J.*, no. 5, p. 32)

[3]*Ullāsita*, observes P.L.S. "is one of the 15 *gamaka-s* but is not associated here with *kampa* which is an essential feature of *gamaka*. It is described as the order of ascent in fast tempo". (*I.M.J.*, no. 5, p. 32)

[4]*Salambita*—lit. elongated. 'S' points out that it is also read *pralambita* in certain MSS. PLS observes, "The analogy of the sound of water in a half-filled jar can be perceived in singing with very deep breath and with extra vigour. It cannot be perceived in fast tempo nor are all singers capable of demonstrating it". (*I.M.J.*, no. 5, p. 32)

[5]*Avaskhalita*—lit. drawn away from the right path. P.L S. elucidates, "This implies an abrupt descent, and then again a sudden ascent from *mandra* e.g. paa a s+a s ss ma ga ri ni dha pa paa a s s s ." (*I.M.J.*, no. 5, p. 32)

[6]Just as the flame cannot be touched for more than an instant, and the hand automatically returns to its previous position, so also in the case of *troṭita* the octave note is touched for on instant only, in order to revert to the original note (i.e. the starting point of the brief ascent). P.L.S. demonstrates it as for example Saaaa Śa+Sa (*I.M.J.*, no. 5, p 32).

[7]PLS demonstrates it as for example, sasasa ninini dhadhadha papapa..

10-12. *Niḥsṛta* (outflow), *bhrāmita* (in cyclic motion) and *dīrghakampita* (long shaken) these three are significant by their names[1] (157 b)

13. *Pratigrāhyollāsita* is that which projects and withdraws[2] (the notes) like the delightful playing ball which is thrown up to be caught again and again. (157 c-158 b)

14. *Alambavilambaka* is preceded by the fast tempo and succeded by the slow one towards the end[3]. (158 c d)

15. *Troṭitapratīṣṭa* is that where (the tonal movement) is discontinued in the higher or the lower register and is resumed in the other (i.e. the lower or the higher register respectively). (159)

16. *Praṣṛtākuñcita* is the *sthāya* in which the volume[4] is increased and then reduced. 160 a b)

17. *Sthira*: The (*sthāya*) wherein the notes of the *sthāyivarṇa* (steady pattern of tonal movement) are shaken is called *sthira*[5]. (160 c d)

18. *Sthāyuka*: The *sthāya* that is formed by staying on one, two or three notes at a time, is considered to be *sthāyuka*[6]. (161)

19. *Kṣipta* is that (*sthāya*) which is extended[7] in the higher register. (162 a)

20. *Sūkṣmānta* ends in reduced volume[8]. (162 b)

[1]P.L.S. elucidates these three on the basis of *Saṅgītasudhā* vide III, 229 and 230 as under:

(i) *Niḥsṛta:* This seems to imply the 'flowing out' of *svara-s* from a particular point e.g. saaa+ga ma pa ni sa gaaaa a s+a s s.

(ii) *Bhrāmita:* This may be interpreted as the cyclic movement of notes bearing the analogy of a merry-go-round; e.g. ma ni dha ma ma ni dha ma ma ni ni ma ni ni dha ma etc.

(iii) *Dīrghakampita:* "This obviously refers to long shakes". (*I.M.J.*, no. 5, pp. 32, 33)

[2]Comp. P.L.S. who says, "Where notes are thrown out like a ball and are again, caught up; e.g. in sa maa ma ma saa sa, ri paa pa pa ri ri, ga dhaa dha dha gaa ga."

[3]Comp. P.L.S. who says, "That which is sung or played first in *druta laya* and then in *vilambita laya.* This can find a place in a composition or in *gatibheda* (e.g. 1/4, 1/2, 1) or in tonal embellishments."

[4]*Dhvani* is literally, (musical) sound.

[5]P.L.S. interprets it as "*Kampa* in *sthāyi varṇas* i.e. repeated or constant shake on solitary *svara-s.*" (*I.M.J.*, no. 5, p. 33)

[6]Comp. with the interpretation of P.L.S. who says, "Staying on one, two or three *svara-s* and then proceeding forward, e.g. sa a ri i i ga a a, or sa ri i i, ga ma a a, ma pa a a, or sa ri ga a a ri ga ma a a etc." (*I.M.J.*, no. 5, p. 33). The word *sthāyuka* lit. means stationary, enduring, prolonged)

[7]*Kṣipta*—lit. thrown. P.L.S. identifies it with the modern *phenk* (Hindi). (cf. *I.M.J.* no. 5, p. 33)

[8]'S' interprets that it is more volume in the beginning and less in the end. P.L.S. associates intensity or volume with it and observes, "This is very much similar to No. 16 above in this group viz. *Praṣṛtākuñcita*, but the latter implies the extra broadening (of volume) in the beginning whereas this may begin in the normal intensity". (*I.M.J.*, no. 5, p. 34). *Sūkṣmānta* literally means that which becomes slender towards the end.

(ii) तत्र सङ्कीर्णलक्षणाः स्थायाः

शब्दः प्रकाशते येषु धृतिभृत्यादिवर्जितः ॥१६२॥
स्वभावादेव शब्दस्य प्रकृतिस्थस्य ते मताः ।
येषु सूक्ष्मीकृताः शब्दास्ते कलायाः प्रकीर्तिताः ॥१६३॥
भृशं प्राणप्रतिग्राह्या ये स्युराक्रमणस्य ते ।
ते स्थाया घटनाया ये शिल्पिना घटिता इव ॥१६४॥
सुखदास्तु सुखस्य स्युश्चालिजंक्केति कीर्तिता ।
स्थायास्तदन्विताश्चालेरंशो जीवस्वरो मतः ॥१६५॥
तत्प्राधान्येन ये गीताः स्थाया जीवस्वरस्य ते ।
वेदध्वनिनिभध्वानाः स्थाया वेदध्वनेर्मताः ॥१६६॥
अन्तःसारो घनत्वस्य यथार्थः शिथिलो मतः ।
दुष्करोऽवघटः प्रोक्तः प्लुतोऽत्यन्तविलम्बितः ॥१६७॥
रागेणेष्टः स्वपूर्त्यर्थं रागेष्ट इति कीर्तितः ।
स स्यादपस्वराभासो भात्यपस्वरवत्तु यः ॥१६८॥
स्तब्धः स्थायस्तु बद्धः स्याद्बहुत्वं मधुरध्वनेः ।
यस्मिन् कलरवस्यासौ छान्दसोऽचतुरप्रियः ॥१६९॥
सुकराभास इत्युक्तो दुष्करः सुकरोपमः ।
घण्टानादवदायातस्तारान्मन्द्रं तु संहितः ॥१७०॥
लघुर्गुरुत्वरहितो ध्रुवकाभोगयोस्तु यः ।
अन्तरे सोऽन्तरो वक्रो यथार्थः सुकरस्तु यः ॥१७१॥
तारे दीप्तप्रसन्नोऽसौ सुकरः कोमलध्वनिः ।
प्रसन्नमृदुरित्युक्तो गुरुरन्वर्थनामकः ॥१७२॥
ह्रस्वः स्तोकः परौ द्वौ तु स्यातामन्वर्थनामकौ ।
शब्दशारीरगुणतः सुकरः सुस्वरोऽथवा ॥१७३॥
यः कस्यचिन्न सर्वेषां सोऽसाधारण उच्यते ।
सदृशो यस्तु सर्वेषामसौ साधारणः स्मृतः ॥१७४॥
न वाञ्छति वहन्यादिर्यः स्वनिर्वाहहेतवे ।
उच्यते स निराधारः सुकरो दुष्करोपमः ॥१७५॥

(ii) The indistinctly defined obscure *sthāya-s:*

1. *Prakṛtistha-śabda:* The *sthāya-s* in which the (musical) sound is manifested naturally without the effort (to adjust it) by reduction or by increase (of volume)[1], are considered to pertain to *prakṛtistha-śabda* (natural voice). (162-163 b)

2. *Kalā*: The *sthāya-s* in which the tonal intensity is reduced are said to be related to *kalā*[2] (163 d).

3. *Ākramaṇa*: The (*sthāya-s*) that can be taken (i.e. produced) only with a great effort of *prāṇa* (vital breath) appertain to *ākramaṇa.* (164 a b)

4. *Ghaṭanā*: The *sthāya-s* that are formulated as though by an artisan pertain to *ghaṭanā*[3]. 164 c d)

5. *Sukha*: Those that are comforting are known to be related to *sukha*[4] (comfort). (165 a b).

6. *Cāli* is known as *jakkā*. The *sthāya-s* incorporating it pertain to *cāli*[5]. (165 b c)

7. *Jīvasvara*: *Aṁśa* (the fundamental note) is considered to be *jīvasvara* (the vital tone). The *sthāya-s* that are sung with its predominance are related to *jīvasvara*[6]. (165 d-166 b)

8. *Vedadhvani*: The *sthāya-s* that sound like the vedic chant are considered to pertain to *vedadhvani*[7]. (166 c d)

9. *Ghanatva* is inherent intensity (*antaḥsāra*) and the *sthāya-s* having it, pertain to *ghanatva*[8] (167 a)

10. *Śithila* is considered to be significant by its name[9] i.e. loose. (167 b)

11. *Avaghaṭa* is said to be difficult of performance. (167 c)

12. *Pluta* is extremely prolonged (i.e. in very slow tempo). (167 d)

[1]*Dhṛti* and *bhṛtī* are interpreted by 'S' as *ākuñcana* (overall reduction) and *pūraṇa* (filling) of volume. Comp. this with P.L.S. who elucidates it as—"where the notes are produced with normal intensity without extra force or softness". (*I.M.J.*, no. 5, p. 34)

[2]P.L.S. explains the *sthāya-s* pertaining to *kalā* as "implying artificial reduction of intensity". (cf. *I.M.J.*, no. 5, p. 34)

[3]*Ghaṭanā*—lit. formulation in this context.

[4]P.L.S. interprets it as "pleasant to the ear", and thereby distinguishes it from *rakti* which is not only pleasant but also delightful to the mind i.e. that which imparts an emotional colour to it. (cf. *I.M.J.*, no. 5, p. 34)

[5]Śārṅgadeva does not obviously define it, but he has resolved to give brief or indistinct definitions only. It seems it was quite well known in his time as it was called *jakkā* among the common folk.

[6]*Aṁśa* is obviously used in the sense of the fundamental note here, and not as in verse 133 ante.

[7]P.L.S. elucidates similarity to the Vedic chant i.e. *vedadhvani* as, "either staying too long on a note or moving around two or three notes for a long time'; (cf. *I.M.J.*, no. 5, p. 35).

[8]P.L.S. interprets *antaḥsāra* as "fulness or richness of voice". *Ghanatva* literally means density or solidity.

[9]*Śithila*—lit. loose, is interpreted by 'S' as the counterpart of *ghanatva.*

13. *Rāgeṣṭa*: (The *sthāya* that) is desirable for the completion of the *rāga* is known as *rāgeṣṭa*[1]. (168 a b)

14. *Apasvarābhāsa*. That (*sthāya*) which appears to be (but is not) like *apasvara*[2] would be *apasvarābhāsa*[3]. (168 cd)

15. *Baddha*[4] is the motionless *sthāya*. (169 a)

16. *Kalarava*: The profusion of sweet sounds in (a *sthāya*) appertains to *kalarava*[5] (169 b c)

17. *Chāndasa* appeals to the uninitiated.[6] (169 d)

18. *Sukarābhāsa* is said to be that (*sthāya*) which, even though difficult (of rendering), resembles[7] an easy (task). (170 a b)

19. *Saṁhita* is the one that is spread from the higher to the lower register like the sound of *ghaṇṭā*[8] (bell). (170 cd)

20. *Laghu* is devoid of *gurutva*[9] (heaviness). (171 a)

21. *Antara* is that (*sthāya*) which is between *dhruva* and *ābhoga*.[10] (171 b c)

[1]Literally rendered it would read, "(That which) is desired by the *rāga* for its own completion, is said to be *rāgeṣṭa*.

[2]*Apasvara* is defined by the author as (a blemish of) singing with an omitted note (of a *rāga*) vide 35 b ante. Most probably here too the author is using the word in this technical sense, as it becomes clear from his expression *bhāti* (appears) *apasvara-vat* (like *apasvara*). That is, the *apasvarābhāsa* appears, not as *apasvara* but, like *apasvara* i.e. resembling *apasvara*. In other words, *Apasvarābhāsa* bears the appearance of resemblance and not identity with *asasvāra*. 'S' interprets it as "that (*sthāya*) which (while actually) being in tune, appears to be out of tune".

[3]*Apasvara*—lit. unwanted note (*apa*+*svara*), and *apasvara*+*ābhāsa*, lit. means the appearance of the unwanted note (*apasvara*+*ābhāsa*)

[4]'S' interprets *stabdha* (motionless) in the sense of *nigalita iva* i.e. stagnating as it were. P.L.S. elucidates by saying that, "this implies a standstill position of a note e.g. when a note is prolonged and movement seems to be absent (though physically a single tone also implies a succession of vibration)". (cf. *I.M.J.*, on. 5, p. 35).

[5]'S' interprets the *bahutva* (profusion) of sweetness of tone negatively as "the absence of the lack of sweet sound (tone)." P.L.S. elucidates *kalarava*: "*Bahutva* (abundance) of sweet *dhvani* (tones) can be explained in melodic music in terms of the simultaneous tones of many instruments or voices produced in unison or in octave", (cf. *I.M.J.*, no. 5, p. 36). Obviously, the phrase *madhuradhvaniḥ* (of sweet sound or sounds or tones) implies the interpretation of *bahutva* in terms of number. The word *dhvani* has been rendered in its literal sense as 'sound' in order to include voice and instrumentation. Actually, it implies musical sound.

[6]*Acatura-priya*—lit. dear to the undiscriminative audience. P.L.S. refers to the demonstration of rivalry between a vocalist or an instrumentalist on the one hand and the drum accompanist (*tablā-vādaka*) on the other as an example of *chāndasa-priya*.

[7]*Upamaḥ*—lit. resembling or similar, but the implication is, "that which is difficult yet appears to be easy".

[8]The simile of the bell is given to illustrate the decreasing intensity of the resulting overtones when a bell is struck.

[9]*Gurutva*—lit. means heaviness; its meaning as applied to music here is not clear. P.L.S. conjectures that being devoid of *gurutva* "may mean either the use of *laghu* (short) syllables in abundance or an easy flowing way of singing or playing".

[10]*Dhruva* and *ābhoga* are the sections of *prabandha*, a melodic composition which is to be dealt with in the next chapter.

22. *Vakra* is significant by itself (i.e. twisted). (171 d)

23. *Dīptaprasanna* is that which is easily[1] (employed) in the higher register. (171 d-172 a)

24. *Prasannamṛdu* is that which is easy (to produce) and of tender tones.[2] (172 b c)

25. *Guru* is significant by its name[3] (i.e. heavy). (172 d)

26. *Hrasva* is short.[4] ((173 a)

27-28. *Śithilagāḍha* and *dīrgha*: The following two (viz. *śithilagāḍha*[5] and *dīrgha*[6]) are significant by their names. (173 a b)

29. *Asādhāraṇa* is said to be that which by virtue of the excellence of voice and *śārīra*,[7] is easily accessible to or remains in tune[8] in the case of a rare (musician) but not in the case of all[9] (musicians). (173 c-174 b)

30. *Sādhāraṇa* is known to be that which is similarly accessible to all.[10] (174 c d)

[1]'S' reads *sakala* (full) in stead of *sukara* (easy) and consequently interprets it as, "that which appears fully in the high register is *dīpta-prasanna*." This is supported by *Saṅgītasudhā* (III 250).

[2]P.L.S. opines that "*mṛdu* should be taken here to stand for *mandra*, i.e. easy flowing and tender tones in '*mandra*' are applied here." (cf. *I.M.J.*, no. 5, p. 37)

[3]*Guru* is lit. heavy or dense, in contradiction with *laghu* described earlier (no. 20 above). Accordingly, P.L.S. conjectures that it may stand for an abundance of long syllables or a sense of heaviness in tone-production. (cf. *I.M.J.*, no. 5, p. 37)

[4]P.L.S. infers shortness of duration (cf. *I.M.J.*, no. 5, p. 37). 'S' interprets it as 'dwarfish'.

[5]*Śithila-gāḍha* seems to be an intermediate variety in-between *śithila* and *gāḍha* which seems to be the same as *ghanatva* from the cryptic definition given. *Śithila* lit. means loose or slack and *gāḍha* lit. means thick. Comp. P.L.S. who elucidates it as "that which has both *śithilatā* (slackness) and *gāḍhatā* or *sabalatā* (force)," vide *I.M.J.*, no. 5, p. 37. However, it cannot be considered to be a mixture of the two, since in that case it would have been included in the category of *miśra* (mixed) *sthāya-s*.

[6]*Dīrgha* is lit. long, and P.L.S. interprets it to be the opposite of *hrasva* (short) and therefore signifying length of duration (cf. *I.M.J.*, no. 5, p. 37).

[7]*Śārīra*—lit. pertaining to the body, it is a technical term already defined as the capability of voice inherent in the body for the delineation of a *rāga* even without any practice. Thus, it may well be considered to be one of the prominent factors that go to constitute a musical genius.

[8]*Susvara*—lit. of good tone, technically signifies the ability of producing the appropriate tone without a fault; or, alternatively, as 'S' interprets it "that which is free from *apasvara*", which has been defined by the author as (a blemish of) singing an omitted note.

[9]The purport is that the *sthāya* called *asādhāraṇa* (lit. uncommon) requires extraordinary excellence of voice, capacity for singing and precision of tone production, and is therefore not easily approachable for all. It can be rendered by a very few extra-ordinarily gifted musicians.

[10]That is why it is called *asādhāraṇa* (lit. common). This may be understood in contradiction with the *asādhārana* described above.

31. *Nirādhāra*: The (*sthāya*) that does not require *vahanī*[1] etc. for discharging its function is called *nirādhāra*[2] (supportless). (175 a b c)

32. *Duṣkarābhāsa* is said to be that (*sthāya*) which, even though easy (to produce), is like[3] a difficult one. (175 f-176 a)

33. *Miśraka* is so called because of being a (product of) mixture.[4] (176 b)

(घ) मिश्रस्थायाः

दुष्कराभास इत्युक्तो मिश्रणान्मिश्रको मतः ।
आनन्त्यान्नैव शक्यन्ते भेदा मिश्रस्य लक्षितुम् ॥१७६॥
दिक्प्रदर्शनमात्रार्थमुच्यन्ते तेषु केचन ।

यो यस्मिन् बहुलः स्थायः स तेन व्यपदिश्यते ॥१७७॥

साम्ये तु मिश्रनामैव स त्विदानीं प्रपञ्च्यते ।
तिरिपान्दोलितो लीनकम्पितः कम्पिताहतः ॥१७८॥
तिरिपस्फुरितो लीनस्फुरितः स्फुरिताहतः ।
लीनकम्पितलीनश्च त्रिभिन्नकुरुलाहतः ॥१७९॥
प्लावितोल्लसितवलिर्वलिहुम्फितमुद्रितः ।
नामितान्दोलितवलिर्वलिनामितकम्पितः ॥१८०॥
आन्दोलितप्लावितकसमुल्लासितन्नामितः ।
तिरिपान्दोलितवलित्रिभिन्नकुरुलोऽपरः ॥१८१॥

[1]*Vahanī* has already been defined (vide 114 c-118 b ante) as the shaking (of notes) either in the ascent or in the descent, and also in the *sañcārī* (*varṇa*) with a constant tremor. Many of its subvarieties are mentioned. This is considered to be a well known *sthāya*.

[2]*Nirādhāra* implies, "that which does not stand in need of anything external to itself." That is why P.L.S. observes that "it seems to be the opposite of *apekṣita* (vide 142 d-150 b). It can be conceived as the last phrase in a particular section which brings about a sense of completeness and which does not require any other phrase for its completeness." (cf. *I.M.J.*, no. 5, p. 38) 'S' includes the *gamaka-s* such as *vali, humphita* and the like as signified by *ādi* (etc.) of the text.

[3]*Duṣkaropama*—lit. like a difficult one, implies a similarity of outward appearance. Obviously, this is the opposite of *sukarābhāsa* (lit. appearing to be easy). (Vide 170 a b ante). Comp. P.L.S. who interprets it as an "artificial rendering of a piece so as to give it an air of being very difficult." (cf. *I.M.J.*, no. 5, p. 38)

[4]The mixed varieties also include the fifteen *gamaka-s* among them. These are being dealt with by the author as a separate category.

त्रिभिन्नलीनस्फुरितप्लावितान्दोलितः परः ।
वहनीढालयोर्ढालवहन्योः शब्दढालयोः ॥१८२॥
वहनीयन्त्रयोच्छायायन्त्रयोः शब्दयन्त्रयोः ।
वहनीच्छाययोर्यन्त्रवाद्यशब्दभवः परः ॥१८३॥
तीक्ष्णप्रेरितकस्तीक्ष्णप्रेरितः स्वरलङ्घितः ।
ढालशब्दोत्थयन्त्रोत्थवाद्यशब्दभवः परः ॥१८४॥
ढालच्छाया यन्त्रवाद्यशब्दशब्दभवोऽपरः ।
प्रलम्बितावस्खलितस्त्राटितोल्लासितः परः ॥१८५॥
संप्रविष्टोत्प्रविष्टश्च संप्रविष्टतरङ्गितः ।
प्रतिग्राह्योल्लासितश्चोत्क्षिप्तालम्बविलम्बकः ॥१८६॥
स्यात् त्रोटितप्रतीष्टोत्प्रविष्टनिःसरणः परः ।
दीर्घकम्पितसूक्ष्मान्तभ्रामितस्थायुकोऽन्यकः ॥१८७॥
वहाक्षराडम्बरजः प्रसृताकुञ्चितस्थिरः ।
भ्रामितक्षिप्तसूक्ष्मान्ततरङ्गितविलम्बितः ॥१८८॥
एते षट्त्रिंशदन्येऽपि विज्ञातव्या दिशानया ।

(d) The mixed (*miśra*) *sthāya-s*.

Since the varieties of mixed *sthāya-s* are infinite, it is not possible to indicate them (all). However, in order to indicate the direction[1] (i.e., to illustrate), some of them are related here. (176-177 b)

Whatsoever (mixed variety) is dominated by whichever (*sthāya*), it is named after that.[2] Where (the constituents are) equal, the name *miśra*[3] alone is (applied). Thus, it (*miśra sthāya*) is now formulated (as under): (177 c-178 b)

[1]*Dik-pradarśana-mātrā-rtham*—lit. "only for indicating the direction", implies the author proposes to briefly indicate the process of their formation and name a few of them by way of illustration.

[2]That is, the resultant mixture of combination is known by the name of the predominating *sthāya* e.g. *śabda-miśra*, *ḍhāla-miśra* and so on.

[3]Such as, *tiripāndolita* (*tiripa*+*āndolita*) and so on, where two are equally mixed, it becomes a bi-mixture (*dviyogaja*), with three it is tri-mixture (*triyogaja*) and with four it is a mixture of four (*caturyogaja*) and so on. In this way thirty-six varieties are spoken of.

1. *Tiripāndolita*
2. *Līnakampita*
3. *Kampitāhata*
4. *Tiripasphurita*
5. *Līnasphurita*
6. *Sphuritāhata*
7. *Līnakampitalīna*[1]
8. *Tribhinnakurulāhata*
9. *Plāvitollāsitavali*
10. *Valihumphitamudrita*
11. *Nāmitāndolitavali*
12. *Valināmitakampita*
13. *Āndolitaplāvitakasamullāsitannāmita*
14. *Tiripāndolitavalitribhinnakurula*
15. *Tribhinnalīnasphuritaplāvitāndolita*
16. *Of vahanī and ḍhāla (or) ḍhāla and vahanī*[2]
17. *Of śabda and ḍhāla*
18. *Of vahanī and yantra*
19. *Of chāyā and yantra*
20. *Of śabda and yantra*
21. *Of vahanī and chāyā*
22. *Of yantra and vādyaśabda*
23. *Tīkṣṇaprerita*[3]
24. *Tīkṣṇapreritasvaralaṅghita*
25. *Of ḍhāla, śabda, yantra, and vādyaśabda*
26. *Of ḍhāla, chāyā, yantra, vādyaśabda and śabda*
27. *Pralambitāvaskhalita*
28. *Troṭitollāsita*
29. *Sampraviṣṭotpraviṣṭa*
30. *Sampraviṣṭotaraṅgita*
31. *Pratigrāhyollāsitotkṣiptālambavilambaka*[4]
32. *Troṭitapratīṣṭotpraviṣṭaniḥsaraṇa*

[1]The name '*līna-kampita-līna*' sounds somewhat strange. A mixture implies the combination of different *sthāya-s*, so the repetition of *līna* is quite unintelligible. Probably some other name might have been there in the original.

[2]The text enumerates the combination of *vahanī* and *ḍhāla* twice keeping both in the first and the second position respectively. However, it appears that the author means to offer the choice of both the practices as the form of one combination.

[3]The text *tīkṣṇa-preritakastīkṣṇapreritaḥ-svaralaṅghitaḥ* in the Ad. ed. has been modified to read as *tīkṣṇapreritasvaralaṅghitaḥ*, as obviously the *visarga* at the end of *prerita* is misplaced due to some scribal error.

[4]Ad. ed. reads it as *utkṣiptālambavilambakaḥ* which isolates *utkṣipta* from the compound. The text has therefore been corrected accordingly.

33. *Dīrghakampitasūkṣmāntabhrāmitasthāyuka*
34. *Of vahākṣarāḍambara*
35. *Prasṛtākuñcitasthira*
36. *Bhrāmitakṣiptasūkṣmāntatarangita-vilambita* (178 c-188)

These are thirtysix (mixed *sthāya-s*). Similarly, others can also be conceived accordingly. (189 a b)

Mixed (*miśra*) *sthāya-s* are formed by intermixing two or more of the *sthāya-s* already mentioned in the last two (a-b) categories. Śārṅgadeva has mentioned the names of 36 mixed *sthāya-s* only, though he has also indicated the possibility of forming many more on this pattern. "*Saṅgītarāja* mentions 66 varieties further sub-divided as follows according to the number of varieties mixed into one viz., *dviyogaja*—29, *triyogaja*—16, *caturyogaja*—10, *pañcayogaja*—5 and *ṣaṭsaṁyogaja*—6=66" (cf. P.L.S., *I.M.J.*, no. 5, p. 38).

In the history of Indian music, Śārṅgadeva is the first author who has dealt comprehensively with the *sthāya-s*. Though, neither Mataṅga nor Bharata has mentioned this concept in their treatment of the music theory of their times, Premlata Sharma (henceforth referred to as P.L.S.), in her article, "The concept of *Sthāya* in Indian *Saṅgītaśāstra*" (cf. *I.M.J.*, no. 3, 1965) opines that, the origin of this concept and the tradition of performance built upon it during the 12th and the 13th century can be traced to their texts. As she observes, "*Sthāya* or *ṭhāya* is a very important concept of Indian *Saṅgītaśāstra*, which has almost fallen completely into oblivion. It is akin to *gamaka*, but has a much wider scope, embracing all aspects of musical tone and its embellishments". Apart from Śārṅgadeva, Pārśvadeva who is considered to be his contemporary, has dealt with *sthāya-s* in his *Saṅgītasamayasāra*. Some of the later writers have also dealt with *sthāya-s*, notably Raghunathabhūpa in his *Saṅgīta Sudhā*, Kumbha in his *Saṅgītarāja*, and Tulajadhipa in his *Saṅgītasārāmṛita*; but they have more or less reproduced the version of *Saṅgītaratnākara*. (cf. P.L.S., *I.M.J.*, no. 3, 1965)

Tracing the origin of the concept of *sthāya* P.L.S. in her article (already mentioned) concludes that, "*Sthāya* was evolved through an analysis of the various elements contributing to variety in tonal rendering".

The important and wide prevalence of *sthāya-s* in the practice of rendering *rāga-s* is obivious from the very fact that Śārṅgadeva details ninetysix *sthāya-s* many of which are very well defined.

The author has classified the *sthāya-s* primarily in three categories viz. (i) *prasiddha*, (well known), (ii) *aprasiddha*, (obscure), and (iii) mixed. The first category is further subdivided into two classes viz. (i) the well known and (ii) significant by name. The names of the latter are so designed as to suggest their function.

The *aprasiddha* (obscure) *sthāya-s* are further subdivided as distinctly defined and indistinctly defined ones. Firstly, the author proceeds to deal with those twenty *sthāya-s* that are obscure i.e. which are not so well-known, and yet are distinctly defined. In other words, the form and the function of these *sthāya-s* is quite definitely known though they can be said to be not so popular in the author's time as those of the former category.

As already mentioned, the obscure (*aprasiddha*) *sthāya-s* are further subdivided by the author into two classes viz. the distinctly defined and the indistinctly defined. The author, having dealt with the first category, proceeds to deal with the second one. It will appear that the difinitions of those *sthāya-s* are vague and indistinct and merely point out a certain characteristic feature, more or less inferred from their names in general terms. Therefore, they are not, properly speaking, to be considered as definitions; and yet they offer an insight into their essential feature and give us an idea about their individual function in the context of *rāga-s*.

(xii) आलप्तिस्तद्भेदाश्च

(क) आलप्तिलक्षणम्, भेदद्वयोद्देशश्च

रागालपनमालप्तिः प्रकटीकरणं मतम् ॥१८९॥

सा द्विधा गदिता रागरूपकाभ्यां विशेषणात् ।

(xii) *Ālapti* and its types (189 c-202)

(a) The definition of *ālapti*:

Ālapti is the vocalization of *rāga* which is considered to be (the process of) manifesting it. That[1] is said to be twofold as qualified by *rāga* and *rūpaka*. (189 c-190 b)

(ख) रागालप्तिः

रागालप्तिस्तु सा या स्यादनपेक्ष्यैव रूपकम् ॥१९०॥

स्वस्थानैः सा चतुर्भिः स्यादिति गीतविदो विदुः ।

यत्रोपवेश्यते रागः स्वरे स्थायी स कथ्यते ॥१९१॥

ततश्चतुर्थो द्व्यर्धः स्यात् स्वरे तस्मादधस्तने ।

चालनं मुखचालः स्यात् स्वस्थानं प्रथमं च तत् ॥१९२॥

द्व्यर्धस्वरे चालयित्वा न्यसनं तद् द्वितीयकम् ।

[1]'That' refers to *ālapti*.

स्थायिस्वरादष्टमस्तु द्विगुणः परिकीर्तितः ॥१९३॥
द्व्यर्धं द्विगुणयोर्मध्ये स्थिता अर्धस्थिताः स्वराः ।
अर्धस्थिते चालयित्वा न्यसनं तु तृतीयकम् ॥१९४॥
द्विगुणे चालयित्वा तु स्थायिन्यासाच्चतुर्थकम् ।
एभिश्चतुर्भिः स्वस्थानै रागालप्तिर्मता सताम् ॥१९५॥
स्तोकस्तोकैस्ततः स्थायैः प्रसन्नैर्बहुभङ्गिभिः ।
जीवस्वरव्याप्तिमुख्यै रागस्य स्थापना भवेत् ॥१९६॥

(b) *Rāgālapti:*

Indeed *rāgālapti* is entirely independent of *rūpaka.*[1] It (arises) by four *svasthāna-s*[2] (steps) as known to the vocal experts.[3] (190 c-191 b)

The note in which the *rāga* is established is said to be steady (*sthāyi*).[4] The fourth from it would be halfway (*dvyardha*).[5] Sounding of the note just below[6] it would be (called) *mukhacāla*; and that forms the first *svasthāna.*[7] (191 c-192)

[1]*Rāgālapti* is said to be entirely independent of *rūpaka,* because it is entirely free from the rules and regulations of *nibaddha* (composed) *gāna* (music) which is called *Prabandha, vastu* or *rūpaka* (cf. *S.R.*, IV.4-6)

[2]*Svasthāna-s* are explained in the following few verses. 'K' describes them as resting points in the rendering of a *rāga*. 'S' considers them to be the integral parts of *ālapti* (the *avayava-s* of *ālapti*).

[3]'S' sees a reference to Bharata and others in this expression.

[4]'K' elucidates, "the fundamental note (*aṁśa*), whichever in whatever *rāga* (even other than *ṣaḍja*), on which the *rāga* is settled, because it imparts stability to it is called the steady note (*sthāyin*)."

[5]The fourth note from the steady in ascent is halfway to the eighth note which completes the octave. Thus, the note which is fourth from the steady divides the octave into two, and since the eighth note is twice the first (i.e. the steady) in pitch, it (the fourth) is called *dvayardha*, dividing the octave in two halves. So, the expression has been translated as 'half way' to octave. *Dvyardha* technically means the half of the double (pitch). 'K' also points out that the range of a *svasthāna*, as defined here, includes the omitted notes as well. Thus the fourth note from the steady, *ṣaḍja* for instance, would be *madhyama*. Even if *ṛṣabha* is omitted in a certain *rāga*, it will remain the fourth note for the purpose of rendering *ālapti* and the arrangement of *svasthāna-s* in it.

[6]'K' observes that the expression 'the note below it' is suggestive. It includes all the notes in between the steady and the halfway notes; not only that, but it also includes the notes below the steady in the lower octave up to its half, for he argues that if the interpretation of text is limited to one note only, the *rāga* cannot be projected at all.

[7]The first *svasthāna* is technically knows as *mukhacāla* (lit. that which moves the mouth) in other words, the initial range of voice production. 'K' presents the purport as follows: "Beginning from the steady and considering the fourth note (from it) as the uppermost limit (which is not to be touched), rendering the intervening notes and returning to the steady as the final note constitutes the first *svasthāna*.

The second (*svasthāna*) consists in sounding the halfway (note) and (similarly) returning[1] (to the steady). The eighth note from the steady is known to be double (in pitch). The notes obtaining in-between the halfway note[2] and the double (pitch)—note are *ardhasthita*[3] (the other half) notes. The rendering of these (*ardhasthita*) notes and their return[4] forms the third (*svasthāna*). The fourth consists in rendering the eighth and returning to the steady as its final note. (193-195 b)

According to the learned, the (rendering) of these four *svasthāna-s* makes for *rāgālapti*. The delineation of *rāga* takes place thereafter through the use of small *sthāya-s* having clarity and various artful turnings[5] and permeated predominantly by the vital tone[6]. (195 c-196)

Ālapti is equated with the *ālapanam* of *rāga*, and not with *rāgālāpa* which has been defined vide *S.R.*, II.2.23 c-24 which essentially portrays the characteristic features of a *rāga* such as the initial note, the fundamental note, the pitch range and so on. The word *ālapti* is derived from the root *ā+lap*, to speak, to address, to converse etc. Likewise, the other two words viz. *ālāpa* and *ālapanam* are also derived from the same root. 'K' contends that since those three words are derived from the same root by applying different suffixes, there is a technical difference in their connotation. *Ālāpa* of masculine gender denotes predominantly the projection. (*āvirbhāva*) of the *rāga; ālapti*, of feminine gender, denotes predominantly the concealment of the *rāga*, and *ālapanam*, of neuter gender denoted both without any stress on either of the two aspects through which a *rāga* is manifested. He therefore argues that *ālāpa* and *ālapti* cannot be equated, though they can both be explained in terms of *ālapanam*.

Thus *ālapti* implies the manifestation of *rāga* through the vocalisation of its essential features, by employing different melodic phrases and tonal patterns.

Kallinātha, however, points out that apart from this general character which *ālapti* shares with *ālapa* and *ālapanam*, its specific function lies in temporarily obscuring the identity of *rāga* by taking resort to the *sañcāra-s*

[1]'K' elucidates "it implies taking the previous notes as said above and including the fourth note as well in the rendering of the *ālapti* and then returning to the steady." This is the range in which the rendering of *ālapti* attains its second *svasthāna*. 'S' supports the views of 'K'.

[2]That is, the fourth note from the steady.

[3]*Ardhasthita* lit. the notes situated in the (other) half excluding the eighth i.e. the fifth, sixth and the seventh.

[4]According to 'K' the *nyāsa* is in the steady (*sthāyin*). It seems to be the rule with every *svasthāna*, that the final note has to be the steady.

[5]*Bahubhaṅgi—Bhaṅgi* is an artful curve or turning. The whole phrase indicates the use of various types of such artistic devices.

[6]*Jīvasvara* (lit. the vital tone) is the fundamental note. The *sthāya-s* are so conceived as to bring about a very frequent use and profusion of the vital tone.

(movements) that are common to other *rāga-s* as well. He elucidates this phenomenon on the analogy of Devadatta entering and sitting in the royal court. He says that, when a member of the royal court, Devadatta for instance, enters the court, he is marked distinctly as so and so; but when he takes his seat among his colleagues he loses his personal identity and becomes one among many. However, if he rises again with some purpose, he is again recognised as so and so. Thus, according to him the function of *ālapti* is to manifest the *rāga* through the alternation of projection and concealment of its identity (cf. P.L.S., Introduction to *Bhāvaraṅgalaharī*, vol. II of Balwantrai Bhatt, pp. 3-5).

This *ālapti* is twofold according to its affiliation viz. *rāgālapti* and *rūpakā'apti*, the former being associated with *rāga* and the latter with *rūpaka*. *Rūpaka* is defined in the next chapter (IV.4-6) as another name for *prabandha* (a type of melodic composition). While *ālapti* is defined here, *rūpaka* is dealt with in the next chapter, but its *ālapti* is treated by the author in the present context.

(ग) रूपकालप्तिः

रूपकस्थेन रागेण तालेन च विधीयते ।
या प्रोक्ता रूपकालप्तिः सा पुनर्द्विविधा भवेत् ॥१९७॥
प्रतिग्रहणिकैकान्या भञ्जनीत्यभिधीयते ।
विधाय स्थायमालप्ते रूपकावयवो यदि ॥१९८॥
प्रतिगृह्येत सा प्रोक्ता प्रतिग्रहणिका बुधैः ।
भञ्जनी द्विविधा ज्ञेया स्थायरूपकभञ्जनात् ॥१९९॥
यदा तत्पदमानेन स्थायो रूपकसंस्थितः ।
नानाप्रकारः क्रियते सा ज्ञेया स्थायभञ्जनी ॥२००॥
तैः पदैस्तेन मानेन समग्रं रूपकं यदि ।
अन्यथा चान्यथा गायेदसौ रूपकभञ्जनी ॥२०१॥

(c) *Rūpakālapti:*

Definition:

That[1] which is constituted in the framework of *rāga* and *tāla* of a *rūpaka* is said to be *rūpakālapti*. That again is twofold. One is called *pratigrahaṇikā* and the other, *bhañjanī*. (197-198 a b)

[1]'That' stands for *ālapti*, 'the *ālapti* which'. . .

(i) *Pratigrahaṇikā*:

Having rendered[1] *sthāya*[2] (constituent part) of *ālapti*,[3] if an integral part[4] of *rūpaka* is resumed,[5] it[6] is called *pratigrahaṇikā* by the experts. (198 c-199 b)

(ii) *Bhañjanī*:

Bhañjanī is known to be twofold as it (lit.) breaks either *sthāya*[7] or *rūpaka*. (199 c-d)

When a *sthāya*[8] built in a *rūpaka*[9] is presented in various ways,[10] keeping the original measure of the respective *pada-s*,[11] it is known as *sthāya-bhañjanī*. (200)

If, however, one sings the entire *rūpaka* in quite different ways, keeping its original measure with original *pada-s*[12] it is (called) *rūpaka-bhañjanī*. (201)

[1] *Vidhāya*—lit. 'having laid down' i.e. having sung to begin with

[2] *Sthāya* in this context has a specific meaning. It refers, according to 'S', to the *svasthāna* of *rāgālapti*, which is a constituent part of it.

[3] By *ālapti*, what is meant here, according to 'K', is *rāgālapti*. This interpretation is supported by Siṁhabhūpāla's interpretation of *sthāya* as related in note 2 above.

[4] *Rūpakāvayava* is identified by P.L.S. with *muṁh* or *mukhḍā* of the modern Hindustani music. Accordingly, she interprets *pratigrahaṇikā*, in the modern context, to be the action comprising the singing of *ālāp-tān*, *bahalāvā* and such other devices that manifest the *rāga* time and again only in order to catch upon the *muṁh* or *mukhḍā*. Thus, she observes that most of the contemporary music involving *tāla* is of the order of *pratigrahaṇikā* (cf. Introduction to *Bhāvaraṅgalaharī* of B. Bhatt, pp. 5 & 6).

[5] *Pratigrahaṇa*—lit. 'taking back', implies the idea of releasing or giving up, and then taking back. That is why it has been rendered as 'resumed' instead of 'taken'.

[6] The pronoun 'it' refers to the entire process of rendering *ālapti*.

[7] In this context the word *sthāya* has quite a different meaning. 'K' interprets it as a part or section (*ekadeśa*) of *prabandha* (i.e. *rūpaka*) and 'S' also elucidates it as an *avayava* (a constituent part) of *prabandha*.

[8] *Sthāya*, in this context, is defined by 'K' as *prabandhaikadeśa* i.e. a section of *prabandha*, and by 'S' as the *avayava* (a constituent part) of *prabandha*.

[9] *Rūpakasaṁsthita* qualifies *sthāya* to the purport that it should form an integral part of *rūpaka* (i.e. *prabandha*).

[10] *Nānāprakāra* i.e. a particular section of *rūpaka* is rendered in different ways as 'S' elucidates it (*anekabhaṅgikaḥ*). 'K' says, it implies creative effort based on the genius of the performer (vocalist or instrumentalist).

[11] *Pada* is defined by 'K' as the subdivision of *vidārī* (a section) in the above context; while, by the measure of *pada-s*, he says, is meant the rest-period (of time) involved in a particular *kriyā* of (*tāla*).

[12] That is, the *pada-s* as defined in note 11 above. 'K' explains it on the analogy of meaningful words (*pada-s*) of a sentence that are related to each other in order to make a sentence, and are not used independently. The *pada-s* taken to be the sub-divisions of *vidārī* (a section) are employed in an integral form, and not independently. Comparing and identifying *rūpaka-bhañjanī* with the contemporary practice called '*bandiś-lauṭānā* or *ulṭānā*' a rare device of modern music, P.L.S. describes *pada* as significant in the context of vocal as well as instrumental music, and as constituted of words or phrases imitating the particular soundings of musical instruments (such as *nom tom*, *diri diri* etc.) set in the pattern of a section of *prabandha* (cf. Introduction to *Bhāvaraṅgalaharī*, II, p. 6).

(घ) आलप्तेः सामान्यलक्षणम्

वर्णालङ्कारसंपन्ना गमकस्थायचित्रिता ।
आलप्तिरुच्यते तज्ज्ञैर्भूरिभङ्गिमनोहरा ॥२०२॥

(d) The general definition of *ālapti*:

Ālapti is described by the experts as enriched by *varṇa* and *alaṅkāra*, variegated by *gamaka* and *sthāya*, and rendered charming by many tactful turnings.[1] (202)

Rūpaka is another name for *prabandha*, a musical composition to be dealt with in chapter IV. *Rūpakālapti* is the particular *ālapti* that is relevant to the singing of *prabandha-s* and essentially differs from *rāgālapti* in so far as it is set in the framework of *rāga* and *tāla* of *prabandha*.

(xiii) वृन्दम्, तद्भेदाश्च

(क) वृन्दलक्षणम्

गातृवादकसंघातो वृन्दमित्यभिधीयते ।
उत्तमं मध्यममथो कनिष्ठमिति तत् त्रिधा ॥२०३॥

(xiii) The ensemble (*vṛnda*) and its types: (203-223)

(a) The definition:

A company[2] of vocalists[3] and instrumentalists is called an ensemble[4] (*vṛnda*). (203 a b).

(ख) गायनवृन्दम्

चत्वारो मुख्यगातारो द्विगुणाः समगायनाः ।
गायन्यो द्वादश प्रोक्ता वांशिकानां चतुष्टयम् ॥२०४॥

[1]This definition applies to all the varieties of *ālapti*. *Bhaṅgi*, in this context, is identified by P.L.S. with "the modern *ḍhuranmuran*, which she elucidates as *joḍ—toḍ* (i e. joints and partings)", the devices that provide for a zigzag rendering. (cf. Introduction to *Bhāvaraṅgalaharī*, II, p. 6).

[2]*Saṅghāta*—lit. close union or (intimate) association.

[3]Singers as well as songstresses.

[4]*Vṛnda*—lit. a large number, group or heap, is here used in the sense of a group.

मार्दङ्गिकास्तु चत्वारो यत्र तद्वृन्दमुत्तमम् ।
मध्यमं स्यात्तदर्धेन कनिष्ठे मुख्यगायनः ॥२०५॥
एकः स्यात् समगातारस्त्रयो गायनिकाः पुनः ।
चतस्रो वांशिकद्वन्द्वं तथा मार्दलिकद्वयम् ॥२०६॥
उत्तमे गायनीवृन्दे मुख्यगायनिकाद्वयम् ।
दश स्युः समगायन्यो वांशिकद्वितयं तथा ॥२०७॥
भवेन्मार्दलिकद्वन्द्वं मध्यमे मुख्यगायनी ।
एका स्यात् समगायन्यश्चतस्रो वांशिकास्तथा ॥२०८॥
इतो न्यूनं तु हीनं स्याद्यथेष्टमथवा भवेत् ।
उत्तमाभ्यधिकं वृन्दं कोलाहलमितीरितम् ॥२०९॥

(b) The (vocal) ensemble:

It[1] is threefold—the ideal[2], the average, and the mini (203 c d).

(1) The best ideal ensemble:

The ensemble with four leading singers, eight following singers, twelve songstresses, four flutists and four drummers[3] is said to be ideal. (204-205 b)

(2) The average[4] is half of it.[5] (205 c).

(3) In the mini, there is one leading singer, three following singers, four songstresses, two flutists and two drummers. (205 d-206).

(4) In the ideal female vocal ensemble, there are two leading songstresses, ten following songstresses, two flutists and two drummers. (207-208 a)

(5) In the average (female vocal ensemble) there is one leading songstress, four following songstresses, one flutist and one drummer.[6] (208 b c d)

(6) Anything less than that[7] or at (one's) discretion makes a mini (female vocal ensemble). (209 a b)

[1]It signifies the band which is classified as ideal, average and small according to the number of vocalists and instrumentalists constituting it.

[2]The classification is based on the number of participants and is characterised as the best of all (*uttama*), medium, (*madhyama*) and small (*kaniṣṭha*) signifying the ideal, the average and the mini ensembles.

[3]*Mārdaṅgika*—lit. one who plays the *mṛdaṅga* which is a type of drum. Though it is thus restricted in its signification, it has been rendered as 'drummer' for want of a more specific word in English.

[4]*Madhyama*—lit. medium.

[5]Half of the personnel of the ideal one i.e., two leading singers, four following singers, six female singers, two flutists and two drummers.

[6]*Vāṁśikāḥ* of the text lit. means flutists, but since the drummer is not mentioned, 'S' interprets this plural to include one flutist and one drummer.

[7]'That' refers to the medium size average female vocal band.

(7) If the ensemble exceeds even the ideal one it is called *kolāhala*[1] (lit. uproar). (209 c d)

(ग) गायनवृन्दगुणा:

मुख्यानुवृत्तिर्मिलनंताललीनानुवर्तनम् ।
मिथस्त्रुटितनिर्वाहस्त्रिस्थानव्याप्तिशक्तिता ॥२१०॥
शब्दसादृश्यमित्येते प्रोक्ता वृन्दस्य षड् गुणाः ।

(c) The excellences of the (vocal) ensemble:

The following six excellences are spoken of with regard to the ensemble: a (sympathetic) following[2] of the leading singer(s), uniformity,[3] keeping of *tāla* and *laya* (rhythm), covering of each other's errors, the ability of operating in the range of three registers, and the similarity of voice.[4] (210-211 b)

(घ) कुतप:

आह वृन्दविशेषं तु कुतपं भरतो मुनिः ॥२११॥
ततस्य चावनद्धस्य नाट्यस्येति त्रिधा च सः ।
ततस्य कुतपे ज्ञेयो गायनस्य परिग्रहः ॥२१२॥
वीणा घोषवती चित्रा विपञ्ची परिवादिनी ।
वल्लकी कुब्जिका ज्येष्ठा नकुलोष्ठी च किंनरी ॥२१३॥
जया कूर्मी पिनाकी च हस्तिका शततन्त्रिका ।
औदुम्बरी च षट्कर्णः पौणो रावणहस्तकः ॥२१४॥
सारङ्ग्यालपनीत्यादेस्ततवाद्यस्य वादकाः ।
वांशिकाः पाविका-पाव-काहला-शङ्खवादकाः ॥२१५॥
मुहरीभृङ्गवाद्याद्यास्तथा तालधरा वराः ।
कुतपे त्ववनद्धस्य मुख्यो मार्दङ्गिकस्ततः ॥२१६॥
पणवो दर्दुरो डक्का मण्डिडक्का च डक्कुली ।

[1] *Kolāhala*—lit. 'a loud and confused noise', an uproar, suggests that such a big ensemble would be unwieldy.

[2] *Anuvṛtti*—lit. 'an attitude of following' i.e., of singing after the leading singer(s).

[3] *Milanam* is explained by 'S' as the absence of dissimilarity in singing.

[4] 'S' interprets *śabda-sādṛśyam* (lit. similarity of sound or words) as the extreme absence of dissimilarity of words. *Śabda* can be interpreted both as sound and as words; perhaps both are implied.

पटहः करटा ढक्का ढवसो घडसस्तथा ॥२१७॥

हुडुक्का डमरू रुञ्जा कुडुक्का कुडुवा तथा ।

निःसाणस्त्रिवली भेरी तुम्बकी बोम्बडी तथा ॥२१८॥

पट्टवाद्यं पटः कम्रा झल्लरीभाणसेल्लुकाः ।

जयघण्टा कांस्यतालो घण्टा च किरिकिट्टकम् ॥२१९॥

वाद्यानामेवमादीनां पृथग्वादकसंचयः ।

वराटलाटकर्णाटगौडगुर्जरकोङ्कणैः ॥२२०॥

महाराष्ट्रान्ध्रहम्मीरचोलैर्मलयमालवैः ।

अङ्गवङ्गकलिङ्गाद्यैर्नानाभिनयकोविदैः ॥२२१॥

अङ्गहारप्रयोगज्ञैर्लास्यताण्डवकोविदैः ।

विचित्रस्थानकप्रौढैर्विषमेषु सुशिक्षितैः ॥२२२॥

नाट्यस्य कुतपः पात्रैरुत्तमाधममध्यमैः ।

कुतपानाममीषां तु समूहो वृन्दमुच्यते ॥२२३॥

॥इति श्रीमदनवद्यविद्याविनोदश्रीकरणाधिपतिश्रीसोढलदेवनन्दननिःशङ्क-

श्रीशार्ङ्गदेवविरचिते सङ्गीतरत्नाकरे प्रकीर्णकाध्यायस्तृतीयः ॥

(d) The *kutapa*:

The sage Bharata has spoken of a special ensemble called *kutapa*,[1] which is threefold viz. as related to the stringed instruments, the membranous instruments and drama.[2] (211 c-212 b)

The ensemble of the stringed instruments is known to be constituted of

[1] *Kutapa*—signifies a group of musicians, dancers or actors. (cf. *N.S.*, XXVIII 4-6)

[2] The classification of *kutapa* in three types is not exclusive, rather it indicates the predominance of that particular type of instrument by which it is named. That is, in the ensemble of stringed instruments, the drums and the flutes are also employed, but it is the former that predominate.

Bharata has classified the musical instruments into four categories viz. stringed, membranous, wind and solid. Even these can be grouped into two broad categories on the basis of their function viz. the *svara* or *gīta vādya-s* i.e. the tone or melody instruments and the *tāla vādya-s*, the instruments of musical time and rhythm. It seems the *tata kutapa* (the ensemble of stringed instruments) is predominantly constituted of the tone-instruments and the *avanaddha kutapa* (the ensemble of the covered instruments) is made prominently of the *tāla*-instruments. The third type is a mixed variety with a very specific purpose, actors being prominent, the singers' company[1] consisting of the players of such stringed instruments as *vīṇā, ghoṣavatī, citrā, vipañcī, parivādinī, vallakī, kubjikā, jyeṣṭhā nakuloṣṭhī, kinnarī, jayā, kūrmī, pinākī, hastikā, śatatantrī, audumbarī, ṣaṭkarṇa, pauṇa, rāvaṇahasta, sāraṅgī* and *ālapanī*,[2] and also those of flute, *pāvikā, pāvā, kāhalā, śaṅkha, muharī* and the horn instruments alongwith the best *tāla* keepers.[3] (212 c-216 b)

In the ensemble of the drums[4] the main player is that of *mṛdaṅga*, and his company is distinguished by the players of *paṇava, dardura, ḍakkā, maṇḍiḍakkā, ḍakkulī, paṭaha, karaṭā, ḍhakkā, ḍhavasa, ghaḍasa, huḍukkā, ḍamarū, ruñjā, kuḍukkā, kuḍuvā, niḥsāṇa, trivalī, bherī, tumbakī, bombaḍī, paṭṭavādya, pataḥ, kamrā, jhallarī, bhāṇa, sellukā, jayaghaṇṭā, kāṅsyatāla, ghaṇṭā* and *kirikiṭṭa*. (216 c-220 b)

The theatrical ensemble is constituted by the different experts of *abhinaya* (acting) drawn from (different regions such as) *varāṭa, lāṭa, karṇāṭa, gauḍa, gurjara, koṅkaṇa, mahārāṣṭra, āndhra, hammīra, caula, malaya, mālava, aṅga, vaṅga* and *kaliṅga* etc.,[5] specialists of *aṅgahāra*[6] (dance movements) and the *lāsya*[7] and *tāṇḍava* (forms of dancing), (artists) mature in variegated static poses (*sthānaka*)[8] and by those who are well trained in the complex formations[9] (of dance). (220 c-223 a)

(This is three-fold) according to the best, the average and the dull members (constituting it). (223 a b)

[1]*Parigraha*—lit. a group of followers or attendants; technically signifies a band of associates.

[2]Some of these stringed instruments are described in Chapter VI and will be dealt with in their due context.

[3]The *kutapa* of the stringed instruments consists mainly of those instruments, but it also includes the wind instruments and the *tāla* instruments of the solid (*ghana*) category for keeping musical time.

[4]'S' interprets the text quite differently. He says that verses 215 & 216 a b describe an alternative ensemble which is obviously based on wind instruments. But 'K' includes the wind and the *tata* instruments in the orchestra of the stringed instruments. He says that since the wind instruments such as the flute are tone instruments and so are creative of song, they share this quality with the stringed instruments and are therefore included in the *tata kutapa* (stringed orchestra). The passage has been translated accordingly.

[5]These are the Sanskrit names of different regions of India as known to the medieval authors.

[6]*Aṅgahāra* signifies the action of displaying more than five *karaṇa-s* (synchronised movement of hands and feet) in a single action in the art of dancing.

[7]*Lāsya* and *tāṇḍava* signify two distinct styles of dancing. These are dealt with in Chapter VII.

[8]*Vicitrasthāna* variegated *sthānaka-s* such as *ālīḍha* and others spoken of in Chapter VII. *Sthāna* signifies the static pose in dancing.

[9]*Viṣameṣu* refers to such difficult dance patterns as *maṇḍala* and others described in Chapter VII.

The group of these *kutapa-s* is called *vṛnda.*[1] (223 c d)

It is difficult to relate the concept of *vṛnda* (group) with its modern forms such as band, the orchestra and so on because of its unique features. Two concepts are presented here: one is based on the size of the band which includes vocalists and instrumentalists and is primarily made up of musicians, and the other is based on its function which has a reference to a theatrical performance and which is attributed to Bharata. However, the peculiar feature of both these concepts that differentiates them from the contemporary forms is their vocal orientation.

[1]The joint operation of the three ensembles goes to constitute *vṛnda* according to Bharata.

Chapter IV

The Prabandha-s

चतुर्थः प्रबन्धाध्यायः

प्रथमप्रकरणम्

उपोद्घातः

(i) गीतलक्षणम्, तद्भेदाश्च

(क) गीतलक्षणम्

रञ्जकः स्वरसंदर्भो गीतमित्यभिधीयते ।

SECTION 1

Introductory

(i) The definition and classification of *gīta*: (1-4 b)

(a) The definition of *gīta*:

A delightful arrangement of notes is called *gīta*.[1] (1 a-b)

(ख) गीतस्य भेदद्वयम्

गान्धर्वं गानमित्यस्य भेदद्वयमुदीरितम् ॥१॥

(b) The classification of *gīta*:

Its twofold classification into *gāndharva* and *gāna*[2] is well known. (1 c-d)

[1]*Gītam* is the nominative singular of *gīta*. The case-endings have been ignored in the English version. So also *gāna* is given for *gānam* and *gāndharva* for *gāndharvam*. The word *gīta* lit. means that which 'is sung'.

[2]*Gāna*—The technical difference between the two concepts of *gāndharva* and *gāna* is clearly and briefly brought out by 'K' when he indentifies the former with *mārga* and the latter with *deśī* music. Thus, *gāna* signifies regional forms of music which did not strictly follow the norms of the *mārga* music. However, there are other subtle differences pointed out by Abhinavagupta but for whose explanation the distinction between the two concepts could not have been known.

(ग) गान्धर्वलक्षणम्

अनादिसंप्रदायं यद्गन्धर्वैः संप्रयुज्यते ।
नियतं श्रेयसो हेतुस्तद्गान्धर्वं जगुर्बुधाः ॥२॥

(c) The definition of *gāndharva*:

The ancient tradition[1] practised by the *gandharva-s* in accordance with definite rules[2], which is the means[3] of attaining the supreme good,[4] is declared by the wise to be *gāndharva*.[5] (2)

(घ) गानलक्षणम्

यत्तु वाग्गेयकारेण रचितं लक्षणान्वितम् ।
देशीरागादिषु प्रोक्तं तद्गानं जनरञ्जनम् ॥३॥
तत्र गान्धर्वमुक्तं प्रागधुना गानमुच्यते ।

(d) The definition of *gāna*:

However, that[6] which is composed by a master composer[7] in accordance with the features spoken of about the *deśī rāga-s* etc.[8] and (that) which is the delight of people is (called) *gāna*. (3)

Of these (two) the *gāndharva*[9] has already[10] been spoken of, now (therefore) *gāna* is being expounded. (4 a-b)

Chapter IV is entitled "*Prabandhādhyāya*" (lit. the Chapter pertaining

[1] *Anādi* of the text literally means 'beginningless' which it appears is a figurative usage to indicate the immemorable antiquity of the tradition under reference. *Sampradāya* is the line of teacher-disciple transmission of knowledge.

[2] *Niyatam*—Well defined in terms of *grāma*, *mūrcchanā*, *jāti* and so on.

[3] *Hetu*—lit. a cause instrumental to an effect.

[4] *Śreyas* is defined by 'S' as, "prosperity in this world and merit for the other as well as emancipation from the bondage of suffering." In other words, the *good* that is enjoyed at every level of existence i.e. the supreme good.

[5] 'K' elucidates that whatever forms of music have been expounded in the first two chapters from *jāti-s* to the *bhāṣā-s* constitute *gāndharva*. The *Deśi Rāga-s* and the compositional forms that are going to be described in this chapter constitute *gāna*.

[6] That 'form of music' or 'vocal composition' in the context.

[7] *Vāggeyakāra*—one who composes not only the musical form (*geya*) but also the verbal context (*vāk*) of the song. *Gāna* is composed by any master composer (i.e. a human being) but in contrast with it, *gāndharva* is considered to be of divine origin handed down through a beginningless tradition.

[8] 'S' includes the *rāgāṅga* etc. among *'deśī rāga-s* and by "etc." he interprets the singer's own improvisation and innovations.

[9] *Gāndharva* has been said by Bharata to be endearing to the gods (cf. *N.S.* G.O.S., IV, Ch. XXIIIV, sl. 9, p. 6). *Gāna* is distinguished from it as endearing to the people.

[10] The melodic structures dealt with in the first two chapters are referred to, as explained in note 9 above.

to the *Prabandha-s*). *Prabandha* is one of the three technical names for the *nibaddha* (structured) form of music as it will presently be defined; but since *nibaddha-gāna* (structured music) is a form of *gīta* (music), the author begins the chapter with the definition and the classification of *gīta*. It is notable that he has defined *saṅgīta* as the threefold art of *gīta*, *vādya*, and *nṛtya* (cf. *S.R.*, I.1.21). *Gīta* may therefore be interpreted as vocal music or melody. The classification of *gīta* as *gāndharva* and *gāna* may or may not be applicable to instrumental music, but surely here it is presented in the context of vocal music. However, *gīta*, as defined here, in some sense seems to include *vādya* as well, though perhaps that may not quite imply what we understand as the instrumental music today.

Gīta is classified in two main categories viz. *gāndharva* and *gāna*, the former representing a pre-historical tradition derived from divine sources and the latter indicating a historical development based on the pattern of popular and regional taste. 'K' straightaway identified *gāndharva* with *mārga* and *gāna* with *Deśī*. Bharata has used the term *gāndharva* to denote either the science of music (*saṅgītaśāstra*) or music (cf. *N.S.*, G.O.S. XXVIII, 8 & 11). 'K' however elucidates that the forms of melodic structures expounded in chapters 1 and 2 ante viz. from *jāti-s* to *antarabhāṣā-s* constitute *gāndharva*, and the forms such as the *rāgāṅga-s* etc., and what he is going to expound now viz. the *prabandha-s* constitute *gāna*. Thus, it would appear that the *gāndharva* form of music was considered to be out of date during Kallinātha's time, since it had acquired inflexibility and other worldly sanctity long ago.

At present, however, the author is concerned with *gāna* i.e. the *deśī* form of music which was popular and had a regional variety and colour of its own. But it is not necessary to accept the equation of *mārga* with *gāndharva* and *deśī* with *gāna*; for, the two classifications are quite different in the scope of what they are supposed to classify. Thus, whereas the concepts of *mārga* and *deśī* classify *saṅgīta* which, in terms of Śārṅgadeva, includes *gīta*, *vādya* and *nṛtya*, the concepts of *gāndharva* and *gāna* are employed in the present context to classify *gītam* (music in general) only.

(ii) गानभेदद्वयम्

निबद्धमनिबद्धं तद् द्वेधा निगदितं बुधैः ॥४॥

बद्धं धातुभिरङ्गैश्च निबद्धमभिधीयते ।
आलप्तिर्बन्धहीनत्वादनिबद्धमितीरिता ॥५॥

सा चास्माभिः पुरा प्रोक्ता निबद्धं त्वधुनोच्यते ।
संज्ञात्रयं निबद्धस्य प्रबन्धो वस्तु रूपकम् ॥६॥

(ii) Classification of *gāna*: (4 c-6)

The sages have declared it[1] to be twofold viz. *nibaddha*[2] (composed) and *anibaddha*[3] (improvised). (4 c-d)

That[4] which is composed of *dhātu-s*[5] (sections) and *aṅga-s*[6] (integral parts) is called *nibaddha*.[7] *Ālapti* being free from such structural limitations is known as *anibaddha*,[8] and that has already been dealt with by us. *Nibaddha* is now being expounded. *Nibaddha* has three names viz. *prabandha, vastu* and *rūpaka*. (5-6)

Gīta is classified as *gāndharva* and *gāna*, and *gāna* is here further classified or distinguished into two types viz. *nibaddham* (that which is structured or composed) and *anibaddhaṁ* (uncomposed or improvised). *Ālapti* is the instance of the latter and has been dealt with in chapter III (See 189 c-202). Now, the author proposes to deal with, what he calls, *nibaddha-gāna* which is popularly known by three names that probably emphasise three different aspects of the same melodic structure, though practically they are synonyms. As Kumbhā explains (cf. *S. Rāj.* II, 4.2.4-6), the name *prabandha* (*pra+bandha* lit. well-knit) emphasises the fact of the composition being well-knit, strongly built with secure structure; and in this sense *prabandha* is analogous to the *bandiś* of modern Hindustani music. *Rūpaka*, ordinarily means drama, or among the figures of speech, metaphor. In the first sense it is defined as that (action) in which the characteristics of the hero of the plot such as Rāma etc. are superimposed upon an actor and so on. In metaphor too certain characteristics of one are transposed upon the other. Thus, *rūpaka* as such refers to a situation (of drama) or a condition (of similarity). Even though *prabandha-s* are sung independently of any dramatic context, they do refer either to a situation that implies a particular emotion or a condition that has reference to a situation in life in general through the verbal text. Thus, the name *rūpaka* emphasises the emotive element of *prabandha*. Similarly, *vastu* is defined as the substratum of *dhātu-s* (sections) and *aṅga-s* (integral parts); in other words, 'that which

[1]The pronoun 'it' refers to *gāna* of the previous verse.

[2]*Nibaddha*-(*ni+baddha*=bound) literally means organised or structured.

[3]*Anibaddha*, similarly means the absence of the structuring design or organised delineation.

[4]'That' stands for *gāna*.

[5]*Dhātu* is defined in the next topic as an *avayava* (lit. a limb) of *prabandha* (a name for *nibaddha-gāna*) personified as man. In terms of composition it forms a section in it.

[6]*Aṅga* is also to be shortly defined as a part of the human organism, a metaphorical personification of *prabandha*.

[7]*Nibaddha* is difficult to render into English precisely. As already pointed out, it is structured on a certain pattern that endows it with more or less a definite compositional form.

[8]*Anibaddha* mostly consists of *ālapti* which is free from such structural limitations as are naturally involved in a compositional pattern. The word denotes a negative concept with reference to *nibaddha*.

is observed to be the *constituted* as related to the *constituents*'. *Vastu*, in this sense, is analogous to the *cīz.* of the modern Hindustani music (cf. *S. Rāj*, II.4.2.3-6 and Premlata Sharma's Introduction to *Bhāvaraṅgalaharī*, part I, p. 15).

Thus, *vastu* emphasises the unity of *prabandha*, and so all the three names have their own significance as well. But these three names are also used in order to distinguish the *prabandha-s* on the basis of different number of sections and integral parts that go to constitute them. For example, Nārāyaṇadeva specified that a composition that is set in four sections and six integral parts is *prabandha*, that which is set with three sections and five integral parts is *vastu* and the one that comprises two sections and two integral parts is called *rūpaka* (cf. *Saṅgītanārāyaṇa*, 1, pp. 305-306). He is of course very specific about all the three; but Kumbhā, who is much earlier, makes a general statement about *vastu* and *rūpaka* having any number as sections and integral parts though he is similarly specific about *prabandha*.

(iii) धातव:

प्रबन्धावयवो धातुः स चतुर्धा निरूपितः ।
उद्ग्राहः प्रथमस्तत्र ततो मेलापकध्रुवौ ॥७॥
आभोगश्चेति तेषां च क्रमाल्लक्ष्माभिदध्महे ।
उद्ग्राहः प्रथमो भागस्ततो मेलापकः स्मृतः ॥८॥
ध्रुवत्वाच्च ध्रुवः पश्चादाभोगस्त्वन्तिमो मतः ।
ध्रुवाभोगान्तरे जातो धातुरन्योऽन्तराभिधः ॥९॥
स तु सालगसूडस्थरूपकेष्वेव दृश्यते ।
वातपित्तकफा देहधारणाद्धातवो यथा ॥१०॥
एवमेते प्रबन्धस्य धातवो देहधारणात् ।
तत्र मेलापकाभोगौ न भवेतां क्वचित्क्वचित् ॥११॥

(iii) The *dhātu-s* (Sections): (7-11)

Dhātu is the structural element[1] of *prabandha* and is shown[2] to be four-

[1]*Avayava* of the text lit. means a limb and is used in accordance with the metaphor of the *prabandha-puruṣa* (personified *prabandha*), but actually the underlying idea, as it is elucidated in verse 10 c-11 b, is that the *dhātu-s* constitute the structural elements of *prabandha* as the three humours hold the physiological balance of the human body. They are thus balancing elements and in a composition function as sections.

[2]*Nirūpitaḥ*, lit. exhibited or illustrated.

fold viz. the first is *udgrāha*,[1] then (follows) *melāpaka*[2], *dhruva*[3] and *ābhoga*[4]. These will now be defined seriatim. (7-8 b)

Udgrāha is the first section, then *melāpaka*[5]; placed thereafter is *dhruva* which is (so called) because it is fixed[6], while *ābhoga* is considered to be the last section. Another *dhātu*[7] that arises in-between *dhruva* and *ābhoga* is called *antara*[8] and is observed[9] in *rūpaka-s* (structured melodic compositions) of *sālagasūḍa*[10] only. (8 c-10 b)

Just as the three humours viz. wind, bile and phlegm are (considered to be) *dhātu-s*,[11] since they support the body so also because these[12] support the structure of *prabandha* they too are (called) *dhātu-s*. (10 c-11 b)

But, however, of these[13] *melāpaka* and *ābhoga* may not occur in certain cases[14]. (11 c d)

Prabandha is divided, as a general rule, into four sections viz. *udgrāha* (the starter), *melāpaka* (the joinder), *dhruva* (the invariable) and *ābhoga* (the concluding section). In certain cases a section called *antara* (the intermediary) is also introduced in addition to these four in-between *dhruva* and *ābhoga*. There is no rule appertaining to the introduction of *antara* as such, but it is mentioned as a fact of observed phenomenon of musical practice.

[1] *Udgrāha*, lit. the point of lifting i.e. the starting point or that of catching hold of.

[2] *Melāpaka*, lit. one that joins (two parts) i.e. the joinder.

[3] *Dhruva*, lit. fixed or invariable i.e. essential.

[4] *Ābhoga*, lit. completion i.e. concluding section.

[5] *Melāpaka*, lit. the joinder, that which joins; it unites the *udgrāha* with *dhruva*.

[6] 'K' interprets *dhruvatva* of the text as *nityatva* i.e. on account of its being *nitya* (permanent), in other words, 'indispensable since, when less than four *dhātu-s* are provided in a *prabandha*, the *udgrāha* and *dhruva* cannot be eliminated.

[7] Although four *dhātu-s* only have been spoken of as a rule (vide verse 7 ante) this fifth one is optionally provided in certain specific melodic structures viz. the *rūpaka-s* classified under *sālagasūḍa* such as *dhruva*, *maṇṭha* etc.

[8] *Antara*, lit. 'that which is placed in-between', according to 'K' is to be sung in-between *dhruva* and *ābhoga*, after *dhruva* has been sung in many cycles (towards the end of its climax).

[9] 'K' interprets *dṛśyate* of the text in the sense that even in the case of the *prabandha-s* of *sālagasūḍa* such as *dhruva*, *maṇṭha* etc., *antara* has to be sung where it is seen to have been traditionally sung, and not everywhere. Thus, he says, in case of *dhruva*, since such a practice is not observed (lit. seen) it is not to be sung, but in case of *maṇṭha* for example, it has to be sung because it is traditionally observed to have been sung.

[10] The *sālagasūḍa prabandha-s* are to be defined by the author shortly in this chapter.

[11] The three humours of the body *vāta*, *pitta* and *kapha* are called *dhātu-s* in *Āyurveda*. The author is here trying to give a semantic derivation of the word *dhātu* on the analogy of its use in *Āyurveda*.

[12-13] That is, the four *dhātu-s*.

[14] In certain cases where only three *dhātu-s* are provided; as 'K' informs us, everywhere *melāpaka* is eliminated and where only two *dhātu-s* are provided, everywhere it is the *melāpaka* and *ābhoga* that are dropped.

Even though *prabandha* is said to be divided into four sections, as a general rule, every *prabandha* need not have as many as four sections. Some times *melāpaka* is eliminated, and some times *melāpaka* and *ābhoga* both are eliminated. It has already been noticed that the three names for the structured melody viz. *prabandha*, *vastu* and *rūpaka* are associated by some with the number of sections and integral parts that go to constitute it. Our author too classifies *prabandha* on this basis.

In modern Hindustani Music, the *khyal-s* generally have two parts called *sthāyī* and *antarā*, and *dhrupad-s* have four viz. *sthāyī*, *antarā*, *sañcārī* and *ābhog*. In the latter case however, the last two sections are hardly distinguished from each other since they are not marked by the re-introduction of the first line of *sthāyī* in-between them. The two can, in terms of the division of *prabandha* into four sections, in fact be considered as one. The *sthāyī* and *antarā* may roughly be considered analogous to *dhruva* and *ābhoga*. Thus, the two sections called *udgrāha* and *melāpaka* of the fourfold division spoken of as above, have become outmoded in the present context. The present *antarā* must not be confused with the ancient *antara* which was designed to interlink *dhruva* and *ābhoga* in certain specific cases (Also see P.L.S. Introduction to *Bhāvaraṅgalaharī*, p. 16).

(iv) धातुसङ्ख्यानुसारेण प्रबन्धभेदाः

स द्विधातुस्त्रिधातुश्च चतुर्धातुरिति त्रिधा ।

(iv) Classification of *prabandha-s:* (12 a b)

That[1] (*prabandha*) is threefold viz. as constituted of two, three or four *dhātu-s*. (12 a b)

(v) प्रबन्धाङ्गानि

अङ्गानि षट् तस्य स्वरश्च बिरुदं पदम् ॥१२॥
तेनकः पाटतालौ च प्रबन्धपुरुषस्य ते ।
भवन्त्यङ्ग वदङ्गानि, मङ्गलार्थप्रकाशके ॥१३॥
तत्र तेनपदे नेत्रे, स्तः पाटबिरुदे करौ ।
कराभ्यामुद्भवात् कार्यं कारणत्वोपचारतः ॥१४॥

[1]'That' implies the *prabandha* as defined and elucidated in the foregoing portion of the text viz. structured melodic composition based on two to four *dhātu-s*.

प्रबन्धगतिहेतुत्वात् पादौ तालस्वरौ मतौ ।
स्वराः षड्जादयस्तेषां वाचकाः सरिगादयः ॥१५॥
स्वराभिव्यक्तिसंयुक्ताः स्वरशब्देन कीर्तिताः ।
बिरुदं गुणनाम स्यात्ततोऽन्यद्वाचकं पदम् ॥१६॥
तेनेतिशब्दस्तेनः स्यान्मङ्गलार्थप्रकाशकः ।
ओं तत्सदिति निर्देशात्तत्त्वमस्यादिवाक्यतः ॥१७॥
तदिति ब्रह्म तेनायं ब्रह्मणा मङ्गलात्मना ।
लक्षितस्तेन तेनेति पाटो वाद्याक्षरोत्करः ॥१८॥
तालस्तालप्रकरणे सप्रपञ्चो निरूप्यते ।

(v) The *aṅga-s* (integral parts) of *prabandha-s:* (12 c-19 b)

That[1] (*prabandha*) has six *aṅga-s* (integral parts) viz. *svara, biruda, pada, tena, pāṭa* and *tāla*[2]*;* like the parts (of the body) they are the integral parts of the configuration[3] of *prabandha.* (12 c-13 c)

Of these (six *aṅga-s*) *tena* and *pada* reflecting[4] auspiciousness and meaning (respectively) are its two eyes, *pāṭa* and *biruda* are the two hands, because they are produced by the hand, the cause being figuratively taken for the effect[5]; and *tāla* and *svara* are considered to be the two feet as they are

[1]Here, the pronoun 'that' is indicative of the *prabandha* as spoken of in 12 a b c viz. with two, three or four *dhātu-s.*

[2]All these six terms i.e. the names of the six *aṅga-s* (integral parts) are to be explained by the author presently, in this topic (vide 15 c-18 b).

[3]The expression '*prabandha-puruṣa*' of the text is metaphorical. Here *prabandha* is conceived on the analogy of a person (a human being). Just as arms, feet, eyes and ears etc. are the parts of a person's body, so also *svara, pada, tena* etc. are the parts of *prabandha,* the embodiment of a melodic structure. The metaphor is well placed in the context of Sanskrit diction, or far that matter, of the Indian literary tradition.

[4]Literally, *tena* and *pada* are said to be *maṅgala-prakāśaka* and *arthaprakāśaka* i.e., the reflectors of auspiciousness and meaning. The word *prakāśaka* lit. means that which brings to light i.e. which manifests, or causes to manifest. Thus *tena* and *pada* are respectively indicative of the auspicious words and the meaning or the emotional content of the composition. So metaphorically, they are said to be the eyes of the *prabandha-puruṣa.*

[5]*Pāṭa-s* are produced mostly from *avanaddha* (covered) instruments which are played upon by the hands. Thus, the *pāṭākṣara-s* (*pāṭa-* syllables) are the product (effect) of the hands which may be conceived as their immediate cause. *Biruda-s* as explained by 'S' are also indirectly related to hands being composed as the part and parcel of the delineation of *pada.* 'K' suggests that *biruda-s* are said to be hands because the acts of philanthropy are performed by hands and these acts are praised; so here the cause is imposed on the effect. Thus both, *pāṭa* and *biruda* are said to be the hands of the *prabandha-puruṣa.* Though in actual fact they are only the products, they are figuratively named by their causes.

the cause of movement[1] in *prabandha*. (13 d-15 b)

The notes *ṣaḍja* etc. briefly spoken of as *sa*, *ri*, *ga* etc. along with their tonal manifestation[2] are known by the word *svara*. *Biruda* is the name (given to) qualities or excellences,[3] and whatever is other than that in the text (of the song) is *pada*. The word *tena* is indicative by itself[4] of an auspicious object[5] for the word *tat* refers to Brahman (the Supreme Being) as evidenced by such *śruti*-passages as *Om tat sat* (that alone is true), *tat tvam asi* (thou art that) etc. *Tat* (in these passages) stands for *Brahman*. Therefore[6] (*tena*), this (*prabandha*) being characterised[7] by that (*tena*) *Brahman* which is the very essence of auspiciousness, it is (significantly called as) *tena*. *Pāṭa* is the group of sound-syllables (arising out) of (some) musical instruments,[8] and *tāla* will be elucidated in detail in the chapter on *tāla*.[9] (15 c-19 b)

If the various *prabandha-s* are classified on the basis of the number of *dhātu-s* constituting them, it is natural to accept that such a classification be illustrated by the enumeration of different *prabandha-s* under the three classes, but the author does not seem to do so. 'S' explains that it is so because this detail with regard to the number of *dhātu-s*, is given by the author in describing the characteristic features of the particular *prabandha-s*.

[1]'K' elucidates that even though *tāla* and *svara* pervade the entire body of *prabandha* from the very beginning to the end, yet they are considered to be parts constituting the whole structure in a specific sense. He says, "just as the sense of touch pervades the entire body, yet it is considered to be one of the five senses; likewise *tāla* is also considered to be one of the six parts: *svara* on the other hand is manifested (in melody) through the succession of individual notes sa, ri, ga etc. and as such it constitutes a part, just as even though space is all prevading, but only the space enclosed by the eardrum is said to be ear for its quality of sound perception.

[2]That is, their articulation in musical sound.

[3]*Guṇa* is difficult to translate precisely. Here it means a good quality, since *biruda* lit. means a panegyric.

[4]The translation is a free rendering of the free text into English bringing out the meaning. The literal version would be, *tena* is (the same) as the word *tena* which is indicative of an auspicious meaning (or object). *Artha* in the expression *maṅgalārtha-prakāśaka* precisely means (in this context), the reference of the word (*tena* in this case). The purport is that *tena* signifies auspiciousness by its very name, since it is associated with Brahman, the Supreme Being in the *śruti*-passages of the *Upaniṣada* which form a part of parcel of the scriptures and have a mystical signification of so naming this integral part (*aṅga*) of the *prabandha*.

[5]Object of consciousness, by implication.

[6]The word *tena* has been used three times in verse 18, in quite different senses. That is why it has been indicated in the brackets. Here, for example, it is used as the instrumental singular of the pronoun *tat* which refers to the noun Brahman by context.

[7]*Lakṣita* lit. means marked or indicated.

[8]The *pāṭākṣara-s* are dealt with in the *Vādyādhyāya* i.e. Chapter VI on instrumental music.

[9]That is, in Chapter V entitled, *Tālādhyāya*.

The author is also going to present a classification of *prabandha-s* based on the *prabandha-jāti-s* i.e. the families of *prabandha-s* distinguished by the number of *aṅga-s* (integral parts) constituting them. He is, therefore, explaining the concept of *aṅga-s*, here, on the analogy of a human being endowed with the eyes, two hands and two feet, symbolising the functions of perceiving and willing (i.e. responding from a conscious purpose in view), acting (producing and consuming), and moving (to and fro). Thus, metaphorically conceiving *prabandha* to be an embodiment of structured melody, its six integral parts viz. *tena*, *pada*, *pāṭa*, *biruda*, *tāla* and *svara* are said respectively to be its two eyes, two hands and two feet. Since the expression is metaphorical its implications may not be stretched too far, for obtaining a clear and precise account of the related concepts. Moreover, the terms employed technically are explained by the author in some detail.

(vi) प्रबन्धजातयः

मेदिन्यथानन्दिनी स्याद्दीपनी भावनी तथा ॥१९॥
तारावलीति पञ्च स्युः प्रबन्धानां तु जातयः ।
अङ्गैः षडादिभिर्द्व्यन्तैः केषांचन मते श्रुतिः ॥२०॥
नीतिः सेना च कविता चम्पूरित्युदितास्तु ताः ।

(vi) The *jāti-s* (families) of the *prabandha-s:* (19 c-21 b)

Indeed there are five *jāti-s* (families) of the *prabandha-s* viz. *medinī*, *ānandinī*, *dīpinī*, and *tārāvalī*, (Constituted as they are) by six to two integral parts (*aṅga-s*). According to some they are known as *śruti*, *nīti*, *senā*, *kavitā* and *campu*. (19 c-21 b)

This, in fact, presents a classification of *prabandha-s* into five families, based on the number of integral parts that constituted them. These are conceived as under:

The *Jāti-s* of the *Prabandha-s*[1]

Sl. No.	*Name of the Jāti*	*No. of the integral parts*	*Other names*
1.	*Medinī*	6	*Śruti*
2.	*Ānandinī*	5	*Nīti*
3.	*Dīpinī*	4	*Senā*
4.	*Bhāvanī*	3	*Kavitā*
5.	*Tārāvalī*	2	*Campu*

[1]That is 6, 5, 4, 3 and 2 respectively.

The significance of the other nomenclature is clearly brought out by 'S', who says: "*Śruti* signifies the six *aṅga s* of the *Veda* viz. *śikṣā*, *jyotiṣ*, *nirukta*, *kalpa*, *chanda* and *vyākaraṇa*; *nīti* is based on five factors viz. the initiative, manpower and material resources, appropriation of time and space, prevention of calamity and fulfilment of the objective; *senā* has four wings viz. elephants, horses, chariots and infantry; *kavitā* (poetry) has three elements viz. talent (of expression), proficiency and practice; and *campu* (mixed form of writing) has two elements viz. prose and poetry.

Thus, these names primarily signify the numbers 6, 5, 4, 3 and 2 and do not seem to have any other relation in terms of their connotation to the *prabandha-jāti-s*.

(vii) प्रबन्धभेदाः

अनिर्युक्तश्च निर्युक्तः प्रबन्धो द्विविधो मतः ॥२१॥
छन्दस्तालाद्यनियमादाद्यः स्यान्नियमात् परः ।
पुनः प्रबन्धास्त्रिविधाः सूडस्था आलिसंश्रयाः ॥२२॥
विप्रकीर्णाश्च,

(vii) The classification of *prabandha-s:* (21 c-23 b)

Prabandha is considered to be twofold viz. *aniryukta* (unspecified) and *niryukta* (specified), no particular *tāla* or *chanda* (metre) etc.[1] being specified in the former, but the latter being regulated as such.[2] (21 c-22 b)

Again[3] the *prabandha-s* are threefold viz. *sūḍa-s*[4], *āli-s*[5] and *viprakīrṇa-s*. Of these the *sūḍa* is being described in the first instance. (22 c-23 b)

Here we have two other classifications of *prabandha-s*, one based on the distinction of specified and unspecified *tāla*, metre etc. and the other on technical considerations which are presently to be described. The second classification is actually used by the author in his description of the various *prabandha-s*.

[1]That is, it is specified in case of certain *prabandha-s* that only a particular *tāla* such as *caccatpuṭa* (to be elucidated in Chapter V) and so on, a particular metre such as *triṣṭup* and so on and likewise a particular section of an integral part, a particular *rasa*, *rāga* or *bhāṣā* etc. are to be employed, then it is called *niryukta* (specified), but if no such specification is there, then it is *aniryukta* (unspecified), etc., (*ādi*) of the text according to 'K' is indicative of the other elements referred to above apart from *tāla* and *chanda*.

[2]As such i.e. with specification in the above terms.

[3]'Again' implies that this one is a different classification.

[4–5]*Sūḍastha* and *ālisaṁśraya* of the text literally means subsisting in the *sūḍa* and based on *āli*.

(viii) त्रिविधप्रबन्धभेदानामुद्देशः

(क) तत्र सूडप्रबन्धोद्देशः

तत्रादौ सूडलक्षणमुच्यते ।
एलाकरणढेङ्कीभिर्वर्तन्या झोम्बडेन च ॥२३॥
लम्भरासैकतालीभिरष्टभिः सूड उच्यते ।

(viii) Enumeration of the varieties of the three classes of *prabandha-s:* (23 c-33 b)

(a) Enumeration of the varieties of *sūḍa:*

Sūḍa (prabandha) is said to be (formed) by eight (melodies) viz. *elā, karaṇa, dheṅkī, vartanī, jhombaḍa, lambha, rāsaka* and *ekatālī.* (23 c-24 b)

(ख) आलिसंश्रितप्रबन्धोद्देशः

वर्णो वर्णस्वरो गद्यं कैवाडश्चाङ्कचारिणी ॥२४॥
कन्दस्तुरगलीला च गजलीला द्विपद्यपि ।
चक्रवालः क्रौञ्चपदः स्वरार्थो ध्वनिकुट्टनी ॥२५॥
आर्या गाथा द्विपथकः कलहंसश्च तोटकम् ।
घटो वृत्तं मातृका च ततो रागकदम्बकः ॥२६॥
पञ्चतालेश्वरस्तालार्णव इत्येषु कश्चन ।
सूडक्रमस्थो मध्ये चेदसावालिक्रमो भवेत् ॥२७॥
सूडालिक्रमसंबन्धाद् द्वात्रिंशदिति कीर्तिताः ।

(b) Enumeration of the varieties of *āli:*

The series of *āli* is (constituted by) *varṇa, varṇa-svara, gadya, kaivāḍa, aṅkacāriṇī, kanda, turagalīlā, gajalīlā, dvipadī, cakravāla, krauñcapada, svarārtha, dhvanikuṭṭanī, āryā, gāthā, dvipathaka, kalahaṁsa, toṭaka, ghaṭa, vṛtta, mātṛkā, rāgakadambaka, pañcatāleśvara, tālārṇava* and any other form of the series of *sūḍa* that happens to be amidst them.[1] Due to the combination of the *sūḍa* and *āli* series, they (*prabandha-s*) are known to be thirtytwo. (24 c-28 b)

[1]That is, amongst the series of *āli-prabandha-s.*

(ग) विप्रकीर्णप्रबन्धोद्देश:

ततोऽन्ये विप्रकीर्णास्तान् प्रसिद्धान् कतिचिद् ब्रुवे ॥२८॥
श्रीरङ्गः श्रीविलासः स्यात् पञ्चभङ्गिरतः परम् ।
पञ्चाननोमातिलकौ त्रिपदी च चतुष्पदी ॥२९॥
षट्पदी वस्तुसंज्ञश्च विजयस्त्रिपथस्तथा ।
चतुर्मुखः सिंहलीलो हंसलीलोऽथ दण्डकः ॥३०॥
झम्पटः कन्दुकः स्यात् त्रिभङ्गिर्हरविलासकः ।
सुदर्शनः स्वराङ्कः श्रीवर्धनो हर्षवर्धनः ॥३१॥
वदनं चच्चरी चर्या पद्धडी राहडी तथा ।
वीरश्रीर्मङ्गलाचारो धवलो मङ्गलस्तथा ॥३२॥
ओवी लोली ढोल्लरी च दन्ती षट्त्रिंशदित्यमी ।

(c) Enumeration of the varieties of *viprakīrṇa:*

Apart from these[1], (there) are the *viprakīrṇa-s*, some of the well known of which, I am to mention as under:

These are thirtysix viz. *śrīraṅga, śrīvilāsa, pañcabhaṅgi, pañcānana, umātilaka, tripadī, catuṣpadī, ṣaṭpadī, vastu, vijaya, tripatha, caturmukha, siṁhalīla, haṁsalīla, daṇḍaka, jhampaṭa, kanduka, tribhaṅgi, haravilāsa, suddrśana, svarāṅka, śrīvardhana, harṣavardhana, vadana, caccarī, caryā, paddhaḍī, rāhaḍī, vīraśrī, maṅgalācāra, dhavala, maṅgala, ovī, lolī, ḍhollarī* and *dantī.*[2] (28 c-33 b)

'*Sūḍa*' is explained by 'K' as a regional term denoting a group of compositions that have been enumerated in the text. It is pointed out by 'K' that the names of some of these eight compositions are literally significant, while some have acquired significance by usage. 'S' elucidates, "The eight viz. *elā* etc. constitute *mārga-sūḍa* and the *prabandha-s* subsisting therein are (said to be) *sūḍastha.*" *Mārga-sūḍa* implies what is called *śuddha-sūḍa* which becomes significant in contrast with *sālagasūḍa* (to be explained subsequently in this chapter vide verse 331).

'*Āli*' literally means a line, a row, a streak, and compounded with the word *krama* (lit. order), the name *ālikrama* seems to imply a series of *prabandha-s* that were probably sung in a row. Similarly, the *prabandha-s* enumerated as *sūḍa-prabandha-s* constitute a series of *sūḍa-s* (*sūḍakrama*). Thus we have in fact two series of *prabandha-s* that were probably sung in a row viz. the series of *sūḍa-prabandhas* and the series of *āli-prabandha-s*.

[1]That is, the *sūḍa* and the *āli-prabandha-s*.
[2]'S' reads *dhvani* instead of *dantī*.

24 *prabandha-s* enumerated in the text constitute the series of *āli-prabandha-s.* In addition to these if any *prabandha* from the series of *sūḍa* is sung along with these, that too becomes an *āli-prabandha*. Thus, the total number of *āli-prabandha-s* counted in association with the *sūḍa-s* is (8+24=32) thirtytwo.

The *viprakīrṇa-s* (lit. isolated or scattered) seem to be complete and independent compositions, sung by themselves without any necessary supplementation.

द्वितोयप्रकरणम्

सूडप्रबन्धाः

(i) एलाप्रबन्धाः

(क) सामान्यलक्षणम्, केचिद्विशेषाश्च

(१) सामान्यलक्षणम्

अङ्घ्रौ खण्डद्वयं सानुप्रासमेकेन धातुना ॥३३॥
ततः प्रयोगस्तदनु पल्लवाख्यं पदत्रयम् ।
द्वे स्तो विलम्बिते तत्र तृतीयं द्रुतमानतः ॥३४॥
एवं पादत्रयं गेयमुद्ग्राहे तुल्यधातुकम् ।
केवलं तु तृतीयेऽङ्घ्रौ संबोधनपदान्वितः ॥३५॥
प्रयोगोऽन्यो विधातव्यो न पल्लवपदस्थितिः ।
अमुं प्रयोगं मेलापं प्राहुः सोमेश्वरादयः ॥३६॥
स्तुत्यनामाङ्कितो मध्यविलम्बितपदत्रयः ।
ध्रुवस्ततस्तत्र पूर्वमेकधातु पदद्वयम् ॥३७॥
भिन्नधातु तृतीयं स्यादाभोगस्तदनन्तरम् ।
गेयो वाग्गेयकारेण स्वाभिधानविभूषितः ॥३८॥
पुनर्गीत्वा ध्रुवे त्यागो ग्रहस्तु विषमो भवेत् ।
एलासामान्यलक्ष्मैतत् पूर्वाचार्यैरुदीरितम् ॥३९॥
मण्ठद्वितीयकङ्कालप्रतितालेषु कश्चन ।
तालोऽस्यां त्यागसौभाग्यशौर्यधैर्यादिवर्णनम् ॥४०॥
एलानां बहवः सन्ति विशेषास्तेषु केचन ।
व्युत्पत्तये निरूप्यन्ते मतङ्गादिमतोदिताः ॥४१॥

SECTION-2

Sūḍa-Prabandha-s

(i) The *elā-prabandha-s:* (33 c-132 b)

(a) General description and other features: (33 c-65)

(1) General description: (33 c-41)

In the first step (*pāda*), there are two parts[1] sung in the same tonal structure[2] with alliteration[3], followed by *prayoga*[4] and thereafter by the three *pada-s* (syllabic-cum-tonal phrases), (together) called *pallava*, two of which are in slow (tempo)[5] and the third one is in the fast measure.[6] (33 c-34)

***Udgrāha* has to be sung in three steps (*pāda-s*) of equal[7] tonal import[8] with the provision that another *prayoga* consisting in the words of address[9] is to be employed, and that there is no need for the *pada-s* of *pallava* (in it). Someśvara and others[10] declare this *prayoga* to be *melāpaka*. (35-36)**

Thereafter, *dhruva* is (sung) with three *pada-s* in medium and slow tempo,

[1]We have three terms viz. *pāda, padu* and *khaṇḍa*. *Pāda* and *khaṇḍa* have been rendered into English as step, and part respectively. The words *pada* seems to be used is a technical sense with manifold shades of connotation, and it has not been translated. Primarily, it denotes a word that is grammatically meaningful. Literally, it can also mean a verbal phrase, but in the context in which it has been used here, it also means a musical phrase. So, essentially, *pada* implies a literary piece of composition (i.e. a fragment of it) or a verb at phrase used as a vehicle for the musical phrase. Since a complex idea is implied in this word, it has not been translated, but roughly it may be rendered as syllabic-cum-tonal phrase.

Pāda, on the other hand, stands for a foot or a quarter of a verse. Here *pada* froms a part of *pāda*, and *khaṇḍa* a section of *pada*.

[2]In this context we have to be familiar with two terms viz. *dhātu* and *mātu* which signify the tonal and the verbal structure of a melody. What is implied here is that the first *pada* is to be divided into two parts of the same *dhātu* but of a different *mātu*, the tonal structure being the same, the verbal structure is to be different.

[3]*Anuprāsa* (alliteration) is defined as *varṇasāmyam*, similarity of letters.

[4]*Prayoga* has been explained in the comments. As a technical term, it has not been possible to translate it.

[5–6]*Vilambita* (*laya*) and *druta* (*laya*) are to be defined in chapter V on *tāla*.

[7]'*Tuya*' implies 'equal' and not similar.

[8]*Dhātu* is generally rendered as section of a song in this chapter. But when the word is used in contradistinction with *mātu* it signifies the tonal structure, form or pattern as against the verbal structure or form of the song.

[9]*Sambodhana-pada*—words of address or calling.

[10]*Someśvara* is the auther of the *Ratnāvalī*.

marked[1] by an adorable[2] name. The first two *pada-s* have to be in one tonal (*dhātu*) and the third in a different one. (37-38 a).

Thereafter,[3] *ābhoga* which is embellished by the master composer (*vāggeyakāra*) with his own name, has to be sung. (38 b-d)

Having repeated, (the song) is concluded in *dhruva*.[4] The commencement (*graha*) in this case is *viṣama*. Such is the general description of *elā* as enunciated[5] by the ancient teachers. (39)

Any *tāla* from amongst *maṇṭha, dvitīya, kaṅkāla* and *pratitāla* (may be used) in it.[6] Generosity, altruism, bravery, fortitude etc.[7] may be the subjects of description. (40)

There are many forms of *elā*, but only a few typical ones are demonstrated here as expounded by Mataṅga's school, for the sake of a clear conception. (41)

Now, the author, having described the general features of the *prabandha* form of singing, proceeds to describe in detail the characteristic features of the various individual *prabandha-s* named under the three classes of *sūḍa*, *āli* and *viprakīrṇa* Naturally, he takes up the eight types of *sūḍa* viz. *elā*, *karaṇa*, *dheṅkī* etc. in the first instant.

To begin with he describes the structure and the technique of singing the *udgrāha* which is to be sung in three steps. According to 'K' a step (*pāda*) consists in singing five *pada-s*. In the first step, the first *pada* is to be sung in two parts which are so balanced as to be of the same tonal structure (*dhātu*) i.e., in other words, they have to be of a different verbal structure (*mātu*). The second one is to be sung by way of *prayoga* which, according to 'K', Śārṅgadeva has been defined as, "the *ālāpa* or *ālapti* with *gamaka-s* devoid of words." The third which would otherwise be like the first is specified to be different from it in so far as its *prayoga* consisting of words of address is cast in another *dhātu* and it has no need for the three *pada-s* of *pallava*; i.e., in other words, the *udgrāha* has 12 *pada-s* in all, 5 in the first step, five in the second and 2 in the third.

He further elucidates that those who consider *elā-prabandha* to be of the three sections (*dhātu-s*), for them its *udgrāha* has twelve *pada-s*, but those who consider it to be of four sections (*dhātu-s*), they count eleven of them as forming the *udgrāha* and one as *melāpaka*. The following names are assigned to these *pada-s* (vide verses 43-44 of this chapter):

[1]*Aṅkita*, literally means marked, imprinted, but the purport seems to be that stanzas are distinctly marked by a praiseworthy name.

[2]*Stutya* lit. worthy of adoration, veneration or praise.

[3]That is, after singing *dhruva*.

[4]'S' reads *dhruvam* instead of *dhruva*.

[5]Lit. 'said by'.

[6]That is, in *elā*.

[7]Etc. may refer to other virtues such as religiosity, humility, and so on,

The twelve *pada-s* of *udgrāha*

Sl. no. of pada	*1st Step*	*2nd Step*	*3rd Step*
1.	*Kāma*	*vikārī*	*gītaka*
2.	*manmathavat*	*māndhātā*	*cita* (*añcita*)
3.	*kānta*	*sumati*	—
4.	*jita*	*śobhī*	—
5.	*matta* (*mitra*)	*suśobhī*	—

Here 'K' seems to raise a controversy. He says, or so he obviously seems to argue that, since the *prayoga* also forms a *pada*, and a *pada* (by its very definition in grammar) has to be a meaningful word, it is rightly ordained that the *prayoga* of the third step should consist of the words of address, though he suggests, these words are to be placed at the end of the extended melody. But, by the same logic, he maintains that the *prayoga-s* of the first and the second steps should also consist of the words of address, though the author has not explicitly mentioned this to be so. However, the text does not necessarily warant such an interpretation, since it can very well mean that these two *prayoga-s* are free of words and the third one consists of the words of address by way of exception; and it finds mention because of its being an exception, while the other two find no such mention being the expression of the rule which is that *prayoga* has to be free from meaningful syllables.

But, in fact the difficulty pointed out by Kallinātha seems to have arisen in his mind by the restricted sense in which he reads the word *pada*. Bharata, for example, does not consider it necessary for *pada* to be a meaningful word; he includes *śuṣkākṣara-s* i.e. meaningless syllables in *pada*; and even Śārṅgadeva has spoken of these as *Brahmaprokta-pada-s*. In musical parlance *pada* implies not only a syllabic but also a tonal phrase, the latter is, of cource based on the former. The syllabic phrase may or may not be meaningful. Even if the words of address are meaningful grammatically in a technical sense, they do not actually convey any relationship or meaning. The author has suggested the use of the words of address not perhaps because they are meaningful but because they provide some scope for the extension of melody.

Moreover, it may be noted that, whereas 'K' thinks that the two parts of the first step (*khaṇḍadvaya*) constitute one *pada* viz. *kāma* (cf.p. 215), according to 'S' these two parts constitute 2 *pada-s* viz. *kāma* and *manmathavat* (cf. p. 221). Consequenty (as it is discussed elsewhere), for 'K' the *prayoga* consists of a *pada* (p. 216) though not composed of any meaningful words, but composed of the words of address of call and so on. But for 'S' it is just a formation of tonal shakes '*gamaka-sandarbharūpaḥ*'.

After the *udgrāha* or the *udgrāha* and the *melāpaka, dhruva* is sung in three *pada-s* in which, as interpreted by 'K', the name of a praiseworthy or ideal character, a hero, a king, the favourite god and so on may somewhere be taken. The text says that these three *pada-s* which from a unit have to be sung in the medium and the slow tempo. Because it is laid down in the text that the first two *pada-s* have to be of one *dhātu* and the third of another, 'K' infers that the first two *pada-s* are to be sung in the medium tempo and the third one in the slow tempo. The three *pada-s* of *dhruva* are respectively called *vicitra, vāsava* and *mṛdu.*

The *pada* of the *ābhoga* is called sucitra. The *elāprabandha* is therefore to be sung in sixteen *pada-s* which are detailed in the following chart.

The sixteen *pada-s* of elā.

Dhātu (*Section*)	*Pada* (*step*)	*S. no. of pada*	*Name of the pada*	*Remarks*
Udgrāha	First	1	*kāma*	
		2	*Manmathavat*	
		3	*kānta*	
		4	*jita*	
		5	*matta**	*named as *mitra* by 'K'
	Second	6	*vikārī*	
		7	*māndhātā*	
		8	*sumati*	
		9	*śobhī*	
		10	*suśobhi*	
	Third	11	*gītaka*	
*(*Melāpaka*)		12*	**ucita***	*according to Someś-vara it forms *melāpaka* making *elā* a four sec-tional *prabandha.*
Dhruva		13	*vicitra*	
		14	*vāsava*	
		15	*mṛdu*	
Ābhoga		16	*sucitra*	**named as *añcita* by 'K'

When the *ābhoga* has been sung, according to 'K's version, all the sixteen *pada-s* may again be sung and the song be concluded in the beginning of the 13th *pada* in *dhruva.* But 'S' has a different reading of the text which has *dhruvam* instead of *dhruva.* He, therefore, interprets the text as follows: "Again, after *ābhoga,* having sung *dhruva* the song may be concluded." Obviously, according to him it is the *dhruva* that has to be sung again and not the entire 16 *pada-s* i.e., the whole of the song. And then, in K's interpretation the difficulty is about the conclusion, i.e. if the sung is to be concluded in the beginning of *dhruva* in the 13th *pada,* after repeating it wholly, how are we to arrive at it?, by singing right from the first *pada* or directly by singing the 13th *pada?*; for, in the former case we have no mandate from the author to sing any portion thrice. The reading of 'S' is therefore to be considered equally, if not more, creditable.

Elucidating the expression *pūrvācāryaiḥ* of the text, 'S' interprets it to mean as "said by Bharata and others." It is not understood how he brings in Bharata in this context for the *prabandha-s* are classified by Śārṅgadeva as a form of *gāna* which he says is characterised like *deśī rāga-s.* As such they are not known to Bharata. It seems, he is only referring to the school of Bharata, for it is Mataṅga who speaks of *prabandha-s* at length.

(२) केचिद्विशेषाः

(क) वर्णानां देवताः

अकारे दैवतं विष्णुरिकारे कुसुमायुधः ।
लक्ष्मीर्लकार एलानामिति वर्णेषु देवताः ॥४२॥

(2) Other features: (42-65)

(a) The presiding deities of the syllables of *elā:*

Among the (three) letters of *elā*, viṣṇu (resides) in the sound *a, kāma*[1] (cupid) in the sound *i*,[2] and *lakṣmī* in the sound *l*.[3] (42)

(ख) एलापदनामानि

कामम‍न्मथवत्कान्तजितमत्तविकारिणः ।
मान्धातृसुमती शोभिसुशोभी गीतकोचितौ ॥४३॥
विचित्रो वासवमृदु सुचित्रा इति षोडश ।
नामान्येलापदानां स्युः षोडशानामनुक्रमात् ॥४४॥

(b) The names of the *pada-s* in *elā:*

The sixteen names for the *pada-s* of *elā* respectively are *kāma, manmathavat, kānta, jita, matta*,[4] *vikārī, māndhātā, sumati, śobhī, suśobhī, gītaka, ucita*,[5] *vicitra, vāsava, mṛdu* and *sucitra.* (43-44)

[1]*Kusumāyudha* is an epithet of Kāmadeva, the god of conjugal love, for he is known to wield the bow and arrow of flowers.
[2]*a* (अ) in conjunction with *i* (इ) makes *e* (ए).
[3]The vowel *ā* is covered by the short *a*.
[4]'K' names it as *mitra*.
[5]'K' names it as *añcita*.

(ग) पददेवताः

पद्मालया पत्रिणी च रञ्जनी सुमुखी शची ।
वरेण्या वायुवेगा च वेदिनी मोहिनी जया ॥४५॥
गौरी ब्राह्मी च मातङ्गी चण्डिका विजया तथा ।
चामुण्डेलापदेष्वेताः क्रमात् षोडश देवताः ॥४६॥

(c) The presiding deities of the *pada-s* of *elā:*

The sixteen deities of the *pada-s* of *elā* are respectively as follows: *Padmālayā, patriṇī, Rañjanī, sumukhī, śacī, vareṇyā, vāyuvegā, Vedinī, Mohinī, Jayā, Gaurī, Brāhmī, Mātaṅgī, Caṇḍikā, Vijayā* and *Cāmuṇḍā.* (45-46)

(घ) पदस्थाः प्राणाः

समानो मधुरः सान्द्रः कान्तो दीप्तः समाहितः ।
अग्राम्यः सुकुमारश्च प्रसन्नौजस्विनाविति ॥४७॥
मान्धात्रादिपदेषु स्युः प्राणा दश दशस्विमे ।
समानोऽल्पाक्षरध्वानो मधुरः स्वल्पनादया ॥४८॥
अल्पमूर्छनया युक्तः सान्द्रस्तु निविडाक्षरः ।
अल्पध्वनिस्तारगतिः कान्तः कान्तध्वनिर्मतः ॥४९॥
दीप्तस्तु दीप्तनादः स्यात् स्थायिस्थस्तु समाहितः ।
अग्राम्योऽक्षरनादानामावृत्त्या समुदाहृतः ॥५०॥
सुकुमारो वर्णनादमूर्छनाकोमलत्वतः ।
प्रसन्नः स्यात् पदस्थानस्वरादीनां प्रसादतः ॥५१॥
ओजोबहुल ओजस्वीत्येभिः सर्वगुणैर्युताः ।
एलाः श्रोतुः प्रयोक्तुश्च धर्मकामार्थसिद्धिदाः ॥५२॥

(d) The allocation of *prāṇa-s* among the *pada-s* of *elā:* (47-52)

The ten *prāṇa-s*[1] of the ten *pada-s* beginning with *māndhātā*[2] are (called)

[1]*Prāṇa* is literally translated as vital breath, but here the word seems to have been used somewhat metaphorically. It may be noticed that though the number of *prāṇa-s* is said to be ten, their names are not identical with the ten forms of *prāṇa* spoken of earlier (cf. 1.2. 6?-69 ante). These names, as they are defined here, have a musical significance.

[2]That is, from *māndhātā* to *sucitra,* leaving aside the first six ones. 'K' however says that, "these ten *prāṇa-s* permeate all the sixteen *pada-s.* How is that? Some of them being of the same *dhātu,* one, two or even three of them are animated by the same *prāṇa* e.g. the *prāṇa* of *manmathavat* and *māndhātā,* i.e. the *prayoga* in the first and second step is the same viz. *samāna* because of the same *dhātu* in the two. Similarly, in the two sets

samāna, *madhura*, *sāndra*, *kānta*, *dīpta* *samāhita*, *agrāmya*, *sukumāra*, *prasanna* and *ojasvī*. (47-48 b) These are defined as under:

(i) *Samāna* sounds[1] with scanty syllables (48 c)

(ii) *Madhura* is (produced) by a short[2] *mūrcchanā* having a small sound.[3] (48-49 a)

(iii) *Sāndra* has close-knit syllables[4] with a small sound[5] and in the high range[6] (49 b c).

of three stanzas of the *pallava* of the second and the first steps, viz. *sumati*, *śobhī* and *suśobhī* on the one hand and *kānta*, *jita* and *matta* on the other, the corresponding couples being of the equal *dhātu* (tonal import) are permeated respectively by the three *prāṇa-s* viz. *madhura*, *sāndra* and *kānta*. And then in the third step, the second part of the first *pada* sung in the same *dhātu* as the first two *pada-s* sung in two parts in the first step, these three have the fifth *prāṇa* viz. *dīpta* in common. Thus, these eleven stanzas have five *prāṇa-s*, and thereafter in the twelfth stanza onwards five other *prāṇa-s* such as *samāhita* etc. may be understood." And then he goes on to argue that 'only in this manner can the twelfth *pada* have *samāhita prāṇa*, not in the ordinary course.' He probably thinks it necessary in the application of the text '*prayogonyo vidhātavya*' (cf. 36 ante) as pointed out by him. In this way, he applies the use of ten *prāṇa-s* to the ten types of *pada-s*, rather than the ten *pada-s*.

Though on the one hand his interpretation is plausible, the text would hardly seem to be warranting it. Perhaps another plausible explanation may have to be sought for not assigning any *prāṇa-s* to the first six *pada-s*.

[1]*Dhyāna* is a noun, but has in English been converted into a verb, as often in Sanskrit the names (nouns) are indicative of functions (verbs). 'K' explains why *samāna* has few words (*alpākṣaratva*). He says, "because it is involved in the stanza (*pada*) pertaining to *prayoga*". And then elucidating his statement he says, "from the character of the *prayoga* of the third step (*pāda*) it is inferred that the character of the *prayoga* of the first and the second steps would be such as to include some words that are not the words of address or calling etc. (*asambodhanātmaka*). Its (i.e. of *samāna*) being short sounding is based on its (of the *pada*) being the *prayoga*. Thus, this *prāṇa* named as *samāna* is to be associated with the two stanzas viz. *manmathavat* and *māndhātṛ* pertaining to the *prayoga* of the first and the second steps (*pāda-s*).

[2]*Alpa-mūrcchanā* according to 'S' implies an incomplete *mūrcchanā* such as *ṣāḍavu* and so on. 'K' explains it as *tānīkaraṇam* i.e. the process of what may be called, tanification, the formation of *tāna-s* out of non-*tāna-s*, which he elucidates as consisting in "pronouncing (singing) the first note, passing on to the last note in the ascending or descending order and merely touching the other notes in-between". This also explains, according to him, the expression *svalpa-nāda*, having small sound. And he supports his contention by the assertion that "this *prāṇa* (*madhura*) should be associated with the first stanzas of the *pallava* in the first and the second steps (*pāda-s*) viz. *kānta* and *sumita* which are of slow tempo.

[3]*Svalpa-nāda* has been translated as 'a small sound' for *nāda* in this context has been used in the sense of sound being the material of music.

[4]'K' infers that the verbal content (*mātu*) is relatively more than the tonal content (*dhātu*) because the syllables are closely employed.

[5]*Alapadhvaniḥ*—Here *dhvani* is used in the sense of sound as the material of music. 'K' points out the purport by referring to the relatively greater verbal than tonal content.

[6]*Tāragati* is interpreted by 'K' as "that which has access (*gati*) to the high (*tāra*)

(iv) *Kānta* is considered to be of a lovely sound.[1] (49 d)

(v) *Dīpta* has brilliant sound.[2] (50 a)

(vi) *Samāhita,* however, is that which abides with the steady tone pattern (*sthāyī-varṇa*). (50 b)

(vii) *Agrāmya* is known by (the association of) the repetition of syllables[3] and sounds. (50 c-d)

(viii) *Sukumāra* is (characterised) by the softness of the syllable[4] tones and *mūrcchanā-s*.[5] (51 a-b)

(ix) *Prasanna* is (so called) because of the clarity[6] of the *pada,* the registers and the tones etc. (51 c-d)

(x) *Ojasvī* is vigorous.[7] (52 a)

Endowed with these excellences, the *elā-s* fulfil the three ends of human endeavour viz. virtue (*dharma*), desire (*kāma*) and wealth (*artha*)—both of

register. 'S' interprets it as permeating the high register. It is notable that whereas 'K' considers *alpadhvanistārgatiḥ* as qualifying *sāndra*, 'S' considers it as qualifying *kānta*, the next one. In keeping with his own interpretation, considering the second stanza of the *pallava-s* of the first and the second steps (*pāda-s*) viz. *jita* and *śobhī* to be relatively higher than their previous stanzas (*pada-s*), 'K' considers their dependence on *sāndra* as meaningful

[1]*Kānta-dhvaniḥ* lit. having lovely sound. 'K' defines loveliness of sound (or voice) explaining it as *ramaṇīya,* beautiful. *Kānta* according to 'K' is to be associated with the last (third) *pada-s,* of the *pallava-s* of the first and the second steps viz. *matta* and *suśobhī*, sung in the fast tempo.

[2]'S' interprets *dīpta* as *tīvra-nāda* (lit. sharp tone) but not in contradistinction with a flat tone. *Tīvra,* thus means 'of a high pitch'. 'K' says, it is called *dīpta* (lit. kindled or stimulated, excited) because of high pitch and perfection of tone.

[3]*Akṣara-nāda* (lit. sound of letters) may also imply the singing of syllables. 'K' suggests the repetition of letters of the words forming part of the *pada-s* in a chain, the last one of the preceding being sung as the first one of the succeeding word. Also, it means the repetition of the tones associated with those particular letters. Thus, as 'K' interprets, the *prāṇa* named *agrāmya* (not uncultivated) associated with such twofold repetition of syllables and tones sung with them is employed in the first *pada* of *dhruva* viz. *citra,* which is sung in the medium tempo.

[4]*Varṇa* lit. the sound of the *varṇa-s* (letters of alphabet). In this context *varṇa* does not mean tone pattern, it rather implies the cumulative musical impact of the syllables woven into the melody, which may be soft or harsh and so on.

[5]'K' interprets *mūrcchanā-s* as *tāna-s* and associates the *prāṇa* called *sukumāra* with the second stanza of *dhruva* viz. *vāsava,* sung in the medium tempo.

[6]According to 'K', the clarity of the *pada-s* consists in their being so composed as to signify their meaning immediately. By clarity of registers and tones is meant the distinctness of tonal form and so on, while 'etc.' implies note-series (*tāna*) and shakes (*gamaka*). He associates this *prāṇa* with the third stanza of *dhruva* viz. *mṛdu* which is sung in the slow tempo.

[7]*Ojo-bahula*—rich or profuse in *ojas* (vigour). *Ojas* is defined by 'K' and 'S' as repeated use of *samāsa* (compounds) and 'K' interprets it to be in the words of stanzas as well as in the note-series (*tāna-s*), or even in the combinations of notes that do not form a note-series.

the listener as well as of the performer. (52 c-d)

(ङ) एलाभेदाः

गणमात्रावर्णदेशविशिष्टास्ताश्चतुर्विधाः ।

गणः समूहः स द्वेधा वर्णमात्राविशेषणात् ॥५३॥

गुरुर्लघुरिति द्वेधा वर्णोऽनुस्वारसंयुतः ।

सविसर्गो व्यञ्जनान्तो दीर्घो युक्तपरो गुरुः ॥५४॥

वा पदान्ते त्वसौ वक्रो द्विमात्रो मात्रिको लघुः ।

ऋजुर्लिपौ भ्रे ष्के ष्पे च रहोर्योगे स वा लघुः ॥५५॥

ए ओ इं हिं पदान्ते वा प्राकृते लघवो मताः ।

पदमध्येऽप्यपभ्रंशे हुं हे ऊ ए इमित्यमी ॥५६॥

(e) The types of *elā:*

These[1] are of four types specified[2] by *gaṇa-s,*[3] *mātrā-s,*[4] *varṇa-s*[5] and regions. (53 a-b)

Gaṇa is a group which is two-fold, as qualified by *varṇa* or *mātrā*; *varṇa* is twofold viz. *guru* (long) and *laghu*[6] (short). *Guru* is (the syllable) that has *anusvāra* or *visarga*, that ends in a consonant, that has a long vowel, that precedes a conjunction or optionally[7] that is at the end of the foot (of a verse).[8]

[1]That is, the *elā* songs spoken of in the previous verse (52 ante).

[2]lit. 'qualified by.'

[3-5]In Sanskrit verse, a quarter or a *pāda* is regulated either by the number of syllables called *varṇa* (or *akṣara*) or by syllabic instants called *mātrā*. In the metres that are based on *varṇa*, balance is regulated by the pattern of short (*laghu*) and long (*guru*) syllables organised into *gaṇa-s*. The metres based on syllabic instants are regulated by the number of *mātrā-s* in a *pāda*. The former are called *vārṇika* and the latter are known as *mātrika chanda-s*. Then there are metres that are based only on the number of syllables.

The *elā-s* based on the groups (*gaṇa-s*) of *varṇa-s* are known as *gaṇa-elā-s*; *elā-s* based on groups of *mātrā-s* are called *mātrā-elā-s*, and *elā-s* based on the number of syllables only are called *varṇa-elā-s*.

[6]A *laghu* at the end of the foot of a verse is optionally taken to be a *guru* according to the exigency of the metre.

[7]*Laghu* is not defined here, but 'S' says that by implication any syllables devoid of the above characteristics is to be considered *laghu*.

[8]This refers to *guru*.

This is zig-zag[1] and of two *mātrā-s* and *laghu* is of one *mātrā* and straight[2] in the script. This,[3] however, in conjunction with[4] the syllable *bhra* the guttural spirant,[5] the labial spirant,[6] the combination of the letters *r* and *h*,[7] optionally becomes *laghu*.[8] The (syllables) *e*, *o*, *iṁ* and *hiṁ* in *Prakṛta*,[9] when at the end of a foot of a verse, are treated as *laghu* so also, the (syllables) *huṁ*, *he*, *ū*, *e* and *iṁ* in *Apabhraṁśa*[10] in the middle of a *pada*. (54-56)

(च) वर्णगणा:

तत्र वर्णगणो वर्णैस्त्रिभिरष्टविधश्च सः ।
मस्त्रिगुः पूर्वलो यः स्यान्मध्यलो रोऽन्तगुस्तु सः ॥५७॥
तोऽन्तलो मध्यगो जः स्याद्गादिर्भस्त्रिलघुस्तु नः ।

(f) *Varṇa-gaṇa-s* (the syllabic groups)

Of (the two types of *gaṇa-s*), *varṇagaṇa* (syllabic group) is (formed) by three syllables. It is eight-fold[11]-*ma* (*gaṇa*) has three *guru-s*,[12] *ya* (*gaṇa*) has *laghu* in the beginning,[13] *ra* (*gaṇa*) has *laghu* in the middle,[14] *sa* (*gaṇa*) has *guru* in the end,[15] *ta* (*gaṇa*) has *laghu* in the end,[16] *ja* (*gaṇa*) has *guru* in the middle,[17] *bha* (*gaṇa*) has *gura* in the beginning[18] while *na* (*gaṇa*)[19] has three

[1] *Vakra* is lit. curved or zig-zag. It refers to notation. *Guru* is written like the letter S.

[2] *Laghu* is written like a straight (perpendicular) line.

[3] This' stands for *laghu* just defined.

[4] That is, preceded by the syllable *bhra* and so on.

[5] That is, *jihvāmūlīya* written as ≍

[6] That is, *upadhmānīya* also written as ≍

[7] That is, *repha* over *h*.

[8] Normally, it would be *guru*, but optionally it becomes *laghu*.

[9] *Prakṛta* is a name of a language, generally thought to have been derived from Sanskrit.

[10] *Apabhraṁśa* is also a similar language, further removed from Sanskrit. These syllables also are considered to be *laghu*.

[11] That is, *ma-gaṇa*, *ya-gaṇa*, *ra-gaṇa*, *sa-gaṇa*, *ta-gaṇa*, *ja-gaṇa*, *bha-gaṇa*, and *na-gaṇa*.

[12] That is, SSS—a *guru* in the beginning, the middle and in the end.

[13] That is, a *laghu* followed by two *guru-s* e.g. ISS

[14] That is, a *laghu* preceded and followed by a *guru* e.g. SIS

[15] That is, a *guru* preceded by two *laghu-s* e.g. IIS

[16] That is, a *laghu* preceded by two *guru-s* e.g. SSI

[17] That is, a *guru* preceded and followed by a *laghu* e.g. ISI

[18] That is, a *guru* followed by two *laghu-s* e.g. SII

[19] That is, having a *laghu* in the beginning, in the middle and in the end, e.g. III

laghu-s.[1] (57-58 a b)

(छ) वर्णगणदेवता:, फलानि च

इत्येषां देवता भूमिजलाग्निमरुतोऽम्बरम् ॥५८॥
सूर्यचन्द्रसुराधीशाः क्रमात् कुर्यु फलानि ते ।
श्रीवृद्धिनिधनस्थानभ्रंशनिर्धनतारुजः ॥५९॥
कीर्तिरायुश्च वर्ण्यस्य श्लोकगीतादियोगतः ।

(g) The deities and the fruits appertaining to the *varṇa-gaṇa-s:*

Their deities respectively are—earth, water, fire, air, space, sun, moon and Indra[2] who bestow upon the subject,[3] through the verse or the song employed, the (following) respective fruits viz. wealth, destruction, loss of position, poverty, affliction of disease, fame and longevity. (58 c-60 b)

(ज) वर्णवर्गाणां देवता: फलानि च

सोमो भौमो बुधो जीवः शुक्रः सौरी रविस्तमः ॥६०॥
क्रमादकचटानां तपयशानां च देवताः ।
वर्गाणां स्युः फलान्येषामायुः कीर्तिरसद्यशः ॥६१॥
संपत् सुभगता कीर्तिमान्द्यं मृत्युश्च शून्यता ।
प्रयोगे श्लोकगीतादौ स्तुत्यस्योक्तानि सूरिभिः ॥६२॥

(h) The deities and the fruits appertaining to the classes of *varṇa-s* (letters):

The deities of the (eight classes) of letters (of the alphabet) viz. the vowels beginning with *a*, the five groups of consonants beginning with *k*, *c*,

[1]The above description of *gaṇa-s* may be illustrated as under:

Varṇa—gaṇa-s (syllabic groups)

S. no.	*Name of the gaṇa*	*Description*	*Symbolic representation.*
1.	*ma-gaṇa*	group of three *guru-s.*	SSS
2.	*ya-gaṇa*	a *laghu* followed by two *guru-s.*	ISS
3.	*ra-gaṇa*	a *laghu* in between two *guru-s*	SIS
4.	*sa-gaṇa*	two *guru-s* followed by a *laghu*	SSI
5.	*ta-gaṇa*	two *laghu-s* followed by a *guru*	IIS
6.	*ja-gaṇa*	a *guru* in between two *laghu-s*	ISI
7.	*bha-gaṇa*	a *guru* followed by two *laghus*	SII
8.	*na-gaṇa*	group of three *laghu-s*	III

[2]*Surādhīśa* lit. means the chief of gods.

[3]*Varṇya* is interpreted by 'S' as 'hero' (*nāyaka*). Lit. it signifies the object of description.

ṭ, t, and p, the semi-vowels beginning with y, and the sibilants beginning with ś[1] respectively are—Moon, Mars, Mercury, Venus, Jupiter, Saturn, Sun and darkness, and their resultant effects respectively are longevity, fame, bad name, wealth, good luck, decline of fame, destruction,[2] and delusion,[3] as associated by the wise with the subject in the context of a verse, a song and so on. (60 c-62)

(झ) मात्रागणाः

मात्रा कला लघुर्लः स्यात्तद्गणाश्छपचास्तदौ ।
स्युः षट्पञ्चचतुस्त्रिद्विसंख्यमात्रायुताः क्रमात् ॥६३॥

यथा—ऽऽऽ इति छगणः; ऽऽ। इति पगणः; ऽऽ इति चगणः; ऽ। इति तगणः; ऽ इति दगणः; । इति पञ्च मात्रागणाः ॥

अत्युक्तायास्तु चत्वारो भेदा रतिगणा मताः ।
किंतु तत्र लपूर्वा ये तेष्वादावधिको लघुः ॥६४॥
एवं मध्याभवा भेदाः प्रतिष्ठायास्तु षोडश ॥६५॥

यथा—ऽऽ; ।ऽ; ऽ।; ।।; इति रतिगणाः ॥

यथा—ऽऽऽ; ।ऽऽ; ऽ।ऽ; ।।ऽ; ऽऽ।; ।ऽ।; ऽ।।; ।।।; इति कामगणाः ॥

यथा—ऽऽऽऽ; ।ऽऽऽ; ऽ।ऽऽ; ।।ऽऽ; ऽऽ।ऽ; ।ऽ।ऽ; ऽ।।ऽ; ।।।ऽ; ऽऽऽ।; ।ऽऽ।; ऽ।ऽ।; ।।ऽ।; ऽऽ।।; ।ऽ।।; ऽ।।।; ।।।।; इति बाणगणाः ॥

[1]The different classes of the letters of the alphabet are indicated as under:

Classes of the letters of the alphabet

S. No.	*Indicated class of letters*	*The letters of alphabet comprehended*	*Specific quality of the class*
1.	Beginning with *a*	*a, ā, i, ī, u, ū, ṛ, ṝ, ḷ, e, ai, o, au.*	Vowels
2.	Beginning with *k*	*k, kh, g, gh, ṅ.*	Consonants
3.	Beginning with *c*	*c, ch, j, jh, ñ.*	Consonants
4.	Beginning with *ṭ*	*ṭ, ṭh, ḍ, ḍh, ṇ.*	Consonants
5.	Beginning with *t*	*t, th, d, dh, n.*	Consonants
6.	Beginning with *p*	*p, ph, b, bh, m.*	Consonants
7.	Beginning with *y*	*y, r, l, v*	Semi Vowels
8.	Beginning with *ś*	*ś, ṣ, s.*	Sibilants

[2]*Mṛtyu*, lit. 'death'.

[3]*Śūnyatā*, lit. voidness, blankness of mind; is interpreted by 'S' as *moha* (delusion).

(i) The *mātrā-gaṇa-s* (measure groups):

Mātrā is (also called) *kalā*, *laghu* and *la*,[1] its five groups viz. *cha* (*gaṇa*), *pa* (*gaṇa*), *ca* (*gaṇa*), *ta* (*gaṇa*) and *da* (*gaṇa*) with six, five, four, three and two *mātrā-s*[2] (unit-measures) respectively are written as follows: (63)

S S S	*cha-gaṇa*
S S I	*pa-gaṇa*
S S	*ca-gaṇa*
S I	*ta-gaṇa* and
S	*da gaṇa*

These are the five *mātrā-gaṇa-s*.

The four varieties of *atyuktā*[3] are called *rati-gaṇa-s*, with the provision that those (of the *gaṇa-s*) among them that commence with a *laghu*, take an extra *laghu* in the commencement. Likewise, the eight varieties created out of *madhyā*[4] are known as *kāmagaṇa-s*, as also the sixteen varieties (obtained) from *pratiṣṭhā*[5] are (called) *bāṇa-gaṇa-s*. (64-65)
They are illustrated as under:

(i) *Rati-gaṇa-s:* SS, IS, SI, II.
(ii) *Kāma-gaṇa-s:* SSS, ISS, SIS, IIS, SSI, ISI, SII, III.
(iii) *Bāṇa-gaṇa-s:* SSSS, ISSS, SISS, IISS, SSIS, ISIS, SIIS, IIIS, SSSI, ISSI, SISI, IISI, SSII, ISII, SIII, IIII.

(ख) गणैला

(१) लक्षणम्, तद्भेदाश्च

तत्र वर्णगणैर्जाता गणैला परिकीर्तिता ।
सा भवेत् त्रिविधा शुद्धा संकीर्णा विकृता तथा ॥६६॥
शुद्धा चतुर्विधा नादावती हंसावती तथा ।
नन्दावती च भद्रावत्यथासां लक्ष्म कथ्यते ॥६७॥
गणादिनियमस्त्वासामङ्घ्रिखण्डद्वयाश्रयः ।

[1] *la* is the abbreviated form of *laghu*.

[2] Obviously two *mātrā-s* are counted for the sign of a *guru*(*s*) and one for that of *laghu* (I).

[3] *Atyuktā* is a group of metres with two syllables in a foot (*pāda*) as defined by 'K'. 'S' describes it as a group of metres with two *laghu-s*. These groups are said to be four which are called *rati-gaṇa-s* when duly modified.

[4–5] *Madhyā* and *Pratiṣṭhā* are groups of metres like those of *Atyuktā*, having three and four syllables respectively for each foot.

(b) *Gaṇa-elā* (66-94 b).

(1) Definition and classification:

From amongst these,[1] (that which is) produced by *varṇa-gaṇa-s* (syllabic groups) is known as *gaṇa-elā*.[2] It is threefold viz. *śuddhā*,[3] *saṅkīrṇā*,[4] and *vikṛtā*.[5] *Śuddhā* is fourfold viz. *nādāvatī*, *haṁsāvatī*, *nandāvatī* and *bhadrāvatī*. These are now to be defined. The rule regarding *gaṇa* etc. however, is applicable in their case to the (first) two parts of the step.'[6] (66-68 b)

(२) शुद्धाया भेदा:

(क) नादावती

नादावती पञ्चभिर्भैर्नान्तैः स्याट्टक्कमण्ठयोः ॥६८॥
ऋग्वेदोत्था सिता विप्रा कैंशिकीं वृत्तिमाश्रिता ।
पाञ्चालीरीतिर्भारत्याः प्रीत्यै श्रृङ्गारवर्धनी ॥६९॥

(2) The varieties of *śuddhā* (pure).

(a) *Nādāvatī:*

Nādāvatī is (composed) by five *bha*-(*gaṇa-s*) followed by a *na* (*gaṇa*) in the end and is (sung) in *ṭakka* (*rāga*) with *maṇṭha* (*tāla*). Derived from the *Ṛgveda*, bright, belonging to the *Brāhmaṇa* caste, couched in *kaiśikī vṛtti*[7] and *pāñcālī*[8] *rīti*, it is (sung) to propitiate *Bhāratī*[9] and to stimulate the sentiment of conjugal love. (68 c-69)

[1]That is, the *varṇa-gaṇa-s* and the *mātrā-gaṇa-s*.

[2]The pronoun (that) stands for *elā* which is implied in the context.

[3]*Śuddhā* lit. means standard or pure.

[4]*Saṁkīrṇā* lit. means mixed.

[5]*Vikṛtā* lit. means modified.

[6] S' infers that apart from the first two parts of the first step the rest of the song is to be sung freely i.e. it is not governed by that rule.

[7]The concept of *vṛtti* seems to have many facets. Bharata simply conceives it as action of four types in the context of drama viz. *sāttvatī*, *ārabhaṭī*, *bhāratī*, and *kaiśikī* (mental, violent, vocal and graceful). The grammarians speak of *abhidhā-vṛtti* (conventional power or function of word) and *lakṣaṇā-vṛtti* secondary power or function of word). Some experts in poetics, accordingly held that *vṛtti* is nothing but the function or the action of the sound value of recurring letters, which helps in the presentation of a particular aesthetic configuration (*rasa*). cf. K.C. Pandey, *Indian Aesthetics*, pp. 457-59. 'K' defines *vṛtti* in its generic sense as "verbal, mental and physical activity conducive to human endeavour (*puruṣārtha*)". He also defines the four types of *vṛtti* specifically, which may be seen in his commentary on verses 66-76 of this chapter.

[8]*Rīti* signifies diction which is fourfold viz. *vaidarbhī*, *gauḍī*, *pāñcālī* and *lāṭī*. 'K' defines *rīti* in its generic sense as "the delineation or composition of words (and phrases) loaded with excellence". He also defines the four types of *rīti* specifically which could be seen in his commentary on verses 66-76 of this chapter.

[9]*Bhāratī* is a name of Sarasvatī, the goddess of learning and fine arts.

(ख) हंसावती

रगणैः पञ्चभिः सान्तैः प्रोक्ता हंसावती बुधैः।
द्वितीयताले हिन्दोले क्षत्रिया यजुरुद्भवा ॥७०॥
लोहितारभटीं वृत्तिं लाटीं रीतिं च संश्रिता।
रौद्रे रसे चण्डिकायाः प्रीतये विनियुज्यते ॥७१॥

(b) *Haṁsāvatī:*

Haṁsāvatī is described by the specialists (as constituted) by five *ra-gaṇa-s* followed by a *sa-gaṇa* in the end. It is (sung) in *rāga hindola* with *dvitīya tāla*. Belonging to the *kṣatriya* (warrior) caste, derived from the *Yajurveda*, it is red in colour and is couched in *ārabhaṭi vṛtti* and *lāṭī rīti*. It is employed in the sentiment of wrath[1] (and) for the propitiation of Caṇḍikā.[2] (70-71)

(ग) नन्दावती

पञ्चभिस्तगणैर्जान्तैरेला नन्दावती मता।
प्रतितालेन सा गेया रागे मालवकैशिके ॥७२॥
सामवेदोद्भवा पीता वैश्या सात्त्वतवृत्तिजा।
गौडी च रीतिरिन्द्राण्याः प्रीत्यै वीररसाश्रया ॥७३॥

(c) *Nandāvatī:*

The *elā* (called) *nandāvatī* is believed to be (formed) by five *ta-gaṇa-s* followed by a *ja-gaṇa* in the end. It is sung in *rāga mālava-kaiśika* with *prati-tāla*. Arising from the *Sāma-veda*, of yellow colour and *vaiśya*[3] caste, couched in *sāttvatī vṛttī* and *gauḍī rīti*, it is employed to propitiate *Indrāṇī*[4] and is based on the sentiment of heroism.[5] (72-73)

[1]*Raudra* of the text.

[2]*Caṇḍikā* is the name of the destructive aspect of the mother goddess *Durgā*.

[3]*Vaiśya* is the third caste, *Brāhmaṇa* (the priestly class) and *kṣatrīya* (the warrior class) being the first two. This class includes not only the merchants but also the peasants—all those who have economic holdings.

[4]*Indrāṇī* is the designation of the wife of *Indra* the chief of gods.

[5]*Vīra* of the text.

(घ) भद्रावती

भद्रावती पञ्चभिर्मैर्यान्तैः कङ्कालतालतः ।
ककुभेऽथर्ववेदोत्था कृष्णा शूद्रा च भारतीम् ॥७४॥
वृत्तिं वैदर्भरीतिं च श्रिता बीभत्ससंभृता ।
वाराहीदेवताप्रीत्यै शार्ङ्गदेवेन कीर्तिता ॥७५॥

(d) *Bhadrāvatī:*

Bhadrāvatī is (composed) by five *ma* (*gaṇa-s*) followed by one *ya* (*gaṇa*) in the end. It is (sung) in *rāga kakubha* with *kaṅkāla tāla.* Arisen from the *Atharvaveda,* black in colour, belonging to the *śūdra*[1] caste, it is couched in *bhāratī vṛtti* and *vaidarbhī rīti.* Endowed with the sentiment of abhorence[2] it is (employed) for the propitiation of the goddess *Vārāhī*[3] as declared by Śārṅgadeva. (74-75)

(३) संकीर्णेला

बहुधा संकरादासां संकीर्णा बहुधा मताः ।
अप्रसिद्धास्तु ता लक्ष्ये तेन नेह प्रपञ्चिताः ॥७६॥

(3) *Saṅkīrṇā* (mixed)

Many mixed (*saṅkīrṇā*) varieties are (obtained) by intermixing these[4] in various ways, but since they are not so well known in practice, they are not dealt with herein. (76)

(४) विकृतैला

शुद्धाः स्युर्विकृतास्तिस्र आद्या गणविकारतः ।
वासवी संगता त्रेता चतुरा बाणसंज्ञिका ॥७७॥
एकद्वित्रिचतुष्पञ्चविकारात् पञ्चधेति ताः ।

(4) *Vikṛtā* (modified):

The first three varieties of *śuddhā*[5] (*elā*) become ***vikṛtā*** **modified** (*elā*) by

[1]*Śūdra* is the fourth caste consisting of labourers and **menial workers.**
[2]*Bībhatsa* of the text.
[3]*Vārāhī* is the name of *lakṣmī*, the consort or power of ***Viṣṇu.***
[4]That is, the *śuddhā gaṇa-elā-s.*
[5]That is, ***nādāvatī, haṁsāvatī*** and ***nandāvatī.***

the modification of their *gaṇa-s*. These are fivefold each[1] viz, *vāsavī, saṅgatā, tretā, caturā* and *bāṇā* (formed) respectively by the modification of one, two, three, four and five (*gaṇa-s*). (77-78 c)

(क) वासवी

प्रत्येकं वासवी पञ्चविधा रामा मनोरमा ॥७८॥
उन्नता शान्तिसंज्ञा च नागरेत्युच्यते बुधैः।
गणानां प्रथमादीनां विकारात् पञ्चमावधि ॥७९॥

(a) *Vāsavi:*

Vāsavi is fivefold viz. *rāmā, manoramā, unnatā, śānti* and *nāgarā* (formed) respectively by the modification of the first to the fifth *gaṇa*,[2] as described by the wise. (78 c-79)

(ख) संगता

रमणीया च विषमा समा लक्ष्मीश्च कौमुदी।
कामोत्सवा नन्दिनी च गौरी सौम्या ततः परम् ॥८०॥
रतिदेहेति दशधा संगता गदिता बुधैः।
आद्यस्य स्युर्द्वितीयादिसहितस्य विकारतः ॥८१॥
चतस्रस्ता द्वितीयस्य तृतीयादियुजस्त्रयम्।
विकारेण तृतीयस्य चतुर्थादियुजो द्वयम् ॥८२॥
तुर्यपञ्चमयोस्त्वेका, लक्ष्म तासां क्रमादिति।

[1]Each of these three has five varieties.

[2]That is 1, 2, 3, 4 and 5th *gaṇa* respectively, viz. by the modification of first *gaṇa* we have *ramā*, by that of the second, we have *manoramā*, by that of the third, *unnatā*, by that of the fourth, *śānti* and by that of the fifth *gaṇa*, we have *nāgarā*. It may be noted that *vāsavī* is formed by the modification of one *gaṇa*.

'K' points out the implication of the text *'pañcamāvadhiḥ'* according to which the process of modification is to be carried on up to the fifth *gaṇa* only. He says that, if even the sixth i.e. the last *gaṇa* also were to be modified, it would not be possible to keep the identity of the song within the range of recognition. He further points out that the rule "deprived of their characteristic features excepting the *nyāsa* they become modified" etc. spoken of earlier (vide *S.R.*, 1.7.3), also applies in this case by implication. And accordingly, even though the last *gaṇa* of *nādāvatī* cannot at all be modified, yet because in case of *haṁsāvatī* and *nandāvatī* the modification of *sa-gaṇa* and *ja-gaṇa* is possible, the author has excluded the last *gana* from the process of modification as a general rule.

(b) *Saṅgatā:*

Saṅgatā[1] is declared by the experts to be tenfold viz. *ramaṇīyā, viṣamā, samā, lakṣmī, kaumudī, kāmotsavā, nandinī, gaurī, saumyā,* and *ratidehā.* These are characterised respectively as follows:

(i) Four of them by the modification of their first (*gaṇa*) in conjunction with their second and so on[2];

(ii) Three (others) by the modification of their second (*gaṇa*) in conjunction with the third and so on[3];

(iii) Two (others) by the modification of their third (*gaṇa*) in conjunction with the fourth and so on[4] and

(iv) One only by the (modification) of the fourth and the fifth *gaṇa-s* (in conjunction),[5] (80-83 b)

(ग) त्रेता

त्रेता दशविधा प्रोक्ता मङ्गला रतिमङ्गला ।।८३।।
कलिका तनुमध्या च वीरश्रीर्जयमङ्गला ।
विजया रत्नमाला च गुरुमध्या रतिप्रभा ।।८४।।
आद्याक्षरेण ग्रहणं प्रथमादेरिहेष्यते ।
प्रद्वित्रिणां प्रद्विचानां प्रद्विपानां प्रचत्रिणाम् ।।८५।।
प्रत्रिपाणां प्रचपानां द्वित्रिचानां द्विपत्रिणाम् ।
द्विचपानां चत्रिपाणां विकृतेः स्युः क्रमादिमाः ।।८६।।

[1] *Saṅgatā* is formed by the modification of two *gaṇa-s*.
[2] That is, the second, the third, the fourth and the fifth one respectively.
[3] That is, the third, fourth and the fifth one respectively.
[4] That is, the fourth and the fifth respectively.
[5] The varieties of *saṅgatā* may be understood from this chart.

The varieties of *saṅgatā*

S. no.	*Name of the variety*	*Formed by the modification of the gaṇa-s in conjunction*
1.	*Ramaṇīya*	First and second
2.	*Viṣamā*	First and third
3.	*Samā*	First and fourth
4.	*Lakṣmī*	First and fifth
5.	*Kaumudī*	Second and third
6.	*Kāmotsavā*	Second and fourth
7.	*Nandinī*	Second and fifth
8.	*Gaurī*	Third and fourth
9.	*Saumyā*	Third and fifth
10.	*Ratidehā*	Fourth and fifth

(c) *Tretā:*

Tretā[1] is said to be tenfold viz. *maṅgalā, rati-maṅgalā, kalikā, tanumadhyā, vīraśri, jayamaṅgalā, vijayā, ratnamālā, gurumadhyā,* and *ratiprabhā.* The first syllable hereunder is indicative of the first (second, third) etc. These are formed respectively by the modification of the first, second and third (*gaṇa-s*) viz., the first, second and fourth (*gaṇa-s*); the first, second and fifth (*gaṇa-s*), the first, fourth and third (*gaṇa-s*); the first, third and fifth (*gaṇa-s*); the first, fourth and fifth (*gaṇa-s*); the second, third and fourth (*gaṇa-s*); the second, third and fifth (*gaṇa-s*); the second fourth and fifth (*gaṇa-s*) and the third, fourth and fifth (*gaṇa-s*). (83 c-86)

(घ) चतुरा

त्यक्त्वैकैकं गणं त्वाद्याच्चतुर्णां स्याद्विकारतः ।
चतुरा पञ्चधा तत्र प्रथमा तूत्सवप्रिया ॥८७॥
महानन्दाथ लहरी जया च कुसुमावती ।

(d) *Caturā:*

Caturā[2] is fivefold viz. *utsavapriyā, mahanandā, laharī, jayā* and *kusumāvatī* which are formed respectively by the modification of four (of the five) *gaṇa-s*, leaving aside one each (in turn)[3] from the first (*gaṇa*) onwards. (87-88 b)

[1]*Tretā* is formed by the modification of three *gaṇa-s* in the following ten varieties:

The varieties of *tretā*

S. no.	*Name of the variety*	*Formed by the modification of the gaṇa-s in conjunction*
1.	*Maṅgalā*	First, second and third
2.	*Ratimaṅgalā*	First, second and fourth
3.	*Kalikā*	First, second and fifth
4.	*Tanumadhyā*	First, third and fourth
5.	*Vīraśrī*	First, third and fifth
6.	*Jayamaṅgalā*	First, fourth and fifth
7.	*Vijayā*	Second, third and fourth
8.	*Ratnamālā*	Second, third and fifth
9.	*Gurumadhyā*	Second, fourth and fifth
10.	*Ratiprabhā*	Third, fourth and fifth

[2]*Caturā* is formed by the modification of four *gaṇa-s*.

[3]That is, by sparing the 1st, 2nd, 3rd, 4th and the 5th *gaṇa-s* in turn from the process of modification. In other words, by the modification of four out of the five modificable

(ङ) बाणा

आद्यात् पञ्चविकारेण बाणा स्यात् पार्वतीप्रिया ॥८८॥

(e) *Bāṇā:*

Bāṇā is (formed) by the modification of five *gaṇa-s* right from the beginning[1] (the first one), which is (also called *pārvatī-priyā* (88 c d)

(Thus) each of these nādāvati etc. has thirty-one[2] varieties making ninety-three in all. (89 a-c)

(५) अन्ये भेदाः

प्रत्यकमेकर्त्रिशत्ते नादावत्यादिषु स्थिताः ।
भेदास्त्रिनवतिर्युक्ता अन्ये पञ्चदश त्विमे ॥८९॥
सावित्री पावनी वातसावित्री त्रिविधा मता ।
संगता सवितुः क्षिप्ते पवनस्य गणे क्रमात् ॥९०॥
द्वितीये चाद्यभेदाभ्यां द्विविधा वासवी मता ।
नादावत्यामिमे भेदा हंसावत्यामपि त्रिधा ॥९१॥
व्योमजा वारुणी व्योमवारुणी चेति संगता ।
तद्दैवत्यगणोपेता तदा स्याद्वासवी द्विधा ॥९२॥
नन्दावत्यां वह्निजा च वारुणी वह्निवारुणी ।
तद्गणैः संगता त्रेधा तथा द्वेधा च वासवी ॥९३॥
इत्येते विकृता भेदा अष्टोत्तरशतं मताः ।

gaṇa-s sparing one in each case commencing with the first *gaṇa*. These are illustrated in the following chart.

The varieties of *Caturā*

S. no.	*Name of the variety*	*Formed by the modification of gaṇa-s in conjunction*
1.	*Utsavapriyā*	Second, third, fourth and fifth
2.	*Mahānandā*	First, third, fourth and fifth
3.	*Laharī*	First, second, fourth and fifth
4.	*Jayā*	First, second, third and fifth
5.	*Kusumāvatī*	First, second, third and fourth

[1]That is from the *bha-gaṇa* onwards.

[2]The no. 31 is comprised of 5 varieties of *vāsavī*, ten of *saṅgatā*, ten of *tretā*, five of *caturā* and one *bāṇā* (5 + 10 + 10 + 5 + 1 = 31). 31 varieties are spoken of in case of each of the three *elā-s* viz. *nādāvatī* (by the modification of *bha-gaṇa*), *haṁsāvatī* (by the modification of *ra-gaṇa*) and *nandāvatī* (by the modification of *ta-gaṇa*).

(5) Other varieties:

Besides,[1] there are fifteen others formed as under:

(i) *Saṅgatā*[2] is considered to be threefold viz. *sāvitrī*, *pāvanī*, *vātasāvitrī* (formed) by the respective displacement of its[3] two *bha* (-*gana-s*), two *ja*[4] (-*gaṇa-s*), two *sa*[5] (-*gaṇa-s*), and by one *ja-gaṇa* and one *sa*[6] (-*gaṇa*). (90-91 a)

(ii) *Vāsavī* is considered to be twofold by the first two varieties.[7] (91-92)

These[8] are the variations of *nādāvatī*. (91 c)

In *haṁsāvatī* also *saṅgatā* has three variations viz. *vyomajā, vāruṇī* and *vyomavāruṇī* when (similarly) treated by *ta* and *ya* (-*gaṇa-s*).[9] Then *vāsavī* too is twofold.[10] (91 c-92)

In *nandāvatī* as well *saṅgatā* is threefold viz. *vahnijā*, *vāruṇī* and *vahnivāruṇī* (formed) respectively by their *gana-s*,[11] and similarly, *vāsavī* is twofold.[12] (93)

Thus,[13] the varieties of *vikṛtā* (modified) *elā* are considered to be one hundred and eight (in all). (94 a b)

[1]That is, apart from the 93 spoken of above.

[2]*Saṅgatā* itself is formed out of *nādāvatī* by the modification of two of its *gaṇa-s*.

[3]The pronoun 'it' refers to *saṅgatā*.

[4]Lit. by the two *gaṇa-s* having the sun for their deity i.e. *ja-gaṇa*.

[5]Lit. the two *gaṇa-s* having air for their deity i.e. *sa-gaṇa*.

[6]Lit. the text *dvitīya ca* would mean 'in the second'. 'K' interprets—"one *bha* (-*gaṇa*) having been displaced by *sa-gaṇa* and the other having been replaced by *ja-gaṇa*, it is called *vātasāvitrī*, a modification of *saṅgatā*." 'S' merely says that the two *bha* (-*gaṇa-s*) are displaced by both (i.e. the *ja* and the *sa*) *gaṇa-s*. In other words, he does not indicate the order in which they displace the two *bha-gaṇa-s*.

[7]The two modifications of *vāsavī*, spoken of here, are caused through the variation of the first two of the three variations of *saṅgatā* mentioned above. Since *vāsavī* is modified by one *gaṇa*, there are only two variations possible in it viz. *sāvitrī* and *pāvanī* formed respectively by the displacement of *bha-gaṇa* by *ja-gaṇa* and *sa-gaṇa*.

[8]Thus, the three variations of *saṅgatā* and two of *vāsavī* make five other modifications of *nādāvatī elā*.

[9]*Saṅgatā* is formed by the modification of two *gaṇa-s*. In *haṁsāvatī* when two *ra* (-*gaṇa-s*) are replaced by two *ta* (-*gaṇa-s*), two *ya* (-*gaṇa-s*) and both *ta* and *ya* (one each) *vyomajā*, *vāruṇī* and *vyomavāruṇī* respectively are formed. Literally, *taddaivatyagaṇopetā* would mean, 'when it (*saṅgatā*) takes resort to the *gaṇa-s*, having space and water as deities'.

[10]That is, in *haṁsāvatī elā*, *vāsavī* has two variations viz. *vyomajā* and *vāruṇī* formed by the replacement of *ra-gaṇa* respectively by *ta* (-*gaṇa*) and *ya* (-*gaṇa*).

[11]The procedure of formation is the same as in *nādāvatī* and *haṁsāvatī*. In the case of *nandāvatī* two *ta* (-*gaṇa-s*) are replaced by two *ra* (-*gaṇa-s*), two *ya* (-*gaṇa-s*) and both *ra* and *ya* (*gaṇa* one each) respectively to produce *vahnijā*, *vāruṇī* and *vahnīvāruṇī*.

[12]*Vāsavī* is formed by the replacement of ta (-*gaṇa*) by *ra* (-*gaṇa*) respectively to produce *vahnijā* and *vāruṇī*.

[13]'K' observes that because *ma* (-*gana*) cannot possibly be modified, the author seems to suggest the non-availability of the variations of *bhadrāvatī*.

(ग) मात्रैला

मात्रागणैस्तु मात्रैला सा च ज्ञेया चतुर्विधा ॥९४॥
रतिलेखा कामलेखाबाणलेखा तथापरा ।
चन्द्रलेखेति तत्राद्ये पादे रुद्राः कला यदि ॥९५॥
द्वितीये च तृतीये तु मात्रा दश तथा भवेत् ।
रतिलेखा रतिगणै कामलेखा तु मान्मथैः ॥९६॥
द्विगुणाभिः कलाभिः स्यान्मात्रात्रैगुण्यतो भवेत् ।
वाणलेखा बाणगणैश्चन्द्रलेखा तु मिश्रितैः ॥९७॥
गणैश्चतुर्गुणकलाश्चतस्त्रोऽन्या ब्रुवेऽधुना ।
आद्येन्दुमत्यथो ज्योतिष्मती पश्चान्नभस्वती ॥९८॥
वसुमत्यपि तत्रेन्दुमती छैः पञ्चभिः सतैः ।
पञ्चभिः पैः सचगणैराहुर्ज्योतिष्मतीं बुधाः ॥९९॥
त्रिभिश्चैः पगणेनापि छाद्यन्ता स्यान्नभस्वती ।
सा स्याद्वसुमती यस्यां दपचाः पत्रयं छतौ ॥१००॥
नादावत्यादयो मात्राश्चाद्यैः स्वगणभङ्गजैः ।
गणाः पञ्च त्रिमात्रोऽन्ते गणाः सप्तान्तिमो लघुः ॥१०१॥
गणाः सप्त लघुश्चान्ते त्रिमात्रोऽन्ते गणाष्टकः ।
लक्ष्माणीति क्रमात्सासामित्यूचे सव्यसाचिना ॥१०२॥
एकद्वित्रिचतुष्पञ्चमात्रावृद्धिर्यदाङ्घ्रिषु ।
तदा विचित्रमात्रैलास्ता जगाद धनञ्जयः ॥१०३॥
नन्दिनी चित्रिणी चित्रा विचित्रेत्यभिधानतः ।
रतिलेखादयः प्रोक्ताः क्रमादनियतैर्गणैः ॥१०४॥
एलयोराद्ययोरङ्घ्री व्यत्ययस्तावयुजाविह ।

(c) *Mātrā-elā:* **(94 c-105 b)**

Mātrā-elā **is (formed) by the *mātrā-gaṇa-s* (measure groups), and it is known to be fourfold viz. *ratilekhā, kāmalekhā, bāṇalekhā and candralekhā.* (94 c-95 c)**

In *ratilekhā* the first *pāda*[1] is composed of eleven *mātrā-s* (units) and so also the second,[2] while[3] the third consists of ten (*mātrā-s*) arranged in *rati-*

[1]The *udgrāha* (of the *elā*) has three steps i.e. *pāda-s* (cf. verse 35-36 ante). The first step is to be composed in 11 *mātrā-s*.

[2]The second step too is likewise to be composed in eleven *mātrā-s*.

[3]The third step is to be composed differently i.e. in ten *mātrā-s*. All the three steps together are composed by (11 + 11 + 10) = 32 *mātrā-s*.

gaṇa-s.[1] *Kāmalekhā* is (composed) by *kāmagaṇa-s*[2] with double[3] the number of *mātrā-s*. *Bāṇalekhā* is (composed) by *bāṇagaṇa-s* with triple[4] number of the *mātrā-s*, while *candralekhā* is (composed) by a mixture[5] of (these) *gaṇa-s* utilising four times[6] the number of *mātrā-s*. (95 c-98 a)

I shall now relate four others viz. *indumatī*, *jyotiṣmatī*, *nabhasvatī* and *vasumatī*. Of these, *indumatī* is (composed) with five *cha*[7] (*gaṇa-s*) along with *ta*[8] (*-gaṇa-s*). *Jyotiṣmatī* is declared by the experts to be (composed) with five *pa*[9] (*-gaṇa-s*) along with a *ca*[10] (*-gaṇa*). *Nabhasvatī* has one *cha* (*-gaṇa*) in the beginning followed by one *pa* (*-gaṇa*) and one *cha* (*-gaṇa*) in the end. *Vasumatī* has one *da*[11] (*-gaṇa*), one *pa* (*-gaṇa*) and *ca* (*-gaṇa*) followed by three *pa* (*-gaṇa-s*), one *cha* (*-gaṇa*) and one *ta* (*-gaṇa*). (98 b-100)

Nādāvatī and others[12] (become) *mātrā* (*elā-s*) by commencing with *ca-gaṇa-s*[13] constituted out of the disintegration of their own *gaṇa-s*,[14] they being defined by Arjuna as respectively consisting of five (*ca*) *gaṇa-s* ending with three *laghu-s*,[15] seven (*ca*) *gaṇa-s* ending with one *laghu*,[16] seven (*ca*) *gaṇa-s*

[1]The *rati-gaṇa-s* have been illustrated vide 63-65 ante.

[2]*Manmatha* lit. 'pertaining to *Manmatha* i.e. *kāma*'.

[3]That is, (22 + 22 + 20) = 64 *mātrā-s* with reference to 32 of *rati-lekhā*.

[4]That is, (33 + 33 + 30) = 96 *mātrā-s*; triple with reference to 32 of *ratilekhā*.

[5]Mixture of the *ratigaṇa-s kāmagaṇa-s* and *bāṇagaṇa-s* in their due measure.

[6]That is, (44 + 44 + 40) = 128; four times 32 of *ratilekhā*.

[7]*Cha* is a *mātrāgaṇa* of six *mātrā-s*.

[8]*Sataiḥ* (*sa* + *taiḥ*) lit. accompanied by *ta* (*gaṇa-s*). The use of the plural is notable. *Ta* is a *mātrāgaṇa* of three *mātrā-s*; 'S' interprets that, "*ta*—(*gaṇa*) has to be placed at the end of the five *cha* (*gaṇa-s*)". This is corroborated by 'K' who says that, "because of the *apradhānatva* (not being primary) of *ta* (*gaṇa*) it has to be kept at the end."

[9]*Pa* (*gaṇa*) has five *mātrā-s*.

[10]*Sacagaṇaiḥ* (lit. accompanied with *ca*—*gaṇa-s*) may be understood in the light of the above note (no. 11). *Ca-gaṇa* is of four *mātrā-s*.

[11]*Da* (*-gaṇa*) has two *mātrā-s*.

[12]The *gaṇa-elā-s* already spoken of vide verses 67-75 ante are referred to, the others being *haṁsāvatī*, *nandāvatī* and *bhadrāvatī*.

[13]The *mātrā-gaṇa-s* spoken of vide verse 63 ante are referred to; *cha-gaṇa* has four *mātrā-s*.

[14]Own *gaṇa-s* means the *gaṇa-s* respectively pertaining to them as *gaṇa-elā-s* i.e. *nādāvatī* has five *bha-s* followed by a *na*, *haṁsāvatī* has five *ra-s* followed by a *sa*, *nandāvatī* has five *ta-s* followed by a *ja* and *bhadrāvatī* has five *sa-s* followed by a *pa* (*gaṇa*). Their disintegration implies the breaking up of their *guru-s* into *laghu* units. Thus, for example *nādāvatī* has five *bha-s* followed by one *na* which means SII × 5 = 20 *laghu-s* + 3 *laghu-s* = 23 *laghu-s*. Now, from these 23 *laghu-s*, as it will presently be shown, *mātrā-elā nādāvatī* is reconstituted by five *ca-gaṇas* followed by three *laghus* (4 × 5 + 3) = 23.

[15]The five *bha-s* and one *na* of *nādāvatī* break into 23 *laghus* which are rearranged into five *ca-s* (of four *mātrā-s*) of *mātrā-gaṇa-s* and three *laghu-s* placed at the end. If this constitutes one step (*aṅghri*) or its two parts together, according to 'S', it forms *nādāvatī* as a *mātrā-elā*.

[16]Of *haṁsāvatī*, the five *ra-s* and one *sa* (SIS × 5 + IIS i.e. 5 × 5 + 4 = 29) when broken become 29 *laghu-s*, and when they are reorganised into seven *ca-s* (of 4 *mātrā-s*) with one *laghu* in the end, become *mātrā-elā*.

ending with one *laghu*[1] and eight (*ca*) *gaṇa-s* ending with three *laghu-s.*[2] (101-102)

Arjuna[3] has (also) ordained that by the increase of one, two, three, four or five *mātrā-s* in each of the steps (*pāda-s*) these[4] (*elā-s*) become *vicitra-mātrā-elā-s.*[5] (103)

Ratilekhā and others,[6] by (the use of) an indefinite arrangement of *gaṇa-s*,[7] are respectively called by the names *nandini*, *citriṇi*, *citrā* and *vicitrā*, (for example) in case of the first two of these,[8] the order of the first and the third steps (*pāda-s*) is to be reversed. (104-105 b)

(घ) वर्णैला

गणमात्राद्यनियता वर्णैला वर्णसंख्यया ॥१०५॥
षडक्षरादङ्घ्रिखण्डादेकोनत्रिंशदक्षरम् ।
यावदेकैकवृद्ध्यैलाश्चतुर्विंशतिरीरिताः ॥१०६॥
प्रथमा मधुकर्युक्ता सुस्वरा करणी ततः ।
चतुर्थी सुरसा प्रोक्ता पञ्चमी तु प्रभञ्जनी ॥१०७॥
षष्ठी मदनवत्युक्ता शशिनी च प्रभावती ।
मालती ललिताख्या च मता भोगवती ततः ॥१०८॥
ततः कुसुमवत्याख्या कान्तिमत्यपरा भवेत् ।
ततः कुमुदिनी ख्याता कलिका कमला तथा ॥१०९॥
विमला नलिनीसंज्ञा कालिन्दी विपुला ततः ।
विद्युल्लता विशाला च सरला तरलेति ताः ॥११०॥
तत्रान्त्या वर्णमात्रैला द्वादशेत्यपरे जगुः ।

[1]Of *nandāvatī*, the given *ta-s* and one *ja* (SSI × 5 + ISI i.e. 5 × 5 + 4 = 29) when broken become 29 *laghu-s*, which when rearranged into seven *ca-s* and one *laghu* as shown above (note 19) make for *mātrā-elā nandāvatī*.

[2]In the case of *bhadrāvatī*, its five *ma-s* along with one *ya* (SSS × 5 + ISS i.e. 6 × 5 + 5 = 35) when broken become 35 *laghu-s* which when restructured as 8 *ca-s* with 3 *laghu-s* at the end, make for the *mātrā-elā bhadrāvatī*.

[3]Dhanañjaya is another name for Arjuna whose school is well known.

[4]That is, the *mātrā-elā-s*.

[5]*Vicitra* lit. 'variegated i.e. of an added element of variety.'

[6]*Ratilekhā*, *kāmalekhā*, *bāṇalekhā* and *candralekhā* are defined in terms of the number of *mātrā-s* and *gaṇa-s* vide verses 94 c-98a ante.

[7]That is, if *rati-lekhā* etc are employed without observing the rule with regard to the arrangement of *gaṇa-s*, but observing duly the number of *mātrā-s* in them, they are transformed into what are called *nandini* etc.

[8]*Iha* lit. 'here' refers to the four *elā-s nandinī* etc. which are originally *ratilekhā* etc.

मण्ठद्वितीयकङ्कालप्रतितालेषु कश्चन ॥१११॥
तालस्तासु विधातव्यो रागादिनियमो न तु ।
रमणी चन्द्रिका लक्ष्मीः पद्मिनी रञ्जनी तथा ॥११२॥
मालती मोहिनी सप्त मतङ्गेन प्रकीर्तिताः ।
यतिमात्रेण भिन्नास्ता इत्यस्माभिर्न दर्शिताः ॥११३॥

(d) *Varṇa-elā*: (105 c-113)

Not being determined by *gaṇa*, *mātrā* etc.,[1] *varṇa-elā* is (composed) on the basis of the number of syllables (*varṇa-s*). Augmenting a part of a step (*pāda*)[2] (consisting) of six syllables, one by one up to twenty-five syllables,[3] twenty-four *elā-s* are known to be (formed). (105 c-106)

Of these,[4] the first is said to be *madhukarī*, followed by *susvarā*, *karaṇī*, *surasā*, which is said to be the fourth, *prabhañjani* the fifth, *madanavatī* which is said to be the sixth, *śaśini* and *prabhāvati*, *mālati* and the one called *lalitā*, then comes[5] *bhogāvatī*, and thereafter the one called *kusumāvatī* and the other (called) *kāntimatī*, then the one known as *kumudini kalikā*, and *kamalā*, *vimalā* and the one called *nalinī*, *kālindī*, and thereafter *vipulā*, *vidyullatā*, *viśālā*, *saralā* and *taralā*. (107-110)

Of these,[6] the last twelve are also called by some as '*Varṇa-mātrā-elā*'.

In these[7] (*elā-s*) any one *tāla* from amongst *maṇṭha*, *dvitiya*, *kaṅkāla* and *pratitāla* may be employed, while the rule pertaining to *rāga*[8] etc. is not to be applied. (111 a-112 b)

[1]Unlike the *gaṇa-elā* and the *mātrā-elā*, the structure of the *varṇa-elā* is determined by the number of syllables in a part of a step (*pāda*) detailed in the following few verses.

[2]A *pāda* has two (*khaṇḍa-s*) parts.

[3]That is, a section has six syllables at least and twenty-nine syllables at the most, in between we have twenty-two other varieties having seven, eight, nine etc. . . . . up to twenty-eight syllables. Thus from six syllables per part of a *pāda* to twenty-nine syllables we get twenty-four varieties in all.

[4]These 24 varieties of *varṇa-elā* are enumerated with 6 syllables in a part as in the first one.

[5]*Mata* lit. means 'is considered to be'.

[6]The *elā-s* named from 13th to 24th above, or as 'S' puts it, "the *varṇa-elā-s* formed by 18 to 29 syllables per part, (i.e. 12 *elā-s*) arise from the *mātrā-elā-s*; therefore, in the view of some experts, they are called *varṇa-mātrā-elā-s*. In these, both the syllables (*varṇa-s*) as well as the *mātrā-s* are counted.

[7]That is, in the *varṇa-elā-s*.

[8]'K' observes that from the present statement of the author it seems that with regard to *varṇa-elā-s*, the injunction laying down a particular *tāla*, *rāga*, *rasa*, *rīti*, *vṛtti* and deity in the case of *nādāvatī* etc. is not applicable and that the inference is that it is applicable to all other types of *elā-s*, *śuddhā* as well as *vikṛtā*, even though the only distinction noted in them is in terms of *gaṇa-s* and *mātrā-s*. Cf. Mataṅga's *Bṛ. D.*, 466 who says, "Here, the rule pertaining to *tāla*, *rasa* and *rāga* does not apply, but only the rule with regard to *varṇa* (applies); that is why it is called *varṇa-elā*."

Matanga[1] has spoken of seven other (*elā-s*) viz. *ramaṇī*, *candrikā*, *lakṣmī*, *padmini*, *rañjanī*, *mālati* and *mohini* which are differentiated only by the spacing[2] of words, and as such are not indicated by us. (112 c-113)

(ङ) देशैला

कर्णाटलाटगौडान्ध्रद्राविडानां तु भाषया।

देशाख्यैला बुधैः पञ्च प्रोक्ता मण्ठादितालतः ॥११४॥

(e) *Deśa-elā:* (114-132 b)

Five *deśa-elā-s*[3] are recognised[4] by the experts, composed as they are in the language of *karṇāṭa*,[5] *lāṭa*,[6] *gauḍa*,[7] *āndhra* and *drāviḍa*[8] which are associated with *manṭha* and other[9] *tāla-s*. (114)

(१) कर्णाटैला

कर्णाटैलादिमध्यान्तवर्त्यनुप्रासभूषिता।

नादावत्यादिका एव कर्णाटीरपरे विदुः ॥११५॥

षट्प्रकारत्वमेतासां वक्ष्यमाणैर्विशेषणैः।

ब्रह्मणः पूर्ववदनाज्जन्म शंभुर्गणाधिपः ॥११६॥

आद्याङ्घ्री आद्यनुप्रासौ रत्यन्तं मदनद्वयम्।

प्रत्येकं च तयोरादिमध्यप्रासस्तृतीयकः ॥११७॥

चतुष्कामो रतिप्रान्तः सुलेखा स्यात्तदादिमा।

दक्षिणास्याज्जनुर्यस्याः सावित्री देवता हरिः ॥११८॥

गणाधिपश्चतुष्कामं प्रत्यकं चरणद्वयम्।

[1]Cf. *Bṛ. D.*, 477-84.

[2]'K' observes that in this context *yati* signifies *pada-vichedaḥ* lit. 'breaking of compound words into their constituent elements.'

[3]The word *deśī* in this context clearly implies the meaning 'regional.'

[4]*Prokta* (of the text) means, 'spoken of.'

[5]*Karṇāṭa* includes (modern) Mysore, Coorg, Canara etc. *Karṇāṭa* is another name for *Kuntaladeśa*.

[6]*Lāṭa* represents southern Gujarat including Khāndesh.

[7]*Gauḍa*, the whole of Bengal.

[8]*Drāviḍa*, part of the Deccan from Madras to Seringapatam and cape Camorine. (for 3-6 above cf. Nandu Lal Dey, *The Geographical Dictionary of Ancient and Medieval India*).

[9]Other *tāla-s* referred to are—*dvitīya*, *kaṅkāla* and *pratitāla*.

आदिमध्यस्थितप्रासं त्रिप्रासोऽङ्घ्रिस्तृतीयकः ॥११९॥
अष्टौ कामाः कामलेखा प्रोक्ता हंसावती च सा।
पश्चिमाद्वदनाज्जन्म ब्रह्मा यस्या गणाधिपः ॥१२०॥
गायत्री देवताप्यादिमध्यप्रासास्त्रयोऽङ्घ्रयः।
पृथक्चतुःस्मरा नन्दावती सा स्वरलेखिका ॥१२१॥
जन्मोत्तरास्याद्गन्धर्वो गणेशः षट् च मान्मथाः।
बाणान्ताः पादयोर्यस्याः प्रत्येकं स्युस्तृतीयके ॥१२२॥
अष्टौ कामा आदिमध्यप्रान्तप्रासास्त्रयोऽङ्घ्रयः।
भद्रावती भद्रलेखा सा स्यात् कर्णाटसंमता ॥१२३॥
पञ्च कामा रतिश्चैका कामोऽन्ते चरणत्रये।
प्रत्येकं तासु चेदेताश्छन्दस्वत्योऽखिला मताः ॥१२४॥
गणादेर्न्यूनताधिक्यादेलाभासा इमा मताः।
यदेकस्य द्वयोरङ्घ्रयोस्त्रयाणां चान्ततः कृतम् ॥१२५॥
अङ्घ्रिपूर्त्यै तदन्यच्चेत्तृतीयाङ्घ्रिमितं पदम्।
शिखापदं तत्तृतीये त्वङ्घ्रौ मेलापकादयः ॥१२६॥

(1) *Karṇāṭa-elā:*

Karṇāṭa-elā is embellished by alliteration running through the beginning, the middle and the end of it. Others[1] hold that *nādāvati*[2] etc. are *karṇāti-s*.[3] These are sixfold as characterised by the following qualities. (115-116 b)

Nādāvatī, the first one is (known as) *sulekhā*. Born of the eastern face[4] of Brahmā, with Śiva[5] as the presiding deity of its *gaṇa-s*, its first two *pāda-s* begin with alliteration and each of them has two *kāmagaṇa-s* followed by one *ratigaṇa*. Their third *pāda*, however, has alliteration in the beginning and the middle (parts), with four *kāmagaṇa-s* followed by one *ratigaṇa* (in the end). (116 c-118 b)

[1]Other experts hold this view. It seems that the author himself does not hold this view.

[2]That is the four *śuddhā elā-s*, the other three being *haṁsāvatī*, *nandāvatī* and *bhadrāvatī*.

[3]That is, *karṇāṭa-elā-s*.

[4]Brahmā, the creative aspect of the Hindu trinity has four faces in four directions.

[5]Śambhu is another name for Śiva, the destructive aspect of the Hindu trinity.

Haṁsāvati is called *kāmalekhā*. Born of the southern face of Brahmā, with Sāvitrī as its deity and Hari[1] as the presiding deity of its *gaṇa-s*, its first two steps (*pāda-s*) are composed with alliteration in the beginning and the middle (parts) and have four *kāmagaṇa-s* each; while its third step (*pāda*) has alliteration in the three (parts)[2] and eight *kāmagaṇa-s*. (118 c-120 d)

Nandāvatī is known as *svaralekhikā*. Born of the western face (of Brahmā) with Gāyatrī as its deity[3] and Brahmā as the presiding deity of its *gaṇa-s*, it has alliteration in the beginning and the middle (parts) of all the three steps (*pāda-s*) with four *kāmagaṇa-s* in each. (120 c-121)

Bhadrāvati is called *bhadralekhikā* and duly considered as *karṇāṭa-elā*. Born of the northern face (of Brahmā) with Gāndharva as the presiding deity of its *gaṇa-s*,[4] it has six *kāmagaṇa-s* followed by one *bāṇa-gaṇa* in each of its first two steps (*pāda-s*) and eight *kāmagaṇa-s* in its third step (*pāda*), the three having alliteration in the beginning, middle and in the end. (122-123)

If, however, five *kāmagaṇa-s* followed by one *ratigaṇa* and one *kāmagaṇa* in the end are (provided) in each of the three steps (*pāda-s*) of these,[5] all of them are known to be *chandasvatīs*. (124)

These[6] are again known as *elā-ābhāsa-s*[7] by the decrease or increase in their *gaṇa* etc.[8] (125 a b)

In the event of providing[9] towards the end of the first, the second or the third step (*pāda*), if another[10] *pāda* equal in measure with the third *pāda* is added after that[11] it is (called) *śikhāpada* and is followed by *melāpaka* etc.[12] (125 c-126)

[1]Hari is another name for Viṣṇu, the existence aspect of the Hindu trinity.

[2]That is, the beginning, the middle and the end.

[3]Brahmā as the presiding deity of the *gaṇa-s* is mentioned before Gāyatrī as the deity in the text.

[4]*Gandharvo gaṇeśaḥ* is interpreted by 'S' as "*Gandharva* is the deity and *Gaṇeśa* is the presiding deity of the *gaṇa-s*." But the text does not seem to warrant such an interpretation. The word '*gaṇeśa*', as it is, should be interpreted as *gaṇānām īśaḥ* i.e. the presiding diety of *gaṇa-s* which qualifies *gandharva*. It is true that the deity as distinct from the presiding deity of *gaṇa-s* is not indicated in this case, but the same is the case with *sulekhā*.

[5]That is, the *karṇāṭa-elā-s*.

[6]That is, the *chandasvatī-s*.

[7]Lit. the apparent *elā-s*.

[8]*Ādi* i.e. 'etc.' refers to *mātrā-s* according to 'K'.

[9]*Yadantataḥ kṛtam* of the text is interpreted by 'K' as referring to *kāmo'-nte caraṇa-traya* of 124 b i e. to the *kāmagaṇa* provided in the end in respect of *chandasvatī elā-s*.

[10]*Anyatva*, 'otherness', according to 'K' consists in the increase or decrease of *gaṇa-s*.

[11]That is, after the third step (*pāda*) is sung. In other words, the extra *pāda* is to be added at the end of the 3rd *pāda* before singing the *melāpaka*.

[12]Etc. refers to *dhruva* and *ābhoga*.

(२) लाटी एला, अन्याश्च

प्रान्तप्रासा तु लाटी स्याद्भूयो रसविराजिता ।
गमकप्रासनिर्मुक्ता गौडी त्वेकरसा मता ॥१२७॥
नानाप्रयोगरागांशरसभावोत्कटान्ध्रिका ।
भूरिभावरसोत्कर्षा द्राविडी प्रासवर्जिता ॥१२८॥
तत्तल्लक्ष्मयुतस्तासु पादस्तुर्यो निबध्यते ।
तदैता गदिताः सर्वाश्छन्दस्वत्यः पुरातनैः ॥१२९॥
द्वावङ्घ्री प्रासहीनौ स्तस्तृतीयः प्राससंयुतः ।
ध्रुवाभोगौ च तेषु स्युश्चतस्रो यतयः पृथक् ॥१३०॥
वर्णैलावत् परं यस्यां सा वस्त्वेला निरूपिता ।

(2) *Lāṭi* and other *elā-s:*

Lāṭī has alliteration in the end (portions) and is saturated with many *rasa-s. Gauḍi* which is devoid of *gamaka-s* (shakes) and alliteration is believed to have one *rasa* only. *Āndhrikā is forceful with various prayoga-s,*[1] elements of *rāga-s,*[2] *rasa-s* (sentiments) and *bhāva-s* (mental states of being). *Drāviḍī* is saturated with many *rasa-s* and *bhāva-s* and is devoid of alliteration. (127-128)

If the fourth step (*pāda*, composed) with the respective characteristic features of these[3] *elā-s* is enjoined to them, they are called *chandasvati-s* by the ancients. (129)

Wherein,[4] the first two steps (*pāda-s*) are devoid of alliteration, the third (step) *pāda* is composed in alliteration and each of them[5] has four *yati-s*[6]

[1]'S' interprets *prayoga* as *gamaka* (shake).

[2]*Rāgāṁśa* implies specific pieces of melodic patterns. The word *aṁśa* is used in two different contexts by the author viz. as a factor characterising the *jāti-s* i.e. in the sense of the fundamental note (cf. *S.R.* I, 7.32-24) and in the context of *sthāya-s* where *rāgāṁśa* implies a particular formation of tones as imported from one *rāga* into another (usually from a parent *rāga* or vice versa) for creating a delightful effect (cf. K. on *S.R.*, III, 133). One wonders in what particular sense the word has actually been used by the author, in this context.

[3]The fourth step (*pāda*) added on to the three steps (*pāda-s*) in the case of these *elā-s* is to be so composed as to bear the characteristic features of that particular *elā* to which it is added. Thus, as pointed out by 'K' the *chandasvatī-s* of these four *elā-s* beginning with *lāṭī* have to be different from those of *karṇāṭaka-elā-s* spoken of in the verse 124 above.

[4]That is, the *elā* being defined as *vastu-elā*.

[5]Three or four steps (*pāda-s*) as the case may be.

[6]*Yati* has been defined by 'K' as *viccheda* 'a split or pause'.

(pauses) and the rest (of the features) are like (those of) *varṇa-elā*, that is illustrated as *vastu-elā.* (130-131 b)

(३) एलास्य सम्पूर्णा संख्या

षट्पञ्चाशद्युतं प्रोक्तमित्येलानां शतत्रयम् ।।१३१।।

अनन्तत्वात्तु संकीर्णा न संख्याति हरप्रियः ।

(3) The total number of the varieties of *elā:*

Thus, three hundred and fifty-six[1] *elā-s* in all have been mentioned. The *saṅkīrṇa* (mixed) *elā-s*, however, being infinite in number, have not been enumerated by the devotee of Lord Śiva.[2] (131 c-132 b)

(ii) करणप्रबन्धः

अष्टधा करणं तत्र स्वराद्यं पाटपूर्वकम् ।।१३२।।

वन्धादिमं पदाद्यं च तेनाद्यं बिरुदादिमम् ।

चित्राद्यं मिश्रकरणमित्येषां लक्ष्म कथ्यते ।।१३३।।

(ii) The *Karaṇa-prabandha-s:* (132 c-144)

Karaṇam is eightfold viz. *svara-karaṇam*, *pāṭa-karaṇam*, *bandha-karaṇam*, *pada-karaṇam*, *tena-karaṇam*, *biruda-karaṇam*, *citra-karaṇam* and *miśra-karaṇam*. These are now being defined.[3] (132 c-133)

(क) स्वरकरणम्

यत्रोद्ग्राहध्रुवौ सान्द्रस्वरबद्धौ पदैः पुनः ।

आभोगस्तत्र नाम स्याद्गातुर्नेत्रोग्रहः पुनः ।।१३४।।

इष्टस्वरेऽशे न्यासः स्याद्रासस्तालो द्रुतो लयः ।

करणं स्वरपूर्वं तत् तद्वदन्यान्यपि स्फुटम् ।।१३५।।

किन्तु तेषां स्वरस्थाने भेदकानि प्रचक्ष्महे ।

[1]The number 356 is arrived as under:—

(i)	*Śuddhā-elā-s*	4
(ii)	*Vikṛtā-elā-s*	108
(iii)	*Mātrā-elā-s*	20
(iv)	*Varṇa-elā-s*	24
(v)	*Varṇa-mātrā-elā-s*	12
(vi)	*Deśākkhyā-elā-s*	10
	Total number of *elā-s*	178

All these 178 *elā-s* become *chandasvatī elā-s* doubling the number $178 \times 2 = 356$.

[2]*Harapriya* is an apithet of the author.

[3]Lit., the text may be rendered as "Their characteristic features are now described."

(a) *Svara-karaṇam:*

Wherein the *udgrāha* and *dhruva* are composed with close-knit *svara-s* (solfa-syllables) and the *ābhoga* with *pada-s*[1] mentioning the names of the singer[2] and the hero,[3] the commencement[4] is made by a discretionary note,[5] the ending[6] with the fundamental note (*aṁśa*) and the *tāla* (is) *rāsa* (with) fast tempo; that (indeed) is *svara-karaṇam.* (134-135 c)

The other (*karaṇa-s*) may likewise be construed;[7] however, the differences in regard to their position[8] of *svara* will be described by us. (135 d-136 b)

(ख) पाटकरणम्

स्वरैः सहस्तपाटैस्तु स्यात् पाटकरणं ध्रुवम् ॥१३६॥
क्रमव्यत्यासभेदेन तद् द्विधा परिकीर्तितम् ।

(b) *Pāṭa-karaṇam*[9] is definitely (produced) by *svara-s* accompanied by *hasta-pāṭa-s.*[10] It is known to be twofold viz. by regular order and by reverse order.[11] (136 c-137 b)

(ग) बन्धकरणम्

स्वरैर्मुरजपाटैर्यत् तद्बन्धकरणं मतम् ॥१३७॥

[1]The word *pada* is used in the technical sense of an *aṅga* (integral part) of the *prabandha* as defined vide sl. 12-19 ante.

[2]*Gātṛ*, lit. 'singer', is interpreted by 'S' as *vāggeyakāra,* since by and large the singer is also the composer in Indian classical music. But, since the author has not himself used this term specifically, it has not been rendered as 'master composer'.

[3]The hero of a song is meant.

[4]*Graha* lit. means 'the initial note' but 'K' says that in this context it has to be taken as the commencement of the song.

[5]*Iṣṭa-svara* lit. the note of choice.

[6]*Nyāsa* lit. means the final note, but 'K' says that in this context it means the last note of the song.

[7]*Sphuṭam* lit. 'clear,' the implication being that they could be construed on the pattern of *svara-karaṇam.*

[8]*Svarasthāna* in this context, implies the placing of the *aṅga* (integral part) *svara* i.e. the solfa-syllables differently in the different varieties of this *prabandha.* In the *svara-karaṇam,* the *svara-s* i.e. the solfa-syllables are to be sung in *udgrāha* and *dhruva,* but in the other following varieties which are otherwise to be similarly constituted, they are to be sung differently as explicitly described by the author in each case e.g., with *hasta-pāṭa-s* in *pāṭa-karaṇam,* with *muraja-pāṭa-s* in *bandha-karaṇam* and so on. K's interpretation throughout is based on the assumption that specific instructions are provided by the author with regard to *udgrāha* and *dhruva.*

[9]'K' interprets the whole verse on even the idea involved in it by saying that, "*udgrāha* is sung by *svara-s* while *dhruva* is sung by *hasta-pāṭa-s* in a regular order; and in reverse order, the *udgrāha* is sung with *hasta-pāṭa-s* and *dhruva* with *svara-s.*"

[10]*Hasta-pāṭa-s* are the sound syllables arising out of such instruments as *paṭaha* (belonging to the class of drums *avanaddhavādya-s*) in the patterns such as *nāgabandha* and others dealt with in chapter VI.

[11]See note 9 above.

(c) *Bandha-karaṇam* is considered to be that which is (composed) with *svara-s* accompanied by *muraja-pāṭa-s.*[1] (137 c d)

(घ) पदकरणम्

स्वरैः पदैश्च बद्धं यत् करणं तत् पदादिमम् ।

(d) *Pada-karaṇam* is that which is composed with *svara-s*, as also with *pada-s.*[2] (138 a b)

(ङ) बिरुदकरणम्

यत् स्वरैर्बिरुदैर्बद्धं करणं बिरुदादि तत् ॥१३८॥

(e) *Biruda-karaṇam* is that which is composed with notes and *biruda-s.*[3] (138 c d)

(च) तेनकरणम्

स्वरैः सतेनकैर्यत्तु तत् तेनकरणं मतम् ।

(f) *Tena-karaṇam* is considered to be that which is (composed) with *svara-s* and *tenaka-s.*[4] (139 a b)

(छ) चित्रकरणम्

स्वरैः सकरपाटैर्यन्निबद्धं मुरजाक्षरैः ॥१३९॥

पदैस्तच्चित्रकरणमभिधत्ते हरप्रियः ।

(g) *Citrakaraṇam*—That which is composed with notes accompanied by *hastapāṭa-s* (syllabic sounds of *paṭaha*), *muraja pāṭa-s* (syllable sounds of

[1]*Muraja-pāṭa* is identified by 'S' with *mṛdaṅga-pāṭa* i.e. the syllabic sounds emanating from *mṛdaṅgam*. It is interpreted by 'K' as "in *bandha-karaṇa, udgrāha* is by notes and *dhruva* by *muraja-pāṭa-s*".

[2]According to 'K's interpretation, "In *pāda-karaṇam,* the *udgrāha* is by *svara-s* (notes) and *dhruva* by the *pada-s.*"

[3]*Biruda* lit. means a panegyric laudatory poem. Technically, *biruda* is an integral part (*aṅga*) of *prabandha* (cf 12 c-13 b ante). 'K' interprets the text as, "In *biruda-karaṇam,* the *udgrāha* is by the *svara s* and *dhruva* by the *biruda.*"

[4]*Tena,* which is technically an integral part of *prabandha* consists of auspicious words. According to 'K's 'interpretation, *Tenakaraṇam* is that in which the *udgrāha* is by notes and the *dhruva* is by *tenaka-s.*"

mṛdaṅga) and *pada-s*, is nâmed by the devotee of Śiva[1] as *citra-karaṇam*.[2] (139 c-140 b)

(ज) मिश्रकरणम्

स्यान्मिश्रकरणं बद्धं स्वरैः पाटैः सतेनकैः ॥१४०॥

(h) *Miśra-karaṇam* is that which is composed with notes, *pāṭa-s*[3] and *tenaka-s*.[4] (140 c d)

(झ) त्रय उपभेदाः

मङ्गलारम्भ आनन्दवर्धनं कीर्तिपूर्विका ।
लहरीति त्रिधा तानि प्रत्येकं गानभेदतः ॥१४१॥

(i) *Three sub-varieties*

Every one of these is threefold viz. *maṅgalārambha*, *ānandavardhana* and *kīrtilaharī* according to differences in singing.[5] (141)

(१) मङ्गलारम्भः

द्विरुद्ग्राहं ध्रुवाभोगौ सकृद्गीत्वा पुनः सकृत् ।
गीयेते चेद्ध्रुवोद्ग्राहौ मङ्गलारम्भकस्तदा ॥१४२॥

(1) *Maṅgalārambha*—If the *udgrāha* is sung twice and then *dhruva* and *ābhoga* once, followed by *dhruva* and *udgrāha* once, then it becomes *maṅgalārambha*. (142)

(२) आनन्दवर्धनम्

उद्ग्राहध्रुवकौ प्राग्वद्ध्रुवार्धं पश्चिमं ततः ।
आभोगध्रुवकोद्ग्राहाः सकृदानन्दवर्धने ॥१४३॥

[1]That is, the author viz. *Śārṅgadeva*.

[2]According to 'K's' interpretation, *Citrakaraṇam* is that in which the *udgrāha* is composed with *svara-s* and *hastapāṭa-s* and *dhruva* with *muraja-pāṭa-s* and *pada-s*.

[3]*Pāṭa* is the general term signifying the syllabic sounds of instruments.

[4]According to the interpretation of 'K', in *miśra-karaṇa* the *udgrāha* is composed of the notes, the *pāṭa-s* and the *tenaka-s*, and the *dhruva* is also similarly constituted.

[5]*Gānabhedataḥ* is interpreted by 'S' as *gānaprakārabhedāt* i.e. due to the difference in the manner of singing which is specified in the text in terms of repetition of some sections of the composition.

(2) *Ānandavardhana*—In *ānandavardhana*, *udgrāha* and *dhruva* are (sung) as in the previous[1] one followed by the second half of the latter,[2] and then are (sung) *ābhoga*, *dhruva* and *udgrāha* once. (143)

(३) कीर्तिलहरी

उद्ग्राहस्य द्वितीयार्धं ध्रुवार्धस्थानगं यदि ।

इतरत् पूर्ववत् कीर्तिलहरी कीर्तिता तदा ।।१४४।।

(3) *Kīrtilaharī*—The other details remaining the same,[3] if the second half of *udgrāha* is sung in place of half[4] of *dhruva* then it is known as *kīrtilaharī*. (144)

(iii) ढेङ्कीप्रबन्धः

(क) लक्षणम्

द्विर्गीत्वोद्ग्राहपूर्वार्धमुत्तरार्धं सकृत् ततः ।

मेलापकः प्रयोगात्मा न वा स्यात्तावुभावपि ।।१४५।।

अतालौ ढेङ्किकाताले कङ्काले वा विलम्बिते ।

लयान्तरेऽन्यतालेन ध्रुवाभोगौ ध्रुवस्त्विह ।।१४६।।

त्रिखण्डस्तत्र खण्डे द्वे गीयेते समधातुनी ।

तृतीयमुच्चमेष द्विराभोगस्तु सकृत् ततः ।।१४७।।

पुनर्गीत्वा ध्रुवे न्यासो यस्यां सा ढेङ्किका मता ।

(iii) *Dheṅkī-prabandha:* (145-152 b)

(a) The characteristic features.

Wherein,[5] having sung the first half of the *udgrāha* twice, and then the second half of it once, the *melāpaka* composed with *prayoga* (*gamaka-s*) is (sung) optionally, both[6] of them being either without any *tāla* or in the

[1]That is, the *maṅgalārambha* i.e. twice *udgrāha* and once *dhruva*.
[2]That is, *dhruva*.
[3]That is, the same as in case of the previous one viz. *anandavardhana*.
[4]It is not clearly or explicitly stated in the text as to what particular half (the first or the second) is meant, but from the context it seems that the second half may be implied.
[5]That is, the *prabandha* which is being defined viz. *Dheṅkī*.
[6]'Both' refers to *udgrāha* and *melāpaka*, the latter in case it is sung.

slow[1] *dheṅkikā* or *kaṅkāla tāla*; and wherein *dhruva* and *ābhoga* are in a different tempo[2] and *tāla*,[3] *dhruva* being in three parts of which the first two are sung with equal tonal content[4] while the third one is high,[5] and when this[6] is (sung) twice followed by *ābhoga* once, the (whole[7]) being repeated before its completion in *dhruva*,[8] it is considered to be *dheṅkikā*. (145-148 b)

(ख) ढेङ्कीभेदा:

चतुर्धा ढेङ्किका मुक्तावली स्याद् वृत्तबन्धिनी ।।१४८।।
युग्मिनी वृत्तमाला च तासां लक्ष्माण्यमून्यथ ।
अभावश्छन्दसां वृत्तं वृत्ते वृत्तानि च क्रमात् ।।१४९।।
त्रिधा तिस्रो द्वितीयाद्या वर्णिका गणिका तथा ।
मात्रिका वर्णजैर्वृत्तैर्गणजैर्मात्रिकैरपि ।।१५०।।
दशापि स्युः पुनस्त्रेधा समालंकरणा तथा ।
विषमालंकृतिश्चित्रालंकृतिर्लक्षणानि तु ।।१५१।।
समालङ्कारसंख्या च विषमा मिश्रिता क्रमात् ।

(b) Varieties of *Dheṅkī*:

Dheṅkikā[9] is fourfold viz. *muktāvalī*, *vṛtta-bandhinī*, *yugminī* and *vṛttamālā*. Their characteristic features respectively are—devoid of metres, (composed) in one metre, two metres and many metres.[10] The three (of these) *vṛtta-bandhinī* and others are threefold each viz. *varṇikā*, *gaṇikā* and *mātrikā*

[1]The slow tempo is implied. Two alternatives are provided here viz. (i) they are sung without any *tāla* whatsoever, (ii) they are sung either in the slow *dheṅkikā tāla* or in the slow *kaṅkāla tāla*.

[2]*Laya* has roughly been rendered as 'tempo' but actually the word tempo or speed does not adequately represent the concept as it will be fully explained in Chapter V. In this context, the expression 'a different tempo' implies any other but the slow i.e. either the middle or the fast tempo.

[3]The implication is that any *tāla* other than *dheṅkikā* and *kaṅkāla* can be used.

[4]*Samadhātuni*—lit. 'of equal (*tulya*) *dhātu*' which is interpreted by 'S' as *sama-geya* i.e. of the same value or measure in terms of tonal element.

[5]That is, higher with reference to the first two parts, as interpreted by 'S'.

[6]'That' refers to *dhruva*.

[7]The whole *prabandha* as defined above.

[8]In the first part of *dhruva* according to 'K'.

[9]*Dheṅkikā* is the same as *dheṅkī*.

[10]That is, *muktāvalī* is not composed in metre i.e. in verse; *vṛttabandhinī* is composed in one metre, *yugminī* in two metres.

(composed as they are) by metres formed by *varṇa-s*[1] (syllables), *gaṇa-s*[2] (groups) and *mātrā-s* (measures).[3] Again all these ten are threefold viz. *samālaṅkaraṇā, viṣamālaṅkṛti* and *citrālaṅkṛti* which are characterised by *sama;*[4] *viṣama*[5] and *miśra*[6] *alaṅkāra-s* (figures of speech). (148 c-152 b)

(iv) वर्तनीप्रबन्धः

स्वराद्यकरणस्येव वर्तन्या लक्ष्म किंत्विह ॥१५२॥
रासकादन्यतालः स्याल्लयो ज्ञेयो विलम्बितः ।
द्विरुद्ग्राहो ध्रुवाभोगौ सकृन्मोक्षो ध्रुवे भवेत् ॥१५३॥
कङ्काले प्रतिताले च कुडुक्के द्रुतमण्ठके ।
रचिता चेत् तदा ज्ञेया वर्तन्येव विवर्तनी ॥१५४॥

(iv) *Vartanī-prabandha:* (152 c-154)

The character of *vartani* is not of the *svara-karaṇam*[7] but here[8] the *tāla* is other than *rāsaka*, tempo (*laya*) is known to be slow, *udgrāha* is (sung) twice and *dhruva* and *ābhoga* once, while the ending[9] is done in *dhruva*. However, if *vartanī* is set in *kaṅkāla, pratitāla, kuḍukkā* or *druta-maṇṭhaka tāla-s*, it is then known as *vivartanī*. (152 c-154)

[1]The metres that are formed on the basis of the number of syllables (*varṇa-s*) are so called.

[2]The metres based on groups (*gaṇa-s*) are so called.

[3]The metres based on the number of units (*mātrā-s*) are so called.

[4–6]'K' says, "By *alaṅkāra*, we should understand figures of speech known as *prāsa, anuprāsa* and *yamaka* etc., the *śabdālaṅkāra-s*"; he also indicates the connection of the words *sama, viṣama* and *miśra* with even and odd numbers, but he does not elaborate the relationship of these numbers with any constituent of the text of the song. 'S', on the other hand, considers the figures of speech based on meaning, *arthālaṅkāra s,* such as simile (*upamā*) and so on as *sama*, the *alaṅkāra-s* associated with odd numbers (probably the *śabdālaṅkāra-s*) as *viṣama* and their mixture as *miśra*. This seems to be quite enigmatic because such a classification of *alaṅkāra-s* is unheard of in the treatises on poetics. 'K's' indication could perhaps be construed as being related to the even or odd number of the steps (*pāda-s*) of the song in which the *prāsa, anuprāsa* etc. occur.

[7]*Svarakaraṇam* is one of the eight *karaṇa-prabandha-s* spoken of vide verses 134-135 c ante. The author says that the general characteristic features of *vartani* are the same as those of *svarakaraṇa-prabandha* with certain differences which he is pointing out now.

[8]That is, in *vartanī*, the differentiating features are being pointed out.

[9]*Mokṣa* lit. 'release' refers to *nyāsa* (the finale of the song) or the final note.

(v) झोम्बडप्रबन्धः

(क) लक्षणम्

द्विर्यत्रोद्ग्राहपूर्वार्धमुत्तरार्धं सकृत् ततः।
मेलापकः प्रयोगाख्यः स वा स्याद् द्विस्ततो ध्रुवः ॥१५५॥
आभोगं तु सकृद्गीत्वा ध्रुवे न्यासः स झोम्बडः।
निःसारुकः कुडुक्कश्च त्रिपुटप्रतिमण्ठकौ ॥१५६॥
द्वितीयो गारुगी रासयतिलग्नाड्डतालिकाः।
एकतालीत्यमी ताला झोम्बडे नियता दश ॥१५७॥
केचिन्मण्ठमपीच्छन्ति नैष लक्ष्येषु लक्ष्यते।

(v) *Jhombaḍa-prabandha-s:* (155-168)

(a) The characteristic features:

Wherein the first half of *udgrāha* is sung twice, than the second half once, optionally followed by *melāpaka* full of *gamaka-s* (shakes), and then, singing *dhruva* twice and *ābhoga* once in the final set in *dhruva*, it is *ihombaḍa* (155-156 b)

These are the ten *tāla-s* prescribed for *jhombaḍa: niḥsāruka, kuḍukkā, tripuṭa, pratimaṇṭhaka, dvitīya, gārugi, rāsa, yatilagna, aḍḍatāla*[1] and *ekatāli.* Some[2] also include *maṇṭha tāla*, but it is not observed in actual practice.[3] (156 c-158)

(ख) झोम्बडभेदाः

तारजोऽतारजश्चेति झोम्बडो द्विविधो मतः ॥१५८॥
तारो ध्वनिस्थानकं स्यात् तद्युतस्तारजो मतः।
स चतुर्धा स्थानकस्योद्ग्राहादिषु निवेशने ॥१५९॥
अतारजस्तारहीनः सर्वोऽप्येष द्विधा मतः।
त्रिधातुश्च चतुर्धातुरिति भूयो भवेद् द्विधा ॥१६०॥
प्रभूतगमकः स्तोकगमकश्चेत्यमी स्फुटाः।
प्रायोगिकः क्रमाख्यश्च ततः क्रमविलासकः ॥१६१॥

[1] *Aḍḍatālikā* of the text is otherwise known as *aḍḍatāla.*
[2] He is obviously referring to the view of some earlier writers.
[3] Since it is not observed to be in actual practice, 'S' interprets that the author's intention is to forbid its use.

चित्रो विचित्रलीलश्चेत्यमी स्युः पञ्चधा पृथक् ।
चतुराद्यष्टपर्यन्तं गणनिष्पादिताः क्रमात् ॥१६२॥
मातृकः श्रीपतिस्तद्वत् सोमो रुचिरसंगतौ ।
ते लक्ष्येष्वप्रवृत्तत्वादस्माभिर्न प्रपञ्चिताः ॥१६३॥
विनियोगवशादेषां त्रयोदश भिदाः पृथक् ।
उपमारूपकश्लेषैर्ब्रह्मा वीरविलासयोः ॥१६४॥
विष्णुश्चक्रेश्वरो वीरे बीभत्से चण्डिकेश्वरः ।
नरसिंहोऽद्भुतरसे भैरवस्तु भयानके ॥१६५॥
हास्यशृङ्गारयोर्हंसः सिंहो वीरभयानके ।
विप्रलम्भे तु सारङ्गः शेखरः करुणे रसे ॥१६६॥
सम्भृङ्गारे पुष्पसारः शृङ्गारे परिकीर्तितः ।
रौद्रे प्रचण्डो नन्दीशः शान्ते धीरैरुदीरितः ॥१६७॥
गद्यजाः पद्यजा गद्यपद्यजा इति ते त्रिधा ।
झोम्बडा इति संख्याता वियच्चन्द्रशराग्नयः ॥१६८॥

(b) Varieties of *Jhombaḍa:*

Jhombaḍa is considered to be twofold viz. *tāraja*[1] and *atāraja*.[2] *Tāra* is tonal range;[3] being associated with that, it is considered to be *tāraja* (born of the high pitch-range). This[4] is of four types according to the entry of the high pitch-range into *udgrāha* etc.[5] *Atāraja* is devoid of the high pitch-range. All this[6] is again considered to be twofold viz. composed of three sections (*dhātu-s*) and four sections. Again these two become twofold viz. (associated) with many *gamaka-s* and with few *gamaka-s*, and so these[7]

[1] *Tāraja* lit. 'born of *tāra*' i.e. of the high range.

[2-3] *Atāraja* accordingly is that which is not *tāraja* The word *tāra* refers to the high register as interpreted by 'S'. He says "the tone produced or arising from the high register is *tāra*." *Atāraja* is indicative of the other two registers But otherwise *tāra* in the ancient terminology is generally understood with reference to *mandra* 'the low'. Thus, the concepts of *tāra* and *mandra* signify a relative tonal value of pitch.

[4] That is, *tāraja*.

[5] *Tāraja jhombaḍa* is considered to be of four types according to the association of the high range with *udgrāha*, *dhruva*, *melāpaka* and *ābhoga* respectively.

[6] That is, the fivefold *jhombaḍa* as described in the foregoing portion.

[7] 'K' enumerates them as follows:

Four of the *tāraja-s* with four sections, three of the *tāraja-s* with three sections (in the absence of *melāpaka*), one of *atāraja* of four sections and one of *atāraja* of three sections making nine in all. Each of these being twofold we get 18 *sphuṭa* (clear) *jhombaḍa-s*. But since each of these is fivefold, there are ninety *jhombaḍa-s* in all.

(eighteen) are obviously clear. Each one of them is fivefold viz. *prāyogika*, *krama*, *kramavilāsaka*, *citra* and *vicitralila* composed respectively of four, five, six, seven and eight[1] *gaṇa-s*. (159-162)

Others like *mātṛka*, *śrīpati*, *soma*, *rucira* and *saṅgata* are not dealt with by us as they are not current in practice. (163)

Governed by the mode of being employed, each one of these[2] has thirteen varieties. (The *jhombaḍa* composed) with simile, metaphor and pun[3] is (called) *brahmā*, with the sentiment of heroism as combined with grace[4] (it is called) *viṣṇu*, with *heroism*[5] *cakreśvara*, with disgust[6] *candikeśvara*, with marvel[7] *narsiṁha*, with terror[8] *bhairava*, with mirth[9] coupled with conjugal love *haṁsa*, with heroism in combination with terror[10] *siṁha*, with conjugal love in separation[11] *sāraṅga*, with pathos coupled with conjugal love[12] *śekhara*, with conjugal love[13] it is known as *puśpasāra*, with wrath[14] *pracaṇḍa*, and with tranquility[15] it is declared by the wise to be *nandīśa*.[16] (164-167)

These are three-fold-composed in prose, in verse and in both prose and poetry. Thus, the *jhombaḍa*-variations are enumerated to be three thousand five hundred and ten.[17] (168)

[1]As per the text, it would read—"from four to eight *gaṇa-s* respectively".

[2]That is, the ninety varieties mentioned above (in note 10).

[3]*Upamā*, *rūpaka* and *śleṣa* of the text. These are defined in many works on poetics, and 'K' quotes from one of them accordingly, "*upamā* signifies an identical quality in different objects e g., the face is beautiful like the moon; *rūpaka* signifies the identity of the standard and the object of comparison, e g , the face is itself the moon; and *śleṣa* is that wherein a sentence, a word bears more than one meaning e.g., *rājā* which stands for king and also for the moon in Sanskrit."

[4]*Vīra-vilāsayoḥ* of the text is interpreted by 'K' as referring to the sentiment of *sambhoga śṛṅgāra* (erotic enjoyment of conjugal love) since *vilāsa* (graceful movements of maidens), he argues, is an *anubhāva* (a response) of *śṛṅgāra* (conjugal love). Moreover *vīra*, the sentiment of heroism, is separately mentioned by the author in the next breath.

[5]*Vīra* of the text.

[6]*Bībhatsa* of the text.

[7]*Adbhuta* of the text.

[8]*Bhayānaka* of the text.

[9]*Hāsya* of the text.

[10]*Vīra-bhayānaka* of the text.

[11]*Vipralambha* of the text.

[12]*Karuṇa-śṛṅgāra* of the text.

[13]*Śṛṅgāra* of the text.

[14]*Raudra* of the text.

[15]*Śānta* of the text.

[16]Thus, in all, we have 90×13=1170 varieties of *jhombaḍa-s*.

[17]We have already arrived at the no. 1170 above (in note 16). All of these are three-fold, so 1170×3=3510. The expression "*viyaccandraśarāgnayaḥ*" of the text is explained by 'K' as follows:

Viyat=0, *candra*=1, *śara*=5 and *agni*=3 all to be written from right to the left.

(vi) लम्भप्रबन्धः

(क) लक्षणम्

उद्ग्राहो द्विः सकृद्वैकखण्डो द्विशकलोऽथवा ।
यत्र ध्रुवो द्विर्वाभोगो ध्रुवे मुक्तिः स लम्भकः ॥१६९॥
भागोऽस्मिञ्झोम्बडेऽप्यूर्ध्वं ध्रुवादुद्ग्राहसंनिभः ।
ध्रुवाभोगध्रुवा गेयास्तत इत्यूचिरे परे ॥१७०॥

(vi) *Lambha-prabandha-s:* (169-175 b)

(a) The characteristic features:

Wherein *udgrāha* is (sung) twice or once, either as one piece or in two parts, *dhruva* (is sung) twice followed optionally by *ābhoga*[1] and the ending is in *dhruva*, it is *lambhaka*.

Others have, however, said that in this[2] as well as in *jhombaḍa* a piece[3] similar[4] to *udgrāha* may be sung after *dhruva*[5] followed by *dhruva*, *ābhoga* and *dhruva*.[6] (169-170)

(ख) लम्भभेदाः

उद्ग्राहस्तालशून्यश्चेत् स स्यादालापलम्भकः ।
स प्रलम्भो ध्रुवस्थाने यत्रोद्ग्राहोऽन्यधातुकः ॥१७१॥
यत्र भागो भवेल्लम्भे भागलम्भः स भण्यते ।
त्रिश्चतुष्पञ्चवारं वा भिन्नोद्ग्राहसमन्वितः ॥१७२॥

[1]'S' interprets the text in a slightly different way. The portion *dhruva dvirvābhoga* is rendered by him as, "*dhruva* is (sung) once or twice and so also the *ābhoga*.

[2]That is, in *lambha*.

[3]*Bhāga* is interpreted by 'S' as *prabandāvayava* i.e., an integral part of the *Prabandha*.

[4]'K' interprets *sannibha* (lit. similar) of the text as—'of the same tonal value'.

[5]The text has been translated according to the interpretation of 'S'. According to 'K', it would read as follows: "In this as well as *jhombada*, the second part of *dhruva* should be similar to *udgrāha* in tonal value."

[6]Since, according to 'K', no additional piece is to be sung after *dhruva*, but only the tonal value of the second part of it is to be made equal to *udgrāha* when it is followed by *dhruva*, *ābhoga* and *dhruva*, in effect *dhruva* is sung twice, as per his interpretation, which is followed by *ābhoga* once and then *dhruva* once before the song is ended in the first part of *dhruva*. It seems, 'S' had a different text, because he says that the additional piece sung after *dhruva* is to be followed by *dhruva* and *ābhoga* and optionally by *dhruva*. This option is not provided for in the printed text of the Adyar edition.

ध्रुवको गीयते यत्र स लम्भपदमुच्यते ।
ध्रुवभेदेऽनुलम्भोऽसौ द्विभेदे तूपलम्भकः ॥१७३॥
एते त्रयोऽप्यनाभोगा विलम्भस्तु स उच्यते ॥
उद्ग्राहा बहवो यस्मिन् ध्रुवाभोगविवर्जिताः ॥१७४॥
एते सालगसूडस्थैस्तालैराकलिता मताः ।

(b) Varieties of *lambha:*

When *udgrāha* is devoid of *tāla*, it becomes *ālāpalambhaka*; when *dhruva* is substituted by an *udgrāha* of a different tonal element,[1] it is *pralambha*; where a piece[2] is added to *lambha*, it is said to be *bhāgalambha*. Where *dhruva* is sung three, four or five times with different[3] *udgrāha-s*, it is called *lambhapada*; with difference in *dhruva* it is *anulambha*,[4] with difference in both,[5] however, it is *upalambhaka*; and these[6] three are devoid of *ābhoga*. *Vilambha* is said to be that in which there are many[7] *udgrāha-s* unaccompanied by *dhruva* and *ābhoga*. These[8] are considered to be set in the *tāla-s* of the *sālaga-sūḍa*[9] (*prabandha-s*). (171-175 b)

[1]*Anyadhātuka* is interpreted by **'S'** as *visadṛśa-geya* i.e. of dissimilar tonation or tonal composition. 'K' explains as follows: "In *lambhaka*, when in the place of *dhruva* i.e. after *udgrāha*, if another *udgrāha* of the same verbal but a different tonal composition is sung, then that variation is called *pralambha*." This has quite a few interesting implications. First of all, it becomes clear that another *udgrāha* is to be sung in place of *dhruva*, and that *dhruva* is obviously not to be sung. This is an example of a *prabandha* where even *dhruva* can be omitted, which is not permitted as a general rule (see verse 12 ante). However, this does not mean that we are confronted with a *prabandha* having only one section (*dhātu*) for while describing *lambhapada*, *anulambha* and *upalambha* varieties of *lambha*, it is said that these are devoid of *ābhoga* (172-173) which implies that the other varieties of *lambha* are not probably devoid of *ābhoga* in spite of the fact that *ābhoga* is not mentioned about them, since a full description of the structure of the song is not provided by the author. So instead of having the usual two *dhātu-s* (sections) *udgrāha* and *dhruva*, we here have *udgrāha* (two) and *ābhoga*.

[2]'K' interprets as follows: "Wherein, as compared to other *lambha* compositions, having sung the first part of *udgrāha* in equal tone-content, if in its second part, the second part of *dhruva* is sung, it is called *bhāga-lambha*, as significant by its name."

[3]That is, when one and the same *dhruva* is sung every time with a different *udgrāha*.

[4]That is, when one and the same *udgrāha* is sung every time with a different *udgrāha*.

[5]That is, when every time a different *udgrāha* is sung with a different *dhruva*.

[6]That is, *lambhapada*, *anulambha* and *upalambha*. 'K' ovserves that from this provision, it is obvious that *ābhoga* is to be sung in case of other variations of *lambha*.

[7]'K' infers that the many *udgrāha-s* indicate a differenee in the verbal composition.

[8]These eight *lambhaka-s* described above.

[9]These will be described in their appropriate context.

(vii) रासकप्रबन्धः

(क) लक्षणम्

यो झोम्बडगतं लक्ष्म गमकस्थानकैर्विना ॥१७५॥
भजते रासकः सोऽयं रासतालेन गीयते ।

(vii) *Rāsaka-prabandha-s:* (175 c-179)

(a) The Characteristic features:

Rāsaka is characterised by the features of *jhombaḍa* except that it is devoid of *gamaka*-formations and is sung in *rāsaka tāla* (175 c-176 b).

(ख) रासकभेदा:

गणैर्वर्णैश्च मात्राभिः केचिदेनं त्रिधा जगुः ॥१७६॥
स्याद्रासवलयो हंसतिलको रतिरङ्गकः ।
चतुर्थस्तत्र मदनावतारश्छगणादिजाः ॥१७७॥
षडक्षरङ्घ्रित्रिंशदक्षरावधिवर्णजाः ।
पञ्चविंशतिराख्यातास्चरणादष्टमात्रिकात् ॥१७८॥
षष्टिमात्रावधिप्रोक्तास्त्रिपञ्चाशत्तु मात्रिकाः ।
लक्ष्ये प्रसिद्धिवैधुर्यात्तेष्वस्माकमनादरः ॥१७९॥

(b) Varieties of *rāsaka:*

According to some, it is threefold viz. (composed) with *gaṇa-s* (group), *varṇa-s* (syllables) and *mātrā-s* (units). Of these[1] from *cha-gaṇa* etc.[2] are derived *rāsavalaya, haṁsatilaka, ratirangaka* and *madanâvatāra*, the fourth one. Those composed of *varṇa-s* (syllables) are said to be twenty-five, beginning with six syllables to a step (*pāda*) and progressively increasing to thirty,[3] while the *mātrikās*[4] are said to be fifty-three arising (progressively)

[1]That is, of these three types in the case of the first one viz. composed of *gaṇa-s*.

[2]That is, from *cha-gaṇa* is derived *rāsavalaya* as stated in the text and by inference it may be construed that from *pa-gaṇa* is derived *haṁsatilaka*, from *ca-gaṇa* is derived *ratiranga* and from *ta-gaṇa* is derived *madanâvatāra*. It is notable that all the *gaṇa-s* mentioned here are *mātṛka gaṇa-s*

[3]That is, in the first case there are six syllables to a step, and next one has seven, and the next eight and so on, up to thirty syllables per step.

[4]*mātrika-s* are those that are derived from the *mātrā-s*. Here too, if in the first case a foot of a verse has eight *mātrā-s*, the next one has nine, and the following one has ten and so on till sixty.

from eight *mātrā-s* to sixty *mātrā-s* to a step (*pāda*). Because these are out of vogue, we have not paid much attention to them. (176 c-179)

It is notable that Śārṅgadeva keeps in view the *lakṣya*, the prevalent practice of his time, in devoting his attention and space. He is not a mere compiler of available data; he is a very skil ful editor too. Nevertheless, he preserves the sophistication of a modern musicologist in presenting a historical perspective by mentioning, however briefly, the obsolete forms as well. This speaks volumes for his ability of combining brevity of expression with the perspective, details and the lucidity of presentation.

(viii) एकतालीप्रबन्धः

द्विरुद्ग्राहो ध्रुवोऽपि द्विराभोगध्रुवकौ ततः ।
गीत्वा न्यासो यत्र सा स्यादेकताल्येकतालिका ॥१८०॥
अस्यामालापमात्रेण केचिदुद्ग्राहमूचिरे ।

इत्येकतालीप्रबन्धः
॥ इति सूडप्रबन्धनिरूपणम् ॥

(viii) *Ekatālī-prabandha:* (180-181 b)

Wherein *udgrāha* and *dhruva* are sung twice followed by *ābhoga* and *dhruva* once and then the ending,[1] it is *ekatāli* composed in *ekatāla.*[2] According to some, the *udgrāha* in this (song) is to be sung in *ālāpa* only.[3] (180-181 b)

तृतीयप्रकरणम्

आलिप्रबन्धाः

(i) वर्णप्रबन्धः

बिरुदैर्वर्णतालेन वर्णः कर्णाटभाषया ॥१८१॥
तालत्रैविध्यतस्तस्य त्रैविध्यं गदितं बुधैः ।

[1]*Nyāsa* (the completion of the song) is not indicated explicitly in the text. 'K' says, ''since *dhruva* is near at hand, it has to be done with *dhruva*'' probably that is so in most of the cases, but 'S' places it in *udgrāha* expicitly ruling out *ābhoga* and *dhruva.*

[2]Name of *tāla*.

[3]The implication is that verbal text is not used. However, as 'K' infers, it also implies that according to the first opinion verbal text is necessary in *udgrāha.*

SECTION 3

Āli-prabandha-s

(i) *Varṇa-prabandha:* (181 c-182 b)

Varṇa is composed in the *Karṇāṭa* language with *biruda-s* (panegyrics) set to *varṇa tāla.* It is declared by the experts to be threefold according to the three variations of its *tāla.*[1] (181 c-182 b)

(ii) वर्णस्वरप्रबन्धः

स्वरैः पाटैः पदैस्तेनै रचना वाञ्छितक्रमात् ॥१८२॥
यस्य स्यात्तेनकैर्न्यासः स वर्णस्वर उच्यते ।
स्वरादेरादिविन्यासभेदादेष चतुर्विधः ॥१८३॥

(ii) *Varṇa-svara-prabandha:* (182 c-183)

The (*prabandha*) that is composed with *svara-s* (solfa-syllables), *pāṭa-s* (instrumental syllabic sounds) *pada-s* and auspicious words (*tenaka-s*) placed in any order at will, is called *varṇa-svara.* It is fourfold according to the distinction of the *svara*[2] etc. being the first (part) of the composition.[3] (182 c-183)

Having characterised the *sūḍa-prabandha-s,* now the author proceeds to describe the characteristic features of the *prabandha-s* that are known as *āli-krama prabandha-s.* He commences with *varṇa.*

(iii) गद्यप्रबन्धः

गद्यं निगद्यते छन्दोहीनं पदकदम्बकम् ।
तत् षोढोत्कलिका चूर्णं ललितं वृत्तगन्धि च ॥१८४॥
खण्डं चित्रं च तेषां च प्रभवः सामवेदतः ।

[1] *Varṇa-tāla* with its there variations will be described in Chapter V.

[2] The four *aṅga-s* (integeral parts) *svara, pāṭa, pada* and *tena. Nyāsa* in this context, does not mean the ending, but the placement of different *aṅga-s.*

[3] That is, the first varieties would be composed with *svara* in the beginning, the second with *pāṭa* in the beginning, the third with *pada* in the beginning and the fourth with *tanaka* in the beginning, there being no rule fixing the position of the remaining three in each case.

(iii) *Gadya-prabandha:* (184-198)

Gadya (lit. prose) is said to be a non-metrical composition of words.[1] It is sixfold viz. *utkalikā, cūrṇa, lalita, vṛttagandhi, khaṇḍa* and *citra.* They have originated from the *Sāmaveda.* (184-185 b)

(क) गद्यभेदा:

(१) उत्कलिका

गातव्योत्कलिका वीरे रक्ता रुद्राधिदेवता ॥१८५॥
गौडीयरीतिरुचिरा वृत्तिमारमटीं श्रिता ।

(a) Variations of *gadya:* (185 c-192 b)

(1) *Utkalikā*—To be sung in the context of heroism, *utkalikā* is red (in colour) and is presided by Śiva.[2] Beatutified by *gauḍī rīti,* it is composed in *ārabhaṭi vṛtti.* (185 c-186 b)

(२) चूर्णम्

चूर्णं शान्ते रसे पीतं गातव्यं ब्रह्मदैवतम् ॥१८६॥
वैदर्भरीतिसंपन्नं सात्त्वतीं वृत्तिमाश्रितम् ।

(2) *Cūrṇa*—To be sung in (the context of) the sentiment (*rasa*) of tranquillity, *Cūrṇa* is of yellow (colour), has *Brahmā* for its presiding deity, is couched in *vaidarbhi rīti* and depends on *sāttvatī vṛtti.* (186 c-187 b)

(३) ललितम्

सितं मदनदैवत्यं शृङ्गाररसरञ्जितम् ॥१८७॥
ललितं कैशिकीं वृत्तिं पाञ्चालीं रीतिमाश्रितम् ।

(3) *Lalita*—Sparkling white, with cupid for its presiding deity, *lalita* is saturated in the sentiment of conjugal love and is composed[3] in *kaiśikī vṛtti* and *pāñcāli rīti.* (187 c-188 b)

[1] *Pada-kadambakam* lit. a cluster of words.
[2] Rudra is a name of Śiva.
[3] *Āśritam* lit. 'depends upon'.

(४) वृत्तिगन्धि

वृत्तगन्धि रसे शान्ते पीतं च मुनिदैवतम् ॥१८८॥
पाञ्चालरीतौ भारत्यां पद्यभागविमिश्रितम् ।

(4) *Vṛttagandhi* is (employed) in the sentiment of tranquillity, is yellow, has *muni* (sage) for its presiding deity and is set in *pāñcāli rīti* and *bhārati* (*vṛtti*) composed with a mixture of verse portion.[1] (188 c-189 b)

(५) खण्डम्

खण्डं गणेशदैवत्यं सात्त्वतीं वृत्तिमाश्रितम् ॥१८९॥
श्वेतं हास्यकृदारब्धं वैदर्भीभङ्गिसंभवम् ।

(5) *Khaṇḍa* has Gaṇeśa as the presiding deity, is composed in *Sāttvatī vṛtti*, is white and arises with the beauty of *vaidarbhī* (*rīti*) oriented in (the sentiment of) mirth. (189 c-190)

(६) चित्रम्

शृङ्गारे वैष्णवं चित्रं चित्रकैशिकवृत्तिजम् ॥१९०॥
वैदर्भ्या रचितं रीत्या नानारीतिविचित्रया ।

(6) *Citra* is (employed) in (the sentiment of) conjugal love, has Viṣṇu for its deity, arises from the variegated[2] *kaiśikī vṛtti*, is composed in *vaidarbhī rīti*, picturesque by (the touch of) different *rīti-s*. (190 c-191 b)

(७, ८) वेणी, मिश्रञ्च

वेणी मिश्रमिति प्राहुरन्ये भेदद्वयं परम् ॥१९१॥
वेणी सर्वैः कृता मिश्रं चूर्णकैर्वृत्तगन्धिभिः ।

(7, 8) Two other varieties viz. *veṇi* and *miśra* are said to be there.[3] *Veṇī* is produced by all (the above six) and *miśra* by *cūrṇaka* and *vṛttagandhi*. (191 c-192 b)

[1]As a general rule *gadya prabandha* is primarily a non-metrical composition.

[2]'K' elucidates that in this case *kaiśikī* is variegated by the intermingling of other *vṛtti-s* such as *bhāratī* etc.

[3]'S' opines that the author is presenting another view according to which these two other varieties are also recognised.

(ख) षड्गतय:

द्रुता विलम्बिता मध्या द्रुतमध्या तथा परा ॥१९२॥
गतिर्द्रुतविलम्बा स्यात् षष्ठी मध्यविलम्बिता ।
इति गद्यस्य षट् प्रोक्ता गतयः पूर्वसूरिभिः ॥१९३॥
लघुभिर्बहुलैरल्पैः समैराद्यत्रयं क्रमात् ।
पृथग्लत्वे मिश्रैस्तु लगैस्तद्वत् परं त्रयम् ॥१९४॥
प्रत्येकं गतिषट्केन षट्त्रिंशद्गद्यजा भिदाः ।

(b) The six speeds (*gati-s*) of *gadya:* (192 c-195 b)

Six speeds pertaining to *gadya* (*prabandha*) have been spoken of by the ancient seers viz. fast, slow, middle, fast-middle, and then fast-slow and middle-slow, the sixth.[1] (192 c-193)

The first three (of these) are (achieved) respectively by many *laghu-s*, a few *laghu-s* and equitable *laghu-s*.[2] When *laghu-s* and *guru-s* are arranged separately, (the result is) the same.[3] The other three[4] (respectively) are (achieved) by the mixture of *laghu-s* and *guru-s*.[5] Thus, each one of them[6]

[1]The six speeds (*gati-s*) pertain respectively to the six varieties of *gadya* i.e., fast (*druta*) for *utkalikā*, slow (*vilambita*) for *cūrṇa*, middle (*madhya*) for *lalita* and so on as pointed out by 'S', and as it can be inferred from the numbering of the last one.

[2]That is by compressing many *laghu-s* (the unit measures) *druta* (fast) speed is gained which is employed in *utkalikā*; by spreading the time units to a few *laghu-s* slow tempo is gained which is applicable to *cūrṇa*, and by balancing the division of time equitably i.e. neither too slow nor too fast, we get the middle speed which is employed in *lalita*. 'K' significantly remarks that the incidence of *guru* in these should be understood in relation to that of *laghu*, i.e. the fast tempo is gained by many *laghu-s* and few *guru-s*, the slow tempo is achieved through few *laghu-s* and many *guru-s* and middle tempo is obtained with equal number of *laghu-s* and *guru-s*.

[3]The other three speeds viz. fast-middle, fast-slow and middle slow.

[4]The purport is that while the first three speeds viz. fast, slow and middle can be obtained both ways i.e by arranging the *laghu-s* and *guru-s* separately as also by arranging them together, the last three viz. fast-middle, fast-slow, and middle-slow can only be achieved by the mixture of *laghu-s* and *guru-s*. *Tadvat* of the text informs that even while one wishes to obtain the first three speeds by arranging the *laghu-s* and *guru-s* separately, one has to do so by observing their ratio, as indicated earlier.

[5]The two commentators differ in their interpretation of verse 194 c d. According to 'K', the purport is that, "In the first half, having employed all the *laghu-s*, if in the second half *laghu-s* and *guru-s* are used equitably mixed as before, it becomes *druta-madhya* i.e. fast-middle speed. But if having employed all *laghu-s* in the first half, only *guru-s* are used in the second it becomes *druta-vilambita* i.e. middle-slow speed. Similarly, having in the first half used *guru-s* and *laghu-s* equitably, if in the other half only *guru-s* are used, it becomes *madhya-vilambita* i.e. middle-slow speed." According to 'S' "*pṛthaksṭhitair-laghubhirvṛttagandhi*, by *guru-s* standing separately it is *khaṇḍa*, and by the mixed ones it is *Citra*." Obviously he does not elaborate.

[6]That is, each one of the six varieties beginning with *utkalikā*.

being sixfold on account of variation in speed, there are thirty-six varieties of *gadya* (*prabandha*). (194-195 b)

(ग) गद्यप्रबन्धानां सामान्यलक्षणानि

प्रणवाद्यमतालं च गमकैरखिलैर्युतम् ॥१९५॥
वर्णैश्चातालशब्दानां स्वरैरन्तेऽन्तरान्तरा ।
प्रबन्धाङ्कं सतालं च पदद्वन्द्वं पृथक् ततः ॥१९६॥
द्विर्गीत्वा गीयते यत्र प्रयोगोऽपि विलम्बितः ।
गातृनाम सतालं च सतालं वर्ण्यनाम च ॥१९७॥
विलम्बितेन मानेन पुनरप्यविलम्बितम् ।
गीत्वा विलम्बितालेन न्यासो गद्यं तदिष्यते ॥१९८॥

(c) Common characteristic features of *gadya-prabandha-s*: (196 c-198)

Wherein the *udgrāha*[1] is commenced with (the singing of) *oṅkāra*,[2] and being devoid of *tāla*, it is enriched by all the *gamaka-s*[3] (shakes) and *varṇa-s*[4] (patterns of tonal movement) interspersed by (solfa) notes at the end of words not set to *tāla*, followed by a couple of *pada-s* bearing the name of the *prabandha* and set in *tāla*, each of which is sung twice, as also the *prayoga*[5] in the slow tempo; and wherein this is followed by singing in *tāla*, the names of the singer[6] and the hero[7] in slow tempo and then

[1]'S' reads *prabandhakam* instead of *prabandhāṅkam* and interprets it as the *udgrāha*. His interpretation has been followed in rendering the text into English. 'K' also thinks that the portion without *tāla* is to be taken as *udgrāha*, the two *pada-s* with *tāla* as *dhruva* and *prayoga* etc. with *tāla* as *ābhoga*.

[2]*Praṇava* is another name for *oṅkāra*.

[3]'K' elucidates that all types of *gamaka-s* such as *tiripa* etc. are meant.

[4]'K' elucidates that the four *varṇa-s* (pattern of tonal movement) viz. *sthāyī* (steady) etc. are meant. His interpretation has been followed in the translation. But 'S' interprets *varṇa* in the sense of "syllables of the words of *pada* (*padākṣaraiḥ yuktam*)".

[5]*Prayoga* is defined by 'S' as *gamaka-sandarbha* i.e. a piece full of *gamaka-s* (shakes). 'K' points out that the use of indeclinable *api* in 117 b rendered as 'as well' in the translation indicates that the *prayoga* too is composed in the same *tāla* as the two *pada-s* spoken of earlier, and that they too are set in the slow tempo like it.

[6]*Gātṛ*, lit. singer, is also the composer as pointed out by 'K' in this context. He says that this may be set in the same *tāla* as that of *prayoga* but in a different tempo, or in another *tāla* altogether.

[7]*Varṇya* is interpreted by 'S' as *nāyaka* or the hero. Lit. *varṇya* means the object of description.

repeated in the fast tempo,[1] ending with the *tāla* associated with the slow tempo,[2] it is said to be *gadya.* (195 c-198)

(iv) कैवाडप्रबन्धः

पाटैः स्यातां ध्रुवोद्ग्राहौ कैवाडे न्यसनं ग्रहे।
सार्थकैरर्थहीनैश्च पाटैः स द्विविधो मतः ॥१९९॥
स शुद्धैर्मिश्रितैः पाटैः शुद्धो मिश्र इति द्विधा।

इति कैवाडप्रबन्धः।

(iv) *Kaivāḍa-prabandha:* (199-200 b)

The[3] *udgrāha* and *dhruva* in *kaivāḍa*[4] are (constituted) by *pāṭa-s* (instrumental syllabic sounds), while the ending (*nyāsa*) is (done) in *udgrāha.*[5] It is considered to be twofold according to the *pāṭa-s*[6] being meaningful

[1]*Avilambitam* lit. 'not slow', may include the middle tempo as well, but 'K' thinks that fast is suggested 'K' also opines that it is not clear what is indicated to be repeated, and hence he concludes that the entire *prabandha* is to be repeated. However 'S' thinks that the names of the singer and the hero only are meant to be repeated.

[2]'K' thinks that since the *tāla* associated with the first two (which constitute *dhruva*) was in slow tempo, the ending (third) has to be done in that same *tāla.*

[3]The text mentions *dhruva* first due to the exigency of metre, but as 'K' points out, since the song cannot commence without *udgrāha,* it has to be mentioned first. It has therefore been put in due order.

[4]'K' elucidates the significance of the name *kaivāḍa.* He says, "since *kaivāḍa* is dominated by *kara-pāṭa-s* (to be defined in chapter VI) it is named by a vernacular word that produces the same impact in spirit."

[5]*Graha* of the text is identified by 'S' and 'K' as the *udgrāha* since *graha* is that with which one commences. But in this context, it is not to be confused with the initial note.

[6]'K' seems to interpret that each of the two varieties of *kaivāḍa* is further of two types—*śuddha* and *miśra,* yielding four in all. But 'S' thinks that, "the meaningful sound syllables (*pāṭa-s*) constitute the first variety and the meaningless sound syllables make for the second, and it is the latter (the second one) which is of two types i.e., composed purely of *pāṭa-s* (*śuddha*) and composed of *pāṭa-s* mixed with the six (*aṅga-s* or integral parts) such as *svara* etc."

On the other hand the purity (*śuddhatva*) of *pāṭa-s* is understood by 'K' in quite different terms. He says, "Purity of *pāṭa-s* consists in the sound syllables produced by the mouth and the instruments, not being mixed together; if they get mixed, the *pāṭa-s* become *miśra* (mixed). The *pāṭa-s* however are the sound syllables that represent the strokes on an instrument. Thus, what has been said by 'K' as quoted above, seems to be relevant in the context of a performance where only the singer can sing the *pāṭa-s* and the instrument may or may not produce them at the same time; but so far as the text is concerned, it can hardly be applicable.

and meaningless. That[1] (again) is twofold *śuddha* and *miśra* (constituted) respectively by unmixed (*śuddha*) and mixed *pāṭa-s*. (199-200 b)

(v) अङ्कचारिणीप्रबन्धः

वीररौद्राश्रितैर्बद्धा बिरुदैरङ्कचारिणी ॥२००॥
वर्ण्यनामाङ्किताभोगा तालेनेष्टेन गीयते ।
वासवी कलिका वृत्ता ततो वीरवती भवेत् ॥२०१॥
वेदोत्तरा जातिमती षट्प्रकारेति सा मता ।
एकद्वित्रिचतुष्पञ्च तालाः स्युर्बिरुदानि तु ॥२०२॥
अष्टौ षोडश तद्वच्च द्वात्रिंशद् द्वयधिका क्रमात् ।
पञ्चाशच्च चतुर्युक्तं शतमाद्यासु पञ्चसु ॥२०३॥
नियमो जातिमत्यां तु न तालबिरुदाश्रयः ।

इत्यङ्कचारिणीप्रबन्धः ।

(v) *Aṅkacāriṇī-prabandha:* (200 c-204 b)

Aṅkacāriṇī is composed in any choice *tāla* with *biruda-s*[2] (panegyrics) based on the sentiments of heroism[3] and wrath,[4] with its *ābhoga* indicating the name of the hero.[5] It is considered to be of six varieties viz. *vāsavi*, *kalikā*, *vṛttā*, *vīravati*, *vedottarā* and *jātimati*. The first five of these are respectively associated with one, two, three, four and five *tāla-s* and also

[1] 'That' may refer either to the twofold *kaivāḍa* as interpreted by 'K', or to the second variety thereof viz., the meaningless *pāṭa-s* which alone are considered to be two-fold according to 'S' viz., *śuddha* and *miśra*.

[2] The panegyrices, as pointed out by 'K', have specifically to be based on the *vīra* and *raudra rasa-s* i.e. the sentiments of heroism and wrath, and not on any others, their scope being so restricted.

[3] 'K' opines that three types of *vīra* (valour) are implied in this context viz., *dāna-vīra* (valiant in philanthropy), *dayā-vīra* (valiant in compassion), and *yuddha-vīra* (valiant in battle). Obviously, he has not taken into account the fourth variety of *vīra* that is traditionally accepted viz. *dharma-vīra* (valiant in virtue).

[4] *Raudra* of the text.

[5] 'K' thinks that the names of the *vāggeyakāra* and *prabandha* too are implied.

with eight, sixteen, thirty-two, fifty-two and one hundred four *biruda-s.*[1] There is no regulation of *tāla* and *biruda* in *jātimati.* (200 c-204 b)

(vi) कन्दप्रबन्धः

(क) लक्षणम्

कर्णाटादिपदैः पाटैर्बिरुदैस्तालवर्जितः ॥२०४॥
आर्यागीतौ रसे वीरे कन्दः स्यात् पाटमुक्तिकः ।

(vi) *Kanda-prabandha-s:* (204 c-209 b)

(a) Characteristic features:

Kanda is composed of *pada-s* of *Karṇāṭa* and other[2] languages with *pāṭa-s*[3] and *biruda-s*;[4] it is devoid of *tāla,*[5] is sung in *āryāgīti,*[6] depicts heroism[7] and ends with *pāṭa-s.*[8] (204 c-205 b)

[1]The five varieties of *aṅkacāriṇī* will be composed as under:

S. No.	*Name of the variety*	*No. of tāla-s*	*No. of biruda-s*
1.	*Vāsavī*	1	8
2.	*Kalikā*	2	16
3.	*Vṛttā*	3	32
4.	*Vīrāvalī*	4	52
5.	*Vedottarā*	5	104

[2]*Ādi* of the text is indicative of other regional languages. *Kandu* is sung in what may be called *deśī bhāṣā-s*.

[3]The sound syllables of instruments.

[4]The panegyrics.

[5]'K' observes that though *kanda* is said to be devoid of *tāla* (*tālasvarūpeṇa śūnyaḥ*) it does not mean that it is devoid of the regulation of *tāla* (*na tālaniyama-śūnyaḥ*). The difference between *tālasvarūpa* and *tāla-niyama* is not elucidated by him.

[6]*Āryāgīti* is not any of the *gīti-s* spoken of in chapter I or II i.e. the *pada* or *svara gīti-s*; it is the name of a metre in which the first half is equal to the second one. It has also to be distinguished from *āryā* metre which has 30 *mātrā s* in the first half and 28 in the second, in so far as this has 30 *mātrā-s* each in both of its halves. 'K' elucidates that, "In such an *āryā-gīti*, the *udgrāha* may be done in the first half, singing the *pada-s*, and *dhruva* may be executed in the second half, singing *pāṭa-s* and *biruda-s*."

[7]*Vīra* implies valour.

[8]'K' elucidates that the ending has to be made after having commenced the second half with *pāṭa-s*.

(ख) भेदाः

पवनो रविसंज्ञश्च धनदो हव्यवाहनः ॥२०५॥

सुरनाथः समुद्रश्च वरुणः शशिशैलकौ ।

मधुमाधवनामानौ ततोऽपि मकरध्वजः ॥२०६॥

जयन्तो मधुपश्चाथ शुकसारसकेकिनः ।

हरिश्च हरिणो हस्ती कादम्बः कूर्मको नयः ॥२०७॥

विनयो विक्रमोत्साहौ धर्मार्थौ काम इत्यमी ।

एकोनत्रिंशदाख्याताः कन्दभेदाः पुरातनैः ॥२०८॥

त्रिंशाद् गुरोराद्विगुरोः क्रमादेकैकभङ्गतः ।

इति कन्दप्रबन्धः ।

(b) Varieties of *Kanda:*

Twenty-nine varieties of *kanda* are mentioned by the ancients viz. *pavana, ravi, dhanada, havyavāhana, suranātha, samudra, varuṇa, śāśi, śaila, madhu, mādhava, makaradhvaja, jayanta, madhupa, śuka, sārasa, kekī, hari, hariṇa, hasti, kadamba, kūrma, naya, vinaya, vikrama, utsāha, dharma, artha* and *kāma*; these are formed respectively by the progressive breaking[1] of one *guru* from the thirtieth to the second, one by one. (205 c-209 b)

(vii) हयलीलाप्रबन्धः

हयलीलेन तालेन हयलीला द्विधा च सा ॥२०९॥

गद्यजा पद्यजा चेति पद्यजा तु चतुर्विधा ।

पूर्वार्धमुत्तरार्धं वा द्वे वा तालयुतं यदि ॥२१०॥

आर्यायाः स्युस्तदा तिस्रश्चतुर्थी त्वादिमे दले ।

स्वरैः पदैस्तु बिरुदैः सतालै रचिता मता ॥२११॥

केचित्तु हयलीलेन छन्दसा तां विदुर्बुधाः ।

इति हयलीलाप्रबन्धः ।

[1]Breaking of *guru-s* signifies the process in which the *guru-s* are split into their constituent *laghu-s*.

(vii) *Hayalila-prabandha:* (209 c-212 b)

Hayalīla[1] is composed in *hayalīla tāla*[2] and it is twofold viz. *gadyaja*[3] and *padyaja.*[4] *Padyaja,* is however, fourfold. Three are (formed) respectively, when the first half of *āryā*[5] or the second half of it or both of the halves are associated with *tāla,*[6] while in the fourth the first half is composed in *tāla* with *svara-s, pada-s* and *biruda-s.*[7] Some of the experts, however, know it as (associated) with *Hayalīla* metre.[8] (209 c-212 b)

(viii) गजलीलाप्रबन्धः

तालेन गजलीलेन गजलीला निगद्यते ।।२१२।।
छन्दोहीनेतरल्लक्ष्म हयलीलागतं मतम् ।

इति गजलीलाप्रबन्धः ।

(viii) *Gajalila-prabandha:* (212 c-213 b)

Gajalīla is said to be (set) in *gajalīka tāla.* Apart from (the specification with regard to) the metre, it follows the characteristics of *hayalīla* in all other respects.[9] (212 c-213 b)

(ix) द्विपदीप्रबन्धः

शुद्धा खण्डा च मात्रादिः संपूर्णेति चतुर्विधा ।।२१३।।
द्विपदी करुणाख्येन तालेन परिगीयते ।

[1]*Haya-līla* lit. 'the sport of the horse', seems to be a metaphorical expression.

[2]*Hayalīla tāla* is also known as *turaga-līla, turaga* as well as *aśva* being the synonyms of *haya*. It will be defined in Chapter V.

[3]*Gadyaja* lit. 'arising out of prose'.

[4]*Padyaja* lit. 'arising out of verse'. *Padya* is defined as 'that (composition) which is organised into stanzas or feet (*pāda*)'.

[5]Obviously *hayalīla prabandha* is ordinarily composed in *āryā* metre.

[6]The implication is that the other half remains devoid of *tāla,* as pointed out by 'K'.

[7]*Svara-s* (notes), *pada-s* and *biruda-s* (panegyrics) are the *aṅga-s* (integral parts) of *prabandha*.

[8]This metre is alternatively used and is constituted of na, ja, bha, ja, bha, ja, bha *gaṇa-s* and *laghu* and *guru* in a *pāda* (foot), as elucidated by 'K'. The purport is that the four varieties are formed as stated above excepting that instead of *āryā, hayalīla* is employed.

[9]*Gajalīla* differs from *Hayalīla,* as explained by 'K', only in so far as it cannot be set in *hayalīla* metre; in every other respect it resembles *hayalila,* and thus is fivefold. 'S' too supports this interpretation.

पादे छः पञ्च भा गोऽन्ते जौ स्तः षष्ठद्वितीयकौ ॥२१४॥
चतुर्भिरीदृशैः पादैः शुद्धा द्विपदिकोच्यते ।
अर्धान्तेऽन्ये स्वरानाहुः खण्डा स्याच्छुद्धयार्धया ॥२१५॥
षष्ठेनैकेन गुरुणा मात्राद्विपदिका मता ।
ज्ञेया शुद्धैव संपूर्णा गुरुणान्तेऽधिकेन तु ॥२१६॥
पुनश्चतुर्धा द्विपदी मानवी चन्द्रिका धृतिः ।
तारेति मानवी छेन तद्वयेन कृताङ्घ्रिका ॥२१७॥
पद्वयं तगणश्चान्ते लगौ चेच्चन्द्रिका मता ।
छगणेन चतुर्मात्रैस्त्रिभिश्च धृतिरुच्यते ॥२१८॥
तारा छेन चतुर्भिश्च यगणैरन्तिमे गुरौ ।

इति द्विपदीप्रबन्धः ।

(ix) *Dvipadī-prabandha-s:* (213 c-219 b)

Dvipadī, which is sung with the *tāla* called *karuṇa*,[1] is fourfold viz. *śuddhā*, *khaṇḍā*, *mātrā* and *sampūrṇā*. (213 c-214 b)

Śuddhā dvipadī is composed in four *pada-s* (steps) each comprising a *cha*[2] (*gaṇa*), five *bha*[3] (*gaṇa-s*) with a *guru* in the end and *ja*[4] (*gaṇa*) in the second and the sixth (place).[5] Others[6] introduce (solfa) notes at the end of the (first) half.[7] (214 c-215 c)

Khaṇḍā is composed of half the *śuddhā*.[8] If the sixth (*gaṇa*) is substituted by one *guru* it is said to be *mātrā-dvipadī*. *Śuddhā* is itself known as *sampūrṇā* if augmented by one *guru* towards the end.[9] (215 d-216)

Dvipadī is again[10] fourfold viz. *mānavī*, *candrikā*, *dhṛti* and *tārā*. *Mānavī*

[1] *Karuṇa* will be defined in Chapter V.

[2] *Cha* is a *mātrā gaṇa* of six *mātrā-s* (units).

[3] *Bha* is a *varṇa-gaṇa* with *guru* in the beginning.

[4] *Ja* has *guru* in the middle.

[5] Thus, the *pāda* will consist of a *cha* (*-gaṇa*), a *ja* (*-gaṇa*), five *bha* (*-gaṇa-s*) a *ja-gaṇa* and a *guru* in the end. And *śuddhā* has four such *pāda-s*.

[6] That is, some other masters. Obviously Śārṅgadeva does not contribute to this view.

[7] That means after singing two *pāda-s*.

[8] This is the literal translation of the text and 'S' interprets accordingly that *khaṇḍā* is composed of two *pāda-s* of *śuddhādvipadī* But 'K' elucidates the purport differently. He says, "Of the four *pāda-s* mentioned above, if the first two are composed as per the rule laid down and the last two are not governed by it, then it becomes *khaṇḍā*." However, the name *khaṇḍā* literally means 'partly executed.'

[9] 'K' interprets this as the augmentation of every *pāda* by one *guru*.

[10] 'Again' denotes another classification.

is (composed) by a *cha (-gaṇa)*[1] and two *ta (-gaṇa-s)*[2] in a *pāda.*[3] If it[4] has two *pa* (-*gaṇa-s*)[5] and a *ta* (-*gaṇa*)[6] ending with a *laghu* and a *guru*, it is said to be *candrikā*. With a *cha* (-*gaṇa*) and three (-*gaṇa-s*) of four *mātrā-s*,[7] it[8] is called *dhṛti*. *Tārā* has one *cha* (-*gaṇa*), four *ya* (-*gaṇa-s*) and a *guru* at the end (of each *pāda*).[9] (217-219 b)

(x) चक्रवालप्रबन्धः

पूर्वपूर्वाक्षरव्राते योऽन्त्यो वर्णचयः स चेत् ॥२१९॥
उत्तरोत्तर संघादौ चक्रवालस्तदोच्यते ।
गद्यपद्यप्रभेदेन स द्विधा गदितो बुधैः ॥२२०॥

इति चक्रवालप्रबन्धः ।

(x) *Cakravāla-prabandha:* (219 c-220)

If the group of the last syllables[10] of the preceding word[11] is also the beginning of the succeeding word,[12] in a series,[13] it is called *cakravāla*. It is declared by the wise to be twofold viz. *gadya* (prose) and *padya* (verse). (219 c-220)

(xi) क्रौञ्चपदप्रबन्धः

पदैः स्वरैः क्रौञ्चपदः प्रतितालेन गीयते ।
स्वरन्यासः स तन्नाम्ना छन्दसा मुक्तकोऽथवा ॥२२१॥

इति क्रौञ्चपदप्रबन्धः ।

[1]*Cha* is the *gaṇa* of six *mātrā-s*.

[2]*Ta*, as pointed out by 'K' in this context refers to the *varṇa-gaṇa* of five *mātrā-s* with a *laghu* in the end.

[3]'K' reminds us that it has four *pāda-s*.

[4]That is, if a *pāda* has such and such . . .

[5]*Pa-gaṇa* has five *mātrā-s*.

[6]'K' opines that there too it is a *varṇa gaṇa*.

[7]That is either *bha-gaṇa* or *ja-gaṇa*.

[8]It is implied that this is the measure of one *pāda* only.

[9]"Of each *pāda*" is implied by the text *kṛtāṅghrika* in 217 d above as pointed out by 'K', who also says that even though it has four *pāda-s*, the name *dvipadī* (having two feet) is significant as the composition is divided into two parts.

[10]*Varṇacayaḥ* of the text literally means a group of *varṇa-s* i.e. letters.

[11]'K' interprets *akṣaravrāta* (lit. a group of letters) as *padam* i.e. a word.

[12]Similarly *saṅgha* is also interpreted as *pada*, a word.

[13]The repetition of *pūrva* and *uttara* in the text, as pointed out by 'K', gives the impression of a series of words.

(xi) *Krauñcapada-prabandha:* 221

Krauñcapada is sung with *svaras* (solfa notes) and *pada-s*[1] set to *pratitāla.*[2] It has its ending with *svara*[3] and is (composed) in *krauñcapada* metre or it is non-metrical.[4] (221)

(xii) स्वरार्थप्रबन्धः

यत्र स्वराक्षरैरेव वाञ्छितोऽर्थोऽभिधीयते ।
स स्वरार्थो द्विधा शुद्धो मिश्रस्तैः शुद्धमिश्रितैः ॥२२२॥
ग्रहन्यासोऽस्य भूयोऽसौ सप्तधैकादिकैः स्वरैः ।
क्रमोत्क्रमाभ्यां बहुशो भिद्यन्ते द्विस्वरादयः ॥२२३॥

इति स्वरार्थप्रबन्धः ।

(xii) *Svarārtha-prabandha:* (222-223)

Wherein the desired meaning is expressed through the note-names[5] themselves, that is *svarārtha.* It is twofold viz. *śuddha* and *miśra,* (composed) with standard and mixed[6] (notes). It ends in *graha.*[7] Again[8] it is

[1]*Svara* and *pada* constitute the integral parts (*aṅga-s*) of *prabandha.* 'K' elucidates that here *udgrāha* has to be done with solfa notes and *dhruva* with *pada,* and accordingly they have been placed in this order in the English version.

[2]*Pratitāla* is defined by 'K' as having a *laghu* and two *druta-s.* This will be dealt with in Chapter V.

[3]Thar is, as 'K' interprets it, the song is completed after *udgrāha* is taken up (again),

[4]*Krauñcapada* metre is composed by *bha, ma, sa, bha,* 4 *na-s* and a *guru* in a *pāda.* 'K' opines that *ābhoga* may be done with *pada-s.* Alternatively, it is *muktaka* which is interpreted both by 'K' and 'S' as 'devoid of metre.'

[5]*Svarākṣara*—solfa notes *sa, ri' ga* etc. indicative of the names of the notes *ṣaḍja, ṛṣabha, gāndhāra* etc.

[6]Standard (*śuddha*) and modified (*vikṛta*) notes together.

[7]*Graha-nyāsa* of the text is interpreted by 'K' as *graha nyāsaḥ asya* i.e. its *nyāsa* (ending) is with the *graha.* Elsewhere 'K' has interpreted *graha* in the context of *prabandha-s* as *udgrāha.* 'S' however reads this phrase in conjunction with the previous one and accordingly interprets that, "It is twofold *śuddha* and *miśra* according to, as in terms of *graha* and *nyasa* whether it composed with standard or mixed notes." However, 'K's' interpretation seems to be more probable and therefore the translation of the text has been based on that.

[8]'K' says *bhūyaḥ* (again) indicates that each of the two varieties viz. *śuddha* and *miśra* is sevenfold.

sevenfold viz. (composed) with one to seven notes.[1] Of these the bi-tones[2] and others are further divided into many[3] varieties by the alternation of their order. (222-223)

(xiii) ध्वनिकुट्टनीप्रबन्धः

ध्रुवोद्ग्राहौ भिन्नतालौ मण्ठकङ्कालवर्जितौ ।
यस्यां समासु मात्रासु यतिर्मेलापको न च ॥२२४॥
तालद्वयेन सा गेया ढेङ्कीवद् ध्वनिकुट्टनी ।
इति ध्वनिकुट्टनीप्रबन्धः ।

(xiii) *Dhvanikuṭṭanī-prabandha:* (224-225 b)

Wherein *dhruva* and *udgrāha* are set in different *tāla-s*[4] but not in *maṇṭha* and *kaṅkāla*, and the *yati*[5] (caesura) is of equal measure and there is no *melāpaka*, it is *Dhvanikuṭṭani*, sung in two *tāla*-s like *dheṅkī*.[6] (224-225 b)

(xiv) आर्याप्रबन्धः

(क) लक्षणम्

अर्धान्ते चरणान्ते वा स्वरान् न्यस्यार्धमादिमम् ॥२२५॥
द्विरार्याछन्दसो गीतं सकृद्गीतं दलान्तरम् ।
यत्राभोगे गातृनाम सार्या स्याद् ग्रहमुक्तिका ॥२२६॥

[1]Here the meaning of the song is expressed through the words constituted of solfa syllables. The purport is that if one note-name e.g. *sa* when expressive of a certain meaning is used, it becomes one variety; similarly, when two notes are so used it becomes another variety and so on till seven notes produce seven varieties. That is how it is elucidated by 'K'.

[2]'K' points out that since these varieties are mixed, they must need at least two notes to reverse their order.

[3]These varieties cannot properly be counted as they are too numerous. The purport is that since they are not well known in practice, they are not being defined in detail.

[4]That is, the *tāla* employed in *udgrāha* should not be used in *dhruva* and vice versa.

[5]'K' takes *yati* in the sense of *padavirati* i.e. caesura, which according to the text, he says should be of equal number of *mātrā-s* (unit measures). But 'S' interprets *yati* as, *yati tāla* to be employed with equal *mātrā-s* (unit measures). But, since the author has already spoken of *tāla* in the previous line barring *maṇṭha* and *kaṅkāla*, it is less likely that 'S' may be right in his interpretation.

[6]'K' elucidates that as *Dheṅkī* is sung alternatively with two *tāla-s* in two different tempos (cf. 146 ante), so also *dhvanikuṭṭani* is to be sung.

(xiv) *Āryā-prabandha:* (225 c-231 b)

(a) Characteristic features of *Āryā:*

Having delineated the (solfa) notes at the end of the (first) half or of the *pāda* (of *āryā*), wherein the first half of the *āryā* metre is sung twice and the other half is sung once, the name of the singer[1] being in the *ābhoga*, it is *āryā* (*prabandha*) which ends in *graha.*[2] (225 c-226)

(ख) भेदाः

लक्ष्मीः स्याद् वृद्धिबुधी च लीला लज्जा क्षमा तथा।
दीर्घा गौरी ततो राजी ज्योत्स्ना छाया च कान्तिका ॥२२७॥
मही मतिस्ततः कीर्तिरथ ज्ञेया मनोरमा।
स्याद्रोहिणी विशाला च वसुधा शिवया सह ॥२२८॥
हरिणी चाथ चक्राख्या सारसी कुररी तथा।
हंसी वधूरिति प्रोक्ता आर्याः षड्विंशतिः क्रमात् ॥२२९॥
षष्ठादन्यैर्गणैः सर्वगुरुभिः प्रथमा, पराः।
एकादिगुरुभङ्गेण क्रमाल्लक्ष्माण्यमूनि तु ॥२३०॥
छन्दोलक्षणतो ज्ञेयाः शेषा भूरितरा भिदाः।

इत्यार्याप्रबन्धः।

(b) Varieties of *Āryā*:

There are twenty-six varieties of *āryā* respectively called *lakṣmī, vṛddhi, buddhi, līlā, lajjā, kṣamā, dīrghā, gaurī, rājī, jyotsnā, chāyā, kānti, mahī mati, kīrti, manoramā, rohiṇī, viśālā, vasudhā, śivā, hariṇi, cakrā, sārasi, kurarī, haṁsī* and *vadhū.* The first[3] (of these) is composed of *gaṇa-s* having all *guru-s* excepting the sixth[4] (*gaṇa*) and the others are (formed) by the progressive splitting of a *guru*[5] (into two *laghu-s*), such being their respective character. Its many other variations may be understood from their metrical definitions.[6] (227-231 b)

[1]'K' reminds us that the names of the hero and the *prabandha* are also understood to be taken along with that of the singer. Though *gātṛ* lit. means a singer, since in this context he is not different from the composer, it is the *vāggeyakāra,* who is actually implied.

[2]*Graha* means *udgrāha.*

[3]That is, *lakṣmī.*

[4]Because, by definition the sixth *gaṇa* is eigher *ja-gana* or *na-gaṇa* with two or three *laghu-s* respectively and therefore can not have all *guru-s.*

[5]That is, one *guru* is split in the case of *vṛddhi,* two in the case of *buddhi* and so on.

[6]*Āryā* metre has nine varieties and the author seems to refer to them.

(xv) गाथाप्रबन्धः

आर्यैव प्राकृते गेया स्यात् पञ्चचरणाथवा ॥२३१॥

त्रिपदी षट्पदी गाथेत्यपरे सूरयो जगुः ।

इति गाथाप्रबन्धः ।

(xv) *Gāthā-prabandha:* (231 c-232 b)

If *āryā* is sung in *prākṛta*[1] or with five feet[2] or according to other experts, with three[3] or six feet[4] (*pada-s*) it is called *gāthā.* (231 c-232 b)

Āryā-prabandha is obviously based on *āryā* metre in which the first and the third quarters must each contain 12 *mātrā-s* or syllabic instants (one being allotted to a short vowel and two to a long one) the second 18 and the fourth 15. The metre is divided in two halves, each consisting of two quarters or *pada-s.* In terms of *gaṇa-s*, the first half has seven *gaṇa-s* with a *guru* at the end. Here it is provided that the sixth of these *gaṇa-s* may either be a *ja-gaṇa* or a *na-gaṇa* with a *laghu* at the end, since by rule the odd numbers of *gaṇa-s* i.e. 1st, 3rd, 5th or 7th *gaṇa-s* canot be *jagaṇa-s.* Every *gaṇa*, in this context is of four *mātrā-s* and not of the usual three since it is a *mātrāvṛtta.* The first half is indicated as under:

SS	SS	IIS	SS	SII	ISI	IIS	S
1	2	3	4	5	6	7	*guru*

The *āryā* has nine varieties viz. *pathyā*, *vipulā*, *capalā*, *mukhacapalā*, *jaghanacapalā*, *gīti*, *upagīti* and *udgīti* apart from *āryā*. These varieties are differentiated by the arrangement of *yati-s* (pauses) and the order of *gaṇa-s.* However, the varieties that have been named here are formed in the following way. The first one i.e. *lakṣmī* it composed of (*gaṇa-s*) having all *guru-s* excepting the sixth *gaṇa* since, as explained above, it cannot have all *guru-s* in *āryā*. The rest of the varieties from 2nd to 26th are formed by

[1]*Aryaiva* ('*āryā* itsel') is read by 'S' as *āryāvad* ('like *āryā*'). This, however, does not make much difference. The purport is that if a *prākṛta* composition is sung in *āryā*, it is called *gāthā* So, the inference drawn by 'K' is that *āryā* has to be sung in Sanskrit only.

[2]Alternatively, if there is no change of language in the verbal composition, then the change in the number of *pada-s* (feet) transforms *āryā* into *gāthā*. Here it is suggested that it may have five quarters or three or six. 'S' reads *pañce-ca-gaṇathavā* and accordingly, interprets the text as "alternatively, if it has five *ca-gaṇa-s*, then it is twofold viz. *tripadī* (with three quarters) and *ṣaṭpadī* (with six feet)".

[3]*Tripadī* lit. 'having three feet'.

[4]*Ṣaṭapadī* lit. 'having six feet'. When *pāda* forms a quarter or a part of the *prabandha* it has been rendered as 'step' but when it froms a quarter or part of a metre, it has been rendered as a 'foot'.

the breaking of one to 25 *guru-s* (each into two *laghu-s*) progressively. In other words, by breaking one *guru* into two *laghus*, *vṛddhi* is formed, by the breaking of two *guru-s*, *buddhi* is formed and similarly, by splitting three *guru-s*, *līlā* is formed and so on.

Here, *udgrāha* is to be sung in the first half and *dhruva* in the second half of *āryā*.

(xvi) द्विपथप्रबन्धः

(क) लक्षणम्

छन्दसा द्विपथेन स्याद् द्विपथः स्वरमुक्तिकः ॥२३२॥
तालहीनः सतालो वा,

(xvi) *Dvipatha-prabandha:* (232 c-241)

(a) General features:

Dvipatha (*prabandha*) is composed in *dvipatha* metre[1] with the ending in *svaras* (solfa notes). It is not set to *tāla* or (alternatively) may be set to a *tāla*.[2] (232 c-233 a)

(ख) भेदाः

स च ज्ञेयश्चतुर्विधः ।
स्वरैरेकोऽन्यः प्रयोगैः सोभयानुभयौ परौ ॥२३३॥
प्राकृते दोहसंज्ञोऽसौ तस्य भेदा नव त्विमे ।
सारसो भ्रमरो हंसः कुररश्चन्द्रलेखकः ॥२३४॥
कुञ्जरस्तिलको हंसक्रीडोऽप्यथ मयूरकः ।
त्रयोदशायुजि समे मात्रा द्वादश सारसे ॥२३५॥
ओजेऽङ्घ्रौ मनवो मात्रा भ्रमरे रवयः समे ।
मात्राः पञ्चदशायुग्मे हंसे युग्मे त्रयोदश ॥२३६॥
त्रयोदशायुजि कलाः कुररे मनवो युजि ।
ओजे कलाश्चन्द्रलेखे तिथयो रवयः समे ॥२३७॥

[1] *Dvipatha* is another name for *dodhaka* which is called *dohā* or *doha* in Prakrit. It has three *bha-gaṇa-s* with two *guru-s* at end i.e. SII SII SII SS.

[2] Any *tāla* which is not defined or particularly indicated.

त्रयोदशायुजि कलाः कुञ्जरे तिथयः समे ।
मात्राः पञ्चदशायुग्मे तिलके मनवः समे ॥२३८॥
त्रयोदशासमे हंसक्रीडे युग्मे कलाः कलाः ।
यद्येषामर्धयोरन्ते पञ्चादिलघुभिः शिखा ॥२३९॥
तं शिखाद्विपथं प्राहुर्मयूरमपि सूरयः ।
एतेषु व्यत्ययेनापि चरणानां स्थितिर्भवेत् ॥२४०॥
भवन्त्येकादिपादानां सकृद्द्विर्गानभेदतः ।
द्विपथा भूरिभेदास्ते लक्ष्या लक्ष्येषु सूरिभिः ॥२४१॥
इति द्विपथप्रबन्धः ।

(b) Varieties of *dvipatha*:

It is known to be fourfold i.e., one is composed in notes (only),[1] the other is (formed) with *prayoga*[2] and the other two with and without both[3] respectively. (233 b-d)

This[4] called *doha* in Prakrit,[5] and these are its nine varieties: *sārasa, bhramara, haṁsa, kurara, candralekha, kuñjara, tilaka, haṁsakrīḍa* and *mayūra*. (234-235 b)

Sārasa has thirteen *mātrā-s*[6] in the odd and twelve in the even (feet).[7] In *bhramara* the odd[8] (feet) have fourteen[9] and the even (feet) have twelve[10]

[1]Wherein *udgrāha* and *dhruva* are composed in *svara-s* only.

[2]The second variety likewise according to 'K' (i.e. *udgrāha* and *dhruva*) is composed by *prayoga-s*. 'S', as usual, interprets *prayoga* as *gamaka*.

[3]That is, the third variety, according to 'K' is composed of both *svara-s* and *prayoga-s*, the former being used in *udgrāha* and the latter in *dhruva*. The fourth is without both i.e. devoid of *svara-s* and *prayoga-s*. 'K' infers that in the case of the fourth, *udgrāha* and *dhruva* are composed with *pada-s* (words). He also suggests that in every case *ābhoga* is done with *pada-s*.

[4]'This 'refers to *dvipatha*.

[5]Prakrit is an ancient language of the people of India. It is derived from Sanskrit according to some, and is a parallel tongue of the common folks according to others. However, the form in which it is available in literary works, supports the first view, since it is very closely related to Sanskrit.

[6]*Mātrā* is of one *laghu akṣara* (short syllable) in prosody but in *mārga tāla* it is of five *laghu-akṣara-s*.

[7]That is, the first and third *pāda-s* are of thirteen *mātrā-s* and the second and the fourth *pāda-s* are of twelve *mātrā-s*.

[8]As explained above, 'odd' refers to the Ist and the 3rd and 'even' to the 2nd and the 4th feet. This may be understood throughout.

[9]*Manu-s* are known to be 14. So the number 14 is thereby indicated.

[10]The suns are known to be 12 (perhaps after the twelve months of the year). So, the number 12 is thereby indicated.

mātrā-s. *Haṁsa* has fifteen in the odd and thirteen *mātrā-s* in the even (feet). In *kurara* there are thirteen *mātrā-s*[1] in the odd and twelve in the even (feet). *Candralekha* has fifteen[2] *mātrā-s*[3] in the odd and twelve in the even (feet). *Kuñjara* has thirteen in the odd and fifteen *mātrā s* in its even quarters. In the odd (feet) *haṁsakrīḍa* has thirteen *mātrā-s* and in the even feet, it has sixteen.[4] (235 c-239 b)

If in these,[5] *śikhā*[6] is (provided) to the extent of five *laghu-s* or so[7] at the end of their two halves,[8] then it[9] is called *śikhādvipatha* and also *mayūra* by the experts. The feet[10] in these can also be arranged in reverse order.[11] (239 c-240)

Many more varieties of *dvipatha* are (formed) by singing the first and other steps (*pāda-s*) once and twice and so on,[12] these should be demonstrated by the experts through practical examples. (241)

(xvii) कलहंसप्रबन्धः

छन्दसः कलहंसस्य पादैरन्ते स्वरान्वितैः ।
कलहंसः स्वरे न्यासो गेयो झम्पादितालतः ॥२४२॥
वर्णजो मात्रिकश्चेति कलहंसो द्विधा मतः ।
गद्यात्मा चेत् स्वरान् गीत्वा ततः पदनिवेशनम् ॥२४३॥

इति कलहंसप्रबन्धः ।

[1]*Kalā* refers to *mātrā*.

[2]The *tithi-s* signify the lunar days of a lunar calendar.

[3]The second *kalā* in 239 b refers to the sixteen phases of the moon. *Kalā* also means a phase of the moon. So, the number 16 is thereby indicated.

[4]These varieties of *doha*.

[5]The idea of *śikhā* has already been introduced by the author in the context of *śikhāpadum* vide verse 126 ante But as 'K' points out and also as provided in the text, the extent of *śikhā* in this context is restricted to 5 *laghu-s* or six or even seven so as to form a part of the total length of the *pāda* concerned.

[6]'K' interprets it as "five, six or seven, but in any case, less than a *pāda*."

[7]'K' elucidates that it can be anywhere in-between or at the end of a *pāda*.

[8]That is, such a *doha* which itself is a variety of *dvipatha*.

[9]The odd and the even feet.

[10]These *śikhādvipatha-s*.

[11]That is, the number of *mātrā-s* prescribed for the odd (Ist odd 3rd) feet may be exchanged with that of the even (second and fourth) feet. Thus, more varieties can be created.

[12]That is, if the first foot is sung once and the other feet are sung twice, it makes for one variety; if the second is sung once and the first is sung twice and so on we get another variety.

(xvii) *Kalahaṁsa-prabandha:* (242-243)

Kalahaṁsa is composed in *kalahaṁsa* metre[1] and its *pāda*-endings are set in solfa notes. It is sung with *jhampā* and such other *tāla-s*[2] and ends in *svara.*[3] (242)

Kalahaṁsa is believed to be twofold viz. based on *varṇa*[4] and depending on *mātrā-s*;[5] but if it is composed in prose,[6] the verbal text may be introduced after singing solfa notes. (243)

(xviii) तोटकप्रबन्धः

तोटकच्छन्दसा न्यस्तस्वरोऽङ्घ्रयन्ते तु तोटकः ।
ननु वृत्ते वक्ष्यमाणे पुनरुक्तोऽत्र तोटकः ॥२४४॥
सत्यं किंतु मते येषां वृत्तं वृत्ताख्यवृत्ततः ।
तन्मते तोटकस्येह नैवास्ति पुनरुक्तता ॥२४५॥

इति तोटकप्रबन्धकः ।

[1]'K' defines *haṁsa* metre as follows, which he says is also called *kalahaṁsa.*
"In a foot of *jagatī* class with twelve syllables, if the 2nd, 4th, 6th, 7th, 10th and the 12th syllables are *guru-s* then it is called *haṁsa. Haṁsa* is also *kalasaṁsa.* "However, *Chandomañjari* of Gangādāsa classifies *kalahaṁsa* under *atijagati* i.e. *praharṣiṇī* and defines it as the metre which has *sa-gaṇa, ja-gaṇa,* 2 *sagaṇa-s* and one *guru* in one pāda, and this is illustrated as:

IIS	ISI	IIS	IIS	S
sa	ja	sa	sa	g *(guru)*

(cf. *Chandomañjari*, pp. 67, 68—Chowkhamba Sanskrit Series no. 115, 1948)

[2]*Jhampā tāla* will be defined in chapter V. The implication of other *tāla-s,* as brought out by 'K' is that such *deśī tāla-s* that are of the same measure in terms of *mātrā-s* can be used.

[3]'K' elucidates that the notes accociated with the first *pāda* may be sung again for a while and the song ended with them. The end here signifies the *nyāsa* of the text. *Svara* in this context signifies the solfa notes.

[4]*Varṇaja* lit. 'born of *varṇa*'. 'K' interprets *varṇaja* as *padya* (verse), but 'S' interprets it as "that which is composed of *varṇa-gaṇa-s* (syllabic groups)."

[5]*Mātrika* lit. 'pertaining to *mātrā*' is interpreted by 'K' as *gadya* (prose) and as "based on *mātrika-gaṇa-s* (unit measure groups)" by 'S'. But it seems K's interpretation is more consonant with the second line of the verse.

[6]According to 'K' if *kalahaṁsa* is composed in verse then the definition given above will apply to it; but if it is in prose then only the number of *mātrā-s* will be taken into consideration which has to be the same in both the varieties i.e. *varṇaja* and *mātrika*; however, they will not be grouped in *gaṇa-s.*

(xviii) *Toṭaka-prabandha:* (244-245)

Toṭaka is (composed) in *toṭaka* metre[1] and is laid with solfa notes at the end of the *pāda* (foot). But indeed, being included in *vṛtta,* which is presently to be defined, here, *toṭaka* seems to be[2] a repetition.[3] True, but it is not at all a repetition here, in the view of those who characterise *vṛtta* (*prabandha*) by *vṛtta* metre.[4] (2 4-245)

(xix) घटप्रबन्धः

तेनैरर्धं द्विपद्यर्धं घटस्तेनकमुक्तिकः ।
इति घटप्रबन्धः ।

(xix) *Ghaṭa-prabandha:* (246 a b)

Half of *ghaṭa* is (composed) with *tena-s*[5] and half in *dvipadī.*[6] It ends with *tenaka-s.*[7] (246 a b)

[1]*Toṭaka* (metre) has four *sa-gaṇa-s* in a (quarter *pāda*) and is illustrated as:

IIS	IIS	IIS	IIS
sa	sa	sa	sa

[2]*Nanu* of the text introduces a doubt and a question which is clarified and answered by the author in the next verse. The sense of the experssion "seems to be" is implied in the construction of the original text.

[3]The contention is that since by definition *vṛtta* (see verse 246 c d) can be sung by any metre, also includes *toṭaka* and therefore to speak of a *prabandha* exclusively composed in that metre is superfluous and a repetition.

[4]The objection raised in the previous verse is admitted to be valid only partially i.e, in case *vṛtta* (*prabandha*) is allowed to be composed in any metre whatsoever. But since there is also a view, quoted by the author (vide verse 247 c d), that it should be composed in *vṛtta* metre specifically, it cannot be said to be a repetition on the part of the author since he has to accommodate every recognised viewpoint in his treatise.

That is how the author meets on, in fact, forestalls a possible objection. But 'K' points out that the objection does not really arise, for if *toṭaka* were to be considered as included or covered by *vṛtta* because it could be composed in any metre, then other *prabandna-s* based on metres such as *kanda*, *turagalīla*, *krauñcapāda*, *dvipatha* etc would also be considered to be repetitions Thus according to 'K', the objection could only be half accepted and therefore is better rejected.

[5]*Tena* is an integral part (*aṅga*) of *prabandha* and consists of auspicious words.

[6]'K' points out that the expression 'half' is a relative term. Half of what? If the text is interpreted to mean that the first half consists of *tena-s*, the question is half of what? And he suggests that the answer lies in the next word i.e. half of *dvipadī*, *Dvipadī* has been defined (see 214 c d ante) as having a *cha-gaṇa* and five *bha-gaṇa-s* with a *guru* in the end in a *pāda*. So, the number of *mātrā-s* required for half of *dvipadī*, composed with verbal text makes for its other half, 'K' also draws our attention to an alternative view in *dvipadī* according to which solfa notes are sung at end of the half of the *pāda* (cf. 215 c d ante). He suggests that there too such an alternative use of solfa notes, though not explicitly provided, may be taken as understood.

[7]*Tenaka* is the same as *tena*.

(xx) वृत्तप्रबन्धः

छन्दसा येन केनापि तालेनेष्टेन गीयते ॥२४६॥
वृत्तं तस्य च पादान्ते वृत्तान्ते वा स्वरान् क्षिपेत् ।
स्वरहीनं तदित्यन्ये वृत्तं छन्दसि चापरे ॥२४७॥
छन्दश्चित्यां विचेतव्याश्छन्दसां बहवो भिदाः ।

इति वृत्तप्रबन्धः ।

(xx) ***Vṛtta-prabandha:*** **(246 c-248 b)**

Composed in any metre whatsoever, *vṛtta* is sung with any choice *tāla* and solfa notes are introduced either at the end of a *pāda* or the *vṛtta*.[1] According to others, it[2] is devoid of solfa notes, while according to some it is (composed) in *vṛtta* metre (only). Many other metrical variations may be discerned from *chandaściti*.[3] (246 c-248 b)

(xxi) मातृकाप्रबन्धः

एकैकमातृकावर्णपूर्वकाणि पदानि चेत् ॥२४८॥
क्रमेण परिगीयन्ते मातृका, सा त्रिधा मता ।
दिव्या च मानुषी दिव्यमानुषी चेति, तत्र तु ॥२४९॥
दिव्या संस्कृतया वाचा मार्गतालैश्च गीयते ।
मानुषी प्राकृतगिरा देशीतालैश्च निर्मिता ॥२५०॥
उभयोर्मिश्रणादुक्ता मातृका दिव्यमानुषी ।
अनिबद्धा निबद्धा च द्विधा सा गद्यपद्यजा ॥२५१॥
सर्वमन्त्रमयी ह्येषा सर्वसिद्धिप्रदायिनी ।
गातव्या नियतैर्नित्यं गीर्वाणगणवल्लभा ॥२५२॥

इति मातृकाप्रबन्धः ।

[1]The whole of *vṛtta prabandha* is implied.
[2]'It' refers to *vṛtta prabandha.*
[3]*Chandoviciti,* as pointed out by 'K', is a work on prosody. In the text it is written as *chandaściti*.

(xxi) *Mātṛkā-prabandha*: (248 c-252)

If *pada-s* composed in order to commence progressively by the letters of alphabet[1] are sung seriatim, it is (called) *mātṛkā* which is threefold viz. *divyā*,[2] *mānuṣī*[3] and *divyamānuṣī*.[4] (248 b-249 d).

Of these *divyā* is composed in the Sanskrit language and is sung with *mārga tāla-s*,[5] *mānuṣī* is produced in the Prakrit tongue with *deśī tāla-s*; while the *mātṛkā* formed out of the mixture of the two is called *divya-mānusī*. (249 d-251 b)

Mātṛkā is again twofold viz. *anibaddha* (non-metrical) and *nibaddha* (metrical) according to whether it is composed in prose or verse.[6] (251 c d)

This (*prabandha*) commands the power of all the sacred chants (*mantra-s*) and is capable of bestowing every accomplishment. Endearing to the host of gods, it is to be sung regularly by the qualified (ones).[7] (252)

(xxii) रागकदम्बप्रबन्धः

नन्द्यावर्तः स्वस्तिकश्च द्विधा रागकदम्बकः ।

चतुर्वृत्तश्चतुस्तालो रागराजिविराजितः ॥२५३॥

नन्द्यावर्तो भवेत्तस्य तालमानद्वयेन वा ।

उद्ग्राहेणाथवा न्यासो गद्येनैनं परे जगुः ॥२५४॥

तालेनैकेन केचित्त्, स्वस्तिको द्विगुणस्ततः ।

अब्जपत्रोऽब्जगर्भश्च भ्रमराम्रेडिते मते ॥२५५॥

केषांचित् पूर्वपूर्वस्माद् द्विगुणः स्यात् परः परः ।

इति रागकदम्बप्रबन्धः

(xxii) *Rāgakadamba-prabandha:* (253-256 b)

Rāgakadambaka (lit. 'cluster of *rāga-s*') is twofold viz. *nandyāvarta* and *svāstika*. *Nandyāvarta* is composed of four *vṛtta-s*[8] set to four *tāla-s* and is

[1]Verse beginning a, ā, i, ī, and so on up to *ha* numbering fifty-two in all.

[2]*Divyā* lit., 'heavenly'.

[3]*mānuṣī* lit., 'human' (female).

[4]*Divyamānuṣī*—a combination of heavenly and human qualities.

[5]Such as *caccatpuṭa* and so on dealt within chapther V.

[6]*Anibaddha* is composed in prose, and *nibaddha* in verse.

[7]'S' interprets *niyataiḥ* as 'those who are pure and attentive'.

[8]'*Vṛtta*' does not stand for any particular metre, but for *mātsī* in general.

embellished by a series of *rāga-s.*[1] Its completion (*nyāsa*) is done with two cycles of *tāla*[2] or with *udgrāha*. Others, however, hold that it may be (composed) in prose, and some others, say that it is set to one *tāla* only. (253-255 a)

Svastika is double[3] that.[4] According to some, *abjapatra*[5] (i.e. *svastika*) is twofold viz. *abjagarbha*[6] and *bhramarāmreḍita*, each being double the preceding one.[7] (255 b-256 b)

It is difficult to be certain about the interpretation regarding the varieties of *svastika* (i.e. 255 c to 256 b), since 'K' and 'S' too give very divergent views. The above translation does not accept either of the two views in toto, neither does it neglect either of them entirely; it is based on the consideration of both the interpretations.

'K' interprets this portion as under:

Svastika is double *nandyāvarta* i.e., it has eight *vṛtta-s*, eight *tāla-s* and eight *rāga-s*. *Svastika* is itself called *abjapatra* i.e. it is another name for *svastika*. Now, every succeeding variety is double the preceding one; so, *abjagarbha* is double of *abjapatra* i.e , it has sixteen *vṛtta-s*, *tāla-s* and *rāga-s*. Then *bhramara* is double of *abjagarbha* i.e., it has 32 *vṛtta-s*, *tāla-s* and *rāga-s*. Again *āmreḍita* is double of *bhramara* and so it has 64 *vṛtta-s*, *tāla-s* and *rāga-s*. He considers *abjapatra* also to be a variety of *svastika* and therefore, there are four varieties of *svastika* for him.

However, 'S' finds only two varieties of *svastika* here viz. *abjapatra* and *bhramarāmreḍita*. *Abjagarbha*, he says, is included in *abjapatra*. Accordingly he interprets that "*abjapatra* has sixteen (twice the number of *svastika*) *vṛtta-s* and sixteen *tāla-s* and *bhramarāmreḍita* has 32 *vṛtta-s* and *tāla-s*, since each is double its preceding one".

Obviously, both differ in their view of the number of varieties of *svastika*, 'K' considering them to be four, works out 64 *vṛtta-s* and *tāla-s* for the last variety, and 'S', considering them to be two, works out 32 *vṛtta-s* and *tāla-s* for his last variety. But normally 'K' seems to think that *abjapatra* is another name for *svastika*.

[1] 'K' elucidates that each *vṛtta*, as it is set to a different *tāla*, is sung in a different *rāga*, or even the *rāga* may be changed at each *pāda* or each half *vṛtta* or a full *vṛtta*.

[2] That is, as pointed out by 'K', whatever *tāla* is employed in whatever *vṛtta*, it is used in two cycles at the end.

[3] *Nandyāvarta* has four *vṛtta-s* and four *tāla-s*, so *svastika* would have double that number i.e. eight *vṛtta-s* and eight *tāla-s*.

[4] That refers to *nandyāvarta*.

[5] *Abjapatra* lit. lotus leaf, is taken by 'K' as another name for *svastika*.

[6] *Abjagarbha* lit. the womb of lotus, is a variant of *abjapatra* with double the number of *vṛtta-s* and *tāla-s*.

[7] In other words, if *abjapatra* has eight *vṛtta-s* and eight *tāla-s*, *abjagarbha* and *bhramarāmreḍita* would respectively have 16 and 32 *vṛtta-s* and *tāla-s* each.

Now, it seems that the contention of 'S' that the varieties are two, is a better interpretation of the text in view of the dual number *mate.* So we have taken *abjapatra* as a synonym of *svastika* as elucidated by 'K' and have considered *abjagarbha* (included by 'S' in *abjapatra*) and *bhramarāmreḍita* as its two varieties with sixteen and thirty-two *vṛtta-s* and *tāla-s* and *rāga-s* respectively.

It is notable that 'K' refers to Gopāla Nāyaka in this context. Gopāla Nāyaka is considered to be a famous court musician of Alauddin Khilji in the middle of the 14th century or so and was a celebrated singer of *prabandha-s* (cf. *Baiju aur Gopāl* by Prabhu Dayal Mital, Sāhitya Sansthān, Mathura, pp. 34-36).

(xxiii) पञ्चतालेश्वरप्रबन्धः

(क) लक्षणम्

आलापः प्रागतालः स्यात् पृथग्द्विः पदपञ्चकम् २५६॥

चच्चत्पुटेन तेनैव स्वराः पाटास्ततः परम् ।

द्विचच्चत्पुटमानेन पाटैः पटहसंभवैः ॥२५७॥

कार्योऽन्तरस्ततश्चाचपुटेन पदपञ्चकम् ।

तद्वत्तेन स्वराः पाटास्तद्द्विमानेन चान्तरः ॥२५८॥

हुडुक्कपाटैस्तदनु षट्पितापुत्रकेण च ।

पृथक् पदानि पञ्च द्विस्तेनैव स्वरपाटकम् ॥२५९॥

तद्द्विमानाच्छङ्खपाटैरन्तरः स्यात्ततस्तु षट् ।

प्रत्येकं द्विपदानि स्युः संपक्वेष्टाकतालतः ॥२६०॥

ततस्तद्वत् स्वराः पाटास्तद्द्विमानेन चान्तरः ।

कांस्यतालोद्भवैः पाटैरुद्घट्टेन पदानि षट् ॥२६१॥

प्राग्वत्तथा स्वराः पाटाः पाटैर्मुरजसंभवैः ।

अन्तरः पूर्ववत्तस्मादाभोगश्चाविलम्बितः ॥२६२॥

प्रबन्धनाम्ना प्राङ्मानं नेतृनामाथ मङ्गलम् ।

वाक्यमालापके न्यासः पञ्चतालेश्वरो भवेत् ॥२६३॥

(xxiii) *Pañcatāleśvara-prabandha:* (256 c-264)

(a) The characteristic features:

In *pañcatāleśvara* initially there is *ālāpa*[1] which is devoid of *tāla* and is followed by a composition[2] of five *pada-s* that are sung separately[3] twice with *caccatpuṭa tāla*[4] in which[5] solfa notes and *pāṭa-s*[6] (instrumental sound syllables) are also sung thereafter. (256 c-257 b)

Then, *antara*[7] is introduced with *pāṭa-s* of *paṭaha*[8] in the measure of two *caccatpuṭa-s.*[9] (257 c-258 a)

Thereafter a composition of five *pāda-s* is sung likewise[10] along with the solfa notes and *pāṭa-s* followed by *antara* in double measure[11] with the *pāṭa-s* of *huḍukkā.*[12] (258 b-259 a)

[1]It has been specifically said that the *ālāpa* should be free of *tāla*. But *ālāpa* is free of *tāla* by its very definition; what then is the need for this specification? It is pointed out by 'K' and 'S' that it has been so specified to exclude it from the rest of the song for which *tāla* is prescribed. 'K' particularly elucidates that *ālāpa*, in this context, implies *rāgālāpa* and not *gamakālāpa* which also goes by the name *ālāpa*.

[2]*Padapañcakam* signifies a unit of five verses. The unifying factor might be the use of the same metre, for in their verbal content they are said to be different and also, as interpreted by 'K' (if we accept his interpretation), they have to be sung in a different melodic structure.

[3]'K' gives a very specific interpretation to *pṛthak* of the text over here. The purport, as brought out by him, is that all the five verses are to be sung in different melodic structures and separately followed by the singing of solfa notes and *pāṭa-s* (syllabic sounds of musical instruments).

[4]*Caccatpuṭa* is defined as having two *guru-s*, one *laghu* and one *pluta*, (see Chapter V).

[5]That is by *caccatpuṭa tāla.*

[6]*Pāṭa-s*: This is perhaps the only *prabandha* wherein *pāṭa-s* of different instruments are separately specified and required to be used at different steps. This is notable.

[7]*Antara* has been defined as an extra *dhātu* (section) of the *prabandha* which is introduced in between *dhruva* and *ābhoga* (cf. 9 c d ante). But it was ordained that *antara* is generally used among the *rūpaka-s* of the *sālaga-sūḍa prabandha-s* (cf. 10 a b ante). Thus, here it seems to be an exception of usage.

[8]*Paṭaha* is an instrument in the category of drums i.e. (*avanaddha vādya-s* or covered instruments). It is notable that it is in the case of *antara* only that particular types of *pāṭa-s* are specifically prescribed. Elsewhere, it is understood that *pāṭa-s* of any instrument or their mix may be used. 'K' elucidates that the *pāṭa-s* of *paṭaha* are elsewhere described as constituted by the syllabic sounds of gutturals (i.e. k, kh, g and gh) excepting the nasal, lingual (ṭ, ṭh, ḍ, ḍh, ṇ) and dentals (t, th, d, dha, n) and r and h. Thus, on this basis 'K' infers that it is only in the case of the *pāṭa-s* of *antara* that the rule pertaining to the repetition of the *tāla*-cycle is applicable, and not in case of the *pāṭa-s* sung elsewhere.

[9]*Dvicaccatpuṭamāna* is interpreted by 'K' as the two cycles (*āvartana-s*) of *caccatpuṭa*.

[10]That is, as described above in 256 d-257 b.

[11]That is, in two cycles of *caccatpuṭa* as explained above (see note 9).

[12]'K' elucidates, on the strength of the author's own definition of the *pāṭa-s* of *huḍukkā* given by him subsequently, that they are constituted by the *pāṭa-s* of *paṭaha* excepting the syllabic sound of *deṁ* and as augmented by that of m and jh (see note 8).

Then five verses (are sung) separately twice with *ṣaṭpitāputraka*[1] (*tāla*) along with solfa notes and *pāṭa-s* in the same *tāla* followed by *antara* (sung) with the *pāṭa-s* of *śaṅkha*[2] in double measure.[3] (259 b-260 b)

Thereafter, six *pada-s* are to be (sung) each separately and twice with *sampakveṣṭāka*[4] *tāla* followed by solfa notes and *pāṭa-s* and then the *antara* with *pāṭa-s* of bronze cymbals[5] (*kāṁsya tāla*) in double measure. (260 b-262 c)

Then six verses (*pada-s*) with *udghaṭṭa tāla* (are to be sung) on the former pattern[6] followed by solfa notes and *pāṭa-s* as well as the *antara* sung with the *pāṭa-s* of *muraja* as before.[7] (261 d-262 c)

After that, comes *ābhoga* in the fast[8] tempo using the previous *tāla*[9] and indicating the names of the *prabandha* and (its) hero, and is sung alongwith an auspicious sentence.[10] The song is concluded with *ālāpa*. (262 d-263)

(ख) भेदा:

वीरावतार: श्रृङ्गारतिलकश्चेति स द्विधा ।
वीरश्रृङ्गारयोस्तेन प्रीयन्ते सर्वदेवता: ॥२६४॥

इति पञ्चतालेश्वरप्रबन्ध: ।

(b) Varieties of *pañcatāleśvara:*

This[11] (*prabandha*) is twofold viz. *virāvatāra* and *śṛṅgāratilaka* sung in (the context of) the sentiments of heroism and conjugal love respectively.

[1]*Ṣaṭpitāputraka* is another *mārga-tāla* described in Chapter V.

[2]'K' informs us that the *śaṅkha-pāṭa-s* are *ghuṁ, ghuṁ, thoṁ, digi* etc. with many letters.

[3]That is, the two cycles of *ṣaṭpitāputraka*.

[4]Likewise *sampakveṣṭāka* is yet another *mārga-tāla* and is defined in Chapter V.

[5]Syllables like *ṭaṭa, kaṭa* etc. according to 'K'.

[6]That is, separately and twice.

[7]That is, in two cycles of *udghaṭṭa*.

[8]*Avilambita*, lit. not slow, would ordinarily include the medium tempo as well; but as 'K' points out, the implication is that of fast tempo.

[9]That is, *udghaṭṭa*.

[10]'K' points out that an auspicious sentence implies the use of *tena*, one of the integral parts of *prabandha*. The purport according to him is that auspicious words may be used or words expressive of auspiciousness may be used. He further says that the word *tena* which signifies Brahman may be used once or more than once to make up for the sentence. 'S' seems to have a different reading altogether. He probably reads *vākyamelapakenyāsaḥ* instead of *vākyamālāpaka-nyāsaḥ* as printed in Ad. ed. of *S.R.* (text). Therefore, according to his text it would mean "the song may be concluded with *melāpaka*, rich with *prayoga-s* and (composed) in the from of a sentence".

[11]This refers to *pañcatāleśvara*.

All the gods are pleased by it.[1] (264)

Pañcatāleśvara, as its name indicates, is based on five *tāla-s*, viz. *caccatpuṭa, cācapuṭa, ṣaṭpitāputraka, sampakveṣṭāka* and *udghaṭṭa*. All these are *mārga tāla-s*. Since *prabandha-s* belong to *deśī* music, it is notable that *mārga tāla-s* are also employed in the composition and singing of certain *prabandha-s*. It is also notable that *pāṭa-s*, *svara-s* (solfa notes) and *tena-s* are fully utilised here. The singing of *maṅgala*, an auspicious composition, towards the end is interpreted by Kallinātha as a *tena*.

(xxiv) तालार्णवप्रबन्धः

तालार्णवो भूरितालः स द्वेधा गद्यपद्यतः ।

इति तालार्णवप्रबन्धः ।

इत्यालिप्रबन्धनिरूपणम् ।

(xxiv) *Tālārṇava-prabandha:* (265 a b)

Tālārṇava[2] is composed in many *tāla-s* and is twofold viz. based on prose and verse respectively. (265 a b)

चतुर्थप्रकरणम्

विप्रकीर्णप्रबन्धनिरूपणम्

(i) श्रीरङ्गप्रबन्धः

तालै रागैश्चतुर्भिः स्याच्छ्रीरङ्गोऽन्ते पदान्वितः ॥२६५॥

इति श्रीरङ्गप्रबन्धः ।

SECTION 4

Viprakīrṇa-prabandha-s

(i) *Śrīraṅga prabandha:* (265 c d)

Śrīraṅga is (composed) in four *rāga-s* set to four *tāla-s* employing verbal

[1]The purport is that all the gods are pleased through singing *pañcatāleśvara.* 'It' stands for the singing of *pañcatāleśvara.*

[2]*Tālārṇava* lit. means an ocean of *tāla-s*. Thus, obviously it is based on many *tāla-s*.

structures (*pada-s*) towards the end.[1] (265 c d)

(ii) श्रीविलासप्रबन्धः

स्वरान्तः श्रीविलासः स्यात्तालै रागैश्च पञ्चभिः ।

इति श्रीविलासप्रबन्धः ।

(ii) *Śrīvilāsa-prabandha:* (266 a b)

Śrīvilāsa is sung with five *rāga-s* set to five *tāla-s*[2] employing solfa notes (*svara-s*) at the end. (266 a b)

(iii-v) पञ्चभङ्गिपञ्चाननोमातिलकप्रबन्धाः

तेनकान्तः पञ्चभङ्गिः, पाटैः पञ्चाननोऽन्तिमैः ।।२६६।।
रागाभ्यामपि तालाभ्यां स्यादुमातिलकः पुनः ।
बिरुदान्तस्त्रिभिस्तालै रागैः सर्वाङ्गिका इमे ।।२६७।।
इति पञ्चभङ्गिपञ्चाननोमातिलकप्रबन्धाः ।

(iii-v) *Pañcabhaṅgi, pañcānana* and *umātilaka prabandha-s* (266 c-267)

Pañcabhaṅgi employs *tenaka-s* (auspicious phrases) in the end, while *pañcānana* ends with *pāṭa-s* (syllabic sounds of musical instruments); but both are (composed) in two *rāga-s* set to three *tāla-s* with *biruda-s* (panegyrics) in the end. These[3] are complete with all the integral parts (*aṅga-s*). (266 c-267)

(vi) त्रिपदीप्रबन्धः

आद्यौ द्विद्विगणौ पादौ तृतीयश्च चतुर्गणः ।
चतुर्थस्त्रिगणः पादेष्वेकादश गणा इमे ।।२६८।।

[1]The text has been translated in accordance with the interpretation of 'K'. He says that each of the four *rāga-s* is related to respective *tāla-s*, but he does not mention the details of this relation. He further asserts that, "since it is said subsequently in the text that these (five *prabandha-s*) have all the integral parts (*aṅga-s*), it is understood that before employing *pāda-s* at the end, the rest of the *aṅga-s* such as *svara* etc. have to be sung in their due order. Thus, in every *rāga*, six *aṅga-s* are envisaged by keeping the *pada-s* at the end."

According to 'S', "*Śrīraṅga* is that which is composed in four *rāga-s* and four *tāla-s* with *pada-s* at the end."

[2]Interpreted as in the case of *Śrīraṅga*, explained above.

[3]That is, these first five *prabandhas*.

रतेः षष्ठश्च दशमः शेषाः स्युर्मान्मथा गणाः ।
गीत्वाद्यपादौ तदनु किंचिच्छेषं तृतीयकम् ॥२६९॥
ततः समग्रं तं गीत्वा चतुर्थो यदि गीयते ।
तदा स्यात् त्रिपदी तालहीना कर्णाटभाषया ॥२७०॥
इति त्रिपदीप्रबन्धः ।

(vi) *Tripadī-prabandha:* (268-270)

The first two *pāda-s* (feet) of *tripadī* have two *gaṇa-s* each; the third consists of four and the fourth of three *gaṇa-s*. Thus, (the four) *pāda-s* have eleven *gaṇa-s* of which the sixth and the tenth are *rati-gaṇa-s*[1] and the rest are *manmatha-gaṇa-s*. (268-269 b)

If, after singing the first two *pāda-s*, the third is sung partially in the first instance and fully thereafter and is followed by the fourth *pāda*, then it becomes *tripadī* which is (composed in the *karṇāṭa*[2] language and is devoid of *tāla*. (269 c-270)

(vii) चतुष्पदीप्रबन्धः

समे षोडश मात्राः स्युः पादे पञ्चदशायुजि ।
यस्यां भिन्नार्थयमकावर्धौ सा तु चतुष्पदी ॥२७१॥
स्वरतेनकसंयुक्ता तेनकन्यासससंयुता ।
इति चतुष्पदीप्रबन्धः ।

(vii) *Catuṣpadī-prabandha:* (271-272 b)

Wherein the even (i.e. the second and the fourth) *pāda-s* (feet) are the sixteen syllabic instants (*mātrā-s*) and the odd ones (i.e. the first and the third) have fifteen (*mātrā-s*) each with its two halves (embellished) by *yamaka-s*[3] of different import; associated with solfa notes (*svara-s*) and auspicious phrases (*tenaka-s*), it ends with the latter. (271-272 b)

[1] *Rati-gaṇa-s* and *kāma-gaṇa s* are illustrated vide verses 61-65 ante. *Manmatha* is another name for *kāma*.

[2] *Karṇāṭa* is a name of a region in South India. It is variously identified with modern Maharashtra, Mysore, Kanara and so on. (cf. *The Geographical Dictionary of Ancient and Mediaeval India* of Nando Lal Dey). Its language may be called *karṇāṭī* or *karṇāṭiki*.

[3] *Yamaka* is a figure of speech somewhat akin to alliteration. *Yamaka* implies the repetition of letters or words of different import in different feet (*pāda-s*) of a verse. Now, 'K' raises apparently a legitimate question that while the repeated words or letters of the two halves have to be of a different import even by the very definition of *yamaka* the specific mention that is made in the text to this effect would be redundant. And he answers the question to the purport that it is meaningful for those who consider *yamaka* to be in the repetition of words or letters of no different import or meaning (*artha*) but of a different implication or significance (*tātparya*).

(viii) षट्पदीप्रबन्धः

षष्ठस्तृतीयस्त्रिगणः पृथग् द्विद्विगणाः परे ॥२७२॥
चत्वारश्चरणा बाणप्रान्तौ षष्ठतृतीयकौ ।
शेषास्तु मान्मथगणा यस्यां सा षट्पदी मता ॥२७३॥
कर्णाटभाषया तालवर्जिता नादमुक्तिका ।
भेदा वेद्यास्त्रिपद्यादेश्छन्दोलक्ष्मणि भूरयः ॥२७४॥
इति षट्पदीप्रबन्धः ।

(viii) *Ṣaṭpadī-prabandha:* (272 c-274)

Wherein the sixth and the third[1] steps (*pāda-s*) have three *gaṇa-s* and the other four (*pāda-s*) have two *gaṇa-s* each, of which the last (*gaṇa*) of the former (i.e. the sixth and the third *pāda-s*) is the *bāṇa-gaṇa*[2], while the rest[3] are *kāma-gaṇa-s*, it is considered to be *ṣaṭpadī*. Composed in the *karṇāṭā* language and devoid of *tāla*, it ends with *nāda*.[4] (272 c-274 b)

The many varieties of *tripadī* and others[5] may be seen in the treatises on prosody. (274 c d)

(ix) वस्तुप्रबन्धः

मात्रा पञ्चदशाद्येऽङ्घ्रौ तृतीये पञ्चमे तथा ।
सूर्यास्तुर्ये द्वितीये च स्वरपाटान्तमादिमम् ॥२७५॥
अपरं स्वरतेनान्तमर्धं तदनु दोधकः ।
यस्य स्यात्तेनके न्यासस्तद्वस्तु कवयो विदुः ॥२७६॥
इति वस्तुप्रबन्धः ।

[1]*Ṣaṭpadī* literally means, 'having six feet'; of the six quarters the sixth and the third have three *gaṇa-s* each and the other four *pāda-s* i.e. the first, second, fourth and the fifth have two *gaṇa-s* each.

[2]Of the three *gaṇa-s* each of the sixth and the third *pāda-s*, the first and the second *gaṇa* would be a *kāma-gaṇa*, only the third one is prescribed to be the *bāṇa-gaṇa*.

[3]That is, the first two *gaṇa-s* of the sixth and the third *pāda-s* and the two *gaṇa-s* each of the other four *pāda-s*. In other words, of the fourteen *gaṇa-s* of the sixth *pāda-s* put together all, but the seventh and the fourteenth (which are said to be *bāṇa-gaṇa-s* vide note above), are *kāma-gaṇa-s*.

[4]'K' elucidates *nāda* in this context to imply the *sthāyī* (steady) note sung in pure tone without articulation such as of the solfa notes (sa, ri, ga, ma etc). For *sthāyī svara*, see 3.191 ante.

[5]That is *catuṣpadī* and *ṣaṭpadī* apart from *tripadī*, the varieties of these *prabandha-s* being based obviously on the respective metres employed.

(ix) *Vastu-prabandha:* (275-276)

Wherein the first step (*pāda*) has fifteen *mātrā-s* (syllabic instants) as also the third and the fifth and the second and the fourth have twevlve each, while the first half[1] ends with solfa notes (*svara-s*) and syllabic sounds of musical instruments (*pāṭa-s*), the second one with solfa notes (*svara-s*) and auspicious phrases (*tenaka-s*) and is followed by a stanza in *dodhaka*[2] ending in *tenaka*, it is known to the wise to be *vastu*. (275-276)

(x) विजयप्रबन्धः

यत्र तेनैः स्वरैः पाटैः पदैर्विजयतालतः ।
गीयते विजयस्तेनैर्न्यासः स विजयो मतः ॥२७७॥
इति विजयप्रबन्धः ।

(x) *Vijaya-prabandha:* (277)

Where a victory is sung by auspicious phrases (*tena-s*), solfa notes (*svara-s*), syllabic sounds of musical instruments (*pāṭa-s*) and verbal texts (*pada-s*) set to *vijaya-tāla*[3] and ending with *tena-s* (auspicious phrases), that (song) is considered to be *vijaya* (*prabandha*). (277)

(xi) त्रिपथप्रबन्धः

पादत्रयं त्रिपथके पाटैश्च बिरुदैः स्वरैः ।
इति त्रिपथप्रबन्धः ।

(xi) *Tripatha-prabandha:* (278 a b)

Tripatha has three steps (*pāda-s*) (composed respectively) with the syllabic sounds of musical instruments (*pāṭa-s*) panegyrics (*biruda-s*) and solfa notes (*svara-s*). (278 a b)

(xii) चतुर्मुखप्रबन्धः

स्वरैः पाटैः पदैस्तेनैर्वर्णैः स्थाय्यादिभिः क्रमात् ॥२७८॥
चत्वारश्चरणा गेया ग्रहे न्यासश्चतुर्मुखे ।
इति चतुर्मुखप्रबन्धः ।

[1]According to 'K', here the first two *pāda-s*, as per general practice, constitute the first half and the last three *pāda-s* constitute the second half.

[2]*Dodhaka* has already been explained as having three *bha-gaṇa-s* with two *guru-s*.

[3]*Vijaya tāla*, as mentioned by 'K', is later defined as *'pluta* and *laghu'*. *Vijaya* lit. means victory, in which sense as well it is used in the second line of the verse. (277)

(xii) *Caturmukha-prabandha:* (278 c-279 b)

The four steps (*pāda-s*) of *caturmukha* are sung with solfa notes (*svara-s*), syllabic sounds of musical instruments (*pāda-s*), verbal texts (*pada-s*) and auspicious phrases (*tena-s*) whice are (set) in the steady and other[1] tone-patterns (*varṇa-s*) respectively. It ends in *udgrāha*.[2] (278 c-279 d)

(xiii) सिंहलीलप्रबन्धः

स्वरैः पाटैश्च बिरुदैस्तेनकैर्यो विरच्यते ।।२७९।।
सिंहलीलेन तालेन सिंहलीलः स उच्यते ।
इति सिंहलीलप्रबन्धः ।

(xiii) *Siṁhalīla-prabandha:* (279 c-280 b)

That which is composed of solfa notes (*svara-s*), syllabic sounds of musical instruments (*pāṭa-s*), panegyrics (*biruda-s*) and auspicious phrases (*tenakas*) and is set in *siṁhalīla tāla*,[3] is said to be *siṁhalīla*. (279 c-280 b)

(xiv) हंसलीलप्रबन्धः

स्वनामतालके हंसलीलेऽङ्घ्री पदपाटकैः ।।२८०।।
इति हंसलीलप्रबन्धः ।

(xiv) *Haṁsalīla-prabandha:* (280 c b)

The two steps (*pāda-s*) in *haṁsalīla* are composed respectively with *pada-s* and the syllabic sounds of the musical instruments (*pāṭa-s*) and are set in *haṁsalīla tāla*.[4] (280 c d)

[1]That is, the first *pāda* is sung with *svara-s* and the steady tone-pattern (*varṇa*), the second with *pāṭa-s* and the ascending tone-pattern, the third with *pada-s* and the descending tone-pattern and the fourth *pada* with *tena-s* and the circulatory (*sañcārī*) tone-pattern.

[2]*Graha* in this context is interpreted by 'K' as *udgrāha* and rightly so.

[3]*Siṁhalīla tāla* is defined in Chapter V.

[4]*Haṁsalīla tāla* is defined in Chapter V.

(xv) दण्डकप्रबन्धः

पदैः स्वरैर्दण्डकेनच्छन्दसा दण्डको मतः ।
तस्य भूरितरा भेदाश्छन्दोलक्ष्मणि भाषिताः ॥२८१॥
इति दण्डकप्रबन्धः ।

(xv) *Daṇḍaka-prabandha:* (281)

Daṇḍaka is known to be composed with *pada-s* and solfa notes (*svara-s*) in *daṇḍaka*[1] metre. Its many varieties[2] are described in the works on prosody. (281)

(xvi) झम्पटप्रबन्धः

झम्पटच्छन्दसा गेयः क्रीडातालेन झम्पटः ।
इति झम्पटप्रबन्धः ।

(xvi) *Jhampaṭa-prabandha:* (282 a b)

Jhampaṭa is sung in *jhampaṭa* metre[3] with *krīḍā tāla.*[4] (282 a b)

(xvii) कन्दुकप्रबन्धः

पदैः पाटैश्च बिरुदैः कन्दुकः परिगीयते ॥२८२॥
इति कन्दुकप्रबन्धः ।

(xvii) *Kanduka-prabandha:* (282 c d)

Kanduka is sung with *pada-s,* syllabic sounds of musical instruments (*pāṭa-s*) and panegyrics (*biruda-s*). (282 c d)

(xviii) त्रिभङ्गिप्रबन्धः

स्वरैः पाटैः पदैरुक्तस्त्रिभङ्गिः स च पञ्चधा ।
एकस्त्रिभङ्गितालेन वृत्तेनान्यस्त्रिभङ्गिना ॥२८३॥

[1]*Daṇḍaka* is defined, as also quoted by 'K', as having two *na-gaṇa-s* followed by seven *ra-gaṇa-s* and is illustrated as under:

na	na	ra	ra	ra	ra	ra	ra	ra
III	III	SIS	SIS	SIS	SIS	SIS	SIS	SIS

Thus it has twenty-seven syllables in a *pada.*

[2]Such as *caṇḍavṛṣṭiprapāta* and *pracita* etc.

[3]*Jhampaṭa* as pointed out by 'K', is a variety of *gāthā* meter having three *pāda-s* (feet).

[4]*Krīḍā tāla* is defined in Chapter V.

तालै रागैस्त्रिभिर्यद्वा यद्वा वृत्तत्रयान्वितः।
यद्वा देवत्रयस्तुत्या तालद्वैगुण्यमुक्तकः ॥२८४॥
इति त्रिभङ्गिप्रबन्धः।

(xviii) *Tribhaṅgi-prabandha:* (283-284)

Tribhaṅgi is said to be (composed) of solfa notes (*svara-s*), syllabic sounds of musical instruments (*pāṭa-s*) and *pada-s*, and is fivefold viz. (i) (sung) with *tribhaṅgi tāla*[1], (ii) (composed) in *tribhaṅgi* metre[2], (iii) (sung) with three *tāla-s* and *rāga-s*, (iv) (sung) with three metres, and (v) (sung) in the propitiation of the three gods.[3] It ends with two cycles of *tāla.* (283-284)

(xix) हरविलासप्रबन्धः

पदैः सबिरुदैः पाटैस्तेनैर्हरविलासकः।
इति हरविलासप्रबन्धः।

(xix) *Haravilāsa-prabandha:* (285 a b)

Haravilāsa-prabandha is (sung) with *pada-s* associated with panegyrics (*biruda-s*),[4] syllabic sounds of musical instruments (*pāṭa-s*) and auspicious phrases (*tena-s*). (285 a b)

(xx) सुदर्शनप्रबन्धः

पदैश्च बिरुदैस्तेनैर्निर्दिशन्ति सुदर्शनम् ॥२८५॥
इति सुदर्शनप्रबन्धः।

(xx) *Sudarśana-prabandha:* (285 c d)

They indicate *sudarśana* by *pada-s,* panegyrics and auspicious phrases (*tena-s*). (285 c d)

[1]To be defined in Chapter V.
[2]*Tribhaṅgi* is a variety of *gāthā* metre, as pointed out by 'K'.
[3]Probably the trinity of Brahmā, Viṣṇu and Śiva.
[4]According to 'K', as the word '*birudaiḥ*' (panegyrics) qualifies *padaih*, the *pada-s* as associated with *biruda-s* may be sung as one part of the song in the first instance and then *pāṭa-s* and *tena-s* may be sung as another part.

(xxi) स्वराङ्कप्रबन्धः

पदैः स्वरैश्च बिरुदैरुद्ग्राहादित्रयं क्रमात् ।
एकद्वित्राश्च तालाः स्युः स्वराङ्के न्यसनं स्वरैः ॥२८६॥
इति स्वराङ्कप्रबन्धः ।

(xxi) *Svarāṅka-prabandha:* (286)

In *svarāṅka*, the *udgrāha* etc.[1] are sung with *pada-s*, solfa notes (*svara-s*) and panegyrics (*biruda-s*) respectively with one, two and three *tāla-s*. It ends with solfa notes. (286)

(xxii) श्रीवर्धनप्रबन्धः

श्रीवर्धनः स्याद्बिरुदैः पाटैरपि पदैः स्वरैः ।
तालमानद्वयन्यासो निःशङ्केन प्रकीर्तितः ॥२८७॥
इति श्रीवर्धनप्रबन्धः ।

(xxii) *Śrīvardhana-prabandha:* (287)

Śrīvardhana is (sung) by panegyrics (*biruda-s*) as also the syllabic sounds of the musical instruments (*pāṭa-s*) and *pada-s* and solfa notes (*svara-s*). Śārṅgadeva has declared its ending with two cycles of the *tāla.* (287)

(xxiii) हर्षवर्धनप्रबन्धः

पदैश्च बिरुदैर्हर्षवर्धनः स्वरपाटकः ।
इति हर्षवर्धनप्रबन्धः ।

(xxiii) *Harṣavardhana-prabandha:* (288 a b)

Harṣavardhana is (sung) with *pada-s* and panegyrics (*biruda-s*) as also solfa notes (*svara-s*) and the syllabic sounds of musical instruments (*pāṭa-s*).[2] (288 a b)

[1] 'K' understands *melāpaka* and *dhruva* as the other two, while 'S' takes *dhruva* and *ābhoga* instead.

[2] 'K' offers no comments. 'S' says that *harṣavardhana* is composed of *pada-s* and *biruda-s* only. The text clearly suggests that it also has *svara-s* and *pāṭa-s*. Kumbhā describes it as having five integral parts (*aṅga-s*) viz. *pada*, *biruda*, *svara*, *pāṭa* and *tāla* in this very order (cf. *S. Raj*, vol. II, 2.4.4,12).

(xxiv) वदनप्रबन्धः

छपद्वयं दो वदनं स्वरपाटयुतान्तरम् ॥२८८॥
तथोपवदनं प्रोक्तं छगणाच्चदतैर्युतम् ।
तथैव वस्तुवदनं छयुगाद्द्चतैः कृतम् ॥२८९॥
इति वदनप्रबन्धः ।

(xxiv) *Vadana-prabandha:* (288 c-289)

Vadana is (composed) of a *cha-gaṇa,*[1] two *pa-gaṇa-s* and a *da-gaṇa* followed by an *antara*[2] full of solfa notes (*svara-s*) and the syllabic sounds of musical instruments (*pāṭa-s*). Similarly,[3] *upavadana* is formed with a *cha-gaṇa*, a *ca-gaṇa*, a *da-gaṇa*, and a *ta-gaṇa*; and likewise,[4] with a couple of *cha-gaṇa-s*, a *da-gaṇa*, a *ca-gaṇa* and a *ta-gaṇa*, *vastuvadanam* is composed.[5] (288 c-289)

(xxv) चच्चरीप्रबन्धः

रागो हिन्दोलकस्तालश्चच्चरी बहवोऽङ्घ्रयः ।
यस्यां षोडशमात्राः स्युर्द्वौ द्वौ च प्राससंयुतौ ॥२९०॥
सा वसन्तोत्सवे गेया चच्चरी प्राकृतैः पदैः ।
चच्चरीच्छन्दसेत्यन्ये क्रीडातालेन वेत्यपि ॥२९१॥
घत्तादिच्छन्दसा वा स्याच्छन्दोलक्ष्मोदिताभिधा ।
इति चच्चरीप्रबन्धः ।

(xxv) *Caccari-prabandha:* (290-292 b)

Where many steps (*pāda-s*) of sixteen syllabic instants (*mātrā-s*) each are composed in alliteration in sets of two in *rāga hindola* with *caccari tāla caccari* is sung in *prākṛta pada-s* in the spring festival. (290-291 b)

[1]That is according to the interpretation of 'S'. However, according to 'K' the text implies two *cha-gaṇa-s* and two *pa-gaṇa-s*. It is also possible that 'S' might have had a slightly different reading in his MS.

[2]'K' interprets *antara* to mean *dhruva* here, being in the midst of *udgrāha* and *ābhoga* and not the *antara* that arises between *dhruva* and *āboga*. 'S' interprets it as the middle portion.

[3-4]That is, with *svara-s* and *pāṭa-s* forming the *antara*.

[5]'S' reminds us here that *cha-gaṇa* has six *mātrārs* (syllabic instants), *ca-gaṇa* has four, *ta-gaṇa* has three and *da-gaṇa* has two *mātrā-s* each.

According to others, it is (sung) in *caccarī* metre or with *krīḍā-tāla*,[1] or with *ghattā* and other metres described in treatises on prosody that lend their names to it.[2] (291 c-292 b)

(xxvi) चर्याप्रबन्धः

पद्धडीप्रभृतिच्छन्दाः पादान्तप्राससशोभिता ॥२९२॥
अध्यात्मगोचरा चर्या स्याद् द्वितीयादितालतः।
सा द्विधा छन्दसः पूर्त्या पूर्णापूर्णा त्वपूर्तितः ॥२९३॥
समध्रुवा च विषमध्रुवेत्येषा पुनर्द्विधा।
आवृत्त्या सर्वपादानां गीयते सा ध्रुवस्य वा ॥२९४॥
इति चर्याप्रबन्धः।

(xxvi) *Caryā-prabandha:* (292 c-294)

Caryā is (composed) in such metres as *paddhaḍī*,[3] is embellished by alliteration towards the end of its *pāda-s* and is full of spiritual import. It is (sung) with *dvitiya* and other *tāla-s*. (292 c-293 b)

It is twofold *pūrṇa* (complete) and *apūrṇa* (incomplete), accordingly as the metre is completed or not completed. Again it is two-fold viz. *samadhruva* and *viṣamadhruva*[4] as it is sung by the repetition of all the *pāda-s* (feet) or of *dhruva* only. (293 c-294)

(xxvii) पद्धडीप्रबन्धः

चरणान्तसमप्रासा पद्धडीच्छन्दसा युता।
बिरुदैः स्वरपाटान्तै रचिता पद्धडी मता ॥२९५॥
इति पद्धडीप्रबन्धः।

[1] *Krīḍā-tāla* is to be defined in Chapter V.

[2] That is, this very *caccarī*, takes on the name of the particular metre in which it is composed.

[3] 'K' defines *paddhaḍī* metre as having sixteen *mātrā-s* in each foot (*pāda*).

[4] *Samadhruva* lit. means, 'having an equal *dhruva*' while *viṣamadhruva*, means, 'having an unequal *dhruva*'. 'K' thinks that *dhruva*, in this context is related to *udgrāha* since that is the other correlate. Accordingly, if *dhruva* and *udgrāha* happen to be equal, that *prabandha*-variety of *caryā* is *samadhruva*, but if it happens to be smaller or greater than *udgrāha* then it is *viṣamadhruva*. However, 'S' interprets differently. According to him if all the steps (*pāda-s*) are repeated, it is called *samadhruva*, but if only *dhruva* is repeated it is called *viṣamadhruva*. The translation represents this interpretation of the text.

(xxvii) *Paddhaḍi-prabandha:* (295)

With the *pada*-endings equally (adorned) with alliteration *paddhaḍi* is considered to be composed in *paddhaḍi* metre with panegyrics (*biruda-s*) ending with solfa notes (*svara-s*) and syllabic sounds of musical instruments (*pāṭa-s*).[1] (295)

(xxviii) राहडीप्रबन्धः

यत्र वीररसेन स्यात् संग्रामरचितस्तुतिः ।
बहुभिश्चरणैः सात्र राहडी परिकीर्तिता ॥२९६॥
राहडीप्रबन्धः ।

(xxviii) *Rāhaḍi-prabandha:* (296)

Rāhaḍi is known to be composed of many steps (*pāda-s*) with battle description (arousing) the sentiment of heroism. (296)

(xxix) वीरश्रीप्रबन्धः

पदैश्च बिरुदैर्बद्धा वीरश्रीरिति गीयते ।
इति वीरश्रीप्रबन्धः ।

(xxix) *Viraśri-prabandha:* (297 a b)

Viraśrī is sung as composed with *pada-s* and panegyrics (*biruda-s*). (297 a b)

(xxx) मङ्गलाचारप्रबन्धः

यस्तु गद्येन पद्येन गद्यपद्येन वा कृतः ॥२९७॥
कैशिक्या मङ्गलाचारः स निःसारुः स्वरान्वितः ।
इति मङ्गलाचारप्रबन्धः ।

(xxx) *Maṅgalācāra-prabandha:* (297 c-298 b)

Maṅgalācāra is composed either in prose or verse or in both. It is sung in *kaiśikī*[2] *rāga* with *niḥsāru tāla* and solfa notes (*svara-s*). (297 c-298 b)

[1] 'K' interprets that in the first half *biruda-s* with *svara-s* may be sung and in the second *biruda-s* with *pāṭa-s* may be sung.

[2] 'K' points out that *kaiśikī* is a *bhāṣā-rāga* of *śuddha-pañcama*.

(xxxi) धवलप्रबन्धः

त्रिविधो धवलः कीर्तिर्विजयो विक्रमस्तथा ।।२९८।।
चतुर्भिश्चरणैः षड्भिरष्टभिश्च क्रमादसौ ।
विषमे तु छयुग्मं स्यात् तो वा दो वाधिकः समे ।।२९९।।
तदा स्यात् कीर्तिधवलो विजये त्वाद्यतुर्ययोः ।
दौ द्वौ षष्ठे द्वितीये च शेषौ द्वौ छेन पेन वा ।।३००।।
प्रथमे चास्त्रयो दः स्यात् तृतीये दास्त्रयस्तु च ।
तुर्यद्वितीययोश्चैतत् पञ्चमे सप्तमे तथा ।।३०१।।
षष्ठेऽष्टमे दाश्चत्वारो यस्यासौ विक्रमो मतः ।
आशीर्भिर्धवलो गेयो धवलादिपदान्वितः ।।३०२।।
यदृच्छया वा धवलो गेयो लोकप्रसिद्धितः ।
इति धवलप्रबन्धः ।

(xxxi) *Dhavala-prabandha:* (298 c-303 b)

Dhavala-prabandha is threefold viz. *kirti*, *vijaya* and *vikrama* having four, six and eight *pāda-s* (steps) respectively. (298 c-299 b)

If the odd (e.g. the first and the third *pāda-s*) have a couple of *cha-gaṇa-s*[1] and the even (e.g. the second and the fourth *pāda-s*) have either a *ta-gaṇa* or a *da-gaṇa* in addition,[2] it becomes *kīrtidhavala*. (299 c-300 a)

The first, second, fourth and the sixth *pāda-s* of *vijaya* have two *da-gaṇa-s* each and the other two (i.e. the third and the fifth *pāda-s*) have one *cha-gaṇa* or *pa-gaṇa* in addition. (300 b c d)

Wherein, the first step (*pāda*) has three *ca-gaṇa-s* and one *da-gaṇa* and the third has three *da-gaṇa-s*, the fourth and the second have these[3] (very *gaṇa-s*), and likewise[4] the fifth and the seventh too, while the sixth and the eighth have four *da-gaṇa-s*, it is considered to be *vikrama*. (301-302 b)

Dhavala is sung with (words of) blessings employing the word *dhavala*[5] or such other words (of similar import). *Dhavala* is sung even at discretion[6] according to the popular tradition. (302 c-303 b)

[1] *Cha-gaṇa* has six *mātrā-s*, therefore each *pāda* would have twelve.

[2] *Ta-gaṇa* has three and *da-gaṇa* has two *mātrā-s* respectively, so each of these *pāda-s* would have fifteen or fourteen *mātrā-s*.

[3] According to 'K' it means that the fourth *pāda* has three *ca-gaṇa-s* and one *da-gaṇa* and the second *pāda* has three *da gaṇa-s*. 'S' does not elaborate it.

[4] 'K' interprets that the fifth has the same as the fourth and the seventh has the same as the second *pāda* has, and 'S' agrees.

[5] *Dhavala* lit. means bright or clean, pure.

[6] That is, not necessarily in keeping with the above prescribed rules.

(xxxii) मङ्गलप्रबन्धः

कैशिक्यां बोट्टरागे वा मङ्गलं मङ्गलैः पदैः ॥३०३॥
विलम्बितलये गेयं मङ्गलच्छन्दसाथवा ॥
इति मङ्गलप्रबन्धः ।

(xxxii) *Maṅgala-prabandha:* (303 c-304 b)

Maṅgala is composed with auspicious words[1] and is sung in *kaiśiki* or *boṭṭa rāga* in slow tempo, or alternatively in the *maṅgala* metre.[2] (303 c-304 b)

(xxxiii) ओवीप्रबन्धः

खण्डत्रयं प्रासयुतं गीयते देशभाषया ॥३०४॥
ओवीपदं तदन्ते चेदोवी तज्ज्ञैस्तदोदिता ।
त्रयाणां चरणानां स्युरेकाद्यावृत्तितो भिदाः ॥३०५॥
आदिमध्यान्तगैः प्रासैरेकाद्यैश्च पदे पदे ।
छन्दोभिर्बहुभिर्गेया ओव्यो जनमनोहराः ॥३०६॥
इत्योवीप्रबन्धः

(xxxiii) *Ovī-prabandha:* (304 c-306)

Ovī, as described by the experts, is sung in a local dialect in three parts full of alliteration and employing the word *ovī* at the end. (304 c-306 b)

Varieties (of *ovī*) are (obtained) by the repetition of one or more of its three steps (*pāda-s*) separately and by (providing) alliteration in its words variously in the beginning, the middle and the end of one or more of its *pāda-s*. Popular among the people, *ovi* is sung in many metres. (305 c-306)

(xxxiv) लोलीप्रबन्धः

सानुप्रासैस्त्रिभिः खण्डैर्मण्डिता प्राकृतैः पदैः ।
प्रान्ते लोलीपदोपेता लोली गेया विचक्षणैः ॥३०७॥
इति लोलीप्रबन्धः ।

(xxxiv) *Lolī-prabandha:* (307)

Composed in Prakrit verse, *loli* is sung by the experts in three parts embellished with alliteration employing the word *loli* at the end. (307)

[1]Such as *śaṅkha*, *cakra* and *abja* etc. pointed out by 'K'.
[2]'K' quotes its definition as having five *ca-gaṇa-s* in each *pāda*,

(xxxv) ढोल्लरीप्रबन्धः

दोहदः स्याद्यदा प्रान्ते प्रोल्लसड्ढोल्लरीपदः ।
ढोल्लरी नाम सा प्रोक्ता लाटभाषाविभूषिता ॥३०८॥
इति ढोल्लरीप्रबन्धः ।

(xxxv) *Ḍhollari-prabandha:* (308)

When *dohada*[1] is furnished with the word *ḍhollari* in the end, it is called *ḍhollari* (if) embellished (i.e. composed) in *lāṭī*[2] (language). (306)

(xxxvi) दन्तीप्रबन्धः

अनुप्रासप्रधानं चेत् खण्डत्रयसमन्वितम् ।
दन्तीपदान्वितं प्रान्ते तदा दन्ती निगद्यते ॥३०९॥
इति दन्तीप्रबन्धः ।

अनुक्ताभोगवस्तूनां पदैराभोगकल्पना ।
ओव्यादयस्तु चत्वारो भवन्त्याभोगवर्जिताः ॥३१०॥
इति विप्रकीर्णप्रबन्धाः ।

(xxxvi) *Dantī-prabandha:* (309)

If (a *prabandha*) excelling in alliteration has its three parts provided with the word *danti* at the end, it is said to be *dantī*. (309)

Among these *prabandha-s* however *ābhoga* has not been mentioned; it may be understood to be composed of *pada-s*. However, the four *prabandha-s* such as *ovī* and these following it are devoid of *ābhoga*. (310)

[1]*Dohada* has already been spoken of vide 308 ante.

[2]*Lāṭī* is the language of the *Lāṭa* region which roughly corresponds to southern Gujarat including Khandesh, also identified by some with central Gujarat or the whole of Gujarat (cf. *The Geographical Dictionary of Ancient and Mediaeval India* by Nundo Lal Dey).

पञ्चमप्रकरणम्

सालगसूडप्रबन्धनिरूपणम्

उपोद्घातः

शुद्धश्छायालगश्चेति द्विविधः सूड उच्यते ।
एलादिः शुद्ध इत्युक्तो ध्रुवादिः सालगो मतः ॥३११॥
छायालगत्वमेलादेर्यद्यप्याचार्यसंमतम् ।
लोके तथापि शुद्धोऽसौ शुद्धसादृश्यतो मतः ॥३१२॥
जात्याद्यन्तरभाषान्तं शुद्धं प्रकरणान्वितम् ।
तत्रोक्तः शुद्धसूडः प्राक् सालगस्त्वधुनोच्यते ॥३१३॥
आद्यो ध्रुवस्ततो मण्ठप्रतिमण्ठनिसारुकाः ।
अड्डतालस्ततो रास एकतालीत्यसौ मतः ॥३१४॥

SECTION 5

Sālagasūḍa Prabandha-s

Introductory: (311-314)

Sūḍa is said to be twofold viz. *śuddha*[1] and *chāyālaga*.[2] *Śuddha*, as constituted by *elā* and other (*prabandha-s*) has already been described,[3] while *dhruva* and others[4] are considered as *sālaga* (*sūḍa*). Though, according to Bharata[5] the (group of *prabandha-s* beginning with) *elā* is conceived

[1]*Śuddha* is defined by 'K' as that which is established in practice as per the rules laid down in theory.

[2]*Chāyālaga*, as elucidated by 'K', is the imitation of *śuddha*. He explains the word *chāyālaga* as a compound of *chāyā* (similarity) and *laga* (lit. that which follows) i.e. the *prabandha* which is structurally similar to the *śuddha prabandha* and follows its rendering. It seems that *chāyālaga* is structurally similar to *śuddha-sūḍa* but technically is not so rigid in the observance of its rules in performance.

[3]The eight *prabandha-s* enumerated vide 23 c-24 b ante i.e. from *elā* to *ekatālī* constitute *śuddha sūḍa*; and these have already been elaborated.

[4]The seven melodies enumerated vide verse 314 i.e. from *dhruva* to *ekatālī* constitute *sālagasūḍa*. The name *sālaga* is a regional modification of *chāyālaga* and is used as a synonym.

[5]*Ācārya* refers to Bharata, as also it is interpreted by the commentators. As a matter of fact 'S' explicitly identifies *ācārya* with Bharata but 'K' refers to him implicitly. The purport of the commentators' elucidation seems to be that there is an apparent contradiction in the author's statement when he says that *ācārya* (presumably Bharata) considers the group of *prabhandha-s* beginning with *elā* to be *chāyālaga*. How is it then

to be *chāyālaga*, in the contemporary practice,[1] because of its similarity with the *śuddha* (forms), it is (considered) *śuddha*. The (structural melodic forms) described (in the text) from *jāti* to *antarabhāṣā*,[2] as also the *prakaraṇa* songs[3] constitute the *śuddha*. In this context, the *śuddha sūḍa* has already been described and it is the *sālagasūḍa* that is being dealt with. (311-313)

The first (among the *sālagasūḍa prabandha-s*) is *dhruva* followed by *maṇṭha*, *pratimaṇṭha*, *niḥsāruka*,[4] *aḍḍatāla*,[5] *rāsa* and *ekatālī*: so it is thought.[6] (314)

Sūḍa is classified as *śuddha* and *chāyālaga*, which expression is by itself significant. The author has himself pointed out the fact that Bharata considered even *śuddha sūḍa prabandha-s* such as *elā* and others to be *chāyālaga* reflecting, in his opinion the nonconformity of *sūḍa prabandha-s* to *jāti-gāna* and allied forms of *mārga*-music. But he elucidates that it being so in his time the *elā* and other *prabandha-s* had acquired the same inflexible adherence to the rules, and were thus in contradistinction with *chāyālaga sūḍa-prabandha-s*, similar in structure and design to the *śuddha* (*mārga*) form of music. Thus, the *śuddha-sūḍa-s* are distinguished from the *chāyālaga prabandha-s* on the basis of similarity in structure and the technical rules of performance. However, it could be deduced from what he writes on the whole that, the *sālagasūḍa prabandha-s* do not follow the rules of *śuddha* music rigidly, though they retain some structural similarity with the *śuddha-sūḍa*. It is notable that 'K' defines *śuddha* as *śāstrokta-niyama-pravartita* i.e. promulgated in accordance with the rule of theory.

(i) ध्रुवप्रबन्धः

(क) लक्षणम्

एकधातुर्द्विखण्डः स्याद्यत्रोद्ग्राहस्ततः परम् ।
किंचिदुच्चं भवेत् खण्डं द्विरभ्यस्तमिदं त्रयम् ॥३१५॥

that he classifies them as *śuddha* in the contemporary practice? The author himself, elucidate the commentators, explains that it is because of similarity of form.

It is a settled fact that Bharata does not speak of *prabandha-s* and therefore he cannot be an authority for *elā* etc. being considered as *śuddha*. To Śārṅgadeva, whatever is spoken of by Bharata is included in *śuddha*, but that is not the case in this context. Hence, by implication, they should be considered to be *sālaga*. However, since the group of *elā* and other *prabandha-s* referred to here as *śuddha* were strictly regulated, they were assigned to the category of *śuddha* on the analogy of *jāti* etc.

[1]*Loke* (lit. in the world of) performance in contradistinction with theory.

[2]Thus, the *śuddha* includes the *jāti-s*, the *kapāla* and *kambala gāna-s*, the *gīti-s*, the *grāma-rāga-s*, the *uparāga-s*, the *bhāṣā-s*, the *vibhāṣā-s*, the *antarabhāṣā-s* and the *prakaraṇa gīta-s*.

[3]The fourteen *prakaraṇa* and other *gītaka-s* are given in *tālādhyāya* i.e. Chapter V.

[4]Also called *niḥsāru*. Ad. ed. reads *nisāruka*.

[5]Ad. ed. reads *aḍutāla*. *Addatālī* is the name appearing in *S.R.* Chapter V.

[6]That is, it (*sālagasūḍa*) is classified into seven *prabandha-s*.

ततो द्विखण्ड आभोगस्तस्य स्यात् खण्डमादिमम् ।
एकधातु द्विखण्डं च खण्डमुच्चतरं परम् ॥३१६॥
स्तुत्यनामाङ्कितश्चासौ क्वचिदुच्चकखण्डकः ।
उद्ग्राहस्याद्यखण्डे च न्यासः स ध्रुवको भवेत् ॥३१७॥

(i) *Dhruva-prabandha:* (315-332 b)

(a) The characteristic features:

In *dhruva,* the *udgrāha* consists of two parts having identical tonal structure,[1] (which is) followed by another part[2] in a somewhat higher range (of notes), the three parts being sung twice. Then *ābhoga* is rendered in two parts, the first of which has two portions[3] of identical tonal structure and the second is higher (in pitch-range). The name of the hero is indicated in *ābboga*[4] which, according to some,[5] is partially sung in a higher pitch-range. It[6] is concluded with the first part of the *udgrāha.* (315-317)

(ख) भेदाः

एकादशाक्षरात् खण्डादेकैकाक्षरवर्धितैः ।
खण्डैः ध्रुवाः षोडश स्युः षड्विंशत्यक्षरावधि ॥३१८॥
जयन्तशेखरोत्साहास्ततो मधुरनिर्मलौ ।
कुन्तलः कामलश्चारो नन्दनश्चन्द्रशेखरः ॥३१९॥
कामोदो विजयाख्यश्च कंदर्पजयमङ्गलौ ।
तिलको ललितश्चेति संज्ञाश्चैषां क्रमादिमाः ॥३२०॥
आदितालेन शृङ्गारे जयन्तो गीयते बुधैः ।
स नेतृश्रोतृगातृणामायुःश्रीवर्धनो मतः ॥३२१॥
ऋद्धिसौभाग्यदो वीरे निःसारौ शेखरो भवेत् ।
प्रतिमण्ठेन हास्ये स्यादुत्साहो वंशवृद्धिकृत् ॥३२२॥
मधुरो भोगदो गेयः करुणे हयलीलया ।

[1]The implication seems to be that the two parts are composed in a different verbal structure.

[2]'S' identifies this third part as *antara.*

[3]*Khaṇḍa* as used here actually implies an *upa-khaṇḍa* i.e. a subsection or a portion of the *khaṇḍa* (part) spoken of earlier in this verse.

[4]The pronoun *asau* is used for *ābhoga* as elucidated by 'S'.

[5]*Kvacid* lit. 'somewhere' is interpreted by 'S' as 'according to some'. It may be noted that it is already provided (vide verse 316) that the second part of *ābhoga* is to be sung in a higher pitch-range.

[6]It refers to *dhruva.*

क्रीडातालेन श्रृङ्गारे निर्मलस्तनुते प्रभाम् ॥३२३॥
लघुशेखरतालेन कुन्तलोऽभीष्टदोऽद्भुते ।
कामलो विप्रलम्भे स्याज्झम्पातालेन सिद्धिदः ॥३२४॥
हर्षोत्कर्षप्रदश्चारो वीरे निःसारुतालतः ।
नन्दनो वीरश्रृङ्गार एकताल्येष्टसिद्धिदः ॥३२५॥
वीरे हास्ये च श्रृङ्गारे प्रतिमण्ठेन गीयते ।
अभीष्टफलदः श्रोतृगातॄणां चन्द्रशेखरः ॥३२६॥
प्रतिमण्ठेन श्रृङ्गारे कामोदोऽभीष्टकामदः ।
हास्ये द्वितीयतालेन विजयो नेतुरायुषे ॥३२७॥
हास्यश्रृङ्गारकरुणेष्वादितालेन गीयते ।
कन्दर्पो भोगदो नॄणां श्रीसदाशिवसंमतः ॥३२८॥
क्रीडातालेन श्रृङ्गारे वीरे च जयमङ्गलः ।
जयोत्साहप्रदः पुंसां ध्रुवकस्तिलकाभिधः ॥३२९॥
रसे वीरे च श्रृङ्गार एकताल्या प्रगीयते ।
प्रतिमण्ठेन श्रृङ्गारे ललितः सर्वसिद्धये ॥३३०॥
स्याद्वर्णनियमः सर्वखण्डे खण्डद्वये तथा ।
यथोक्तान् यो जयन्तादीन् गायेन्निपुणया धिया ॥३३१॥
सर्वक्रतुफलं तस्येत्यवोचन्मुनिसत्तमः ।
इति ध्रुवप्रबन्धः ।

(b) The varieties of *dhruva:*

Sixteen *dhruva-s*[1] are obtained by successively adding one syllable to the initial eleven syllables upto the maximum of twenty-six syllables to each part (*khaṇḍa*). They are respectively named *jayanta, śekhara, utsāha, madhura, nirmala, kuntala, kāmala, cāra, nandana, candraśekhara, kāmoda, vijaya, kəndarpa, jayamaṅgala, tilaka* and *lalita.* (318-320)

(These are described as under):

1. *Jayanta* is sung by the sages in *ādi-tāla* in the context of conjugal love (*śṛṅgāra*). It is believed that it prolongs the lifespan and increases the prosperity of the hero, the listener and the singer.[2] (321)

2. *Śekhara* is (sung) in *niḥsāru* (*tāla*) in (the context of) heroic sentiment (*vira*) and bestows accomplishment and fortune. (322 a b)

[1]The varieties of *dhruva prabandha* are meant.

[2]*Gātā*, lit. The singer, also stands for the composer. Incidentally, it may be remarked that the specific merit of singing these particular variations of *dhruva* is also mentioned by the author.

3. *Utsāha* is (sung) in *pratimaṇṭha* (*tāla*) in the context of mirth (*hāsya*), and it advances the family line. (322 c d)

4. *Madhura* is sung with *hayalīla-tāla* in (the expression of) pathos. It bestows worldly enjoyment. (323 a b)

5. *Nirmala* is (sung) with *krīḍā tāla* in (the context of) conjugal love; it spreads glory. (323 c d)

6. *Kuntala* is (sung) with *laghuśekhara tāla* in (the expression of) astonishment or wonder (*adbhuta*). (324 a b)

7. *Kāmala* is (sung) with *jhampā tāla* in (portraying) love in separation (*vipralambha*); it bestows attainment. (324 c d)

8. *Cāra* is (sung) with *niḥsāru tāla* in the heroic sentiment; it endows gladness and upliftment. (325 a b)

9. *Nandana* is (sung) with *ekatālī* (*tāla*) in (the expression of) heroism and conjugal love; it bestows desired attainment. (325 c d)

10. *Candraśekhara* is sung with *pratimaṇṭha tāla* in (the expression of) heroism, mirth and conjugal love; it bestows desired rewards upon the listener as well as singer. (326)

11. *Kāmoda* is (sung) with *pratimaṇṭha tāla* in (the sentiment of) conjugal love; it fulfils the most desired object. (327 a b)

12. *Vijaya* is sung with *dvitīya tāla* in (the expression of) mirth, it bestows longevity upon the hero (*netā*). (327 c d)

13. *Kandarpa*, having the approbation of sadāśiva is (sung) with *ādi-tāla* in the (context of) mirth, conjugal love and pathos, and it affords wordly enjoyments to people. (328)

14. *Jayamaṅgala* is sung with *krīḍā tāla* in (the context of) conjugal love and the heroic sentiment. (329 a b)

15. *Tilaka*—the variety of *dhruva* called *tilaka* is sung with *ekatāli* (*tāla*) in (the context of) heroic sentiment and conjugal love; it inspires enthusiasm in men and bestows victory upon them. (329 c-330 b)

16. *Lalita* (is sung) with *pratimaṇṭha tāla* in (the context of) conjugal love for every attainment. (300 c d)

The rule pertaining to the (use of) syllables[1] may be applied to all the parts (*khaṇḍa-s*) or to two only. (331 a b)

Whoever sings the *jayanta* and other *prabandha-s*[2] by the prescribed method with an efficient mind, to him accrues the reward of (performing) all the sacrifices; so it is declared by Bharata.[3] (331 c-332 b)

A reference may be made to Section IV of Chapter I (verse 90-91) wherein the *śuddha tāna-s* (combinational note-series) are linked with the names of vedic sacrifices and are said to yield the very same fruits to the

[1]The rule prescribed vide verse no. 318.

[2]The sixteen variations of *dhruva* are meant.

[3]As it has already been pointed out, Bharata does not mention any *prabandha-s*, but this statement has been ascribed to him on the basis that whatever musical forms were strictly regulated were ultimately traced to Bharata in their origins.

users of those *tāna-s*. Here, the same line of thinking is extended to the *dhruva-prabandha-s*. Each of them is capable of producing a particular benefit for the listeners, the singer and the hero as well, not only in terms of worldly prosperity and so on, but also in terms of *adṛṣṭa* (the unforeseen) results that are usually obtainable through the performance of vedic sacrifices. In other words, the term *chāyālaga* becomes significant as the reflection of *śuddha sūḍa* even in this respect, since *śuddha* as such being *gāndharva* i.e. strictly regulated, is capable of *adṛṣṭa-phala* (unforeseen other-worldly results). (cf. 'K' on verse 332)

(ii) मण्ठप्रबन्धः

(क) लक्षणम्

द्वियत्येकविरामं वा यस्योद्ग्राहाख्यखण्डकम् ॥३३२॥
ततः खण्डं ध्रुवाख्यं द्विस्ततो वैकल्पिकोऽन्तरः ।
तं गीत्वा ध्रुवमागत्य वाभोगो गीयते सकृत् ॥३३३॥
ध्रुवे न्यासस्ततः प्रोक्तः स मण्ठो मण्ठतालतः ।

(ii) *Maṇṭha-prabandha:* (332 c-338 b)

(a) The characteristic features:

Wherein the section called *udgrāha* is provided with either two pauses (*yati-s*[1]) or one stop (*virāma*),[2] the section called *dhruva* is (sung) twice followed optionally by *antara*; and wherein having sung that and having returned to *dhruva*, if the *ābhoga* is sung once and the conclusion is set in *dhruva* (by a singer), it is said to be *maṇṭha*. It is (sung) with *maṇṭha-tāla*. (332 c-334 b)

(ख) भेदाः

जयप्रियो मङ्गलश्च सुन्दरो वल्लभस्तथा ॥३३४॥
कलापः कमलश्चेति षड्भेदा मण्ठके मताः ।
षट्प्रकारो मण्ठतालो रूपकं तेन भिद्यते ॥३३५॥
वीरे जयप्रियो गेयो मण्ठेन जगणात्मना ।
मङ्गलो भेन शृङ्गारे सुन्दरः सेन तद्रसे ॥३३६॥
वल्लभो रेण करुणे कलापो नगणेन तु ।

[1] *Yati*, in this context, is not used in relation to *tāla* but it signifies a metrical pause, a caesura provided within a part (*khaṇḍa*) of a song.
[2] *Virāma* (lit. a stop) is similarly used in the sense of a pause.

विरामान्तेन गातव्यो रसे हास्ये विचक्षणैः ॥३३७॥
विरामान्तद्रुतद्वंद्वाल्लघुना कमलोऽद्भुते ।
इति मण्ठप्रबन्धः ।

(b) The varieties of *maṇṭha:*

Six varieties of *maṇṭha* are accepted viz. *jayapriya*, *maṅgala*, *sundara*, *vallabha*, *kalāpa* and *kamala*. *Maṇṭha tāla* (too) is of six varieties by which the *prabandha*[1] is distinguished. (334 c-335)

(These are defined as under):

1. *Jayapriya* is sung with the *maṇṭha* (*tāla*) having a *ja-gaṇa*,[2] in the (context of) heroic sentiment. (336 a b)
2. *Maṅgala* is (sung) with (*maṇṭha tāla* having) a *bha-gaṇa* in the context of conjugal love. (336 c)
3. *Sundara* is with *sa-gaṇa*[3] in the same[4] *rasa* (aesthetic delight). (336 d)
4. *Vallabha* is with *ra-gaṇa* in pathos. (337 a)
5. *Kalāpa* is sung by the experts with a *na-gaṇa* ending with *virāma*[5] in (the context of) mirth. (337 b-d)
6. *Kamala* is with two *druta-s*[6] having a *virāmānta* and a *laghu* in the sentiment of wonder. (338 a b)

(iii) प्रतिमण्ठप्रबन्धः

मण्ठवत् प्रतिमण्ठादेर्लक्ष्मोद्ग्राहादिकं मतम् ॥३३८॥
तथाप्येषां विशेषस्तु प्रत्येकं प्रतिपाद्यते ।
तत्र च प्रतिमण्ठेन तालेन प्रतिमण्ठकः ॥३३९॥
चतुर्धा सोऽमरस्तारो विचारः कुन्द इत्यपि ।
अमरो गुरुणैकेन शृङ्गारे स विधीयते ॥३४०॥
विरामान्तद्रुतद्वंद्वाल्लघुद्वंद्वेन जायते ।

[1]*Rūpaka* is another name for *prabandha*. The purport seems to be that the six varieties of *maṇṭha-tāla* form the distinguishing feature of the six varieties of *maṇṭha-prabandha*.

[2]*Maṇṭha-tāla* is described fully in Chapter V (see verses 277-278). It has a *ja-gaṇa* (ISI), or *bha gaṇa* (SII), or *sa-gaṇa* (IIS) etc. in the beginning which is followed by four *laghu-s* arranged as a *guru* and two *laghus* and so on, differently in different varieties (of *maṇṭha*) which is said to be of ten types.

[3]That is, in *maṇṭha-tāla* with a *sa-gaṇa*.

[4]That is, conjugal love.

[5]A measure of time in *deśī-tāla-s* (Chapter V).

[6]*Druta* is a measure of time in *tāla* equal to half of *laghu*.

तारारव्यः प्रतिमण्ठोऽसौ रसयोर्वीररौद्रयोः ॥३४१॥
लघुत्रयाद्विरामान्ताद्विचारः करुणे भवेत् ।
कुन्दो विराममध्येन लत्रयेणाद्भुते भवेत ॥३४२॥
ते शृङ्गारेऽपि चत्वारो गीयन्ते लक्ष्मवेदिभिः ।
इति प्रतिमण्ठप्रबन्धः ।

(iii) *Pratimaṇṭha-prabandha:* (338 c-343 b)

The character of *udgrāha* and other sections of *pratimaṇṭha* is similar[1] to that described in *maṇṭha*, yet certain specifications are being laid down in each case. (338 c-339 b)

To begin with, *pratimaṇṭha* is sung with *pratimaṇṭha tāla.*[2] It is fourfold viz. *amara*, *tāra*, *vicāra* and *kunda.* (339 c-340)

(These are defined as under):

1. *Amara* is (sung) with one *guru* and is employed (in the context of) conjugal love. (340 c d)

2. *Tāra-pratimaṇṭha* arises with two *druta-s* ending with *virāma*[3] followed by two *laghu-s*; it is (sung) in (the expression of) the sentiments of heroism and wrath. (341)

3. *Vicāra* is (sung) with three *laghu-s* ending with a *virāma* in (the expression of) pathos. (342 a b)

4. *Kunda* is sung with three *laghu-s* having the middle with *virāma* and is (used in the context of) wonder. (342 c d)

According to the experts, these four varieties are also sung in (sentiment of) conjugal love. (343 a b)

(iv) निःसारुकप्रबन्धः

बद्धो निःसारुतालेन प्रोक्तो निःसारुको बुद्धैः ॥३४३॥
वैकुन्दानन्दकान्तारा: समरो वाञ्छितस्तथा ।
विशालश्चेति स प्रोक्तः षड्विधः सूरिशार्ङ्गिणा ॥३४४॥
द्रुतद्वंद्वाल्लघुद्वंद्वाद्वैकुन्दो मङ्गले भवेत् ।

[1]*Pratimaṇṭha* has the same general features as *maṇṭha* but it is distinguished by *pratimaṇṭha tāla* which it employs, and by the *rasa-s* with which its varieties are associated.

[2]*Pratimaṇṭha tāla* is defined in Chapter V (296 a) as having a *sa-gaṇa* or a *bha-gaṇa* i.e. IIS, SII.

Pratimaṇṭha tāla is composed of *sa gaṇa* or *bha-gaṇa* as shown above and in any case has one *guru* and two *laghu-s* arranged in a different order.

[3]*Virāma*, in this context, signifies a measure of time used in *deśī tāla-s* which is equivalent to half of the unit to which it is applied e.g., *druta virāma* means half the measure of *druta* being added to *druta*.

कुर्यादानन्दमानन्दे विरामान्तद्रुतद्वयात् ।।३४५।।
कान्तारो लगुरुभ्यां स्याद्विप्रलम्भे स गीयते ।
लघुद्वयाद्विरामान्तात् समरो वीरगोचरः ।।३४६।।
लघुत्रयाद् द्रुतद्वंद्वाद्वाञ्छितो वाञ्छितप्रदः ।
संभोगे स्याद्विशालाख्यो लाद् द्रुतद्वयतो लघोः ।।३४७।।

इति निःसारुकप्रबन्धः ।

(iv) *Niḥsāruka-prabandha:* (343 c-347)

Niḥsāruka is composed in *niḥsāru tāla* as spoken by the wise. (343 c d)

Śārṅgadeva has declared it to be sixfold viz. *vaikunda, ānanda, kāntāra, samara, vāñchita* and *viśāla.* (344)

(These are described as under):

1. *Vaikunda* is (sung) with two *druta-s* and two ***laghu-s*** on auspicious occasions. (345 a b)

2. *Ānanda*[1] is done with two *druta-s* ending with a *virāma*, in blissful enjoyment. (345 c d)

3. *Kāntāra* is sung with a *laghu* and a ***guru*** in (the context of) love in separation. (346 a b)

4. *Samara*[2] is (sung) with two *laghu-s* ending with a *virāma* in the heroic situation. (346 c d)

5. *Vāñchita* is (sung) with three *laghu-s* followed by two *druta-s*; it bestows the desired (fruit). (347 a b)

6. *Viśāla* is (sung) by one *laghu* and two *druta-s* followed by a *laghu* in (the context of) the union of lovers. (347 c d)

(v) अड्डतालप्रबन्धः

अड्डतालेन तालेनाड्डतालः परिकीर्तितः ।
निःशङ्कश्शङ्कशीलाश्च चारोऽथ मकरन्दकः ।।३४८।।
विजयश्चेति स प्रोक्तः षोढा सोढलसूनुना ।
लगुरुभ्यां द्रुतद्वंद्वान्निःशङ्को विस्मये भवेत् ।।३४९।।
लघोर्द्रुतद्वयेन स्याच्छङ्कः शृङ्गारवीरयोः ।
शान्ते शीलो विरामान्तद्रुतद्वंद्वाल्लघोर्भवेत् ।।३५०।।
द्रुतद्वन्द्वाल्लगाभ्यां स्याच्चारो वीरेऽद्भुते रसे ।

[1]'S' says that *ānanda* is popularly known as *rūpaka*.
[2]According to 'S' *samara* is popularly known as *jambunāla*.

शृङ्गारे मकरन्दः स्याद् द्रुतद्वंद्वात् परे गुरौ ॥३५१॥
विजयाख्यो रसे वीरे द्रुताभ्यां लघुना भवेत् ।
इति अड्डतालप्रबन्धः ।

(v) *Aḍḍatāla-prabandha:* (348-352 b)

Aḍḍatāla is known to be (composed) in the *tāla* called *aḍḍatāla.*[1] (348 a b)

The son of Sodhala[2] has declared it to be sixfold viz. *niḥśaṅka, śaṅka, śīla, cāra, makaranda* and *vijaya.* (348 c-349 b)

(These are now described as under):

1. *Niḥśaṅka* is (sung) with a *laghu* and a *guru* followed by two *druta-s* in (the expression of) astonishment. (349 c d)
2. *Śaṅka* is (sung) with one *laghu* and two *druta-s* in (the context of) conjugal love and heroic sentiment. (350 a b)
3. *Śīla* is (sung) with a couple of *druta-s* ending with a *virāma* and followed by a *laghu* in the context of tranquillity. (350 c d)
4. *Cāra* is (sung) with a couple of *druta-s* followed by a *laghu* and a *guru* in (the context of) conjugal love. (351 a b)
5. *Makaranda* is (sung) with a couple of *druta-s* followed by two *guru-s* in (the context of) conjugal love. (351 c d)
6. *Vijaya* is (sung) with two *druta*-s and one *laghu* in the heroic sentiment. (352 a b)

(vi) रासकप्रबन्धः

रासको रासतालेन स चतुर्धा निरूपितः ॥३५२॥
विनोदो वरदो नन्दः कम्बुजश्चेति शार्ङ्गिणा ।
आलापान्तध्रुवपदाद्विनोदः कौतुके भवेत् ॥३५३॥
ध्रुवादालापमध्यात्तु वरदो देवतास्तुतौ ।
खण्डमाद्यं द्विखण्डस्योद्ग्राहस्यालापनिर्मितम् ॥३५४॥
यस्यासौ रासको नन्दो गीयतेऽभ्युदयप्रदः ।
आलापादेर्ध्रुवपदात् कम्बुजः करुणे भवेत् ॥३५५॥
सर्वेषु रासकेष्वेषु द्विखण्डोद्ग्राहकल्पना ।
इति रासकप्रबन्धः ।

[1]*Aḍḍatāla* is defined in Chapter V (205 d and 206 a b) as having one *druta* followed by two *laghu-s* under the name of *aḍḍatāla,* also called by some as *tripuṭa.*

[2]That is, Śārṅgadeva, the author.

(vi) *Rāsaka-prabandha:* (352 c-356 b)

Rāsaka is (composed) with *rāsa tāla*; it is demonstrated by Śārṅgadeva as fourfold viz. *vinoda*, *varada*, *nanda* and *kambuja*. (352 c-353 b)

(These are described as under):

1. *Vinoda* has *ālāpa* (sung) at the end of the verbal content of *dhruva* (*dhruvapada*); it (expresses) the feeling of curiosity. (353 c d)

2. *Varada* has *ālāpa* in the midst of *dhruva* and is (sung) in the propitiation of gods. (354 a b)

3. *Nanda* is the *rāsaka* in which there are two sections (*khaṇḍa-s*) of which the first comprises *ālāpa*; it bestows prosperity. (354 c-355 b)

4. *Kambuja* has *ālāpa* in the beginning of *dhruva*; it is (expressive of) pathos. (355 c d)

In all the *rāsaka-s*, the *udgrāha* is conceived in two parts (*khaṇḍa-s*). (356 a b)

(vii) एकतालीप्रबन्धः

एकताली भवेत्तालेनैकताल्या त्रिधा च सा ।।३५६।।
रमा च चन्द्रिका तद्वद्विपुलेत्यथ लक्षणम् ।
सकृद्विरतिरुद्ग्राहोऽन्तरस्त्वक्षरनिर्मितः ।।३५७।।
यस्यामसौ रमा सा च गातृश्रोत्रोः श्रिये भवेत् ।
उद्ग्राहो द्विदलो यस्यामालापरचितोऽन्तरः ।।३५८।।
घनद्रुता घनयतिर्घनानुप्रासयोगिनी ।
चन्द्रिका सैकताली स्याद् भूरिसौभाग्यदायिनी ।।३५९।।
आलापपूर्वकोद्ग्राहा विपुलानन्ददायिनी ।
आलापो गमकालप्तिरक्षरैर्वजिता मता ।।३६०।।
सैव प्रयोगशब्देन शार्ङ्गदेवेन कीर्तिता ।

इत्येकतालीप्रबन्धः

इति सालगसूडप्रबन्धाः

(vii) *Ekatālī-prabandha:* (356 c-361 b)

Ekatālī is composed in *ekatālī tāla*; it is threefold viz. *ramā*, *candrikā* and *vipulā*. They are defined (as follows). (356 c-357 b)

1. *Ramā* is that wherein the *udgrāha*, having two pauses,[1] is sung once,

[1]This has been translated according to the interpretation of 'S' who seems to have had a different reading. 'K', as also the text of Ad. ed. reads *Sakṛdvirati* but 'S' seems to read *sakṛddviyati*.

while the *antara*[1] is composed of words;[2] it is for the prosperity of the singer and the listener. (357 c-358 b)

2. *Candrikā* is that wherein *udgrāha* has two parts and the *antara*[3] consists of *ālāpa*. It employs many *druta-s*, pauses (*yati-s*) and is rich in alliteration. It bestows immense fortune. (358 c-359)

3. *Vipulā* is that (wherein) *ālāpa* is done before *udgrāha*; it is extremely delightful. (360 a b)

The singing of *gamaka-s* (shakes) in *ālapti* without (employing) words is considered to be *ālāpa*. This has also been called *prayoga* by Śārṅgadeva. (360 c-361 b)

षष्ठप्रकरणम्

प्रबन्धानामुत्तमादिविभागः

(क) रूपकविभागः

(i) उत्तमरूपकम्

गुणान्वितं दोषहीनं नवं रूपकमुत्तमम् ॥३६१॥
रागेण धातुमातुभ्यां तथा താललयौडुवैः ।
नूतनै रूपकं नूत्नं रागः स्थायान्तरैर्नवः ॥३६२॥
धातू रागांशभेदेन मातोस्तु नवता भवेत् ।
प्रतिपाद्यविशेषेण रसालंकारभेदतः ॥३६३॥
लयग्रहविशेषेण तालानां नवता मता ।
तालविश्रामतोऽन्येन विश्रामेण लयो नवः ॥३६४॥
छन्दोगणग्रहन्यासप्रबन्धावयवैर्नवैः ।
औडुवापरपर्याया रचना नवतां व्रजेत् ॥३६५॥

SECTION 6

Criteria of Critical Evaluation of *Prabandha-s*

(a) Critical classification of *Rūpaka:* (361 c-373)

(i) *Uttama-rūpaka-s:* (361 c-365)

The best *rūpaka-s* embody excellences,[4] are free from faults[5] and are

[1] 'K' argues that the use of the word *tu* in the text shows that *antara* here refers to a part of *dhruva*.

[2] From this 'K' infers that *udgrāha* consists of *ālāpa*.

[3] According to 'K' *antara* means a part of *dhruva*.

[4] The excellences of singing as described vide verses 374-379 b of this section.

[5] The faults or the blemishes of singing as described vide verses 379 c-380 of this section.

(marked by) novelty. (361 c d)

A *rūpaka* acquires novelty by employing new *rāga-s*, new tonal and verbal structures, new *tāla-s*, tempo and specific compositions (*auḍuva-s*). (362 a c)

Rāga gains novelty by employing different *sthāya-s*,[1] the tonal structure (becomes new) by inducting some of the aspects of other *rāga-s*[2] and the novelty of verbal structure is obtained by modifying the subject matter, and through different *rasa-s* and figures of speech employed. (362 d-363)

Novelty of *tāla-s* consists in the special tempo[3] (*laya*) and *graha*[4] (commencement). The tempo (*laya*) becomes new by (patterns of) rest other than those inherent in *tāla*. (364)

The specific composition, also in other words called *auḍuva*, gains novelty by employing new elements of *prabandha* such as metre, *gaṇa*, the *graha*[5] and the conclusion (*nyāsa*).[6] (365)

(ii) मध्यमरूपकम्

रूपकं त्रिविधं ज्ञेयं परिवृत्तं पदान्तरम् ।
भञ्जनीसंश्रितं चेति शार्ङ्गदेवेन कीर्तितम् ॥३६६॥

(ii) *Madhyama-rūpaka:* (366)

Rūpaka[7] is known to be threefold viz. *parivṛtta*, *padāntara* and *bhañjanīsaṁśrita*; so is it declared by Śārṅgadeva. (366)

[1] *Sthāya* is defined as *gītāvayava* i.e. a constituent part of the melody. The *sthāya*-have been dealt with in Chapter III.

[2] *Rāgāṁśa*, as defined by 'K' refers to the constituent parts of any other *rāga*, used as a specific part of a *rāga*.

[3] *Laya* is threefold viz. the slow, middle and fast.

[4] *Graha* too is threefold viz. *sama* (even), *atīta* (past) and *anāgata* (unarrived), cf. Chapter V for further details.

[5] *Graha* in the context of *prabandha* implies *udgrāha*, through in a *rāga* or *jāti* it means initial note.

[6] *Nyāsa* similarly is the final note, but in the context of *prabandha* it means conclusion of the composition.

[7] The *uttama* (best) *rūpaka* has been spoken of in verse 361 c d ante. 'K' enumerates these three *rūpaka-s* (366) as belonging to the category of *madhyama*. The text merely states that *rūpaka* is threefold etc. not specifying them anyway either as *uttama* or *madhyama*. On the other hand 'S' speaks of threefold best *rūpaka*. We have followed the interpretation of 'K' in our classification.

(iii) अधमरूपकम्

खल्लोत्तारानुसारौ तु रूपकेष्वधमौ मतौ ।

इति रूपकप्रबन्धः ।

(iii) *Adhama-rūpaka:* (367 a b)

Khalottāra and *anusāra* are rather considered as the inferior *rūpaka-s.* (367 a b)

(These varieties are described as follows):

(iv) मध्यमरूपकभेदाः

(१) परिवृत्तरूपकम्

रूपकं पूर्वसंसिद्धं स्वस्थानेन नवेन यत् ॥३६७॥
यद्वा रागेण तालेन कृतं तत् परिवृत्तकम् ।
यत्र स्थायिनि यत्स्थानं रूपकं रचितं पुरा ॥३६८॥
तत् स्वस्थानं तदन्यत्त्वं स्थाय्यन्यपरिवर्तनम् ।
परिवृत्तं रागतालपरिवर्तभवं स्फुटम् ॥३६९॥

इति परिवृत्तरूपकम् ।

(iv) Varieties of *madhyama-rūpaka:* (367 c-371)

(1) *Parivṛtta-rūpaka:*

If a pre-established *rūpaka* is modified by a new *svasthāna*[1] or a (new) *rāga* or *tāla*, it is *parivṛtta* (367 c-368 b)

Svasthāna is that *sthāna*[2] (range) in which the *rūpaka* is originally composed on the basis of a particular *sthāyi* (steady note). That (*svasthāna*) becomes different through a change in factors other than the *sthāyi* (steady note).[3] Thus, *parivṛtta* clearly emerges from a change in *rāga* and *tāla*. (368 c-369)

[1]*Svasthāna* is a term that we first came across in Chapter 3 (verse 191) in the sense of 'step of *rāgālapti*' (there being four such steps). But here the word *svasthāna* is not used in that sense. Here it is used by the author in a different sense which is elucidated by him in verses 368 c-369 b.

[2]*Sthāna*—register.

[3]According to 'S' the editor of Ad. ed. of *S.R.* has reconstructed the text as स्थाय्यन्यपरिवर्तनम्, cf. Anandashrama ed. स्थाय्येव परिवर्तनम् ।

(२) पदान्तररूपकम्

तस्मिन्नेव रसे रागे ताले च रचितं भवेत् ।
मातुस्थायविचित्रत्वाद् गुणोदारं पदान्तरम् ।।३७०।।
इति पदान्तररूपकम् ।

(2) *Padāntara-rūpaka:*

When the excellence (of a pre-established *rūpaka*) is enhanced by varying its verbal structure and the *sthāya-s*, retaining the same *rāga*, *rasa* and *tāla*, it is *padāntara*. (370)

(३) भञ्जनीसंश्रितरूपकम्

केनापि रूपकं गीतं निजादन्येन धातुना ।
येन तस्यान्यधातुत्वाद्भञ्जनीसंश्रितं मतम् ।।३७१।।
इति भञ्जनीसंश्रितरूपकम् ।

(3) *Bhañjanisaṁśrita-rūpaka:*

If a *rūpaka* leaving aside its tonal structure (*dhātu*), takes resort to another *dhātu*, because of having a different *dhātu*, it is called *bhañjanī-saṁśrita*. (371)

(v) अधमरूपकभेदाः

(१) खल्लोत्तारररूपकम्

प्राग्रूपकगताः स्थायाः स्थानान्तरगता यदि ।
मात्वन्तरेण रच्यन्ते खल्लोत्तारस्तदा भवेत् ।।३७२।।
इति खल्लोत्ताररूपकम् ।

(v) Varieties of *adhama-rūpaka:* (372-373)

(1) *Khallottāra-rūpaka:*

When the *sthāya-s* of the original *rūpaka* are transferred in to another verbal structure (*mātu*) and a different *sthāna*, it becomes *khallottāra.* (372)

(२) अनुसाररूपकम्

रागे ताले च तत्रैव किंचिद्धातुविलक्षणः ।
मात्वन्तरेणानुसारो गुणोत्कर्षविवर्जितः ।।३७३।।
इत्यनुसाररूपकम् ।

(2) *Anusāra-rūpaka:*

The *rāga* and *tāla* (of the original *rūpaka*) remaining the same, if there be a slight novelty (i.e. variation) in the tonal structure (*dhātu*) with a different verbal structure (*mātu*) it (the *rūpaka*) becomes *anusāra*; it is devoid of heightened excellence. (373)

(ख) गीतगुणदोषाः

(i) गीतगुणाः

व्यक्तं पूर्णं प्रसन्नं च सुकुमारमलंकृतम् ।
समं सुरक्तं श्लक्ष्णं च विकृष्टं मधुरं तथा ॥३७४॥
दशैते स्युर्गुणा गीते तत्र व्यक्तं स्फुटैः स्वरैः ।
प्रकृतिप्रत्ययैश्चोक्तं छन्दोरागपदैः स्वरैः ॥३७५॥
पूर्णं पूर्णाङ्गगमकं प्रसन्नं प्रकटार्थकम् ।
सुकुमारं कण्ठभवं त्रिस्थानोत्थमलंकृतम् ॥३७६॥
समवर्णलयस्थानं सममित्यभिधीयते ।
सुरक्तं वल्लकीवंशकण्ठध्वन्येकतायुतम् ॥३७७॥
नीचोच्चद्रुतमध्यादौ श्लक्षणत्वे श्लक्ष्णमुच्यते ।
उच्चैरुच्चारणादुक्तं विकृष्टं भरतादिभिः ॥३७८॥
मधुरं धुर्यलावण्यपूर्णं जनमनोहरम् ।
इति गीतगुणाः ।

(b) The excellences and blemishes of song (*gīta*): (374-380)

(i) The excellences of song: (374-379 b)

The ten excellences of singing (*gīta*)[1] are *vyakta*, *pūrṇa*, *prasanna*, *sukumāra*, *alaṅkṛta*, *sama*, *surakta*, *ślakṣṇa*, *vikṛṣṭa* and *madhura*.[2] (374-375 a)

(These are defined as follows):

1. *Vyakta* (manifest) is that in which the basic words[3] along with the prefixes or suffixes are pronounced (i.e. sung) with clear and distinct notes. (375 b c)

[1] *Gīta* (i.e. in vocal melody) seems to refer to the tonal as well as the verbal, as also the rhythmic structure.

[2] Since all these terms are presently being defined, their literal meanings are not indicated in English.

[3] *S. Rāj* reads it as *vyutkṛṣṭam* which seems to reflect its function more clearly (*S. Rāj*, II. 2.3.55).

2. *Pūrṇa* (perfect) is complete with integral parts (*aṅga-s* of *prabandha*) and is enriched by shakes (*gamaka-s*). (375 d-376 a)

3. *Prasanna* (clear) has lucidity of meaning. (376 b)

4. *Sukumāra* (delicate) is produced in the throat. (376 c)

5. *Alaṅkṛta* (embellished) arises from the three registers (*sthāna-s*). (376 d)

6. *Sama* (equipoised) is so called for it obtains a happy correlation among tone-patterns (*varṇa-s*),[1] tempo (*laya*) and the registers. (377 a b)

7. *Surakta* (delightful) embodies unity of the sounds of *viṇā*, flute and the throat. (377 c d)

8. *Ślakṣṇa* (smooth) is indicative of smoothness (of movement) between the low and the high (tones) and the fast and the middle tempo and so on. (378 a b)

9. *Vikṛṣṭa* (raised) is so called by Bharata and others because it is pronounced (sung) in high tones. (378 c d)

10. *Madhura* (sweet) is full of incomparable beauty and is enchanting for people. (379 a b)

(ii) गीतदोषा:

दुष्टं लोकेन शास्त्रेण श्रुतिकालविरोधि च ।।३७९।।
पुनरुक्तं कलाबाह्यं गतक्रममपार्थकम् ।
ग्राम्यं संदिग्धमित्येवं दशधा गीतदुष्टता ।।३८०।।

इति गीतदोषाः ।

।। इति श्रीमदनवद्यविद्याविनोदश्रीकरणाधिपतिश्रीसोढल-
देवनन्दननिःशङ्कश्रीशार्ङ्गदेवविरचिते संगीत-
रत्नाकरे प्रबन्धाध्यायश्चतुर्थः ।।

(ii) The blemishes of song: (379 c-380)

Melodic fault is tenfold viz. (1) being defective by peoples' (popular) standard, (2) being defective by critical[2] standard, (3) being inappropriate[3] in *śruti-s*, and (4) time,[4] (5) by repetition, (6) by violating the *kalā-s*,[5] (7) by transgressing proper order,[6] (8) being devoid of meaning, (9) being indecent or uncultured, and (10) being confused. (379 c-380)

[1] *Varṇa* could also mean syllables of the song text.

[2] *Śāstra*, here means a body of rules incorporating criteria of critical evaluation.

[3] That is imperfection in the use of *śruti-s*, or, as 'S' interprets it, 'short of *śruti-s*.'

[4] Some *rāga-s* are assigned to particular seasons or periods of time during the day. Violation of this prescription may be implied.

[5] *Kalā* has different meanings, but here it may imply the pattern of *tāla*, in the sense of the basic unit of time-measure in *tāla*.

[6] The order could be related to melody, rhythm, text etc.

Half-line Śloka-Index

अंशांशश्चेति यो रागे 181
अंशोंऽशान्तरसंचारात् 181
अकारे दैवतं विष्णुः 227
अक्षराडम्बरो येषु 187
अखण्डितस्थितिः स्थान॰ 4
अग्राम्यः सुकुमारश्च 228
अग्राम्योऽक्षरनादानाम् 228
अङ्गं कर्णाटबङ्गालम् 106
अङ्गबङ्गकलिङ्गाद्यै॰ 206
अङ्गहारप्रयोगज्ञै॰ 206
अङ्गानि षट् तस्य 215
अङ्गैः षडादिभिर्द्वचन्तैः 218
अङ्घ्रिपूर्त्यै तदन्यच्चेत् 249
अङ्घ्रौ खण्डद्वयं सानु॰ 222
अड्डुतालस्ततो रासः 308
अड्डुतालेन तालेन 316
अतारजस्तारहीनः 259
अतारमध्यमा पाप॰ 97
अतारा प्रार्थने मन्द्र॰ 135
अतालौ ढेङ्किकाताले 256
अतिदीर्घप्रयोगाः स्युः 181
अति सूक्ष्मः कृशो भग्नः 168
अत्युक्तायास्तु चत्वारः 234
अत्रोच्यते परित्यागात् 158
अथ ग्रन्थेन संक्षिप्त॰ 1
अथ प्रकीर्णकं कर्ण॰ 145
अथ रागाङ्गभाषाङ्ग॰ 14
अथाधुनाप्रसिद्धानाम् 16
अध्यात्मगोचरा चर्या 303
अनन्तत्वात्तु संकीर्णाः 252
अनादिसंप्रदायं यत् 210
अनिबद्धा निबद्धा च 287
अनिर्युक्तश्च निर्युक्तः 219
अनुकार इति प्रोक्तः 151
अनुक्ताभोगवस्तूनाम् 307
अनुच्छिष्टोक्तिनिर्बन्धः 146
अनुप्रासप्रधानं चेत् 307
अनुरक्तेस्तु जनकः 166
अनुस्वानविहीनत्वम् 169
अनेकस्थायसंचारः 150
अन्तःसारो धनत्वस्य 190
अन्त्येऽह्नः प्रहरे गेयः 43
अन्तरः पूर्ववत्तस्मात् 290
अन्तरे सोऽन्तरो वक्रः 190
अन्यच्छायाप्रवृत्तौ ये 178
अन्यथा चान्यथा गायेत् 201
अन्यस्तु मधुरस्निग्ध॰ 159
अन्यूनशिक्षणे दक्षः 151
अन्येषां सूक्ष्मभेदानाम् 161
अन्योपरागजा ताभ्यः 12
अपरं स्वरतेनान्तम् 296
अपरः स्निग्धमधुर॰ 159
अपस्थानस्य ते स्थायाः 181
अपस्थानस्य निकृतेः 174
अपेक्षितश्च घोषश्च 174
अप्रसिद्धास्तु ता लक्ष्ये 238
अब्जपत्रोऽब्जगर्भश्च 288
अभावश्छन्दसां वृत्तम् 257
अभिव्यक्तिर्यत्र दृष्टा 19
अभीष्टफलदः श्रोतृ॰ 311
अमरो गुरुणैकेन 314
अमुं प्रयोगं मेलापम् 222

अरूक्षो दूरसंश्राव्यः 166
अर्धस्थिते चालयित्वा 199
अर्धान्ते चरणान्ते वा 279
अर्धान्तेऽन्ये स्वरानाहुः 276
अल्पत्वस्य बहुत्वस्य 19
अल्पध्वनिस्तारगतिः 288
अल्पमूर्छनया युक्तः 228
अवधानं गुणैरेभि० 146
अवरोहिणि वर्णे 48
अवरोहिप्रसन्नान्तः 22
अवरोहिप्रसन्नान्त० 19
अवरोह्यादिवर्णेन 66
अवस्खलति यो मन्द्रात् 187
अविरुद्धस्य माधुर्य० 158
अव्यवस्थित इत्युक्तः 156
अशेषभाषाविज्ञानम् 146
अष्टधा करणं तत्र 252
अष्टाविति त्रिमिश्रस्य 160
अष्टोपरागास्तिलकः 8
अष्टौ कामा आदिमध्य० 249
अष्टौ कामाः कामलेखा 249
अष्टौ षोडश तद्वच्च 272
अस्यामालापमात्रेण 265

आक्षिप्तिका स्वरपद० 19
आकण्ठकुण्ठनं स स्यात् 165
आडिल्ल एष एव स्यात् 158
आडिकामोदिका तज्जा 101
आडिकामोदिका नाग० 16
आदितालेन शृङ्गारे 310
आदिमध्यस्थितं प्रासम् 249
आदिमध्यान्तगैः प्रासैः 306
आद्यस्य स्युर्द्वितीयादि० 239
आद्याक्षरेण ग्रहणम् 240
आद्याङ्घ्री आद्यनुप्रासौ 248
आद्यात् पञ्च विकारेण 242
आद्येन्दुमत्यथो ज्योति० 244
आद्यो ध्रुवस्ततो मण्ठ० 308
आद्यौ द्विद्विगुणौ पादौ 294
आनन्त्यान्नैव शक्यन्ते 194
आन्दोलितप्लावित० 194
आन्धाल्युपाङ्गं मल्हारः 118
आपञ्चमं तारमन्द्रा 107
आभीरिका मधुकरी 9
आभोगं तु सकृद् गीत्वा 259
आभोगध्रुवकोद्ग्रोहाः 255
आभोगस्तत्र नाम स्यात् 252
आभोगश्चेति तेषां च 213
आयत्तकण्ठस्तालज्ञः 150
आभासेन विना यत्र 181
आरोहिणि प्रसन्नादि० 37
आरोहिणि प्रसन्नाद्ये 80
आरोहिणि प्रसन्नान्ता० 43
आरोहिण्युत्प्रविष्टः स्यात् 187
आर्या गाथा द्विपथकः 220
आर्यागीतौ रसे वीरे 273
आर्यायाः स्युस्तदा तिस्रः 274
आर्येव प्राकृते गेया 281
आलप्तिरुच्यते तज्ज्ञै० 203
आलप्तिर्बन्धहीनत्वात् 211
आलापः प्रागतालः स्यात् 290
आलापपूर्वकोद्ग्राहा 318
आलापादेर्ध्रुवपदात् 317
आलापान्तध्रुवपदात् 317
आलापो गमकालप्तिः 318
आवृत्त्या सर्वपादानाम् 303
आशीर्भिर्धवलो गेयः 305
आह वृन्दविशेषं तु 205

इतरत् पूर्ववत् कीर्ति० 256
इतरेषां च रागाणाम् 156
इति गद्यस्य षट् प्रोक्ताः 269
इति गौडास्त्रयः षड्जे 6
इति भाषा, विभाषे द्वे 9

इति षण्णवतिः स्थायाः 175
इतो न्यूनं तु हीनं स्यात् 204
इत्येते विकृता भेदाः 242
इत्येषां देवता भूमि० 233
इष्टस्वरेंऽशे न्यासः स्यात् 252

ईर्ष्यायां विनियोक्तव्या 127

उक्ताश्चतस्रो गुर्जर्यः 16
उच्चैरुच्चारणादुक्तम् 323
उच्यते स निराधारः 190
उज्ज्वलो गदितश्चोक्षः 182
उज्ज्वलोऽयमिति प्रोक्तः 166
उत्क्षिप्योत्क्षिप्य निपतन् 187
उत्तमं मध्यममथो 203
उत्तमाभ्यधिकं वृन्दम् 204
उत्तमे गायनीवृन्दे 204
उत्तमोत्तम इत्युक्तः 159
उत्तरोत्तरसंघादौ 277
उत्प्रविष्टो निःसरणः 174
उत्सवे विनियोक्तव्यः 43
उद्ग्राहः प्रथमस्तत्र 213
उद्ग्राहः प्रथमो भागः 213
उद्ग्राहध्रुवकौ प्राग्वत् 255
उद्ग्राहस्तालशून्यश्चेत् 262
उद्ग्राहस्य द्वितीयार्धम् 256
उद्ग्राहस्याद्यखण्डे च 310
उद्ग्राहा बहवो यस्मिन् 63
उद्ग्राहेणाथवा न्यासः 288
उद्ग्राहो द्विः सकृद् वैक० 262
उद्ग्राहो द्विदलो यस्याम् 318
उद्घुष्टो विरसोद्घोषः 155
उद्दीपने नियोक्तव्या 132
उद्भटे नटने काम० 137
उद्भटे नटने गेयः 35
उद्भूतः कौशिकीषड्ज० 37
उन्नता शान्तिसंज्ञा च 239

उपमा रूपकं श्लेषैः 260
उभयोर्मिश्रणादुक्ता 287
उल्लासितः प्लावितश्च 171
उल्लासितः स तु प्रोक्तः 172

ऊर्ध्वं प्रसारितः क्षिप्तः 187

ऋग्वेदोत्था सिता विप्रा 236
ऋजुर्लिपौ भ्रे ष्के ष्पे च 231
ऋद्धिसौभाग्यदो वीरे 310
ऋषभांशः पञ्चमान्तः 122
ऋषभोऽल्पो निगन्यासः 57
ऋषभोऽस्यामपन्यासः 117

ए ओ इं हि पदान्ते वा 231
एकः स्यात् समगातारः 204
एक एव तु यो गायेत् 151
एकतालीत्यमी तालाः 259
एकताली भवेत्ताले 318
एकद्विन्त्राश्च तालाः स्युः 301
एकद्विन्त्राश्चतुष्पञ्च 238, 244, 272
एकधातु द्विखण्डं च 310
एकधातुर्द्विखण्डः स्यात् 309
एकलो यमलो वृन्द० 151
एकस्त्रिभङ्गितालेन 299
एकादशाक्षरात् खण्डात् 310
एकादिगुरुभङ्गेण 280
एका स्यात् समगायन्य० 204
एकैकमातृका वर्ण० 287
एकैकस्मिन् स्वरे स्थित्वा 187
एकोऽन्यो घनगम्भीर० 160
एकोनत्रिंशदाख्याताः 274
एतत्संमिश्रणादुक्तः 158
एतेऽधुना प्रसिद्धाः स्यु० 17
एते त्रयोऽप्यनाभोगाः 263
एते द्वन्द्वजभेदाः स्युः 160
एते षट्त्रिंशदन्येऽपि 195

एते सालगसूडस्थैः 263
एतेन घननिःसार० 158
एतेषां मिश्रणान्मिश्र० 172
ऐतेषु व्यत्ययेनापि 283
एभिश्चतुर्भिः स्वस्थानैः 199
एरण्डकाण्डनिःसारः 168
एलयोराद्ययोरङ्घ्री 244
एलाकरणढेङ्कीभिः 220
एलादिः, शुद्ध इत्युक्तः 308
एलानां बहवः सन्ति 222
एलाः श्रोतुः प्रयोक्तुश्च 228
एलासामान्यलक्ष्मैतत् 222
एवं पादत्रयं गेयम् 222
एवं मध्याभवा भेदाः 234
एवं षणवतिर्भाषाः 10
एवमेते प्रबन्धस्य 213
एषा भाषाङ्गमन्येषाम् 135

ओं तत्सदिति निर्देशात् 216
ओजक्रीन्द्रक्रियौ नाग० 15
ओजे कलाश्चन्द्रलेखे 282
ओजेऽङ्घ्रौ मनवो मात्राः 282
ओजोबहुल ओजस्वी० 228
ओवीपदं तदन्ते चेत् 306
ओवी लोली ढोल्लरी च 221
ओव्यादयस्तु चत्वारः 307
ओहाटी कम्पितैर्मन्द्रैः 4

औडुवापरपर्याया 319
औदुम्बरी च षट्कर्णः 205

ककुभेऽथर्ववेदोत्था 238
कङ्काले प्रतिताले च 258
कथं तयोर्मिश्रणं स्यात् 158
कन्दस्तुरगलीला च 220
कन्दर्पो भोगदो नृणाम् 311
कफजः खाहुलः स्निग्धः 158
कम्पितः कम्पनाज्ज्ञेयः 155
करणं स्वरपूर्वं तत् 252
कराभ्यामुद्भवात् कार्ये 215
कराली गदितः सद्भिः 155
कराली विकलः काकी 155
करुणः श्रोतृचित्तस्य 165
कर्णाटभाषया ताल० 296
कर्णाटलाटगौडान्ध्र० 248
कर्णाटादिपदैः पाटैः 273
कर्णाटाद्याः सजातीयाः 181
कर्णाटैलादिमध्यान्त० 248
कर्णाटो देशवालश्च 17
कलहंसः स्वरे न्यासः 284
कलापः कमलश्चेति 313
कलिका तनुमध्या च 240
कश्चित् स्यान्मधुरस्निग्ध० 159
कांस्यतालोद्भवैः पाटैः 290
काकक्रूररवः काकी 155
काकलीकलितो गेयः 81
काकल्यन्तरयुक्तश्च 66
काकल्यन्तरसंयुक्तः 22, 35, 51, 69
काकल्या कलितः 72
काकोलिकाख्यः काकोलः 168
काण्डारणा प्रसिद्धैव 182
कान्तारो लगुरुभ्यां स्यात् 316
काममन्मथवत्कान्त 227
कामलो विप्रलम्भे स्यात् 311
कामोत्सवा नन्दिनी च 239
कामोदलक्षणोपेता 113
कामोदा सिंहलीच्छाया 17
कामोदोपाङ्गमाख्याता 113
कामोदो विजयाख्यश्च 310
काम्भोजी मध्यमग्रामा 9
कारणांश्च कार्यांश० 181
कारणांशस्त्वसौ राम० 181
कारणे कार्यरागांशः 181
कार्मारव्याश्च कैशिक्याः 24

कार्योऽन्तरस्ततश्चाच० 290
कार्श्यं कार्कश्यमित्याद्यैः 169
किंचिदुच्चं भवेत् खण्डम् 309
किन्तु तत्र लपूर्वा ये 234
किन्तु तेषां स्वरस्थाने 252
कीर्तितो मधुरो लीन० 160
कीर्तिरायुश्च वर्ण्यस्य 233
कुञ्जरस्तिलको हंस० 282
कुट्टिकारोऽन्यधातौ तु 147
कुतपानाममीषां तु 206
कुतपे त्ववनद्धस्य 205
कुन्तलः कामलश्चारः 310
कुन्दो विराममध्येन 315
कुरुलो वलिरेव स्यात् 171
कुर्यादानन्दमानन्दे 316
कृच्छ्रोन्मीलन्मन्द्रतारः 168
कृशो भग्न इति प्रोक्तः 168
केचित्तु हयलीलेन 274
केचिन्मण्ठमपीच्छन्ति 259
केनापि रूपकं गीतम् 322
केवले तु तृतीयेऽङ्घ्रौ 222
केषांचित् पूर्वपूर्वस्मात् 288
केषांचिन्मतमाश्रित्य 14
कैशिकीकार्मारवीभ्याम् 30
कैशिकीजातिजः षड्ज० 63
कैशिकी त्रावणी तानो० 9
कैशिक्यां बोट्टरागे वा 306
कैशिक्या मङ्गलाचारः 304
कोकिलापञ्चमो रेव० 8
कोमलः प्रसृतः स्निग्ध० 174
कोमलः स्निग्धनिःसारः 159
कोमलोऽन्वर्थनामैव 165
कोलाहला टक्कभाषा 114
कौन्तली द्राविडी सैन्ध० 16
क्रमव्यत्यासभेदेन 253
क्रमादकचटानां त० 233
क्रमाद्वच्छेत् प्लावितस्तु 172
क्रमेण परिगीयन्ते 287
क्रमोत्क्रमाभ्यां बहुशः 278
क्रियाङ्गत्रितयं राम० 16
क्रियापरो युक्तलयः 150
क्रीडातालेन शृङ्गारे 311

खञ्जनी गुर्जरी गौडी 10
खण्डं गणेशदैवत्यम् 268
खण्डं चित्रं च तेषां च 206
खण्डत्रयं प्रासयुतम् 306
खण्डमाद्यं द्विखण्डस्य 317
खण्डैध्रुवाः षोडश स्युः 310
खम्भाइतिस्तदंशान्ता 112
खल्लोत्तारानुसारौ तु 321
खाहुलोन्मिश्रनाराटे 159

गणः समूहः सद्वेधा 231
गणमात्राद्यनियता 246
गणमात्रावर्णदेश० 231
गणा पञ्च त्रिमात्रोऽन्ते 244
गणाः सप्त लघुश्चान्ते 244
गणादिनियमस्त्वासाम् 235
गणादेर्न्यूनताधिक्यात् 249
गणाधिपश्चतुष्कामम् 248
गणानां प्रथमादीनाम् 239
गणैर्वर्णैश्च मात्राभिः 264
गणैश्चतुर्गुणकलाश्च 244
गतारमन्द्रः कामोदः 124
गतिर्द्रुतविलम्बा स्यात् 269
गद्गदध्वनिरव्यक्त० 155
गद्यं निगद्यते छन्दो० 266
गद्यजा पद्यजा गद्य० 260
गद्यजा पद्यजा चेति 274
गद्यपद्यप्रभेदेन 277
गद्यात्मा चेत् स्वरान् गीत्वा 284
गमकप्रासनिर्मुक्ता 251
गमद्विगुणिता मन्द्र० 94

गमन्द्रा चोत्सवे गेया 99
गम्भीरमधुरध्वाना 182
गम्भीरोच्चतरो रूक्षः 160
गांशं सान्तं च शृङ्गारे 106
गाढः शैथिल्यनिर्मुक्तः 182
गाढस्तु प्रबलो दूर० 165
गाढैस्त्रिस्थानगमकै० 4
गाढो ललितगाढश्च 174
गातव्या नियतैर्नित्यम् 287
गातव्योत्कलिका वीरे 267
गातृनाम सतालं च 270
गातृबादकसंघातः 203
गात्रस्य गात्रे नियताः 182
गात्रोपशमयोः काण्डा० 174
गान्धर्वं गानमित्यस्य 209
गान्धारगतिका वेर० 15
गान्धारतिरिपोपेतः 120
गान्धारपञ्चमो भिन्न० 8
गान्धारबहुलो मन्द्र० 120
गान्धारमन्द्रा करुणे 89
गान्धारवल्ली कच्छेल्ली 10
गान्धारांशग्रहन्यासः 90, 124
गान्धारांशग्रहा धान्ता 139
गान्धाराल्पः काकलीयुक् 84
गान्धारीमध्यमापञ्च 60
गान्धारीरक्तगान्धारी 90
गापन्यासा दीर्घरिमा 100
गायत्री देवताप्यादि० 249
गायन्यो द्वादश प्रोक्ताः 203
गाल्पः पूर्णः सषड्जादि० 52
गाल्पः प्रसन्नमध्येन 54
गाल्पः षड्जग्रहन्यासां० 102
गीतयः पञ्च शुद्धा च 4
गीतस्यातिशयाधानात् 151
गीते तथाविधः स्थायः 187
गीत्वाद्यपादौ तदनु 295
गीत्वा न्यासो यत्र सा स्यात् 265
गीत्वा विलम्बितालेन 270
गीयतामृषभान्तांशा 111
गीयते चेद् ध्रुवोद्ग्राहौ 255
गुणान्वितं दोषहीनम् 319
गुणैः कतिपयैर्हीनः 150
गुणैरेभिः पञ्चदश० 165
गुरुर्लघुरिति द्वेधा 231
गुर्जर्येव रिकम्प्रा स्यात् 111
गृहिणां च प्रवेशादौ 102
गेयं नासिकया गायन् 156
गेयः कर्णाटगौडस्तु 120
गेयः शरदि तज्जाता 95
गेयोऽह्नः प्रथमे यामे 22, 30
गेयोऽह्नः पश्चिमे यामे 46
गेयो द्राविडगौडोऽयम् 120
गेयो निर्वहणे यामे 24
गेयो वाग्गेयकारेण 222
गोली नादान्तरी नीलो० 15
गौडपञ्चमकः षड्जे 6
गौडस्तदङ्गं निन्यासः 80
गौडी च रीतिरिन्द्राण्याः 237
गौडीयरीतिरुचिरा 267
गौरी ब्राह्मी च मातङ्गी 228
ग्रहन्यासोऽस्य भूयोऽसौ 278
ग्रहांशन्यासगान्धारा 92
ग्रहांशन्यासषड्जश्च 52
ग्रहांशन्यासषड्जान्या 134
ग्रहांशमन्द्रताराणाम् 19
ग्राम्यं सन्दिग्धमित्येवम् 324
ग्रीष्मेऽह्नः प्रथमे यामे 60
ग्रीष्मे प्राक् प्रहरे गेयः 72

घटनायाः सुखस्यापि 175
घटो वृत्तं मातृका च 220
घण्टानादवदायातः 190
घत्तादिच्छन्सा वा स्यात् 302
घनतास्निग्धताकान्ति० 169

घनद्रुता घनयति० 318
घनलनः पीवरोच्च० 160
घनस्वरोऽवरोहे स्यात् 187
घनोऽपरस्तु मधुर० 159

चक्रवालः क्रौञ्चपदः 220
चच्चत्पुटादितालेन 19
चच्चत्पुटेन तेनैव 290
चच्चरीच्छन्दसेत्यन्ये 302
चतस्रः पञ्चमे भिन्ने 9
चतस्रस्ता द्वितीयस्य 239
चतस्रोऽनुक्तजनका 10
चतस्रोऽन्तरभाषाः स्युः 10
चतस्रो वांशिकद्वन्द्वम् 204
चतुःषष्ट्यधिकं ब्रूते 17
चतुराद्यष्टपर्यन्तम् 260
चतुरा पञ्चधा तत्र 241
चतुर्गीतिगतं लक्ष्म 4
चतुर्थस्तत्र मदनाव० 264
चतुर्थस्त्रिगणः पादे० 294
चतुर्थी सुरसा प्रोक्ता 246
चतुर्धा ढेङ्किका मुक्ता० 257
चतुर्धा सैन्धवी तत्र 131
चतुर्धा सोऽपरस्तारः 314
चतुर्भिरीदृशैः पादैः 276
चतुर्भिश्चरणैः षड्भिः 305
चतुर्भेदो भवेच्छब्दः 158
चतुर्मुख सिंहलीलः 221
चतुर्वृत्तश्चतुस्तालः 288
चतुर्विधा मतङ्गोक्ता 12
चतुस्त्रिंशदिमे रागाः 16
चतुष्कामो रतिप्रान्तः 248
चत्वारश्चरणा गेयाः 297
चत्वारश्चरणा बाण० 296
चत्वारो मुख्यगातारः 203
चन्द्रप्रियः पूर्वयामे 84
चन्द्रलेखेति तत्राद्ये 244
चन्द्रिका सैकताली स्यात् 318
चरणान्तसमप्रासा 303
चामुण्डैलापदेष्वेताः 228
चारुसंचारिवर्णश्च 116
चालनं मुखचाल. स्यात् 198
चित्राद्यं मिश्रकरण० 252
चित्रो विचित्रर्लालश्च 260
चिरं स्थित्वाग्निवत्तारम् 187
चूर्ण शान्ते रसे पीतम् 267

छगणेन चतुर्मात्रैः 276
छन्दःप्रभेदवेदित्वम् 146
छन्दश्चित्यां विचेतव्याः 287
छन्दस्तालाद्यनियमा० 219
छन्दसः कलहंसस्य 284
छन्दसा द्विपथेन स्यात् 282
छन्दसा येन केनापि 287
छन्दोगणग्रहन्यास० 319
छन्दोभिर्बहुभिर्गेया 306
छन्दोलक्षणतो ज्ञेयाः 280
छन्दोहीनेतरल्लक्ष्म 275
छपद्वयं दो वदनम् 302
छागवद्वहनीं कुर्वन् 155
छान्दसः सुकराभासः 175
छाया काकुः षट्प्रकारा 177
छायानट्टा तु नट्टैव 113
छायाप्रतापोपपदे 16
छायायास्ते मताः स्थायाः 178
छायालगत्वमेलादेः 308
छायावेलावली वेला० 112
छेवाटी पिञ्जरीत्येका 10
छेवाटी सैन्धवी कोला० 9

जन्मोत्तरा स्याद् गन्धर्वः 249
जयघण्टा कांस्यतालः 206
जयन्तशेखरोत्साहाः 310
जयन्तो मधुपश्चाथ 274

जयप्रियो मङ्गलश्च 313
जया कूर्मी पिनाकी च 205
जयोत्साहप्रदः पुंसाम् 311
जातो नैषादिनीषड्ज० 48
जात्याद्यन्तरभाषान्तम् 308
जीवस्वरव्याप्तिमुख्यैः 199
ज्ञं या शुद्धेव संपूर्णा 276

झम्पटः कन्दुकः स्यात् 221
झम्पटच्छन्दसा गेयः 299
झोम्बकस्तुम्बकी वक्री 155
झोम्बडा इति संख्याताः 260

टक्कः सांशग्रहन्यासः 77
टक्ककैशिकहिन्दोल० 8
टक्कभाषा वेगरञ्जी 101
टक्कभाषैव ललिता 129
टक्काङ्गटक्कवत्तारैः 80

डोम्बक्री सावरी वेला० 16

ढालच्छायायन्त्रवाद्य० 195
ढालशब्दोत्थयन्त्रोत्थ० 195
ढालो मुक्ताफलस्येव 177
ढोल्लरी नाम सा प्रोक्ता 307

तं गीत्वा ध्रुवमागत्य 313
तं शिखाद्विपथं प्राहुः 283
तच्छारीरमिति प्रोक्तम् 169
तज्जा गुर्जरिका मान्ता 77
तज्जा डोम्बकृतिः सांशा 95
तज्जा देशी रिग्रहांशः 89
तज्जा धन्नासिका षड्ज० 86
तज्जा रामकृतिर्वीरे 114
तज्जा वराटिका सैव 104
तज्जा वेलावली तार० 99
तज्जा समस्वरा नट्टा 106
तज्जा स्फुरितगान्धारा 92
ततः कुमुदिनी ख्याता 246
ततः कुसुमवत्याख्या 246
ततः खण्डं ध्रुवाख्यं द्विः 313
ततः प्रयोगस्तदनु 222
ततः समग्रं तं गीत्वा 295
ततश्चतुर्थो द्व्यर्धःस्यात् 198
ततस्तद्वत् स्वराः पाटा० 290
ततस्य चावनद्धस्य 205
ततो द्विखण्ड आभोगः 310
ततोऽन्ये विप्रकीर्णास्तान् 221
तत्तल्लक्ष्मयुतस्तासु 251
तत् सुशारीरमित्युक्तम् 169
तत्र गान्धर्वमुक्तं प्राक् 210
तत्र च प्रतिमण्ठेन 314
तत्र तेनपदे नेत्रे 215
तत्र पूर्वप्रसिद्धानाम् 14
तत्र मेलापकाभोगौ 213
तत्र वर्णगणैर्जाता 235
तत्र वर्णगणो वर्णैः 232
तत्रादौ ग्रामरागाणाम् 17
तत्रान्त्या वर्णमात्रैला 246
तत्रोक्तं लक्ष्म वागानाम् 174
तत्रोक्तः शुद्धसूडः प्राक् 308
तत्प्राधान्येन ये गीताः 190
तत् षोढोत्कलिका चूर्णम् 266
तत् स्वस्थानं तदन्यत्त्वम् 321
तथाप्येषां विशेषस्तु 314
तथैव वस्तुवदनम् 302
तथोपवदनं प्रोक्तम् 302
तदा विचित्रमात्रैला 244
तदा स्यात् कीर्तिधवलः 305
तदा स्यात् त्रिपदी 295
तदिति ब्रह्म तेनायम् 216
तदैता गदिताः सर्वा० 251
तद्गणैः संगता त्रेधा 242
तद्दैवत्यगणोपेता 242

तद्द्विमानाच्छङ्कपाटैः 290
तद्भवा सावरी धान्ता 97
तद्भाषा दाक्षिणात्या स्यात् 117
तद्युक्तास्तु गतेः स्थायाः 180
तद्युक्ता भजनस्य स्युः 180
तद्वद्बाणगणा भेदाः 234
तद्वृत्तेन स्वराः पाटाः 290
तन्मते तोटकस्येह 285
तस्य भूरितरा भेदाः 299
तस्य भेदास्तु तिरिपः 171
तस्मिन्नेव रसे रागे 322
तानाम्ब्राहेरिका दोह्या 9
ताने तानोद्भवा भाषा 10
तारजोऽतारजश्चेति 259
तारधा मन्द्रषड्जा च 117
तारमन्द्रोऽयमाषड्ज० 123
तारषड्जग्रहः षड्जे 124
तारषड्जग्रहांशश्च 24
तारसांशग्रहो मान्तः 84
ताराख्यः प्रतिमण्ठोऽसौ 315
तारा छेन चतुर्भिश्च 276
तारानुध्वनिमाधुर्य० 169
तारावलीति पञ्च स्युः 218
तारेति मानवी छेन 276
तारे दीप्तप्रसन्नोऽसौ 190
तारो ध्वनिस्थानकं स्यात् 259
तालत्रैविध्यतस्तस्य 265
तालद्वयेन सा गेया 279
तालमानद्वयन्यासः 301
तालविश्रामतोऽन्येन 319
तालस्तालप्रकरणे 216
तालस्तासु विधातव्यः 247
तालहीनः सतालो वा 282
तालार्णवो भूरितालः 293
तालेन गजलीलेन 275
तालेनैकेन केचित्तु 288
तालै रागैश्चतुर्भिः स्यात् 293
तालै रागैस्त्रिभिर्यद्वा 300
तालोऽस्यां त्यागसौभाग्य० 222
तिरिपास्फुरितो लीन० 194
तिरिपान्दोलितवलि० 194
तिरिपान्दोलितो लीन० 194
तिर्यगूर्ध्वमधस्ताच्च 178
तिलको ललितश्चेति 310
तीक्ष्णप्रेरितकस्तीक्ष्ण० 195
तुम्बकी तुम्बकाकारो० 155
तुम्बुरा षड्जभाषा च 10
तुर्यद्वितीययोश्चैतत् 305
तुर्यपञ्चमयोस्त्वेका 239
तृतीयमुच्चमेष द्वि० 256
ते ग्रन्थविस्तरत्रासात् 161
ते च शब्दस्य ढालस्य 174
तेनकः पाटतालौ च 215
तेनकान्तः पञ्चभङ्गिः 294
तेनेतिशब्दस्तेनः स्यात् 216
तेनैरर्धं द्विपद्यर्धम् 286
ते लक्ष्येष्वप्रवृत्तत्वात् 260
ते शृङ्गारेऽपि चत्वारः 315
तेषां तु स्थायवागेषु 172
ते स्थाया घटनाया ये 190
तैः पदैस्तेन मानेन 201
तोऽन्तलो मध्यगो जः स्यात् 232
तोटकच्छन्दसा न्यस्त० 285
तोड्येव ताडिता गाल्पा 110
तौर्यत्रितयचातुर्यम् 146
त्यक्त्वैकैकं गणं त्वाद्या० 241
त्रयाणां चरणानां स्युः 306
त्रयोदशायुजि कलाः 282, 283
त्रयोदशायुजि समे 282
त्रयोदशासमे हंस० 283
त्रवणा भिन्नषड्जस्य 94
त्रवणा मध्यमा शुद्धा 10
त्रिंशाद् गुरोराद्विगुरोः 274
त्रिखण्डस्तत्र खण्डे द्वे 256

त्रिधा तिस्रो द्वितीयाद्या 257
त्रिधातुश्च चतुर्धातुः 259
त्रिपदी षट्पदी गाथा 281
त्रिभिन्नलीनस्फुरित॰ 195
त्रिभिन्नस्तु त्रिषु स्थाने॰ 171
त्रिभिश्चैः पगणेनापि 244
त्रिविधो धवलः कीर्तिः 305
त्रिश्चतुष्पञ्चवारं वा 262
त्रिषु त्रिष्वथवा स्थायः 187
त्रिषु स्थानेष्वेकरूप॰ 165
त्रिस्थानगमकप्रौढिः 146
त्रिस्थानघनगम्भीर॰ 158, 160
त्रिस्थानलीननिःसार॰ 160
त्रिस्थानशोभी गम्भीर॰ 159
त्रिस्थानोऽन्यस्तु मधुर॰ 159
त्रिस्थानो मनसो यस्तु 165
त्रीण्युपाङ्गानि पूर्णाटी 16
त्रेता दशविधा प्रोक्ता 240

दक्षिणा गुर्जरी कम्प्र॰ 111
दक्षिणास्याज्जनुर्यस्याः 248
दधानः कन्धरामूर्ध्वा 155
दन्तीपदान्वितं प्रान्ते 307
दश स्युः समगायन्यो 204
दशापि स्युः पुनस्त्रेधा 257
दशैते स्युर्गुणा गीते 323
दिक्प्रदर्शनमात्रार्थं॰ 194
दिनस्य केशवप्रीत्यै 63
दिनस्य पश्चिमे यामे 41
दिनस्य प्रथमे यामे 26
दिनस्य मध्यमे यामे 37
दिव्या च मानुषी दिव्य॰ 287
दिव्या संस्कृतया वाचा 287
दीर्घकम्पितसूक्ष्मान्त॰ 195
दीर्घा गौरी ततो राजी 280
दीप्तस्तु दीप्तनादः स्यात् 228
दुष्कराभास इत्युक्तः 194
दुष्करोऽवघटः प्रोक्तः 190
दुष्टं लोकेन शास्त्रेण 324
दूरश्रवणयोग्यस्तु 166
देवक्रीरित्यथोपाङ्ग॰ 16
देशाख्यैला बुधैः पञ्च 248
देशीमार्गाश्रयं वक्ति 145
देशीरागतया प्रोक्तम् 14
देशीरागादिषु प्रोक्तम् 210
देशीरागादिहेतूनाम् 17
देशीरागेष्वभिज्ञानम् 146
दोहदः स्याद्यदा प्रान्ते 307
दौ द्वौ षष्ठे द्वितीये च 305
द्रुतगीतविनिर्माणम् 146
द्रुततुर्यांशवेगेन 171
द्रुतद्वन्द्वाल्लघुद्वन्द्वात् 315
द्रुतद्वन्द्वाल्लगाभ्यां स्यात् 316
द्रुतपूर्वो विलम्बान्तः 187
द्रुतस्यान्वर्थनामानः 181
द्रुतार्धमानवेगेन 171
द्रुता विलम्बिता मध्या 269
द्वावङ्घ्री प्रासहीनौ 251
द्विगुणाभिः कलाभिः 244
द्विगुणे चालयित्वा तु 199
द्विग्रामः ककुभस्त्रिंशत् 6
द्विचच्चत्पुटमानेन 289
द्विचपानां चत्रिपाणाम् 240
द्वितीयताले हिन्दोले 237
द्वितीये च तृतीये तु 244
द्वितीये चाद्यभेदाभ्याम् 242
द्वितीयो गारुगी रास॰ 259
द्विपथा भूरिभेदास्ते 283
द्विपदी करुणाख्येन 275
द्वियत्येकविरामं वा 313
द्विरार्याछन्दसो गीतम् 279
द्विरुद्ग्राहं ध्रुवाभोगौ 255
द्विरुद्ग्राहो ध्रुवाभोगौ 258
द्विरुद्ग्राहो ध्रुवोऽपि द्विः 265

द्विर्गीत्वा गीयते यत्र 270
द्विर्गीत्वोद्ग्राहपूर्वार्ध० 256
द्विर्यत्नोद्ग्राहपूर्वार्धम् 259
द्विश्रुती संगतौ तत्र 139
द्वेस्तो विलम्बिते तत्र 222
द्व्यर्धद्विगुणयोर्मध्ये 199
द्व्यर्धस्वरे चालयित्वा 198

धग्रहांशः पञ्चमान्तः 72
धग्रहो धैवतीषड्ज० 35
धनिभ्यां गमपैर्भूरि० 99
धनिसैर्वलिता धांश० 94
धन्यासांशग्रहा भाषा 100
धन्यासांशग्रहा भूरि० 97
धन्यासांशग्रहो मन्द्र० 118
धन्यासी देशिदेशाख्या 16
धपत्यक्तं रसे वीरे 102
धांशग्रहः पञ्चमान्तः 95
धांशग्रहो मध्यमान्तः 69
धांशन्यासग्रहा तार० 113
धांशषड्जग्रहन्यासा 74
धांशो मान्तस्तथा गौड० 35
धांशो मान्तो रिपत्यक्तः 69
धातुमातुविदप्रौढः 146
धातुर्विमलकण्ठत्वात् 166
धातू रागांशभेदेन 319
धाद्यन्तांशा कम्प्रषड्जा 99
धीरैरुद्भटचारीक० 54
धीरैर्वीरोत्सवे प्रोक्ता 129
धैवतांशग्रहन्यास० 123, 137
धैवतांशग्रहन्यासा 99
धैवतीमपि तद्धेतुम् 54
धैवत्या मध्यमायाश्च 137
धैवत्यार्षभिकावर्ज० 80
ध्रुवको गीयते यत्र 263
ध्रुवत्वाच्च ध्रुवः पश्चात् 213
ध्रुवभेदेऽनुलम्भोऽसौ 263
ध्रुवस्ततस्तत्र पूर्वम् 222
ध्रुवादालापमध्यात्तु 317
ध्रुवाभोगध्रुवा गेयाः 262
ध्रुवाभोगान्तरे जातः 213
ध्रुवाभोगौ च तेषु स्युः 251
ध्रुवे न्यासस्ततः प्रोक्तः 313
ध्रुवोद्ग्राहौ भिन्नतालौ 279

नट्टनारायणश्चेति 8
नट्टा कर्णाटबङ्गालः 16
नट्टोपाङ्गं निषादेन 113
ननु रूक्षगुणो बोम्बः 158
ननु वृत्ते वक्ष्यमाणे 285
नन्दनो वीरशृङ्गारे 311
नन्दावती च भद्राव० 235
नन्दावत्यां वह्निजा च 242
नन्दिनी चित्रिणी चित्रा 244
नन्द्यावर्तः स्वस्तिकश्च 288
नन्द्यावर्तो भवेत्तस्य 288
नरसिंहोऽद्भुतरसे 260
न वाञ्छति वहन्या० 190
नागध्वनिं तदुद्भूतम् 102
नाट्यस्य कुतपः पात्रै० 206
नातिस्थूलो नातिकृशः 165
नादावती पञ्चभिर्भेर्ना० 236
नादावत्यादयो मात्रा० 244
नादावत्यादिका एव 248
नादावत्यामिमे भेदाः 242
नानाप्रकारः क्रियते सा 201
नानाप्रयोगरागांश० 251
नामसाम्यं तु कासांचित् 12
नामान्येलापदानां स्युः 227
नामितान्दोलितवलि० 194
नामितो मिश्रितः पञ्च० 171
नाराटखाहुलोन्मिश्र० 159
नाराटबोम्बकौ बोम्ब० 159
नाराटे बोम्बभेदाः स्यु० 160

नाराटो बोम्बकस्तु स्यात् 158
निःशङ्कशङ्कशीलाश्च 316
निःशङ्को निखिलम् राग० 1
निःसाणस्त्रिवली भेरी 206
निःसारतारूक्षताभ्याम् 159
नि सारता विस्वरता 169
निःसाररूक्षोऽन्यो लीन० 160
निःसारुकः कुडुक्कश्च 259
निःसारोच्चतरस्थूलः 159
निःसारोच्चैस्तरोऽन्यस्तु 160
निकृतेः करुणायाश्च 181
निगतारो मन्द्रहीन· 124
निगाल्पो मध्यमन्यासः 18
नितारा रिबहुस्तार० 131
निबद्धमनिबद्धं तत् 211
निमन्द्रा मध्यमव्याप्ता 108
निमीलको मतो गायन् 155
नियतं श्रेयसो हेतु० 210
नियमो जातिमत्यां तु 272
नियुक्ता सर्वभावेषु 128
निषादांशग्रहन्यास० 120
नीचोच्चद्रुतमध्यमादौ 323
नीतिः सेना च कविता 218
नूतनै रूपकं नूत्नम् 319
नोक्ते करणवर्तन्यौ 19
न्यासांशमध्यमस्तार० 66

पञ्च कामा रतिश्चैका 249
पञ्चतालेश्वरस्ताला० 220
पञ्चधा ग्रामरागाः 3
पञ्चभिः पैः सचगणैः 244
पञ्चभिस्तगणैर्जन्तिः 237
पञ्चमस्य विभाषा स्यात् 136
पञ्चमांशग्रहन्यास 46, 116
पञ्चमांशग्रहन्यासा 99, 117, 118
पञ्चमादेव सौराष्ट्री 128
पञ्चमेनोज्झिता मन्द्र० 111
पञ्चमोत्पन्नगमक० 134
पञ्चमो मध्यमग्रामः 6
पञ्चविंशतिराख्याताः 264
पञ्चविंशतिरित्येते 155
पञ्चाननोमातिलकौ 221
पञ्चाशच्च चतुर्युक्तम् 272
पटहः करटा ढक्का 206
पट्टवाद्यं पटः कम्रा 206
पणवो दर्दुरो ढक्का 205
पथि भ्रष्टे वनभ्रान्ते 52
पदमध्येऽप्यपभ्रंशे 231
पदैः पाटैश्च बिरुदैः 299
पदैः सबिरुदैः पाटैः 300
पदैः स्वरैः क्रौञ्चपदः 277
पदैः स्वरैर्दण्डकेन 299
पदैः स्वरैश्च बिरुदैः 301
पदैश्च बिरुदैर्बद्धा 304
पदैश्च बिरुदैर्हर्ष० 301
पदैश्च बिरुदैस्तेनैः 300
पदैस्तच्चित्रकरण० 254
पद्धडीप्रभृतिच्छन्दाः 303
पद्मालया पत्रिणी च 228
पद्वयं तगणश्चान्ते 276
पन्यासांशग्रहा माप० 127
परचित्तपरिज्ञानम् 146
परितोऽर्धभृते कुम्भे 187
परिवृत्तं रागताल० 321
परुषोच्चैस्तरः स्थूलः 158
पवनो रविसंज्ञश्च 274
पश्चिमाद्वदनाज्जन्म 249
पाञ्चालीरीतिर्भारत्याः 236
पाटैः स्यातां ध्रुवोद्ग्राहौ 271
पादत्रयं त्रिपथके 297
पादे छः पञ्च भा गोऽन्ते 276
पान्तांशादिः समनिपैः 136
पान्ता सरिपमैर्भूरिः 135
पुनः प्रबन्धास्त्रिविधाः 219

पुनरुक्तं कलाबाह्यम् 324
पुनर्गीत्वा ध्रुवे त्यागः 222
पुनर्गीत्वा ध्रुवे न्यासः 256
पुनर्द्विधा स्थिरा वेगा० 177
पुनश्चतुर्धा द्विपदी 276
पूर्णं पूर्णाङ्गमकम् 323
पूर्णस्तल्लक्षणो देशी 83
पूर्वपूर्वाक्षरव्राते 277
पूर्वरङ्गे प्रयोक्तव्यः 66
पूर्वार्धमुत्तरार्धं वा 274
पृथक्चतुःस्मरा नन्दा० 249
पृथक् पदानि पञ्चद्वि० 290
पृथग्लगत्वे मिश्रैस्तु 269
पोता भाषा शकामेके 10
पौराली मालवा कालि० 10
प्रकृतिप्रत्ययैश्चोक्तम् 323
प्रकृतिस्थस्य शब्दस्य 175
प्रचुरः कोमलो गाढः 165
प्रणवाद्यमतालं च 270
प्रतिगृह्येत सा प्रोक्ता 201
प्रतिग्रहणिकैकान्या 201
प्रतिग्राह्योल्लासितः स्यात् 187
प्रतिग्राह्योल्लासितश्च 174
प्रतिग्राह्योल्लासितश्चो० 195
प्रतितालेन सा गेया 237
प्रतिपाद्यविशेषेण 319
प्रतिमण्ठेन शृङ्गारे 311
प्रतिमण्ठेन हास्ये स्यात् 310
प्रतिपाणां प्रचपानाम् 240
प्रत्येकं गतिषट्केन 269
प्रत्येकं च तयोरादि० 248
प्रत्येकं तासु चेदेता० 249
प्रत्येकं द्विपदानि स्युः 290
प्रत्येकं वासवी पञ्च० 239
प्रत्येकमेकत्रिंशत्ते 242
प्रथमं त्रोटयित्वैक० 187
प्रथमा मधुकर्युक्ता 246
प्रथमे चास्त्रयो दः स्यात् 305
प्रद्वित्रिणां प्रद्विचानाम् 240
प्रबन्धगतिहैतुत्वात् 216
प्रबन्धगाननिष्णातः 150
प्रबन्धनाम्ना प्राङ्मानम् 290
प्रबन्धाङ्कं सतालं च 270
प्रबन्धावयवो धातुः 213
प्रबन्धोऽङ्गानि षट् तस्य 215
प्रभूतगमकः स्तोक० 259
प्रभूतप्रतिभोद्भेदभाक्त्वम् 146
प्रभूतभाग्यविभवैः 169
प्रयोक्तव्यो महाकाल० 137
प्रयोगे श्लोकगीतादौ 233
प्रयोगोऽन्यो विधातव्यः 222
प्रयोज्यः पश्चिमे यामे 102
प्रयोज्या रणरणके 134
प्रयोज्या ललिते स्नेहे 130
प्रयोज्या सर्वभावेषु 132
प्रयोज्यो वीरकरुणे 48
प्रलम्बितावस्खलित० 195
प्रलम्बितोऽवस्खलित० 174
प्रवेशे तुर्ययामेऽह्नः 137
प्रसन्नः स्यात् पदस्थान० 228
प्रसन्नमध्यारोहिभ्याम् 95
प्रसन्नमध्यालंकारः 48, 52, 63, 90
प्रसन्नमध्येनारोहि० 32, 35, 51
प्रसन्नमृदुरित्युक्तः 190
प्रसन्नादियुतो दान० 26
प्रसन्नाद्यन्तकलिता० 74
प्रसन्नाद्यवरोहिभ्याम् 57, 60, 102
प्रसन्नाद्ये न संचारि० 72
प्रसन्नान्तान्वितश्चारु० 77
प्रसन्नान्तावरोहिभ्याम् 84
प्रसारी गीयते तज्ज्ञैः 155
प्रसिद्धा ग्रामरागाद्याः 14
प्रसृतः प्रसरोपेतः 182
प्रसृताकुञ्चितः स्थायः 187

प्रहर्षे विनियोक्तव्यः 69
प्राकृते दोहसंज्ञोऽसौ 282
प्राग्यामे करुणे गेयः 28
प्राग्रूपकगताः स्थायाः 322
प्राग्वत्तथा स्वराः पाटाः 290
प्रान्तप्रासा तु लाटी स्यात् 251
प्रान्ते लोली पदोपेता 306
प्रायोगिकः क्रमाख्यश्च 259
प्रियस्मृतौ नियोगोऽस्याः 117
प्रेरितस्तीक्ष्ण इत्युक्ताः 174
प्लावितोल्लासितवलि० 194

बङ्गालस्तारमध्यस्थ० 122
बङ्गालोंऽशग्रहन्यास० 122
बद्धं धातुभिरङ्गैश्च 211
बद्धो निःसारुतालेन 315
बन्धादिमं पदाद्यं च 252
बहुधा संकरादासाम् 238
बहुभिश्चरणैः सात्र 304
बहुलो येषु नादः स्यात् 180
बाङ्गाली माङ्गली हर्ष० 10
बाणलेखा बाणगणै० 244
बाणान्ताः पादयोर्यस्याः 249
बिरुदं गुणनाम स्यात् 216
बिरुदान्तास्त्रिभिस्तालैः 16
बिरुदैः स्वरपाटान्तैः 303
बिरुदैर्वर्णतालेन 265
बुधैरुद्भटचारीक० 86
बोट्टः स्यात् पञ्चमीषड्ज० 43
बोम्बको मिश्रकश्चेति 158
बोम्बयुक्तो मध्यमः 159
ब्रह्मणः पूर्ववदनात् 248

भजते रासकः सोऽयम् 264
भजनस्य स्थापनायाः 174
भञ्जनी द्विविधा ज्ञेया 201
भञ्जनीसंश्रितं चेति 320
भद्रावती पञ्चभिर्मै 238
भद्रावती भद्रलेखा 249
भयानके च बीभत्से 35
भयानके च वीरादौ 32
भयानके सबीभत्से 72
भल्लातिका च मल्हारी 17
भवन्ति बहवो भेदाः 159
भवन्त्यङ्गवदङ्गानि 215
भवन्त्येकादिपादानाम् 283
भवेन्मार्दलिकद्वन्द्वम् 204
भवेल्ललितगाढस्तु 182
भागोऽस्मिञ्झोम्बडेऽप्यूर्ध्वम् 262
भावनापञ्चमो नाग० 8
भावनीति विभाषाः स्युः 9
भावकश्चेति गीतज्ञाः 151
भाषाः सप्तदश ज्ञेयाः 10
भाषाः स्युरथ देवार० 9
भाषाः स्युर्वेसरी चूत० 9
भाषाङ्गत्वेऽप्युपाङ्गत्वम् 114
भाषाङ्गाण्यथ भावक्री० 15
भाषा मुख्या स्वराख्या च 12
भाषाणां जनकाः पञ्च 8
भाषाश्चतस्र सौवीरे 9
भाषास्तिस्रो वेदवती 10
भाषास्त्रयोदश ज्ञेयाः 10
भाषा हर्षपुरी षड्ज० 136
भाषे द्वे द्राविडीत्येका 9
भिन्नधातु तृतीयं स्यात् 222
भिन्नपञ्चम इत्येते 6
भिन्नषड्जश्च षड्जाख्ये 6
भिन्नषड्जेऽपि ललिता 130
भिन्ना वक्रैः स्वरैः सूक्ष्मैः 4
भीतो भयान्वितो गाता 155
भूरीतरा ममन्द्रा च 128
भूरिभावरसोत्कर्षा 251
भृशं प्राणप्रतिग्राह्याः 190
भेदा वेद्यास्त्रिपद्यादे० 296

भेदास्त्रिनवतिर्युक्ता 242
भैरवी भैरवोपाङ्गम् 113
भैरव्यंशः, समां जातिम् 181
भ्रामितक्षिप्तसूक्ष्मान्त० 195

मकरक्रीत्रिनेत्रक्री० 15
मग्रहांशा स्वल्पषड्जा 97
मङ्गलारम्भ आनन्द० 255
मङ्गलो भेन शृङ्गारे 313
मण्ठद्वितीयकङ्काल० 222, 247
मण्ठवत्प्रतिमण्ठादेः 314
मण्डिता मनिधैस्तत्र 109
मतङ्गादिमताद् ब्रूमः 19
मतङ्गोक्ता तारमन्द्र० 134
मत्यक्तान्दोलितसपा 112
मधुमाधवनामानौ 274
मधुरं धुर्यलावण्य० 323
मधुरः कीर्तितस्तारः 165
मधुरस्निग्धगम्भीर० 159
मधुरी भिन्नपौराली 10
मधुरो भोगदो गेयः 310
मधुरो मृदुगम्भीर० 160
मध्यमं स्यात्तदर्धेन 204
मध्यमग्रामरागोऽयम् 60
मध्यमग्रामसम्बन्धः 74
मध्यमांशग्रहन्यासः 40
मध्यमांशग्रहन्यासा 68
मध्यमादिर्मग्रहांशा 62
मध्यमादिर्मालवश्री० 16
मध्यमापञ्चमीजातः 28, 116
मध्यमापञ्चमीजाति० 46
मध्यमापञ्चमीजातो 54
मध्यमापञ्चमीजात्योः 71
मध्यमापञ्चमी धैव० 95
मध्यमे कैशिकीजातः 122
मध्यमे नर्तगान्धार० 6
मध्यमेन निषादेन 112
मध्यस्थरागौ सादृश्य० 181
मध्यस्थांशस्तयोरंशः 181
मध्ये मध्ये स्वरान् भूरीन् 178
मनसा तद्गतेनैव 181
मन्द्रभूरिः ससञ्चारी 30
मन्द्रे ध्वनिः स घोषः स्यात् 182
मन्यासः काकलीयुक्तः 54
मन्यासो मन्द्रषड्जांश० 60
मन्यासो रूपसाधारः 48
ममन्द्रा तारगान्धारः 101
मल्हारी तदुपाङ्गं स्यात् 118
मस्त्रिगुः पूर्वलो यः 232
महानन्दाथ लहरी 241
महामाहेश्वरेणोक्तः 151
महाराष्ट्रान्ध्रहम्मीर० 206
महाराष्ट्री च सौराष्ट्री 16
मही मतिस्ततः कीर्तिः 280
मातुस्थायविचित्रत्वात् 322
मातृकः श्रीपतिस्तद्वत् 260
मात्रा पञ्चदशाद्येऽङ्घ्रौ 296
मात्राः पञ्चदशायुग्मे 282, 283
मात्रा कला लघुर्लः स्यात् 234
मात्रागणैस्तु मात्रैला 244
मात्रिका वर्णजैर्वृत्तैः 257
मातवन्तरेण रच्यन्ते 322
मातवन्तरेणानुसारः 322
माधुर्यधुर्यध्वनयः 151
मानुषी प्राकृतगिरा 287
मान्तोऽल्पगः काकलिमान् 43
मान्धातृसुमती शोभि० 227
मान्धात्रादिपदेषु स्युः 228
मार्गं देशीं च यो वेत्ति 149
मार्दङ्गिकास्तु चत्वारः 204
मार्दवाघूर्णितः प्रोक्तः 182
मालती मोहिनी सप्त 247
मालती ललिताख्या च 246
मालवः पञ्चमान्तश्च 8

मालवः पञ्चमान्तोऽथ 6
मालवा तस्य भाषा स्यात् 138
मालवी तानवलिता 9
मालवे कैशिकेऽप्यस्ति 132
मिथस्त्रुटितनिर्वाह० 205
मिलिता मुग्धबोधाय 160
मिश्रकोऽनवधानश्च 155
मिश्रश्चैतेऽपि संकीर्णाः 175
मिश्रस्य भेदाश्चत्वारः 159
मुक्तशब्दप्रतिग्राह्याः 177
मुखमुद्रणसंभूतः 172
मुख्याः षडिति शेषाः स्युः 12
मुख्यानुवृत्तिमिलनम् 205
मुदे रुद्रस्य वर्षासु 77
मुहरी शृङ्गवाद्याद्याः 205
मृदुस्त्रिस्थानगम्भीरः 159
मृष्टो मधुरचेहाल० 165
मेघरागः सोमरागः 8
मेघरागो मन्द्रहीनः 123
मेदिन्यथानन्दिनी स्यात् 218
मेलापकः प्रयोगाख्यः 259
मेलापकः प्रयोगात्मा 256

यः कस्यचिन्न सर्वेषाम् 190
यतिमात्रेण भिन्नास्ताः 247
यत्तु कम्पनमारोहि० 177
यत्तु वाग्गेयकारेण 210
यत्र गङ्गातरङ्गन्ति 187
यत्र तैनैः स्वरैः पाटैः 297
यत्र ध्रुवो द्विर्वाभोगः 262
यत्र भागो भवेल्लम्भे 262
यत्र वीररसेन स्यात् 304
यत्र स्थायिनि यत्स्थानम् 321
यत्र स्वराक्षरैरेव 278
यत्स्वरैर्बिरुदैर्बद्धम् 254
यत्राभोगे गातृनाम 279
यत्रोपवेश्यते रागः 198
यत्रोद्ग्राहध्रुवौ सान्द्र० 252
यथोक्तान् यो जयन्तादीन् 311
यदा तत्पदमानेन 201
यदृच्छया वा धवलः 305
यदेकस्य द्वयोरङ्घ्र्योः 249
यद्येषामर्धयोरन्ते 283
यद्वा देवत्रयस्तुत्या 300
यद्वा रागेण तालेन 321
यस्तु गद्ये न पद्ये न 304
यस्मिन् कलरवस्यासौ 190
यस्य स्यात्तेनके न्यासः 296
यस्य स्यात्तेनकैर्न्यासः 266
यस्यां भिन्नार्थयमका० 295
यस्यां षोडशमात्राः स्युः 302
यस्यां समासु मात्रासु 279
यस्यामन्तर्विशन्तीव 177
यस्यामसौ रमा सा च 318
यस्यासौ रासको नन्दः 317
या प्रोक्ता रूपकालप्तिः 201
या रागस्य निजच्छाया 177
यामद्वये मध्यमेऽह्नः 32
यावदेकैकवृद्ध्यैला० 246
याष्टिके त्रावणी भाषा 135
युक्ताः कोमलया कान्त्या 181
युग्मिनी वृत्तमाला च 257
येन तस्यान्यधातुत्वात् 322
ये यन्त्रेष्वेव दृश्यन्ते 177
येषु सूक्ष्मीकृताः शब्दाः 190
येषूपशान्तिः क्रियते 182
येष्वंशो दृश्यते स्थायाः 181
यो झोम्बडगतं लक्ष्म 264
यो यस्मिन् बहुलः स्थायः 194
यो वेत्ति केवलं मार्गम् 149

रक्तहंसः कोल्लहासः 8
रक्तेरुत्कर्षतो रक्ते 181
रक्तेर्द्रुतस्य शब्दस्य 174

रगणैः पञ्चभिः सान्तैः 237
रचिता चेत् तदा ज्ञेया 258
रञ्जकः स्वरसन्दर्भः 209
रञ्जनाद्रागता भाषा॰ 14
रतिदेहेति दशधा 239
रतिलेखा कामलेखा 244
रतिलेखादयः प्रोक्ताः 244
रतिलेखा रतिगणैः 244
रतेः षष्ठश्च दशमः 295
रमणी चन्द्रिका लक्ष्मीः 247
रमणीया च विषमा 239
रमा च चन्दिका तद्वत् 318
रम्यमातुविनिर्माता 146
रसभावपरिज्ञानम् 146
रसाविष्टस्तु रसिकः 151
रसे वीरे च शृङ्गारे 311
रागमग्ना वाद्यशब्दाः 177
रागरागाङ्गभाषाङ्ग॰ 150
रागस्यातिशयाधानम् 180
रागस्यावयवः स्थायः 174
रागाङ्गाण्यष्ट, गाम्भीरी 15
रागान्तरस्यावयवः 181
रागाभिव्यक्तिशक्तत्वम् 169
रागाभ्यामपि तालाभ्याम् 294
रागालपनमालप्तिः 198
रागालप्तिस्तु सा या स्यात् 198
रागे ताले च तत्रैव 322
रागे नानाविधा काकुः 178
रागेण धातुमातुभ्याम् 319
रागेणेष्टः स्वपूर्त्यर्थम् 190
रागेष्टोऽपस्वराभासः 175
रागो हिन्दोलकस्तालः 302
रासकादन्यतालः स्यात् 258
रासको रासतालेन 317
राहुप्रियोऽद्भुते हास्ये 90
रिगमैर्ललितैस्तार॰ 130
रिग्रहांशो मध्यमान्तः 86
रितारा रिधभूयिष्ठा 77
रिधत्यक्तां पमन्द्रां च 107
रिन्यासांशग्रहः क्वापि 74
रिपत्यक्ता तु तोड्येव 110
रिपापन्याससंयुक्ता 131
रिमन्द्रतारा स्फुरिता 111
रिर्वाजिता गपाल्पा च 86
रिषड्जाभ्यधिका धीरैः 107
रिहीनांशग्रहन्यास॰ 115
रिहीना सगधैस्तारा 128
रिहीनो वा मध्यमान्तः 28
रीतिः कर्णाटिका लाटी 15
रूक्षः स्निग्धत्वनिर्मुक्तः 168
रूक्षनिःसारपीनश्च 160
रूक्षस्फुटितनिःसार॰ 168
रूक्षोऽन्यस्तु मृदुस्निग्ध॰ 159
रूपकं तद्वदेव स्यात् 19
रूपकं त्रिविधं ज्ञेयम् 320
रूपकं पूर्वसंसिद्धम् 321
रूपकस्थेन रागेण 201
रूपयौवनशालिन्यः 151
रोषद्वेषपरित्यागः 146
रौद्रे प्रचण्डो नन्दीशः 260
रौद्रे रसे चण्डिकायाः 237

लक्षितस्तेन तेनेति 216
लक्ष्माणीति क्रमात्तासाम् 244
लक्ष्माधुना प्रसिद्धानाम् 60
लक्ष्मीः स्याद् वृद्धिबुद्धी 280
लक्ष्मीर्लंकार एलानाम् 227
लक्ष्ये प्रसिद्धिवैधुर्यात् 264
लगुरुभ्यां द्रुतद्वन्द्वात् 316
लघिष्ठडमरुध्वान॰ 171
लघुद्वयाद्विरामान्तात् 316
लघुभिर्बहुलैरल्पैः 269
लघुत्रयाद् द्रुतद्वन्द्वात् 316
लघुत्रयाद् विरामान्तात् 315

लघुर्गुरुत्वरहितः 190
लघुशेखरतालेन 311
लघोर्द्रुतद्वयेन स्यात् 316
लम्भरासैकतालीभिः 220
लयग्रहविशेषेण 319
लयतालकलाज्ञानम् 146
लयान्तरेऽन्यतालेन 256
ललितं कैशिकीं वृत्तिम् 267
लवनी, तद्युजः स्थायाः 177
लहरीति त्रिधा तानि 255
लीन आन्दोलितवलि॰ 171
लीनकम्पितलीनश्च 194
लीनत्रिस्थानरूक्षोच्च॰ 160
लीनस्तु द्रुतवेगेना॰ 171
लोके तथापि शुद्धोऽसौ 308
लोहितारभटीं वृत्तिम् 237

वक्री वक्रीकृतगलः 155
वक्रो दीप्तप्रसन्नश्च 175
वदनं चच्चरी चर्या 221
वराटलाटकर्णाट॰ 206
वराटी गुर्जरी गौड॰ 16
वराटी द्राविडी भूरि॰ 109
वराटी सैन्धवी भूरि॰ 109
वराट्यः षडितिच्छाया॰ 16
वरेण्या वायुवेगा च 228
वरो वस्तुकविर्वर्ण॰ 147
वर्णजो मातृकश्चेति 284
वर्णानां स्युः फलान्येषाम् 233
वर्णालंकारसंपन्ना 203
वर्णैलावत् परं यस्याम् 251
वर्णैश्चातालशब्दानाम् 270
वर्णो वर्णस्वरो गद्यम् 220
वर्ण्यनामाङ्कितामोगा 272
वलिर्या गमकेषूक्ता 177
वलिर्विविधवक्रत्व॰ 171
वलौ वहे वहन्यां च 182
वल्लकी कुब्जिका ज्येष्ठा 205
वल्लभो रेण करुणे 313
वल्लाता तदुपाङ्गं स्यात् 115
वसन्ते प्रहरे तुर्ये 81
वसुमत्यपि तत्रेन्दु॰ 244
वहनीच्छाययोर्यन्त्र॰ 195
वहनीढालयोर्ढाल॰ 195
वहनीयन्त्रयोश्छाया॰ 195
वहनी येषु ते स्थायाः 177
वहनी साथ संचारि॰ 177
वहनी स्यात् पुनर्द्वेधा 177
वहन्त इव कम्पन्ते 187
वहाक्षराडम्बरजः 195
वहाक्षराडम्बरयो 174
वांशिकाः पाविका-पाव॰ 205
वाक्यमालापके न्यासः 290
वागानामापि केषांचित् 174
वाङ्मातुरुच्यते गेयम् 146
वाचं गेयं च कुरुते यः 146
वातपित्तकफा देह॰ 213
वाद्यशब्दस्य यन्त्रस्य 174
वाद्यानामेवमादीनाम् 206
वा पदान्ते त्वसौ वक्रः 231
वाराहीदेवताप्रीत्यै 238
वासवी कलिका वृत्ता 272
वासवी संगता त्रेता 238
विकलः स तु यो गायेत् 155
विकारीमध्यमोद्भूतः 66
विकारेण तृतीयस्य 239
विचित्रस्थानकप्रौढैः 206
विचित्रो वासवमृदु 227
विजयश्रीः क्रियाङ्गाणि 16
विजयश्चेति स प्रोक्तः 316
विजयाख्यो रसे वीरे 317
विजया रत्नमाला च 240
विदधानोऽधिकं धातुं 146
विद्यादानेन तपसा 169

विद्युल्लता विशाला च 246
विधाय स्थायमालप्तेः 201
विनयो विक्रमोत्साहौ 274
विनियुक्तः प्रतिमुखे 22
विनियुक्तो गर्भसन्धौ 19
विनोदो वरदो नन्दः 317
विप्रकीर्णश्च तत्रादौ 219
विप्रलम्भे कञ्चुकितः 46
विप्रलम्भे तु सारङ्गः 260
विप्रलम्भे प्रयोक्तव्यः 63
विप्रलम्भे भवेद् भुञ्छी० 112
विभाषा ककुभे भोग० 99
विभाषा पल्लवी भास० 10
विभाषा मालवाभिन्न० 9
विभाषे द्वे तु काम्भोजी 10
विभाषे पार्वती श्रीकण्ठ० 10
विमला नलिनी संज्ञा 246
वियुक्तबन्धने गेया 117
विरसापस्वराव्यक्त० 155
विरसो नीरसो वर्ज्य० 155
विरामान्तद्रुतद्वन्द्वात् 314
विरामान्तेन गातव्यः 314
विरुद्धगुणताक्षेप० 158
विलम्बितलये गेयम् 306
विलम्बितेन मानेन 270
विलसत्काकलीकोऽपि 74
विशालश्चेति स प्रोक्तः 315
विषमालंकृतिश्चित्रा० 257
विषमे तु छयुग्मं स्यात् 305
विष्णुश्चक्रेश्वरो वीरे 260
वीणा घोषवती चित्रा 205
वीणावंशादियन्त्रोत्था 178
वीररौद्राद्भुतरसः 24, 57, 74, 86, 122
वीररौद्राद्भुतरसे 77
वीररौद्राश्रितैर्बद्धा 272
वीरशृङ्गारयोस्तेन 292
वीरश्रीर्मङ्गलाचारः 221
वीरहास्ये निर्वहणे 51
वीरावतारः शृङ्गार० 292
वीरे जयप्रियो गेयः 313
वीरे रौद्रे रसे गेयः 19
वीरे रौद्रेऽद्भुते गेयः 37
वीरे हास्ये च शृङ्गारे 311
वृत्तं तस्य च पादान्ते 287
वृत्तगन्धि रसे शान्ते 268
वृत्तिं वैदर्भरीतिं च 238
वेगवद्भिः स्वरैर्वर्ण० 4
वेगस्वरा रागगीति० 4
वेगे द्रुततृतीयांश० 171
वेगेन प्रेरितैरूर्ध्वम् 187
वेणीमिश्रमिति प्राहुः 268
वेणी सर्वैः कृता मिश्रम् 268
वेदध्वनिनिभध्वानाः 190
वेदध्वनेर्घनत्वस्य 175
वेदोत्तरा जातिमती 272
वेलावल्याश्च गुर्जर्याः 181
वेसरे षाडवः षड्ज० 40
वेसरे षाडवे भाषे 10
वैकुन्दानन्दकान्ताराः 315
वैदर्भीरीतिसम्पन्नम् 267
वैदर्भ्या रचितं रीत्या 268
वैरञ्जी मध्यमग्राम० 9
व्यक्तं पूर्णं प्रसन्नं च 323
व्युत्पत्तये निरूप्यन्ते 222
व्योमजा वारुणी व्योम० 242

शङ्कराभरणौ घण्टा० 15
शकमिश्रेति षट्तिस्रः 9
शकाद्या वलितेत्येका 10
शब्दः प्रकाशते येषु 190
शब्दशारीरगुणतः 190
शब्दसादृश्यमित्येते 205
शब्दानामधमः प्रोक्तः 159
शब्दानुशासनज्ञान० 146

शरीरं क्षेत्रमित्युक्तम् 177
शान्ते शीलो विरामान्त० 316
शाङ्गदेवेन गदितः 124
शाङ्गदेवेन गदिता 109
शाङ्गदेवेन निर्णीत० 114
शालवाहनिका टक्के 9
शिक्षाकारोऽनुकारश्च 151
शिखापदं तत्तृतीये 249
शुकप्रियः पूर्वयामे 66
शुद्धच्छायालगाभिज्ञः 150
शुद्धच्छायालगौ रागौ 156
शुद्धपञ्चमभाषा स्यात् 127
शुद्धभिन्ना च वाराटी 9
शुद्धमध्यमया सृष्टः 52
शुद्धश्छायालगश्चेति 308
शुद्धसाधारितः षड्ज० 6
शुद्धाः सप्तेति भिन्नाः स्युः 6
शुद्धाः स्युर्विकृतास्तिस्रः 238
शुद्धा खण्डा च मात्रादिः 275
शुद्धा चतुर्विधा नादा० 235
शुद्धादिगीतियोगेन 4
शुद्धाभीरी रगन्ती च 12
शुद्धा मालवरूपा च 10
शृङ्गारहासयोः सन्धौ 116
शृङ्गारे मकरन्दा स्यात् 317
शृङ्गारे वैष्णवं चित्रम् 268
शेषास्तु मान्मथगणाः 296
श्रीशंकरप्रियेणोक्तः 165
श्रुतिन्यूनाधिकत्वेन 177
श्रोत्रनिर्वापको मृष्टः 165
श्रीवर्धनः स्याद् विरुदैः 301
श्रीवृद्धिनिधनस्थान० 233
श्रीकण्ठिका च बाङ्गाली 10
श्रीरङ्गः श्रीविलासः स्यात् 221
श्रीरागनट्टौ बङ्गालौ 8
श्लक्ष्णस्तु तैलधारावत् 166
श्वेतं हास्यकृदारब्धम् 268
षट्पञ्चाशद्युतं प्रोक्तम् 252
षट्पदी वस्तुसंज्ञश्च 221
षट्प्रकारो मण्ठतालः 313
षट्प्रकारत्वमेतासाम् 248
षडक्षराङ्घ्रितस्त्रिंशत् 264
षडक्षरादङ्घ्रिखण्डात् 246
षड्जग्रहांशापन्यासः 30
षड्जग्रहांशो मन्यासः 26, 32
षड्जग्रामसमुत्पन्नः 6
षड्जग्रामे मन्द्रहीनः 122
षड्जग्रामे रेवगुप्तः 86
षड्जधौ संगतौ तत्र 138
षड्जमध्यमया जातः 18
षड्जमध्यमया सृष्टः 22, 32, 77, 84, 102
षड्जमध्यमिकोत्पन्नः 26
षड्जमन्द्रा प्रयोक्तव्या 134
षड्जर्षभांशग्रहः स्यात् 57
षड्जांशग्रहणन्यासा 129
षड्जांशग्रहणन्यासाम् 107
षड्जादिमूर्छनः पूर्णः 26
षड्जादिमूर्च्छनो दान० 30
षड्जाद्यन्तात्र संवादः 104
षड्जे धैवतिकोद्भूतः 123
षड्जे षाड्जीभवः षड्ज० 123, 124
षड्जे षाड्जीसमुद्भूतम् 121
षड्जे स्याद्रूपसाधारः 6
षड्जोदीच्यवतीजातः 69
षष्टिमात्रावधिप्रोक्ताः 264
षष्ठस्तृतीयस्त्रिगणः 296
षष्ठादन्यैर्गणैः सर्व० 280
षष्ठी मदनवत्युक्ता 246
षष्ठेऽष्टमे दाश्चत्वारः 305
षष्ठेनैकेन गुरुणा 276
षाडवादेव बङ्गालः 69
षाड्जीधैवतिकोत्पन्नः 51

संकीर्णा देशजा मूला 12
संगतासवितु: क्षिप्ते 242
संचारिवर्णरुचिर: 69
संचारिणि प्रसन्नादि० 28
संज्ञात्रयं निबद्धस्य 211
संदश्य दशनान् गायन् 155
संदष्टोद्घुष्टसूत्कारि० 155
संपत्सुभगताकीर्ति० 233
संपूर्ण: शान्तशृङ्गार० 41
संपूर्णो मध्यमन्यास: 22
संप्रविष्टोत्प्रविष्टश्च 195
संभोगे विनियोक्तव्य: 81
संभोगे स्याद् विशालाख्य: 316
स एवान्दोलित: षड्जे 120
स येषु ते स्युर्ढालस्य 177
सकाकलीक: षड्जादि० 63
सकाकलि: पञ्चमान्त: 37
सकृद् विरतिरुद्ग्राह: 318
सगतारा षड्जमन्द्रा 131
सगतारोत्सवे हास्ये 115
स चतुर्धा स्थानकस्य 259
सजातीयांशक: स स्यात् 181
स तु सालगसूडस्थ० 213
सत्यं किन्तु मते येषाम् 285
सदृशांशो यथा नट्टा० 181
सदृशांशो विसदृश: 181
सदृशो यस्तु सर्वेषाम् 190
सद्वितीयो यमलक: 151
सद्विधातुस्त्रिधातुश्च 215
सधमन्द्रा मभूयिष्ठा 114
स नेतृगातृश्रोतृणाम् 310
सन्यासांशग्रहं मन्द्र० 121
सन्यासांशग्रहा गेया 115
सन्यासांशग्रहा तार० 104
सन्यासांशग्रहा मन्द्र० 106
सन्यासांशग्रहा सान्द्रा 131
सन्यासांशा धग्रहा च 108
स प्रलम्भो ध्रुवस्थाने 262
समं सुरक्तं श्लक्ष्णं च 323
समध्रुवा च विषम० 303
समन्द्रा कौन्तली तत्र 108
समन्द्रा निगनिर्मुक्ता 132
समवर्णलयस्थानम् 323
समशेषस्वरं वीरे 121
समस्वरा तारमन्द्र० 65
समस्वरा रितारा च 127
समस्वरोऽन्य: कामोद: 124
समालंकारं संख्या च 257
समानोऽल्पाक्षरध्वान: 228
समानो मधुर: सान्द्र: 228
समेतरस्वरा गेया 74
समेतरस्वरा मन्द्र० 68
समे षोडश मात्रा: स्यु: 295
सरल: कोमलो रक्त: 182
सर्वक्रतुफलं तस्य 311
सर्वमन्त्रमयी ह्येषा 287
सर्वस्थानोत्थगमके० 150
सर्वेषामपि रागाणाम् 17
सर्वेषु रासकेष्वेषु 317
सविलासास्ति गीतस्य 180
सविसर्गो व्यञ्जनान्त: 231
स शुद्धैर्मिश्रितै: पाटै: 271
सशृङ्गारे पुष्पसार: 260
ससौवीरौ मध्यमे तु 6
स स्यादपस्वराभास: 190
स स्वरार्थौ द्विधा 278
सांशग्रहान्ता माने 101
सांशग्रहान्ता सौराष्ट्री 128
सा गीतालप्तिसंबन्ध० 177
सा चास्माभि: पुरा प्रोक्ता 211
सा त्वन्यरागकाकुर्या 177
सादृश्यशून्ययोरंशो० 181
सा देशकाकुर्या रागे 177
सा द्विधा गदिता राग० 198

सा द्विधा छन्दसः पूर्वा 303
साधारणीति शुद्धा 4
साधारणो निराधारः 175
साधारिता च गान्धारी 9
सानुप्रासैस्त्रिभिः खण्डैः 306
सा भवेत् त्रिविधा 235
सामवेदोद्भवा पीता 237
साम्ये तु मिश्रनामैव 194
सारङ्ग्यालापिनीत्यादेः 205
सारसो भ्रमरो हंसः 282
सारौहिसप्रसन्नान्त: 46
सारोही सप्रसन्नादिः 40, 137
सार्थकैरर्थहीनैश्च 271
सार्वभौमोत्सवे गेयः 69
सावरोहिप्रसन्नान्तः 24
सा वसन्तोत्सवे गेया 302
सावित्री पावनी वात० 242
सा स्याद्वसुमती यस्याम् 244
सिंहलीलेन तालेन 298
सितं मदनदैवत्यम् 267
सिरालभालवदनग्रीवः 155
सुकराभास इत्युक्तः 190
सुकुमारं कण्ठभवम् 323
सुकुमारो वर्णनात् 228
सुखदास्तु सुखस्य स्युः 190
सुदर्शनः स्वराङ्गः श्री० 221
सुदेशिको विदग्धानाम् 182
सुरक्तं वल्लकीवंश० 323
सुरनाथः समुद्रश्च 274
सुसंप्रदायो गीतज्ञैः 150
सूडक्रमस्थो मध्ये 220
सूडालिक्रमसंबन्धात् 220
सूर्यचन्द्रसुराधीशाः 233
सूर्यास्तुर्ये द्वितीये च 296
सैन्धवी दाक्षिणात्याऽऽन्ध्री 9
सैन्धवी पञ्चमेऽप्यस्ति 131
सैन्धवी भिन्नषड्जेऽपि 132
सैव प्रतापपूर्वा स्यात् 112
सैव प्रयोगशब्देन 318
सोऽवस्खलित इत्युक्तः 187
सोत्फुल्लेत्युदिता यस्याम् 177
सोमरागः स्मृतो वीरे 123
सोमो भौमो बुधो जीवः 233
सौराष्ट्री पञ्चमी वेग० 9
सौवीरः ककुभष्टक्कः 8
सौवीरा तद्भवा मूल० 104
स्तब्धः स्थायस्तु बद्धः स्यात् 190
स्तुत्यनामाङ्कितश्चासौ 310
स्तुत्यनामाङ्कितो मध्य० 222
स्तोकस्तोकैस्ततः स्थायैः 199
स्थानत्रयव्याप्तियुक्तः 168
स्थानभ्रष्टः समः प्राप्तुम् 155
स्थापयित्वा स्थापयित्वा 180
स्थायः स्थायेन पूर्वेण 182
स्थायादिष्ववधानेन 156
स्थायानां गुणभेदेन 174
स्थाया नानाविधां भङ्गीम् 181
स्थायास्तदन्विताश्चालैः 190
स्थायिवर्णस्थितिः कम्पः 187
स्थायिस्वरादष्टमस्तु 199
स्थायुकः क्षिप्तसूक्ष्मान्ता० 175
स्निग्धः श्लक्ष्णो रक्तियुक्त० 165
स्निग्धकोमलगम्भीर० 159
स्निग्धकोमलनिःसार० 159
स्निग्धत्रिस्थाननिःसारः 160
स्फूर्जन्निर्जवनो हारि० 150
स्यातां कन्दर्पदेशाख्यौ 8
स्यात् त्रोटितप्रतीष्टोऽपि 174
स्यात् त्रोटितप्रतीष्टोऽसौ 187
स्यात् प्रतापवराटी तु 109
स्यात् त्रोटितप्रतीष्टोत्प्र० 195
स्याद् वर्णनियमः सर्व० 311
स्याद्देशक्षेत्रयन्त्राणाम् 177
स्याद्रासवलयो हंस० 264

स्याद्रोहिणी विशाला च 280
स्यान्मिश्रकरणं बद्धम् 255
स्युः षट्पञ्चतुस्त्रिद्वि॰ 234
स्युर्वराट्या उपाङ्गानि 108
स्वनामतालके हंस॰ 298
स्वभावादेव शब्दस्य 190
स्वरः पूर्णश्रुतिस्तारे 178
स्वरः स्याद्येषु ते स्थायाः 182
स्वरतेनकसंयुक्ता 295
स्वरदेशाख्यया ख्याता 12
स्वरन्यासः स तन्नाम्ना 277
स्वरमग्रिममाहत्य 171
स्वरस्य कम्पो गमकः 171
स्वरहीनं तदित्यन्ये 287
स्वराः षड्जादयस्तेषाम् 216
स्वराणां नमनादुक्तः 172
स्वरादेरादिविन्यास॰ 266
स्वराद्यकरणस्येव 258
स्वरान्तः श्रीविलासः स्यात् 294
स्वरान्तरस्य रागे स्यात् 177
स्वराभिव्यक्तिसंयुक्ताः 216
स्वरैः पदैश्च बद्धं यत् 254
स्वरैः पदैस्तु बिरुदैः 274
स्वरैः पाटैः पदैरुक्तः 299
स्वरैः पाटैः पदैस्तेनैः 266, 297
स्वरैः पाटैश्च बिरुदैः 298
स्वरैः सकरपाटैर्यत् 254
स्वरैः सतेनकैर्यत्तु 254
स्वरैः सहस्तपाटैस्तु 253
स्वरैर्मुरजपाटैर्यत् 253
स्वरैरेकोऽन्यः प्रयोगैः 282
स्वस्थानं तदपस्थानम् 181
स्वस्थानैः सा चतुर्भिः स्यात् 198

हंसी वधूरिति प्रोक्ता 280
हकारौकारयोगेन 4
हतस्वरवराटी च 16
हतस्वरा धमन्द्रा कं॰ 109
हयलीलेन तालेन 274
हरिणी चाथ चक्राख्या 280
हरिश्च हरिणी हस्ती 274
हर्षोत्कर्षप्रदश्चारः 311
हास्यशृङ्गारकरुणे 311
हास्यशृङ्गारयोरेष 54
हास्यशृङ्गारयोर्हंसः 260
हास्ये द्वितीयतालेन 311
हिन्दोलको रिधत्यक्तः 80
हिन्दोलभाषा गौडी स्यात् 134
हिन्दोलभाषा छेवाटी 115
हिन्दोलोऽष्टौ वेसरास्ते 6
हिन्दोले पिञ्जरी भाषा 106
हीनो वेगविलम्बाभ्याम् 182
हुडुक्कपाटैस्तदनु 290
हुडुक्का डमरू रुञ्जा॰ 206
हृदयंगमहुंकार॰ 172
हृद्यशब्दः सुशारीरः 150
हृद्या कण्ठ्या शिरस्या च 177
हृष्यकामूर्छनोपेता 116
हेमन्ते प्रथमे यामे 69
ह्रस्वः शिथिलगाढश्च 175
ह्रस्वः स्तोकः परौ द्वौ तु 190

Word-Index

अंशः (जीवस्वरः) 190
अंशः (रागालापलक्षणे) 19
अंशः (स्वर-करणे) 252
अंशः (आडिकामोदिकायाम्) 101
अंशः (आन्धाल्याम्) 117
अंशः (आम्रपञ्चमे) 124
अंशः (ककुभे) 95
अंशः (कर्णाटबङ्गाले) 106
अंशः (कोलाहलायाम्) 104
अंशः (खम्भाइत्याम्) 112
अंशः (गान्धारपञ्चमे) 90
अंशः (गुर्जर्याम्) 77
अंशः (गौडकृतौ) 107
अंशः (गौडकैशिके) 37
अंशः (गौडकैशिकमध्यमे) 32
अंशः (गौडपञ्चमे) 35
अंशः (गौडे) 80
अंशः (टक्ककैशिके) 137
अंशः (टक्के) 77
अंशः (डोम्बकृतौ) 95
अंशः (तृतीयसैन्धव्याम्) 132
अंशः (तोडिकायाम्) 68
अंशः (त्रवणायाम्) 94
अंशः (त्रावण्याम्) 135
अंशः (देशाख्यायाम्) 92
अंशः (देश्याम्) 89
अंशः (द्राविडगौड्याम्) 120
अंशः (द्राविड्याम्) 139
अंशः (द्वितीयकामोदायाम्) 124
अंशः (द्वितीयगौड्याम्) 134
अंशः (द्वितीयललितायाम्) 130
अंशः (द्वितीयसैन्धव्याम्) 131
अंशः (द्वितीयसौराष्ट्र्याम्) 128
अंशः (धन्नास्याम्) 86
अंशः (नट्टायाम्) 106
अंशः (नर्ते) 54
अंशः (पिञ्जर्याम्) 106
अंशः (प्रथमकामोदायाम्) 124
अंशः (प्रथमगौडे) 134
अंशः (प्रथममञ्जर्याम्) 99
अंशः (प्रथमसैन्धव्याम्) 131
अंशः (प्रथमसौराष्ट्र्याम्) 128
अंशः (बङ्गाले) 69
अंशः (बाङ्गाल्याम्) 100
अंशः (बोट्टे) 43
अंशः (भम्माणपञ्चमे) 52
अंशः (भम्माण्याम्) 136
अंशः (भिन्नकैशिकमध्यमे) 26
अंशः (भिन्नकैशिके) 30
अंशः (भिन्नताने) 28
अंशः (भिन्नपञ्चमे) 72
अंशः (भिन्नषड्जे) 69
अंशः (भैरवे) 69
अंशः (भैरव्याम्) 113
अंशः (भोगवर्धन्याम्) 99
अंशः (मध्यमग्रामरागे) 60
अंशः (मध्यमषाडवे) 122
अंशः (मध्यमादौ) 62
अंशः (मल्हारे) 118
अंशः (मल्हार्याम्) 118
अंशः (मालवकैशिके) 63
अंशः (मालवश्रियाम्) 65

अंशः (मालवायाम्) 138
अंशः (मेघरागे) 123
अंशः (रगन्त्याम्) 97
अंशः (रामकृतौ) 107, 114
अंशः (रूपसाधारे) 48
अंशः (रेवगुप्ते) 86
अंशः (वराट्याम्) 74, 104
अंशः (वराट्युपाङ्गेषु) 108
अंशः (वल्लातायाम्) 115
अंशः (वेलावल्याम्) 99
अंशः (वेसरषाडवे) 40
अंशः (शके) 51
अंशः (शुद्धकैशिकमध्यमे) 84
अंशः (शुद्धकैशिके) 24
अंश (शुद्धपञ्चमे) 116
अंशः (शुद्धभैरवे) 123
अंशः (शुद्धसाधारिते) 18
अंशः (श्रीरागे) 121
अंशः (षड्जकैशिके) 57
अंशः (षड्जग्रामरागे) 22
अंशः (षाडवे) 60
अंशः (सोमरागे) 123
अंशः (हिन्दोले) 80
अंशग्रहन्यासषड्जः (प्रथमबङ्गालः) 122
अंशग्रहन्यासषड्जा (छेवाटी) 115
अंश — (स्थायः) 174, 181
अंशांशः (स्थाये) 181
अकचटतपयशाः (वर्णवर्गाः) 233
अकारः (एलापदे) 227
अक्षरनिर्मित—(अन्तरः) 318
अक्षरवर्जिता (आलप्तिः) 318
अक्षरव्रातः (चक्रवाले) 277
अक्षराडम्बर—(स्थायः) 174, 187
अखण्डितस्थितिः (गौडी गीतिः) 6
अग्निः (रगणदेवता) 233
अग्राम्यः (प्राणः, एलायाम्) 228
अग्रिमप्रहरः (अह्नः, शुद्धपञ्चमे) 116
अङ्कचारिणी (आलिसंश्रितप्रबन्धः) 220, 272
अङ्ग—(पात्रम्) 206
अङ्गम् (निबद्धे, प्रबन्धे) 211, 215, 218
अङ्गहारः (कुतपे) 206
अङ्घ्रिः (एलायाम्) 222, 244, 248
अङ्घ्रिः (चच्चर्याम्) 302
अङ्घ्रिः (तोटके) 285
अङ्घ्रिः (द्विपथे) 283
अङ्घ्रिः (वस्तुप्रबन्धे) 296
अङ्घ्रि—(पूर्तिः) 249
अङ्घ्रिः (हंसलीले) 298
अचतुरप्रियः (स्थायः) 190
अड्डतालः (सालगसूडः) 308, 316
अड्डतालिका (तालः, अड्डताले) 316
अड्डतालिका (तालः, झोम्बडे) 259
अतारज—(झोम्बडः) 259
अतारमध्यमा (रगन्ती) 97
अतारा (त्रावणी) 135
अत्युक्ता (छन्दोजातिः) 234
अथर्ववेदोत्था (भद्रावती) 238
अद्भुत—(रसः, आम्रपञ्चमे) 124
अद्भुत—(रसः, कमलमण्ठे) 314
अद्भुत—(रसः, कुन्तले) 311
अद्भुत—(रसः, कुन्दप्रतिमण्ठे) 315
अद्भुत—(रसः, गान्धारपञ्चमे) 90
अद्भुत—(रसः, गौडकैशिके) 37
अद्भुत—(रसः, नरसिंहझोम्बडे) 260
अद्भुत—(रसः, भम्माणपञ्चमे) 52
अद्भुत—(रसः, भिन्नकैशिके) 30
अद्भुत—(रसः, भिन्नकैशिकमध्यमे) 26
अद्भुत—(रसः, मालवकैशिके) 63
अद्भुत—(रसः, रूपसाधारे) 48
अद्भुत—(रसः, शुद्धकैशिके) 24
अद्भुत—(रसः, षड्जकैशिके) 57
अद्भुत—(रसः, षड्जग्रामरागे) 22
अद्भुत—(रसः, सौवीरे) 102

अधम—(मिश्रशब्दः) 159
अधम—(वाग्गेयकारः) 146
अधम—(गायनः) 151, 155
अधम—(पात्रम्, कुतपे) 206
अधम—(रूपकम्) 321
अधुनाप्रसिद्ध—(रागाः) 16, 17, 60
अध्यात्मगोचरा (चर्या) 303
अनवधानः (गायनः) 155
अनादिसम्प्रदायम् (गान्धर्वम्) 210
अनिबद्ध—(गानम्) 210
अनिबद्धा (मातृका) 287
अनिर्युक्त—(प्रबन्धः) 219
अनुकारः (गायनः) 151
अनुक्तजनका (विभाषा, अन्तरभाषा) 10
अनुक्रीः (क्रियाङ्गम्) 15
अनुलम्भः (लम्भभेदः) 263
अनुच्छिष्टोक्तिः (वाग्गेयकारे) 146
अनुप्रासः (एलायाम्) 222
अनुप्रासः (कर्णाटैलायाम्) 248
अनुप्रासः (दन्त्याम्) 307
अनुप्रासः (लोल्याम्) 306
अनुवर्तनम् (ताललीन-, वृन्दगुणः) 205
अनुसार—(रूपकम्) 321, 322
अनुस्वानविहीनता (शारीरदोषः) 169
अन्त—(अनुप्रासः, कर्णाटैलायाम्) 248
अन्त—(प्रासः, ओव्याम्) 306
अन्तः (न्यासः, ककुभे) 95
अन्तः (न्यासः, कर्णाटबङ्गाले) 106
अन्तः (न्यासः, खम्भाइतौ) 112
अन्तः (न्यासः, गुर्जर्याम्) 77
अन्तः (न्यासः, गौडकैशिके) 37
अन्तः (न्यासः, गौडपञ्चमे) 35
अन्तः (न्यासः, डोम्बकृतौ) 95
अन्तः (न्यासः, त्रावण्याम्) 135
अन्तः (न्यासः, द्राविड्याम्) 139
अन्तः (न्यासः, द्वितीयसौराष्ट्र्याम्) 128
अन्तः (न्यासः, पिञ्जर्याम्) 106
अन्तः (न्यासः, प्रथमकामोदायाम्) 124
अन्तः (न्यासः, प्रथमसौराष्ट्र्याम्) 128
अन्तः (न्यासः, भम्माण्याम्) 136
अन्तः (न्यासः, भिन्नपञ्चमे) 72
अन्तः (न्यासः, भिन्नषड्जे) 69
अन्तः (न्यासः, भैरवे) 69
अन्तः (न्यासः, मालवकैशिके) 63
अन्तः (न्यासः, रामकृतौ) 114
अन्तः (न्यासः, रेवगुप्ते) 86
अन्तः (न्यासः, वेलावल्याम्) 99
अन्तः (न्यासः, शुद्धकैशिके) 24
अन्तः (न्यासः, शुद्धकैशिकमध्यमे) 84
अन्तः (न्यासः, सोमरागे) 123
अन्तः (न्यासः, सौवीर्याम्) 104
अन्तःसारः (घनत्व-स्थायः) 190
अन्तःसारता (शब्दस्य) 166
अन्तरः (गौडपञ्चमे) 35
अन्तरः (रूपसाधारे) 57
अन्तरः (वेसरषाडवे) 40
अन्तरः (षड्जग्रामरागे) 22
अन्तरः (धातुः, प्रबन्धे) 213, 290, 313 318
अन्तरः (स्थायः) 175, 190
अन्तरभाषा 9, 10, 308
अन्तर्निःसारता (शब्दस्य) 158
अन्तिम—(प्रहरः, मालवकैशिके) 63
अन्तिम—(मूर्छनः, भिन्नतानः) 28
अन्त्य—(प्रहरः, बोट्टे) 43
अन्यरागकाकुः (स्थाये) 177
अपन्यासः (आन्धाल्याम्) 117
अपन्यासः (कैशिक्याम्) 127
अपन्यासः (छेवाट्याम्) 114
अपन्यासः (दाक्षिणात्यायाम्) 116
अपन्यासः (द्वितीयसैन्धव्याम्) 131
अपन्यासः (बाङ्गाल्याम्) 100
अपन्यासः (भिन्नकैशिके) 30
अपन्यासः (भोगवर्धन्याम्) 99

अपन्यासः (मध्यमषाडवे) 122
अपन्यासः (रगन्त्याम्) 97
अपन्यासः (षड्जग्रामरागे) 22
अपन्यासः (रागालापलक्षणे) 19
अपभ्रंशः 231
अपस्थानवराटी (उपाङ्गम्) 109
अपस्थान—(स्थायः) 175, 181
अपस्वरः (गायनः) 155
अपस्वराभासः (स्थायः) 174, 190
अपार्थकम् (गीतम्) 324
अपूर्णा (चर्या) 303
अपेक्षितः (स्थायः) 174, 182
अब्जगर्भः (स्वस्तिकभेदः) 288
अब्जपत्रम् (स्वस्तिकभेदः) 288
अभिधानम् (वाग्गेयकारलक्षणे) 146
अभिनयः (कुतपे) 206
अभीष्टदः (कुन्तलः) 311
अभीष्टकामदः (कामोदः) 311
अभीष्टफलदः (चन्द्रशेखरः) 311
अभ्युदयप्रदः (नन्दः) 317
अमरः (प्रतिमण्ठभेदः) 314
अम्बरम् (तगणदेवता) 233
अम्बाहेरी (टक्कभाषा) 9
अयुक्—(अङ्घ्रिः, द्विपथे) 282, 283
अयुक्—(पादः, चतुष्पद्याम्) 295
अर्थः (कन्द भेदः) 274
अर्थः (स्वरार्धे) 278
अर्थहीन—(पाटः, कैवाडे) 271
अर्धबेसरी (मालवकैशिकभाषा) 10
अर्धस्थित—(स्वराः) 199
अर्धान्तम् (आर्यायाः) 279
अलङ्कारः (आलप्तौ) 203
अलङ्कारः (प्रसन्नमध्यः, गान्धारपञ्चमे) 90
अलङ्कारः (प्रसन्नमध्यः, भम्माणपञ्चमे) 52
अलङ्कारः (प्रसन्नमध्यः, मालवकैशिके) 63
अलङ्कारः (प्रसन्नमध्यः, रूपसाधारे) 48
अलङ्कारः (वाग्गेयकारलक्षणे) 146
अलङ्कृतम् (गीतम्) 323
अलम्बविलम्बः (स्थायः) 174, 187
अल्प—(गः, नर्ते) 54
अल्प—(गः, बोट्टे) 43
अल्प—(गः, भम्माणपञ्चमे) 52
अल्प—(गः, मालवपञ्चमे) 46
अल्प—(धैवतः, मालवकैशिके) 63
अल्प—(निगौ, शुद्धसाधारिते) 18
अल्प—(पञ्चमः, टक्के) 77
अल्प—(रिः, भिन्नताने) 28
अल्प—(रिः षड्जकैशिके)
अल्प – (रिपौ, रूपसाधारे) 48
अल्पत्वम् (रागालापलक्षणे) 19
अवक्र—(स्वराः, शुद्धागीतौ) 4
अवधटः (स्थाय) 175, 190
अवधानम् (गायनगुणः) 150, 156
अवधानम् (वाग्गेयकारगुणः) 146
अवधान—(स्थायः) 174, 181
अवनद्ध—(कुतपः) 205
अवमर्श—(सन्धिः, शुद्धपञ्चमे) 116
अवयवः (प्रबन्धस्य) 213
अवयवः (रागस्य, स्थायः) 174
अवयवः (रूपक-) 201
अवरोहि—(वर्णः, मध्यमग्रामरागे) 60
अवरोहि—(वर्णः, रूपसाधारे) 48
अवरोहि—(वर्णः, वहन्याम्) 177
अवरोहि—(वर्णः, शुद्धकैशिकमध्यमे) 84
अवरोहि—(वर्णः, शुद्धकैशिके) 24
अवरोहि—(वर्णः, शुद्धसाधारिते) 19
अवरोहि—(वर्णः, षड्जकैशिके) 57
अवरोहि—(वर्णः, षड्जग्रामरागे) 22
अवरोहि—(वर्णः, सौवीरे) 102
अवरोह्यादि—(वर्णः, षाडवे) 66
अवस्खलित—(स्थायः) 174, 187
अव्यक्तः (गायनः) 155
अव्यवस्थित—(गायनः) 155
अशेषभाषा (वाग्गेयकारलक्षणे) 146

असंकीर्णलक्षणाः (स्थायाः) 174, 175
असह्यशः (चादिवर्णवर्गफलम्) 233
असम --(अङ्घ्रिः, द्विपथे) 283
असाधारणः (स्थायः) 175, 190
अहन् (गौडकैशिकमध्यमे) 32
अहन् (गौडपञ्चमे) 35
अहन् (भिन्नकैशिके) 30
अहन् (मध्यमग्रामरागे) 60
अहन् (मालवपञ्चमे) 46
अहन् (शुद्धकैशिके) 24
अहन् (षड्जग्रामरागे) 22

आक्रमण -(स्थायः) 175, 190
आचार्यः 308
आजिः (नर्तविनियोगे) 54
आजिः (रेवगुप्तविनियोगे) 86
आडिकामोदिका (अधुनाप्रसिद्धरागः) 16
आडिकामोदिका (भाषाङ्गम) 101
आडिल्लः (खाहुलः) 158
आदिः (ग्रहः, भम्माण्याम्) 136
आदिः (ग्रहः, वेलावल्याम्) 99
आदिः (ग्रहः, सौवीर्याम्) 104
आदि—(अनुप्रासः, कर्णाटैलायाम्) 248, 249
आदि -(प्रासः, ओव्याम्) 306
आदितालः (कन्दर्पे) 311
आदितालः (जयन्ते) 310
आदिम—(प्रहरः, शुद्धसाधारिते) 19
आद्या--(मूर्छना, टक्के) 77
आद्या -(मूर्छना, शुद्धकैशिकमध्यमे) 84
आधानम् (गीतस्य) 151
आनन्दः (विपुलायाम्) 318
आनन्दः (आनन्दे) 316
आनन्दः (निःसारुभेदः) 315, 316
आनन्दवर्धनम् (मिश्रकरणम्) 255
आनन्दिनी (प्रबन्धजातिः) 218
आन्दोलितः (गमकः) 171
आन्दोलितः (देशगौडः) 120
आन्दोलितसपा (भुच्छी) 112
आन्दोलिता (खम्भाइतिः) 112
आन्धालिका (पञ्चमविभाषा) 9, 117
आन्ध्र -(पात्रम्) 206
आन्ध्र—(एला) 248, 251
आन्ध्री (टक्कविभाषा) 9
आन्ध्री (पञ्चमभाषा) 9
आभीरिका (मालवकैशिकभाषा) 10
आभीरिका (सौवीर-विभाषा) 9
आभीरी (पञ्चमभाषा) 9
आभीरी (मुख्या भाषा) 12
आभोगः (प्रबन्धे) 213, 222, 251, 252, 255, 256, 258, 259, 262, 263, 265, 272, 279, 290, 307, 310, 313
आभोगः (स्थाये) 190
आम्रपञ्चमः (रागः) 8, 124
आम्रेडितम् (स्वस्तिकभेदः) 288
आयुः (आदिवर्णवर्गफलम्) 233
आयुः (नगणफलम्) 233
आयुः (नेतुः, विजये) 311
आयुःश्रीवर्धनः (जयन्तः) 310
आरभटी (वृत्तिः, उत्कलिकायाम्) 267
आरभटी (वृत्तिः, हंसावत्याम्) 237
आरोहि—(वर्णः, ककुभे) 95
आरोहि—(वर्णः, गौडकैशिकमध्यमे) 32
आरोहि—(वर्णः, गौडकैशिके) 37
आरोहि—(वर्णः, गौडपञ्चमे) 35
आरोहि -(वर्णः, टक्ककैशिके) 137
आरोहि—(वर्णः, बोट्टे) 43
आरोहि—(वर्णः, भम्माणपञ्चमे) 52
आरोहि—(वर्णः, मालवकैशिके) 63
आरोहि—(वर्णः, मालवपञ्चमे) 46
आरोहि—(वर्णः, रूपसाधारे) 51
आरोहि—(वर्णः, वहन्याम्) 177
आरोहि -(वर्णः, वेसरषाडवे) 40
आरोहि—(वर्णः, स्थाये) 187

आरोहि—(वर्णः, हिन्दोले) 80
आर्या (आलिसंश्रितप्रबन्धः) 14, 220, 279-81
आर्या (छन्दः) 279
आर्या—(हयलीलायाम्) 274
आर्यागीतिः (कन्दे) 273
आलपनम् (राग-) 198
आलप्ति—(वहनी) 177
आलप्तिः (अनिबद्धम्) 198, 201, 203, 211
आलप्तिः (गायकगुणे) 150
आलप्तिः (राग-) 19
आलापः (पञ्चतालेश्वरे) 290
आलापः (प्रयोगे) 318
आलापनिर्मित—(उद्ग्राहखण्डम्) 317
आलापपूर्वक—(उद्ग्राहः) 318
आलापमध्य—(ध्रुवपदम्) 317
आलापरचित—(अन्तरः) 318
आलापलम्भः (लम्भभेदः) 262
आलापादि—(ध्रुवपदम्) 317
आलापान्त—(ध्रुवपदम्) 317
आलापिनी (कुतपे) 205
आलिक्रम—(प्रबन्धाः) 220
आलिसंश्रय—(प्रबन्धाः) 219
आवृत्तिः (ओव्याम्) 306
आवृत्तिः (चर्यायाम्) 303
आशीः (धवले) 305
आर्षभिका (रेवगुप्तजमका) 86
आहतः (गमकः) 171
आक्षिप्तिका 19
आहता (प्रतापवेलावली) 112

इकारः (एलापदे) 227
इन्दुमती (मात्रैला) 244
इन्द्रश्रीः (पूर्वप्रसिद्धक्रियाङ्गम्) 15
इन्द्राणी (नन्दावती-देवता) 237
इष्टसिद्धिदः (नन्दनः) 311
इष्टस्वरः (ग्रहः) 252
ईर्ष्या (कैशिक्याम्) 127

उचितः (एलापदनाम) 227
उचितः (स्थायः) 174, 182
उचितज्ञता (वाग्गेयकारगुणः) 146
उच्चतरः (शब्दः) 159, 160
उच्चैरुच्चारणम् (गीते) 323
उच्चैस्तरः (शब्दः) 158
उत्कटः (निग-, सोमरागः) 123
उत्कट—(स्वराः, प्रथमललितायाम्) 129
उत्कलिका (गद्यभेदः) 266, 267
उत्तमः (मिश्रशब्दः) 159
उत्तम—(ध्रुवभेदः) 310
उत्तम—(पात्रम्, कुतपे) 206
उत्तम—(रूपकम्) 319
उत्तम—(वृन्दम्) 203, 204
उत्तमोत्तमः (मिश्रशब्दः) 159
उत्तरायता (मूर्छना, टक्ककैशिके) 137
उत्तरायता (मूर्छना, भिन्नषड्जे) 69
उत्तरार्धम् (आर्यायाः) 274
उत्तरास्यम् (ब्रह्मणः) 249
उत्पली (पूर्वप्रसिद्धभाषाङ्गम्) 15
उत्प्रविष्टः (स्थायः) 174, 187
उत्फुल्ला (वहनी) 177
उत्सवः (कैशिक्याम्) 127
उत्सवः—(छेवाट्याम्) 115
उत्सवः—(प्रथममञ्जर्याम्) 99
उत्सवः—(बोट्टे) 43
उत्सवः—(भम्माण्याम्) 136
उत्सवः—(महाराष्ट्रगुर्जर्याम्) 111
उत्सवप्रिया (चतुराभेदः) 241
उत्साहः (कन्दभेदः) 274
उद्ग्राहः (प्रबन्धे) 213, 222, 252, 255, 256, 258, 259, 262, 263, 265, 271, 279, 288, 301, 309, 313,

317, 318
उद्घट्ट—(तालः, पञ्चतालेश्वरे) 290
उद्दीपनम् (चतुर्थसैन्धव्याम्) 132
उद्दीपनम् (बाङ्गाल्याम्) 100
उद्घुष्टः (गायनः) 155
उद्भटः (गायनः) 155
उद्भटचारीमण्डलम् (नर्ते) 54
उद्भटचारीमण्डलम् (रेवगुप्ते) 86
उद्भटनटनम् (गौडपञ्चमे) 35
उद्भटनटनम् (टक्ककैशिके) 137
उन्नता (वासवीभेद) 239
उपचारः (कार्ये, कारणस्य) 215
उपमा (ब्रह्मोतिझोम्बडभेदे) 260
उपरागाः 8
उपरागजा (भाषा) 12
उपलम्भः (लम्भभेदः) 263
उपवदनम् (वस्तुभेदः) 302
उपशम—(स्थायः) 174, 182
उपस्थानवराटिका (अधुनाप्रसिद्धोपाङ्गम्) 16
उपाङ्गत्वम् (रामकृतेः) 114
उपाङ्गम् (गायकगुणे) 150
उपाङ्गम् (छायानट्टा) 113
उपाङ्गम् (देशीरागवर्गः) 14, 16
उपाङ्गम् (मल्हारः) 118
अपाङ्गम् (वराट्याः) 108
उपाङ्गम् (वल्लाता) 115
उपाङ्गम् (सिंहलीकामोदा) 113
उमातिलकः (विप्रकीर्णप्रबन्धः) 5, 221, 294
उरु-पा (प्रथमवराटी) 109
उरुमध्यमा (त्रावणी) 135
उल्लासितः (गमकः) 171, 172
उल्लासितः (स्थायः) 174, 187
उशनस् (देवता, वेसरषाडवे) 41

ऋग्वेदोत्था (नादावती) 236
ऋद्धिसौभाग्यदः (शेखरः) 310
ऋषभांशः (मध्यमषाडवे) 122
ऋषभान्तांशा (महाराष्ट्रगुर्जरी) 111

एकता (वल्लकी-वंश-कण्ठ-ध्वनीनाम्) 323
एकताली (तालः, एकताल्याम्) 265, 318
एकताली (तालः, झोम्बडे) 259
एकताली (तालः, तिलके) 311
एकताली (तालः, नन्दने) 311
एकताली (सालगसूडः) 308, 318
एकताली (सूडप्रबन्धः) 220, 265
एकधातु (उद्ग्राह-खण्डद्वयम्) 309
एकरसा (गौडी एला) 251
एकल—(गायनः) 151
एला (सूडप्रबन्धः) 220, 222, 227, 228, 237, 244, 246, 248, 251, 252
एलादि—(शुद्धसूडः) 308
एलाभासाः 249

ओज—(अङ्घ्रिः, द्विपथे) 283
ओजस्वी: (पूर्वप्रसिद्धक्रियाङ्गम्) 15
ओजस्वी (प्राणः, एलायाम्) 228
ओवी (विप्रकीर्ण-प्रबन्धः) 33, 221, 306, 307
ओवीपदम् (ओव्याम्) 306
ओहाटी (गौडीगीतौ) 4

औडुव—(रचना) 319
औडुवम् (रागालाप-लक्षणे) 19
औडुवम् (रूपके) 319
औदुम्बरी (कुतपे) 205

ककुभः (ग्रामरागः) 95, 99
ककुभः (भाषाजनकः) 8, 9
ककुभः (रागः, भद्रावत्याम्) 238
ककुभः (साधारणग्रामरागः, उभयग्रामिकः) 6
कङ्काल—(तालः, एलायाम्) 222, 247
कङ्काल—(तालः, ढेङ्कीप्रबन्धे) 256

कङ्काल—(तालः, ध्वनिकुट्टन्याम्) 279
कङ्काल—(तालः, भद्रावत्याम्) 238
कङ्काल—(तालः, वर्तन्याम्) 258
कच्छेल्ली (भिन्नषड्जभाषा) 10
कञ्चुकि-प्रवेशः (टक्ककैशिके) 137
कञ्चुकी (मालवपञ्चमे) 46
कण्ठः (गायकगुणे) 150
कण्ठकुण्ठनम् (पुंसाम्) 165
कण्ठभवम् (गीतम्) 323
कण्ठ्या (वहनी) 177
कनिष्ठ—(वृन्दम्) 203, 204
कन्दः (आलिसंश्रितप्रबन्धः) 220, 273, 274
कन्दर्पः (ध्रुवभेदः) 310, 311
कन्दर्पः (रागः) 8
कन्दुकः (विप्रकीर्णप्रबन्धः) 17, 221, 299
कफः (धातुः) 213
कफजः (खाहुल-शब्दः) 158
कमलः (मण्ठभेदः, मण्ठताल-भेदश्च) 313, 314
कमला (वर्णैला) 246
कम्पः (स्थाये) 187
कम्पः (स्वरस्य, गमके) 171
कम्पनम् (गमके) 172
कम्पनम् (गात्रशब्दयोः) 155
कम्पनम् (स्थाये) 177
कम्पित—(गमकः) 171
कम्पित—(गायनः) 155
कम्पित—(स्वराः) 4
कम्पिता (छायानट्टा) 113
कम्प्रधा (कौन्तली वराटी) 108
कम्प्रधैवता (सिंहलीकामोदा) 113
कम्प्रपञ्चमा (तोडी) 68
कम्प्रपसा (हतस्वरवराटी) 109
कम्प्रमध्यमा (दक्षिणगुर्जरी) 111
कम्प्रमन्द्रमा (छायावेलावली) 112
कम्प्रषड्जा (वेलावली) 99
कम्प्रसा (प्रथमवराटी) 109
कम्बुजः (रासकभेदः) 317
कम्प्रा (कुतपे) 206
करः (पाटः, बिरुदम्, प्रबन्धपुरुषस्य) 215
करटा (कुतपे) 206
करणम् (आलापभेदः) 19
करणम् (सूडप्रबन्धः) 220, 252-55
करणी (वर्णैला) 246
करपाटः (चित्रकरणे) 254
करभः (गायनः) 155
कराली (गायनः) 155
करुण—(तालः, द्विपद्याम्) 275
करुण—(रसः, ककुभे) 95
करुण—(रसः, कन्दर्पे) 311
करुण – (रसः, कम्बुजे) 317
करुण—(रसः, गान्धारपञ्चमे) 90
करुण—(रसः, गौडकैशिके) 37
करुण—(रसः, देश्याम्) 89
करुण—(रसः, द्वितीयसौराष्ट्र्याम्) 128
करुण—(रसः, भिन्नताने) 28
करुण—(रसः, मधुरे) 310
करुण—(रसः, वल्लभमण्ठे) 313
करुण—(रसः, विचार-प्रतिमण्ठे) 315
करुण—(रसः, शब्दे) 165
करुण—(रसः, शेखर-झोम्बडे) 260
करुण—(रसः, सावर्याम्) 97
करुणा—(स्थायः) 174, 181
कर्णाट—(एला) 248
कर्णाट—(गौडः, अधुनाप्रसिद्धोपाङ्गम्) 17, 120
कर्णाट—(पात्रम्) 206
कर्णाटबङ्गालः (भाषाङ्गम्) 16, 106
कर्णाटभाषा (त्रिपद्याम्) 295
कर्णाटभाषा (वर्णप्रबन्धे) 265
कर्णाटभाषा (षट्पद्याम्) 296
कर्णाटसंमता (एला) 249
कर्णाटादिपदम् (कन्दे) 273

कर्णाटादि—(रागाः, स्थाये) 181
कर्णाटिका (पूर्वप्रसिद्धरागाङ्गम्) 15
कलरव—(स्थायः) 175, 190
कलहंसः (आलिसंश्रित-प्रबन्धः) 17, 220, 284
कलहंस—(छन्दः) 284
कलहः (कोलाहलायाम्) 114
कला (ताले) 146
कला (मात्रापर्यायः) 234, 244, 282, 283
कला—(स्थायाः) 175, 190
कलापः (मण्ठभेदः, मण्ठ-तालभेदश्च) 313
कलाबाह्यम् (गीतम्) 324
कलाशास्त्रम् (वाग्गेयकारगुणे) 146
कलिका (अङ्कचारिणी-भेदः) 272
कलिका (त्रेता-भेदः) 240
कलिका (वर्णेला) 246
कलिङ्ग—(पात्रम्) 206
कविता (प्रबन्धजातिः) 218
कश्यपः (नर्ते) 54
कांस्यताल—(पाटाः, पच्चतालेश्वरे) 290
कांस्यतालः (कुतपे) 206
काकली (गान्धारपञ्चमे) 90
काकली (गौडकैशिकमध्यमे) 32
काकली (गौडकैशिके) 37
काकली (गौडपञ्चमे) 35
काकली (नर्ते) 54
काकली (बोट्टे) 43
काकली (भम्माणपञ्चमे) 52
काकली (भिन्नकैशिके) 30
काकली (भिन्नकैशिकमध्यमे) 26
काकली (भिन्नताने) 28
काकली (भिन्नपञ्चमे) 72
काकली (मध्यमग्रामरागे) 60
काकली (मालवकैशिके) 63
काकली (मालवपञ्चमे) 46
काकली (रूपसाधारे) 48
काकली (वेसरषाडवे) 40
काकली (शुद्धकैशिकमध्यमे) 84
काकली (शुद्धकैशिके) 24
काकली (षड्जग्रामरागे) 22
काकली (सौवीरे) 102
काकली (हिन्दोले) 81
काकल्यन्तरौ (टक्के) 77
काकल्यन्तरौ (टक्ककैशिके) 137
काकल्यन्तरौ (भिन्नषड्जे) 69
काकल्यन्तरौ (वेसरषाडवे) 40
काकल्यन्तरौ (शुद्धपञ्चमे) 116
काकल्यन्तरौ (षाडवे) 66
काकित्वम् (शारीरदोषः) 169
काकी (गायनः) 155
काकुः (गायकगुणे) 150
काकुः (वाग्गेयकारगुणे) 146
काकुः (स्थाये) 177, 178
काकोली (शब्दः) 168
काण्डारणा—(स्थायः) 174, 182
कादम्बः (कन्दभेदः) 274
कान्तः (प्राणः, एलायाम्) 228
कान्तजितः (एलापदनाम) 227
कान्तारः (निःसारुभेदः) 315, 316
कान्तिः (शारीरगुणः) 169
कान्तिका (आर्यभेदः) 28
कान्तिमती (वर्णेला) 246
कामः (एला-पदनाम) 227
कामः (कन्दभेदः) 274
कामगणः 234, 248, 249
कामग्रस्त—(नटनम्, टक्ककैशिके) 137
कामलः (ध्रुवभेदः) 310, 311
कामलेखा (कर्णाटैला) 249
कामलेखा (मात्रैला) 244
कामादि-दैवतः (शुद्धपञ्चमः) 116
कामोत्सवा (संगता भेदः) 239
कामोदः (उपाङ्गमूलम्) 113
कामोदः (ध्रुवभेदः) 310, 311

कामोदः (रागः, द्विविधः) 8
कामोदासिंहली (अधुनाप्रसिद्धोपाङ्गम्) 17
काम्भोजी (ककुभ-भाषा) 9
काम्भोजी (मालवकैशिकविभाषा) 10
कारणरागः (स्थाये) 181
कारणांशः (स्थाये) 181
कार्कश्यम् (शारीरदोषः) 169
कार्मारवी (जातिः, भिन्नकैशिक-जनका) 30
कार्मारवी (जातिः, शुद्धकैशिक-जनका) 24
कार्यरागः (स्थाये) 181
कार्यांशः (स्थाये) 181
कार्श्यम् (शारीरदोषः) 169
कालविरोधि (गीतम्) 324
कालिन्दी (भिन्नषड्जविभाषा) 10
कालिन्दी (वर्णेला) 246
काहला (कुतपे) 205
किन्नरी (कुतपे) 205
किरणावली (अनुक्तजनका अन्तरभाषा) 10
किरिकिट्टकम् (कुतपे) 206
कीर्ति—(धवलः, धवलभेदः) 305
कीर्तिः (आर्याभेदः) 280
कीर्तिः (कादि-वर्ग-फलम्) 233
कीर्तिः (भगणफलम्) 233
कीर्तिमान्द्यम् (पादिवर्ग-फलम्) 233
कीर्तिलहरी (मिश्रकरणम्) 256
कुञ्जरः (द्विपथकभेदः) 282, 283
कुट्टिकारः (वाग्गेयकारः) 147
कुडुक्क—(तालः, झोम्बडे) 259
कुडुक्क—(तालः, वर्तनीप्रबन्धे) 258
कुडुक्का (कुतपे) 206
कुडुवा (कुतपे) 206
कुतपः 205, 206
कुन्तलः (ध्रुवभेदः) 310, 311
कुन्दः (प्रतिमण्ठभेदः) 314, 315
कुब्जिका (कुतपे) 205
कुमुदक्री (पूर्वप्रसिद्धक्रियाङ्गम्) 15
कुमुदिनी (वर्णेला) 246
कुररः (द्विपथकभेदः) 282
कुररी (आर्याभेदः) 280
कुरुलः (गमकः) 171
कुशारीरम् 169
कुसुमवती (वर्णेला) 246
कुसुमायुधः (दैवतम्, एलायाम्) 227
कुसुमावती (चतुरा-भेदः) 241
कूर्मकः (कन्दभेदः) 274
कूर्मी (कुतपे) 205
कृशः (शब्दः) 165, 168
कृष्णा (भद्रावती) 238
केकी (कन्दभेदः) 274
केटिः (शब्दः) 168
केणिः (शब्दः) 168
केतुः (देवः, मालवपञ्चमे) 49
केशवः (देवः, मालवकैशिके) 63
कैवाडः (आलिसंश्रितप्रबन्धः) 220, 271
कैशिक—(वृत्तिः, चित्रे) 268
कैशिकः (भिन्नग्रामरागः) 6
कैशिकककुभः (रागः) 8
कैशिकमध्यमः (भिन्नग्रामरागः) 6
कैशिकी (जातिः, गौडकैशिकजनका) 37
कैशिकी (जातिः, द्वितीयबङ्गालजनका) 122
कैशिकी (जातिः, भिन्नकैशिकजनका) 30
कैशिकी (जातिः, मालवकैशिकजनका) 63
कैशिकी (जातिः, शुद्धकैशिकजनका) 24
कैशिकी (जातिः, षड्जकैशिकजनका) 57
कैशिकी (जातिः, षड्जकैशिकमध्यमजनका) 84
कैशिकी (पञ्चमभाषा) 9, 127
कैशिकी (रागः, मङ्गलाचारे) 304
कैशिकी (रागः, मङ्गले) 306
कैशिकी (वृत्तिः, नादावत्याम्) 236
कैशिकी (वृत्तिः, ललिते) 267
कोकिलापञ्चमः (उपरागः) 8
कोङ्कण—(पात्रम्) 206
कोमलः (शब्दः) 158, 160, 165

कोमलः (स्थायः) 174, 182
कोमलकान्तिः (स्थाये) 181
कोलाहल—(वृन्दम्) 204
कोलाहलः (अधुनाप्रसिद्धरागाङ्गम्) 16, 80
कोलाहलः (स्थाये) 181
कोलाहला (टक्कभाषा) 9, 114
कोल्लहासः (रागः) 8
कौतुकम् (विनोदे) 317
कौन्तली (वराटी, अधुनाप्रसिद्धोपाङ्गम्) 16, 108
कौमुदी (संगता-भेदः) 239
कौशली (भिन्नपञ्चमविभाषा) 9
क्रमविलासः (झोम्बडभेदः) 256
क्रमव्यत्यासः (पाटकरणे) 253
क्रमाख्यः (झोम्बडभेदः) 259
क्रमोत्क्रमः (स्वरार्थप्रबन्धे) 278
क्रिया (गायकगुणे) 150
क्रियाङ्गम् (गायकगुणे) 150
क्रियाङ्गम् (देशीरागवर्गः) 150
क्रीडा – (तालः, चच्चर्याम्) 302
क्रीडा—(तालः, जयमङ्गले) 311
क्रीडा – (तालः, झम्पटे) 299
क्रीडा –(तालः, निर्मले) 311
क्रौञ्चपदः (आलिसंश्रितप्रबन्धः) 11, 220, 277
क्षत्रिया (हंसावती) 237
क्षमा (आर्या-भेदः) 280
क्षिप्तः (विकृतगणः) 242
क्षिप्तः (स्थायः) 175, 187
क्षेत्रकाकुः (स्थाये) 177, 178
क्षेत्रम् (शरीरम्) 177

खञ्जनी (मालवकैशिकभाषा) 10
खण्डः (एलायाम्) 222
खण्डः (ओव्याम्) 306
खण्डः (दन्त्याम्) 307
खण्डः (ध्रुवप्रबन्धे) 309, 310, 311
खण्डः (लोल्याम्) 306
खण्डम् (गद्यभेदः) 266, 268
खण्डा (द्विपदी) 275, 276
खम्भाइतिः (उपाङ्गम्) 112
खल्लोत्तार—(रूपकम्) 321, 322
खाहुलः (शब्दभेदः) 158, 159
खुत्ता (वहनी) 177

गङ्गातरङ्गः (स्थाये) 187
गजलील—(तालः) 275
गजलीला—(आलिसंश्रितप्रबन्धः) 8, 220, 275
गणः (मात्रा-) 231, 244
गणः (वर्ण-) 231, 239, 241, 242, 246, 264, 294, 295
गण—(एला) 231
गणज - (वृत्तम्) 256
गणभङ्गः (गणैलायाम्) 244
गणविकारः (गणैलायाम्) 238
गणाधिपः (कर्णाटैलायाम्) 248, 249
गणिका (ढेङ्की) 257
गणेश - (दैवत्यम्, खण्डम्) 268
गणैला 235
गतक्रमम् (गीतम्) 324
गतारमन्द्रः (प्रथमकामोदा) 124
गतारा (सावरी) 97
गतिः (गद्ये) 269
गति – (स्थायः) 174, 180
गद्य – (चक्रबालः) 277
गद्य—(तालार्णवः) 293
गद्य -- (मङ्गलाचारः) 304
गद्यजः (झोम्बडः) 260
गद्यजा (मातृका) 287
गद्यजा (हयलीला) 274
गद्य-पद्य—(मङ्गलाचारः) 304
गद्य-पद्यजः (झोम्बडः) 260
गद्यम् (आलिसंश्रितप्रबन्धः) 220, 266,

269
गद्यात्मा (कलहंसः) 284
गन्धर्वः (गणेशः, कर्णाटैलायाम्) 249
गन्धर्वः (गान्धर्वप्रयोक्ता) 210
गपदुर्बलः (षाडवः) 66
गपाल्पा (धन्नासी) 86
गर्भसन्धिः (शुद्धसाधारिते) 19
गमकः 171, 174, 177
गमकः (आलप्तौ) 203
गमकः (गायकगुणे) 150
गमकः (रासके) 317
गमकप्रासनिर्मुक्ता (गौडी एला) 251
गमकबहुला (प्रथमगौडी) 134
गमकसंयुता (छेवाटी) 115
गमकाः (प्रथमसैन्धव्याम्) 131
गमकान्विता (कोलाहला) 114
गमकान्विता (प्रथमसौराष्ट्री) 128
गमकालप्तिः (प्रयोगे) 318
गमद्विगुणिता (त्रवणा) 96
गमन्द्रा (प्रथममञ्जरी) 99
गमन्द्रा (वेलावली) 99
गमोत्कटा (प्रथममञ्जरी) 99
गम्भीरः (शब्दः) 158, 159, 160
गवर्जिता (आन्धाली) 117
गहीना (मल्हारी) 118
गांशम् (कर्णाटबङ्गालम्) 106
गांशा (पिञ्जरी) 106
गाढ—(गमकाः) 4
गाढः (शब्दः) 165
गाढः (स्थायः) 174, 182
गाता 155
गाता (चन्द्रशेखरः) 311
गाता (जयन्ते) 310
गाता (रमायाम्) 318
गात्र—(स्थायः) 174, 182
गातृ—(नाम, आर्यायाम्) 279
गातृ—(नाम, करणे) 252
गातृ—(नाम, गद्ये) 270, 279
गाथा (आलिसंश्रितप्रबन्धः) 220, 281
गानभेदः (द्विपथे) 283
गानभेदः (मिश्रकरणे) 254
गानम् (गीतभेद) 209, 210
गान्धर्वम् (गीतभेदः) 209, 210
गान्धर्वः (मार्गदेशी-ज्ञाता) 149
गान्धारगतिका (पूर्वप्रसिद्धभाषाङ्गम्) 15
गान्धारपञ्चमः (ग्रामरागः) 90
गान्धारपञ्चमः (भाषाजनकः) 8, 10
गान्धारपञ्चमः (साधारण-ग्रामरागः, मध्यमग्रामे) 6
गान्धारपञ्चमी (टक्कभाषा) 9
गान्धारबहुलः (द्राविडगौडः) 120
गान्धारवल्ली (भिन्नषड्जभाषा) 10
गान्धारांशग्रहन्यास (आम्रपञ्चमः) 124
गान्धारांशग्रहन्यासः (गान्धारपञ्चमः) 90
गान्धारांशग्रहा (द्राविडी) 139
गान्धाराल्प. (शुद्धकैशिकमध्यमः) 84
गान्धारी (जातिः, गान्धारपञ्चमजनका) 90
गान्धारी (जातिः, मध्यमग्रामरागजनका) 60
गान्धारी (गान्धारपञ्चमभाषा) 10
गान्धारी (भिन्नषड्जभाषा) 10
गान्धारी (सौवीरभाषा) ,
गापन्यासा (छेवाटी) 115
गापन्यासा (बाङ्गाली) 100
गापन्यासा(भोगवर्धनी) 99
गाम्भीरी (पूर्वप्रसिद्धभाषाङ्गम्) 151
गाम्भीर्यम् (शारीरगुणः) 169
गायत्री (देवता, कर्णाटैलायाम्)
गायनः (गुणदोषनिरूपणे) 150, 151, 155
गायनः (ततकुतपे) 205
गायनी 151
गायनी—(वृन्दम्) 204
गायनी (वृन्दे) 203, 204
गाल्पः (सौवीरः) 102
गाल्पा (तुरुष्कतोडी) 110

गारुगि—(तालः, झोम्बडे) 259
गीत—(गतिः, स्थाये) 180
गीत – (गुणाः) 323
गीत—(दुष्टता) 324
गीत—(वहनी) 177
गीतकः (एला-पद-नाम) 227
गीतम् (गीतज्ञनिरूपणे) 151
गीतम् (वाग्गेयकारगुणे) 146
गीतम् (स्थाये) 187
गीतम् (लक्षितम्) 209
गीतिः (आर्या, कन्दे) 273
गीतिः (ग्रामरागाश्रयभूताः; पञ्च) 3, 4
गीर्वाणगणवल्लभा (मातृका) 287
गुणः (गायकस्य) 150
गुणः (गीतस्य) 323
गुणः (वाग्गेयकारस्य) 146
गुणः (वृन्दस्य) 205
गुणः (शब्दस्य) 158, 165
गुणः (शारीरस्य) 169
गुणनाम (बिरुदम्) 216
गुणभेदः (स्थायेषु) 174, 175
गुणान्वित—(रूपकम्) 319
गुणोत्कर्षवर्जित (रूपकम्) 322
गुणोदार—(पदान्तरम्) 322
गुरुः (आर्यायाम्) 280
गुरुः (गद्ये) 269
गुरुः (स्थायः) 175, 190
गुरु—(वर्णः) 231
गुरुञ्जिका (पूर्वप्रसिद्धोपाङ्गम्) 16
गुरुदैवतः (षड्जग्रामरागः) 22
गुरुभङ्गः (आर्यायाम्) 280
गुरुमध्या (त्रेताभेदः) 240
गुर्जर—(पात्रम्) 206
गुर्जरी (अधुनाप्रसिद्ध-रागाङ्गम्) 16, 77
गुर्जरी (चतुर्विधा, अधुनाप्रसिद्धोपाङ्गम्) 16
गुर्जरी (टक्कविभाषा) 9
गुर्जरी (पञ्चमभाषा) 6
गुर्जरी (मालवकैशिकभाषा) 10
गुर्वाज्ञा (आडीकामोदिकायाम्) 101
गृहि—(प्रवेशः, सौवीरे) 102
गेयम् (गायनदोषे) 156
गेयम् (धातुः) 146
गोली (पूर्वप्रसिद्धभाषाङ्गम्) 15
गौडः (अधुनाप्रसिद्धरागाङ्गम्) 16, 80
गौडः (चतुर्विधः, अधुनाप्रसिद्धोपाङ्गम्) 17
गौड – (एला) 248, 257
गौड—(पात्रम्) 206
गौडकृतिः (अधुनाप्रसिद्धक्रियाङ्गम्) 16, 107
गौडकैशिकः (गौडग्रामरागः, मध्यमग्रामे) 6, 37
गौडकैशिकमध्यमः (गौडग्रामरागः, षड्जग्रामे) 6, 32
गौडत्वादि—(जातिः) 181
गौडपञ्चमः (गौडग्रामरागः, षड्जग्रामे) 6, 35
गौडी (गीतिः) 4
गौडी (मालवकैशिकभाषा) 10
गौडी (रीतिः, उत्कलिकायाम्) 265
गौडी (रीतिः, नन्दावर्त्याम्) 237
गौडी (मालवकैशिकभाषा) 134
गौडी (हिन्दोलभाषा) 10, 139
गौरी (आर्याभेदः) 280
गौरी (देवता, एलापदे) 228
गौरी (संगता-भेदः)
ग्रहः (आलापलक्षणे) 19
ग्रहः (उद्ग्राह—नामान्तरम्) 271, 279, 297
ग्रहः (गायकगुणे) 150
ग्रहः (रागलक्षणे) 18-139
ग्रहः (आडिकामोदिकायाम्) 101
ग्रहः (आन्धाल्याम्) 117
ग्रहः (आम्रपञ्चमे) 124
ग्रहः (ककुभे) 95
ग्रहः (कोलाहलायाम्) 114
ग्रहः (गान्धारपञ्चमे) 90

ग्रहः (गुर्जर्याम्) 77
ग्रहः (गौडे) 80
ग्रहः (गौडकृतौ) 107
ग्रह (गौडकैशिके) 37
ग्रहः (गौडकैशिकमध्यमे) 32
ग्रहः (गौडपञ्चमे) 35
ग्रहः (टक्के) 77
ग्रहः (टक्ककैशिके) 137
ग्रहः (तृतीयसैन्धव्याम्) 132
ग्रहः (तोडिकायाम्) 68
ग्रहः (त्रवणायाम्) 94
ग्रहः (त्रावण्याम्) 135
ग्रहः (देशाख्यायाम्) 92
ग्रहः (देश्याम्) 89
ग्रहः (द्राविडगौडे) 120
ग्रहः (द्राविड्याम्) 139
ग्रहः (द्वितीयकामोदे) 124
ग्रहः (द्वितीयगौड्याम्) 134
ग्रहः (द्वितीयललितायाम्) 130
ग्रहः (द्वितीयसैन्धव्याम्) 131
ग्रहः (द्वितीयसौराष्ट्र्याम्) 128
ग्रहः (धन्नास्याम्) 86
ग्रहः (नट्टायाम्) 106
ग्रहः (नर्ते) 54
ग्रहः (प्रथमगौडे) 134
ग्रहः (प्रथममञ्जर्याम्) 99
ग्रहः (प्रथमललितायाम्) 129
ग्रहः (प्रथमसैन्धव्याम्) 131
ग्रहः (प्रथमसौराष्ट्र्याम्) 128
ग्रहः (बङ्गाले) 69
ग्रहः (बङ्गाल्याम्) 100
ग्रहः (बोट्टे) 43
ग्रहः (भम्माणपञ्चमे) 52
ग्रहः (भिन्नकैशिकमध्यमे) 26
ग्रहः (भिन्नकैशिके) 30
ग्रहः (भिन्नताने) 28
ग्रहः (भिन्नपञ्चमे) 72
ग्रहः (भिन्नषड्जे) 69
ग्रहः (भैरव्याम्) 113
ग्रहः (भोगवर्धन्याम्) 9
ग्रहः (मध्यमग्रामरागे) 60
ग्रहः (मध्यमादौ) 62
ग्रहः (मल्हारे) 118
ग्रहः (मल्हार्याम्) 118
ग्रहः (मालवकैशिके) 63
ग्रहः (मालवायाम्) 138
ग्रहः (मेघरागे) 123
ग्रहः (रगन्त्याम्) 97
ग्रह (रामकृतौ) 107
ग्रहः (रूपसाधारे) 48
ग्रह (रेवगुप्ते) 86
ग्रहः (वराट्याम्) 74, 104
ग्रहः (वराट्युपाङ्गेषु) 108
ग्रहः (वल्लातायाम्) 115
ग्रहः (वेसरषाडवे) 40
ग्रहः (शके) 51
ग्रहः (शुद्धकैशिकमध्यमे) 84
ग्रहः (शुद्धकैशिके) 24
ग्रहः (शुद्धपञ्चमे) 116
ग्रहः (शुद्धभैरवे) 123
ग्रहः (शुद्धसाधारिते) 18
ग्रहः (श्रीरागे) 137
ग्रहः (षड्जकैशिके) 57
ग्रहः (षड्जग्रामरागे) 22
ग्रहः (षाडवे) 66
ग्रहः (सोमरागे) 123
ग्रहः (हिन्दोले) 80
ग्रहः (विषम-, एलायाम्) 222
ग्रहः (स्वर-करणे) 252
ग्रहः (स्वरार्थे) 278
ग्रहन्यास (औडुवे) 319
ग्रहमुक्तिका (आर्या) 279
ग्रहांशन्यासगान्धारा (देशाख्या) 92
ग्रहांशन्यासधैवतः (मेघरागः) 123

ग्रहांशन्यासधैवता (आडिकामोदिका) 101
ग्रहांशन्यासधैवता (मालवा) 138
ग्रहांशन्यासपञ्चमा (द्वितीयसैन्धवी) 131
ग्रहांशन्याससप्तमः (द्राविड-गौडः) 120
ग्रहांशपः (बोट्टः) 43
ग्रहांशन्यासषड्जा (द्वितीयगौडी) 134
ग्रहांशसः (गौडकैशिकः) 37
ग्रहांशसा (त्रावणी) 135
ग्राम्यम् (गीतम्) 324
ग्रामरागाः 6, 14, 17
ग्रामरागाः (पञ्चधा) 3, 6
ग्रीष्मः (गौडपञ्चमे) 35
ग्रीष्मः (भिन्नपञ्चमे) 72
ग्रीष्मः (मध्यमग्रामरागे) 60
ग्रीष्मः (शुद्धपञ्चमे) 116

घटः (आलिसंश्रितप्रबन्धः) 220, 286
घटना—(स्थायः) 175, 190
घडसः (कुतपे) 206
घण्टा (कुतपे) 206
घण्टारवः (पूर्वप्रसिद्धरागाङ्गम्) 15
घत्तादि—(च्छन्दः, चच्चर्याम्) 302
घनः (शब्दः) 158-60, 165, 166
घनता (शारीरगुणः) 169
घनत्व—(स्थायः) 175, 190
घनद्रुता (चन्द्रिका) 318
घनयतिः (चन्द्रिका) 318
घनानुप्रासः (चन्द्रिकायाम्) 318
घोषः (स्थायः) 174, 182
घोषवती (कुतपे) 205

चः (मात्रागणः) 234, 244, 302, 305
चक्रवालः (आलिसंश्रितप्रबन्धः) 220, 277
चक्रा (आर्याभेदः) 280
चक्रेश्वरः (झोम्बडभेदः) 260
चच्चत्पुट—(तालः, पञ्चतालेश्वरे) 290
चच्चत्पुटादि—(तालः, आक्षिप्तिकायाम्) 19
चच्चरी (छन्दः, चच्चरीप्रबन्धे) 302
चच्चरी (तालः, चच्चरीप्रबन्धे) 302
चच्चरी (विप्रकीर्णप्रबन्धः) 221, 302
चण्डिका (देवता, एलापदे) 228
चण्डिका (हंसावती-देवता) 237
चण्डिकेश्वरः (झोम्बडभेदः) 260
चतुरा (गायनी) 151
चतुरा (विकृतगणैला) 238, 241
चतुराननः (देवता, भिन्नषड्जे) 69
चतुर्थ—(स्वस्थानम्) 199
चतुर्धातुः (प्रबन्धः) 215, 259
चतुर्मुखः (विप्रकीर्णप्रबन्धः) 221, 297
चतुष्पदी (विप्रकीर्णप्रबन्धः) 221, 295
चन्द्रः (भगणदेवता) 233
चन्द्रप्रियः (शुद्धकैशिकमध्यमः) 84
चन्द्रलेखः (द्विपथकभेदः) 282
चन्द्रलेखा (मात्रैला) 244
चन्द्रशेखरः (ध्रुवभेदः) 310, 311
चन्द्रिका (एकताली-भेदः) 318
चन्द्रिका (द्विपदीभेद) 276
चन्द्रिका (मतङ्गोक्तवर्णैला) 247
चम्पूः (प्रबन्धजाति) 218
चर्या (विप्रकीर्ण-प्रबन्धः) 221, 303
चरणः (धवले) 305
चरणः (मङ्गले) 306
चरणः (राहड्याम्) 304
चरणान्तम् (आर्यायाः) 279
चरणान्त—(प्रासः, पद्धड्याम्) 303
चाचपुट—(तालः, पञ्चतालेश्वरे) 290
चातुरी (वाग्गेयकारगुणे) 146
चामुण्डा (देवता, एलापदे) 228
चारः (अड्डतालभेदः) 316
चारः (ध्रुवभेदः) 310, 311
चालि—(स्थायः) 175, 190
चित्र—(करणम्) 252, 254
चित्रः (झोम्बडभेदः) 260
चित्रम् (गद्यभेदः) 266, 268

चित्रा (कुतपे) 205
चित्रा (विचित्र-मात्रैला) 244
चित्रालंकृति—(ढेङ्की) 257
चित्रिणी (विचित्रमात्रैला) 244
चित्रिता (आलप्तिः) 203
चूतमञ्जरी (हिन्दोलभाषा) 9
चूर्णकम् (गद्यभेदः) 268
चूर्णम् (गद्यभेदः) 266, 267
चेहालः (शब्दः) 165
चोल—(पात्रम्) 206
चोक्षः (स्थायः) 174, 182

छः (मात्रागणः) 234, 244, 276, 302, 305
छन्दः (ओव्याम्) 306
छन्दः (कलहंस-) 284
छन्दः (गीते) 323
छन्दः (घत्तादि-) 302
छन्दः (चच्चरी) 302
छन्दः (झम्पट-) 299
छन्दः (तोटक-) 285
छन्दः (दण्डक-) 299
छन्दः (द्विपथ-) 282
छन्दः (प्रबन्धे) 219, 274
छन्दः (वाग्गेयकारगुणे) 146
छन्दश्चितिः 287
छन्दस्वती (कर्णाटैला) 249
छन्दस्वती (देशैला) 251
छन्दोगणः (औडुवे) 319
छन्दोलक्षणम् (आर्यायाः) 280
छन्दोलक्ष्म 296, 299, 302
छन्दोहीन—(गद्यम्) 266
छन्दोहीना (गजलीला) 275
छबिमान् (शब्दः) 165, 166
छवि—(स्थायः) 174, 181
छान्दस—(स्थायः) 175, 190
छाया—(आर्याभेदः) 280
छाया—(पूर्वप्रसिद्धभाषाङ्गम्) 15
छाया—(स्थायः) 174, 177, 178
छायातोडी (अधुनाप्रसिद्धोपाङ्गम्) 16, 110
छायानट्टा (अधुनाप्रसिद्धोपाङ्गम्) 17, 113
छायामात्रा (याष्टिकोक्तभाषा-भेदः) 12
छायालग—(रागः) 156
छायालग (प्रबन्धः) 150
छायालग—(सूडः, एलादिः) 308
छायालगत्वम् (एलादेः) 308
छायावेलावली (अधुनाप्रसिद्धोपाङ्गम्) 16, 112
छेवाटी (टक्क भाषा) 9, 115
छेवाटी (हिन्दोलभाषा) 10

ज (वर्णगणः) 232, 237, 276
जक्का (चालिः, स्थायः) 190
जगणः (मण्ठतालः) 313
जनमनोहरम् (गीतम्) 323
जनमनोहरा (ओवी) 306
जनरञ्जनम् (गानम्) 210
जयघण्टा (कुतपे) 206
जयन्तः (कन्दभेदः) 274
जयन्तः (ध्रुवभेदः) 310
जयप्रियः (मण्ठभेदः, मण्ठतालभेदश्च) 313
जयमङ्गलः (ध्रुवभेदः) 310, 311
जयमङ्गला (त्रेता-भेदः) 240
जया (कुतपे) 205
जया (चतुराभेदः) 241
जया (देवता, एलापदे) 228
जयोत्साहप्रदः (जयमङ्गलः) 311
जलम् (यगणदेवता) 233
जातिः (गौडत्वादि-) 181
जातिः (गौडपञ्चमजनका) 35
जातिः (प्रबन्धः-) 218
जातिः (मालवकैशिकजनका) 63
जातिः (मालवपञ्चमजनका) 46
जातिः (वेसरषाडव—जनका) 40

जातिः (षड्कैशिकजनका) 57
जातिमती (अङ्कचारिणी) 272
जात्यादि—(शुद्ध-प्रकरणम्) 308
जीवः (टादिदेवता) 233
जीवस्वर—(व्याप्तिः, आलप्तौ) 199
ज्येष्ठा (कुतपे) 205
ज्योतिष्मती (मात्रैला) 244
ज्योत्स्ना (आर्याभेदः) 280

झम्पट - (च्छन्दः) 299
झम्पटः (विप्रकीर्ण-प्रबन्धः) 221, 299
झम्पस्तालः-(कामले) 311
झम्पादि—(तालः, कलहंसे) 284
झल्लरी (कुतपे) 206
झोम्बकः (गायनः) 155
झोम्बडः (सूडप्रबन्धः) 220, 259. 260, 262, 264

टक्कः (कोलाहला—जनकः) 114
टक्कः (भाषाजनकः) 8, 9
टक्कः (ललिताजनकः) 129
टक्कः (वेगरञ्जी —जनकः) 101
टक्कः (वेसर—ग्रामरागः, षड्जग्रामे) 6, 77, 80
टक्कः (सौराष्ट्री—जनकः) 128
टक्क—(रागः, नादावत्याम्) 236
टक्ककैशिकः (भाषाजनकः) 8, 9
टक्ककैशिकः (वेसर-ग्रामरागः, उभयग्रामिकः) 6, 137
टक्कसैन्धवः (उपरागः) 8

डक्का (कुतपे) 205
डक्कुली (कुतपे) 205
डमरू (कुतपे) 206
डोम्बक्री(अधुनाप्रसिद्ध—भाषाङ्गम्) 16, 95

ढक्का (कुतपे) 206
ढवसः (कुतपे) 206
ढाल—(स्थायः) 174, 177
ढेङ्किका—(तालः, ढेङ्कीप्रबन्ध) 256
ढेङ्की (सूडप्रबन्धः) 220, 256, 257, 279
ढोल्लरी—(पदम्, ढोल्लर्याम्) 307
ढोल्लरी (विप्रकीर्ण-प्रबन्धः) 35, 221, 307

तः (मात्रागणः) 234, 244, 276, 302, 305
तः (वर्णगणः) 232, 237
तत्—(ब्रह्मन्) 216
तत (कुतपः) 205
तत—(वाद्यम्, कुतपे) 205
तनुमध्या (त्रेता-भेदः) 240
तपस्वि—(प्रवेशः, सौवीरे) 102
तपस् (सुशारीरलाभे) 169
तमः (शादि-वर्ग-देवता) 233
तरङ्गिणी (पूर्वप्रसिद्धभाषाङ्गम्) 15
तरङ्गित – (स्थायः) 174, 187
तरला (वर्णैला) 246
ताडितः (मन्द्र-, तुरुष्कगौडः) 120
ताडिता (गुर्जरी) 77
ताडिता (तुरुष्कतोडी) 110
ताडिता (दक्षिणगुर्जरी) 111
ताडिता (मल्हारी) 118
ताडिता (महाराष्ट्रगुर्जरी) 111
ताण्डवम् (कुतपे) 206
तानः (भाषाजनकः) 8, 10
तानः (भिन्नग्रामरागः, मध्यमग्रामे) 6
तानवलिता (टक्कभाषा) 9
ताना (टक्कभाषा) 9
तानोद्भवा (तान-भाषा) 10
तानोद्भवा (पञ्चमभाषा) 9
तारः (आलापलक्षणे) 19
तारः (प्रतिमण्ठभेदः) 314, 315
तार—(समनिपाः, भम्माण्याम्) 136
तारगान्धारधैवता (प्रथमललिता) 129

तारगान्धारपञ्चमा (नट्टा) 106
तारगान्धारा (आडिकामोदिका) 101
तारज—(झोम्बडः) 259
तारधा (आन्धाली) 117
तारधा (वेलावली) 99
तारधैवता (नट्टा) 106
तारधैवता (वराटी) 74
तारपा (द्वितीयसैन्धवी) 131
तारमध्यमः (ग्रहः, षाडवे) 66
तारमध्यमः (श्रीरागे) 121
तारमध्यस्थ—(पञ्चमः, द्वितीयबङ्गाले) 122
तारमध्यस्थ—(मध्यमः, सोमरागे) 123
तारमन्द्रः (आषड्जगान्धारम्, शुद्धभैरवे) 123
तारमन्द्र—(रिगमाः, ललितायाम्) 130
तारमन्द्रगा (भोगवर्धनी) 99
तारमन्द्रगान्धारा (भैरवी) 113
तारमन्द्रषड्जः (मालवश्रियाम्) 65
तारमन्द्रषड्जा (द्वितीयगौडी) 134
तारमपा (हर्षपुरी) 136
तारषड्जग्रहः (प्रथमकामोद्याम्) 124
तारषड्जग्रहांशः (शुद्धकैशिकः) 24
तारषड्जग्रहांशः (शुद्धसाधारितः) 18
तारसधा (वराटी) 104
तारसप्तमः (मल्हारः) 118
तारसांशग्रहः (शुद्धकैशिकमध्यमे) 84
तारस्वराः (कोलाहले) 80
ताराः (निपमधैवताः, दाक्षिणात्यायाम्) 117
तारा (द्विपदी) 276
तारा (सगधैः, प्रथमसौराष्ट्री) 128
तारानुध्वनिः (शारीरगुणः) 169
तारावली (प्रबन्धजातिः) 218
तालः (आक्षिप्तिकायाम्) 19
तालः (गायकगुणे) 150
तालः (गायकदोषे) 155
तालः (प्रबन्धाङ्गम्) 215, 216, 219, 222, 246, 252, 256, 258, 259, 263, 265, 270, 272-76, 279, 282, 287, 290, 293, 301, 303, 310, 311, 313-19
तालः (रूपकस्थः) 201
तालः (रूपके) 319, 322
तालः (वाग्गेयकारगुणे) 146
तालधरः (कुतपे) 205
ताल-राग-त्रयम् (त्रिभङ्गी) 300
ताल-लीनानुवर्तनम् (वृन्दगुणः) 205
तालार्णवः (आलिसंश्रितप्रबन्धः) 220, 293
तिरिपः (गमकः) 171
तिरिपः (गमकः, द्राविडगौडे) 120
तिलकः (उपरागः) 8
तिलकः (द्विपदी-भेदः) 282, 283
तिलकः (ध्रुवभेदः) 310, 311
तीक्ष्णः (स्थायः) 174, 178
तुम्बकी (कुतपे) 206
तुम्बकी (गायनः) 155
तुम्बुरा (भिन्नषड्जभाषा) 10
तुरगलीला (आलिसंश्रित-प्रबन्धः) 220, 274
तुरुष्कगौडः (उपाङ्गम्) 120
तुरुष्कतोडी (अधुनाप्रसिद्धोपाङ्गम्) 16, 110
तुर्यप्रहरः (हिन्दोले) 81
तुर्ययामः (अह्नः, टक्ककैशिके) 137
तुल्याखिल—(स्वरः, प्रथमबङ्गालः) 122
तृतीय—(स्वस्थानम्) 199
तेन—(करणम्) 252, 254
तेन—(शब्दः) 216
तेन(कः) (प्रबन्धाङ्गम्) 215, 216, 252, 254, 255, 266, 286, 294-98, 300
तोटक—(च्छन्दः) 285
तोटकम् (आलिसंश्रितप्रबन्धः) 220
तोडिका (तोडी) (अधुनाप्रसिद्धरागाङ्गम्) 16, 68
तोडी (द्विप्रकारा, अधुनाप्रसिद्धोपाङ्गम्) 16
तौरुष्क – (गौडः, अधुनाप्रसिद्धोपाङ्गम्) 17
तौर्यत्रितयं (वाग्गेयकारगुणे) 146

त्यक्तपञ्चमा (खम्भाइतिः) 112
त्यक्तरक्तिता (शारीरदोषः) 169
त्यक्तरिः (भम्माणी) 136
त्याग — (वर्णनम् एलायाम्) 222
त्रवणा (टक्कभाषा) 9, 94
त्रवणा (भिन्नषड्जभाषा) 10
त्रवणोद्भवा (टक्कभाषा) 9
त्रावणी (पञ्चमभाषा) 9, 135
त्रिधातुः (झोम्बडः) 259
त्रिधातुः (प्रबन्धः) 215
त्रिनेत्रक्रीः (पूर्वप्रसिद्धक्रियाङ्गम्) 15
त्रिपथः (विप्रकीर्णप्रबन्धः) 221, 297
त्रिपदी (गाथा) 281
त्रिपदी (विप्रकीर्ण-प्रबन्धः) 221, 294, 295
त्रिपद्यादि - (प्रबन्धाः) 296
त्रिपुट - (तालः, झोम्बडे) 25
त्रिभङ्गि—(तालः, त्रिभङ्गौ) 299
त्रिभङ्गिः (विप्रकीर्ण-प्रबन्धः) 221, 299
त्रिभङ्गि—(वृत्तम्, त्रिभङ्गौ) 299
त्रिभिन्नः (गमकः) 171
त्रिमिश्र—(भेदाः, शब्दस्य) 160
त्रिवली (कुतपे) 206
त्रिस्थान—(गमकाः) 4
त्रिस्थानः (शब्दः) 158-60, 165
त्रिस्थान-व्याप्ति - (शक्तिता, वृन्दगुणः) 205
त्रिस्थानोत्थ (गीतम्) 323
त्रेता (विकृतगणैला) 238, 240
त्रोटित—(स्थायः) 174, 187
त्रोटितप्रतीष्टः (स्थायः) 178,187

दः (मात्रागणः) 234, 244, 302, 305
दण्डक — (च्छन्दः) 299
दण्डकः (विप्रकीर्णप्रबन्धः) 221, 299
दन्ती—(पदम्, दन्त्याम्) 307
दन्ती (विप्रकीर्णप्रबन्धः) 221, 307
दर्दुरः (कुतपे) 205
दक्षिणा (गुर्जरी, अधुनाप्रसिद्धोपाङ्गम्) 16, 111
दक्षिणास्यम् (ब्रह्मणः) 248
दलम् (आर्यायाः) 274
दाक्षिणात्या (पञ्चमभाषा) 9, 117
दाक्षिणात्या (भिन्नषड्जभाषा) 10
दानवीर—(रसः, भिन्नकैशिकमध्यमे) 26
दानवीर—(रसः, भिन्नकैशिके) 30
दिनम् (भिन्नकैशिकमध्यमे) 26
दिनम् (मालवकैशिके) 63
दिनम् (वेसरषाडवे) 41
दिव्यमानुषी (मातृका) 287
दिव्या (मातृका) 287
दीपकः (पूर्वप्रसिद्धरागाङ्गम्) 15
दीपनी (प्रबन्धजातिः) 218
दीप्तः (प्राणः, एलायाम्) 228
दीप्तप्रसन्नः (स्थायः) 175, 190
दीर्घः (स्थाय) 175, 190
दीर्घकम्पितः (स्थायः) 174, 187
दीर्घरिमा (बाङ्गाली) 100
दीर्घा (आर्याभेदः) 280
दुर्गाशक्तिः (आचार्यः) 54
दुर्बल—(स्वरौ, षाडवे) 66
दुष्कराभासः (स्थायः) 175, 190, 194
दुष्टः (शब्दः) 168
दुष्टता (गीत-) 324
दूषणम् (शारीरस्य) 169
देवक्कृतिः (क्रियाङ्गम्) 108
देवक्रीः (अधुना-प्रसिद्धक्रियाङ्गम्) 16
देवता—(स्तुतिः, वरदे) 317
देवता (अकचटतपयशेषु) 233
देवता (एलायाम्) 227
देवता (एलापदेषु) 228
देवता (कर्णाटैलायाम्) 248, 249
देवता (खण्डे) 267
देवता (पञ्चतालेश्वरे) 292
देवता (भद्रावत्याम्) 238

देवता (वर्णगणेषु) 233
देवत्रयस्तुतिः (त्रिभङ्गौ) 300
देवारवर्धनी (टक्कविभाषा) 9
देवारवर्धनी (भिन्नषड्जविभाषा) 10
देवारवर्धनी (मालवकैशिकविभाषा) 10
देवालः (पूर्वप्रसिद्धोपाङ्गम्) 16
देश—(एला) 231, 248
देशकाकुः (स्थाये) 177
देशजा (याष्टिकमते भाषाभेदः) 12
देशभाषा (ओव्याम्) 306
देशवाल—(गौडः, अधुनाप्रसिद्धोपाङ्गम्) 17, 120
देशस्थितिः (वाग्गेयकारगुणे) 146
देशस्वभावः (स्थाये) 177
देशाख्य—(रागः) 8
देशाख्य—(रागः, स्थाये) 181
देशाख्या (भाषा) 12
देशाख्या (अधुनाप्रसिद्ध-रागाङ्गम्) 16, 92
देशी (अधुनाप्रसिद्धरागाङ्गम्) 16, 89
देशी (प्रकीर्णके) 145, 149
देशीतालाः (मातृकायाम्) 287
देशीरागाः 14, 17
देशीरागाः (वाग्गेयकारगुणे) 146
देशीरागादिः (गाने) 210
देशीहिन्दोलः (वसन्तपर्यायसंज्ञा) 83
देहधारणम् (धातोः) 213
देहस्था (वहनी) 177
दैन्यम् (डोम्बकृतौ) 95
दोधकः (वस्तुप्रबन्धे) 296
दोषः (गायने) 150, 151
दोषहीन-(रूपकम्) 319
दोहः (द्विपथकनामान्तरम्) 282
दोहदः (दोधकनामान्तरम्) 307
दोह्या (टक्कभाषा) 9
द्राविड—(एला) 248
द्राविड—(गुर्जरी, अधुनाप्रसिद्धोपाङ्गम्) 16, 111
द्राविड—(गौडः, अधुनाप्रसिद्धोपाङ्गम्) 17, 120
द्राविड—(वराटी, अधुनाप्रसिद्धोपाङ्गम्) 16, 109
द्राविडी (टक्ककैशिकविभाषा) 9
द्राविडी (मालवा-विभाषा) 139
द्रुत - (पदम्, एलायाम्) 222
द्रुत—(लयः, स्वरकरणे) 252
द्रुत—(स्थायः) 174, 181
द्रुतः (गमकवेगमानम्) 171
द्रुततर—(स्वराः) 4
द्रुतमध्यम् (गीते) 323
द्रुतमध्या (गतिः, गद्ये) 269
द्रुतविलम्बा (गतिः, गद्ये) 269
द्रुता (गतिः, गद्ये) 269
द्व्यर्धः (स्वरः) 198
द्वन्द्वज —(भेदाः, शब्दस्य) 160
द्विखण्डः (उद्ग्राहः) 317
द्विगुणः (स्वरः) 199
द्विग्रामः (ग्रामरागः) 6
द्वितीय—(तालः, एलायाम्) 222, 247
द्वितीय—(तालः, चर्यायाम्) 303
द्वितीय—(तालः, झोम्बडे) 259
द्वितीय—(तालः, विजये) 311
द्वितीय --(तालः हंसावत्याम्) 237
द्वितीय—(स्वस्थानम्) 198
द्वितीयकामोदः (प्रसिद्धदेशीरागः) 124
द्वितीयसौराष्ट्री (भाषा) 128
द्विदल—(उद्ग्राहः) 318
द्विधातुः (प्रबन्धः) 215
द्विपथ—(च्छन्दः) 282
द्विपथकः (आलिसंश्रितप्रबन्धः) 220, 282, 283
द्विपदी (आलिसंश्रितप्रबन्धः) 220, 275, 276
द्विपदी (घटे) 286
द्वेषः (वाग्गेयकारगुणे) 146

द्व्यर्धः (स्वरः) 198

धग्रहः (गौडकैशिकमध्यमः) 35
धग्रहा (देवकृतिः) 108
धग्रहांशः (भिन्नपञ्चमः) 72
धग्रहांशा (त्रावणी) 135
धनदः (कन्दभेदः) 274
धनञ्जयः (आचार्यः) 244
धनिपाधिका (वराटी) 104
धन्नासी, धन्नासिका (रागाङ्गम्) 86
धन्यकृतिः, धन्यश्रीः (पूर्वप्रसिद्धक्रियाङ्गम्) 15
धन्यासांशग्रहः (मल्हारः) 118
धन्यासांशग्रहा (बाङ्गाली) 100
धन्यासांशग्रहा (भुञ्छी) 112
धन्यासांशग्रहा (रगन्ती) 97
धन्यासांशग्रहा (वराटी) 104
धन्यासी (अधुनाप्रसिद्धरागाङ्गम्) 16
धपत्यक्तः (नागध्वनिः) 102
धपर्वजिता (वेगरञ्जी) 101
ध-भूयसी (छेवाटी) 115
ध-मन्द्रभाक् (ललिता) 130
ध-मन्द्रा (चतुर्थसैन्धवी) 132
ध-मन्द्रा(प्रथमवराटी) 109
ध-मन्द्रा(बाङ्गाली) 100
ध-मन्द्रा(हतस्वर-वराटी) 109
धरि-तारा (प्रथममञ्जरी) 99
धरि-वर्जिता (प्रथमगौडी) 134
धर्मः (कन्दभेदः) 274
धर्मकामार्थसिद्धिदा (एला) 228
धवर्जिता (हर्षपुरी) 136
धवलः (विप्रकीर्णप्रबन्धः) 222, 305
धवलादि—(पदम्, धवले) 305
धांशः (गौडपञ्चमः) 35
धांशः (प्रथमकामोदः) 124
धांशः (भैरव) 69
धांशग्रहः (भिन्नषड्जः) 69
धांशग्रहन्यासा (त्रवणा) 94
धांशन्यासग्रहा (भैरवी) 112
धांशा (वराटी) 74
धातुः (गेयम्) 146, 166
धातुः (देहे) 213
धातुः (निबद्धे, प्रबन्धे) 211, 213, 222
धातुः (रूपके) 319, 322
धातुः (वाग्गेयकारगुणे) 146, 147
धातुविलक्षण—(रूपकम्) 322
धाद्यन्तांशा (वेलावली) 99
धान्ता (डोम्बकृतिः) 95
धान्ता (द्राविडी) 139
धान्ता (सावरी) 97
धापन्यासा (आन्धाली) 117
धारणा (गायने) 150
धृतिः (द्विपदीभेदः) 276
धृतिः (शब्दस्य) 190
धैर्य—(वर्णनम्, एलायाम्) 222
धैवतभूषिता (भिन्नपञ्चम-भाषा) 9
धैवतांशग्रहन्यासः (टक्ककैशिकः) 137
धैवतांशग्रहन्यासः (शुद्धभैरवः) 123
धैवतांशग्रहन्यासा (भोगवर्धनी) 99
धैवतादि—(मूर्छना, ककुभे) 95
धैवतादि—(मूर्छना, गौडपञ्चमे) 35
धैवती (जातिः, ककुभजनका) 95
धैवती (जातिः, गौडपञ्चमजनका) 35
धैवती (जातिः, टक्कजनका) 77
धैवती (जातिः, टक्ककैशिकजनका) 137
धैवती (जातिः, नर्तजनका) 54
धैवती (जातिः, मेघरागजनका) 123
धैवती (जातिः, शकजनका) 51
धैवत्यार्षभिकावर्ज—(जातयः, हिन्दोलजनका 80
ध्रुवः (प्रबन्धे) 213, 222, 251, 252, 255, 256, 258, 259, 262, 263, 265, 271, 279, 303, 310, 313
ध्रुवः (सालगसूडः) 308, 309-11
ध्रुवः (देवता, मध्यमग्रामरागे) 60

ध्रुवकः (स्थाये) 190
ध्रुवत्वम् (ध्रुवस्य) 213
ध्रुवपदम् (रासके) 317
ध्रुवादिः (सालगसूडः) 308
ध्वनिः (कण्ठजः) 151, 158, 166, 168, 169
ध्वनिः (रागः) 8
ध्वनिः (स्थाये) 182
ध्वनि—(स्थायः) 174, 181
ध्वनि—कुट्टनी (आलिसंश्रितप्रबन्धः) 220, 279

नः (वर्णगणः) 232, 236, 313
नकुलोष्ठी (कुतपे) 205
नटनम् (उद्भट-, टक्ककैशिके) 137
नट्ट—(रागः) 8
नट्टनारायणः (रागः) 8
नट्टा (अधुनाप्रसिद्धभाषाङ्गम्) 16, 106, 113
नट्टा (रागः, स्थाये) 181
नन्दः (रासकभेदः) 317
नन्दनः (ध्रुवभेदः) 310, 311
नन्दावती (कर्णाटैला) 249
नन्दावती (गणैला) 242, 244
नन्दावती (शुद्धा गणैला) 235, 237
नन्दिनी (विचित्र-मात्रैला) 244
नन्दिनी (संगता-भेदः) 239
नन्दीशः (झोम्बड-भेदः) 260
नन्द्यावर्तः (रागकदम्बः) 288
नभस्वती (मात्रैला) 244
नयः (कन्दभेदः) 274
नरसिंहः (झोम्बड-भेदः) 260
नर्तः (साधारणग्रामरागः, मध्यमग्रामे) 6, 54
नलिनी (वर्णैला) 246
नव—(तालः, रूपके) 321
नव—(रागः, रूपके) 321
नव—(स्वस्थानम्) 321
नव—(रागः) 319
नव—(रूपकम्) 319
नव—(लयः) 319
नवता (मातोः) 319
नवता (रचनायाः) 319
नागकृतिः (नागक्री, पूर्वप्रसिद्धक्रियाङ्गम्) 15
नागगान्धारः (उपरागः) 8
नागध्वनिः (अधुनाप्रसिद्धभाषाङ्गम्) 16, 102
नागपञ्चमः (उपरागः) 8
नागरा (वासवीभेदः) 239
नाट्य—(कुतपः) 205, 206
नाद—(स्थायः) 174, 180
नादमुक्तिका (षट्पदी) 296
नादान्तरी (पूर्वप्रसिद्धभाषाङ्गम्) 15
नादावती (कर्णाटैला) 248
नादावती (गणैला) 242
नादावती (शुद्धगणैला) 235, 236
नाद्या (वेसरषाडवभाषा) 10
नानारीतिविचित्रा (वैदर्भी) 268
नामितः (गमकः) 171, 172
नाराटः (शब्दः) 158, 160
नाराटखाहुलः (मिश्रशब्दः) 159
नाराटबोम्बकः (मिश्रशब्दः) 159
निःशङ्कः (अड्डतालः) 316
निःशङ्क (ग्रन्थकारः) 1, 32, 160, 301
निःसरणः (स्थायः) 174, 187
निःसारः (शब्दः) 158-60, 168
निःसारता (शब्दस्य) 159
निःसारता (शारीरदोषः) 169
निःसारु(कः) (सालगसूडः) 308, 315, 316
निःसारुक—(तालः, चारे) 311
निःसारुक—(तालः, झोम्बडे) 259
निःसारुक—(तालः, निःसारौ) 315
निःसारुक—(तालः, मङ्गलाचारे) 304
निःसारुक—(तालः, शेखरे) 310
निःसाणः (कुतपे) 206

निष्कृति—(स्थायः) 174, 181
निगतारः (आम्रपञ्चमे) 124
निगनिर्मुक्तः (तृतीयसैन्धवी) 132
निगाल्पः (शुद्धसाधारितः) 18
निजच्छाया (रागस्य) 177
निजादन्य—(धातुः, रूपके) 322
नितारा (सैन्धवी) 131
निधनम् (रगणफलम्) 233
निधभूयसी (तुरुष्कतोड़ी) 110
निन्यासग्रहांशः (गौडः) 80
निपोज्झिता (त्रावणी) 135
निबद्ध—(गानम्) 211
निबद्ध—(मातृका) 287
निभूरिः (कौन्तली वराटी) 108
निमन्द्रा (देवक्कृतिः) 108
निमन्द्रा (देशाख्या) 92
निमन्द्रा (वेगरञ्जी) 101
निराधारः (स्थायः) 175, 190
निर्जवन—(स्थायः) 1 0, 174, 182
निर्धनता (तगणफलम्) 233
निर्मलः (ध्रुवभेदः) 310, 311
निर्युक्त—(प्रबन्धः) 219
निर्वहण—(सन्धिः, रूपसाधारे) 51
निर्वहण—(सन्धिः, शुद्धकैशिकमध्यमे) 84
निर्वहण—(सन्धिः, शुद्धकैशिके) 24
निर्वाजिता (पिञ्जरी) 106
निषादांशग्रहन्यासः (तुरुष्कगौड़ः) 120
निषादिनी (भिन्नषड्जभाषा) 10
नीचोच्चम् (गीते) 323
नीतिः (प्रबन्धजातिः) 218
नीरसः (गायनः) 155
नीलोत्पली (पूर्वप्रसिद्धभाषाङ्गम्) 15
नूतन—(रूपकम्) 319
नूत्न—(धातुः, वाग्गेयकारगुणे) 146
नेता (जयन्ते) 310
नेता (विजये) 311
नेतृनाम (करणसूडे) 252
नेतृनाम (पञ्चतालेश्वरे) 290
नेत्रम् (प्रबन्धपुरुषस्य तेन-पदे) 215
नैषादिनी (जातिः, रूप-साधारजनका) 48
न्यस्या (आन्धाली) 117
न्यसनम् (स्वराङ्के) 301
न्यस्तस्वरः (तोटकः) 285
न्यासः (आलाप-लक्षणे) 19

प्रबन्धनामसहितोल्लेखाः

न्यासः (कलहंसे) 284
न्यासः (चतुर्मुखे) 297
न्यासः (चतुष्पद्याम्) 295
न्यासः (ध्रुवप्रबन्धे) 310
न्यासः (पञ्चतालेश्वरे) 290
न्यासः (मण्ठे) 313
न्यासः (वस्तुप्रबन्धे) 296
न्यासः (विजये) 297
न्यासः (स्वरकरणे) 252
न्यासः (स्वरार्थे) 278
न्यासः (रागलक्षणे) 18-139

रागनामसहितोल्लेखाः

न्यासः (आम्रपञ्चमे) 124
न्यासः (आडिकामोदिकायाम्) 101
न्यासः (आन्धाल्याम्) 117
न्यासः (कर्णाटगौडे) 120
न्यासः (गान्धारपञ्चमे) 90
न्यासः (गौडकृतौ) 107
न्यासः (गौडे) 80
न्यासः (गौडकैशिकमध्यमे) 32
न्यासः (टक्ककैशिके) 137
न्यासः (टक्के) 77
न्यासः (तृतीयसैन्धव्याम्) 132
न्यासः (तोडिकायाम्) 68
न्यासः (त्रवणायाम्) 94
न्यास : (देशाख्यायाम्) 92

न्यासः (देश्याम्) 89
न्यासः (द्राविडगौडे) 120
न्यासः (द्वितीयकामोदायाम्) 124
न्यासः (द्वितीयगौड्याम्) 134
न्यासः (द्वितीयललितायाम्) 130
न्यासः (द्वितीयसैन्धव्याम्) 131
न्यासः (धन्नास्याम्) 86
न्यासः (नट्टायाम्) 106
न्यासः (नर्ते) 54
न्यासः (प्रथमगौडे) 134
न्यासः (प्रथममञ्जर्याम) 99
न्यासः (प्रथमललितायाम्) 129
न्यासः (प्रथमसैन्धव्याम्) 131
न्यासः (बङ्गाले) 69
न्यासः (बाङ्गाल्याम्) 100
न्यासः (भम्माणपञ्चमे) 52
न्यासः (भिन्नकैशिकमध्यमे) 26
न्यासः (भैरव्याम्) 113
न्यासः (भोगवर्धन्याम्) 99
न्यासः (मध्यमग्रामरागे) 60
न्यासः (मध्यमादौ) 62
न्यासः (मल्हारे) 118
न्यासः (मल्हार्याम्) 118
न्यासः (मालवकैशिके) 63
न्यासः (मालवायाम्) 138
न्यासः (मालवश्रियाम्) 65
न्यासः (मेघरागे) 123
न्यासः (रगन्त्याम्) 97
न्यासः (रामकृतौ) 107
न्यासः (रूपसाधारे) 48
न्यासः (वराट्याम्) 74, 104
न्यासः (वराट्युपाङ्गेषु) 107
न्यासः (वल्लातायाम्) 115
न्यासः (वेसरषाडवे) 40
न्यासः (शके) 51
न्यासः (शुद्धपञ्चमे) 116
न्यासः (शुद्धभैरवे) 123
न्यासः (शुद्धसाधारिते) 18
न्यासः (श्रीरागे) 121
न्यासः (षड्जकैशिके) 57
न्यासः (षड्जग्रामरागे) 22
न्यासः (षाडवे) 66
न्यासः (हिन्दोले) 80
न्यासमध्यमा (धन्नासी) 86
न्यासांशग्रहधैवता (चतुर्थसैन्धवी) 132

पः (मात्रागणः) 234, 244, 276, 302, 305
पञ्चचरणा (गाथा) 281
पञ्चतालेश्वरः (आलिसंश्रितप्रबन्धः) 220, 290
पञ्चभङ्गिः (विप्रकीर्णप्रबन्धः) 221, 294
पञ्चमः (त्रावणीजनकः) 135
पञ्चमः (भाषाजनकः) 8, 9
पञ्चमः (शुद्धग्रामरागः, मध्यमग्रामे) 6
पञ्चमः (सैन्धवीजनकः) 131
पञ्चमः (सौराष्ट्रीजनकः) 128
पञ्चमलक्षिता (टक्कभाषा) 9
पञ्चमवर्जिता (देशी) 89
पञ्चमषाडवः (भाषाजनकः) 8, 10
पञ्चमषाडवः (उपरागः) 8
पञ्चमांशग्रहः (भिन्नतानः) 28
पञ्चमांशग्रहन्यासः (शुद्धपञ्चमः) 116
पञ्चमांशग्रहन्यासा (आन्धाली) 11
पञ्चमांशग्रहन्यासा (प्रथममञ्जरी) 99
पञ्चमांशग्रहन्यासा (मल्हारी) 118
पञ्चमादि—(मूर्छना, नर्ते) 54
पञ्चमादि—(मूर्छना, बोट्टे) 43
पञ्चमान्तः (ककुभः) 95
पञ्चमान्तः (गौडकैशिकः) 37
पञ्चमान्तः (भिन्नपञ्चमः) 72
पञ्चमान्तः (मध्यमषाडवः) 122
पञ्चमान्तः (शुद्धकैशिकः) 24
पञ्चमी (जातिः, ककुभजनका) 95

पञ्चमी (जातिः, नर्तजनका) 54
पञ्चमी (जातिः, बोट्टजनका) 43
पञ्चमी (जातिः, भिन्नतानजनका) 60
पञ्चमी (जातिः, मध्यमग्रामरागजनका) 60
पञ्चमी (जातिः, मालवपञ्चमजनका) 46
पञ्चमी (जातिः, शुद्धपञ्चमजनका) 116
पञ्चमी (जातिः, भिन्नपञ्चमजनका) 71
पञ्चमी (टक्कभाषा) 9
पञ्चमोज्झितः (गौडः) 80
पञ्चमोज्झितः (गौडपञ्चमः) 35
पञ्चमोज्झिता (महाराष्ट्रगुर्जरी) 111
पञ्चमोज्झिता (सावरी) 97
पञ्चाननः (विप्रकीर्णप्रबन्धः) 221, 294
पटः (कुतपे) 206
पटहः (कुतपे) 206
पटह—(पाटाः, पञ्चतालेश्वरे) 290
पट्टवाद्यम् (कुतपे) 205, 206
पणवः (कुतपे)205
पत्रिणी (देवता, एलापदे) 228
पथिभ्रष्टः (भम्माणपञ्चमविनियोगे) 52
पद—(करणम्) 252, 254
पदम् (आक्षिप्तिकायाम्) 19
पदम् (गीते) 323
पदम् (प्रबन्धाङ्गम्)215, 216, 252, 254, 266, 270, 273, 274, 277, 284, 287, 290, 293, 297-302, 304-7
पदानि (षोडश, एलायाम्) 227, 228
पदान्तर—(रूपकम्) 320, 322
पदान्तरम् (वाग्गेयकारगुणे) 146
पद्धडी (छन्दः, चर्यायाम्, पद्धड्याम्) 303
पद्धडी (विप्रकीर्ण-प्रबन्धः) 221, 303
पद्मालया (देवता, एलापदे) 288
पद्मिनी (मतङ्गोक्ता वर्णैला) 247
पद्य—(चक्रवालः) 277
पद्य—(तालार्णवः) 293
पद्य—(मङ्गलाचारः) 304
पद्यजः (झोम्बडः) 260
पद्यजा (मातृका) 287
पद्यजा (हयलीला) 274
पद्यभागः (वृत्तगन्धौ) 268
पन्यासांशग्रहा (कैशिकी) 127
पमन्द्रा (गौडकृतिः) 107
परचित्त—(परिज्ञानम्, वाग्गेयकारगुणे)146
परिवर्तनम् (रागतालयोः, रूपके) 321
परिवादिनी (कुतपे) 205
परिवृत्त—(रूपकम्) 320, 321
परुषः (शब्दः) 158
पल्लवाख्य—(पदत्रयम्, एलायाम्) 222
पल्लवी (अनुक्तजनका विभाषा) 10
पवनः (कन्दभेदः) 274
पवन—(गणः, सगणः) 242
प-र्वजितम् (कर्णाटबङ्गालम्) 106
प-र्वजिता (कोलाहला) 114
प-र्वजिता (रामकृतिः) 114
पश्चिम-यामः (मालवपञ्चमे) 46
पश्चिम-प्रहरः (अह्नः, टक्के) 77
पश्चिम-प्रहरः (वेसरषाडवे) 41
पश्चिम-प्रहरः (सौवीरे) 102
पश्चिम-वदनम् (ब्रह्मणः) 249
प-हीना (द्वितीयसौराष्ट्री) 128
पाञ्चाल—(रीतिः, नादावत्याम्) 236
पाञ्चाल—(रीतिः, वृत्तगन्धौ) 268
पाञ्चाल (रीतिः, ललिते) 267
पाञ्चाली (पूर्वप्रसिद्ध-रागाङ्गम्) 15
पाटः (प्रबन्धाङ्गम्) 215, 216, 252-54, 266, 271, 273, 290, 294, 296-303
पाट—(करणम्) 252, 253
पात्रम् (कुतपे) 206
पादः (कर्णाटैलायाम्) 249
पादः (कलहंसे) 284
पादः (चतुष्पद्याम्) 295
पादः (चर्यायाम्) 303
पादः (त्रिपथे) 297

पादः (त्रिपद्याम्) 294, 295
पादः (द्विपथे) 283
पादः (मात्रैलायाम्) 244
पादः (प्रबन्धपुरुषस्य, ताल-स्वरः) 216
पादान्त—(प्रासः, चर्यायाम्) 303
पादान्तम् (वृत्ते) 287
पान्तग्रहांशा (प्रथमसौराष्ट्री) 128
पान्ता (त्रावणी) 135
पान्तांशादिः (भम्माणी) 136
पापन्यासा (रगन्ती) 97
पार्वती (देवता, बाणायाम्) 242
पार्वती (वेसरषाडव-विभाषा) 10
पार्वतीपतिः (देवता, रेवगुप्ते) 86
पार्वतीपतिः (सुशारीरलाभे) 169
पाल्पः (मध्यमषाडवः) 122
पावः (कुतपे) 205
पावनी (संगता-भेदः) 242
पाविका (कुतपे) 205
पिञ्जरी (हिन्दोलभाषा) 10
पित्तम् (धातुः) 213
पित्तोद्भवः (शब्दः) 158
पिनाकी (कुतपे) 205
पीतम् (चूर्णम्) 267
पीतम् (वृत्तगन्धि) 268
पीता (नन्दावती) 237
पीनः (शब्दः) 160
पीवरः (शब्दः) 160
पुनरुक्तम् (गीतम्) 324
पुरुषः (प्रबन्धः) 215
पुलिन्दका (भिन्नषड्जभाषा) 10
पुष्पसारः (झोम्बडभेदः) 260
पूर्णः (गौडकैशिकः) 37
पूर्णः (गौडकैशिकमध्यमः) 32
पूर्णः (भम्माणपञ्चमः) 52
पूर्णः (भिन्नकैशिकमध्यमः) 26
पूर्णः (रूप साधारः) 48
पूर्णः (शकः) 51
पूर्णः (शुद्धकैशिकः) 24
पूर्णः (शुद्धसाधारितः) 18
पूर्णम् (गीतम्) 323
पूर्णश्रुति—(स्वरः, स्थाये) 178
पूर्णा (चर्या) 303
पूर्णाङ्गगमक—(गीतम्) 323
पूर्णाटी (पूर्वप्रसिद्धोपाङ्गम्) 16
पूर्व – (प्रसिद्ध-रागाः) 14
पूर्व-यामः (शुद्धकैशिकमध्यमे) 84
पूर्व-यामः (षाडवे) 66
पूर्वरङ्गः (षाडवे) 66
पूर्ववदनम् (ब्रह्मणः) 248
पूर्वसंसिद्ध—(रूपकम्) 321
पूर्वार्धम् (आर्यायाः) 274
पोता (पञ्चमषाडवभाषा) 10
पौणः (कुतपे) 205
पौरवी (मूर्छना, भिन्नपञ्चमे) 72
पौराली (भिन्नषड्जविभाषा) 10
पौराली (मालवकैशिकभाषा) 10
प्रकटार्थकम् (गीतम्) 323
प्रकृति-प्रत्ययः (गीते) 323
प्रकृतिस्थ-शब्द— (स्थायः) 175, 190
प्रचण्डः (झोम्बडभेदः) 260
प्रचुरः (शब्दः) 165
प्रभञ्जनी (वर्णैला) 246
प्रताप—(वराटिका, अधुनाप्रसिद्धोपाङ्गम्) 16, 109
प्रताप—(वेलावली, अधुनाप्रसिद्धोपाङ्गम्) 16, 112
प्रतिग्रहणिका (रूपकालप्तौ) 201
प्रतिग्राह्योल्लासितः (स्थायः) 174, 187
प्रतितालः (एलायाम्) 222, 247, 277
प्रतितालः (नन्दावत्याम्) 237
प्रतिपाद्यम् (मातौ) 319
प्रतिभा (वाग्गेयकारे) 146
प्रतिमण्ठः (सालगसूडः) 308, 314
प्रतिमण्ठ – (तालः, उत्साहे) 310

प्रतिमण्ठ—(तालः, कामोदे) 311

प्रतिमण्ठ—(तालः, चन्द्रशेखरे) 311

प्रतिमण्ठ—(तालः, झोम्बडे) 259

प्रतिमण्ठ—(तालः, प्रतिमण्ठे) 311

प्रतिमण्ठ—(तालः, ललिते) 311

प्रतिमुख—(सन्धिः, षड्जग्रामरागे) 22

प्रतिष्ठा—(छन्दोजातिः) 234

प्रथम—(कामोदः, प्रसिद्धदेशीरागः) 124

प्रथम—(बङ्गालः, प्रसिद्धदेशीरागः) 122

प्रथम—(मञ्जरी, अधुनाप्रसिद्धभाषाङ्गम्) 16, 99

प्रथम—(यामः, अह्नः, भिन्नकैशिकमध्यमे) 26

प्रथम—(यामः, अह्नः, भिन्नकैशिके) 30

प्रथम—(यामः, भिन्नषड्जे) 69

प्रथम—(यामः, मध्यमग्रामरागे) 60

प्रथम—(यामः, शुद्धकैशिके) 24

प्रथम—(यामः, षड्जग्रामरागे) 22

प्रथम—(सौराष्ट्री भाषा) 128

प्रथम—(स्वस्थानम्) 198

प्रबन्धः (गायकगुणे) 150

प्रबन्धः (निबद्धसंज्ञा) 211, 213, 215, 218, 219

प्रबन्धः (रूपकवर्तनीनिरूपणे) 19

प्रबन्धः (वाग्गेयकारगुणे) 146

प्रबन्ध—(जातिः) 218

प्रबन्ध—(नाम, पञ्चतालेश्वरे) 290

प्रबन्ध—(पुरुषः) 215

प्रबन्धाङ्गम् (गद्ये) 270

प्रबन्धावयवः (ओडुवे) 319

प्रभावती (वर्णैला) 246

प्रभूत-गमकः (झोम्बडः) 259

प्रयोगः (एलायाम्) 222

प्रयोगः (गद्ये) 270

प्रयोगः (द्विपथके) 282

प्रयोगः (लक्षितः) 318

प्रलम्बित—(स्थायः) 174, 187

प्रलम्भः (लम्भभेदः) 262

प्रवेशः (कञ्चुकि-, टक्ककैशिके) 46

प्रवेशः (कञ्चुकि-, मालवपञ्चमे) 46

प्रवेशः (संयत-तपस्वि-गृहिणाम्, सौवीरे) 102

प्रसन्नः (प्राणः, एलायाम्) 228

प्रसन्न—(स्थायाः) 199

प्रसन्नम् (गीतम्) 323

प्रसन्नमध्य—(अलंकारः, ककुभे) 95

प्रसन्नमध्य—(अलंकारः, गान्धारपञ्चमे) 90

प्रसन्नमध्य—(अलंकारः, गौडकैशिकमध्यमे) 32

प्रसन्नमध्य—(अलंकारः गौडपञ्चमे) 35

प्रसन्नमध्य—(अलंकारः, नर्ते) 54

प्रसन्नमध्य—(अलंकारः, भम्माणपञ्चमे) 52

प्रसन्नमध्य—(अलंकारः, मालवकैशिके) 63

प्रसन्नमध्य—(अलंकारः, रूपसाधारे) 48

प्रसन्नमध्य—(अलंकारः, शके) 51

प्रसन्नमृदुः (स्थायः) 175, 190

प्रसन्नादिः (अलंकारः, गौडकैशिके) 37

प्रसन्नादिः (अलंकारः, भिन्नकैशिके) 30

प्रसन्नादिः (अलंकारः, भिन्नकैशिकमध्यमे) 26

प्रसन्नादिः (अलंकारः, भिन्नताने) 28

प्रसन्नादिः (अलंकारः, मध्यमग्रामे) 60

प्रसन्नादिः (अलंकारः, वेसरषाडवे) 40

प्रसन्नादिः (अलंकारः, षड्जकैशिके) 57

प्रसन्नादिः (अलंकारः, सौवीरे) 102

प्रसन्नाद्य—(अलंकारः, भिन्नपञ्चमे) 72

प्रसन्नाद्यन्त—(अलंकारः, रेवगुप्ते) 86

प्रसन्नाद्यन्त—(अलंकारः, हिन्दोले) 80

प्रसन्नान्त—(अलंकारः, टक्के) 77

प्रसन्नान्त—(अलंकारः, बोट्टे) 43

प्रसन्नान्त—(अलंकारः, भिन्नषड्जे) 69

प्रसन्नान्त—(अलंकारः, मालवपञ्चमे) 46

प्रसन्नान्त—(अलंकारः, शुद्धकैशिकमध्यमे) 84

प्रसन्नान्त—(अलंकारः, शुद्धकैशिके) 24

प्रसन्नान्त—(अलंकारः, शुद्धसाधारिते) 19

प्रसन्नान्त—(अलंकारः, षड्जग्रामरागे) 22
प्रसन्नान्त—(अलंकारः, षाडवे) 66
प्रसवः (रागः) 8
प्रसारणम् (गात्रगीतयोः) 155
प्रसारी (गायनः) 155
प्रसृतः (स्थायः) 174, 182
प्रसृताकुञ्चितः (स्थायः) 174, 187
प्रस्फुरत्—(षड्जपञ्चमः, द्राविडगौडः) 120
प्रहर्षः (बङ्गाले) 69
प्राकृतम् 231, 281, 282, 287, 302, 306
प्राक्प्रसिद्ध—(रागः, देशी-) 16
प्राक्—(प्रहरः, भिन्नपञ्चमे) 72
प्राग्—(यामः, भिन्नताने) 28
प्राचुर्यम् (शारीरगुणः) 169
प्राणाः (एलापदेषु) 228
प्रान्त—(प्रासः, कर्णाटैलायाम्) 249
प्रान्त—(प्रासः, लाटैलायाम्) 251
प्रायोगिकः (झोम्बडः) 259
प्रार्थनम् (त्रावण्याम्) 135
प्रार्थना (भैरवे) 69
प्रासः (ओव्याम्) 306
प्रास—वर्जिता (द्राविडी) 251
प्रासा (चरणान्तसम-, पद्धडी) 303
प्रियसम्भाषणम् (प्रथमगौडे) 134
प्रीतिः (महाकालमन्मथ-, टक्ककैशिके) 137
प्रीतिः (सवितुः, रूपसाधारे) 48
प्रेखकः (हिन्दोलनामान्तरम्, भाषाजनकः) 9
प्ररितः (स्थायः) 174, 178
प्रौढः (शब्दः) 158, 165
प्लावितः (गमकः) 171, 172
प्लुतः (स्थायः) 175, 190
प्लुतम् (गमकवेगमाने) 172

फलम् (वर्णगणानाम्) 233
फलम् (वर्णवर्गाणाम्) 233

बङ्ग—(पात्रम्) 206
बङ्गालः (अधुनाप्रसिद्धरागाङ्गम्) 16, 69
बङ्गालः (द्विविधः, रागः) 8
बटुकी (वराटी-नामान्तरम्) 104
बद्धः (स्थायः) 175, 190
बन्धः (गाने) 211
बन्ध—(करणम्) 252, 253
बहु—(निसरिगमाः) 101
बहुत्वम् (रागालाप-लक्षणे) 19
बहुलमध्यमा (सौवीरी) 104
बाङ्गाली (भिन्नषड्जभाषा) 10, 100
बाङ्गाली (मालवकैशिकभाषा) 10
बाण—(गणः, षट्पद्याम्) 296
बाणगणः 234, 244, 249
बाणलेखा (मात्रैला) 244
बाणा (विकृतगणैला) 238, 242
बाह्यषाडवा (वेसरषाडव-भाषा) 10
बिरुद—(करणम्) 252, 254
बिरुदम् (प्रबन्धाङ्गम्) 215, 216, 252, 254 265, 272-74, 294, 297-301, 303, 304
बीभत्स—(रसः, गौडपञ्चमे) 35
बीभत्स—(रसः, चण्डिकेश्वरे) 260
बीभत्स—(रसः, टक्ककैशिके) 137
बीभत्स—(रसः, भद्रावत्याम्) 238
बीभत्स—(रसः, भिन्नपञ्चमे) 72
बीभत्स—(रसः, भिन्नषड्जे) 69
बुद्धिः (आर्याभेदः) 280
बुधः (चादि—वर्णगण—देवता) 233
बृहद्देशी (अनुक्तजनका विभाषा, अन्तरभाषा च) 10
बोट्टः (भाषाजनकः) 8, 10
बोट्टः (रागः, मंगले) 306
बोट्टः (वेसरग्रामरागः, मध्यमग्रामे) 6, 43
बोम्बकः (शब्दः) 158, 160
बोम्बखाहुलः (मिश्रशब्दः) 159
बोम्बडी (कुतपे) 206

ब्रह्म (तेने) 216
ब्रह्मदैवतम् (चूर्णम्) 267
ब्रह्मा (कर्णाटैलाजनकः) 248
ब्रह्मा (गणाधिपः, कर्णाटैलायाम्) 249
ब्रह्मा (झोम्बडभेदः) 260
ब्राह्मी (देवता, एलापदे) 228

भः (वर्णगणः) 232, 236, 238, 276, 313
भक्तिः (सुशारीरलाभे) 169
भग्नः (शब्दः) 168
भङ्गः (गुरोः, आर्यायाम्) 280
भङ्गः (गुरोः, कन्दे) 274
भङ्गी (आलप्तौ) 199, 203
भङ्गी (गायने) 151
भङ्गी (स्थाये) 181
भजन—(स्थायः) 174, 180
भजनम् (गायने) 150
भञ्जनी (रूपकालप्तौ) 201
भञ्जनीसंश्रित (रूपकम्) 320, 322
भद्रलेखा (कर्णाटैला) 249
भद्रावती (कर्णाटैला) 249
भद्रावती (शुद्धा गणैला) 235, 237
भम्माणपञ्चमः (साधारणग्रामरागः, षड्ज-ग्रामे) 6, 52
भम्माणी (पञ्चमविभाषा) 9, 136
भयानक—(रसः, गौडकैशिकमध्यमे) 32
भयानक—(रसः, गौडपञ्चमे) 35
भयानक—(रसः, टक्ककैशिके) 137
भयानक—(रसः, भिन्नपञ्चमे) 72
भयानक—(रसः, भिन्नषड्जे) 69
भयानक—(रसः, भैरवेति-झोम्बडभेदे) 260
भरत—(मुनिः) 205
भरतादयः (गीतगुणे) 323
भल्लातिका (अधुनाप्रसिद्धोपाङ्गम्) 17
भवानीपतिः (देवता, बोट्टरागे) 43
भागलम्भः (लम्भभेदः) 262
भाग्यविभवः (सुशारीरलाभे) 169
भाणः (कुतपे) 206
भारती (नादावती-देवता) 236
भारती (वृत्तिः, भद्रावत्याम्) 238
भारती (वृत्तिः, वृत्तगन्धौ) 268
भावः (वाग्गेयकारे) 146
भावकः (गायनभेदः) 151
भावक्रीः (पूर्वप्रसिद्धक्रियाङ्गम्) 15
भावनापञ्चमः (उपरागः) 8
भावनी (टक्क-विभाषा) 9
भावनी (पञ्चमभाषा) 9
भावनी (प्रबन्ध-जातिः) 218
भावनी (मालवपञ्चम-भाषा) 10
भाषा (कोलाहला) 114
भाषा (कैशिकी) 127
भाषा (छेवाटी) 115
भाषा (टक्कललिता) 129
भाषा (त्रवणा) 94
भाषा (त्रावणी) 135
भाषा (दैशैलासु) 248
भाषा (पिञ्जरी) 106
भाषा (बाङ्गाली) 100
भाषा (मालवा) 138
भाषा (रगन्तिका) 97
भाषा (रूपकनिरूपणे) 19
भाषा (वाग्गेयकारलक्षणे) 146
भाषा (वेगरञ्जी) 101
भाषा (सौराष्ट्री) 128
भाषा (हर्षपुरी) 136
भाषा (ग्रामरागेषु) 9, 10, 12, 14
भाषाङ्गत्वम् (रामकृतेः) 114
भाषाङ्गम् (कैशिकी, मतान्तरेण) 127
भाषाङ्गम् (गायकगुणे) 150
भाषाङ्गम् (त्रावणी, मतान्तरेण) 127
भाषाङ्गम् (देशीरागवर्गः) 14, 15
भाषाजनकाः (पञ्चदशग्रामरागाः) 8
भासमध्यमः (रागः) 8
भासवलिता (अनुक्तजनका अन्तरभाषा) 10

भिन्न—(ग्रामरागाः) 6
भिन्नकैशिकः (भिन्नग्रामरागः) 6, 30
भिन्नकैशिकमध्यमः (भिन्नग्रामरागः) 6, 26
भिन्नतानः (भिन्नग्रामरागः) 6, 28
भिन्नपञ्चमः (भाषाजनकः) 8, 9
भिन्नपञ्चमः (भिन्नग्रामरागः) 71
भिन्नपञ्चमी (ककुभ-भाषा) 9
भिन्नपौराली (हिन्दोलभाषा) 10
भिन्नवलिता (टक्ककैशिकभाषा) 9
भिन्नषड्जः (बाङ्गालीजनकः) 100
भिन्नषड्जः (भाषाजनकः) 8, 10
भिन्नषड्जः (भिन्नग्रामरागः) 6, 69
भिन्नषड्जः (ललिताजनकः) 130
भिन्नषड्जः (सैन्धवीजनकः) 132
भिन्ना (गीतिः) 4
भीत—(गायनः) 155
भुञ्छी (उपाङ्गम्) 112
भुञ्जिका (अधुनाप्रसिद्धोपाङ्गम्) 16
भूमिः (भगणदेवता) 233
भूयसी (धनिस-, त्रवणा) 94
भूयोरसविराजिता (लाटी एला) 251
भूरि—(इतरस्वरा, आन्धाली) 117
भूरि—(धैवतः, रगन्त्याम्) 97
भूरि—(निषादः, द्वितीयगौडे) 134
भूरि—(धनिपमाः, भोगवर्धन्याम्) 99
भूरि—(सरिपमाः, त्रावण्याम्) 135
भूरि-गान्धारा (सैन्धवी वराटी) 109
भूरिनिमन्द्रा (द्राविडी वराटी) 109
भूरिभावरसोत्कर्षा (द्राविडी एला) 251
भूरिसौभाग्यम् (चन्द्रिकायाम्) 318
भूरीतरा (द्वितीयसौराष्ट्री) 128
भृत—(स्थायः) 174, 181
भृतिः (शब्दस्य) 190
भेरी (कुतपे) 206
भैरवः (अधुनाप्रसिद्धरागाङ्गम्) 16, 69, 113
भैरवः (झोम्बड-भेदः) 260
भैरवः (रागः) 8
भैरवः (स्थाये) 181
भैरवी (अधुनाप्रसिद्धोपाङ्गम्) 16
भैरवी (स्थाये) 181
भोगद (कन्दर्पः) 311
भोगदः (मधुरः) 310
भोगवती (वर्णैला) 246
भोगवर्धनी (ककुभ विभाषा) 99
भोगवर्धनी (सौवीर-विभाषा) 9
भौमः (कादि-वर्णवर्ग-देवता) 233
भौमः (देवता, शुद्धकैशिके) 24
भ्रमरः (द्विपथक-भेदः) 282
भ्रमरः (स्वस्तिक-भेदः) 288
भ्रामितः (स्थायः) 174, 187

मः (ग्रहांशः, मध्यमादौ) 62
मः (वर्णगणः) 232
मकरश्रीः (पूर्वप्रसिद्धक्रियाङ्गम्) 15
मकरध्वजः (कन्दभेदः) 274
मकरध्वजः (हिन्दोले) 81
मकरन्दः (अड्डतालः) 316, 317
मग्रहांशा (सावरी) 97
मङ्गलः (मण्ठभेदः, मण्ठताल-भेदश्च) 313
मङ्गलः (विप्रकीर्णप्रबन्धः) 221, 306
मङ्गल—(च्छन्दः, मङ्गले) 306
मङ्गल—(पदम्, मङ्गले) 306
मङ्गलम् (पञ्चतालेश्वरे) 290
मङ्गला (त्रेता-भेदः) 240
मङ्गलाचारः (विप्रकीर्णप्रबन्धः) 221, 304
मङ्गलात्म—(ब्रह्मन्) 216
मङ्गलारम्भः (मिश्रकरणम्) 255
मङ्गलार्थ—(प्रकाशकतेनः, पदम्) 215, 216
मण्ठः—(सालागसूडः) 308, 313
मण्ठ—(तालः, एलायाम्) 222
मण्ठ—(तालः, झोम्बडे) 259
मण्ठ—(तालः, देशैलासु) 248
मण्ठ—(तालः, द्रुत-, वर्तन्याम्) 258
मण्ठ—(तालः, ध्वनिकुट्टन्याम्) 279

मण्ठ —(तालः, नादावत्याम्) 236
मण्ठ—(तालः, वर्णेलासु) 247
मण्ठ—(तालः, षट्प्रकारः, मण्ठे) 313
मण्डिडक्का (कुतपे) 205
मतङ्गः (मुनिः) 19, 130, 134, 222, 247
म-तारा (गौडकृतिः) 107
मतिः (आर्याभेदः) 280
मत्तः (एला-पद-नाम) 227
मत्त –(मातङ्ग-गतिः, स्थाये) 180
म-त्यक्ता (भुञ्छी, उपाङ्गम्) 112
मदन—(गणः) 248
मदन—(दैवत्यम्, ललितम्) 267
मदनवती (वर्णेला) 246
मदनावतारः (रासकभेदः) 264
मधु (कन्दभेदः) 274
मधुकरी (वर्णेला) 246
मधुकरी (सौवीर-विभाषा) 9
मधुपः (कन्दभेदः) 274
मधुरः (ध्रुवभेदः) 310
मधुरः (प्राणः, एलायाम्) 228
मधुरः (शब्दः) 158-60, 165
मधुर—(गमकाः) 4
मधुरम् (गीतम्) 323
मधुरी (ककुभ-भाषा) 9
मधुरी (हिन्दोल-भाषा) 10
मध्य—(अनुप्रासः, कर्णाटैलायाम्) 248, 249
मध्य—(पदम्, एलायाम्) 222
मध्य —(प्रासः, ओव्याम्) 306
मध्य—(यामौ, गौडपञ्चमे) 35
मध्य—(स्थानम्) 158
मध्यमः (अंशग्रहन्यासः, तोडिकायाम्) 68
मध्यमः (ग्रहांशन्यासः, बङ्गाले) 69
मध्यमः (न्यासांशः, षाडवे) 66
मध्यमः (गायनः) 150
मध्यमः (मिश्रशब्दः) 159
मध्यमः (वाग्गेयकारः) 146, 147
मध्य-मः (गुर्जर्याम्) 77
मध्यम—(पात्रम्, कुतपे) 206
मध्यम—(यामद्वयम्, गौडकैशिकमध्यमे) 32
मध्यम—(वृन्दम्) 203, 204
मध्यम-ग्रामः (ग्राम-नाम) 6
मध्यम-ग्रामः (शुद्धग्रामरागः) 6, 60
मध्यमग्रामदेहा (टक्कभाषा) 9
मध्यमग्रामा (ककुभ-भाषा) 9
मध्यमन्यासः (शुद्धसाधारितः) 18
मध्यमन्यासः (षड्जग्रामरागः) 22
मध्यम-व्याप्ता (देवकृतिः) 108
मध्यमषाडवः (देशीरागः) 122
मध्यमस्थांशः (स्थाये) 181
मध्यमा (जातिः, ककुभ-जनका) 95
मध्यमा (जातिः, टक्ककैशिकजनका) 137
मध्यमा (जातिः, नर्तजनका) 54
मध्यमा (जातिः, भिन्नतानजनका) 28
मध्यमा (जातिः, भिन्नपञ्चमजनका) 71
मध्यमा (जातिः, मध्यमग्रामरागजनका) 60
मध्यमा (जातिः, मालवपञ्चमजनका) 46
मध्यमा (जातिः, रेवगुप्तजनका) 86
मध्यमा (जातिः, विकारि-षाडवजनका) 66
मध्यमा (जातिः, शुद्धपञ्चमजनका) 116
मध्यमा (भिन्नषड्जभाषा) 10
मध्यमांशग्रहन्यासः (वेसरषाडवः) 40
मध्यमादिः (अधुनाप्रसिद्धरागाङ्गाम्) 16, 62
मध्यमादिक—(मूर्छनः, वेसरषाडव.) 40
मध्यमादिक—(मूर्छनः, षाडवः) 66
मध्यविलम्बिता (गतिः, गद्ये) 269
मध्यसप्तक—(पञ्चमः, शुद्धपञ्चमे) 116
मध्यस्थरागः (स्थाये) 181
मध्या (गतिः, गद्ये) 269
मध्या (छन्दोजातिः) 234
मनिसभूयसी (देशी) 89
मनोरमा (आर्या-भेदः) 280
मनोरमा (वासवी-भेदः) 239
मन्द्रः (आलापलक्षणे) 19
मन्द्र—(गान्धारषड्जौ, षड्जकैशिके) 57

मन्द्र—(मनिधाः, षड्जकैशिके) 57
मन्द्र --(स्थानम्) 158
मन्द्र (स्वराः) 4
मन्द्रगान्धारः (द्वितीयकामोदः) 124
मन्द्रगान्धारः (मल्हारः) 118
मन्द्रगान्धारः (श्रीरागः) 121
मन्द्रगान्धारा (तोडी) 68
मन्द्र-धग-व्याप्ता (त्रावणी) 135
मन्द्रधैवता (त्रवणा) 94
मन्द्रधैवता (वल्लाता) 115
मन्द्रनिषादा (नट्टा) 106
मन्द्रनिषादा (महाराष्ट्रगुर्जरी) 111
मन्द्रपञ्चमा (छायानट्टा) 113
मन्द्रभूरिः (भिन्नकैशिकः) 30
मन्द्रमध्यः (आम्रपञ्चमः) 124
मन्द्रमध्यमा (मल्हारी) 118
मन्द्रमध्यमा (सावरी) 97
मन्द्रषड्जः (ग्रहांशः, मध्यमग्रामरागे) 60
मन्द्रषड्जा (आन्धाली) 117
मन्द्रषड्जा (भम्माणी) 136
मन्द्रसान्तः (भिन्नकैशिकमध्यमः) 26
मन्द्रहीनः (आम्रपञ्चमः) 124
मन्द्रहीनः (प्रथमबङ्गाल) 122
मन्द्रहीनः (मेघरागः) 123
मन्मथ -(प्रीतिः, टक्ककैशिके) 137
मन्मथवत् (एला-पद-नाम) 227
मन्यासः (गौडकैशिकमध्यमः) 32
मन्यासः (भिन्नकैशिकमध्यमः) 26
मपभूयसी (कैशिकी) 127
मपभूयसी (गौडकृतिः) 107
मपभूयिष्ठा (कोलाहला) 114
ममन्द्रा (आडिकामोदिका) 101
ममन्द्रा (कैशिकी) 127
ममन्द्रा (द्वितीयसौराष्ट्री) 128
ममन्द्रा (वराटी) 74
ममन्द्रा (सिंहलीकामोदा) 113
मयूरः (द्विपथक-भेदः) 282, 283
मरुतः (सगणदेवता) 233
मलय—(पात्रम्) 206
मल्हारः (अधुनाप्रसिद्धोपाङ्गम्) 17, 118
मल्हारी (अधुनाप्रसिद्धोपाङ्गम्) 17, 118
महाकाल-प्रीतिः (टक्ककैशिके) 137
महानन्दा (चतुराभेदः) 241
महामाहेश्वरः (ग्रन्थकारः) 151
महाराष्ट्र --(पात्रम्) 206
महाराष्ट्री (गुर्जरी, अधुनाप्रसिद्धोपाङ्गम्) 16, 111
मही (आर्याभेदः) 280
मांशा (रामकृतिः) 114
माङ्गली (पञ्चमभाषा) 9
माङ्गली (बोट्टभाषा) 10
माङ्गली (मालवकैशिकभाषा) 10
मातङ्गी (देवता, एलापदे) 228
मातुः (रूपके) 319
मातुः (वाक्, वाग्गेयकारकर्मणि) 146, 147
मातु-स्थाय—(विचित्रत्वम्, गुणोदारे) 322
मात्रिक -(वृत्तम्) 256
मात्वन्तरम् (रूपके) 322
माधवः (कन्दभेदः) 274
माधुर्यम् (ध्वनेः, गायन्याम्) 151
माधुर्यम् (शारीरगुणः) 169
माधुर्यमांसलः (नादः, स्थाये) 180
मानः (वेगरञ्ज्याम्)) 101
मानम् (गद्ये) 270
मानम् (पदस्य, भञ्जन्याम्) 201
मानवी (द्विपदी-भेदः) 276
मानुषी (मातृका) 287
मान्तः (गौडपञ्चमः) 35
मान्तः (बोट्टः) 43
मान्तः (भैरवः) 69
मान्तः (शुद्धकैशिकमध्यमः) 84
मान्ता (गुर्जरी) 77
मान्धाता (एला-पद-नाम) 227, 228
मान्मथ—(गणः) 244, 295, 296

मार्गः (प्रकीर्णकनिरूपणे) 145, 149
मार्गतालाः (मातृकायाम्) 287
मार्गत्रयम् (तालस्य, आक्षिप्तिकायाम्) 19
मार्दङ्गिकः (मुख्यः, कुतपे) 205
मार्दङ्गिकः (वृन्दे) 204
मार्दलिकः (वृन्दे) 204
मार्दवम् (शारीरगुणः) 169
मालती (वर्णैला) 246
मालती (वर्णैला, मतङ्गोक्ता) 247
मालव—(पात्रम्) 206
मालवकैशिकः (भाषाजनकः) 8, 10
मालवकैशिकः (वेसर-ग्रामरागः) 6, 63
मालवकैशिकः (द्वितीयगौडी-जनकः) 134
मालवकैशिकः (सैन्धवी-जनकः) 132
मालवकैशिकः (हर्षपुरी-जनकः) 136
मालवकैशिक—(रागः, नन्दावत्याम्) 237
मालबपञ्चमः (भाषाजनकः) 8, 10
मालवपञ्चमः (वेसरग्रामरागः) 6, 46
मालवा (टक्ककैशिकभाषा) 9, 138
मालवा (भिन्नषड्जविभाषा) 10
मालवरूपा (मालवकैशिकभाषा) 10
मालववेसरी (टक्कभाषा) 9
मालववेसरी (त्रिधा, मुख्या भाषा) 12
मालववेसरी (मालवकैशिकभाषा) 10
मालववेसरी (हिन्दोलभाषा) 10
मालवश्रीः (अधुनाप्रसिद्धरागाङ्गम्) 16, 65
मातृकः (झोम्बड-भेदः) 260
मातृका (आलिसंश्रित-प्रबन्धः) 220, 287
मातृका-वर्णः (मातृकायाम्) 287
मात्रा 234, 244, 246, 264, 282, 295, 296
मात्रा (समा, ध्वनि-कुट्टन्याम्) 279
मात्रा—(एला) 231
मात्रा—(गणाः) 231, 234, 244
मात्रा—(द्विपदी) 275, 276
मात्रिक—(कलहंसः) 284
मात्रिका (ढेङ्की-भेदः) 257
मात्रैला 244
मिथस्त्रुटितनिर्वाहः (वृन्दगुणः) 205
मिलनम् (वृन्दगुणः) 205
मिश्रः (स्थायः) 175, 190, 194
मिश्रः (स्वरार्थः) 278
मिश्र—(करणम्) 252, 255
मिश्र—(पाटः, कैवाडे) 271
मिश्र—(स्वराक्षरम्, स्वरार्थे) 278
मिश्रकः (गायनः) 155
मिश्रकः (शब्दः) 158, 160
मिश्रम् (गद्यभेदः) 268
मिश्रितः (गमकः) 171, 172
मुक्तावली (ढेङ्की) 257
मुक्तिः (न्यासः, घटे) 286
मुक्तिः (न्यासः, लम्भे) 262
मुखचालः (प्रथमस्वस्थानम्) 198
मुख-मुद्रणम् (गमके) 172
मुख-सन्धिः (मध्यमग्रामरागे) 60
मुख्यः (मार्दङ्गिकः, कुतपे) 205
मुख्य-गाता (वृन्दे) 203, 204
मुख्य—गायनः (वृन्दे) 204
मुख्य—गायनिका (वृन्दे) 204
मुख्या भाषा (षड्विधा) 12
मुख्यानुवृत्तिः (वृन्दगुणः) 205
मुत् (रुद्रस्य, टक्के) 77
मुद्रितः (गमकः) 171, 172
मुनिः (भरत-) 205
मुनिदैवतम् (वृत्तगन्धि) 268
मुरज—(पाटाः, पञ्चतालेश्वरे) 290
मुरज—(पाटाः बन्धकरणे) 253
मुरजाक्षरम् (बन्धकरणे) 254
मुहरी (कुतपे) 205
मूर्छना (आद्या, टक्के) 77
मूर्छना (आद्या, शुद्धकैशिक-मध्यमे) 84
मूर्छना (एलाप्राणः) 228
मूर्छना (गौडकैशिके) 37
मूर्छना (गौडकैशिकमध्यमे) 32

मूर्छना (गौडपञ्चमे) 35
मूर्छना (धैवतादिः, ककुभे) 95
मूर्छना (नर्ते) 54
मूर्छना (पौरवी,भिन्नपञ्चमे) 72
मूर्छना (बोट्टे) 43
मूर्छना (भम्माणपञ्चमे) 52
मूर्छना (भिन्नकैशिकमध्यमे) 26
मूर्छना (भिन्नताने) 28, 30
मूर्छना (मध्यमग्रामरागे) 60
मूर्छना (मध्यमादिः, षाडवे) 66
मूर्छना (मालवकैशिके) 63
मूर्छना (मालवपञ्चमे) 46
मूर्छना (रूपसाधारे) 48
मूर्छना (वेसरषाडवे) 40
मूर्छना (शुद्धकैशिके) 24
मूर्छना (शुद्धमध्या, हिन्दोले) 80
मूर्छना (षड्जादि-, मालवकैशिके) 63
मूर्छना (षड्जादि-, सौवीरे) 102
मूर्छना (शके) 51
मूर्छना (षड्जकैशिके) 57
मूर्छना (षड्जादि-, शुद्धसाधारिते) 18
मूर्छना (सौवीरी, मध्यमग्रामरागे) 60
मूर्छना (हृष्यका, शुद्धपञ्चमे) 116
मूला (याष्टिकोक्त-भाषाभेदः) 12
मृत्युः (यादि-वर्ण-वर्ग-फलम्) 233
मृदुः (शब्दः) 159, 160
मृदुः (एला-पद-नाम) 227
मृदु—(पञ्चमा, तृतीयसैन्धवी) 132
मृदु— (स्वराः) 4
मृष्टः (शब्दः) 165
मेघरागः (रागः) 8, 123
मेदिनी (प्रबन्धजातिः) 218
मेलापकः (प्रबन्धे) 213, 222, 249, 256, 259, 279
मोहिनी (मतङ्गोक्त वर्णेला) 247
मोहिनी (देवता, एला-पदे) 228
मोक्षः (न्यासः, गायकगुणे) 150
मोक्षः (-न्यासः, गार्तन्याम्) 258

यः (वर्णगणः) 232, 238, 276
यजुरुद्भवा (हंसावती) 237
यतिः (देशैलासु) 251
यतिः (ध्वनिकुट्टन्याम्) 279
यतिः (मण्ठे) 313
यतिः (वर्णैलासु) 247
यतिलग्न—(तालः, झोम्बडे) 259
यदृच्छा (धवले) 305
यन्त्र—(काकुः, स्थाये) 177, 178
यन्त्र— (स्थायः) 174, 177
यमकः (चतुष्पद्याम्) 295
यमदैवतः (ककुभः) 95
यमल—(गायनः) 151
यमल— (प्रथमः, भिन्नकैशिके) 30
यमल—(प्रथमः, भिन्नकैशिकमध्यमे) 26
यामः (पश्चिमः, वेसरषाडवे) 41
यामः (प्रथमः, मध्यमग्रामरागे) 60
यामः (प्रथमः, शुद्धकैशिके) 24
यामद्वयम् (मध्यम-, गौडकैशिकमध्यमे) 32
यामौ (मध्य-, गौडपञ्चमे) 35
याष्टिकः (भाषा-निरूपणे) 8, 12, 135
युक् (अङ्घ्रिः, द्विपथके) 282, 283
युग्मिनी (ढेङ्की-भेदः) 257
युद्धवीर—(रसः, टक्के) 77
यौवनम् (गायन्याम्) 151

रः (वर्णगणः) 232, 237, 313
रक्तगान्धारी (जातिः,गान्धारपञ्चम-जनका) 90
रक्तहंसः (रागः) 8
रक्ता (उत्कलिका) 267
रक्तिः (वेसरागीतौ) 4
रक्तिः (शारीरगुणः) 169
रक्तिः (स्थाये) 174, 181
रक्तियुक्तः (शब्दः) 165, 166

रगन्ती (ककुभभाषा) 9, 97
रगन्ती (मुख्या भाषा) 12
रञ्जकः (गायकभेदः) 151
रञ्जकः (शब्दः) 165
रञ्जकः (स्वरसन्दर्भः) 209
रञ्जनम् (रागे) 14
रञ्जनी (देवता, एला-पदे) 228
रञ्जनी (मतङ्गोक्ता वर्णेला) 247
रणरणकः (द्वितीयगौडः) 134
रतिः (कौन्तली-वराट्याम्) 108
रतिगणः 234, 244, 248, 249, 295
रतिदेहा (संगता-भेदः) 239
रतिप्रभा (त्रेता-भेदः) 240
रतिमङ्गला (त्रेता-भेदः) 240
रतिरङ्गकः (रासक-भेदः) 264
रतिलेखा (मात्रैला) 244
रत्नमाला (त्रेता-भेदः) 240
रमणी (मतङ्गोक्ता वर्णैला) 247
रमणीया (संगता-भेदः) 239
रमा (एकताली-भेदः) 318
रविः (कन्दभेदः) 274
रविः (यादि-वर्णवर्ग-देवता) 233
रविचन्द्रिका (टक्कभाषा) 9
रविदैवतः (शुद्धसाधारितः) 19
रसः (अद्भुत-, आम्रपञ्चमे) 124
रसः (अद्भुत-, टक्के) 77
रसः (अद्भुत-, मध्यमषाडवे) 122
रसः (अद्भुत-, मालवकैशिके) 63
रसः (अद्भुत-, रेवगुप्ते) 86
रसः (अद्भुत-, शुद्धकैशिकमध्यमे) 84
रसः (अद्भुत-, सौवीरे) 102
रसः (अद्भुत-, हिन्दोले) 81
रसः (गायनगुणे) 151
रसः (गौडकैशिके) 37
रसः (गौडकैशिकमध्यमे) 32
रसः (गौडपञ्चमे) 35
रसः (चारे) 316
रसः (नर्ते) 54
रसः (बीभत्सः, भिन्नपञ्चमे) 72
रसः (भम्माणपञ्चमे) 52
रसः (भिन्नकैशिके) 30
रसः (भिन्नकैशिकमध्यमे) 26
रसः (मालवकैशिके) 63
रसः (रूपके) 322
रसः (रूपसाधारे) 48
रसः (रौद्र-, टक्के) 77
रसः (रौद्र-, मालवकैशिके) 63
रसः (रौद्र-, रेवगुप्ते) 86
रसः (रौद्र-, शुद्धकैशिकमध्यमे) 84
रसः (रौद्र-, सौवीरे) 102
रसः (रौद्र-, हिन्दोले) 81
रसः (वाग्गेयकार-गुणे) 146
रसः (विजये) 317
रसः (वीरः, टक्के) 77
रसः (वीरः, नागध्वनौ) 102
रसः (वीरः, मध्यमषाडवे) 102
रसः (वीरः, मालवकैशिके) 63
रसः (वीरः, रेवगुप्ते) 86
रसः (वीरः, शके) 51
रसः (वीरः, शुद्धकैशिकमध्यमे) 84
रसः (वीरः, सौवीरे) 102
रसः (वीरः, हिन्दोले) 81
रसः (शान्त-, सौवीरे) 102
रसः (शुद्धकैशिके) 24
रसः (षड्जकैशिके) 57
रसः (षड्जग्रामरागे) 22
रसः (हास्य-, आम्रपञ्चमे) 124
रसभावोत्कटा (आन्ध्री एला) 251
रसालकारः (मातौ) 319
रसिकः (गायकभेदः) 151
रहः (वेगः, गायनगुणे) 150
रागः (गायनगुणे) 150
रागः (गीते) 323
रागः (रूपके) 201, 319, 322

रागः (स्थायलक्षणे) 174
रागः (स्थाये) 177, 178, 180, 181
रागः (हिन्दोल-, चच्चर्याम्) 302
राग –(आलफ्तम्) 198
राग—(आलप्तिः) 198, 199
राग—(गीतिः, वेसरानामान्तरम्) 4
रागकदम्बः (आलिसंश्रितप्रबन्धः) 220, 288
राग-काकुः (स्थाये) 177
राग-राजिः (रागकदम्वे) 288
रागविवेकः 1
रागस्थापना (आलप्तौ) 199
रागाः (उमातिलके) 294
रागाः (ग्रामरागादिभिन्न-वर्गविशेषः) 8
रागाः (पञ्चानने) 294
रागाः (श्रीरङ्गे) 293
रागाः (श्रीविलासे) 294
रागाः (सामान्यकथने) 17, 156
रागांशभेदः (धातौ) 319
रागाङ्गम् (गायनगुणे) 150
रागाङ्गम् (देशीरागवर्गः) 14, 15
रागालापः (लक्षितः) 19
रागेषुः (स्थायः) 175, 190
राजिः (आर्याभेदः) 280
रामकृतिः (अधुना-प्रसिद्ध-क्रियाङ्गम्) 16, 107
रामकृतिः (अधुना-प्रसिद्धोपाङ्गम्) 17, 114
रामा (वासवीभेदः) 239
रावणहस्तकः (कुतपे) 205
रासः (सूडप्रबन्धः) 220, 264
रास—(तालः, झोम्बडे) 259
रास –(तालः, रासके) 264, 317
रास—(तालः, वर्तनीप्रबन्धे) 258
रास (तालः, स्वरकरणे) 252
रासकः (सालगसूडः) 317
रासवलयः (रासकभेदः) 264
राहडी (विप्रकीर्णप्रबन्धः) 221, 304
राहुप्रियः (गान्धार-पञ्चमः) 90
रि-कम्प्रा (सौराष्ट्रगुर्जरी) 111
रि-ग्रहांशः (रेवगुप्तः) 86
रि ग्रहांशन्यासा (देशी) 89
रि-ग्रहांशा (गुर्जरी) 77
रि-तारा (कैशिकी) 127
रि-तारा (गुर्जरी) 77
रिध-त्यक्तः (हिन्दोलः) 80
रिध-त्यक्ता (गौडकृतिः) 107
रिध-भूयिष्ठा (गुर्जरी) 77
रिप-त्यक्तः (भैरवः) 69
रिप-त्यक्ता (छायातोडी) 110
रिप-त्यक्ता (देवकृतिः) 108
रिप-वर्जितः (तुरुष्कगौडः) 120
रिप-वर्जिता (चतुर्थसैन्धवी) 132
रिप-वर्जिता (प्रताप-वेलावली) 112
रिपोज्झितः (देशवालगौडः) 120
रिपोज्झितः (भिन्नषड्जः) 69
रिपोज्झिता (डोम्बकृतिः) 95
रिपोज्झिता (त्रवणा) 94
रिपोज्झिता (प्रथमललिता) 129
रिपोज्झिता (प्रथमसैन्धवी) 131
रिबहुः (द्वितीयसैन्धवी) 131
रिमन्द्रतारा (द्राविडगुर्जरी) 111
रि-वर्जिता (धन्नासी) 86
रि-वर्जिता (भोगवर्धनी) 99
रि-षड्जाधिका (रामकृतिः) 107
रि-हीनः (भिन्नतानः) 28
रि-हीना (छेवाटी) 115
रि-हीना (प्रथमसौराष्ट्री) 128
रि-हीना (वल्लाता) 115
रीतिः (गौडी, उत्कलिकायाम्) 267
रीतिः (पाञ्चाली, नादावत्याम्) 236
रीतिः (पाञ्चाली, ललिते) 267
रीतिः (पाञ्चाली, वृत्तगन्धौ) 268
रीतिः (पूर्वप्रसिद्ध-रागाङ्गम्) 15
रीतिः (लाटी, हंसावत्याम्) 237

रीतिः (वैदर्भी, चित्रे) 268
रीतिः (वैदर्भी, चूर्णे) 267
रीतिः (वैदर्भी, भद्रावत्याम्) 238
रुक् (जगणफलम्) 233
रुचिरः (झोम्बडः) 260
रुञ्जा (कुतपे) 206
रुद्रः (देवता, टक्के) 77
रुद्रः (देवता, शके) 51
रुद्राधिदेवता (उत्कलिका) 267
रूक्षः (शब्दः) 158-60, 168
रूक्षता (शब्दस्य) 159
रूक्षत्वम् (शारीरदोषः) 169
रूपक—(आलप्तिः) 198, 201
रूपक—(भञ्जनी) 201
रूपकम् (अर्थालंकारः) 260
रूपकम् (आलापप्रकारः, लक्षितः) 19
रूपकम् (निबद्ध-संज्ञा) 211, 213, 319, 320, 321
रूपकस्थ—(तालः) 201
रूपकस्थ—(रागः) 201
रूपम् (गायन्याम्) 151
रूपसाधारः (साधारण-ग्रामरागः) 6, 48
रेवगुप्तः (उपरागः) 8
रेवगुप्तः (ग्रामरागः) 86
रेवगुप्तः (भाषाजनकः, मतान्तरेण) 10
रोषः (वाग्गेयकार-गुणे) 146
रोहिणी (आर्या-भेदः) 280
रौद्रः (रसः, गौडकैशिके) 37
रौद्रः (रसः, प्रचण्डे) 260
रौद्रः (रसः, भम्माणपञ्चमे) 52
रौद्रः (रसः, भिन्नकैशिके) 30
रौद्रः (रसः, भिन्नकैशिकमध्यमे) 26
रौद्रः (रसः, मालवकैशिके) 63
रौद्रः (रसः, रूपसाधारे) 48
रौद्रः (रसः, शुद्धकैशिके) 24
रौद्रः (रसः, शुद्धसाधारिते) 19
रौद्रः (रसः, षड्जकैशिके) 57
रौद्रः (रसः, षड्जग्रामरागे) 22
रौद्रः (रसः, सौवीरे) 102
रौद्रः (रसः, हंसावत्याम्) 237

लकारः (एलापदम्) 227
लक्षणम् (भाषाणाम्) 12
लक्षणान्वितम् (गानम्) 210
लक्ष्म 12, 17, 60
लक्ष्मीः (आर्या-भेदः) 280
लक्ष्मीः (दैवतम्, एलायाम्) 227
लक्ष्मीः (मतङ्गोक्ता वर्णेला) 247
लक्ष्मीः (संगता-भेदः) 239
लक्ष्य-लक्षण—(कोविदाः) 169
लक्ष्यम् (झोम्बडस्य) 260
लक्ष्यम् (द्विपथे) 283
लक्ष्यम् (रासके) 264
लघुः (गद्ये) 269
लघुः (गमकवेगमाने) 171
लघुः (मात्रापर्यायः) 234
लघु—(वर्णः) 237
लघुः (स्थायः) 175, 190
लघुशेखर—(तालः, कुन्तले) 311
लङ्घितस्वराः (प्रथम-सैन्धव्याम्) 131
लज्जा (आर्याभेदः) 280
लम्भः (सूडप्रबन्धः) 220, 262, 263
लम्भ-पदम् (लम्भभेदः) 263
लयः (गायनगुणे) 150
लयः (रूपके) 319
लयः (वाग्गेयकारगुणे) 146
लयग्रहः (ताल-नवतायाम्) 319
ललितः (ध्रुवभेदः) 310, 311
ललितः (स्थायः) 174, 182
लुलितः (स्थायः) 174, 182
ललित—(रिगमाः, ललितायाम्) 130
ललित—(स्वराः, गीतौ) 4
ललित—(स्वराः, प्रथमललितायाम्) 129
ललितगाढः (स्थायः) 174, 182

ललितम् (गद्यभेदः) 266, 267
ललित-स्नेहः (ललितायाम्) 130
ललिता (टक्कभाषा) 9
ललिता (भिन्नषड्जभाषा) 10, 130
ललिता (वर्णेला) 246
लवनी—(स्थायः) 174, 177
लहरी (चतुरा-भेदः) 241
लाट—(एला) 248, 251
लाट—(पात्रम्) 206
लाट-भाषा (ढोल्लर्याम्) 307
लाटी (पूर्वप्रसिद्धरागाङ्गम्) 15
लाटी (रीतिः, हंसावत्याम्) 237
लावण्यम् (गीते) 323
लास्यम् (कुतपे) 206
लीनः (गमकः) 171
लीनः (शब्दः) 158-60
लीला (आर्याभेदः) 280
लोकः (शुद्धसूडे) 308
लोकदुष्ट—(गीतम्) 324
लोकप्रसिद्धिः (धवले) 305
लोली (विप्रकीर्ण-प्रबन्धः) 221, 306
लोली—पदम् (लोल्याम्) 306
लोहिता (हंसावती) 237

वंशवृद्धिकृत् (शेखरः) 310
वक्रः (स्थायः) 175, 190
वक्र—(स्वराः, गीतौ) 4
वक्री (गायनः) 155
वदनम् (विप्रकीर्ण-प्रबन्धः) 221, 302
वधूः (आर्या-भेदः) 280
वनभ्रान्तम् (भम्माण-पञ्चमे) 52
वरः (उत्तम-वाग्गेयकारः) 146, 147
वरदः (रासकभेदः) 317
वराट—(पात्रम्) 206
वराटी (अधुना-प्रसिद्धरागाङ्गम्) 16, 74
वराटी (अधुनाप्रसिद्धोपाङ्गम्, षट्प्रकारा), 16, 108
वराटी, वराटिका (भाषाङ्गम्) 104
वराटी (रागः, स्थाये) 181
तरुणः (कन्दभेदः) 274
वरेण्या (देवता, एलापदे) 228
वर्जितर्षभा (देशाख्या) 92
वर्ज्य-स्वरः (गायनदोषे) 155
वर्णः (अक्षरम्) 264
वर्णः (आलप्तौ) 203
वर्णः (आलिसंश्रितप्रबन्धः) 220, 265
वर्णः (नर्ते) 54
वर्ण (मालवकैशिके) 63
वर्णः (रूपसाधारे) 48
वर्णः (शके) 51
वर्णः (संचारि-, भिन्नपञ्चमे) 72
वर्णः (संचारि-, भिन्नषड्जे) 69
वर्णः (संचारि-, शुद्धपञ्चमे) 116
वर्णः (स्थाय्यादिः) 297
वर्ण—(एला) 231
वर्ण—(गणः) 231, 232, 235
वर्णकविः (वाग्गेयकारः) 147
वर्णचतुष्कम् (रागगीतौ) 4
वर्णचयः (चक्रवाले) 277
वर्णज—(कलहंसः) 284
वर्णज—(वृत्तम्) 256
वर्णतालः (वर्णप्रबन्धे) 265
वर्णनियमः (ध्रुवे) 311
वर्ण-मात्रैला 246
वर्णस्वरः (आलिसंश्रित-प्रबन्धः) 220, 266
वर्णिका (ढेङ्कीभेदः) 257
वर्णैला 246, 251
वर्ण्य—(नाम, अङ्कचारिण्याम्) 272
वर्ण्य—(नाम, गद्ये) 270
वर्ण्यः (श्लोकगीतादौ) 233
वर्तनी (सूडप्रबन्धः) 220, 258
वर्तनी (आलाप-भेदः) 19
वर्षा (टक्के) 77
वर्षा (षड्जग्रामरागे) 22

वलिः (गमकभेदः) 171, 177, 182
वलिता (धनिस-, त्रवणा) 94
वल्लकी (कुतपे) 205
वल्लभः (मण्ठभेदः, मण्ठतालभेदश्च) 313
वल्लाता (उपाङ्गम्) 115
वसन्तः (अधुनाप्रसिद्ध-रागाङ्गम्) 16, 83
वसन्तः (हिन्दोले) 87
वसन्तोत्सवः (चच्चर्याम्) 302
वसुधा (आर्याभेदः) 280
वसुमती (मात्रैला) 244
वस्तु (निबद्ध-संज्ञा) 211
वस्तु (विप्रकीर्ण-प्रबन्धः) 221, 296
वस्तु-कविः (वाग्गेयकारः) 147
वस्तु-वदनम् (वस्तुभेदः) 302
वस्त्वेला 251
वहः (स्थायः) 174, 182, 187
वहनी (स्थायः) 174, 177, 182
वह्निजा (नन्दावती-भेदः) 242
वह्निवारुणी (नन्दावती-भेदः) 242
वांशिकः (कुतपे) 205
वांशिकः (वृन्दे) 203, 204
वाक् (मातुः) 146
वाक्-पटुत्वम् (वाग्गेयकारगुणे) 146
वागः (गमक-नामान्तरम्) 172, 174
वाग्गेयकारः 146, 210, 222
वाञ्छितः (निःसारुभेदः) 315, 316
वाञ्छितप्रदः (वाञ्छितः) 316
वातः (धातुः) 213
वातजः (शब्दः) 158
वातसावित्री (संगता-भेदः) 242
वादकः (कुतपे) 205, 206
वाद्यम् (कुतपे) 206
वाद्यशब्द—(स्थायः) 174, 177
वाद्याक्षरम् (पाटे) 216
वायुवेगा (देवता, एला-पदे) 228
वाराटी (भिन्नपञ्चमभाषा) 9
वाराही (देवता, भद्रावत्याम्) 238
वारुणी (नन्दावती-भेदः) 242
वारुणी (संगता-भेदः) 242
वासरादिम—(प्रहरः, शुद्धसाधारिते) 19
वासवः (एला-पद-नाम) 227
वासवी (अङ्कचारिणी) 272
वासवी (विकृता गणैला) 238, 239, 242
विकलः (गायनः) 155
वकारः (गणैलायाम्) 238, 239, 241, 242
विकारि-मध्यमा (जातिः, षाडव-जनका) 66
विकारी (एला-पद-नाम) 227
विकृता (गणैला) 235, 238, 242
विकृतिः (गणैलायाम्) 240
विकृष्टम् (गीतम्) 323
विक्रमः (कन्दभेदः) 274
विक्रम-धवलः (धवल-भेदः) 305
विचारः (प्रतिमण्ठ-भेदः) 314, 315
विचित्रः (एला-पद-नाम) 227
विचित्र—(मात्रैला) 244
विचित्रत्वम् (मातुस्थाय-) 322
विचित्रलीलः (झोम्बडः) 260
विजयः (अड्डताल-भेदः) 316, 317
विजयः (त्रवणायाम्) 94
विजयः (ध्रुव-भेदः) 310, 311
विजयः (विप्रकीर्ण-प्रबन्धः) 221, 297
विजय—(तालः, विजये) 297
विजय—(धवलः) 305
विजयश्रीः (पूर्वप्रसिद्ध-क्रियाङ्गम्) 16
विजया (देवता, एलापदे) 228
विजया (त्रेता-भेदः) 240
वितालः (गायनदोषे) 155
विदारी (रूपक-नामालाप-भेदे) 19
विद्या-दानम् (सुशारीरलाभे) 169
विद्युल्लता (वर्णैला) 246
विनयः (कन्दभेदः) 274
विनिमीलकः (गायनदोषे) 155
विनियुक्तः (शुद्धसाधारितः) 19

विनियोगः (झोम्बडे) 260
विनोदः (रासकभेदः) 317
विन्यासभेदः (स्वरादेः, वर्णस्वरे) 266
विपञ्ची (कुतपे) 205
विपुला (एकतालीभेदः) 318
विपुला (वर्णेला) 246
विप्रकीर्ण - (प्रबन्धाः) 219, 221
विप्रलम्भः (कान्तारे) 316
विप्रलम्भः (कामले) 311
विप्रलम्भः (भुञ्छ्याम्) 112
विप्रलम्भः (मालवकैशिके) 63
विप्रलम्भः (वेलावल्याम्) 99
विप्रलम्भः (सारङ्गे) 260
विप्रलम्भः (मालवपञ्चमे) 46
विप्रलम्भ—(शृङ्गारः, गौडपञ्चमे) 35
विप्रा (नादावती) 236
विभावनी (मालव-पञ्चम-भाषा) 10
विभाषा (आन्धालिका) 117
विभाषा (ग्रामरागेषु) 9, 10
विभाषा (द्राविडी) 139
विभाषा (भम्माणी) 136
विभाषा (भोगवर्धनी) 99
विमला (वर्णेला) 246
वियुक्त-बन्धनम् (आन्धाल्याम्) 117
विरतिः (उद्ग्राहे) 318
विरसः (गायनः) 155
विरामः (मण्ठताले) 313
विरामान्तः (सगणः, कलापमण्ठे) 314
विलम्बित—(पदम्, एलायाम्) 222
विलम्बित—(मानम्, गद्ये) 270
विलम्बित—(लयः, मङ्गले) 306
विलम्बित—(लयः, वर्तन्याम्) 258
विलम्बिता (गतिः, गद्ये) 269
विलम्भः (लम्भ-भेदः) 263
विवर्तनी (वर्तनी-भेदः) 258
विविधत्व—(स्थायः) 174, 181
विशालः (निःसारु-भेदः) 315, 316
विशाला (आर्याभेदः) 280
विशाला (भिन्नपञ्चम-भाषा) 9
विशाला (वर्णेला) 246
विश्रामः (लये) 319
विषम—(मण्डलादिः, कुतपे) 206
विषम—(ग्रहः, एलायाम्) 222
विषम—(चरणः, धवले) 305
विषम—(ध्रुवा, चर्या) 303
विषमा (संगता-भेदः) 239
विषमालंकृति—(ढेङ्की) 257
विष्णुः (झोम्बड-भेदः) 260
विष्णुः (दैवतम्, एलायाम्) 227
विसदृशांशः (स्थाये) 181
विस्मयः (गान्धारपञ्चमे) 90
विस्मयः (निःशङ्के) 316
विस्वरता (शारीरदोषः) 169
वीणा (कुतपे) 205
वीणावंशादि—(यन्त्रम्) 178
वीर—(रसः, उत्कलिकायाम्) 267
वीर—(रसः, कन्दे) 273
वीर—(रसः, गौडकैशिके) 37
वीर (रसः, चक्रेश्वरे) 260
वीर—(रसः, चन्द्रशेखरे) 311
वीर—(रसः, चारे) 311
वीर—(रसः, जयप्रियमण्ठे) 313
वीर—(रसः, जयमङ्गले) 311
वीर—(रसः, तिलके) 311
वीर—(रसः, देवकृतौ) 108
वीर—(रसः, द्वितीयगौडे) 134
वीर—(रसः, धन्नास्याम्) 86
वीर—(रसः, नन्दावत्याम्) 237
वीर—(रसः, नागध्वनौ) 102
वीर—(रसः, भम्माणपञ्चमे) 52
वीर—(रसः भिन्नकैशिकमध्यमे) 26
वीर—(रसः, मालवकैशिके) 63
वीर—(रसः, रामकृतौ) 114
वीर—(रसः, राहड्याम्) 304

वीर—(रसः, विजये) 317
वीर—(रसः, शुद्धकैशिके) 24
वीर—(रसः, शुद्धसाधारिते) 19
वीर—(रसः, शेखरे) 310
वीर—(रसः, श्रीरागे) 121
वीर—(रसः, षड्जकैशिके) 57
वीर—(रसः, षड्जग्रामरागे) 22
वीर—(रसः, सोमरागे) 123
वीर—(रसः, सौवीरे) 102
वीरकरुण—(रसौ, रूपसाधारे) 48
वीर-रौद्र—(बिरुदम्) 272
वीर-रौद्र—(रसौ, तार-प्रतिमण्ठे) 315
वीर-रौद्राद्भुत—(रसाः, टक्के) 77
वीर-रौद्राद्भुत—(रसाः, रेवगुप्ते) 86
वीर-रौद्राद्भुत—(रसाः, शुद्धकैशिकमध्यमे) 84
वीरगोचरः (समरः) 316
वीरवती (अङ्कचारिणी) 272
वीर-विलासौ (विष्णुझोम्बडे) 260
वीर-शृङ्गार—(रसौ, नन्दने) 311
वीर-शृङ्गार—(रसौ, पञ्चतालेश्वरे) 292
वीरश्रीः (त्रेता-भेदः) 240
वीरश्रीः (विप्रकीर्ण-प्रबन्धः) 221, 304
वीर-हास्य—(रसौ, शके) 51
वीरादि—(रसः, शके) 51
वीराद्भुत—(रसौ, चारे) 316
वीरावतारः (पञ्चतालेश्वरः) 292
वीरोत्सवः (प्रथमललितायाम्) 129
वृत्तगन्धि (गद्यभेदः) 266, 268
वृत्तत्रयम् (त्रिभङ्गी) 300
वृत्तबन्धिनी (ढेङ्की) 257
वृत्तम् (आलि-संश्रित-प्रबन्धः) 220, 285, 287
वृत्तम् (ढेङ्की-प्रबन्धे) 257
वृत्तम् (रागकदम्बे) 288
वृत्तमाला (ढेङ्की) 257
वृत्ता (अङ्कचारिणी) 272
वृत्ताख्य—(वृत्तम्) 285
वृत्तान्तम् (वृत्ते) 287
वृत्तिः (आरभटी, उत्कलिकायाम्) 265
वृत्तिः (आरभटी, हंसावत्याम्) 237
वृत्तिः (कैशिकी, चित्रे) 268
वृत्तिः (कैशिकी, नादावत्याम्) 236
वृत्तिः (कैशिकी, ललिते) 267
वृत्तिः (भारती, भद्रावत्याम्) 238
वृत्तिः (सात्त्वती, खण्डे) 268
वृत्तिः (सात्त्वती, चूर्णे) 267
वृत्तिः (सात्त्वती, नन्दावत्याम्) 237
वृद्धिः (आर्या-भेदः) 151
वृद्धिः (यगणफलम्) 233
वृन्द—(गायनः) 151
वृन्दम् 203-6
वेगः (गमके) 171
वेगमध्यमा (सौवीर-भाषा) 9
वेगरञ्जी (टक्कभाषा) 9, 101, 106
वेगवत्—(स्वराः, गीतौ) 4
वेगाढ्या (वहनी) 177
वेणी (गद्यभेदः) 268
वेदध्वनि—(स्थायः) 175, 190
वेदवती (मालव-पञ्चम-भाषा) 10
वेदिनी (देवता, एला-पदे) 228
वेदोत्तरा (अङ्कचारिणी) 272
वेलावली (अधुना-प्रसिद्ध-भाषाङ्गम्) 16, 99, 112
वेलावली (अधुना-प्रसिद्धोपाङ्गम्, द्विविधा) 16
वेसरषाडवः (भाषाजनकः) 8, 10
वेसरषाडवः (वेसर-ग्रामरागः) 6, 40
वेसरा (गीतिः) 4
वेसरी (टक्कभाषा) 9
वेसरी (हिन्दोलभाषा) 9
वेहारी (पूर्वप्रसिद्ध-भाषाङ्गम्) 15
वैकुन्दः (निःसारु-भेदः) 315
वैदर्भी (भङ्गी, खण्डे) 268
वैदर्भी (रीतिः, चित्रे) 268

वैदर्भी (रीतिः, चूर्णे) 267
वैदर्भी (रीतिः, भद्रावत्याम्) 238
वैरञ्जी (टक्कभाषा) 9
वैरञ्जी (पूर्वप्रसिद्ध-भाषाङ्गम्) 15
वैराग्यम् (भोगवर्धन्याम्) 99
वैश्या (नन्दावती) 237
वैष्णवम् (चित्रम्) 268
वैसादृश्यम् (रागे) 181
व्यक्तम् (गीतम्) 323
व्यक्ताः (स्थायाः) 174
व्योमजा (संगताभेदः) 242
व्योमवारुणी (संगताभेदः) 242

शकः (साधारण-ग्रामरागः) 6, 51
शकमिश्रा (ककुभ-भाषा) 9
शकवलिता (अनुक्तजनका अन्तरभाषा) 10
शका (रेवगुप्त-भाषा) 10
शकादिः (उपरागः) 8
शङ्कः (अड्डताल-भेदः) 316
शङ्करः (देवः, गौडकैशिके) 37
शङ्कराभरणः (पूर्वप्रसिद्ध-रागाङ्गम्) 15
शङ्कित—(गायनः) 155
शङ्खः (कुतपे) 205
शङ्ख—(पाटाः, पञ्चतालेश्वरे) 290
शची (देवता, एला-पदे) 228
शततन्त्रिका (कुतपे) 205
शब्दः (कण्ठः) 158, 159, 165
शब्दः (गायनगुणे) 150
शब्द—(स्थायः) 174, 177
शब्दगुणः (स्थाये) 190
शब्द-सादृश्यम् (वृन्दगुणः) 205
शब्दानुशासनम् (वाग्गेयकार-गुणे) 146
शम्भुः (गणाधिपः, कर्णाटैलायाम्) 248
शरत् (ककुभे) 95
शरीरम् (क्षेत्रम्) 177
शरीरम् (शारीर-लक्षणे) 169
शशिनी (वर्णैला) 246
शशी (कन्दभेदः) 274
शान्त—(रसः, चूर्णे) 267
शान्त—(रसः, नन्दीशे) 260
शान्त—(रसः, वराट्याम्) 104
शान्त—(रसः, वृत्तगन्धौ) 268
शान्त—(रसः, वेसरषाडवे) 41
शान्त—(रसः, शीले) 316
शान्त—(रसः, सौवीरे) 102
शान्तिः (वासवी-भेदः) 239
शाम्भवः (देवता, षड्जकैशिके) 57
शारीर-गुणः (स्थाये) 190
शारीरम् (लक्षितम्) 169
शारीरम् (वाग्गेयकारगुणे) 146
शार्ङ्गदेवः (ग्रन्थकारः) 10, 102, 109, 114, 117, 124, 175, 190, 238, 318, 320
शार्ङ्गी (ग्रन्थकारः) 17, 74, 115, 158
शालवाहनिका (अन्तरभाषा, ककुभे) 9
शास्त्रदुष्ट—(गीतम्) 324
शिक्षा (द्विपथे) 283
शिक्षाकारः (गायकभेदः) 151
शिखापदम् (कर्णाटैलायाम्) 249
शिथिलः (स्थायः) 175, 190
शिथिलगाढः (स्थायः) 175, 190
शिरस्या (वहनी) 177
शिवः (देवः, भम्माणपञ्चमे) 52
शिवः (देवः, भिन्नताने) 28
शिवः (देवः, भिन्नकैशिके) 30
शिवक्री: (पूर्वप्रसिद्ध-क्रियाङ्गम्) 15
शिव-प्रियः (सौवीरः) 102
शिवा (आर्या-भेदः) 280
शिशिरः (गौडकैशिके) 37
शिशिरः (भिन्नकैशिके) 30
शिशिरः (मालवकैशिके) 63
शिशिरः (शुद्धकैशिके) 24
शीतांशुः (देवः, गौडकैशिक-मध्यमे) 32
शीलः (अड्डताल-भेदः) 316

शुकः (कन्दभेदः) 274
शुक्रः (तादि-वर्ण-गण-देवता) 233
शुक्रप्रियः (षाडवः) 66
शुद्ध —(ग्रामरागाः) 6
शुद्ध—(पाटः, कैवाडे) 271
शुद्ध—(रागाः, गायनदोषे) 156
शुद्ध —(रागाः, स्थाये) 181
शुद्ध—(सूडः, एलादि-) 308
शुद्ध—(सूडः, गायनगुणे) 150
शुद्ध—(स्वराक्षरम्) 278
शुद्ध—(स्वरार्थः) 278
शुद्धकैशिकः (शुद्ध-ग्रामरागः) 6, 24
शुद्धकैशिक-मध्यमः (शुद्धग्रामरागः) 6, 84
शुद्धपञ्चमः (भाषाजनकः) 9, 127
शुद्धपञ्चमः (शुद्धग्रामरागः) 6, 116
शुद्धभिन्ना (भिन्नपञ्चम-भाषा) 9
शुद्धभैरवः (देशीरागः) 123
शुद्धमध्यमा (जातिः, भम्माण-पञ्चमजनका) 52
शुद्धमध्या (मूर्छना, हिन्दोले) 80
शुद्ध-वराटिका (अधुनाप्रसिद्धभाषाङ्गम्) 16
शुद्ध-सादृश्यम् (एलादेः) 308
शुद्ध-साधारितः (शुद्ध-ग्रामरागः) 6, 19
शुद्धा (गणैला) 235, 238
शुद्धा (गीतिः) 4
शुद्धा (द्विपदी) 275, 276
शुद्धा (भिन्नषड्जभाषा) 10
शुद्धा (मालवकैशिकभाषा) 10
शुद्धा (मुख्या भाषा) 12
शुद्धादि—(रागाः) 4
शूद्रा (भद्रावती) 238
शून्यता (शादि-वर्णगण-फलम्) 233
शृङ्गः (कुतपे) 205
शृङ्गार—(रसः, भ्रमरे) 314
शृङ्गार—(रसः, कन्दर्पे) 311
शृङ्गार—(रसः, कर्णाटबङ्गाले) 106
शृङ्गार—(रसः, कामोदे) 311
शृङ्गार—(रसः, खम्भाइतौ) 112
शृङ्गार—(रसः, गुर्जर्याम्) 77
शृङ्गार—(रसः, चन्द्रशेखरे) 317
शृङ्गार—(रसः, चित्रे) 268
शृङ्गार—(रसः, जयन्ते) 310
शृङ्गार—(रसः, जयमङ्गले) 311
शृङ्गार—(रसः, तिलके) 311
शृङ्गार—(रसः, नर्ते) 54
शृङ्गार—(रसः, निर्मले) 311
शृङ्गार—(रसः, पुष्पसारे) 260
शृङ्गार—(रसः, बोट्टे) 43
शृङ्गार—(रसः, मकरन्दे) 317
शृङ्गार—(रसः, मङ्गल-मण्ठे) 313
शृङ्गार—(रसः, मध्यमग्रामरागे) 60
शृङ्गार—(रसः, मल्हार्याम्) 118
शृङ्गार—(रसः, मालव-पञ्चमे) 46
शृङ्गार—(रसः, ललितगद्ये) 267
शृङ्गार—(रसः, ललितध्रुवे) 311
शृङ्गार—(रसः, वराट्याम्) 74
शृङ्गार—(रसः, वल्लातायाम्) 115
शृङ्गार—(रसः, वेसर-षाडवे) 41
शृङ्गार—(रसः, शुद्धपञ्चमे) 116
शृङ्गार—(रसः, शेखरे) 260
शृङ्गार—(रसः, सर्वप्रतिमण्ठेषु) 315
शृङ्गार—(रसः, सैन्धवी-वराट्याम्) 109
शृङ्गार-तिलकः (पञ्चतालेश्वरः) 292
शृङ्गार-वर्धनी (नादावती) 236
शृङ्गार-वीर-(रसौ, शङ्खे) 316
शेखरः (झोम्बड-भेदः) 260
शेखरः (ध्रुवभेदः) 310
शैलः (कन्द-भेदः) 274
शोभी (एला-पद-नाम) 227
शौरिः (देवता, गौडपञ्चमे) 35
शौरिः (देवता, भिन्नपञ्चमे) 72
शौरि-स्मर-प्रियः (गौडपञ्चमः) 35
शौर्य—(वर्णनम्, एलायाम्) 222
श्रमः (जित-, गायनगुणे) 150

श्रावकः (शब्दः) 165
श्राः (मगण-फलम्) 233
श्रीः (रमायाम्) 318
श्रीकण्ठिका (भिन्नषड्जभाषा) 10
श्रीकण्ठी (वेसरषाडवविभाषा) 10
श्रीकरणाग्रणीः (ग्रन्थकारः) 17, 121
श्रीकरणेश्वरः (ग्रन्थकारः) 106
श्रीपतिः (झोम्बडः) 260
श्रीरङ्गः (विप्रकीर्ण-प्रबन्धः) 221,293
श्रीरागः (रागः) 8, 121
श्रीवर्धनः (विप्रकीर्ण-प्रबन्धः) 221, 301
श्रीविलासः (विप्रकीर्ण-प्रबन्धः) 221, 294
श्रीशंकरप्रियः (ग्रन्थकारः) 165
श्रीशार्ङ्गी (ग्रन्थकारः) 41, 97
श्रीसदाशिवः (पूर्वाचार्यः) 311
श्रीसोढलसुतः (ग्रन्थकारः) 132
श्रुतिः (गायकदोषे) 155
श्रुतिः (प्रबन्ध-जातिः) 218
श्रुतिन्यूनाधिकत्वम् (स्थाये) 177
श्रुति-विरोधि (गीतम्) 324
श्रेयस् (गान्धर्वफलम्) 210
श्रोता (चन्द्रशेखरे) 311
श्रोता (जयन्ते) 310
श्रोता (रमायाम्) 318
श्रोतृचित्तम् (गमके) 171
श्रोतृचित्तम् (स्थाये) 165
श्लक्ष्णः (शब्दः) 165, 166
श्लक्ष्णत्वम् (गीते) 323
श्लक्ष्णम् (गीतम्) 323
श्लेषः (ब्रह्मोति-झोम्बडभेदे) 26
श्लोकगीतादि 233
श्वसिता (पूर्वप्रसिद्ध-भाषाङ्गम्) 15
श्वेतम् (खण्डम्) 268

षट्कर्णः (कुतपे) 205
षट्पदी (गाथा-भेदः) 281
षट्पदी (विप्रकीर्ण-प्रबन्धः) **227, 296**
षट्पितापुत्रकः (तालः, पञ्चतालेश्वरे) **290**
षड्जः (ग्रहांशन्यासः, शके) 51
षड्जः (ग्रहांशान्तः, मालवकैशिके) 63
षड्ज (ग्रामे, द्वितीयकामोदः) 124
षड्ज—(ग्रामे, प्रथमकामोदः) 124
षड्ज—(ग्रामे, प्रथमबङ्गालः) 122
षड्ज—(ग्रामे, मेघरागः) 123
षड्ज—(ग्रामे, रेवगुप्तः) 86
षड्ज—(ग्रामे, श्रीरागः) 121
षड्ज— (ग्रामे, सोमरागः) 123
षड्जकैशिकः (साधारण-ग्रामरागः) 6, 57
षड्जग्रहन्यासा (वराटी) 74
षड्जग्रहन्यासांशः (सौवीरः) 102
षड्जग्रहांशः (गौडकैशिकमध्यमः) 32
षड्जग्रहांशः (भिन्नकैशिकमध्यमः) 26
षड्जग्रहांशन्यासः (द्वितीयकामोदः) 124
षड्जग्रहांशन्यासा (धन्नासी) 86
षड्जग्रहांशान्तः (सोमरागः) 123
षड्जग्रहांशापन्यासः (भिन्नकैशिकः) 30
षड्जग्रामः (ग्राम-नाम) 6
षड्जग्रामः (शुद्धग्रामरागः) 6, 22
षड्जतारः (मेघरागः) 123
षड्जन्यासग्रहांशः (कर्णाटगौडः) 120
षड्जन्यासग्रहांशः (नागध्वनिः) 102
षड्जन्यासग्रहांशः (हिन्दोलः) 80
षड्जन्यासग्रहांशिका (तृतीय-सैन्धवी) 132
षड्जन्यासांशग्रहः (द्वितीयबङ्गालः) 122
षड्जन्यासांशग्रहा (रामकृतिः) 107
षड्जभाषा (भिन्नषड्जे) 10
षड्जमध्यमा (जातिः, गौडकैशिक-जनका) 37
षड्जमध्यमा (जातिः, गौडकैशिकमध्यम-जनका) 32
षड्जमध्यमा (जातिः, गौडपञ्चमजनका) 35
षड्जमध्यमा (जातिः, टक्कजनका) 77
षड्जमध्यमा (जातिः, प्रथमकामोद-जनका) 124

षड्जमध्यमा (जातिः, प्रथमबङ्गालजनका) 122
षड्जमध्यमा (जातिः, बोट्टजनका) 43
षड्जमध्यमा (जातिः, भिन्नकैशिकजनका) 26
षड्जमध्यमा (जाति., रूपसाधार-जनका) 48
षड्जमध्यमा (जातिः, वेसरषाडवजनका) 40
षड्जमध्यमा (जातिः, शुद्धकैशिकमध्यम-जनका) 84
षड्जमध्यमा (जातिः, शुद्धसाधारितजनका) 18
षड्जमध्यमा (जातिः, षड्जग्रामरागजनका) 22
षड्जमध्यमा (जातिः, सौवीरजनका) 102
षड्जमध्यमा (हिन्दोलभाषा) 9
षड्जमन्द्रा (प्रथमगौडी) 134
षड्जमन्द्रा (प्रथमललिता) 129
षड्जमन्द्रा (प्रथमसैन्धवी) 131
षड्जमन्द्रा (हर्षपुरी) 136
षड्जांशग्रहन्यासा (गौडकृतिः) 107
षड्जांशग्रहन्यासा (प्रथमललिता) 129
षड्जादि—(मूर्छना, गौडकैशिके) 37
षड्जादि—(मूर्छना, गौडकैशिकमध्यमे) 32
षड्जादि—(मूर्छना, भम्माणपञ्चमे) 52
षड्जादि—(मूर्छना, भिन्नकैशिके) 30
षड्जादि—(मूर्छना, भिन्नकैशिकमध्यमे) 26
षड्जादि—(मूर्छना, मालवकैशिके) 63
षड्जादि—(मूर्छना, रूपसाधारे) 48
षड्जादि—(मूर्छना, शके) 51
षड्जादि—(मूर्छना, शुद्धकैशिके) 24
षड्जादि (मूर्छना, शुद्धसाधारिते) 18
षड्जादि—(मूर्छना, षड्जग्रामरागे:) 22
षड्जादि (मूर्छना, सौवीरे) 102
षड्जाद्यन्ता (सौवीरी) 104
षड्जोदोच्यवती (जातिः, भिन्नषड्ज-जनका) 69
षाडवः (रागः) 8
षाडवः (वेसरग्रामरागः) 6, 40
षाडवः (शुद्धग्रामरागः) 6, 66, 69
षाडवम् (रागालापलक्षणे) 19

सः (सगणः) 232, 237, 313
संकीर्णा (एला) 252
संकीर्णा (गणैला) 235, 238
संकीर्णा (याष्टिकोक्त-भाषाभेदः) 12
संकीर्णाः (स्थायाः) 175, 190
संगत—(ऋषभ-पञ्चमौ, मालवायाम्) 138
संगतः (झोम्बडभेदः) 260
संगत—(द्विश्रुतिः, त्रावणी) 135
संगत—(द्विश्रुती, द्राविड्याम्) 139
संगत—(षड्जधैवतौ, द्राविड्याम्) 139
संगत—(षड्जधौ, मालवायाम्) 138
संगता—(नादावती-भेदः) 243
संगता—(विकृतगणैला) 238, 239
संग्राम-स्तुतिः (राहड्याम्) 304
संचारि—(वर्णः, गान्धारपञ्चमे) 90
संचारि—(वर्णः, टक्के) 77
संचारि—(वर्णः, नर्ते) 54
संचारि—(वर्णः, भिन्नकैशिके) 30
संचारि—(वर्णः, भिन्नकैशिकमध्यमे) 26
संचारि—(वर्णः, भिन्नताने) 28
संचारि—(वर्णः, भिन्नपञ्चमे) 72
संचारि—(वर्णः, भिन्नषड्जे) 69
संचारि—(वर्णः, वहनी-स्थाये) 177
संचारि—(वर्णः, शुद्धपञ्चमे) 116
संदष्टः (गायनः) 155
संपूर्णः (भिन्नकैशिकः) 30
संपूर्णः (वेसरषाडवः) 41
संपूर्णः (षड्जग्रामरागः) 22
संपूर्णा (द्विपदी) 275, 276
संप्रविष्टकः (स्थायः) 174, 187
संबोधन (पदम्, एलायाम्) 222
संभोगः (हिन्दोले) 81
संयत—(प्रवेशः, सौवीरे) 102

संवादः (रिधयोः, सधयोः, सौवीर्याम्) 104
संस्कृतम् 287
संहितः (स्थायः) 175, 190
सकलस्वरः (बोट्टः) 43
सकाकली (भिन्नकैशिकमध्यमः) 26
सकाकली (भिन्नतानः) 28
सकाकली (शुद्धकैशिकः) 24
सगतारा (छेवाटी) 115
सगतारा (प्रथमसैन्धवी) 131
सगमक —(स्वराः, द्वितीय-सैन्धव्याम्) 131
सगम-तारा (कैशिकी) 127
सगम-मन्द्रा (छेवाटी) 115
सजातीय —(रागाः, स्थाये) 171
सजातीयांशः (स्थाये) 181
सतारा (तोडी) 68
सदृश-रागाः (स्थाये) 181
सदृशांशः (स्थाये) 181
सध-कम्पिता (सैन्धवी वराटी) 109
सध-मन्द्रा (कोलाहला) 114
सन्दिग्धम् (गीतम्) 324
सन्धिः (अवमर्श-, शुद्धपञ्चमे) 116
सन्धिः (निर्वहण-, शुद्धकैशिकमध्यमे) 84
सन्यासांशग्रह —(वराट्युपाङ्गानि, षट्) 108
सन्यासांशग्रहः (श्रीरागः) 121
सन्यासांशग्रहा (नट्टा) 106
सन्यासांशग्रहा (प्रथम-सैन्धवी) 131
सन्यासांशग्रहा (वल्लाता) 115
सन्यासांशग्रहा (हर्षपुरी) 136
सन्यासांशा (देवकृतिः) 108
सप-भूयसी (प्रथमसौराष्ट्री) 128
सभाजयः (वाग्गेयकारगुणे) 146
समः (स्थायः) 174, 182
सम—(अङ्घ्रिः, द्विपथे) 282, 283
सम—(चरणः, धवले) 305
सम—(पादः, चतुष्पद्याम्) 295
सम-(लयम्, गीतम्) 323
सम-गाता (वृन्दे) 204
सम-गायनः (वृन्दे) 203
सम-गायनी (वृन्दे) 204
सम-मन्द्रा (कौन्तली वराटी) 108
सम-मन्द्रा (तृतीय-सैन्धवी) 132
समधातु-(खण्डे, ढेङ्कीप्रबन्धे) 256
समध्रुवा (चर्या) 303
समम् (गीतम्) 323
समरः (निःसारुभेदः) 315, 316
सम-वर्णम् (गीतम्) 323
सम-स्थानम् (गीतम्) 323
सम-स्वरः (द्वितीय-कामोदः) 124
सम-स्वरः (द्वितीय-बङ्गालः) 122
सम-स्वरः (प्रथम-कामोदः) 124
सम-स्वरः (भैरवः) 69
सम-स्वरः (मेघरागः) 123
सम-स्वरः (शुद्धभैरवः) 123
सम-स्वरः (श्रीरागः) 121
सम-स्वरा (आडि-कामोदिका) 101
सम-स्वरा (कैशिकी) 127
सम-स्वरा (देवकृतिः) 108
सम-स्वरा (देशाख्या) 92
सम-स्वरा (नट्टा) 106
सम-स्वरा (भैरवी) 113
सम-स्वरा (मालवश्रीः) 65
सम-स्वरा (वेलावली) 99
समा (मात्रा, ध्वनि-कुट्टन्याम्) 279
समा (संगता-भेदः) 239
समानः (प्राणः, एलायाम्) 228
समालंकरणा (ढेङ्की) 257
समाहितः (प्राणः, एलायाम्) 228
समुद्रः (कन्दभेदः) 274
समेतर-स्वरा (तोडी) 68
समेतर-स्वरा (वराटी) 74
सम्पक्वेष्टाक —(तालः, पञ्चतालेश्वरे) 290
सम्पत् (रादि-वर्णगण-फलम्) 233
सम्प्रदायः (गायन-गुणे) 150
सम्भोगः (विशाले) 316

सरला (वर्णैला) 246
सर्वक्रतु—(फलम्, ध्रुवप्रबन्धे) 311
सर्व-भावा: (तृतीय-सैन्धव्याम्) 132
सर्व-भावा: (प्रथम-सौराष्ट्र्याम्) 128
सर्वमन्त्रमयी (मातृका) 287
सर्वरसा: (प्रथम-सैन्धव्याम्) 131
सर्वसिद्धि: (ललिते) 311
सर्वसिद्धि-(प्रदायिनी, मातृका) 287
सर्वाङ्गिका: (प्रबन्धा:) 294
सर्वाधम: (मिश्रशब्दभेद:) 159
सविता (देव:, रूपसाधारे) 48
सवितृ—(गण:, जगण:) 242
सव्यसाची (मात्रैला-निरूपणे) 244
सांशग्रहन्यास: (टक्क:) 77
सांशग्रहान्ता (द्वितीय-सौराष्ट्री) 128
सांशग्रहान्ता (वेगरञ्जी) 101
सांशा (डोम्बक्रृति:) 95
सात्त्वती (वृत्ति:, खण्डे) 268
सात्त्वती (वृत्ति:, चूर्णे) 267
सात्त्वती (वृत्ति:, नन्दावत्याम्) 237
सादृश्यम् (रागे) 181
साधारण: (स्थाय:) 175, 190
साधारण—(ग्रामरागा:, सप्त) 6
साधारणी (गीति:) 4
साधारिता (सौवीर-भाषा) 9
सानुनासिक: (गायन:) 155
सान्त: (प्रथम-कामोद:) 124
सान्तम् (कर्णाट-बङ्गालम्) 106
सान्ता (पिञ्जरी) 106
सान्ता (रामकृति:) 114
सान्द्र: (प्राण:, एलायाम्) 228
सान्द्र: (शब्द:) 159
सान्द्रा (प्रथम-सैन्धवी) 131
सान्निपातिक: (शब्द:) 158, 160
सामवेद: (गद्य-उत्पत्तौ) 266
सामवेदोद्भवा (नन्दावती) 237
सामीप्यम् (उपाङ्गत्व-निर्णये) 114
सारङ्ग: (झोम्बड-भेद:) 260
सारङ्गी (कुतपे) 205
सारस: (कन्दभेद:) 274
सारस: (द्विपथ-भेद:) 282
सारसी (आर्या-भेद:) 280
सार्थक—(पाट:, कैवाडे) 271
सार्द्रत्वम् (वाग्गेयकार-गुणे) 146
सार्वभौमोत्सव: (भिन्नषड्जे) 69
सालग-सूडस्थ—(रूपकम्) 213
सालग-सूडस्थ—(ताला:, लम्भे) 263
सावरी (आधुनाप्रसिद्ध-भाषाङ्गम्) 16, 97
सावित्री (देवता, कर्णाटैलायाम्) 248
सावित्री (संगता-भेद:) 242
सिंह: (झोम्बड-भेद:) 260
सिंहली-कामोदा (उपाङ्गम्) 113
सिंहलील: (ताल:, सिंहलीले) 298
सिंहलील: (विप्रकीर्ण-प्रबन्ध:) 221, 298
सितम् (ललितम्) 267
सिता (नादावती) 236
सिद्धि: (कामल:) 311
सुकराभास: (स्थाय:) 175, 190
सुकुमार: (प्राण:, एलायाम्) 228
सुकुमारम् (गीतम्) 323
सुख—(स्थाया:) 175, 190
सुखावह: (शब्द:) 165
सुघट: (गायन:) 150
सुचित्रा (एला-पद-नाम) 227
सुदर्शन: (विप्रकीर्ण-प्रबन्ध:) 221, 300
सुदेशिक: (स्थाय:) 174, 182
सुन्दर: (मण्ठभेद:, मण्ठतालभेदश्च) 313
सुभग-गेयम् (वाग्गेयकार-गुणे) 146
सुभगता (तादि-वर्ण-गण-फलम्) 233
सुमति: (एला-पद-नाम 227)
सुमुखी (देवता, एला-पदे) 228
सुरक्तम् (गीतम्) 323
सुरनाथ: (कन्दभेद:) 274
सुरसा (वर्णैला) 246

सुराधीशः (नगणदेवता) 233
सुलेखा (कर्णाटैला) 248
सुशारीरम् (गायकगुणे) 150
सुशारीरम् (लक्षितम्) 169
सुशोभी (एला-पद-नाम) 227
सुस्वरा (वर्णैला) 246
सूक्ष्म — (गमकाः) 4
सूक्ष्मान्तः (स्थायः) 175, 187
सूड—(प्रबन्धः) 308
सूडक्रमस्थ—(प्रबन्धः) 220
सूडस्थ—(प्रबन्धाः) 219
सूत्कारी (गायनः) 155
सूत्रधार —(प्रवेशः, भिन्नपञ्चमे) 72
सूरिशाङ्गी (ग्रन्थकारः) 315
सूर्यः (जगण-देवता) 233
सेना (प्रबन्ध-जातिः) 218
सेल्लुका (कुतपे) 206
सैन्धवी (टक्कभाषा) 9, 131
सैन्धवी (पञ्चमभाषा) 9, 131
सैन्धवी (भिन्नषड्जभाषा) 10, 132
सैन्धवी (मालवकैशिकभाषा) 10, 132
सैन्धवी (वराटी, अधुनाप्रसिद्धोपाङ्गम्) 16, 109
सोढलसूनुः (ग्रन्थकारः) 69, 159
सोढलात्मजः (ग्रन्थकारः) 14, 112
सोमः (आदि-वर्ण-गण-देवता) 233
सोमः (झोम्बड-भेदः) 260
सोमः (देवः, भिन्नकैशिक-मध्यमे) 26
सोमरागः (रागः) 8
सोमेश्वरः (पूर्वाचार्यः) 222
सौकुमार्यम् (शब्दे) 158
सौभाग्य—(वर्णनम्, एलायाम्) 222
सौम्या (संगता-भेदः) 239
सौराष्ट्री (गुर्जरी, अधुना-प्रसिद्धोपाङ्गम्) 16, 111
सौराष्ट्री (टक्कभाषा) 9
सौराष्ट्री (प्रथम-, द्वितीय-) 128
सौरिः (=शनिः, गौड-पञ्चम-देवता) 35
सौरिः (पादि-वर्ण-गण-देवता) 233
सौवीरः (भाषाजनकः) 8, 9
सौवीरः (वेसरग्रामरागः) 6, 102
सौवीरी (मूर्छना, मध्यमग्रामरागे) 60
सौवीरी (मूलभाषा) 104
सौवीरी (सौवीर-भाषा) 9
स्तम्बतीर्थिका (अधुना-प्रसिद्धोपाङ्गम्) 16
स्तुत्यः (श्लोकगीतादौ) 233
स्तुत्य-नाम (एलायाम्) 222
स्तुत्य-नाम (ध्रुवप्रबन्धे) 310
स्तोक-गमकः (झोम्बडः) 259
स्थानम् (गायनगुणे) 150
स्थानम् (गायनदोषे) 155, 156
स्थानकम् (कुतपे) 206
स्थानकम् (रासके) 264
स्थानभ्रंशः (सगणफलम्) 233
स्थानभ्रष्टः (गायनः) 155
स्थान-विच्युतिः (शारीरदोषः) 169
स्थानान्तरगत—(स्थायाः रूपके) 322
स्थापना (रागस्य, आलप्तौ) 199
स्थापना—(स्थायः) 174, 180
स्थायः (आलप्तौ) 199, 201, 203
स्थायः (गायनगुणे) 150
स्थायः (गायनदोषे) 156
स्थायः (रूपकावयवः) 201
स्थायः (लक्षितः) 172
स्थायः 174, 175, 177, 178, 180-82, 187, 190
स्थाय-भञ्जनी 201
स्थाय्यादि—(वर्णः) 297
स्थायान्तरम्—(रागे) 319
स्थायि— (वर्णः, स्थाये) 187
स्थायी (स्वरः, आलप्तौ) 198, 199
स्थायुकः (स्थायः) 175, 187
स्थिरः (स्थायः) 174, 187
स्थिर-कम्पनम् (स्थाये) 177

स्थिरा (वहनी) 177
स्थूल: (शब्द:) 158-60, 165
स्निग्ध: (नाद:, स्थाये) 180
स्निग्ध: (शब्द:) 158-60, 165, 166
स्निग्ध: (स्थाय) 174, 182
स्निग्धता (शारीरगुण:) 169
स्फुट—(स्वरा:, गीते) 323
स्फुटित: (शब्द:) 168
स्फुरित: (गमक:) 171
स्फुरित—(धैवत:, रगन्त्याम्) 97
स्फुरित —(गान्धारा, देशाख्या) 92
स्फुरितर्षभा (द्राविडी वराटी) 109
स्फुरिता (द्राविड-गुर्जरी) 111
स्मर: (देवता, गौडपञ्चमे) 35
स्मर-गण: (कामगणपर्याय:) 249
स्वभावक्री: (पूर्व-प्रसिद्ध-क्रियाङ्गम्) 15
स्वर: (आक्षिप्तिकायाम्) 19
स्वर: (गमके) 171, 172
स्वर: (गायनदोषे) 155
स्वर: (प्रबन्धाङ्गम्) 215, 216, 252-55, 266, 270, 274, 276-79, 282, 284, 285, 287, 290, 294-99, 301-4
स्वर —(करणम्) 252
स्वर—(स्थाय:) 174, 182
स्वरकाकु: (स्थाये) 177
स्वरनामक —(जातय:, हिन्दोलजनका:) 80
स्वरमुक्तिक: (द्विपथक:) 282
स्वरलङ्घित: (स्थाय:) 174, 178
स्वरलेखिका (कर्णाटैला) 249
स्वरवल्ली (भिन्नषड्ज-भाषा) 10
स्वर-सन्दर्भ: (गीते) 209
स्वरा: (स्थाये) 177, 178, 182, 187
स्वरा: (स्फुट-, गीते) 323
स्वराख्या (भाषा) 12
स्वराङ्क: (विप्रकीर्ण-प्रबन्ध:) 221, 301
स्वरादि: (मार्गवेत्ता) 149
स्वरार्ध: (आलिसंश्रित-प्रबन्ध:) 220, 278
स्वल्पषड्जा (सावरी) 97
स्वस्तिक: (रागकदम्ब:) 288
स्वस्थानम् (रागालप्तौ) 198
स्वाभिधानम् (वाग्गेयकारस्य) 222

हंस: (झोम्बड-भेद:) 260
हंस: (द्विपथक-भेद:) 282
हंसक: (पूर्वप्रसिद्ध-रागाङ्गम्) 15
हंसक्रीड: (द्विपथक-भेद:) 282, 283
हंसतिलक: (रासकभेद:) 264
हंसलील: (विप्रकीर्ण-प्रबन्ध:) 221, 298
हंसलील— (ताल:, हंसलीले) 298
हंसावती (कर्णाटैला) 249
हंसावती (गणैला) 242
हंसावती (शुद्धा गणैला) 235, 237
हंसी (आर्या-भेद:) 280
हतपञ्चमा (हतस्वर-वराटी) 109
हतस्वर-वराटी (अधुना-प्रसिद्धोपाङ्गम्) 16, 109
हम्मीर—(पात्रम्) 206
हयलील— (छन्द:, हयलीलायाम्) 274
हयलील—(ताल:, मधुरे) 310
हयलील—(ताल:, हयलीलायाम्) 274
हयलीला (आलि-संश्रितप्रबन्ध:) 274, 275
हरप्रिय: (ग्रन्थकार:) 252, 254
हरविलास: (विप्रकीर्ण-प्रबन्ध:) 221, 300
हरि: (कन्दभेद:) 274
हरि: (गणाधिप:, कर्णाटैलायाम्) 248
हरिण: (कन्दभेद:) 274
हरिणी (आर्याभेद:) 280
हरिप्रिया (वेलावली) 99
हर्ष: (द्राविड-गुर्जर्याम्) 111
हर्ष: (हर्षपुर्याम्) 136
हर्षकारिणी (तोडी) 68
हर्षपुरी (मालवकैशिकभाषा) 10, 135
हर्षवर्धन: (विप्रकीर्ण-प्रबन्ध:) 221, 301
हर्षोत्कर्षप्रद: (चार:) 311

हव्यवाहनः (कन्दभेदः) 274
हस्तपाटः (पाटकरणे) 253
हस्तिका (कुतपे) 205
हस्ती (कन्दभेदः) 274
हारिणाश्वा (मूर्छना, गान्धारपञ्चमे) 90
हास्य—(रसः, आन्ध्रपञ्चमे) 124
हास्य—(रसः, कन्दर्पे) 311
हास्य—(रसः, कलापे) 314
हास्य—(रसः, खण्डे) 268
हास्य—(रसः, गान्धारपञ्चमे) 90
हास्य—(रसः, छेवाट्याम्) 115
हास्य—(रसः, नर्ते) 54
हास्य—(रसः, बोट्टे) 43
हास्य—(रसः, मध्यमग्रामरागे) 60
हास्य—(रसः, मालवपञ्चमे) 46
हास्य—(रसः, विजये) 311
हास्य—(रसः, वेसरषाडवे) 41
हास्य—(रसः, शुद्धपञ्चमे) 116
हास्य—(रसः, शेखरे) 310, 311
हास्य—(रसः, षाडवे) 66
हास्य-शृङ्गार—(रसौ, मध्यमग्रामरागे) 60
हिन्दोलः (भाषाजनकः) 8, 106, 115
हिन्दोलः (वेसर-ग्रामरागः) 6, 80
हिन्दोल—(रागः, चच्चर्याम्) 302
हिन्दोल—(रागः, हंसावत्याम्)'237
हीन—(वृन्दम्) 204
हुंकारः (गमके) 172
हुडुक्क—(पाटाः, पञ्चतालेश्वरे) 290
हुडुक्का (कुतपे) 206
हुम्फितः (गमकः) 171, 172
हृद्या (वहनी) 177
हृष्यका (मूर्छना, मालवपञ्चमे) 46
हृष्यका (मूर्छना, शुद्धपञ्चमे) 116
हेमन्तः (भिन्नषड्जे) 69
ह्रस्वः (स्थायः) 175, 190

Corrigenda

Page	*Line* (*from above*)	*Line* (*from below*)	*Incorrect*	*Correct*
34	8		(vi)	(vii)
39		1	writer	winter
46	6		गेयोऽङ्ग.	गेयोऽङ्गः
91	13		इति रागाङ्गानि	should be read on p. 92 after इति देशाख्या
172	2		क्रमाद्वच्छेत्	क्रमाद्गच्छेत्
187		9	इत्यामिधीयते	इत्यभिधीयते
194	16		य्लावितोल्लसित॰	प्लावितोल्लासित॰
205		12	सारङ्गचालपिनी॰	सारङ्गचालापिनी॰
215		11		add प्रबन्धः, after l. 11
234	14		एवं मध्याभवा भेदाः	add अष्टौ कामगणाः स्मृताः (after)
234	14		प्रतिष्ठायास्तु षोडश	add तद्वद् बाणगणा भेदाः (before)
264	13		षडक्षरङ्घ्रि॰	षडक्षराङ्घ्रि॰
269	6		पृथग्लत्वे	पृथग्लगत्वे
307		5	308 ante	276 ante
315		14	बुद्धैः	बुधैः